Jacopo de'Barbari, *Panoramic View of Venice in 1500*, detail.
(Reproduced by courtesy of the Trustees of the British Museum, London)

VENICE

A Documentary History,
1450–1630

Edited by
David Chambers and Brian Pullan,
with Jennifer Fletcher

Published by University of Toronto Press
Toronto Buffalo London
in association with the Renaissance Society of America

Reprinted by permission of the publisher from David Chambers and
Brian Pullan, *Venice: A Documentary History, 1450–1630* (Oxford UK
and Cambridge USA: Blackwell Publishers, 1992. © 1992 by David Chambers
and Brian Pullan. All rights reserved.)

Printed on acid-free paper

Canadian Cataloguing in Publication Data

Main entry under title:

Venice : a documentary history, 1450–1630

(Renaissance Society of America reprint texts ; 12)
ISBN 0-8020-8424-9

1. Venice (Italy) – History – 697–1508 – Sources.   2. Venice (Italy) –
History – 1508–1797 – Sources.   I. Chambers, David (David Sanderson).
II. Pullan, Brian.   III. Fletcher, Jennifer.   IV. Renaissance Society of
America.   V. Series.

DG677.85.V35 2001   945'.31   C00-933009-7

University of Toronto Press acknowledges the financial assistance to its
publishing program of the Canada Council for the Arts and the
Ontario Arts Council.

University of Toronto Press acknowledges the financial support for its
publishing activities of the Government of Canada through the Book
Publishing Industry Development Program (BPIDP).

Contents

Preface

Tentative plans for this book were laid at the Warburg Institute in December 1985, at a meeting in London of the Venetian Seminar – a peripatetic group which has been getting together at various venues in England and Scotland two or three times a year ever since 1977. Participants felt the need for a collection of texts and documents in translation that would encourage the advanced study of Venetian history and at the same time offer attractive reading, both instructive and entertaining, to anyone with a serious interest in Venice and its past. Many members of the seminar have offered suggestions and some have contributed material found in the course of their researches, much of it previously unpublished in any language. The starting-point of this anthology is the mid fifteenth century, when Venice had consolidated its conquests on the mainland of Italy, thereby adding a second empire to its overseas dominions in Dalmatia, Greece and the eastern Mediterranean, and was approaching the zenith of its power and reputation. The terminus lies about 1630, the year of the great plague, when the population of Venice and its Italian state was sadly depleted and there were unmistakable signs of relative economic decline and loss of political strength.

For practical reasons the work concentrates almost entirely on the domestic history of Venice itself. To give adequate representation to government, society and culture in the Venetian dominions as well, or to provide texts illustrating the complexities of foreign relations and naval and military campaigns, would demand at least one additional volume of large dimensions. War and diplomacy are always present in the background, but the book deals with the impact of war rather than with war as such; and though Venice's dominions are often mentioned incidentally they are not at the centre of the stage. These texts and documents are arranged thematically, with, for example, general descriptions in part I, and sections devoted to authority and government (part II), law, order and social policy (part III), and wealth and its expenditure (part IV); but many individual pieces illustrate more than one theme. They are generally designed to portray the city, its buildings, its setting, its people, its economy and its institutions. They attempt to analyse its constitution and the political behaviour of its ruling order. They seek to establish the purpose and scope of government and the powers of the state. Specific sections of the book set out to reconstruct the religious life of the city, both of clergy and of laity (part V); to identify the characteristics, privileges, institutions and economic activities of the different social orders (part VI) and of the principal foreign communities (part VIII), and to examine the services they rendered to the state; to show how the poor were treated, at least by the more highly organized forms of charity and poor relief (part VII). Finally, there are two sections (parts IX and X) which show how Venice became – despite its mercantile values – a major centre of learning, book production and the arts, and a place where lavish public and private spectacles were presented. Architecture, sculpture and painting are treated in relation to the artists themselves and, above all, to the people and the public bodies which commissioned, paid for, bought, enjoyed, and otherwise supported them.

The editors and contributors are anxious not to offer merely a bland and conventional view of Venice as the just city of Renaissance myth, the city without revolution and almost without change. Nor do they wish to represent Venice crudely in one of its other guises, as the great anti-clerical state of the Counter-Reformation years, defying the Pope, expelling the Jesuits and restraining the Inquisition. Rather they seek to record the shortcomings of government as well as its successes, and to pay suitable attention to protest and disturbance as well as to the preservation of order, to faction and division as well as to unity and harmony. Critical and polemical accounts of the city take their place beside eulogies. There is evidence here of religious belief and behaviour at all levels, and not just of tensions between Church and state. The book tries to deal not just with the making of money and the uses of wealth, but also with the problems of the poor and outcast; not just with the Venetians themselves, but also with resident aliens; not just with the famous gentlemen of Venice, but also with the citizens and craftsmen who formed the second and third estates of Venetian society.

No attempt is made at providing extended commentaries on the documents, although they have been annotated to explain some of their most significant allusions. Most of the precious space is reserved for the texts themselves, and the brief introductions are intended chiefly to establish the reasons for the selections made and to indicate the relationship of the texts to each other. This is a do-it-yourself history of Venice: bibliographies are provided to enable readers to carry out the work of interpretation for themselves. They will notice that the names of people have been given in the form (sometimes variable) in which they occur in the original text, which is very often the Venetian rather than the Italian form (e.g. Zorzi Corner rather than Giorgio Cornaro); but place names, the names of churches, and the names of Venetian magistracies have been standardized and generally presented in their Italian forms, save where there are generally accepted English equivalents. Hence the Doge's chapel is St Mark's, while the district named after it is San Marco; the university town is Padua and not Padova; and Venice's standing-committee of public safety appears as the Council of Ten and not the Consiglio dei Dieci, her principal court of law as the Criminal Court of the Forty and not the Quarantia al Criminal. Unless otherwise stated, all translations are made from originals in Italian or Venetian.

One function of the collection is to demonstrate the uses and possibilities of various types of historical material. Those represented here include observers' descriptions of Venice; chronicles; diaries; letters; myth-making literature and polemical denunciations; legislation; petitions; minute-books of guilds, hospitals and religious brotherhoods; wills; notarial acts; trial records; state budgets; and so forth. Our anthology is intended partly for use by teachers in higher education, and it may help to guide the steps of postgraduate students and to whet their appetites for archival research and the study of manuscripts. Professional historians may find it useful to refer to crucial documents in areas where they claim little expertise themselves: an economic historian may look at texts on the making of books or pictures, an art historian at those on taxes or the making of money. But the book is not designed exclusively for a student audience or solely for an academic one. We hope that it will bring Venice to life for all those interested in reading the words of those who observed it in past centuries, of those who lived in it, and of those who helped to shape its history.

Acknowledgements

We are particularly grateful to our associate, Jennifer Fletcher, who is chiefly responsible for the material concerning the visual arts, and for suggesting and finding illustrations with the co-operation of the Conway Library at the Courtauld Institute. We are deeply indebted to Laura and Giulio Lepschy for their willingness to deal with an endless series of questions about problems of translation. Jill Kraye has given invaluable help with some passages of Latin. Among friends and colleagues who have at different times made helpful suggestions we should especially like to thank Charles Hope and Nicolai Rubinstein; we have been greatly heartened by the sustained interest which members of the Venetian Seminar have shown in the progress of this book. All texts carry at the end the initials (see List of Contributors) of the person or persons who suggested them, with those of the translator if the translator is somebody else. With editorial headnotes, the initials are those of the author, and occasionally those of persons who have helped to annotate the document. Maria Grazia Grandese has been most helpful in obtaining copies of original documents from the Venetian archives, and Nubar Gianighian and Paola Pavanini have been most generous with hospitality and advice while the book was in the making. Many of the contributors will remember with gratitude the assistance they have received over the years from the staff of the archives and libraries of Venice and of the magnificent collection of microfilms at the Fondazione Giorgio Cini.

The editors owe a great deal to those most immediately concerned with the preparation and production of a complicated book: to Graham Eyre, for his painstaking and often ingenious copy-editing, which extends to a remarkable skill in verse; to Ann McCall, for designing the lay-out of the pages; to Ginny Stroud-Lewis, for help with the illustrations; to Janet Pullan, for compiling the index; and to the secretaries of Manchester University History Department for typing voluminous correspondence and labouring at the photocopying machine.

We are grateful to the Controller of Her Majesty's Stationery Office for permission to publish Sir Dudley Carleton's report on Venice in 1612 [I.4], the text of which is Crown copyright; to the American Musicological Society, Inc., for permission to include extracts from R. J. Agee's translations of material in the Strozzi papers in Florence [IX.14, 20], which first appeared in the Society's *Journal* in 1983 and 1985; and to the following for permission to include, in original translations, extracts from the sources listed below: the Archivi di Stato of Mantua, Milan and Venice for numerous materials in their keeping; the Archivio Segreto del Vaticano for several extracts from the writings of the papal nuncios to the Venetian Republic, both published and unpublished; the Biblioteca Nazionale Marciana, Venice, for numerous extracts from manuscripts in their keeping; the Bibliothèque Nationale, for extracts from manuscripts in their Fonds français [II.17(a), VII.2]; the Bodleian Library, Oxford, for an extract from Bodley ms. 911 [III.3(d)]; the British Library for extracts from Additional mss 5471 [VI.3] and 15816 [II.3(b)]; Gaetano Cozzi of the University of Venice for extracts from the writings of Nicolò Contarini [IV.13] and for material on Venetian theatres [IX.21]; the Curia Patriarcale of Venice for a copy of the foundation document of the Venetian magistracy responsible for convents [V.8]; the Direzione Musei Civici of Venice for numerous extracts from manuscripts kept in the Biblioteca Correr, Venice; Pier Cesare Ioly Zorattini of the University of Udine for an extract from his monumental edition of the trials of Jews and judaizers by the Inquisition in Venice [VIII.9]; the Istituto Ellenico di Studi Bizantini e Postbizantini in Venice for documents in the archive of the Scuola di San Giorgio dei Greci in Venice [VIII. 5 and 6]; the Istituzioni di Ricovero e di Educazione [I.R.E.] of Venice for extracts from documents on the history of charity kept in their archives [VII.6(a)–(d)]; Laura Lepschy for an extract from her edition of Santo Brasca's *Viaggio in Terrasanta*; Casa Editrice Leo S. Olschki for an extract from Benedetto Dei's invective against Venice [II.12], first published by G. degli Azzi in the *Archivio storico italiano* for 1952; Benjamin Ravid of Brandeis University, Waltham, Massachusetts, for several extracts from documents on the history of Venetian Jewry [VIII.8, 11, 12, 14]; the *Rivista di Storia della Chiesa in Italia* for extracts from the rule of the Venetian Scuola di San Chiereghino e del Rosario [V.11], first published by A. Niero in that journal for 1961; the Scuola Grande Arciconfraternità di San Rocco, Venice, for extracts from the records of the Scuola kept in their archives [V.13, VII.9(b)]; the Trustees of the National Museums and Galleries on Merseyside, Liverpool Museum, for extracts from the statutes of the ferry station of San Tomà [VI.10]; and Zanichelli Editori for extracts from the volumes of the Diaries of Girolamo Priuli which were published in the new edition of *Rerum Italicarum Scriptores* [III.2(c), III.6(c), IV.12]. Permission has been sought from *La Bibliofilia* for an extract from the business records of Aldus Manutius and Andrea di Asola [IX.13] first published by E. Pastorello in that journal in 1965; from the Fondazione Cini, Venice and the Istituto di Collaborazione Culturale, Rome for extracts from the account book of Lorenzo Lotto [X.8, 9, 21, 22] first published by P. Zampetti in 1969; from Casa Editrice Dott. Antonio Giuffré for an extract from Domenico Morosini's *De Bene Instituta Republica*, edited by C. Finzi in 1969 [II.13]; and from Marsilio Editori for documents on the history of plague [III.4(a), 5(a)] first published in *Venezia e la peste, 1348–1797* in 1979.   D. C., B. P.

List of Abbreviations

ACPV	Archivio della Curia Patriarcale, Venice
ASF	Archivio di Stato, Florence
ASGG	Archivio della Scuola di San Giorgio dei Greci, Venice
ASMn.	Archivio di Stato, Mantua
ASV	Archivio di Stato, Venice
ASVat.	Archivio Segreto del Vaticano
b., bb.	busta, buste
BCV	Biblioteca Correr, Venice
BL	British Library, London
BMV	Biblioteca Marciana, Venice
BN	Bibliothèque Nationale, Paris
cap.	capitulare
cart.	cartella
cl.	classe
DBI	*Dizionario biografico degli italiani*
DMS	*I diarii di Marino Sanuto*, ed. R. Fulin et al., 58 vols, Venice, 1879–1903
DN	Dispacci del nunzio a Venezia alla Segreteria di Stato
DNB	*Dictionary of National Biography*
fasc.	fascicolo
HC	*Hierarchia Catholica Medii et Recentioris Aevi*, ed. C. Eubel et al., 6 vols, Münster and Padua, 1898–1958 (reference is to vols II–III, 1901–11)
IRE	[Archivio degli] Istituti di Ricovero e di Educazione, Venice
NV	*Nunziature di Venezia*, ed. F. Gaeta et al., Rome, 1958–
PRO	Public Record Office, London
Prov. Div.	Provenienze Diverse
reg.	registro
RIS	Rerum Italicarum Scriptores
SP	State Papers

List of Contributors

J. G. B.   James G. Ball, PhD in history, The Warburg Institute, University of London
J. B.   Jane Berdes, DPhil. in musicology, Wolfson College, Oxford
G. B.   George Bull, Director of the Anglo-Japanese Economic Institute; Editor of *International Minds*; translator of Renaissance texts.
D. C.   David Chambers, Reader in Renaissance Studies, The Warburg Institute, University of London
P. C.   Paul Chavasse, graduate in Litterae Humaniores, University of Oxford
R. C.   Ruth Chavasse, Lecturer in Ecclesiastical History, King's College, University of London
C. H. C.   Cecil H. Clough, Reader in Medieval History, University of Liverpool
M. C.   Madeleine Constable, formerly Senior Lecturer in Italian Studies, University of Exeter
A. C.   Alexander Cowan, Senior Lecturer in the Department of Historical and Critical Studies, Newcastle upon Tyne Polytechnic
N. D.   Nicholas Davidson, Lecturer in History, University of Leicester
S. G. D.   Sarah Georgia Davidson, Divisional Director of Laura Ashley Ltd.; graduate in history, University of Manchester
I. F.   Iain Fenlon, Fellow of King's College, Cambridge, and University Lecturer in Music
J. F.   Jennifer Fletcher, Senior Lecturer, The Courtauld Institute of Art, University of London; Slade Professor of Fine Art, University of Oxford, 1991
R. G.   Richard Goy, architect; PhD in history of architecture, University College, London
C. H.   Charles Hope, Lecturer in Renaissance Studies, The Warburg Institute, University of London
J. L.   John Law, Senior Lecturer in History, University College, Swansea
O. L.   Oliver Logan, Lecturer in European History, University of East Anglia, Norwich
M. L.   Martin Lowry, Senior Lecturer in History, University of Warwick, Coventry

R. M. Richard Mackenney, Senior Lecturer in History, University of Edinburgh

R. C. M. Reinhold C. Mueller, Associate Professor of History, University of Venice

R. P. Richard Palmer, formerly Curator of Western Manuscripts, The Wellcome Institute for the History of Medicine, London; now Librarian and Archivist, Lambeth Palace Library

V. P. Victoria Primhak, Ph.D. in history, The Warburg Institute, University of London

B. P. Brian Pullan, Professor of Modern History, University of Manchester

L. D. S. Lidia D. Sciama, MA in English literature, Cornell University, and MLitt. in social anthropology, University of Oxford

M. N. S. Mary Neff Sebastian, PhD in history, University of California at Los Angeles

D. T. Dora Thornton, Assistant Keeper, Department of Medieval and Later Antiquities, British Museum

S. C. W. Susan Connell Wallington, formerly Lecturer in the History of Art, University of Essex

List of illustrations

Part I
General Descriptions

Pilgrims believe with little evidence

*T*HE 'CITY LAUDATION', a long-established genre of writing, with classical antecedents, flourished in fifteenth-century Italy. Venice lent itself well to promotional descriptions of this sort, but also inspired the praises of pious pilgrims and other impressionable travellers. It was celebrated as a miraculous city, not only because of its unique setting in water, but also because it claimed to be a holy place, under St Mark's special protection, and served, incidentally, as the port of passage for those going to Jerusalem. Pilgrims' accounts tend to be over-credulous, though some also display an eye for mundane particulars [e.g. I.2]. But pride of place has been given here to the more secular description [I.1] by the Venetian patrician Marin Sanudo (1466–1536), written in 1493 and slightly revised thereafter, part of a compilation which includes an essay on the origin of Venice, a description of its government, and pieces on miscellaneous other matters. It only survives in a later sixteenth-century copy, and the text long remained unpublished. In a tone of confident superiority, Sanudo rehearses some of the themes which modern historians have labelled 'the myth of Venice'. He virtually provides a literary equivalent to Jacopo de'Barbari's great panoramic view of the city printed in 1500 [see IX.12] and includes in his description a great number of the subjects to be explored more specifically elsewhere in this anthology; it therefore serves excellently as an introduction. It can also be read as a prototype for the historico-topographical guidebook (1581) of that prolific writer Francesco Sansovino (1521–83), son of the sculptor Jacopo Sansovino, who came to Venice in 1527. He is quoted here [I.3] on the practicalities of house-building, drainage, water supply and interior furnishing in Venice.

In contrast with these somewhat ecstatic descriptions are the observations of two foreign ambassadors from the early seventeenth century. The informative if incoherent report in the form of notes by Sir Dudley Carleton, James I's ambassador 1610–16, describes [I.4] a Venice less congenial than it appeared to his better-known predecessor and successor in that post, the antiquarian Sir Henry Wotton. If he did not subscribe here to the puritanical view of Venice as 'a foul stinking sink' of licence and immorality, as it was described by a visitor in 1589 (Wood 1940, pp. 12–13), Carleton was convinced that he was a witness to the degeneracy of the city and the decay of a once-great power. On the other hand, Spain's contemporary ambassador (1607–18) Don Alonso della Cueva,

Marquis of Bedmar, stressed less the internal weaknesses of Venice than its enduring external strength, and part of his account of the city's dominions – not wholly reliable on statistical detail – is included [I.5] as a reminder that Venice had a much wider significance than as just the lagoon metropolis. Bedmar was implicated in the mysterious conspiracy of May 1618 to submit Venice to Spanish rule, by means of a Spanish–Neapolitan naval invasion, and – drawing upon a network of secret agents and informers, some of them noble, from both Venice and the mainland – he may have wished to exaggerate the value of the prize seemingly there for the taking.

BIBLIOGRAPHY *On Sanudo: Sanudo ed. Fulin et al. 1879, i.e.* DMS i *(preface); Sanudo ed. Aricò 1980; Cozzi 1970b; Chambers 1977; Sheard 1977; Finlay 1980. On pilgrims' accounts: Faber ed. Hassler 1843–9; Wey 1850; Newett 1907; Momigliano-Lepschy 1966. On saints' cults: Tramontin et al. 1965. On Francesco Sansovino: Grendler 1969a. On building and physical conditions relating to it: Cessi and Alberti 1934; Howard 1976; MacAndrew 1980; Concina 1989. On Wotton and Carleton:* DNB; *Smith 1907; Lee 1966–7, 1972. On Bedmar: Chiarelli 1925. On the Spanish conspiracy: Raulich 1893; H. F. Brown 1907; Coniglio 1953.* D. C.

1 PRAISE OF THE CITY OF VENICE, 1493

Marin Sanudo, *Laus urbis Venetae*: BCV ms. Cicogna 969, ff. 8v–19r (Sanudo ed. Fulin 1880, pp. 28–66; Sanudo ed. Aricò 1980, pp. 20–39).

This city of Venice is a free city, a common home to all men, and it has never been subjugated by anyone, as have been all other cities. It was built by Christians, not voluntarily but out of fear, not by deliberate decision but from necessity. Moreover it was founded not by shepherds as Rome was, but by powerful and rich people, such as have ever been since that time, with their faith in Christ, an obstacle to barbarians and attackers. And, having described its origin, with God's grace I will describe its site and things worthy of record.

This city, amidst the billowing waves of the sea, stands on the crest of the main, almost like a queen restraining its force. It is situated in salt water and built there, because before there were just lagoons, and then, wanting to expand, firm ground was needed for the building of palaces and houses. These are being constructed all the time; they are built above the water by a very ingenious method of driving piles, so that the foundations are in water. Every day the tide rises and falls, but the city remains dry. At times of very low tides, it is difficult to go by boat to wherever one wants. The city is about 7 miles in circumference; it has no surrounding walls, no gates which are locked at night, no sentry keeping watch as other cities have for fear of enemies; it is so very safe at present, that no one can attack or frighten it. As another writer has said, its

name has achieved such dignity and renown that it is fair to say Venice merits
the title 'Pillar of Italy', 'deservedly it may be called the bosom of all
Christendom'. For it takes pride of place before all others, if I may say so, in
prudence, fortitude, magnificence, benignity and clemency; everyone throughout the world testifies to this. To conclude, this city was built more by divine
than human will. But enough of these preliminary matters: let us turn to the
main subject.

It is, then, a very big and beautiful city, excelling over all others, with houses
and piazze founded upon salt water, and it has a Grand Canal. You can go by
galley from a place called Lido (where there are two fortresses at the port of
Venice; it is about 2 miles away) to St Mark's; from there the Grand Canal,
which is very wide indeed, takes you as far as Santa Chiara, which is almost
where the city begins. And I have seen a galley going up the Canal. On either
side there are houses of patricians and others; they are very beautiful, costing
from 20,000 ducats downwards; as an example I give the palace belonging to
the magnificent Messer Zorzi Corner, most worshipful knight and brother of
the Queen of Cyprus;[1] he bought it in our time for 20,000 ducats. Another one
of great value is the house which formerly belonged to our late most serene
Prince, Francesco Foscari,[2] and now belongs to his heirs. There are many
others, which it would take too long to record; I would say there are more than
[. . .][3] worth upwards of 10,000 ducats, and the rest decreasing in value
between 10,000 and 3000 ducats; there are also a few, but very few, of less
value, which are being rebuilt. And the houses which overlook the said canal are
much sought after, and are valued more highly than the others, particularly
those near Rialto or St Mark's. Property is more valuable in one neighbourhood
than another if it is near to the Piazza. It must be understood that these houses,
or indeed palaces, are built in our particular way, in three or four lofty and
beautiful storeys, on each of which a household can reside very comfortably,
because there are living-rooms, reception rooms and all other amenities. Land
is very expensive, and is worth a great deal of money. There is an infinite
number of houses valued at upwards of 800 ducats, with rooms having gilded
ceilings, staircases of white marble, balconies and windows all fitted with glass.
There are so many glass windows that the glaziers are continually fitting and
making them (they are manufactured at Murano as I will tell below); in every
district there is a glazier's shop. Many of these houses are rented out to whoever

[1] Caterina Corner, widow of James de Lusignan; in 1489 she resigned the kingdom to Venice
and received as compensation the fief of Asolo (near Treviso), scene of Pietro Bembo's Platonic
dialogue *The Asolani*. See also below, VI.1(d).

[2] Doge, 1423–57, associated with the westward expansion of Venetian power in the Milanese
wars [see II.14(a)].

[3] A blank in Sanudo's own text. Such blanks are quite common in his compilations; he evidently
neglected to check and fill them in later.

5

wants them, from one year to a maximum of five years (because by law there can be no leases for a longer period than this) and they are rented out to present-day patricians, some for 100, some for 120 and more ducats a year. These houses, I emphasize, are only for longer terms of residence or occupation; I exclude the others, not available for long tenancy, which are rented out in great number. Almost all the houses, and especially those of a high value (because, as well as on the Grand Canal, there are many beautiful houses in every parish) have a watergate and also a land entrance; for there are innumerable waterways called *rii* which lead out of the Grand Canal and pass through different neighbourhoods. Above them are bridges; in olden times these were made of wood, but now they are being rebuilt in stone. There is also a very large wooden bridge over the Grand Canal; it is very high, strong and wide, and crosses the Canal at Rialto, as I shall describe later.

There are two ways of getting about in Venice: by foot, on the dry land, and by boat. Certain boats are made pitch black and beautiful in shape; they are rowed by Saracen negroes or other servants who know how to row them. Mostly they are rowed with one oar, though Venetian patricians and senators and ladies are usually rowed with two oars. In summer the cabins have a high covering to keep off the sun, and a broad one in winter to keep off the rain; the high ones are of satin, and the low sort green or purple. These small boats are dismantled at night because they are finely wrought and each one is tied up at its mooring. There is such an infinite number of them that they cannot be counted; no one knows the total. On the Grand Canal and in the *rii* one sees such a continual movement of boats that in a way it is a marvel. There is easily room on them for four people, comfortably seated within. The basic cost of one of these boats is 15 ducats, but ornaments are always required, either dolphins or other things, so that it is a great expense, costing more than a horse. The servants, if they are not slaves, have to be paid a wage, usually one ducat with expenses, so that, adding it all up, the cost is very high. And there is no gentleman or citizen who does not have one or two or even more boats in the family, according to household, etc.

The population of the city, according to a census which was made, is about 150,000 souls.[4] There are three classes of inhabitants: gentlemen [nobles] who govern the state and republic, whose families will be mentioned below; citizens; and artisans or the lower class. The gentlemen are not distinguished from the citizens by their clothes, because they all dress in much the same way, except for the senatorial office-holders, who during their term of office have to wear

[4] This round figure is certainly inflated as a total: on the basis of incomplete but more detailed figures recorded also by Sanudo, the population in 1509 has been estimated at about 102,000 excluding the clergy and religious orders. The highest figure recorded under any year up to 1630 is 168,627 in 1563 (Beloch 1961, pp. 5–13).

6

the coloured robes laid down by law. The others almost always wear long black robes reaching down to the ground, with sleeves open to the elbows, a black cap on the head and a hood of black cloth or velvet. Formerly they wore very large hoods, but these have gone out of fashion. They wear trimmings of four sorts – marten, weasel, fox or even sable – which are worn a lot in winter; also skins and furs of vair and sendal. Soled stockings and clogs are worn in all weathers, silk [under]shirts and hose of black cloth; to conclude, they wear black a lot. And when they are in mourning for a dead relative, they wear shoes and a long gown with a hood over the shoulders, but only for a few days before they change back. They also grow beards for some time: three years for the father, two years for the mother, one year for a brother, etc. The majority are merchants and all go to do business on Rialto, as I shall write below. The women are truly very beautiful; they go about with great pomp, adorned with big jewels and finery. And, when some grand lady comes to see Venice, 130 or more ladies go to meet her, adorned with jewels of enormous value and cost, necklaces worth from 300 up to 1000 ducats, and rings on their fingers set with large rubies [*balassi*], diamonds, rubies, sapphires, emeralds and other jewels of great value. There are very few patrician women (and none, shall I say, so wretched and poor) who do not have 500 ducats worth of rings on their fingers, not counting the enormous pearls, which must be seen to be believed. And there are more than 100 of such precious necklaces in the city, as I have said. These ladies of ours during their maidenhood wear veils and long tresses; then they wear a black cape. For the most part they wear silk, and formerly they wore gold cloth, but on account of a decree passed in the Senate they now cannot do so. And, if it were not for the provisions drawn up by the most serene Signoria with regard to their tastes and desires in adornment with jewels and other things, and the regulations enacted, they would be very extravagant. When ladies meet each other (excepting the Doge's wife and daughters, the wives of knights and doctors of learning) precedence is by age, and the same applies to the patricians. They do not uncover their heads except to the Prince, although they exchange polite salutations. At present a much-used form of address to any gentleman in the city is 'Magnificence', and all of them are addressed as 'Missier'. I wanted to write this down because usages vary from city to city and it is sometimes useful to know these things.

Venice is divided into six sestieri [i.e. six districts]: three on one side of the Canal, and three on the other. . . . On the near side, their names are Castello, St Mark's and Canareggio; on the other side are Santa Croce, San Polo and Dorsoduro. I will begin with the first-named, Castello, and write what seems to be worth recording about it.

Castello is the smallest sestier of Venice. It begins where the seat of the Patriarch is, the cathedral church, founded in the time of Doge Maurizio [Galbaio (764–87)], with the acclamation of clergy and people and confirmed by the privilege of the Roman pontiff Adrian.[5] There our most reverend pontiff resides with his canons. There is a beautiful, large church; it has a bell tower covered with white marble and is called San Piero. It is on an island which is linked to Venice by a long wooden bridge. Approaching it by boat, you see the embankment close by, as one can go from St Mark's as far as Castello by a paved embankment overlooking the Canal, where the port is. Many ships are repaired there and new ones built, of immeasurable size. Not being a seafaring man myself, I will leave the job of writing about them to others, though I do know that there are some ships called state ships [*di Commun*] for heavy cargoes. The Arsenal is in this district, and I shall later write what occurs to me about it. In this district there are eleven parish churches named below, not counting monasteries and convents and other religious houses with churches.

St Mark's is the second sestier. It has a very beautiful and rich church, all covered with mosaics representing histories. It is paved with most beautiful stones, and fashioned and inlaid throughout with marble, which is a worthy thing to see. This is the principal church of Venice. It has a chief priest [*primicerius*] (who wears a mitre and carries a pastoral staff) and twenty-four canons.[6] Three Procurators, who are among the foremost patricians of the city,[7] are in charge of it. Every day many masses and religious offices are celebrated. The Doge with the Signoria and the Senate go there to hear divine service. There is a place where jewels are kept, which one can only call the jewel house of the Signoria of Venice; I will not enlarge on this, because the jewels are very well known and of infinite value. The Procurators have custody over them and they are shown to visiting lords or ambassadors, and on the eve and feast day of the Ascension and the eve and feast day of St Mark some of them are displayed for ornament upon the altar of St Mark's. These jewels were stolen in 1449 by a Greek called Stamati, and by God's will they were retrieved without having been damaged at all. Here, at St Mark's, there are two very large piazze, paved all over. Overlooking one of them at one end is the church of St Mark, with its splendid façade, and those four gilded bronze horses brought to this city from Constantinople – a very famous work of art, made in Greece and taken from there first to Rome, then to Constantinople by the Emperor Constantine, thence here; and at the other end of the Piazza is the church of San Gimignano. Beyond this in a small piazza is also the church of San Basso. The other piazza [i.e. the Piazzetta] is near the place where justice is meted out to all and the [law] officers hold session; it leads to the Grand Canal, where, at the mooring-place, there are two very high columns mounted upon several steps. On the top of one [column] is St Theodore and on the other St Mark. In the space between

[5] The bishopric was allegedly founded *c.*774–7 on the island of Olivolo, when Adrian I (772–95) was Pope (Romanin 1853–61, I, 131).

[6] See below, V.3.

[7] See below, II.4.

them judicial sentences are carried out on all robbers, traitors or others, being burnt, hanged or otherwise according to the crime. Here overlooking the Piazza stands the Mint, where ducats and other coins are minted; it is hard at work every day. Here, overlooking the Canal, are the corn warehouses, where that vast crowd of Genoese prisoners were held until they were released and allowed to go free.[8] Then, further back, is the Campanile, a marvellous work with its height, like a tall tower; you go up it by many winding stairs. It was built in 1145 or, according to others, in 1148. Here are the bells which are heard all over the city and also many miles away. In the evening the *marangona* sounds, meaning that all workers can go home at the end of the day; then at one hour after sunset the first bell rings, at one and a half hours the second rings, and at two hours the third; then midnight. And in the morning the *marangona* rings for the start of work, then half way to the third hour, at the third, and at the ninth hours, the *campana*, and the vesper bell. And when there is to be a meeting of the Great Council the bell rings. Enough about this. Overlooking the nearby Piazza [of St Mark] are the Procurators' offices, where there are many ducats deposited of the trust funds administered by the nine [Procurators], foremost among the city's patricians; these offices have recently been rebuilt; then come the houses of the Procurators. It should be noted that the Campanile of St Mark formerly had a gilded top, and in the evening of [. . .] August 1483 a thunderbolt burnt it, and at the same time [another one] hit the bell tower of the Friars Minor [Frari], which was shattered.

Leaving the Piazza, you go towards Rialto by a street called Merceria, with shops on each side. Here is all the merchandise that you can think of, and whatever you ask for is there. And when it is decorated – because all [visiting] lords want to see it – it is one of the finest streets in Venice. Thus you proceed towards the Rialto Bridge, which was first erected in 1458 and completed in May in the form it now has[9] with shops upon it, which because of their good position are with chains, so that it can be raised and thus divide Venice into two parts. And always when a great lord visits the city the state barge [*bucintoro*] with the Prince and Signoria passes through it, because for the most part they lodge in the house of the Duke of Ferrara,[10] which overlooks the Grand Canal in the neighbourhood of San Giacomo dell'Orio; because they must pass by this bridge, it is raised for the day. The present bridge is of wood and was built and completed on 11 July 1472, having been begun on 6 September 1471. That it took so long to build is a sign that it is a very great work. Near this bridge and overlooking the Grand Canal is the exchange house [*Fondaco*] of the German

[8] 4670 Genoese prisoners were said to have been taken at the relief of Chioggia in June 1380. (Romanin 1853–61, III, 292).

[9] The works in 1458 were only a repair operation to the wooden Rialto Bridge. By 1499 its state was again considered dangerous (Cessi and Alberti 1934, pp. 169, 171).

[10] Eventually the Fondaco dei Turchi [see below, VIII.15].

merchants, where the Germans live and carry on their business.[11] There are brokers appointed for this, and only they can deal with the Germans; and there are three patricians there who draw the money as we shall explain below. They pay 100 gold ducats a month in rent, from which can be understood the prominent position and the size and convenience of the place, being in the middle of Rialto. In this sestier there are sixteen parishes.

Canareggio is the third sestier, and has one of the largest *rii* of the city running through it. It begins at the church of San Gieremia, which overlooks the Grand Canal, and goes towards San Giobbe, thence towards Marghera on the mainland 5 miles away. On both sides of the said *rio* there are beautiful houses and pavements, so that on one side one can walk to where Canareggio begins. The said Canareggio is, as its name suggests, almost a regal canal; and it has a very high bridge, made only of wood, across it. In this sestier there is the newly built church of Santa Maria Nuova, on account of a very ancient Madonna that was on the street there and wrought miracles. And there are so may miracles daily that it is incredible to see all the silver and *ex voto*s there and the throng of people, who have masses said there every day. Here, less than five years ago, the very beautiful church was built from voluntary offerings.[12] It is inlaid with marbles, worked in the ancient manner, with porphyry and serpentine and roofed with lead. There is also a convent of religious ladies of the Franciscan Order, drawn from the Clares' convent at Murano, and they are never seen. These ladies sing divine offices and live off the alms they are given, in thanksgiving for the said miracles which the Virgin Mary works there. And there are thirteen parish churches in the said sestier, excluding the houses of friars and nuns which will be described in the right place.

On the other side of the Grand Canal there are three sestieri to which you can cross by small ferries, and the fare is a small coin [*bagattino*]. Each will be listed below.[13]

Santa Croce, on the other side of the Canal, is the fourth sestier. It contains the church of Santa Croce, where there are priests and an adjacent convent of nuns; in this church there are perpetual indulgences for the souls of the dead. There are ten parish churches in the said [sestier], and it is not only confined to the further part of the Canal, but also spans it, for part of the parish of Santa Lucia is in the Santa Croce sestier. And Murano, which is an island separate from Venice, is counted as part of Santa Croce.

San Polo, the fifth sestier, is so called after the name of the church there, which has a very big, wide and beautiful *campo* where on Wednesday mornings a

[11] See below, VIII.1–3.

[12] Santa Maria dei Miracoli, built 1481–9, the work mainly of Pietro and Antonio Lombardo.

[13] Here, as at other points in the description, Sanudo refers to his many miscellaneous lists, which are copied in a companion manuscript: BCV ms. Cicogna 970 (Sanudo ed. Aricò 1980; on ferries see pp. 49–55). On *bagattini* see VIII.11, n. 10.

market is held, selling everything you could want. Because it is held so frequently, it is not much esteemed by us; it would be quite otherwise in any other city or village were such a beautiful and rich fair held even once a year. On Saturdays there is also a market on St Mark's Piazza, which is much finer than this one. In this sestier is the island of Rialto, which I would venture to call the richest place in the whole world. First of all, overlooking the Canal, is the grain warehouse, large and well stocked, with two doorways and many booths; there are two lords appointed to supervise it, as I shall relate below. Then you come to Riva del Ferro, so called because iron is sold there; where it ends at the Rialto Bridge is the public weighhouse, where all the merchandise for sale has to be weighed, and the reckonings are made of customs and excise duty. Here is the Rialto itself, which is a piazzetta, not very large at all, where everyone goes both morning and afternoon. Here business deals are made with a single word 'yes' or 'no'. There are a large number of brokers, who are trustworthy; if not, they are reprimanded. There are four banks: the Pisani and Lippomani, both patricians, and the Garzoni and Augustini, citizens.[14] They hold very great amounts of money, issue credits under different names, and are called authorized bankers [banchieri creti]; their decisions are binding. They have charge of the moneys of the Camerlenghi.[15] Furthermore, throughout the said island of Rialto there are storehouses, both on ground level and above, filled with goods of very great value; it would be a marvellous thing were it possible to see everything at once, in spite of the fact that much is being sold all the time. Every year goods come in from both east and west, where galleys are sent on commission from the Signoria; they are put in the charge of whoever wants this [responsibility], provided he is a patrician, by public auction. It should be noted that the Venetians, just as they were merchants in the beginning, continue to trade every year; they send galleys to Flanders, the Barbary Coast, Beirut, Alexandria, the Greek lands and Aigues-Mortes. All the galley [fleets] have a captain elected by the Great Council, and the Signoria appoints the galley patrons by auction at Rialto, i.e. according to whoever bids highest for the galleys. Thus we have the galleys for these voyages built at the Arsenal, and then, at the time of sending them forth, according to the Senate's orders, they are auctioned at Rialto. For some of these galleys 3000 ducats and more is paid, and for others only 1 ducat, according to different times and the particular voyage. And in order that galley masters should be found, sometimes the Signoria itself pays those willing to accept a galley. And when, to take an example, there are three galleys, and two of them have found a galley master for

[14] See Lane 1966, esp. pp. 71–80 concerning the failure of the Garzoni in 1499–1500 and of the Agostini (sic) in 1508.
[15] The two Camerlenghi di Comun or Treasurers of the Republic were elected for a sixteen-month term, with senatorial rank (Sanudo ed. Aricò 1980, pp. 110–11, 247–8).

more than a thousand ducats each, then the third is given for only 1 ducat; it is laid down that, if no one bids more, it is given [for this sum]. And then the said galley masters present their sponsors at the office of the Avogadori di Comun[16] and are voted upon in the Senate: that is, whether they are suitable and have invested their full shares. Then their appointments stand, and at once they start business, the captain having been elected. If it seems to the Senate that they are not suitable, and they fall in the voting, a new auction is held at their expense. Noble patricians are put in charge of the said long-distance galleys, called great galleys, after election for each galley by ballot in the Council of the Criminal Court of the Forty[17] from the list of all who want their names to go forward, provided they are over the age of eighteen. They are impoverished gentlemen; there are eight of them to each galley every year. They are paid by the galley master, some more, some less, according to the [particular] voyage, before the fleet departs. They go with the galleys, have their expenses and their cabins (which they rent) and their pay; they are called galley nobles. In addition every ship of 400 to 600 botte capacity takes one of them, and those above 600 take two; every narrow galley usually has two patricians [on board]. This rule was laid down by our revered ancestors, to the end that those who cannot hold offices or governorships, and are without incomes and unable to practise any skilled art, should have this income of 60 ducats and more a year from St Mark, if they remain in this service of bowmanship [*ballestraria*]. And the said *ballestrarie* can be sold, and other patricians sent, provided the place is filled. Enough on this subject. These galleys go on long-distance voyages, they carry merchandise which they exchange and then bring back other goods, and they are hired for both the outward and return journeys; they have their special judges called the Office of the Ten Offices.[18]

On the island of Rialto, these stores and warehouses, of which there are such a great number, pay rent for the most part to [the Procurators of] St Mark's; a high rent is paid for every small piece of space on Rialto, not only for these properties, but for those belonging to various private persons who rent out shops. Such a shop at Rialto may cost about 100 ducats in rent and be scarcely two paces wide or long. Property here is very expensive. Our own family, the Sanudi, can bear witness to this, having an inn called the Bell at the New Fishmarket [*Pescharia Nuova*]. The ground floor is all let out as shops; it is a small place, but from this one building we get about 800 ducats a year in rent, which is a marvellous thing and a huge rent. This is because it is on such a good site; the inn itself brings in 250 ducats, more than the foremost palace in the

---

[16] See below, II.5.

[17] See below, II.6.

[18] Sanudo ed. Aricò 1980, pp. 112, 149. These were three patrician officials, who held office for sixteen months.

city; I daresay it is the best property of its sort in Venice. On Rialto, moreover, are all the skilled crafts; they have their separate streets, as I shall write below.[19]

Here, on the Canal, there are embankments where on one side there are barges for timber, and on the other side for wine; they are rented as though they were shops. There is a very large butchery, which is full every day of good meat, and there is another one at St Mark's. The Fishmarket overlooks the Grand Canal; here are the most beautiful fish, high in price and of good quality. The fish are caught in the Adriatic sea by fishermen, for there is a neighbourhood in Venice called San Niccolò where only fishermen live, and they speak an ancient Venetian dialect called *nicoloto*. It is remarkable to see, that they live in Venice and speak the way they do. Also from various other places, such as Murano, Burano, Torcello, and Chioggia too, fishermen come with their fish to sell it here in the Fishmarket. The names of the fish which are caught and brought here will be listed below.[20] There are also oysters in very large quantities. They bring as much fish here as can be sold in a day and in the evening none is left, the cause of it being that everyone spends, and every one lives like lords. And in this city nothing grows, yet whatever you want can be found in abundance. And this is because of the great turnover in merchandise; everything comes here, especially things to eat, from every city and every part of the world, and money is made quickly. This is because everyone is well-off for money. Here at Rialto it is like a vegetable garden, so much green stuff is brought from nearby places, and such varieties of fruits are on sale, and so cheap, that it is marvellous. But I shall just repeat what I heard from somebody else, who said 'where business is good, good stuff can be had.' And on Rialto the prices of some things are controlled, so that those who buy are not cheated. Mutton, sold at the butchery, cannot be sold for more than 3 soldi a pound, and if short weight is given the butchers are penalized by the lords in charge of them, because there are officials who weigh the meat which has been sold; the fixed price for lamb is [. . .] soldi, for veal [. . .] soldi, for kid goat [. . .] soldi. Item: oil is fixed at 4 soldi to the pound weight, candles at 4 soldi a pound; a barber's charge for hairdressing is the standard 4 soldi; a cartload of wood at all times cannot be more than 28 soldi, and there are loading-officials of the commune so that justice is done fairly to everyone. And for other goods the saying is 'right weight and high price'. Other comestibles are sold as they want, but the Giustizia Vecchia,[21] who are lords with special responsibility, are free to fix a just price on things to eat. Thus the city is governed as well as any city in the world has ever been; everything is well ordered, and this is why the city has survived and grown. Here on Rialto, beneath several inns, is the public brothel[22] of the city, where

[19] Sanudo ed. Aricò 1980, p. 172.
[20] Sanudo ed. Aricò 1980, p. 172.
[21] Sanudo ed. Aricò, pp. 136–7, 266–7.
[22] See below, III.6(a).

the prostitutes are, although there are more in various other places: at St Mark's, San Luca and San Cassano in Carampane; there are brothels to some extent in a number of different neighbourhoods, but as they are not the ones I am describing I will write no more.

On this island of Rialto, near to the church of St John the Evangelist, where there is the relic of the wood of Christ's most holy Cross, there is a bell tower where instead of a bell that is rung [by being pulled] there are two male figures bearing hammers who alternately strike a bell, by a system of counterweights; in this manner, the hours strike, which is a beautiful thing to see.[23] Here lectures are given in philosophy and theology, both in the mornings and afternoons, to whoever wants to go and listen; they are paid for from the funds of St Mark's. At present the lecturer is our own patrician Antonio Corner, a most excellent philosopher, whose fame in various fields of learning is celebrated.[24] Every day he endures a very great burden in the large number of lectures he gives in logic, philosophy and theology, on which account he has been honoured by the Senate with a considerable number of magistracies and offices. This worthy institution the Venetians wanted to have in their city so that whoever wants to acquire the virtues of learning and make himself very scholarly could do so here at Venice without going to study at Padua, where there is such an excellent university, full of scholars from all over the world, maintained at great expense to our Signoria.[25] For those wanting to become doctors, there is a college of physicians at San Luca, and they have authority to confer doctorates in medicine.[26] Also at St Mark's near to the Campanile, there are two very learned humanists who are paid by St Mark's, who give public lectures to whoever wants to hear them without paying any fee. They are men of great fame; at present one of them is Giorgio Valla from Piacenza,[27] a very good grammarian and perfect in Greek, who has translated many works and also written some himself; the other is Marcantonio Sabellico, a great man of letters, who wrote the *Ten Books on Venice*,[28] a great, worthy and copious work; he also lectures. And there is another government stipendiary who gives lectures to the notaries of the Chancery, so that they may become learned; his name is Benedetto

[23] See below, X.2(g).

[24] Antonio Corner (*c*.1445–*c*.1500) was also politically active, serving in the Zonta of the Senate 1493–5; after his appointment as a Provveditore of the Salt Office (1498) he seems to have stopped lecturing (*DBI*).

[25] See Arnaldi and Stocchi 1981–3, III; and below, headnote preceding IX.1.

[26] This body, which did not provide organized teaching, received a privilege to grant degrees from the Emperor Frederick III when he visited Venice in 1469 (Palmer 1983).

[27] See below, III.2(a).

[28] Marcantonio Coccio, known as Sabellicus (*c*.1436–1502), had written on the model of Livy his *Rerum venetarum ab urbe condita*, Venice 1487 [see below, IX.2, 9]. Sanudo omits to mention Sabellicus's *De venetis magistratibus* (1488) and *De venetae urbis situ et vetustate* (1492), to which his own work is a sort of vernacular response.

Brognolo from Legnago, a very learned man, well grounded in learning.[29] There are also teachers in various neighbourhoods, not counting those in private houses, who teach moral philosophy and grammar to patricians' children and others. Here in the said sestier are nine parish churches, not counting monastic houses, and there are no nuns, i.e. convents of nuns, in this district. I have described all the above matters for two reasons: first, that they may be remembered for all time; and, second, to inform those who have not seen our city of Venice. Although there might be many writers, it would not be possible for them to tell everything about the said city and its site.

Dorsoduro is the sixth sestier. Its name is very ancient and it was one of the first islands of Venice to be inhabited, as I have said above. It has eleven parishes, not to mention the monks and friars. Included in this sestier is the Giudecca, which is a part of Venice separated by half a mile on an island where there are very beautiful palaces, churches and monasteries. It is long and not very wide, and has a paved way on the waterfront, so that you can go from one end to the other, i.e. from St John the Baptist's church to San Biagio Catoldo [in Castello], a nunnery. There are various *rii* with bridges over them; you go to and from by ferryboats as I shall tell below.[30] At the beginning of the sestier there is a place called the Punta, opposite St Mark's; here is the overseas customs office, where there are very large warehouses. All galleys, roundships and other types of vessel unload into these warehouses all their merchandise, with the exception of wine, which goes to the control point to be assessed for duty, and salt, which goes to its own warehouses, and corn, which is unloaded in other warehouses of the merchants' choice. If any ship does not unload its goods, the penalty is very severe. These regulations have been made by our government so that the payment of duties shall not be avoided by deception; there are special officials in charge.

This must suffice as a brief description of the sestieri. There are many churches served by priests here in Venice, and religious houses for monks and nuns. The parish priests are elected by the parishioners by ballot, i.e. by those who have property in the parish, and then the election is reported to Rome and confirmed by the Pope. The appointment is for life and the superior authority is the most reverend Patriarch. At the present time this is Thomaso Donato, a Dominican friar or preacher. He was elected by the Senate and confirmed by His Holiness the Pope in place of Maffio Girardi, Patriarch and Cardinal of the Roman Church with the title of St Sergius and Bacchus, who died of old age on the way from Rome, he being exceedingly old.[31] And it has always been the

---

[29] Benedetto Brugnuli (1427–1502) had been teaching in the Chancery school since 1466; he was buried with honour in the Frari (*DBI*).

[30] See below, VI.10.

[31] Maffeo Gherardi, a Camaldolese monk, Patriarch since 1468, had been the sixth incumbent

custom to appoint a patrician who is a member of a religious order; likewise in many bishoprics patricians have been appointed bishops or worthy citizens of our subject towns. Enough about that. Besides the priest in charge of a parish church, there are other priests and their assistants. The number of them varies according to the parish. One thing is common to all parishes, that in all of them a High Mass is sung every day and there are many other Masses, so that all the priests perform a Mass daily unless they are prevented from doing so by some legitimate reason. They also celebrate other offices. And the Patriarch's income is about [. . .] ducats; he has a vicar; he holds his ecclesiastical court at Castello and dispenses justice there to the clergy. He also has jurisdiction over nuns, except in the case of certain convents which have exemption from the Patriarch's jurisdiction, as do the Virgins [*Verzene*], who are under the Doge; the Celestines, who are exempt; and Santa Chiara, which is under the General of the Franciscans. The Patriarch has no authority over friars because they have their generals, but he can enforce the rule. This Patriarch can go about in a friar's habit, as the present one does, with a cross carried before him. He takes precedence over everyone except the Doge, who always goes first, whether on ceremonial occasions or not.

It only remains to mention the Ducal Palace, where our most serene Prince resides. It is at St Mark's and is a most beautiful and worthy building. First of all, [the part of] the Palace where he lives has recently been renovated, the work being finished in 1492, and the Doge has taken up residence there. It overlooks the canal called the *rio* of the Palace. The rebuilding took ten years, because the old Palace, dating from the time of Doge Giovanni Mocenigo, was burnt down in the night.[32] The present one was then begun, which has cost more than 100,000 ducats up to now. The outside walls are all worked over and inlaid with white marble and with stones from all over the world. Inside, the walls on the ground floor are all gilded and inlaid with panelling so that it is a very beautiful sight. There are four gilded chambers – I never saw any more beautiful – which took a very great time and elaborate workmanship apart from the gold and the labour. Excellent rooms are the Hall of Public Audience [Collegio] and the Hall of the Senate, which they are working on at present and will be very worthy. One can therefore compare the Venetians to the Romans (who raised such stately edifices) on account of the buildings, both private and public, being erected at the present time. Indeed it can be said, as another writer has done, that our republic has followed the Romans in being as powerful in military

since 1451, when the bishopric was raised to the status of a patriarchate. He died on 14 September 1492 (*HC*, II 290).

[32] 14 September 1483. It is an exaggeration to suggest that the whole Palace, as rebuilt in the 1420s, was destroyed. Sanudo refers to the east wing, redesigned by Mauro Codussi and including the Doge's apartments, into which Agostino Barbarigo moved in March 1492. He also exaggerates the cost. See Wolters 1983, pp. 19–20.

strength as in virtue and learning. He writes moreover, 'Greece was the seat of learning and powerful in arms; now the Venetians are the learned ones, now the lion is strongly armed.' Here is the very large hall of the Great Council, renovated throughout with paintings by the hand of most excellent masters, among the best and most famous painters to be found today in the whole world: the brothers Gentile and Giovanni Bellini.[33] Their works demonstrate how highly they are to be esteemed. In further proof of this, Mohammed the Ottoman, King of the Turks,[34] sent to Venice some time ago for Gentile, to commission him to do some paintings for him and paint his portrait from life, and he went there and after the Turk's death returned to Venice. And this hall is under constant renovation. On the upper part of its walls are paintings on canvas of the history of Alexander III, the Pope of Rome, and the Emperor Frederick Barbarossa who persecuted him; how he came to this city in disguise and was recognized. This was in 1177, in the time of Doge Sebastiano Ziani, who, in order to help the Pope, set out with the fleet against Otto, son of the forenamed Emperor. He found him in Istria, with a larger and more powerful fleet than ours, and at the Cape of Salbua, near Pirano, he attacked it, broke it up and brought back Otto captive to Venice. The peace was proclaimed, and Frederick himself came to Venice to beg the Pope's forgiveness, and thus at one and the same time the Pope and Emperor were in Venice. And on this occasion the Pope bestowed upon the Prince and his successors certain ceremonial dignities, which will be listed below.[35] He returned to his see of Rome, thanks to the help of the Venetians, who had for so long been waging war, but of others too as one reads in the chronicles. Here in this hall, to return to my original subject, the Great Council meets, as I shall relate below; it has a panelled ceiling all done in gold, which cost more than 10,000 ducats.

Here there are two rooms full of arms for the needs of the city; there are enough to arm a great number of persons. They are called the rooms of the Council of Ten, who have guard over them. Then, going on from here you reach the Palace where justice is administered and the offices are, situated round a central courtyard. Here sit the magistrates deputed to hear cases: you will read about them in my section on the magistrates. Then, below them, are the prisons, very strong and varying according to the prisoner's crimes. They have names, such as 'The Lion', 'The Fresh Jewel', 'The Stronghold', 'The Cramped Rooms' [cameroti], 'The Armoury', and so on. I daresay they are the

[33] Commissions to repaint the historical scenes in the Hall of the Great Council were given in 1474 to Gentile (active c.1460; d. 1507) and in 1478 to Giovanni Bellini (active c.1460; d. 1516). See Lorenzi 1868, pp. 86, 91; tr. in Chambers 1970b, pp. 79–80. These and other painters' works were destroyed in the fire of 1577. See also below, I.2; X.2(a), (e).
[34] Mohammed II the Conquerer, Sultan 1451–81; his portrait in the National Gallery, London, was painted by Gentile in Constantinople in 1479–81 (Thuasne 1888).
[35] See also below, II.3(d).

strongest prisons in Italy, and there is a captain put in charge of them with warders. There is also a prison at Rialto, but not so strong, called 'The Shack' [*caxon*] and in other neighbourhoods in the sestieri there are lock-ups or places where somebody who has been caught wrong-doing can be held overnight until the morning. And Venice has this marvellous custom, that when a malefactor has confessed his crime and deserves to be put to death, according to the sentence passed either by the Giudici di Proprio[36] or by the Councils (though excepting the Council of Ten), it is usual for everything first to be ratified in a hearing before the Prince. And on the day of execution the Prince sends the condemned person the same dinner as he is having himself; then, when the malefactors' bell sounds, the victim comes out accompanied by two friars who comfort him, and by the members of a confraternity dressed in black called San Fantin, who carry a crucifix in front of him. Executions are carried out on all except patricians; for them, there are within the Palace two pink columns between which they are executed, although it very rarely happens, except in some exceptionally serious case. For the most part they are exiled or imprisoned in various cities and strongholds of the Signoria.

At Rialto is the office of the Camerlenghi di Comun, newly built and all inlaid with white marble, worked in the shape of diamonds. Here is the treasury of St Mark; that is to say, the cash from government revenues, kept in a large number of iron chests. Our officials bring the money here every evening, and, if they fail to deliver it, or are robbed in their own offices, then they are obliged to make good the payment. But, if after it is brought here the money is stolen (which would be impossible), the expense and loss is borne by St Mark. Note that here in Rialto two non-noble [*populari*] captains are appointed who take turns to sleep here each night (each for one night at a time) with many officials; during the night some of them are always sent round on patrol with lanterns, to see that no one is breaking in or doing any damage on the said island, on account of the great wealth stored there. The same is done every night round the Piazza of St Mark, and round the Palace and the Procurators' offices.

The Arsenal is truly one of the finest sights imaginable. It covers a great area, about 20 stadii all round. It is situated in the parish of San Martino, surrounded by very handsome walls, and here great galleys for the war fleet are continually being built, with other *fuste* and *gripi*.[37] There is enough space to build a total of [. . .] galleys; there are ready wooden frames, almost completed, the total of which is [. . .], and other *fuste* and *gripe*. Almost a thousand workmen labour here every day and every skill to do with the building of galleys and other ships is to be found here. There are covered building-yards for galleys with water

[36] See below, III.1(a).

[37] Respectively smaller, lighter galleys used for patrols etc. and small merchant vessels which combined sail with oars (Lane 1934, pp. 13, 53).

surrounding them, so that they can be launched and floated. They can then leave the Arsenal and join the Grand Canal at St Mark's, whence they can be rowed by one deck of oarsmen, etc. Here there are a great number of carpenters or shipwrights for the galleys; smiths also work here, making all the iron fittings; in conclusion, whatever is required of every skill is here. There are enormous bombards and catapults of inestimable force, which no city or castle would be strong enough to withstand; recent witness to this are the [strong] places of the Duke of Ferrara, i.e. Figarolo on the Po.[38] And every bombard has its name, such as 'No More Words', 'The Lion', 'The Venetian Woman who Casts down Every Wall and Spike', 'The Little Man', and various other names. Also there are an enormous quantity of hand guns [*spingardi, schiopeti, passavolanti*] which are cast every day, and masters are paid there to cast bombards and suchlike instruments of war. There are eight rooms here all filled with armaments of every sort, and every day new supplies are being made for the defence of fortresses and for arming galleys and other ships. Altogether it is beautiful and marvellous thing to see our Arsenal so well equipped. There are women who make sails, some spinning, others in another set of rooms, sewing; others making ropes. Some do one skilled job, some another; and anyone who is willing to go and work at the Arsenal is taken on and paid at least 10 soldi a day, and this is because there is always work there. It costs our Signoria more than 10,000 ducats a year. The workers are paid every week on Saturdays. They have refreshment breaks in turn, [. . .] times a day; that is, tubs are carried round to provide everyone with a drink. There are guards in charge, and at night there are watchmen to guard against fire, principally on account of the gunpowder. Three patricians are elected by the Great Council to govern the Arsenal, and live in houses there for a term of thirty months. Nearby there is also another arsenal, called the New Arsenal, which has very beautiful and thick towers and walls; it is not yet finished. And here in the Arsenal is kept the *bucintoro*, a marvel, in which the Prince and Senate go to pay honour to any great lord visiting the city; they go to San Clemente or elsewhere, depending on the direction from which the visitor is coming. It is covered with crimson satin, and is rowed from a lower deck. In conclusion, the first master craftsman who planned it was worthy and excellent in ability, because there is no more beautiful structure afloat. It has a gilded prow of the seated figure of Justice, bearing the sword and scales, symbolizing that the Venetians administer justice to all without distinction. On the deck upwards of 200 people can be seated with comfort; sometimes, when a visiting lord comes to Venice, it is adorned with ladies. But about the Arsenal an epigram by Gregorio Typhernas comes to my mind:

[38] Sanudo refers to the successful Venetian bombardment of the fortress of Figarolo in May–June 1482, about which he had written (Sanudo ed. anon. 1829, pp. 17–19, 29).

The illustrious Senate of the Venetians founded this Arsenal.
Here the fleet and its armaments will be secure.
And you, visitor, who have travelled many coasts,
Say, in what place have you seen greater marine power?

Here in this city of Venice there is a regulation that warehouses should be stocked with grain, so that the city may not suffer any hardship. Likewise there are stores of wood, in case of need. Thus there is an abundance of everything except sometimes of fresh water. There are wells in private houses and in all the open spaces of the parishes, but they are used up in times of drought. Hence there are barges taken round full of water for sale, brought from the river Brenta at Lizza Fusina, 5 miles away on the mainland. The water is contained in large chests on the said barges, and they go round shouting 'Water! Water here!' and it is sold at eight buckets a soldo. And it is truly a joke, living in water and having to buy it; were it possible to make fountains here, I think no city in the world would equal Venice. It is conveniently and pleasantly guarded, with certain marshes at the mouths of the rivers and waterways, where places are appointed for the collection of customs duties and issue of receipts. And these are the gateways of Venice. Besides these customs posts, there are along various routes patrol boats of officials who search out smugglers, and this is done because there is no other way of guarding Venice. However, it is wonderful that there is no crime so great or deed so cruel in Venice that it does not come to light without discovery of who has done it. And this is because of the great sums that the Signoria sets on the heads of those who commit some wrong, and it is known if more than one person has been involved. Not only are there rewards fixed for delivering the wanted person alive to the Signoria, but also for delivering him dead, or for killing him on the spot, they can claim the reward from the funds of St Mark.

Here around the city of Venice are the following notable rivers: the Brenta, going to Padua; the Sil, going to Treviso; the mouths of the Po, going to Ferrara, and the Adige, going to Verona, so that it is very convenient for everyone. And the district of Venice is as follows: between Grado and Cavarzere, between which boundaries are the following places: Grado, Caorle, Iesolo, Citta Nuova, Lido Pizolo, Lido Mazor, Lido di Pigneda, Lido di San Nicolò, Malamocho, Torcello, Burano, Mazorbo, Murano and Rialto.

To conclude about the site of Venice: it is a marvellous thing, which must be seen to be believed; its greatness has grown up only through trade, based on navigation to different parts of the world. It is governed by its own statutes and laws, and is not subject to the legal authority of the Empire as everywhere else is. This is because in the year 806 Charlemagne had the Western Empire and another ruler had the Eastern, and [Charlemagne] conceded to the Venetians that they could live under their own laws and obey whichever empire they pleased, and gave them a privilege which, moreover, Pope Leo III confirmed.

And the order with which this holy Republic is governed is a wonder to behold; there is no sedition from the non-nobles (*populo*), no discord among the patricians, but all work together to [the Republic's] increase. Moreover, according to what wise men say, it will last for ever, as appears from this epigram found in the *Supplementum chronicarum*:

> So long as the sea contains dolphins, so long as clear skies contain stars; so long as the moist ground gives forth her pleasant fruits; so long as the human race carries on its generations upon the earth, the splendour of the Venetians will be celebrated for all eternity.   D. C.

2   A PILGRIM'S IMPRESSIONS, 1480
Brasca, Santo, ed. Momigliano-Lepscy 1966, pp. 48–50.

I stayed at Venice until 5 June because the pilgrim galley was not yet fitted out, and during this interval I went sightseeing all over the city. I saw the great church, St Mark's, very beautiful and decorated in mosaic at both upper and lower levels and on the outside. There, on the night of Ascension Day, they show about a palmful of blood, which they say flowed miraculously out of a crucifix. The story is that a gambler had lost his money at play, and in desperation stuck his knife many times into the breast of Christ on a crucifix, and this blood gushed out. When this is shown, all the people and all the Scuole of Venice flock to it, bearing wax candles. And this crucifix is still displayed in the middle of the church, where everyone can clearly see it with the wounds gaping. Part of the treasure is also on display there, and on that day there was a plenary indulgence.

I also visited the church of Santi Giovanni e Paolo and the Scuola di San Marco and the church of San Francesco [*sic* for Santa Maria dei Frari], which are two very large and beautiful churches. In San Francesco are the tombs of the Doges Francesco Foscari[39] and Niccolò Tron,[40] facing each other, and they are the most beautiful tombs in the whole of Venice. I visited the church of San Bartolomeo, where the Sunday sermon is in German, the church of San Francesco della Vigna, and many other churches where they worship with great devotion.

Then I visited from top to bottom the palace of the Signori [*sic*], very splendid and marvellous. On the top floor there is a very large and ornate room, with the seat of the Doge facing towards the sea; it is painted, the relief done in gold, with the history of the victory the Signori had [in 1177] against the Emperor

---

[39] See below, II.14(a).
[40] Doge from November 1471 to July 1473.

curiosity and details importance

Frederick Barbarossa in support of Pope Alexander [III]. In this room they hold meetings of the Great Council, where all the nobles over twenty-five years of age go to the urn to ballot for offices, and in addition on St Barbara's Day they add thirty who are younger but not less than eighteen years old, and approved by the Avogadori. Down a long staircase is the Hall of Audience [Collegio] which is the most beautiful in the whole Palace, but not so large as the first. Here the story of Pope Pius [II] is painted, when he went to Ancona for the expedition against the Turks.[41] Here they grant audiences to ambassadors and other worthy men. On the other side is the Hall of the Senate, who are 140 in number; they receive and discuss all letters about affairs of state, except those concerning some matters in which the Council of Ten intervenes. These Ten have power over all criminal matters, even to have the Doge beheaded, an absolute power if they so choose. And there are many other fine things, which it would take too long to describe.

Then I went to see the Marriage of the Sea, beyond the fortresses, where the Doge was in the *bucintoro* with so many boats of citizens and well-dressed ladies that it was a very great and magnificent sight. Then I went to see the Arsenal, where all the munitions and artillery of the Signoria are kept, every sort of ship, infinite in number, five huge halls full of arms, two halls full of sails where there are always a great number of women sewing the sails. In the Arsenal it is estimated that every year more than 200,000 ducats are spent on labour and materials. Likewise I saw the New Arsenal, in which, when it is finished, there will be 100 great galleys. Then I went to see a Castilian woman born without arms, recently housed in the Piazza of St Mark. This woman eats and drinks with her feet; she sews, cuts and spins with her feet as others do with their hands. It was indeed a prodigious thing to see, and all the people flock to her with many charitable donations. Then I went to see the Campanile of St Mark, where there are seven huge bells, and from where one sees the whole site of the city. Then I went to Murano, where glass is made. This place, small as it is, is no less beautiful than Venice, and there is a very splendid palace, among others, with a very big garden, which belongs to Messer Leonardo Vendramin, son of the former Doge. Then I saw the Corpus Christi Day procession, very solemn and marvellous, in which all the Scuole of Venice took part and all the people with very many wax candles and ornamental devices; behind them came the Prince and all the other noblemen of the government, which lasted from the twelfth until the sixteenth hour [i.e. from about 8 a.m. until noon]. Then I saw the magnificent Messer Antonio Loredan's arrival in Venice; he was away for six years as Captain General of the navy, and he had distinguished himself so

[41] Pius was met at Ancona in August 1464 by Doge Cristoforo Moro, bringing a war fleet, but died before the expedition could proceed. The painting was destroyed in the 1483 fire (Wolters 1983, p. 19).

highly that almost the whole city went to meet him, with such a show of magnificence that it seemed like one of those triumphs that in ancient times were held for the Roman emperors.

Afterwards I went to see the bodily relics of saints in the city, and I was shown all the following, which I saw and touched.

First, in the monastery of Sant'Antonio:

> The arm of St Luke the Evangelist
> The head of St John the Almsgiver
> Part of the arm of St Cecilia, Virgin and Martyr
> A leg bone of St Simon the Apostle
> The thigh bone of St Ursula
> The thigh bone of St Hadrian, Martyr
> A rib of St Stephen, Protomartyr
> A rib of St Martin, the Bishop
> One of the thorns from the crown of thorns of Our Lord Jesus Christ
> [Relics of] St Marina, Virgin; St Christopher, martyr; St Blaise, martyr; St Bernard, the Abbot
> Some wood from the Cross of Our Lord Jesus, and many other relics of holy martyrs

[There follows a list of relics seen in six other churches.]   D. C.

3   SANSOVINO ON BUILDING-MATERIALS AND TECHNIQUES
Sansovino 1581, ff. 140r–142r (ed. Martinioni 1663, pp. 382–5).

Almost all the palaces are on prime sites in the most beautiful areas of the city and for the most part are on the waterside; most of the inhabitants' houses have a waterfront which, apart from convenience for the carriage of goods needed by each family throughout the year, is not so easy to explain. Besides this, every house has a terrace on the roof made of brick or wood: these are called *altane* and are used for hanging out washing in the sun. From them one sees – beyond the long stretches of water – the whole of the surrounding countryside. All the roofs are made of single and double tiles [*coppi doppi*] without any mortar, thus the cost of building is much greater here than on the mainland. Around the roof runs a stone gutter from which the rainwater is drained away by pipes concealed inside the wells where the water is filtered and returns to benefit the people. Because there are no rivers or dry land where it is possible to find springs of fresh water, cisterns are used, in which the water is healthier and easier to digest than fresh water, which is less pure. These wells and cisterns, which are both public and private, are very numerous. For every square or courtyard has its well, made for the most part by the state and on different occasions. Thus it so happened under Doge Foscari that in one year it did not rain from November until the following February, and the Republic had thirty new wells sunk to help the poor and had water transported in barges from the Brenta, and so human skill made good the defects of the season. Now, the foundations of all the buildings are made of the strongest oak piles, which last for ever under the water because of the slimy bed and even bottom of the marsh. These are driven into the earth and then made firm with thick cross-planks. The space in between the piles is filled in with various cements and rubble, which sets and makes the foundations so stable that they support any bulky or tall building without moving a hair's breadth. The bricks, terracotta and mortar come from the territory of Padua, Treviso and Ferrara, but the most praised are those from Padua, because the earth is better and also because the bricks are more seasoned and well baked, and because the bricks and flat tiles are bigger than those from elsewhere, and a boat steered by two persons at the most, by making several journeys, can bring building-materials for every great building. The sands are from the Brenta or the Lido, but the fresh-water sand is best. The wood is brought to us in great quantities by the rivers in the form of timber rafts [zattare] from the mountains of Cadore in Friuli and the Treviso area, the iron from Brescia and from other places in Lombardy; but a beautiful and marvellous building-material is the hard stone which is brought from Rovigno and Brioni, a citadel on the Dalmatian coast. It is white in colour and like marble, but sound and strong, of a kind that resists frost and sun for a very long time. Therefore they make statues from it which are polished with felt to look like marble; then they are rubbed with pumice and resemble marble. Entire church and palace façades are embellished with tall columns as thick and long as one desires, made from single blocks because these Rovigno quarries have an abundance of this kind of stone which writers call Istrian or 'Liburnica'. There are also façades covered with fine marbles, but these are Greek, transported from the islands of the Archipelago and especially from Paros; the latter type is not so white as the common marble, and is very different from the marble from Carrara in Tuscany. Then the stone from Verona is highly valued, because, being red and with various markings, it beautifies buildings, and they make chequered floors for churches and palaces from it, and other works which are very lovely, such as lavabos, fireplaces, cornices and other similar things. . . .

The roofs of the buildings are mainly sloping and four-sided [in quattro acque], which, besides helping the rain water to drain away more easily, is also very decorative. Because of the thickness of the rafters they place one and then leave a space, which pleases the eye as well as strengthening the building, because they support any great weight and the ceilings do not shake when people walk above. The houses are usually built with three floors, not counting the roof. All the bedrooms have fireplaces, but the living-rooms do not, and this is certainly wise, because when one gets out of bed the fire not only dries out the damp that gathers while one sleeps during the night, but it warms up the room and purges it of unhealthy vapours which rise in the air or in other places.

Our ancestors made their rooms *in crocciola* – that is, in the form of a T – which was ugly to see, but this custom has changed. The rooms now run through from front to back, and the window openings are regularly arranged, and the doors likewise, in such a way that every opening is in proportion; and, besides being offered a beautiful view, the eye is free to range unimpeded and the rooms are light and full of sunshine. It should be added that all the windows are covered not with waxed canvas or paper, but with fine white glass mounted in wooden frames and sealed with iron and lead, not only in palaces and houses but in all places, however humble, to the amazement of foreigners. . . .

The façades of the buildings are flush from top to bottom and do not project or have loggias below, or anything to block them, which means that when the weather is wet a man cannot shelter from the rain as in Padua or Bologna, where there are porticos on the ground-floor level. In designing buildings the window of the main room is placed in the middle of the façade, so that onlookers can easily recognize where the room is situated, and at the windows they put projecting balconies bordered by rows of columns; these [balconies] are little more than waist-high and are very useful in summer for taking the cool air.

In the past, although our ancestors were frugal they were lavish in the decoration of their houses. There are countless buildings with ceilings of bedrooms and other rooms decorated in gold and other colours and with stories painted by celebrated artists. Almost everyone has his house adorned with noble tapestries, silk drapes and gilded leather, seat backs [*spalliere*] and other things according to the time and season, and most of the bedrooms are furnished with bedsteads and chests, gilded and painted, so the cornices are loaded with gold. The dressers displaying silverware, porcelain, pewter and brass or damascened bronze are innumerable. In the reception rooms [*sale*] of the great families there are racks of arms with the shields and standards of their ancestors who fought for Venice on land and at sea.

[Francesco thereafter refers to some outstanding palaces, in either Gothic or Renaissance styles. His top four on the Grand Canal are those belonging to the Loredan (now Vendramin-Calergi), attributed to Codussi; the Grimani (at San Luca) by Sanmichele; and the Delfin and Cornaro, both of which were designed by his Florentine father, Iacopo Tatti 'Sansovino' (1486–1570).]

J. F.

4 THE ENGLISH AMBASSADOR'S NOTES, 1612

Notes for a report by Sir Dudley Carleton, probably written in spring 1612: PRO SP 99, file 8, ff. 340–4.

Particular notes of the goverment and state of Venice cum observationibus minimarum rerum, as they come by discourse withowt observacion of time or congruitie

The habit, manner of speach, gesture etc. of the gentlemen of Venice all alike.

Betwixt the old families and the new a perpetual faction.[42] The new are for most in number, the old in welth and dignitie; the new by this meanes carrie away all principal offices in the goverment as the Duke is ever of late chosen amongst them[43] but the old have the love of the people. The opinion of many is that this will be one day the ruin of theyr common wealth.

It may be marvayled how at the death of a Duke the election of a new being to pass through all theyr nominations where every one will advance in what he may his own familie it may notwithstanding be easely foreseene who shall be chosen: but it falls owt in this sort. First all the old families are excluded. Next all Papalini.[44] Then such as have children: and unwillingly they chuse a maried man. They will have one that hath run through the principal offices of the commonwealth withowt any note of misgoverment, and with these circumstances the election is not great but within two or three and of those one for the potencie of his familie and frends is soone distinguished from the other.[45] They have an infinitie of officers. The lest thing hath his superintendent. For example, there is one appointed to oversee the sellers of mellons and pepponi etc. that none doe monopolise the trade, nor play the retaylers to prevent that such as have skill to make special choise doe not rob the markett of the best and then sell them at a dearer rate.

[42] The twenty-four 'old' families, or *lunghi*, were the Badoer, Barozzi, Basegio, Bembo, Bragadin, Contarini, Corner, Dandolo, Dolfin, Falier, Gradenigo, Memmo, Michiel, Morosini, Polani, Querini, Salomon, Sanudo, Soranzo, Tiepolo, Zane, Zen, Zorzi and Zustinian. The sixteen 'new' families, or *curti*, were the Barbarigo, Donà, Foscari, Grimani, Gritti, Lando, Loredan, Malipiero, Marcello, Mocenigo, Moro, Priuli, Trevisan, Tron, Vendramin, and Venier. See Romanin 1853–61, IV, 420; Smith 1907, II, 135; Cozzi 1958, pp. 5–6; Georgelin 1978, pp. 648–9. See also below, II.14(c).

[43] However, in July 1612 the tradition was at last broken by the election of Marcantonio Memmo, who belonged to an 'old' family, as Doge. He was the first member of the group to attain this office since Michele Morosini, who was elected in 1382 and died of plague in the same year. The family of Michele Steno, Doge from 1400 to 1413, is not listed in either group.

[44] Noblemen who had clerical relatives.

[45] Carleton added a marginal note to this paragraph: 'There are case dogale such as have had Dukes and other poore families which have had none; the greater of these shall endevor to keepe downe the less.'

There is a law that all fruterers and herb-men (for woemen sell nothing abroad) must have no covert for theyr shops because the Sun must not be kept from them. The like for such as sell fish; the reason is because such as sell these commodities must be forced to come the sooner in the morning to avoyde the heat, and so sell the cheaper, because if they doe not make quick marketts theyr ware will be mared.

They want no arts in raising monie. Omnes vias pecuniae norunt [they know all the ways of money]. At the making the Fondamento Nuovo, a matter of great charge to fill so much vacant grownd and make it firme against the sea, they had this invention, to force all the barcheroli [boatmen] who carrie the stuff and rubbish of the cittie to Lio (a banck two mile distant from Venice) to bring it to this place. And wheras there was a rate sett downe of two ducats for every bote which caried the sayde stuff to Lio and was usually payde, the barcheroli continued to receave the 2 du. and bringing theyr lode to the fondamento they there discharged it, and left one of the ducats which went to the payment of other workemen. The parties that first payde this monie had no cause to complaine because they payde no more than before and the speedie return of the botes made the busines the sooner dispacht, and the barqueroli were as well pleased because theyr jornie was shortned and they were hindred by no weathers.

The opinion of many is that this state can not long continue according to the rule of preserving iisdem artibus [by the same skills] as of getting, because they here change theyr manners, they are growne factious, vidicative, loose, and unthriftie. Theyr former course of life was marchandising: which is now quite left and they looke to landward buieng house and lande furnishing themselfs with coch and horses, and giving themselfs the goode time with more shew and gallantrie then was wont, and in effect theyr studie is spantalonirsi[46] whereas theyr old manners would promise more assured continuance after the old manner. Theyr wont was to send theyr sonnes uppon gallies into the Levant to accustume them to navigation and to trade. They now send them to travaile, and to learne more of the gentleman than the marchant.

There is greate dowte of restoring of the Jesuits as long as theyr houses and lands rest undisposed of. A proposition now made in November 1611 for the erecting a colledge for the poorer sort of gentlemen in place of the Jesuits to be maintained with theyr revenues. Not past by the secret arts of the Procurator Moccenigo, who doth with great caution advance the Popes affaires: who hath a

---

[46] That is, to shed the character of Pantaloon (from the foolish old Venetian, a stock type in Italian comedy, named after San Pantaleone, a favourite saint in Venice) in favour of something less dull. 'Pantalon' or 'Pantaloon' was a common nickname for Venetians: 'those Pantalons will sooner turne Turkes than Protestants' (John Chamberlain to Dudley Carleton, 5 October 1606: Chamberlain ed. McClure 1939, I, 233).

promise to be created a Cardinal but he waites for the Dogato.[47] In this Popes time who aimes onely at two things: la lunga vita and il buon tempo [to live long and enjoy life]: and this Dukes who is a goode patriot[48] any thing may be done; lett this time pass, there is little to be hoped to be further concluded against Rome.

In matter of trade the decay is so manifest that all men conclude within 20 yeares space here is not one part left of three. The wonted course of bringing Indian marchadise to Alexandria, from thence hether, and from hence transporting it to other parts was the cause of theyr greatnes of trade. These marchandises being now brought about by sea into owr parts hath so changed the case that wheras pepper and other spice was wont to be bought here by owr men, it is now brought from owr ports and here sold.

The Turkie trade which we are now entred into is likewise a hinderance to these marchants and no great profitt to owr men: for some are of opinion owr marchants thrived better when they bought these wares here of these men, partly by reason of the habilitie of this people above owrs in trading, partly by the advantage these have of exchanging commodities by reason they furnish silke and velvets etc. and when they had the trade to themselfs they did manadge it better. Owr men buying all with readie monie make the less gaine.

Touching the point of religion here are many which privatively may be sayde not to be Papists, but positively to say what they be else can not well be, unless I should stile them politici and not so much in publike respects as for theyr privat interests changeing and turning as often as they see cause for theyr particular advancemente. A proofe we have of this in N. C.[49] who being an opposit to the Pope changed his course in an instant. In general the vices of Venice can be supported by no religion but the Roman, and they are so natural that there is no hope of change by consaquent as little hope of change of religion:[50] besides theyr custome being of a race of many sisters to marrie one or two onely and to thrust the other into Covents, in this respect they will have them supported and theyr bastard children doe in like manner fill the cloisters.

In trade there is a manifest decay in Venice, and by consequence of shipping. The decay of trade proceedes of the greatness of the imposts which are 6 in the

---

[47] For the withdrawal and exclusion of the Jesuits from Venice in and after 1606 see below, V.18 and headnote preceding V.14. The academy for poor noblemen was eventually founded in 1619, and its endowments (by Senate decree of 14 March 1620) came to include an assignment of 200 ducats a year from the revenues of the banished Jesuits of Padua (Zenoni 1916, p. 9). Giovanni Mocenigo was appointed Procurator of St Mark's on 4 April 1611; he was never elected Doge.

[48] Pope Paul V and Doge Leonardo Donà, the protagonists of the Interdict of 1606-7 [below, V.17].

[49] Probably Nicolò Contarini, historian of the Republic [below, IV.13] and Doge in 1630-1. See Cozzi 1958; Benzoni and Zanato 1982, pp. 135-442.

[50] Cf. below, V.5 and headnote preceding V.1.

hundreth of all that comes out of the Levant,[51] from whence likewise none but Venetians may bring marchandice which causeth the trade to run so quick in Florence, Genoa and Marcelles to which places all men that will may bring, the impost is very small, and by reason of the exportacion of the same marchandice into the land the Datio[52] is great, wheras here little is brought, and little sold so as the customes are so fayled which were the best revenues of the state that they doe not equal the present charges. The decay of shipping is manifest to the eye there having ben 80 great vessels of above 1000 tun apeece in this port and traffiking these seas where as now not one is to be seene, some being sold others cast away, most taken by pirats, in which these Signori are much condemned of incuriousnes for not providing some sufficient convoy or setting owt some vessels purposely against the Corsari which they never tooke into consideracion, as yf there in they had lost theyr judgments, which commonly fayle first when a ruin doth follow, and it is much marvailed that seeing the world so much changed in the course of trade yet they will not consent to change theyr strict lawes touching the Levant: but of this it is impossible to make impression in the Senat where the maior part ever give theyr balls for continuing that which is receaved by custome against the propositions of such as accomodating theyr counsell according to the times would recommend any new course.

The decay of trade appeares in the fall of the customes which are now come to so low a rate that for many particulars the State doth not as they were wont rent them owt because the decay of theyr meanes should not appeare to Stranger Princes and States with whom they desire to preserve a reputacion of welth. The cariage of commodities directly from the Indies by th'English and Hollanders into owr Northern parts hinders the cumming of these wares to Soria from whence they were usually in times past brought hether, from hence transported over all Christendome. Now, those things are brought from owr parts hether, and such commodeties as silkes and the like that come to Soria are caried by owr ships directly home without coumming to this place at all. From hence it proceedes that even the commodities of this cittie which were wont to be caried into Soria fayle likewise of vent, insomuch that for some yeares past there was 24 thousand and 25 thousand clothes sent thether in a yeare. This last yeare 1611 there was but 15 thousand and the next it is not thought there will be above 10 thousand or 12 thousand,[53] and this trade maintaining many people for the making and working of clothes there is likewise an apparent decrease of the poorer sort there being thought to be 14 or 15 thousand people less then were in Venice within two yeares.

[51] See below, IV.9.

[52] Income from customs and excise duties.

[53] Cf. the series of figures for cloth production in Sella 1968, p. 109 – including 16,079 cloths for 1611, 16,193 for 1612, rising (despite the pessimism which Carleton reports) to 21,740 in 1613.

The gentlemen desirous by the industrie of strangers to make some profit to themselfs seeke to joyne with them in theyr adventures by sea, but they avoyde them all they may – terming them sacks of coles (with allusion to theyr habits as well as theyr qualities) which doe either black, or burne. O e' cuoce o e' tigne [literally: 'either it burns or it stains'].

Touching the treasure of St Marcs, wherof the voice goeth so high as yf it were towards 30 millions, It is a hard matter to make any just computacion: but by reasonable coniecture thus stands the state of it. In the time of the warre with the Turke they were much exhausted and growne into great debts. Those asked a time to be recovered. It is judged that afterwards untill within these 7 or 8 yeares that theyr trade of Soria fayled and the commerce grew dead in this cittie, they putt up yearly 750 thousand crowns.[54] For these later yeares the charge hath exceeded theyr revenues. In the time of the Interdict theyr store was somwhat abated, at what time they having occasion to looke into theyr treasure fownd a great fraude some of theyr bags being fild with stones, which it is thought may succeede againe that being but a casual search. So as the whole matter considered the wiser sort imagine there is not in Zecca [the Mint] above 7 millions.

There are besides ordinarie charges many secret expences belong to this state, as towards Turkie to satisfie those Visirs and Bashas there goe great bribes who otherwise in all likelyhood would turne theyr warrs this way. Besides it is noted of all that have charge of collections or otherwise that may turne to the profit of this State that they rather of late gather for themselfs then for the common stock.

The Venetians doe not suffer any to trade theyr commodities to Tripoli where is the descent into Soria, but there owne citizens uppon confiscacion of goods to all strangers. Heruppon the Flemings have fownd a meanes to carrie owt by stealth as contrabandi great quantitie of clothes which they convay in small botes to Goro,[55] and there having ships at ancor they lade them for Soria, which being discovered by the consul at Aleppo [*marginal note*: the 4th of April 1612] and advertised hether is the chiefe occasion that this Signoria seeks at this present to destroy that port at Goro for which purpose theyr general is sent thether with his gallies.

Whereas other Goverments are ruled by lawes the Venetian hath little other than reason of state to which they doe resort in all occasions as that which gives law to all other lawes, and when in controversies betwixt the Church and them they are assayled and sometime putt to the worst (as in those lately of Ceneda[56]

[54] See below, IV.10, n. 36; IV.13.

[55] On the Po delta, near the border between Venetian territory and the Ferrarese, which formed part of the Papal States. Cf. Benzoni and Zanato 1982, pp. 186–9.

[56] A small town on the plain of Treviso, incorporated since 1866 in the commune of Vittorio Veneto. Sovereignty over the city was disputed by, on the one hand, the Bishop and the Pope, who

and Goro) with texts of civil and Canon lawe, they will not spare to alleadge what is required by reason of state.

Theyr general course in all divisions betwixt other Princes and states is to maintaine a neutrality which doth give them the advantage of time.

There is no apparence that ever religion should be brought into this state or any part of Italy whilst the world rests in peace. Any moving of arms would bring in strangers and amongst those there would come many protestants to spred theyr fayth. There was as much done as could be in a peaceable time by F. P. and F.,[57] the one of which infused his conceits into the other and he preached for two Lents publiquely in Venice touching many points of the Popes autority and some others accidentally of doctrine but it tooke little place.

B. P.

5   THE DOMINIONS OF THE VENETIAN REPUBLIC: A REPORT BY THE SPANISH AMBASSADOR, *c.*1618.
From a report by Don Alonso della Cueva, Marquis of Bedmar (Raulich 1898, pp. 9–19)

good relationship
to majesty
common enemy = Turk

In the unanimous opinion of all men, the Venetian Republic is deemed to be the first and greatest in dignity, power and authority in Italy today, for it founded itself, has always lived in freedom, and has never owed allegiance to any prince. Furthermore, it is the most ancient state in Italy today . . . it has grown so much in the course of time, through a continual influx of people from every quarter, that it has acquired a vast and spacious empire of great wealth and power, both maritime and terrestrial. Hence it can truly be called a great and powerful commonwealth, more amply endowed with population, weapons and riches than is any other state in Italy. Subject to it on the mainland are three whole provinces, Istria, Friuli, and the entire March of Treviso, and in Lombardy it enjoys territory which was formerly part of the Duchy of Ferrara and hence a possession of the Church. Those parts of the body politic [*Membri*], being joined and united together, can give strength to one another when the need arises.

To seaward it has extensive and far-flung possessions, from Venice itself to the island of Crete, and in that stretch of sea called the Adriatic [*sic*] it has, first of all, the kingdom of Crete, and if this were in the hands of a mighty prince

claimed it as recipients of a donation from the Emperor, and on the other hand the Venetian Republic, which claimed it by right of conquest. See Sarpi ed. Cozzi 1969, pp. 468–554.

[57] Fra Paolo (Sarpi), legal consultant (Consultor in Iure) to the Republic, and his assistant and biographer Fra Fulgenzio (Micanzio). See Sarpi ed. Cozzi 1969; Wootton 1983. For Micanzio: Benzoni and Zanato 1982, pp. 733–863.

31

there is no doubt that it alone would be a sufficient curb to the arrogance of our common enemy the Turk. For if a goodly squadron of swift and well-equipped galleys were raised in that kingdom they could, by constantly patrolling the Archipelago, plunder and disrupt the shipping which passes from the much-frequented ports of the Morea to Constantinople. Since the Turks draw from the Morea a vast quantity of grain, munitions and other things essential to that most populous city, it would soon be in deep trouble, suffering a great dearth of victuals, and that would be the surest way of inflicting upon it the worst fate that anyone could contrive.

Further to the east the Republic possesses three other small islands, which are not fertile, but are of the greatest importance for their strength and security, for they serve as protecting walls to the kingdom of Crete.

Apart from this, Venice possesses the islands of Zante, Cefalonia and Corfu, as well as many others scattered through the Gulf, some of them close to the mainland and to the fortresses which are, as they call them, the limbs of Dalmatia, Albania and Schiavonia. But, to tell Your Majesty the truth, they are all for the most part uninhabited and barren, and to put it bluntly, they are more of a wild beasts' lair or a robbers' roost than places of great importance. Hence, excepting the islands I have named, and a few others of repute and profit, the rest serve only to maintain the appearance of a great empire, and in truth entail more loss than gain, because none of them can maintain itself unless vital supplies, and especially foodstuffs, are imported from elsewhere. Hence they are inhabited by sailors, fishermen and great numbers of brigands, who, having committed a thousand acts of plunder, take refuge in the dominions of the Turk, or on the shores close to Trieste, in Segna, Fiume, and other possessions of the Archdukes. I shall not discuss these regions any further, because such discourse would not relate to Your Majesty's interests, but shall turn instead to the mainland possessions of the Venetian Republic. I shall first describe their borders, which on the Lombard side almost all march with Your Majesty's lands and those of the Archdukes, and, to a certain extent, with the Mantovano.

To the east, then, the Republic borders on the Archdukes' lands and on the Adriatic sea.

To the west it borders on the state of Milan.

To the south, it is confined by the borders of the Trentino, and by part of the Milanese and the Mantovano.

To the north, likewise, lies the Trentino, with part of the Grisons, and between them is the Valtelline, the passage of which is vital to the interests of the Venetians, because through the Valtelline they can bring troops from France, Germany, and other North European nations, and if they were deprived of this it would be easy to prevent the Republic from obtaining such aid, which is always most damaging to Italy, both to its government and to its religion.

In all the possessions of the Venetian Republic, both to seaward and to landward, there are some thirty episcopal cities and seventy to eighty fortresses. But, since it is my intention to describe to Your Majesty only those things most relevant to your interests, I will omit the things of the sea and discuss only the mainland of Italy, including the Lombard dominions, which, in the size of their cities, the extent of their population, the fertility of their land, and the abundance of all things vital to man's existence, are equal to any other Italian state. Many of them were formerly annexed to the state of Milan and to other states of the Empire.

The most notable city of Padua is larger than any other city of the Republic, with a circumference of 7 miles, well fortified with ramparts, lakes and deep moats, counterscarps, and other fortifications well adapted to the defence of such an important city; for the possession of Padua was the foundation of the Venetians' ample dominion in Lombardy, and by means of this they applied themselves to the gradual acquisition of the remainder, upon a variety of pretexts and stratagems.

Padua has a splendid university, the best in all Italy, both for its excellent doctors of every profession and for its great concourse of students. Here, too, come great quantities of vegetables, cattle, wool, cloth and fish. On these grounds it can boast of greater prosperity than can all the other cities of Lombardy. However, there are two major causes of damage to the city. First, it is too close to Venice, to which – there being a navigable river to hand – all the things just mentioned, and especially the grain, are removed. Hence it has sometimes proved necessary to export corn from Venice for the assistance of this city, and the reason for this deficiency (here is the second notable affliction) is that the Venetians have for many years largely neglected maritime affairs and have applied themselves instead to huge purchases of land, especially in the Padovano, Trevigiano and Polesine. In this way they have so far expanded by means of purchases, acquisitions, usurpations and confiscations that we can say that three quarters of Paduan territory is now in the hands of Venetian nobles, to the great impoverishment of the Paduans, who in the past used to be generally well endowed with material goods but are now plunged into penury. Indeed in Padua there are only four, or at most six, families with fortunes of 15,000 crowns or perhaps a little more. The rest of them are scarcely worth a thousand, and were it not for the influx of scholars, especially from beyond the Alps, the city would be wretched indeed. In other matters the Venetian nobility exercises its authority with such licence, and in such an overbearing manner, that nowhere is poorer than Padua. Since the masters are by nature altogether haughty and vindictive, the properties of Paduans are confiscated and immediately purchased by Venetians, or else are so sadly reduced in value by the damage they do that as soon as the lands are restored the Paduans feel profound dissatisfaction. . . .

mostly negative of Padua

33

[Accounts follow of Vicenza, Verona, Brescia, Bergamo and Crema.]

These are all the chief components of the Venetian state in Lombardy, and certainly nothing more commodious could be seen or desired, for the cities are among the great ones of Italy for population, wealth and trade, and they not only compare in fertility and abundance of all goods with any other Italian city, but actually surpass all others in the splendour of their buildings and in the extent of their large, populous and wealthy villages, and in everything else that can be achieved by the labour and industry of men. It seems that the subjects are discontented only with their subjection to the insolence of so many noblemen – each of these striving to be recognized as the master and superior and to be respected even in matters at odds with justice and honour, for they claim absolute power and command obedience through the dependence upon them of other nobles who collude or do not wish to oppose them, and so they inflict damage, ruin and poverty. But of this and other details Your Majesty will receive another report. Let me point out only that the Venetians today have a mainland dominion a thousand miles and more in length, which they contrived to acquire by taking advantage of timely leagues and alliances . . . Always championing the cause of Italian liberty, the Republic has invariably succeeded in making some addition to its own possessions. Even so, in the Wars of Ferrara it acquired the Polesine di Rovigo, and so, little by little, all the other states of the sea and land, and so the Republic built up its empire in the same manner as the Turk – that is, out of the quarrels and dissensions of its neighbours and the great number of petty lords, and so with skill rather than ease it succeeded in making them all its prey. Had it won the lordship of Milan, as it strenuously endeavoured to do, the monarchy of all Italy would certainly have fallen to Venice.

Apart from the dominion of Lombardy, the Republic holds three other whole provinces of Italy: [Istria,] Friuli and the March of Treviso. In Istria it has five cities, although these are small ones, and a number of fortresses. The air of Istria is, one may say, pestilential, and hence the countryside is almost totally deserted, but the Republic draws huge profit from its salt, which is made there in vast quantities, as well as dairy produce, meat, wood for fuel and construction, fish, oil, building-stone of the highest quality, and other commodities which are exported to Venice.

In the province of Friuli Venice has two cities, Udine (seat of the Patriarchate which was once at Aquileia) and Cividale del Friuli; the first is on a plain and the second on a mountain, poorly supplied with grain but well-off for lesser crops, animals, dairy produce and wine. In general, this province produces great quantities of wine, which are exported to various parts of Italy, and it also has metal mines in Candore, a mountain fortress on an impregnable site. In this province lies the magnificent fortress of Palma, recently built; constructed as it is with great intelligence and industry, it strikes wonder into all who look upon it, for they see that all conceivable skill and diligence have been applied in order to bring it to perfection.

There still remains the March of Treviso, which contains three small cities. They are headed by Treviso itself, which is on a very strong site, safe from undermining. The March of Treviso enjoys great plenty of corn, fish, wine, wood, animals, dairy produce and fruit, but above all of excellent timber for the use of the Arsenal, for it has a wood 15 miles in length. This province has most notable and beautiful castles, well and truly rich, populous, and given to trade.

Finally, the Republic possesses the Polesine di Rovigo, which, like another Apulia, abounds in corn, vegetables, lesser crops, animals, and fish.

Enough has now been said to Your Majesty about the Republic's possessions, and I shall now mention some points concerning fortresses. The fortifications of the whole Venetian empire are concentrated on two regions alone, i.e. on Lombardy (on the frontiers of the state of Milan), and on the sea, where they are exposed to attack from the Turks. The Republic greatly fears Your Majesty and the Turk, and so all places in Lombardy and on the sea are garrisoned, either heavily or lightly.

In Friuli the fortress of Marano, situated in a marsh, is of great importance. Then we have Palma, Monfalcone, and Osopo and Candore, which are small places with scanty garrisons, but their situation is impregnable, for they are high up in the mountains and set among rocks. For the rest there is no other fortress, and no other garrison.

Let me only say to Your Majesty that in matters relating to the defence of their possessions, in keeping them well supplied with provisions, munitions and victuals for many years, the Venetians have spared no trouble or expense. Hence they are fully secured against invasion, especially in Lombardy, where they are well equipped not only to resist, but to destroy, any powerful army.

B. P.

Republic's possessions
strengths + weaknesses
how they acquired

35

Part II
Authority and Government

'AN INFINITIE OF OFFICERS':
THEORY, DESCRIPTION AND
PANEGYRIC

*T*HIS SECTION *illustrates some of the essential points about the political 'myth of Venice'. The passage describing the Senate [II.1] is almost a classic formulation of this; it comes from an Elizabethan translation of the book which Gasparo Contarini (1483–1542) was drafting in the early 1520s, i.e. during the period of Venice's recovery from the humiliating mainland wars of 1509–17. The completed Latin text of Contarini's treatise on the Venetian system of government, which he praised for its semblance of perfect harmony, was first published in 1543; translations into Italian and other languages soon followed, as did further editions. (Because of the book's wide influence, and because, too, the Senate was so important in Venice's constitutional structure, this item takes precedence here over some of the earlier texts.) From Contarini also comes a passage describing the highest and oldest of the three courts of Forty, the Criminal Court of the Forty, which heard serious criminal cases, but also had a prominent political role as a part of the Signoria [II.6]. Its patrician (non-professional) judges, paid a small salary, served an eight-month term; the practice (since 1455) was for this to follow an eight-month term in the Civil Court of the Forty (this court was subdivided in 1492, to make a separate court just for cases from the mainland). Here Contarini argues that these judicial offices, to which members of the Great Council were elected only for short terms – as were the rest of Venice's 'infinitie of officers' [above, I.4], apart from the Doge and Procurators, who were appointed for life – also enshrined a 'popular' element in the constitution.*

The description of the Pien [Full] Collegio [II.2], which was the supreme executive committee of the Signoria and also determined business in the Senate, is taken from a treatise on Venice c.1500 by an unknown Frenchman, and contains an interesting triple definition of the word 'Signoria' in its Venetian context; the same French writer is also quoted for his uniquely well-informed account of the Chancery [II.9]. The highest appointment, that of Doge or 'most serene Prince' – the more majestic title in use since the early fifteenth century – is illustrated by a variety of texts: the credulous account of an English pilgrim who was in Venice during a vacancy in the office in 1462 [II.3(a)]; some extracts from the new incumbent's promissione *[II.3(b)] – the long list of restrictive obligations that an incoming Doge had to swear to observe; and a letter of 1474 affording some graphic impressions of the excitement, competition and (to some extent) confusion which the election of a Doge generated [II.3(c)]. These documents serve to correct the pilgrim's illusions, but some measure of numinous dignity adhered none the less to the 'most serene Prince', as Francesco Sansovino's description of the Ducal procession illustrates [II.3(d)]. Several passages explaining other high offices are taken from one or other of the accounts of Venice's magistracies by Marin Sanudo (the first, written c.1493 with subsequent revisions, accompanies the late-sixteenth-century copy of his description of Venice [I.1], and the other, which survives in autograph, is dated 1515). The differences of detail between these two versions serve to underline, as does the Doge's* promissione, *updated at every election, that the Venetian constitution was not an ossified but a constantly changing organism. The growth of new statutes and regulations without a simultaneous moulting of the old was, however, a burden on the constitution which complicates any attempt to describe it over a long period.*

Sanudo's description of the Council of Ten, that 'very severe' magistracy [II.7(a)], is followed by extracts from the revised statutes of 1578 [II.7(b)]; these illustrate the exclusive access that the 'Ten' (seventeen in practice) had to highly secret information, and the obvious difficulty of defining any restriction on their power. It was, in spite of the short term of tenure, an excessive power which had led to the erosion of the office of the Avogadori (state prosecutors and guardians of constitutional law) and eventually provoked a constitutional crisis [see II.17(a)]. Both Contarini and Sanudo, as patrician contemporaries and patriots, unquestioningly accepted the Ten as a vital part of the security apparatus, though in most respects they could scarcely have been less alike. Contarini, grave and pious, held many high offices; his book, published three years after his death, attained world celebrity. Sanudo, inquisitive, pedantic, perhaps even paranoidal, never progressed to the higher ranks, and none of his voluminous works was printed until several centuries later. Two variations on the patrician mentality are therefore combined here with other sources to illustrate the chorus of praise that the structure of the Venetian regime generally evoked from the second half of the fifteenth century onwards. The passages about procedures in the Great Council from the treatise written in 1526–7 by the Florentine Donato Giannotti (1492–1573) and from the treatise by the anonymous French writer (II.8(a)–(b)] reflect this wide admiration, as does the frank acknowledgment of Venice's superior constitution [II.10] by one of the most celebrated Florentine political thinkers, Francesco Guicciardini (1483–1540): this comes from his dialogue concerning the best form of government for Florence, written c.1524 but set fictitiously in December 1494, a moment of crisis there after the first collapse of Medici ascendancy.

Finally, attention is drawn to the visual effect of ceremonial processions, festivals and receptions, which were in part contrived to impress foreign visitors and at the same time were intended to strengthen devotion to – or identification with – the regime. The first [II.11(a)] describes the Corpus Christi procession, and the second [II.11(b)] records the elaborate if ephemeral architectural works constructed at short notice for the arrival of King Henri III of France in 1574 – the most splendid and most described visit to Venice of an illustrious foreigner in the sixteenth century.

BIBLIOGRAPHY *In general: E. Besta 1899; Maranini 1931; Chambers 1970a; Finlay 1980. Sanudo ed. Aricò 1980 and Perret 1896 should be consulted for further contemporary texts. On Contarini: Gilbert 1968; Bouwsma 1968. On Lewkenor: McPherson 1988. On the Doge's promissione: Musatti 1888; Graziato 1986. On ceremony: Sansovino 1581, ed. Martinioni 1663; Muir 1981. On Procurators: Mueller, 1971. On the Council of Ten and Avogadori: Cozzi 1973. On later opposition to the Ten: Cozzi 1958; Lowry 1971. On Florentine regard for the Venetian constitution: Gilbert 1968. On the Chancery: Trebbi 1980, 1986; Neff 1981, 1985; Cozzi and Knapton 1986, pp. 141–6. On Henri III's visit: Wolters 1979.*   D. C.

I   CONTARINI'S PICTURE OF PERFECTION: THE SENATE
Contarini (Latin 1st edn 1543) tr. Lewkenor 1599, pp. 64–8.

Every institution and government of man, the neerer it aspireth to the praise of perfection and goodnesse, the nearer shold it imitate nature, the best mother of thinges: for so hath she disposed the order of the whole world, that those things which are devoide of sence and understanding, shoulde bee ruled and governed by those that have sence and knowledge: and therefore in this assemblie of men, (which of us is called Citie) olde men ought to be preferred before the younger sort, as those that are lesse subiect to the perturbations of the minde, and withall having beene of longer life, must needes be of greater experience in the affaires of the world. . . . With this reason therefore was the Senate ordayned and established in this commonwealth of ours, & likewise the councell of the tenne, who in the citie of *Venice* in whose commonwealth (as I said) there is a mixture of the three governments royall, popular & noble, do represent the state of the nobilitie ['*optimatum statum*'], & are (as it were) the meane or the middle, which reconcileth and bindeth together the two extreames, that is, the popular estate represented in the great councell, & the prince bearing a shew of royaltie. . . .

. . . the Senate of *Venice* hath a hundred and twenty lawfull senators, besides many other magistrates that do also obtaine the priviledge and right of Senators, so that now in this time of ours there are above two hundred and twentie that have the authority of using their suffrages in the senate. The lawfull Senators are every yeare created by that assembly of citizens, which (as I have often repeated) is tearmed the Great Councell: Neyther hath this honour any vacation, as the other magistrates have, but they may if their lot fall out, and that the great councell bee therewith pleased (which for the most parte happeneth) continue every yeare in that office. The manner and meane of their election is of us before declared, when we expressed the forme of the whole sessions. There are in the monthes of *August* and *September* in every session sixe Senators elected: which session being in those sessions tenne times removed, make up the number of threescore elected Senators, the other threescore are joyned, or (as it were) ascribed to the former, and they are all chosen together at certain particular sessions. For upon the nine & twentieth day of *September*, the Senate doth assemble, and then every senator and other that hath authority of suffrages, nameth a citizen in the Senate. And the next day early at three a clocke in the morning [*mane ad horam diei tertiam*, i.e. three hours after sunrise], the whole number of citizens commeth into the session house, and then the names being rehearsed by the Secretary of all those citizens, who the day before were named of the Senators, the names of all are put into a potte, and afterwardes taken out by chaunce [*coniecta in urnam omnium nomina sorte educuntur*]. By and by they go to their lottes, of which threescore of those that shall have most lottes in their favour (so that they exceed not the halfe) are that year ascribed in the number of the Senators, but yet in that sort that there may not bee in that last number above two of a kindred: so that in the whole number of lawfull Senators, there cannot in all be above three of a kindred, which ordinance seemeth to have beene established with exceeding wisedom in behalfe of the commonwealth. . . .

Now besides this hundred and twenty lawfull Senators, those of the councell of tenne have in the Senate equall authoritie with the Senators, as also beside the Duke and the other councellors, the councell of the fortie have the like, the judges of capitall and waighty crimes, the maisters over the salt and corne, and the procurers of *S. Marke*, besides many others: so that in our time their number exceedeth two hundred and twenty, who in their offices have all the power and authority of senators. The whole manner of the commonwealths government belongeth to the senate. That which the senate determineth is held for ratified and inviolable. By their authority and advise is peace confirmed and war denounced. The whole rents and receipts of the commonwealth are at their appointment collected and gathered in, and likewise laid out againe and defrayed. If there be any new taxations or subsidies to be laid upon the citizens, they are imposed, & likewise levied by the Senates decree. And if at any time it shall seeme necessary for the good of the commonwealth, to create a new officer or magistrate upon any sodaine urgent occasion, he is by the senate elected. Besides, the Senate by a perpetuall prerogative, hath authority to chuse such Embassadors as are to bee sent to forrain princes, and likewise to create the colledge[1] of those, whose office is to assemble the senate, and to report unto them.   D. C.

2   THE SIGNORIA 'IN PIEN COLLEGIO'
From the French. Extracts from Anon., *Description ou traictié du gouvernement ou régime de la cité et seigneurie de Venise* (Perret 1896, II, 270–4).

In the Collegio first of all is the Doge. Item: six Councillors,[2] three Heads of the Forty, and sixteen Savi. Six of the latter are called the Savi del Consiglio, and are usually from the leading noblemen of the city. Item, five of them are called the Savi di Terraferma, who have the same power as the said Savi del Consiglio but without such authority. Finally, there are another five, who are called the Savi agli Ordini, who in maritime affairs have the same power as the other Savi, but in other matters have no power, and they are usually young men. The said Savi del Consiglio are elected from the Senate by scrutiny, and remain in the said office for six months, and after this they have six months of ineligibility, when they cannot be elected to the said office. They change over in the following way: three of them [are appointed] on 1 October, and serve until the end of March, and on 1 April they are succeeded by another three, who stay in office until the end of September. Another three enter office on 1 January, and three others on 1 July, who remain until the end of December. This change-over is done so that there is always in the Collegio someone who knows and understands matters in hand, because if all the Savi were changed on a single day the Savi who succeeded them would have no understanding of the current business they were dealing with, and as a result everything would have to be begun again, which would mean great loss of time. The Savi di Terraferma are elected from the Senate by scrutiny, remain in office for six months and have three months of ineligibility; they change over as follows: three on 1 October, two on 1 January, three on 1 April and two on 1 July. The Savi agli Ordini are also elected from the Senate by scrutiny and remain for six months in the said office; they have six months of ineligibility and all of them change on 1 October and 1 April. All the Savi have no emoluments, serving without salary. However, holders of these posts can be elected to other offices and magistracies.

[1] That is, the Collegio [see II.2].
[2] The Doge's Councillors, six in number (corresponding to the sestieri of the city), were elected for a term of eight months (Sanudo ed. Arico 1980, pp. 91, 240).

43

In the said Collegio business is conducted as follows. Every day, including holidays, the Councillors and Heads of the Forty go to the Palace at daybreak, and if it is not one of the solemn days when the Doge goes, according to custom, to hear Mass at St Mark's or some other church, as will be told later, the said Councillors and Heads of the Ten hear Mass together with the Doge in a chapel in the Palace, and immediately afterwards they gather for the meeting of the Collegio in the room appointed. At the end of this room is a raised dais on which the Doge sits with his Councillors and the Heads of the Forty, and for an hour or thereabouts they hold public audience and receive the petitions presented to them, and expedite the business contained in the said petitions. Afterwards all the Savi enter the Collegio and take their seats on the dais, i.e. the Savi di Consiglio on the right side, and the Savi di Terraferma on the left, and the Savi agli Ordini in a slightly lower place. After the Savi have entered, the doors are closed and all the letters are read which have been brought in the previous night. The Doge and some of his Councillors first always read most of the letters secretly in the Doge's chamber; however, I said 'some of his Councillors', because if the Doge does not have at least one Councillor with him he may not open any letter addressed to him. After the said letters have been read by the Doge, as mentioned already, they are read again in the full Collegio. . . . The letters which contain anything of importance are reserved for reading in the Senate; letters demanding a reply, and of minor importance, about which the Doge, the Councillors, the Heads of the Forty and all the Savi are agreed, have the reply subsequently dispatched. It is necessary for the minutes of these replies to be signed by the hands of four Councillors; the minutes of all other letters written in the name of the Signoria have to be signed similarly.

And, since I have mentioned the Signoria, it should be known that Signoria can be understood in three ways. The first meaning signifies the whole republic of Venice, and the entire state of the Venetians. The second meaning signifies the whole Collegio, as described here. The third meaning signifies only the Doge and his Councillors and the Heads of the Forty. . . . It must be understood that all the letters written by the said Signoria and by the other councils are written on parchment on the Doge's name and sealed with lead. . . .

Afterwards the said Savi propose by word of mouth or in writing the things which from time to time have to be written or done concerning the city of Venice and the Venetian state, and everything else which is to the profit of the said Signoria, and every matter is discussed in the Collegio, and, if it is of little importance and everyone is in agreement, the said matter is expedited by the Collegio; but, if members of the Collegio differ in their opinions, it has to be referred to the Senate and expedited by that Council. . . . And in these discussions the Collegio often sits until midday, and, if during the time when the Collegio is assembled some prince, lord, ambassador or other notable person wants to have an audience of the Signoria, they are at once taken to the Collegio, and made to sit down behind the Doge on his right-hand side, provided they are persons for whom this place is appropriate. Afterwards they expound and request whatever it is they want, and the Doge then replies as to generalities, and as to their particular proposal or request, he takes time to consult with the Councillors and Savi. . . . And it should be known that when the Doge speaks to Senate or to the Great Council he stands up and faces straight ahead, never moving from his place, but in the Council of Ten and the Collegio he speaks sitting down.   D. C.

3   THE DOGE

(a) Death and election of a Doge noted by a visiting pilgrim, 1462

From the Latin. Wey ed. Williams 1857, pp. 83–6.

On 3 May of that year [1462] the lord Pasquale Malipiero, the very illustrious Doge of Venice, quitted this world,[3] and was laid out in his palace for three days. Then he was taken for burial. At his funeral first arrived all the confraternities, in religious dress with candles and scourges in their hands. Before them crosses and tapers were carried. Then came the parish clergy of Venice, the secular and regular clergy, and lastly the canons of St Mark's with a cross and tapers. Next came two noblemen carrying his arms. Then came his body laid out as follows: on his head he wore his biretta and his face was uncovered; under his head was placed a cushion of cloth of gold. His body was dressed in the golden robe of his office and a cloak. On his feet there were slippers, with golden spurs to one side; on the other side was placed his sword in a gilded scabbard. And with these accoutrements he was buried high up in the wall of the church of the Friars Preachers [Santi Giovanni e Paolo] in Venice.

After his death and burial, the Venetians met to elect a new Doge, summoned by the appointed Councillors. Called to the election were all the eminent nobles, who, on oath, were to choose from among the more noble of those lords firm in the Catholic faith. They themselves had to swear, on pain of losing all their worldly goods, to choose the man who was the wisest, the best provided by circumstances, the staunchest in defence of the faith and the most experienced in the affairs of the world, to serve the city and its dominions. Those 100, with some notaries, were confined to a house from which they were not to emerge

---

[3] The Doge actually died on 5 May 1462. William Wey (c.1407–76), a Fellow of Eton College, was making his second pilgrimage to Jerusalem; he is inaccurate on dates as on many other particulars.

until they had elected forty of the more noble for this honourable task.[4] Then the forty took Communion so that they might elect him whom they believed would be most firm in upholding the Catholic faith and of the greatest benefit to the city of Venice. And the man acknowledged to have the majority of the votes they accepted as their Doge. They will not, on pain of death, reveal the name of the loser. Then he who has the majority and who is elected to the office of Doge is taken to his house. As he is taken by water, the Venetians come up to him saying, 'All your possessions are now ours'; and he says, 'I know that well, but I beseech you to accept between you 100 ducats, and that will content you.' And he gives them the money, and scatters coins as he goes, to clear a way home. And, after he has settled his domestic affairs, he is led by the lords of the city to the Ducal Palace. They make him a knight, and then they robe him in the vestments of his office and place a biretta [*berriculam*] covered in precious stones on his head. And the following Sunday he comes to the church of St Mark, and before him process all the confraternities, one of which puts on a pageant for him. Then come the religious in procession with relics, torches, crosses and canopies. Among them are many children dressed as angels; they are carried on high floats, and they sing to the Doge while the secular clergy sing *Te Deum laudamus*, etc. And thus he leaves the church of St Mark with a great procession, and a multitude of the people. Coming to the Ducal Palace, he stands on the threshold, turning to face the people. Then all the lords climb towards him in reverence to pay their respects. Once all this is over he dines in his Palace, where he will remain for the rest of his life. After his election, ambassadors from the various subject provinces attend him bearing gifts, heartily congratulating him on his elevation to such a dignity.

The Doge elected that year is Cristoforo Moro, a man strong in his Catholic faith. . . .   J. L.

(b) Some restrictive obligations in the *promissione* of Doge Moro, 1462
From the Latin. Selection from 127 clauses in BL Additional ms. 15816.

12 May 1462

Proemium   . . . We, therefore, Cristoforo Mauro [Moro], by the Grace of God Doge of Venice etc., promise to you, the whole Venetian people, great and small, and to your heirs . . . for the rest of the days during which we shall bear the Dogeship, to govern and uphold the state. . . .

---

[4] Wey telescopes the complicated procedural stages of the election; the ultimate electoral college numbered forty-one [see below, II.3(c), 14(b)]. He seems not to have known that the election took place within the Ducal Palace.

councillors can carry out duty of senate

54   And if we shall suffer any temporary impediment, whether on account of illness or any other cause, whereby we are unable to carry out the government of the Doge of Venice in the Ducal Palace, one of our Councillors, whom the said Councillors have elected by a majority vote, must act on our behalf, until we shall be able to exercise the said government. . . .

71   Item, we cannot nor ought we to engage in trade, nor arrange for it to be done by any person in any way, or of any kind, either in or outside Venice, nor must we invest in any partnership; and we shall make our Dogaressa and our sons and nephews, whether or not they are living with us, swear that they will not engage in trade, nor arrange for it to be done by person in any way or of any kind either in or outside Venice, nor invest in any partnership. And similarly our daughters and nieces living with us are held and bound to the observance of all the foregoing. Nor even can we have or keep as associate any notary, page, servant or household retainer who engages in or arranges any commercial business, or who invests anything in a partnership. . . .

83   Moreover, we are obliged every two months to have the present capitulary and *promissio* of the Venetians clearly read out to us, in the right order. . . .

96   Moreover, we cannot nor ought we to go outside the Dogado[5] of Venice, unless by the wish of our Small and Great Councils. Item: we cannot pass through the port of Malamocco or the bishopric of Torcello, unless by the wish of our Small Council or a majority of it. . . .

101   We shall also arrange that, within three months of our entry into the Dogeship, we shall have made two capitularies similar to this one, one of which must be kept in the Chancery and the other in the Procuracy of St Mark's, the third one remaining with us. These three capitularies are secured with our lead seal. . . .

117   Moreover, we are obliged to have an ermine cape [*baverum*], which we must wear at least ten times during the year, and more often if we please, and on those days which shall seem, appropriate to us.

118   We are held and obliged under oath, whenever the Great Council is called, to be present and to stay in it, unless some personal impediment prevents us, and the same we are bound to do whenever the Senate is called.

119   Also, we are held and obliged to give audience with our Councillors at least once a week, and the statutory day for this is Monday. And, if, because of other urgent business, this is not possible, it shall be on the following Tuesday or the next day after that. And this pious and necessary provision must without fail be observed at least once a week.   D. C.

---

[5] Places in the vicinity of the Lagoon, listed by Sanudo at the end of his description [I.1]

Promissione of Christoforo Moro, Doge of Venice (1462–71), extract.
(British Library Add. ms. 15816, f. 5r. Photograph copyright the Conway Library,
Courtauld Institute of Art)

(c) Publication of the new Doge, 1474: an eyewitness report

From a letter to Marquis Ludovico Gonzaga from the Mantuan ambassador, Giacomo di Palazzo, Venice, 15 December 1474: ASMn. Archivio Gonzaga, b. 1432, f. 932.

At the fifth hour [i.e. after sunset] I embarked [at Padua] for Venice, but while transferring to the ferry at Fusina, getting back into the boat at night in the rain, I was in danger of losing the use of my leg from a blow on the shin. I don't know how it will turn out. At the fifteenth hour [probably about 8 a.m.] I reached Venice and found my messenger, who told me that he had heard that the lord Petro Mocenigo had been created Prince, and moreover that they were making preparations for the publication [of his name] at St Mark's in the customary fashion. He told me that he could not talk to any of the people he had been ordered to find, because the doors below the palace, where usually such conversations could be held, had been locked. . . . The messenger returned at about the sixteenth hour with news that the church of St Mark and the whole Piazza were packed with people, and that the newly created Prince was expected to come into the church. Without wasting a moment, I rushed there and made my way through the Piazza with great difficulty, and with even more difficulty managed [to push my way] into the church and to reach the High Altar and enter the chapel adjacent to the Palace. There I found the lords Marcho Cornaro and Marcho Barbarigo, who kept me beside them, while everyone awaited the entrance of the Prince, who after a short while arrived with the forty-one electors who had been shut up together and by whom he had been elected. . . . I accompanied the Prince to the [high] altar, where he knelt without the ducal insignia, and, having offered up the customary prayers at the high altar, he ascended the pulpit outside the choir, in the part of the church nearest to the Palace. Not all of the forty-one could be together in the pulpit; the leading ones came, but not Andrea Vendramin,[6] and the Prince asked for him and he was made to come up, and when he was there [Mocenigo] spoke to him and they embraced, calling for Andrea Leone and Bernardo Giustinian.[7] After a short delay Andrea Leone[8] took off the biretta and proclaimed to the people that Petro Mocenigo had, on account of his virtues, been canonically elected Prince of the whole Republic of Venice, and subsequently the Prince showed himself to the people.   D. C.

[6] A favoured candidate, who was the next Doge to be elected (1476–8).

[7] Bernardo Giustinian (1408–89), statesman and historian, was several times a favoured candidate for the dogeship (Labalme 1969).

[8] Leone was presumably Vice Doge, i.e. the senior Councillor at the time of Doge Nicolò Marcello's death, and so had acted as temporary head of state during the vacancy.

(d) Ceremonial dignity: the Doge's procession

Sansovino 1581, pp. 193–4 (ed. Martinioni 1663, pp. 492–3).

The Prince . . . every year makes various progresses [*andate*] to different parts of the city on certain festal days, solemnized either by the rites of the Church, by public decree for perils averted, or as an act of thanksgiving. The palace officials commonly call them triumphal progresses, because, in addition to the fact that the Doge wears all the insignia of the principate, the Signoria turns out in full, i.e. with the additional persons required for these progresses. Thus on these occasions the body, which the Prince accompanies as head, consists of a variety of persons and magistrates. And they go in order, thus: first, the eighty Banners that were presented by the Pope,[9] then the Silver Trumpets, borne on the shoulders of children, and two by two the heralds [*comandatori*], called by the Romans *praecones*; the latter are always dressed in blue [*turchino*] except for those of the Proprio,[10] with long gowns, wearing on their heads a red biretta with a small gold medal on one side with the emblem of St Mark. In earlier times they each held a staff, but in 1323 this was exchanged for the biretta. And they are created by the Doge, up to the total number of fifty, over whom he has jurisdiction.

Behind these come the pipers and trumpeters, wearing red, all playing harmoniously. They are followed by the Doge's shield-bearers [*scudieri*], two by two, wearing black velvet. Then come six canons [of St Mark's] wearing their pluvials, because it was always the custom of our forebears that temporal matters should be accompanied by religion. Close behind them walk the stewards [*castaldi*] of the Doge, and the secretaries of the Collegio, the Senate and the Council of Ten; then come the Doge's two Chancellors, who are called the Inferior and Ducal [Chancellors], as distinct from the Grand Chancellor, who is in the service of the Republic; and behind them the Grand Chancellor follows. They wear purple [*pavonazzo*] but with the sleeves closed, unlike the Grand Chancellor, who wears senator's robes. Immediately after him comes the Prince's chaplain, with the page [*zago*] who carried the Wax Candle, and the ballot boy [*ballotino*] of the Doge. Then come the Seat and the Cushion, one borne on the right hand and the other on the left, together with the Umbrella. Shortly after them appears the Doge in person, surrounded by the ambassadors of foreign princes. And in triumphal processions he always wears the ermine cape [*bavera*]. After them follow the Councillors and the Procurators of St Mark's two by two (at least, according to the law of 1459), the Avogadori, the Heads of

---

[9] These and the emblems listed below were allegedly presented by Pope Alexander III to Doge Ziani in 1177 (Muir 1981, pp. 103–19).

[10] That is, of the three Giudici (judges) di Proprio. See Glossary.

the Ten, the Savi Grandi, the Savi of War (called Savi di Terraferma), and the other senators and magistrates two by two according to the laws, all wearing crimson-coloured silk with sleeves *alla Ducale*, with a magnificence and grandeur that cannot be surpassed.   D. C.

4   ELDER STATESMEN: THE PROCURATORS OF ST MARK'S
Sanudo, *De . . . magistratibus urbis*: BCV ms. Cicogna 969, ff. 50v–51r (Sanudo ed. Fulin 1880, pp. 112–17; Sanudo ed. Aricò 1980, pp. 104–5).

There are nine Procurators of St Mark's . . . they have six houses overlooking the Piazza, which two members of each Procuracy inhabit. In the time of Doge Foscari three Procurators were added to the others, making nine, three to each Procuracy; these three [additional] Procurators do not have a house on the Piazza, but live in their own houses and receive 60 ducats in rent; and, when a Procurator dies, the next one goes to live at St Mark's, and the newly elected one lives in his own house; this is the rule they observe.

This magistracy is composed of the top nobles [*primi*].[11] The city bestows it upon the oldest and foremost patricians, who deserve most for their services to the state, and it is a ladder to the Dogeship; on most occasions, the Prince is elected from their number. They hold office for life and are paid no salary. Three are called Procurators *di Supra*, that means '[over] the church and treasury of St Mark'; they also have certain testamentary trusts [*commessarie*]. Three are called *di Ultra* or 'beyond the Canal', because they attend to testamentary trusts on the farther side of the Grand Canal, and three are called *di Citra*, or 'on the near side of the Grand Canal', and they too look after trust funds. Their Procuracies have been newly built on the Piazza of St Mark, near to the Campanile, and all three of them have very strong iron doors, where there are sacks of ducats from various trust funds, kept there on deposit. They administer many charitable bequests on behalf of the souls of deceased persons who have entrusted the Procurators with distributing their money for the benefit of their souls, and each one distributes very large sums. They have stewards, financial officers and secretaries [*gastaldi, masseri et cancellieri*]; they have no superior to check their accounts. Each of the three of each Procuracy has a key. They are placed in guardianship over orphans and mentally handicapped people, and they set up trusts on behalf of those who die intestate. They administer the assets and defend [the interests of] minors, appointing themselves as guardians, providers or governors. And many people in their wills

[11] On the *primi della terra* or 'governing circle' among the patriciate see Finlay 1980, pp. 26–7, 59–68 and *passim*.

appoint the Procurators their trustees, in order that their last wishes may be carried out. They have three judges assigned to them, who hear cases every morning at St Mark's . . . and they have their own salaried advocates called the Avocati di Procuratori. In the street processions they take precedence over everyone, the sons of the Prince and others; among themselves, they go in sequence of age, and when they walk with the Signoria a Procurator is paired with a Councillor of the Doge. Three brothers can be Procurators at the same time, and three from the same family: one to each Procuracy. And in my own time I have seen two brothers Procurators, and also two members of one family. They cannot be elected to any office except Captain General of the Sea, Savi of the Collegio, Provveditore in Campo[12] and Doge. . . . They do not come to Rialto, but in the morning and after dinner they go their small loggia [*lozeta*] at San Marco, near to the Campanile,[13] and then either to the Senate or to the Council of Ten if they are members of the Zonta,[14] or to the Collegio, if they are members of that. They go frequently to their Procuracies: because of the alms they distribute, there are always poor people at the doors of the Procuracies awaiting money.   D. C.

5   WATCHDOGS AND PUBLIC PROSECUTORS: THE AVOGADORI DI COMUN, 1515

Sanudo, *De . . . magistratibus urbis* (autograph): BMV ms. Ital., cl. VII, 761 (7959), f. 4r (Sanudo ed. Aricò 1980, p. 240).

They are three; they hold office for a year.[15] They have very great power [*libertà*] and it is a great magistracy. It deals with criminals and can arraign [*intrometter*] and arrest anyone, and have malefactors brought before the Councils, either the Doge and [Six] Councillors or the Criminal Court of the Forty or the Senate, and propose that proceedings be taken against them; and when the proposal is carried by vote, they can propose what charge they wish. And the Councillors

[12] The Provveditori in Campo, elected by the Senate, were patricians who accompanied the Captain General (a professional commander) in war, transmitting to him the Senate's instructions and reporting back to it; by the later fifteenth century they were gaining extensive control over 'support services' and even military responsibilities (Hale and Mallett 1984, pp. 168–80).

[13] This meeting-pavilion, rebuilt after 1537 to the design of Jacopo Tatti (Sansovino), eventually became, according to his son Francesco, less a place of social resort than a sort of guard house, where the Procurators waited after meetings of the Great Council until the rest of the nobility had left the Palace (Pope-Hennessy 1963, pp. 103–5).

[14] See below, II.7(a).

[15] Sixteen months, according to Sanudo's earlier version (Sanudo ed. Aricò 1980, p. 97). On the decline in power of the Avogadori in the early sixteenth century (mainly owing to the Council of Ten), and attempts to revive and to reformulate their role, see Cozzi 1973, esp. pp. 335–7.

and Heads of the Forty and Vice Heads also propose [charges] and whichever proposal receives the most votes is adopted. They attend all Councils, but do not vote except in the Senate and Great Council. They are obliged to hear all complaints of personal assaults and have the power to propose penal sentences and to override conclusions reached by the Councillors with the Councils, and voted resolutions which contravene the laws. They are obliged to ensure that all the laws and resolutions adopted are observed. They write letters to governors [*Rettori*] and impose penalties upon them, and may suspend for a month their acts and those of other judges and officials. They have many other powers, and hear [cases] from the dais of the Great Council and the Senate, [seated] above the Heads of the Ten; and having completed their term of office they go for two years into the Senate, with voting-rights.   D. C.

6   THE COURTS OF THE FORTY
Contarini (Latin 1st edn 1543) tr. Lewkenor 1599, pp. 93–5.

There are in the commonwealthes of *Venice* three Courtes or Colledges, every one consisting of forty judges, two of them are for the judging and determining of civile causes, and the thirde of which wee speake for Capitall, but they are in this sort distributed, that these forty Capitall Judges, so soone as they have finished their lymited time of office, do returne privately into order, and forthwith other forty are chosen into their places by the session of the great Councell, and yet the forty new chosen, doe not presently come to the judging of Capitall causes, but in place of these former Capitall Judges, doth the other Colledge of Forty succeede, that did in the meane space of these eight moneths, exercise the judgement of civile causes within the City. And againe in their place doth succeede the other Colledge of forty, which also in this eight moneths space, had the handling of civil-foreyne causes, and in their place do suceed these last forty newly created. . . .

They have besides three heads or presidentes of their company, which are every two monethes chosen new by Lot, and in their turnes they sit with the Duke and Councellors, and have with them equal authority of making report over of whatsoever they shal please, eyther to the Senate or to the great Councell, the same neverthelesse in such manner as I tolde you before: neyther without reason are these forty yonger men mingled with the Senators, which are for the most part old men in regard that the heate of their nature maketh a temperature with the others coldnesse, yet are not these yonge men equall in number to the olde men, but much fewer, onely inough to put some heat into the cold deliberations of their Senate, which sometimes exceeding & in matters of some nature is necessarie. Besides by this grant of Senatorlike authority to the forty, there may seeme to bee in some sorte a communication of the commonwealths government with the lower and meaner sort of citizens, such as for the most part they are that do exercise this office of the forty, wherin our auncesters have seemed to use & observe a certaine kinde of popular law: for to every of these three Colledges of forty men there is a certain rated allowance of money appointed and given for every day that they shall assemble and meete, and therefore very seldome do those that are rich, require this office, and if they should they would as easily be repulsed. The honor therof being without difficulty granted to the needier sort, provided alwaies, that their life beare with it the fame of an honest conversation, by which meanes the poverty of meane gentlemen is not only in some sort provided for, but also the government and administration of the common wealth, is as well in some sort communicated with the meaner and poorer sorte of Citizens, as with those that are highliest remarkable eyther for riches or nobilitie, which custome hath a reference to the popular estate. By these thinges you may perceive that there appeareth in every parte of the *Venetian* common wealth, that moderation, and temperature, which in the beginning of this worke, I told you our auncesters did so highly indevour to establish.   D. C.

7   STATE SECURITY AND ARBITRARY POWER: THE COUNCIL OF TEN

(a) 'A very severe magistracy'

Sanudo, *De . . . magistratibus urbis*: BCV ms. Cicogna 969, ff. 48r–v (Sanudo ed. Fulin 1880, pp. 98–103; Sanudo ed. Aricò 1980, pp. 98–100).

The Council of Ten is a very severe magistracy of the top nobles [*primi*][16] of the city. They are ten patricians who hold office for a year, and the term of office is meant to be completed unless someone else is elected in their place. The election of the ordinary members begins in the first meeting of the [Great] Council in August, and lasts all through September, and at the end of September they take up office. It is done by election of the bench, and four electoral committees. First three, then two, are elected in August; three and two are elected in September, so that they reach the number of ten. Every month they elect three Heads from among themselves in the following manner: first, they place in an urn ten ballots, three of which are gilded, and the first to select one of these can elect himself, or choose whom he pleases. And, if the first to be eligible is not chosen, the second can be chosen, and likewise the third, so that only one of those eligible can become a Head, and the two others must not be among those who are being elected. They are excluded from being Heads again

[16]   See above, II.4, n. 11.

54

for one month. . . . Also, they choose by lot among themselves two Inquisitors; that is, the seven remaining in the Council select from five ballots of silver and two of gold, and those who select the gold ones are Inquisitors for that month. Moreover, every four months they ballot among themselves for a Treasurer [*cassiere*], who has charge of the funds of the Council of Ten and also the armoury of the Great Council.

This Council of Ten was first created under Doge Piero Gradenigo in 1310, and now, as always, is in very high repute. They preside over three matters: the Republic, that is [to say] its state of peace; the coinage; and sodomy. However, they also have other powers and hear serious cases, and they impose whatever penalty the Council thinks fit. And those who fall into the hands of the Council of Ten cannot defend themselves with lawyers; when they examine a case they block [access to] the Palace, and there are four persons delegated as a committee, a Ducal Councillor, a Head of the Council of Ten, an Avogador and an Inquisitor (and sometimes they double the size of this committee for important cases) and it is they who act for the defence, if they are so willing; and whatever is decided by the Council of Ten is firm and valid, and cannot be revoked except by the said Council of Ten. Present in the Council are also the most serene Prince, the six [Ducal] Councillors and the Ten of the said Council itself, and the Avogadori also enter, but they cannot cast a vote. This Council imposes banishment and exile upon nobles, and has others burnt or hanged if they deserve it, and has authority to dismiss the Prince, even to do other things to him if he so deserves. Long ago in 1355 a Doge's head was cut off by order of this Council, and in 1457 another was dismissed for being incapable of exercising his duties as Doge.[17] This Council of Ten has even imposed the supreme penalty on great lords who have given cause for it: in 1432 it had Count Carmagnuola, who was our Captain General on the mainland, beheaded. There cannot be more than one member of a family in the said Council, and, so that they do not [try to] avoid election, they get exemption for a year after serving before they can be re-elected. They do not receive any salary; they can be elected whether present in the city or absent; and, if elected to an ambassadorship or any other office, they can refuse without paying a fine. Their Heads sit on a dais [*tribunal*] in the Great Council and Senate, and take their place after the Avogadori when they accompany the Signoria. They enter the Collegio when they wish, and, when they enter, the Head of the Forty, the Savi agli Ordini, the Provveditori sopra l'Armar[18] and the Treasurers leave the Collegio. It is laid down that the Council of Ten meets every Wednesday, so that, meeting so often, there should not be a great terror in the city whenever it

[17] Respectively Marino Falier, who was beheaded on 17 April 1355 for alleged conspiracy against the nobility, and Francesco Foscari, who was compelled to abdicate on 1 November 1457 [see below, II.14(a)].

[18] Officials in charge of enrolling crews for war galleys (Lane 1934, p. 147).

is called. And so there is a meeting of the Council of Ten every Wednesday, or at least once a week, and, when the Signoria has given the order for some other Council, and the Heads of the Ten want their Council to meet, the Signoria is obliged to give way to them. They have two notaries and a captain and two officers or foot soldiers. It is, in conclusion, a very terrifying magistracy, and the Council is highly secret. And often, when they have to debate some arduous matters, the seventeen elect various Zonte of twenty or twenty-five of the top nobles, who are not incompatible because they are not related to any member of the said Council of Ten. In these Zonte for the most part Procurators, and others of the top nobles, usually take part. And they have various of these Zonte as occasion demands.   D. C.

(b) Special duties and official secrecy

From the oath taken by members of the Council of Ten, in the Council's revised statutes of 1578 (Romanin 1853–61, VI, 523–33).

(ii)   I am obliged to preserve the confidence which is understood to have been entrusted to me upon each and every matter or question which is read, proposed, considered or discussed in this Council: this is to include letters of every kind, and other writings and reports, whether written or brought before this Council by word of mouth. I am obliged not to disclose the questions themselves, or the names of those who may have spoken for and against them, or the identity of those who have proposed or wished to propose a resolution upon them. I must not reveal a sign or word, by any device, hint or other means, which could be plotted or planned outside the limits of this Council, under pain of immediate dismissal from this or any other office which I may happen to hold, and of exclusion from all the offices, benefits, governorships, councils and secret committees of the state for ten years, this penalty to be imposed on me immediately by the Heads of the said Council. . . .

(x)   If any anonymous note containing information which affects or could affect the general interest of our state should be handed in at the Ducal Palace, in a church or in any other part of the city, the Ducal Councillors are obliged to have the note read to the Heads of the Council of Ten as soon as they have it in their hands, so that appropriate measures can be taken by the said Council if the matter falls within its competence. I shall not, however, concern myself with any note or information which is lodged with or comes in the house of the state Avogadori [di Comun], which concerns individual persons, and which has not been presented by those who lodged the information in the first place. . . .

(xix)   I must take account of the fact that this Council . . . besides decreeing the death penalty against those who have betrayed any city or other place in our dominion to any enemy, is, in any case where one of the said cities, fortresses or strong points has been occupied by our enemies (which Heaven forbid), the authority responsible for inquiring into that crime and for prosecuting and punishing the offenders. Once the event has occurred and our government has received news of it, the Heads of the Council are obliged with all dispatch and no delay to institute a special and accurate inquiry and to report to this Council at the earliest moment to render account and execute justice. The penalty for failure [to do so] is 1000 ducats in gold. . . .   M. L.

8   THE GREAT COUNCIL: PROCEDURE AND FUNCTION

(a) Order of seating

Giannotti ed. Polidori 1850, pp. 66–8.

The day on which the Council has to meet begins, therefore, at the appointed time; the bell starts to ring at noon and does not cease for a whole hour. During that time, every nobleman eligible to sit in the Council must appear in the Hall, into which, as soon as it is locked and the keys have been brought to the dais on which the Doge sits and placed at his feet, no one is allowed to enter except a Councillor, Avogador, Head of the Ten or a Censor.[19] When, therefore, the Great Council has assembled, the Doge comes in with his Councillors, and the three Heads of the [Criminal Court of the] Forty, the three Heads of the Ten, the three Avogadori and the two Censors . . . also come, or have already come, into the said Hall. All except for the Heads of the Forty wear the ducal robes, which are of scarlet cloth and have the sleeves open at the wrist, not like those which we wear privately, which are of black cloth and are closed up to the wrist. The Doge is seated on his dais, which is in the middle of one of the two shorter walls, varying according to season, whether summer or winter . . . on his right hand he has three Councillors and one Head of the Forty, and on his left three Councillors and the other two Heads of the Forty, seated similarly after the Councillors. At the sides of the dais there are two benches with back rests, one to the right, the other to the left of the Doge; on these are seated the Grand Chancellor and the other administrators. And those magistrates whom we have mentioned all take their places: one Avogador (the one appointed for that week) and one of the Heads of the Ten go to sit in the middle of the shorter wall, opposite the Doge, on the second row of benches against the wall, and the

---

[19] The two Censors, elected to one-year terms by the Great Council, were first established in 1517 to guard against illegal electoral practices in the Great Council and Senate, but proved somewhat ineffective (Finlay 1980, pp. xv, 210–15).

Avogador takes the place to the right. The three Auditori Vecchi[20] sit against the longer wall, to the right of the aforesaid Avogador and the Head of the Ten, near the corner with the shorter wall. The two Censors sit against the longer walls, one on one side, one on the other, almost in the middle of the two walls. The other two Avogadori and the Heads of the Ten also take their places against the longer walls, but near to the corner where they meet the wall where the Doge sits; the two Avogadori are on the side to the right of the Doge, the two Heads of the Ten on the other side. And these magistrates sit side by side on the higher of the two rows of benches, and whoever is the older sits on the right. This arrangement makes an impression of great beauty upon anyone entering: the eye is drawn first to the seat of the Doge, which, as we have said, is in a very eminent position; then it travels round the rest of the Hall, honoured by the presence of the foresaid magistrates. Thus, wherever you look, you see grandeur and magnificence.   D. C.

(b) Procedure in election of office-holders
From the French (see II.2). Perret 1896, II, 259–61.

When the said [Great] Council is fully assembled and the doors are shut, the first Chancellor, who is called the Grand Chancellor, reads out all the magistracies and offices which must be filled on that day in the said Council, and he pronounces them in a loud voice so that everyone knows what is to be done. Afterwards the Councillors take as many ballots of silvered copper as (according to their information) there are noblemen present, and add to the said silvered ballots 36 gilded ones, and place them in two urns, i.e. half of the said ballots – gilded as well as silvered – in one urn, and the other half in the other urn. And the said urns are placed one to the right and the other to the left of the dais, and the benches are called out to come to the said urn, according to a lottery drawn by a person appointed for this task. . . . And the said nobles come to the urn one after another, and those who select the gilded ballots come up on the dais and are seated there on a bench facing the Doge, until there are nine of them who have picked the gilded ballots. When this number has been reached, they are sent into a room apart, and thus it continues . . . until there are thirty-six in four different rooms, and each of the said rooms is called ELECTION. In these rooms they have, written down, all the magistrates and officers which are to be appointed on that day, set down in order; in one urn there are also placed the corresponding number of copper ballots numbered according to the said

---

[20] A prestigious and senior magistracy which judged appeals against judgements in civil law cases (Sanudo ed. Aricò 1980, pp. 124–6, 258–9).

58

magistracies and offices. And those who are in the said room draw the said ballots in order of age, and he who has the ballot marked with the number of the first office on it chooses and proposes a name, and writes it down on a piece of paper; he who has the ballot marked with the second number chooses and proposes someone for the second magistracy or office; and the rest of the nine in the said rooms do likewise. And the slips of paper on which the names are written are carried to the dais where the Doge sits, and the names of the four persons proposed for the first office are read out in a loud voice by the Grand Chancellor. The said four are then balloted one after another by everyone in the Great Council who is eligible to vote; ballots made of fabric are used, and red and green voting-urns. These urns are carried up all the benches of the Great Council by appointed persons. And everyone in the Council casts his vote without moving from his seat, and those who place their ballots in the green urn reject the candidate. Afterwards the bearers of the urns come up to the dais and place the ballots which are in the red urns in front of the Councillor who sits on the right hand of the Doge, and those [ballots] in the red urns in front of the Councillors on the left of the Doge. And the said ballots are very carefully counted, and the number of them, both red and green, is checked by the authorized secretaries. . . . And he who has the most ballots in the red urn is elected to the first office, provided always that the ballots in the red urn are more than in the green one – that is to say, more than half the nobles in the Great Council approve and elect him. However, if none of the said nominees has more red than green ballots, no one will be elected to the said magistracy or office and the same election is deferred until another day. After the said four have been balloted, all the others are balloted, four by four, according to their nomination by the foresaid four rooms for the other magistracies or offices. . . . And this method of election is called 'election by four hands', and is very solemn.

There is another manner of electing, which is not so solemn, when the Councillors place only eighteen gilded balls in the urns, and only two elections are made.   D. C.

9   THE CHANCERY
From the French (see II.2), Perret 1896, II, 277–80.

In the Chancery there are, according to the laws and ordinances which govern it, 100 secretaries, fifty 'ordinary' and fifty 'extraordinary', of whom the first and principal member is called the Grand Chancellor.[21] Although not one of the

[21] See also VI.6.

noblemen of Venice, he is always held in great honour and reverence, among both the said nobles and the other people and inhabitants of the city. The said Grand Chancellor normally enters all the Councils and other bodies attended by the Doge, and the other secretaries are ordered and delegated some to write and register what is done in the Senate and likewise in the Council of Ten and the Forty, some what is done in the Collegio. These writings and reports are kept in very good order. The minutes of letters are filed together; the registers of elections made in the Great Council and the Senate are kept separate. The registers of laws, ordinances and other matters decided in the Great Council are also kept separately and, similarly, what is decided in the Senate and the Council of Ten. All matters done secretly are registered apart. The said secretaries also compile *Commemoriali*, registering all the treaties of peace and alliances and other agreements negotiated and concluded by the Signoria. All these registers are on parchment, well written and kept in such order that without difficulty one can find written down all that has happened in the past 400 or 500 years. The secretaries who enter the Council of Ten, who are about four in number, are of greater importance, after the Grand Chancellor, than the others; following them, are those who serve in the Senate, about twenty in number, and these twenty also serve the Signoria and in the Collegio, each of them always has an office to himself, very well organized. Some of the secretaries are sent with the Captain General of the Sea, with the Provveditori in charge of war on land and sea, and also with ambassadors and similar dignitaries, and their office is to write the letters and other matters transacted by the person to whom they are attached. Within the said Chancery there are many persons who are well trained not only in the use of Italian and Latin, but also in Greek and all other languages, so that all the letters written to the Signoria of Venice, in whatever language, are read and interpreted by the staff of the said Chancery without the need to employ anyone from outside.

The said Grand Chancellor is elected by the Great Council by scrutiny of the members; that is to say, everyone selects one name, and all are balloted with [*bouettes*] and ballots as already described,[22] and he who has the most ballots is elected Grand Chancellor, and the other secretaries are elected by the Council of Ten. Nevertheless, the said elections are made on the advice of the said Grand Chancellor, full information about those elected being first provided, and no one is elected unless born in the city of Venice. The Grand Chancellor has 300 ducats a year in salary, and about twelve of the other secretaries each get 200 ducats a year. The others get a lower salary, each according to his rank.

The said secretaries have another source of income, i.e. all those who obtain privileges or concessions of grace, letters and other similar things expedited by the said Chancery, pay for the said expedition a certain sum of money laid down

[22] Cf. above, II.8(b).

by law and ordinance of the Chancery, and this payment amounts each year to a great sum of money. It is placed in a chest apart and is divided between the Chancellor and other members of the Chancery, according to their salary levels. And those who obtain the said privileges and other things mentioned above pay for the seal, which is made of lead, about 16 denari, but if the seal is of silver or gold they pay more according to its value. And the keeper of the said seal or bull earns for the said office about 400 ducats a year; he is appointed by the Doge and remains in office for life. And, because mention has been made above of gold, silver and lead, it should be noted that all letters in the name of the Doge of Venice are written on parchment, and the seal on them is of one of the said metals, but almost always lead. And on one side of the seal is engraved St Mark in the form of a man, and on the other side is written the Doge's name and these words in Latin: [e.g.] *Sebastianus Ziani, Dei gratia Dux venetorum.*

And in order that the said secretaries, including the young ones, should become good and learned clerks, the Signoria employs some great man of learning, who gives daily lessons in grammar and rhetoric to the secretaries, and he has an income from the Signoria of 300 ducats a year; and there are other learned men and doctors paid by the Signoria, who at different times every day teach grammar or rhetoric, and also logic and philosophy and other liberal arts and sciences, including theology; the lowest-paid earn 200 ducats a year, but most of these doctors get 300 ducats a year.   D. C.

10   FLORENTINE ADMIRATION FOR VENICE'S SYSTEM OF GOVERNMENT
Guicciardini, Francesco, ed. Palmarocchi 1932, pp. 106–7.

BERNARDO RUCELLAI   It seems to me that – for an unarmed city – the Venetian government is as fine perhaps as that which any free republic has ever had. Besides the fact that experience demonstrates it – because, having lasted for hundreds of years, flourishing and united as everyone knows, one cannot attribute this to fortune or to chance – there are beyond this many other reasons, all of which will emerge more clearly from the ensuing discussion. And, although it has a different name from the sort of government that we Florentines want to establish, because it is called a government by noblemen and ours will be called a government of the people, it is not on these grounds different in kind. For it is no more than a government in which participates the entire body of those who are eligible to hold office; nor is there a distinction made on account of either wealth or lineage, as is made when the aristocracy [*ottimati*] govern, but all are admitted to everything on equal terms, and they are many in number, perhaps more than with us. And, if the lower classes [*plebe*] do not take part, they do not take part with us either, because an infinite number of artisans, new inhabitants and suchlike people do not enter our Council. And, even though in Venice the ineligible are made eligible to hold office with greater difficulty than with us, this does not arise because its type of government is different, but because, while being of the same kind, they have a different political structure; it is altogether possible for the constitution to be the same, but for the political structure, as one may call an infinite number of their particular rules, not to be always identical. They have known in this manner how to keep their regime in high repute; and they have also been grand in the way they name their citizens, so that, although those they call noblemen are nothing more than private citizens, the name imparts lustre to the bearer, and makes a greater appeal than just 'citizens'. Moreover, if we called ours noblemen, and this name was with us given only to those who are eligible to hold office, you would find that the Venetian government is just as democratic as ours, and that ours is no less aristocratic than theirs. Pagolantonio Soderini has twice been ambassador to Venice, and I believe he will say the same as I do.

PAGOLANTONIO SODERINI   This is all very true. And, although they are richer overall than we are, there are nevertheless many of them who are poor, and in the government the rich are admitted in no greater number than the others. Nor do their riches depend on their different form of government, but on the great extent of their dominion, and the great size of their city and the opportunities [it affords them].

BERNARDO RUCELLAI   There is another widespread misunderstanding, that their unity is owing to the site of the city, which I confess is very useful in preserving the city from wars and foreign invaders, but it was established where it is by those who wished to flee from the barbarian invasions. I think it does little or nothing to keep the city from sedition. For one reads in their histories that in the early times of the Republic, before the government was firmly established, they had much discord and often resorted to arms; yet it was on the same site then as now. In later times there were Doges and others who aspired to tyranny, but they were soon suppressed, because of the good institutions of government. A private citizen can only with difficulty – indeed it is almost an impossibility – reduce a free city to serfdom, unless he be supported by the citizens. It can happen there only with difficulty, because the government is normally loved by those who take part in it, and the political institutions are thriving and well designed to suppress quickly anyone who begins to rise by taking this road [towards tyranny]. And these are the causes of their concord, and not the difficulty of bringing horses there, because to overthrow governments foot soldiers are just as good as cavalry, and one can bring them to Venice just as easily as to other places, and perhaps more easily, because at least there is no need for keys to the city gates in order to admit them, whether by day or night.   D. C.

II   PUBLIC SPECTACLE

(a) The Corpus Christi procession, 1533
DMS, lviii, cols 315–16.

Thursday 12 June 1533 (Corpus Christi Day)

The most serene Prince [Doge Andrea Gritti] came to the church of St Mark's dressed in crimson damask with the orators of the Pope, the Emperor, France, England and Ferrara; Barbarigo the chief priest [*primocerio*] of St Mark's; [Giovanmaria] Pesaro the Bishop of Paphos; [*Giambattista*] Vergerio, the Bishop of Pola; and the lord Sebastian Michiel, Prior of San Giovanni del Tempio. The [Doge's Six] Councillors were all dressed in satin; the Heads of the Forty, the Avogadori, all the Heads and the Censors, excepting the Heads of the Forty, were dressed in silk . . . all of us, forty in number excluding the *ordinari*, were wearing silk, except for one person [unnamed] in scarlet. Sier Stefano Memo, who does not usually appear, was there. The solemn Mass was performed by the Bishop of Veia [Veglia?], then the procession began, which was beautiful, and best of all was the Scuola di San Rocco, which had many fantasies: twelve prophets, in very fine costumes; three floats representing subjects from the Old Testament; two more carrying many silver objects, including a San Rocco, cast in silver up to the head (one of those newly made images, and very beautiful). There were twenty-four gilded torch-holders, three to every set of four candles. Then came the Flagellant Companies [*Scuole di Batudi*] bearing many silver objects in their hands. I will not omit to mention that there were seven Procurators of St Mark's wearing silk [names given]. And the most serene Prince let the procession go round the Palace and came out when it reached the door, and the knight [?unidentified] gave him a hand, but he had difficulty in walking he was so weak. An irregularity [*disordine*] was introduced in that to each of the Councillors and Procurators a pilgrim was allotted. There were altogether [. . .] pilgrims, friars and women going to Jerusalem, among them that Scotsman staying in the house of Sier Nicolò Venier. He has been there for more than fifteen days without eating; he walks barefoot and wants to go to Jerusalem. According to custom, the most serene Prince touched the hand of every pilgrim, and each of them had a wax candle.

D. C.

63

(b) Temporary architecture for the reception of Henri III, King of France, at the Lido, 1574

Della Croce 1574, pp. 12–15.

Situated here on the edge of the Lagoon facing out to sea[23] at the end of the bridge there was a four-sided building, 50 feet wide by 14 feet deep, and 44½ feet [sic] 7 inches high, which was suitable because it had three great openings or rather, as we wish to say, most beautiful triumphal arches, built according to the Roman custom in imitation of the Arch of Septimus at the foot of the Campidoglio. By means of the arch one passed beyond to a loggia which faced it and was built by the honoured and ingenious architect Palladio,[24] supervised by the lords Luigi Mocenigo and Iacomo Contarini, who are most honourable noblemen and possess great spirit. The middle arch is 14 feet wide and 26 feet high, and the two on either side are each 7 feet wide and 14 feet high, so that the four great pilasters which formed the openings were each 6 feet wide. A little above the central opening there was an architrave, frieze and cornice that ran all round the said building, and was 8½ feet high but protected more at the back. . . .

Besides these [inscriptions in honour of the King] the structure was decorated with ten paintings by the hands of the most famous painters Paolo Veronese and Iacomo Tentoretto; two of these were above the two side openings, illustrating the victories won in France against his enemies.[25] On the other side facing the loggia were two pictures. One represented the King's journey to Poland and his arrival there,[26] [showing] the King on horseback with a large entourage and his meeting with some senators and a multitude with palms and olive wreaths in their hands. The other [represented] his coronation, the King kneeling before a bishop. . . .

The loggia, as I have already said, was four-sided, 80 feet long by 40 wide, and the façade facing the arch was completely open with a colonnade made up of ten very beautiful columns imitating marble. . . . From the floor of the loggia

---

[23] By tradition, state visitors were welcomed in front of San Niccolò on the Lido.

[24] Andrea Palladio (1508–80) after 1558 frequently worked in Venice. The appearance of the structures described here is preserved in several engravings and in Vicentino's painting of the entry in the Sala degli Antipregadi in the Ducal Palace.

[25] The battles of Jarnac and Montcour (1569) against the Protestants. Veronese (c.1530–88) had previously worked in Palladio's buildings; Tintoretto (1518–94) was renowned for his speed of execution [cf. below, X.5(c), 17].

[26] Henri III (b. 1551) had been elected in 1573 to the Polish throne, which he abdicated upon the death of his brother, Charles IX. He left Cracow for France on 16 June and wrote from Vienna on 24 June announcing his intention to visit Venice. He arrived on 18 July, staying for ten days of official festivity and sightseeing.

there rose a flight of five steps, and above them hung garlands linked together from which was suspended the royal coat of arms. On each façade at the corner of the building there was a squared pilaster, and on each side of the loggia there was an opening 12 feet wide on the outside of which were two half columns flanking the opening, which was decorated within by ten figures, and in the middle of the opening on the front façade there was a most beautiful altar in a niche, and to the right a baldachin made of embroidered silk drapes coloured purple, white and gold, with the royal throne, and below it a bench backed by a cloth of gold, and on the other part was gilded leather and on the ground in front of the baldachin were lengths of velvet and gold cloth. On the remainder of the floor there were carpets, and below the stairs cloths of blue and yellow covering a large area which formed a square. The figures represented all the virtues attributed to the King. . . . In the middle of the ceiling four winged victories were painted [flying] aloft with palms and wreaths in their hands to crown him, so that it seemed when His Majesty passed beneath that they wished to crown him in recognition of victories that he had won against his enemies, and the rest of the ceiling was not painted for lack of time.   J. F.

DEFECTS, CORRUPTION AND ADVERSE CRITICISM

*I*N REALITY *the Venetian Republic fell far short of the perfection claimed for it, and was subject to much abusive comment both within and outside the city, as this section illustrates. The first passage [II.12] is an extract from one of the most polemical attacks upon Venice ever written, the chauvinistic diatribe of a Florentine merchant and secret agent, Benedetto Dei (1418–92). Full of exaggerations and inaccuracies, Dei's invective nevertheless makes some powerful points, and well conveys the suspicion of Venice's territorial expansion felt by other Italians in the later fifteenth century, outweighing any admiration for the Republic's stability, which Dei, in any case, denied. Internal criticism usually – and prudently – tended to be less about fundamentals than about human failures, but an exception is provided by the ancient Procurator Domenico Morosini (1417–1509), who in 1497 began writing his rambling and inconsistent treatise about an ideal republic. This contains a thinly disguised critique of Venice; Morosini proposed [II.13], among other things, that the first magistrate (or Doge) should hold office for only five years, and that the Great Council should be reconstructed, since the nobility was so full of men too young and rich, or simply too uneducated and profit-motivated, for governmental duties. Both Dei and Morosini effectively stress that the Venetian nobility was no homogeneous caste of ideal rulers, operating an intricate and marvellous mechanism of brakes and balances to attain perpetual harmony. Such defects are confirmed from many other sources, such as a passage [II.14(b)] revealing faction or division between the twenty-four 'ancient' or 'long' families, who traced their prominence back to the ninth century, and the other leading clans, who long conspired to keep the 'ancient' families from the Dogeship [see also I.4].*

That individuals, as Doges, did not match up to expected standards is also exemplified by several cases: the forced abdication of the once-intrepid Francesco Foscari in 1457 [II.14(a)] demonstrates a near-breakdown of the system through inertia at the top; and the financial malpractices of Doge Agostino Barbarigo [II.14(c)] provoked the setting-up, after his death, of a magistracy to inquire into his affairs and exact compensation from his relatives. For all their constitutional limitations, Doges were expected to personify integrity and leadership, but Doge Loredan was criticized for his feebleness during the invasion crisis of 1509 [II.14(d)], and Doge Alvise Mocenigo was blamed [II.14(e)] for most of Venice's misfortunes during the 1570s (though, if an individual Doge could be cast as scapegoat, this was arguably a hidden strength contributed by the 'monarchical' element in the constitution). A rather different, and greater, constitutional danger was implied by the demagogy and largesse in which some Doges indulged, notably Marino Grimani at his election in 1595 [II.14(f)]. Meanwhile, it is clear that, among the nobility in general, abuses were so recurrent that – one may infer – they were virtually ineradicable. Official secrecy was too widely defined to be capable of enforcement even among the Inquisitors of the Council of Ten [II.16], and ingeniously corrupt practices undermined the 'impartial' system of election to offices. But broglio, or the fixing of nominations and elections by lobby intrigues and ballot fiddles, was even praised (though the intention may have been ironical) by the diarist Girolamo Priuli [II.15(a)], who put the case for it as a method of ensuring stability and peace and avoiding patrician faction. That it was officially anathema, but in practice very difficult to eradicate, seems to be proved by the repeated complaints and the exposure of some of its more scandalous forms, which involved cash bribery [II.15(b)–(c)].

In the later sixteenth century a current of opposition set in among the younger patricians (the 'Giovani'). It has been questioned whether this movement really was very radical: its inspiration rested upon supposedly traditional moral, constitutional and religious values, even if its targets were the dominant holders of power and their deference towards Spain, the Jesuits and the Papacy. However, a letter of the French ambassador (II.17(a)) refers succinctly to the crisis of 1582–3, when the younger patricians succeeded in depriving the Council of Ten of some of the powers it had acquired in foreign and financial policy, and a report to the Grand Duke of Tuscany in 1589 indicates strong divisions among the patricians about this trend towards more 'open' government (II.17(b)). Finally, a passage from a private diary notes that a preacher had even dared to attack the judicial activity of the Ten [II.17(c)].

BIBLIOGRAPHY   In general: Romanin 1851–63 (esp. Foscari's deposition: IV, 286–95); Maranini 1931; Gilbert and Cozzi 1973; Finlay 1980. On Florentines' and other Italians' prejudice against Venice: Rubinstein 1973. On Domenico Morosini: Cozzi 1970. On ducal elections and political manoeuvres: Finlay 1978 and 1980, esp. pp. 92–6. On the charges against Agostino Barbarigo: Nani-Mocenigo 1909; Brunetti 1925; Finlay 1980. On Angelo Trevisan: Finlay 1976 and 1980. On broglio and corruption: Finlay, 1980; and (up to 1509) Queller 1986. On the crisis of 1582–3: Cozzi 1958, esp. pp. 2–52; Lowry 1971.   D. C.

12   BENEDETTO DEI'S INVECTIVE AGAINST VENICE, *c.*1472
Dei ed. degli Azzi 1952, pp. 103–13.

I Benedetto Dei reply ... in full, and refute everything you have said, and I shall prove my case by argument and by the witness of your own merchant ambassadors, of your merchants in Florence and your citizens and preaching friars. ...

First of all, Florence is more beautiful than your city of Venice, and more ancient by 540 years. Furthermore we spring from three honourable ancestries: Roman, French and Fiesolan. Just compare your own descent, likewise from three stems: Slavs, Paduans (from the traitorous breed of Antenor), and fishermen from Malamocco and Chioggia. We are the disciples of St John [the Baptist], not of your St Mark, and there is the same difference as between French wool and the wool stuffed into rough mattresses. And in another respect the Florentines are richer and greater than you are: in their 30,000 landed estates belonging to gentlemen, merchants, ordinary citizens and artisans. These provide us with bread, wine, corn, oil, wood, meat, cheese, fruit and vegetables to the annual value of 90,000 ducats, and this represents hard cash for people who have to buy such things, like you Venetians, Genoese, Chiots and Rhodians. Every year proves it, and the all-powerful Florentine people possess this wealth to your contempt and shame. ... We have two guilds, greater and worthier than four of yours put together, namely the wool and cloth guilds ... they export more than the cities of Venice, Genoa and Lucca combined. Witnesses to the truth of this are your merchants who come to Lyons in France, to Bruges, London, Antwerp, Avignon, Geneva, and in Provence to Pésenas and Marseilles, all places where there are large banks and exchanges, worthy merchants with regal warehouses, permanent residences and offices, churches and consuls and rich furnishings. Your agents who go every year to the trade fairs know all this very well; ask them if they have not seen the Medici bank and the Capponi bank ... and a thousand other business houses and banks, which I will not list as I would need a hundred pages, and in all these places they trade and undertake currency transactions with all countries; and there is no trade there in arms or in lambskins or babies' rattles or silk thread for sewing and fringe-making, nor cymbals, Paternoster beads, chaplets or Murano glassware, but it is all big money in brocades and cloth and alum, in huge quantities. ... We are a lot more powerful than you in commerce, because your Signoria has no major trading-post other than Alexandria, for spices, cotton and wax, which commodities we Florentines get at a better price by the routes through Bursia,[27] and in exchange we sell cloth, whereas you pay in gold

---

[27]   Bursa, an important trading post in Asia Minor.

ducats. This I know very well, because I lived for twelve years in that Venice of yours, in the house of Messer Marino Cappello at San Polo, so that I know your power, your government and its revenues and all your ways better than . . . many others who in the past have lived in Venice, in the days before you went bankrupt and lost your reputation and credit, and fell fifteen years behind with your interest payments on public loans, and did all the mad things that you did before giving up the alliance with the Florentine lion [*marzocco*]. You know what honour and reputation you had and always acquired in the days when you were in league and confederation with the Florentines.

Turning to the other chapter of your poisonous and intoxicated letter, which contains so much malice and boastfulness, declaring that you are lords of the sea and land, that you will go on making such false and futile claims, that the state and the Signoria of Venice has ruled for a thousand years without ever changing or making any innovations – you are simply scattering your counterfeit money for those who know no better. I, Benedetto Dei, will prove the contrary, and I declare and will constantly reiterate that the city of Venice has undergone more revolutions and innovations and bloodshed than have the four most violent and warlike cities in Italy – Genoa, Bologna, Perugia and Città di Castello – whose joint tally would not equal a quarter of that of the city of Venice. And, to show that I know very well what I am talking about, let me tell you that I borrowed a book of your chronicles from your own Messer Alvise Gaguoli on St Anthony's Day, the day on which he was put to death and given to the Grand Turk's elephant for a meal, in the presence of your consul Messer Jacomo Barbarigo . . . and you will find in the above chronicles twenty-five bloody events in the history of your Dogeship and Principate. . . . I read of the great happenings and the very great wrongs which you have done to one another, and I also came across things which I will not mention, because to do so needs a thousand pages, so many are the events and revolutions and changes which have occurred in this Venice of yours.

In the above chronicles I read about the innovations and the torture which you gave the son of Francesco Foscari, your Prince and Doge, and I noted the innovation and deprivation when you changed him for another [Doge] and took power away from him, in which you certainly made one of the worst possible mistakes ever made in Italy, to deprive of office such a man, who in his lifetime had been responsible for giving the Signoria of Venice all the lands which you hold in Lombardy, for it was by his merit that they fell to you. You foul traitors of a thousand sets of gallows! This I say, because I found that in the time of his trial you reproached him for being a friend of Cosimo de'Medici and Neri di Gino Capponi, and complained that you were molested by the wars waged in Lombardy during the time of the league with the Florentines. And I also found that you introduced a big innovation when your ballot secretaries falsified the laws and ordinances and gave office to their relatives and friends and anyone

69

whom they favoured, and how you condemned some to death and cut off the hands or gouged out the eyes of others; and that those who fled, such as Andrea da Cà Corner, were declared rebels. I, Benedetto Dei, talked to them in Cyprus and Rhodes, Scios [or Chios?], Candia and Nicosia and everywhere else, and certainly this was very great upheaval and bloodshed for the Venetians. . . . And I found in the above chronicles how you imprisoned and tortured the Pope's sister[28] and the exile you inflicted on your citizens at that time who were in contact with the Duke of Milan and the Florentines.

And after these innovations I also found recorded the mad deeds which the Signoria of Venice performed after the war in the east, and the exile of the Loredan family and all the fine provisions and ordinances you made. I am not at all surprised because I know that with you everything comes from the arse, and nothing from the head: experience makes it all clear to me.   D. C.

13   RADICAL PROPOSALS (*c.*1500) BY AN AGED PATRICIAN (DOMENICO MOROSINI)
Morosini ed. Finzi 1969, pp. 118–19.   *ideal* Venice

But now we come to a matter of the greatest weight in any republic and to which few have paid attention: appointment to offices [*honores*]. For, if it is done according to reason, it is of the utmost value in preserving justice, doing away with endemic dissension and ensuring the permanent survival of the city. But offices are of various sorts in each city. Certain high offices are suited only to the leading nobles well-deserving of the republic; some ordinary and minor offices are commonly committed to the people (or virtually to the people) either by election or lottery, and those of every age and condition are permitted to compete. I do not approve of this for various reasons. For the young and poor are admitted in this competition, and they greatly outnumber the leading nobles [*optimates*]. From them all sorts of evils proceed, as there are always many of this class of men to be found in every city. From this arises bribery, the selling of lawsuits, [the cause,] in my view, of the corrupting and depraving of moral standards; this is the source of factions and sedition, the last and fatal evil in any republic. For among the young not gravity, nor consideration for legal penalties, but only passion, hatred and restlessness thrive. . . . In any republic, there are many rich men, who are powerful and factious, and who are not worthy to hold offices, but who strive after those that they cannot justly obtain and attempt to

---

[28] In 1472 Isabella Zeno, sister of the deceased Paul II (1464–71) – who although a Venetian patrician had been in conflict with the Republic – was imprisoned and banished on grounds of betraying secrets (Pastor ed. Mercati 1932, II, 351, n. 6).

gain them through devious means, so that worthy and meritorious men are most often rebuffed. Nothing is more dangerous and more destructive than this in a free republic. For men of this sort do not govern republics well. . . . Therefore, to guard against this evil, the magistracy should be divided, i.e. the highest should be separated from the rest, and likewise for those councils which they customarily hold in high regard. A few outstanding magistrates should be assigned to a Council of Elders, and the rest relegated to a Council of Juniors. We say 'a few' and only those who are outstanding, because, if you want to adopt the many, you will admit into this Council many uneducated men, who will attend it not from love of dignity, but out of desire for wealth, and so are apt to dishonour rather than to embellish their order. Only a few, therefore, of the magistrates are to be assigned to this order, and the rest are to be left to the 'multitude' . . . but the authority and power of the people (or virtually of the people) resides with the Council of Elders. If it is asked who are and who are not Elders, the age limit should be defined according to the [individual] city and place, but the dividing-line ought not to be less than the age of forty, or, if the 'multitude' is huge, forty-five or fifty.   D. C.

14   INDIGNITIES OF THE DOGESHIP

(a) The deposition of Francesco Foscari, 1457

indw doge not up to standards

From the Latin. ASV Consiglio dei Dieci, Parti miste, filza 15 (1457), f. 140r–v.

22 October [1457]: the Council of Ten with the Zonta

This excellent Council has heard how our most illustrious Prince replies to what was explained to him yesterday and today, according to the decision of the said Council taken by the Lords Councillors and the [Three] Heads of the Council, exhorting and asking him that he be willing to resign for the necessary and most evident convenience of our state and government; also that he should be willing to say definitively what his intention is, and thus clearly and openly be understood. His Sublimity, who did not wish to give any definite reply, asked that the matter be allowed to ride for the time being and things go on as they are, with such detriment and prejudice to our state as everyone knows, because, owing to his absence and personal inability, the affairs of our state and government are daily seen to go from bad to worse. And, unless provision is made, it can be held for certain that in the passage of time we shall expect much greater and more serious inconveniences and dangers, which as true citizens we must avoid with all our powers. Therefore, the motion is proposed by the authority of this Council with the Zonta: let it be agreed that the Lords Councillors and Heads of the Council shall tomorrow morning confer with the most illustrious Prince, saying to him that this Council has now twice sent them to his presence, urging and requesting him to be willing to resign voluntarily and freely, for the necessary good and most evident convenience of our state; and that, because His Sublimity has refused to do so, the Council is firmly persuaded that, to avoid the emergencies and dangers which might develop, it is wholly necessary, as this excellent Council very well understands, to declare to him the decision and resolution of the forenamed Council with the Zontà, that he shall be deposed from the Dogeship and made to leave the Palace within the next eight days. However, he shall be told that he will have every year for the remainder of his lifetime 1500 ducats from our Salt Office from the moneys of our dominion, which will be paid to him in monthly instalments; in addition, whatever remains to him of his salary up to the present day shall be paid to him in instalments by the said Office in six months (as was offered to His Highness). Moreover, it is henceforth resolved that, if the said Prince will not obey this decision of ours within the said term, all his goods will be forfeit and will pass to our possession, and he shall none the less remain deprived. Meanwhile it is also resolved that the matter of electing a new Prince shall proceed by way of the Great Council, according to the usual manner and custom.

For, 28; against, 5; uncertain, 5.   D. C.

(b) Discord over a ducal election: 'old' and 'new' families, 1486

Marin Sanudo, *Vite dei Dogi*: BMV ms. Ital., cl. VII, 531 (7152), ff. 271r–273r.

[*September 1486*]   *ancient families + faction*

There arose in the city a cursed discord between noblemen of the old and new families. This was because members of the Forty-One[29] wanted to elect as Doge Bernardo Giustinian, who was from [one of] the ancient families,[30] and the others could not tolerate that any of these [families] should regain the Dogeship, from which they had been excluded since the 1380s. And they began to arrange for the exclusion [*a far caxer*] of a third of those nominated in the Great Council from the ancient families, especially for the Senate and Council of Ten . . . people talked of nothing else but of these highly important matters, splitting the city into two parties: . . . it was said that there had never been such hatred and party division [*partialità*], and if it continued the city would be in a bad way. It began on the day of the entry into office of the Eleven[31] [five names are given], who wanted to elect a large number from the ancient families to the

[29] The ultimate electoral committee for the Dogeship (Finlay 1980, pp. 92–6).
[30] See above, II.3(b)–(c).
[31] Penultimate electoral committee for the Dogeship (Finlay 1980, pp. 92–6).

Forty-One, although not from the leading families of the city [*primi di la terra*]. . . . And, if God had not provided, great division in the state would have followed. Agostino Barbarigo was elected Doge, but in spite of this they did not calm down; on the contrary, with the ballots in both the Great Council and the Senate they struck out members of the said old families who were nominated, and at the election of the Zonta on 30 September only seven members of the ancient families remained. . . . And already the news was spread through the whole of Italy that there was a great party division between nobles of the old and new families in Venice, as in many Italian cities and particularly in Florence, Siena, Bologna and Genoa; and Signor Lodovico Sforza, who governed Milan, went in person to talk to Marcantonio Morosini, our ambassador.   D. C.

(c) Financial abuses of Agostino Barbarigo: investigations in 1501

DMS, iv, cols 181–2.

Magistry after death to look into

15 December 1501

Since the whole city wanted to hear about the deceased Doge's faults, and his contraventions of his *promissione*, the Great Council was summoned at the petition of three Inquisitors, etc., and there were over 1200 in the Council. And Sier Antonio Loredan, the knight, Inquisitor, took the platform, and delivered an ornate, elegant and moral opening speech expressing detestation of so much horrible, abominable and frightful greed and extortion on the part of the deceased Doge, the selling of justice and the possessions of the treasuries [*camere*] and of our subjects of Piove di Sacco, Rovigo, Padua, Feltre, Cividale and other places. He remained on the dais for four hours, commanding attention wonderfully, without a spit being heard. The case was opened by him with a great display of memory for the main details of all the greedy excesses operated on the Doge's behalf by his son-in-law Sier Zorzi Nani, who died a few days ago, and by his [Zorzi's] sons and many of his esquires [*scudieri*] without any shame ('as Doge and tyrant, my will is thus, my order is thus', etc.), and all proved by every sort of evidence and especially from the account books of Sier Zorzi Nani, removed from his house by order of the Forty, and from the account books of Batista, the former chamberlain, and by stewards and knights and the books of the public customs offices. And the said Antonio Loredan was on the dais until the twenty-fourth hour and still had not finished [railing] against the diabolical Doge, ridden with such detestable avarice and insatiable cupidity. The written evidence is very great: three days are needed to read through it; there are 200 witnesses. The advocates for the Doge were Rigo Antonio and Venereo, doctors of law, and Marin Querini. . . .

[16 December]

In the Great Council, called for the above hearing, the heirs of the Doge, Nani and Pisani,[32] asked the Signoria to reveal the names of the witnesses, in order to contest them, and they did this to prolong matters. And this [plan] was opposed by the Inquisitors, saying that they should be left to complete the opening of the case, and to prove the evidence contained in the account books of Sier Zorzi Nani and others of the Doge's household, Batista the steward and the knights, and that then the names of the witnesses would be given. And it was thus decided by the Signoria. And Sier Antonio Loredan returned to the podium and completed his unfinished speech of the previous day, saying that there were twelve charges of contravention of the *promissione*. Of these twelve he only read out three, which he proved from the account books of the aforesaid Zorzi Nani and others of the household. And the said heirs, having seen that they proceeded by means of the account books, left the Council, not having anything to say in defence and not wishing to be put to shame.

Charges made by the Inquisitors against the deceased Doge

1   That he wanted all the moneys of his salary from the Camerlengo, [income] from the state loan funds [*imprestidi*] of the Monte Vecchio and Monte Nuovo,[33] and the sums levied from the subject cities which come to the Doge, to be paid to him in ducats of the Mint at ½ per cent or even 2 to 3 per cent above par, at the expense of St Mark and the [subject] cities, and be brought to him in silk bags or silver purses; and from this profit they reckon the loss [to the state] exceeds 680 ducats.

2   That everything he received in advance for the banquets he gave, i.e. pheasants, partridges, larks, etc., down to the beef fat [*el seo di bo*] which the Duke of Milan gave to the Signoria, and all the game he was given, he [ordered to be] sold off to the poulterers: this is recorded in Nani's account book.

3   That over 10,000 quarts of wine and malmsey came into his cellar from prelates, lords, noblemen and citizens, and retail wine sold as though for the Arsenal at 31 soldi a quart, exempt from duty; on all this quantity it was found that duty had been paid on only 500 quarts. Some of this wine, it was found, had been noted as sold clandestinely beneath the staircase of the Prisons, and this appears from the said account books.   D. C.

---

[32] Bernardo and/or Paolo Nani, sons of Zorzi, were grandsons of the deceased Doge, and Domenico Pisani was his other son-in-law (Brunetti 1925, pp. 279, 293).

[33] See below, IV.11–13.

(d) Leonardo Loredan's want of leadership in the war crisis, 1509

DMS, viii, cols 265–6.

feebleness

17 May 1509

The whole city was in a state of gloom, and there was much railing against fortune for allowing such a fine army to be wretchedly beaten. They blamed the greed of Alviano,[34] and they wanted him here to give some satisfaction to the people, and they blamed even more the Capitanio,[35] who is worthless, and the *condottieri* and our own troops, who are worth zero; everyone concludes that we have lost this most excellent state. And they greatly blamed the members of the Collegio, who will be noted down and remembered for ever: we are done for, and they did not know what to do, nor have they taken any measures at all. . . .

One sees that God has abandoned us for our sins. It was Ascension Day, but everyone has been weeping, almost no foreigners have come, nobody has been seen in the Piazza, the father figures of the Collegio are at a complete loss, and even more so our Doge, who said nothing and was like a dead man and [thoroughly] wretched.

And the final proposal, discussed by everyone, was to send the Doge in person as far as Verona, to put some heart into our troops and the people, and to make the Councillors go with him; if he should make this move, 500 nobles would go with His Serenity, at their own expense. It was talked about both on the Piazza and on the benches of the Senate. And the members of the Collegio did not want to put the matter to the vote, nor did the Doge offer to go. The proposal was put to his son, and they said, 'The Doge will do as the city requires; however, he is more dead than alive; he is [. . .] years old.' I conclude, these are bad times: we see our ruin ahead, and nobody does anything.

D. C.

[34] Bartolomeo D'Alviano, a long-serving professional commander of Venetian armies, who held the office of Governor General when confronting the invading French army of the League of Cambrai, had insisted against other military opinion that the Venetian army should cross the river Adda; he was taken prisoner at the disastrous battle of Agnadello on 14 May 1509 (Mallett and Hale 1984, *passim*).

[35] Niccolò Orsini, Count of Pitigliano, the Captain General and senior professional commander at Agnadello.

(e) Alvise Mocenigo, scapegoat for misfortunes, 1577

Diary of Francesco di Marco da Molin: BMV ms. Ital., cl. VII, 553 (8812), p. 80.

[On the news of the Doge's illness] all orders of the Republic showed themselves very well content, for everyone remembered how unfortunate had been the time of his Principate, even up to this present moment, for there seemed to be no kind of ill luck or catastrophe that had failed to descend upon our country under his ill-starred auspices. For it had suffered great losses of cities and of whole kingdoms, fires, floods, famines, and at last the most terrible pestilence. Attributing these to his personal fortune, they desired to change their Prince. He was envied by the powerful and by the great noblemen because of his extensive property and wealth, and he was feared on account of his great authority and eloquence. Indeed, he used this authority a trifle more severely than was appropriate to a commonwealth, and to a Republic more inclined to honour its Prince as a representative of itself than to obey him on account of his personal standing.   B. P.

(f) Demagogic tendencies: Marino Grimani's election, 1595

Cronaca Agustini over Savina: BMV, ms. Ital., cl. VII, 134 (8035), f. 368v.

This Doge was elected amid great applause and rejoicing on the part of the people. On the day of his election the people bore away the benches from the Palace and the stalls that had been set up in the Piazza for the Ascension-tide fair, and that evening they even burned the wooden apparatus by the side of the Palace where the torture of the rope is administered, and they seemed to go mad with joy. The previous night there had been an uproar on the quay by the Palace and at its doors, with shouts that they wanted this man for Doge, all of which created some fear and misgiving in the city. The following day he had a huge quantity of bread and wine distributed to the poor, and he had a butt of wine and a sack of bread distributed to all the ferry stations in Venice, so that almost all the bread in the bakeries was distributed to the poor upon his orders. When he was carried about the Piazza he was accompanied by three sons-in-law and a nephew, and with the admiral that made up a party of six, and he threw away a large quantity of money which he was carrying in three silver basins. And the Dogaressa too, with her three daughters, flung down from the balconies of the Palace a large sum of money, in such a way that for a long time afterwards the people cried, 'Viva, viva!' at the tops of their voices every time the Prince put in an appearance. The following night, at San Marco and Rialto, the people made bonfires by burning all the benches and stands or platforms from the palace and all the flooring for the shops around the Piazza – in short, all the wood they could lay their hands on, with immense damage both to the public and to private persons.   B. P.

15   CORRUPT PRACTICES

(a) *Broglio*: a curse or a blessing?   *Method of securing peace + stability*

Diary of Girolamo Priuli: BCV ms. Prov. Div. 252c, vol. 5, ff. 89v–90r.

2 March 1510

This morning the Great Council met to expedite the case of Messer Angelo Trevisan[36] . . . there were 849 noblemen present, and, after one had spoken to the motion, it was put to the vote as was the custom. There were 392 votes against (that is, to absolve him); 401 votes in favour; 49 uncertain. And out of respect for the undecided, and because it was the second [sitting of the] Council, another vote was taken: 405 for the motion, 399 against, 39 uncertain. And nothing was decided, and it was referred to another meeting of the Council: truly a great matter that in this Council the outcome of a case should depend on only five votes. And the Trevisani made great dealings [*pratiche*] and begged all those whom they suspected of having some doubts not to go to the Council, and thus to reduce the vote to a small number; and by these intrigues every evil was done. And these intrigues and supplications will yet be the cause of Venice's ruin, so that because of them I marvel it has lasted so long. On the other hand, some have said that these intrigues, [lobbyings for] offices and magistracies, and these supplications, have been the salvation of the Venetian republic, and the principal cause of [the nobles] not offending in tranquillity, friendship and peace. So that if they were without intrigues, salutations and flattery, within a short time they would be seduced into factions and discord among themselves, as in all cities of the world, and there would be great discord among the Venetian nobility. From this the total ruin of Venice would certainly follow. It is because of these intrigues and lobbyings for magistracies and offices that everyone avoids self-publicity, and likewise they keep secret their enmities, factions and particular interests.   D. C.

[36] The disgraced commander of the naval expedition against Ferrara, defeated in the battle of Polesella, December 1509. In 1500 his brother had been instrumental in the condemnation of Antonio Grimani [cf. below, III.2(c)], who – rehabilitated – now took revenge on Angelo (Finlay 1976, esp. pp. 60–2).

cash bribery

(b) Fraudulent voting in the Great Council, 1519

DMS, xxviii, cols 65, 93–4.

11 November 1519

After dinner the Great Council met and the Grand Chancellor announced that everyone should show their ballots to those who carry the urns [*bussole*]; otherwise the laws would be enforced. And this was done because it is said that many in the Council nowadays put in fistfuls of ballots to assist those who want to remain [as candidates for election], particularly those who spend money for this. Because whoever wants to be honoured must give money to some poor noblemen who are called the Swiss,[37] and the Censors do not want it different from this, nor do they make any proposals. It is the business of the Council of Ten to make a diligent inquiry [to detect] anyone putting in more than one ballot; and, if what is said is true, whoever does such things will, according to the law, have one hand cut off and be banished, etc.

27 November 1519

After dinner the Great Council met, and before going to vote, everyone was sent out, both those who carry the urns and the secretaries extraordinary. Then Gasparo de la Vedoa, secretary to the Council of Ten, took the podium, and read out two decrees passed yesterday in the illustrious Council of Ten with the Zonta. Item (the first matter): in view of a letter delivered to the Councillors, telling of many enormities within our Great Council, and that there are secret arrangements [*intelligentie*] and more than one ballot is cast, and other allegations, as contained in the exordium of the said resolution, it was resolved that whoever wrote the said letter must come within three days to make a full explanation. If such things are found to be true, he will immediately receive 1000 ducats in cash from the treasury of the Council of Ten, and the matter will be kept secret, and he will likewise be absolved of any blame for the said information, the Council moreover having the right to restore the said 1000 ducats to their treasury from the goods of the delinquents. Item: a further decree was read out, seeing that notice had been given of something very abominable, that offices are bought for money payments, before and after election, for government offices, magistracies and councils. This is something against which our ancestors never thought to provide, that, before casting lots, money might be given to our nobles to get elected, and to obtain favour from those elected to positions of dignity. Therefore it should be resolved that whoever gives or receives any money or anything else in order to have offices

---

[37] Presumably an allusion to Swiss mercenaries.

78

etc. [both the one and the other] shall be banished from Venice in perpetuity, nor can any grace be bestowed except by unanimous vote of the Council of Ten and the Zonta. And the person or persons who make the accusation should have 500 ducats from the Council of Ten, as above, and the execution of this law is committed to the Heads of the Council of Ten, the Avogadori and the Censors, and both resolutions shall be published in the first meeting of the Great Council.

Concerning these two decrees, many said there was no substance to the first of them, and that the person who had written the said letter had been put up to writing it, whereas in effect nothing was known; admittedly, in the balloting in the Great Council there is a great variety in the ballots, which is a sign that fistfuls are put in, very largely to help the rich who are nominated and are willing to spend money on the poor nobles. . . .

The other decree is a marvellous way to prevent gifts of money; others in the Council of Ten wanted to make an inquiry into past [abuses], but this was not approved. . . .   D. C.

(c) Misconduct and fraud, 1620
Gian Carlo Sivos, *Delle vite dei Dosi*, IV: BMV ms. Ital., cl. VII, 1818 (9436), f. 191.

In September 1620 there was discovered in the Great Council an affair of the greatest moment. For a number of noblemen had conspired to work together, in the balloting and at the elections, to put up their own candidates for public posts and magisterial offices, and to get them elected even when they had no qualifications, in place of those persons who were well qualified and of great family. They [the conspirators] were detected, and some were arrested and others proclaimed, and then sentenced by the Council of Ten. . . . Four or five of them would go to the urn at the same time, and one would pull out a fistful of ballots, which would always include one or two gilded ballots, whilst the others lined his path, as they say, and concealed him from view. They would then give these ballots to others who were in the plot, and these men would go to the first urn with the golden ballot concealed in their hands, and since they always bore away a gilded ballot rather than a silver one they almost invariably became electors. By this means, too, they laid wagers and made a lot of money and got their friends into magistracies, and did the same for other people too in return for money, for they made them pay well. [They succeeded] in the balloting because they were carrying an enormous quantity of ballots and voting with fistfuls of them, for they undoubtedly had 200 more ballots saying 'Yes' and their competitors 200 more saying 'No'. Monstrous things happened, for people who were almost unqualified and had very little family were elected to magistracies, and the best-qualified noblemen failed to obtain them. This is not surprising, because (if I may say so) the number of noblemen has now so greatly increased that it is almost impossible for everyone to enjoy these offices and magistracies. Only the richest, and those most amply endowed with relatives, can hope to succeed – the more so because, despite these high prices, each of them lives so luxuriously and extravagantly that it seems almost impossible for him to afford it. Small wonder that these unseemly occurrences should arise; they are reasons for the destruction, not the preservation, of commonwealths. However, the most severe penalties were imposed on [the conspirators].

B. P.

16   BREACHES OF OFFICIAL SECRECY

(a) Reports in 1481

From the *Capitular delli Inquisitori di Stato* (Romanin 1853–61, VI, 116–17).

12 July 1481, in the Council of Ten

Some time ago there arose a very great malpractice, whereby our citizens serving in the Senate, Collegio and secret Councils talked with ambassadors and other foreigners in their own houses, and in the churches and squares and on [street] corners; and they recklessly discussed with them public business pertaining to our state, exhorting and encouraging them as they wished, with no slight damage and hurt to our interests.

BE IT [THEREFORE] DETERMINED that no gentleman of ours of the Senate, Collegii and secret Councils, no matter what his rank and status, may confer with, converse with, listen to or advise any foreigner or any ambassador who is not a subject of our Signoria concerning matters pertaining to our state, either in his own house or outside it, except to refer him to our Signoria. He must refer him immediately either to our Signoria or to the Heads of the Ten, if he thinks the matter more appropriate to them; and if he fails to do so he must suffer a penalty of 1000 ducats and two years' exile from Venice and its district. Of this penalty one half shall go to the accuser, who shall be kept secret, and the other half to the treasury of this Council.

And the Heads and the Inquisitors of the Council of Ten shall be bound to enforce and investigate these matters, as shall the Avogadori di Comun; nor may anyone propose the imposition of a lighter penalty, on pain of suffering the above penalty himself.

B. P.

(b) Institution of the Inquisitori di Stato, 1539
Romanin 1853–61, VI, 122–3.

20 September 1539, in the Council of Ten

Despite all the measures taken by this Council, it has still proved impossible to prevent the most important matters dealt with in our secret Councils from being known and published, as we are reliably informed from every quarter: a disgraceful situation, and one cannot imagine anything more harmful and damaging to our state. So we must neglect no possible remedy against so grave an abuse, and

BE IT DETERMINED that, preserving all other resolutions in the matter which do not conflict with this one, at the first session next October of the Council of Ten and Zonta three Inquisitors shall be chosen by scrutiny from those who are members of this Council by any title whatsoever, to deal with anyone who may be charged with offending against our laws and regulations concerning the revelation of secrets. They may not refuse, upon penalty of 500 ducats, even if they hold another office which carries a penalty [for refusal], and they will none the less have to retain that office. They shall serve for one year, and at the end of that term they may be re-elected. They shall be instructed by authority of this Council, and solemnly sworn to make most diligent inquiry against such offenders, and, when all three are in agreement, they must deliver them to the law and condemn them, and must always publish in the Great Council the sentences they impose. And every resolution of theirs shall be just as firm and valid as if it had been passed by this Council [of Ten].

If, indeed, the three Inquisitors are not all of one mind, or if there shall be some case of disclosing secrets so grave that it seems to deserve abnormally heavy punishment, they shall draw up the dossier [*processo*] and present it to the Heads of the Council, who shall be obliged upon their oath and on pain of 1000 ducats to appear the same day and propose to this Council what steps shall be taken to impose appropriate penalties.

The present decree shall be read at the next Senate, and in future shall always be read at the first Senate in October, and, whether it is read or not, it must always have due execution.   B. P.

(a) Powers of the Council of Ten reduced by the younger patricians, 1583
From the French (unreliable Italian translation in Macchi 1849, II, 91–3). Letter from

Hurault de Maisse, French ambassador at Venice, to King Henri III of France, 8 May 1583 (BN Fonds Français 10736, ff. 301r–302r: copy in a seventeenth-century hand).

Sire, these *signori* have in recent days been much occupied about the system of managing the Republic's money; formerly it was within the power of the Council of Ten with the Zonta to appoint the magistrates who bore this duty. Debate about it arose from the moment when the Zonta was dissolved, leaving just the Council of Ten. The question was to decide whether the right of creating the said magistrates rested with the Council of Ten or the Senate. The Prince [Nicolò da Ponte] proposed that it should be a matter for the Ten, but another maintained that it ought to be a function of the Senate. There were many arguments on one side and the other, and it even led to some rather rough talk. In the end it was determined that the Senate should have this power, and will elect the said magistrates, of whom there are three, a depositary and two Provveditori of the Mint, who would have all the management of financial affairs and entry to the Council of Ten. The Prince had only 300 votes in favour of his proposal, and the other had over 900. By this means all the power in the Republic regarding the said financial affairs of the state is entrusted today to the Senate; there is no Zonta [of the Ten] and it will not exist in future. The Council of Ten remains simply what it used to be, with competence just in the cases reserved to it. From now on, there will be no more secret audiences, because everything proposed by ambassadors and others will no longer be addressed to the Council of Ten but to the Senate, which is the sole point [of authority]. This, Sire, can bring some inconvenience to the Republic, because, to tell the truth, regarding money the Ten have only done good, and, regarding the abuses that were committed, certainly these can occur no less in the Senate, it being composed of at least 340 persons, and business to be dealt with there cannot be discharged as secretly as it needs to be without the Zonta. However, to avoid such inconveniences, they have created three Inquisitors of State, to inform themselves about all who speak, write or propagate news, with powers to castigate rigorously anyone who, by word of mouth or in writing, makes himself a propagator of secret matters. Behold, Sire, how this crisis has now been resolved, with the older members of the Republic very angry that the young have forced such changes upon it, and the young, on the other hand, very happy, being liberated (so they say) from the tyranny of the Council of Ten, against which there remains amongst them much secret hostility. We shall see what happens subsequently, but the business seems to be settled although not all are content with it.   D. C.

(b) Open government versus restricted government, 1589
From the report of Raffaele de'Medici to Ferdinando, Grand Duke of Tuscany, 18 April 1589 (Fulin 1865, p. 15).

They take it for granted that Your Highness, out of self-interest and reason of state, will share their intentions,[38] and they fear only that you will be reluctant to confide in them on account of the manner of open government which they employ at the present time in discussing and determining the most important affairs. This is very different from what used to happen many years ago, when public authority was confined to less than twenty senators; now there are some 300 who take part in the public deliberations in the Senate, although less than 200 are entitled to vote. To remove these difficulties, the older and wiser men would like to see the old restricted form of government restored; but, because this method of open government [*questo modo largo*] is immensely pleasing to the generality, no senator would dare to make such a proposal, for fear of becoming universally hated, which is a great disadvantage in this Republic. And Monsignor Priuli, Bishop of Vicenza, talking to me of this matter, said that the need for it was generally recognized, and everyone would be ready to agree to it whenever it was proposed; but that for the aforesaid reason no Venetian nobleman could suggest it, and Your Highness might perhaps arrange for the Pope to take up the matter with the Venetian ambassador resident in Rome. You might say that the Venetian nobility were so fearful on account of these calamities in France, as His Holiness may learn from his own servants, that it would not be surprising if they began to have dealings with the Turks and the Huguenots, in order to create diversions when the need arose, and that all these things happen because when decisions are taken it is the majority that prevails, and not the prudence of the wisest men, who were inclined to proceed with more deliberation and not to appear so strongly moved. Your Highness would thus indicate your concern for the service of Christendom in general and for that of the King of Spain in particular; it seems that the Venetian government is deeply disaffected towards him, and suspects him more deeply than his good intentions deserve and their own prudence demands. You should advise His Holiness that, so as not to reveal any desire to bend them to his own will, he should say that he cannot confide in them or open his mind fully to them as the present times may well demand, unless they give authority to a smaller number of persons with whom one can discuss things more freely. One must not suggest or remind them of the Council of Ten and the Zonta, as before, but mention the matter in the way I have already stated and leave them to do the rest. I have

[38] He refers to the Venetians' desire for a defensive league against Spain, and possibly to assist the King of France to regain authority.

discovered all these sentiments through conversations with these prelates, who because they have no part in the government of the state will venture to speak a trifle more freely than do the other noblemen..... Priuli, the Bishop of Vicenza, was the most open with me.   B. P.

(c) A preacher criticizes the government, 1584

Alvise Michiel, *Memorie pubbliche della Repubblica di Venezia*: BMV ms. Ital., cl. VIII, 811 (7299), ff. 277r–278r.

[March 1584]

The acquittal of Gritti [the Avogador di Comun] gave rise to much talk on the part of several foolish and loose-tongued preachers, who charged the judges of Venice with corruption and bias, implying that Gritti had been released not by justice but by favour.[39] One Fra Theodoro da Bologna, preaching in San Francesco della Vigna, said (in substance, though it took him many words to say it) that the judges of Venice had been corrupted by presents of money, by women, and by children, and for these reasons they took proceedings against him. On 13 March the Council of Ten determined to summon the leading friars of the community of San Francesco and ordered them to tell their preacher that within four days he must leave the city and never again preach in Venice or in any town of its dominion without the permission of the Council of Ten. This was duly done, so that he stopped preaching and left the city, and the sentence appeared much heavier than the crime warranted; but the foolish fellow had said these things in the presence of the papal nuncio and perhaps of more than 4000 persons, while there were many foreigners present, and they made a great show of laughing and enjoying themselves. There were complaints, too, of a Jesuit who preached at the hospital of the Incurabili and of a Capuchin preaching at San Giovanni Nuovo, but [the Ten] did not proceed or take action against them, since the punishment of Fra Theodoro would serve as a warning to all.

The legate went to the Collegio to defend this friar and beg that he be restored to favour, but to no avail, and he was repulsed with very strong words; indeed, he only confirmed the impression that he himself had caused the friar to say these words because he [the nuncio Campeggio] was disgruntled with Venice – for in the past few months rumours had been circulating to the effect that he had been thrashed on more than one occasion on account of women.

B. P.

[39] Rimondo Gritti, Avogador di Comun, had been acquitted by the Council of Ten on charges of accepting bribes in a case involving the commune of Caleppio. Michiel ascribed the accusation to the malice of another Avogador, Zuan Battista Bernardo.

Part III
Law, Order and Social Policy

CRIME AND PUNISHMENT

*J*USTICE *was equivalent to a symbol of the Republic and provided a major iconographical theme for the Ducal Palace, both inside and out; its impartial, unprivileged administration according to the laws of Venice was one of the government's most vaunted qualities. Jurisdiction in criminal matters could, however, be somewhat arbitrary and ruthless; suspects soon discovered the severe limitations upon individual liberty in Venice. The extensive policing-powers conferred upon the 'Lords of the Night' [III.1(a)] and the 'Heads of the Sestieri' permitted forcible entry and arrest on suspicion; cross-examination could involve torture. Punishment was often cruel and barbaric, even if a German pilgrim from Ulm in the 1480s recorded his impression that Venetian prisons were relatively humane [III.3(a)]; and even though a case, at a low social level, in which the plea of insanity was convincing could take up a lot of judicial time and result in the imposition, finally, of a relatively merciful sentence [III.1(c)]. Nevertheless, the ghastly fate of a convicted thief and molester of women who was arrested after chance recognition in the street was typical of exemplary penal rituals [III.1(b)]. The nearest thing to an enlightened programme of penal reform in Venice was only a proposal to substitute galley service for death or mutilation [III.3(c)], on the grounds that this would be healthy, economical and good for the convicts' souls (not least by strengthening Venetian naval forces against the Turks). Moreover, beyond the normal apparatus of law enforcement lurked the almost limitless powers exerted in the name of security by the Council of Ten [II.7(a)], extending to moral as well as political offences, and permitting the accused no resort to a lawyer. A functionary of the Chancery, denounced for breaking official secrets in private gossip, was, for instance, summarily (and inefficiently) hanged at night on the Piazza [III.2(b)]. A foreigner with good connections might perhaps stand a slightly better chance. Such seems to have been the case for Placido Amerino (from Amelia, in the region of Rome), who implicated the leading humanist teacher of the Chancery School in espionage, and on his own behalf composed the eloquent and grovelling appeal to the Ten which is presented here [III.2(a)]; it earned him a relaxation of his stringent conditions of imprisonment in the final*

87

months before his release. A more famous case of treason was that of Antonio Grimani, a noble of the very highest social and political rank. His trial for incompetence in war, i.e. for not engaging the Turkish fleet off the southern coast of Greece in 1499 and not disciplining his subordinate officers, was (as the law permitted, in spite of the attempts to prevent it made by the Grimani family) transferred to the Great Council. It thus took on a public and political hue, with Grimani's supporters and enemies clamouring over his fate [III.2(c)]. The vote went against him, but he recovered from his sentence of exile to be rehabilitated, and even to end as Doge in 1521–3. In contrast to this is the case of Gabriel Emo, who towards the end of the century was condemned to death for his excessive zeal in attacking a Turkish fleet and appropriating presents intended for the Sultan [III.2(d)]. Finally, there was no lack of criticism among foreign observers concerning the shortcomings of Venetian justice. A Welsh visitor, William Thomas, noted the practice of disallowing the plaintiff to speak on his own behalf and the wide discretion left to the non-professional, patrician judges: in fact, he concluded, the entire judicial system was amateurish and corrupted [III.3(b)]. A Florentine observer made similar remarks [III.3(d)], as did a papal nuncio who upheld as superior the administration of justice in Church courts [III.3(e)].

BIBLIOGRAPHY   *In general: Cozzi 1973, 1980–5, 1982; also (though concerning an earlier period) Ruggiero 1980, 1985. On 'ritual punishment': Muir 1981. On prisons: Scarabello 1979. On convict labour in the galleys: Tenenti 1962, 1967; Viaro 1980. On state crimes: Finlay 1976, 1980. For Grimani's trial in detail: Zille 1945.*

D. C.

I   CRIMES OF VIOLENCE AND THEIR PUNISHMENT

(a) The Lords or Officials of the Night

Sanudo, *De . . . magistratibus urbis*: BCV ms. Cicogna 969, f. 6ov (Sanudo ed. Fulin 1880, pp. 179–81; Sanudo ed. Aricò 1980, pp. 129–30).

There are six Officiali di Notte, one for each sestier . . . they must be over thirty, and they hold office for eight months.[1] . . . They hear cases in the morning and after dinner at San Marco, above the prison, where the torture of the rope is [administered]. They arrive at their judgements by means of the balloting-urns, by a majority of not less than four. They go on patrol with their heads of the guard, and the Officiali di Notte go out four days or nights of the week, and on

---

[1] In his later, autograph version Sanudo writes that in 1515 they had to be forty years of age and held office for one year (BMV ms. Ital., cl. VII, 761 (7959), ff. 28r–29r: Sanudo ed. Aricò 1980, p. 26).

the other nights the Heads [*Capi*] of the Sestieri patrol. And they go out armed, with a lantern, in search of weapons and robbers if there are any to be found, and they are also fire officers for the city. And, if they find anyone, they can at their discretion arrest him, i.e. the Signor di Notte of the sestier can put him in the lock-up of that sestier, or else at Rialto, and then send him to San Marco. There must be four in agreement to release him, and only one [vote is needed] to commit him to custody. They have authority to demand that any door in Venice be opened, in order to search for whomever they consider it necessary [to look for], and, if anyone does not open the door, they can take punitive action and break it down. They examine arrested robbers and murderers by means of the rope, and put them on trial, and, having done so, remit them for justice [i.e. sentence] to the Giudici di Proprio.[2] They have jurisdiction concerning those who live in rented accommodation, and can send them to redeem pledges and sell goods at auction; every month one of them makes up the accounts and pays the Officiali. They have jurisdiction over slaves, both male and female, and over gambling and swearing, and can impose fines and imprisonment and also dispense pardons, though no one with a criminal record can receive their grace. They are responsible for enforcing the law against carrying offensive weapons, and if they find offenders can condemn them, except those who have a licence from the Council of Ten. . . . They have a salary from the Signoria, and a cut of the fines that they impose.   D. C.

(b) Ritual execution of an alleged rapist and robber, 1513

DMS, xvi, col. 580.

1 August 1513

This morning in the Criminal Court of the Forty, on the proposal of the Avogador di Comun Sier Zuan Capello and his colleagues, there was sentenced to be quartered tomorrow a certain Gasparo d'Arquà, who prowled around on the pretext of having a trembling-sickness, committing acts so hideous that they make the head reel. This man, for more than a year, had found a trade which brought here many young girls and women from the country and outside the city; and when they were on the road he took them into a certain wood and worked them over, taking any goods and money they had, threatening to kill them, and made off, and the poor ashamed [creatures], having lost their goods, remained there. And he had meted out this treatment to more than eighty, among them eleven young girls who were raped, and sixteen from this city, as [recorded] in the trial. This [rogue] was recognized by one of the women in the

---

[2] See Glossary, under Proprio.

street at San Fantin, and she said to him, 'Here you are, you murderer!' grabbed hold of him and handed him over to the officials. He was held in custody by the Forty and fully confessed everything. Now he has been sentenced to be conveyed tomorrow at noon on a raft up the Grand Canal, in the usual manner, then to be disembarked at Santa Croce and dragged by a horse to San Marco, there to have his head cut off and to be quartered, and the quarters to be hung on the scaffold.   D. C.

(c) Homicide mitigated by insanity: a special case, 1553–4
From the Latin. ASV Signori di Notte al Criminal, reg. 22 (Raspe, 1523–59), f. 123r–v.

(Sestier of Dorsoduro)

Bernardino, boatman of the parish of Santa Margarita, [resident] in the houses of Cha' Marconi, found guilty in the month of June 1553 of wounding the deceased Zoanne Moro, fruit-seller, at Santa Maria of the Carmelites, with a wound in the head from which he died, as [recorded] in the trial on the 30th day of the above month, was summoned by proclamation on the Rialto steps to present himself in person within the limit of eight days.[3] Within the time allowed, the magnificent Lord Lorenzo Contarini, Advocate of the Prisoners,[4] presented him to the Officials of the Night, saying, 'Signori, I deliver to you this man who is crazy [mato]. Your lordships will determine justice.' And it was thereupon decided that he was obviously demented and out of his mind, above all because he said so many things that were nothing to the point; nevertheless he all but confessed to the deed, except that he did not confess that he killed the man, asserting that another Bernardino wounded and killed the aforesaid Zoanne Moro. However, from the depositions of the witnesses examined, the said Bernardino there present was clearly found to have committed the said homicide. The case was referred to the Collegio, some evidence having been submitted by Paula, his wife; and the witnesses on his behalf were examined concerning his dementia and madness. The case was afterwards remitted to the magnificent Giudici di Proprio, who on 6 October 1553 appeared before the Criminal Court of the Forty with the magnificent Lord and the Avogadori and introduced the case, with all the written evidence; and, having heard the defence from the Advocate of the Prisoners, after many different proposals had

---

[3] That is, on pain of perpetual banishment. The entry, from a register of banishment sentences, provides information of a sort that is rare, owing to the loss of trial records for the sixteenth century.

[4] The Avocato di Presonieri (here Advocatus carceratorum), an office created under Doge Francesco Foscari, was elected by the Great Council for a two-year term and paid 10 ducats a month by the Procurators of St Mark's (Sanudo ed. Aricò 1980, pp. 124, 261).

been voted upon, it was decided that the said Bernardino, boatman, should have to serve in the convict galleys, for three years, with half his wages from the Lords Provveditori sopra l'Armare being given monthly to the said Bernardino's wife for the family's living-expenses and food (as recorded in the trial in greater detail).

Note that the forementioned Bernardino, boatman, because he was known to be unfit [*innabilis*] for the galley service, on 3 March 1554 was instead condemned to three years in prison.   D. C.

2   CRIMES OF STATE

(a) An imprisoned foreign agent petitions for clemency, 1497

From the Latin. Petition of Placido Amerino and Giorgio Valla, June 1497: ASV Consiglio dei Dieci, Parti miste, filza 11 (Dalla Santa 1895, pp. 22–3).

14 June 1497. To the Lord Heads, and the most excellent Council of Ten

Most eminent patricians, noble lords, I, Placido Amerino, prostrate myself before your feet.[5] Dejected and shut away in a strong prison cell at your behest, I beg and beseech of you with the utmost supplication and oh so much humility that, if the Council of Ten – that most important of great offices, that most powerful of most important offices, that most pious of most powerful offices – has ever shown any semblance of mercy to anyone in distress (as has very frequently been the case), then may you show the same to me too, troubled and distressed as I am at this time; and, if I seem ever to have wronged you in any way, then be quick to forgive, taking heed of our Lord Jesus Christ – for he, with these most forgiving words, took up and sent away the self-confessed sinner, lying prostrate before his very feet: 'Go forth and sin no more.'[6]

I have been committed to prison for two years by your most equitable laws; for sixteen months I have been deprived of both sun and sky. As a result I am losing my eyesight; almost daily I am racked by pains of the body and intestines, and am burdened by the uneasy apprehension of fever.

Thus I pray that (if it can be done without giving you trouble, and if it is lawful) you restore to me the light of day and my former liberty. And, should I seem to seek too much, then grant me at least a more hospitable dwelling, and a brighter one – which would be no chagrin to you. There I would read a little and write, so that in these two years' captivity I may feel alive for a few hours.

---

[5] He had been accused, as was the humanist Giorgio Valla, of transmitting secrets of Venetian diplomacy to Giangiacomo Trivulzio, the enemy of Venice's then ally Ludovico Sforza 'il Moro', Duke of Milan (on the case see also Gabotto 1891, pp. 201–20). Valla was released much earlier.

[6] John 8:11.

I would sincerely declare, unceasingly both in public and private, in front of no matter whom, that the Ten of Venice were extremely merciful to me. Furthermore, noble lords, as you are like the immortal gods themselves in earthly matters, I beg you not to cease copying them in your conduct: behaviour you will find none too difficult, if indeed mercy is the sole requirement for this. The eloquent poet Claudian expresses this sentiment as he outlines his ideal emperor in the following words:

> Clement above all be; we fail in every faculty
> But one – Mercy alone can raise us to the lofty throne
> Of the immortal Gods.[7]

I know – indeed I have promised myself – that your mercy is no vain hope and that my plea will be heard this far, at least: that I may be imprisoned in a less rigorous place where I am free to dwell awhile on the rightfulness and renown of your most pre-eminent rank and most just power; this is closest to my heart. I pray to the gods that you should now permit this to come about.   R. C.

(b) Execution of a Chancery secretary for breaking official secrets, 1498
DMS, i, cols 917–18.

Monday 26 March 1498

On this day there was a meeting of the Council of Ten with the Zonta, even though there had been one on Saturday; and in the evening, at about three hours of night [i.e. about 9 p.m.] there happened what I shall now write. On the Tuesday morning, 27 March, while I was going as usual to St Mark's, everyone was saying 'Justice has been done.' Thus, when I reached the Piazza, there was our Secretary, Antonio di Lando, aged about seventy, hanging between the two columns. He had access to secret matters, transcribing letters written in cipher, and attending the Senate. All the city marvelled, because nobody had known anything about it, and he was hanged in his long-sleeved official gown, and at night. And the truth of the matter is that this was for having revealed secrets to one Zuan Battista Trevisan, who was formerly in the Chancery, but had been dismissed and was virtually a secretary to the Marquis of Mantua. The way it was discovered was as follows. Antonio di Lando, although he was an old man and had an annual salary of 180 ducats from our Signoria, kept a woman called Laura Troylo, who lived at Santa Trinità, and this Zuan Battista also frequented the place, and in the evening they chatted together in Latin. This Laura told another male friend of hers, Hironimo Amai, one of our non-noble

---

[7] Claudian, *On the Fourth Consulship of the Emperor Honorius* (AD 398), II.276–7.

citizens [*popular nostro*], who hid beneath the bed and listened to these two discussing matters of state and the secrets of the Senate. And the said Laura did not have the courage to go herself and make an accusation against him, but sent the said Hironimo.

The Heads of the Council of Ten were Troylo Malipiero, Antonio Tron and Alvise da Molin, and when the Council had been called it was decided to arrest the two of them and also the said Laura. And so, on Sunday morning, this Antonio (who was lying ill at the said Laura's house) was arrested, and also Zuan Battista, who on Monday was on his way from Mantua in a boat, was seized by the captain and taken to prison. And, once the [Council] meeting was over, the case was delegated to the following: Lorenzo Venier, Councillor; Troylo Malipiero, a Head of the Council of Ten; Niccolò Michiel, Avogador di Comun; and Marco Antonio Moresini, knight and Inquisitor. On Monday morning these closed off almost the whole Palace, and, having examined the case, after dinner proceeded with the trial. And it was a rapid business, for Antonio was hanged in the night, as he was found, and Zuan Battista, not having had access to any secret Council, and because there is no law carrying the death penalty unless one does [have such access], was sentenced to life imprisonment in the fortress of Rethimo [in Crete] with a price on his head of 3000 ducats if taken alive, and 2000 ducats if dead, and if taken alive the sentence is that he should be hanged. And the said Antonio was left all day on the gallows, and in the evening his corpse was cut down and sent away to be buried. And it is worth noting that the said Antonio had been forty years in the Chancery, but he was very poor. He had a wife at Padua, and from the time he was arrested until he was hanged he refused either to eat, to make his confession or to take Communion. And, when he was to be hanged, they had no rope; nor could any be bought because the shops were shut, and they sent to the Arsenal for some pieces of rope, and thus they hanged him. And, while they were hanging him, as related above, he fell and broke an arm, and then he was pulled up again, and the captains did not allow anyone to stay on the Piazza, and not a sound was heard.   D. C.

(c) Antonio Grimani on trial, 1500
Priuli ed. Segre (1912) I, 326–32.

By 11 June [1500] the Great Council had met nineteen times to deal with the case of Antonio Grimani, the Procurator [and Captain General]. These meetings were divided as follows. Eight days were spent in reading out the written evidence and [records of preliminary] hearings. Then Nicolao Michiel, doctor, knight and Avogador del Comun, mounted the rostrum. He had been coerced and begged by members of the Grimani family and their relatives, who have great power in the city, and had been promised money and favours, not to bring the case before the Great Council, because the Grimani [family] saw that the young were very ill disposed towards him, and he wanted the case to be taken to the Senate and judged by the old men, whence he hoped to be acquitted. This Avogador would never, and under no circumstances, consent to such a thing, only to bring him to trial before the Great Council. Now, having mounted the rostrum, he conducted the prosecution of such a culprit with the most abusive and insulting language, basing it upon new accusations but mainly upon eight charges. The first was that, for no other reason but fear and timidity, he had intended not to attack the Turkish fleet . . . ; the second, that in this office he was never willing to punish any [subordinate commanders] . . . but was concerned not to give offence to our nobles, out of a consideration for honours, not wanting to castigate justly those who deserved it, whence every scandal proceeded. . . . And all three Avogadori, truly most sagacious men, expressed themselves very vehemently and with imperious words put great emphasis upon his disobedience and upon his return in his war galley to Venice, hoping by making such a case for the prosecution to condemn him outright. This Avogador Michiel was on his feet for two hours and no longer, and put the above case with brevity.

To him replied Zuan Campezo, a most excellent doctor of both [civil and canon] laws, who was held in the highest repute and has lectured in Padua with a salary of 1000 ducats a year. He took four days over his speech, i.e. two full days and two half days, and he demonstrated to the Council his very great prudence and profound memory, and he struggled with all his power to refute all the charges against the magnificent Captain General Grimani. . . . After all the advocates had spoken, Messer Antonio Grimani, the Procurator, mounted the rostrum as the accused, with very great humanity and great spirit and a long white beard, and truly [the sight] moved the whole Council to pity and tears, considering and remembering the former felicity of such a citizen. And in his speech he strove to demonstrate to the Council how great had been his faith and good service and faith towards the Venetian Republic at all times, showing how, in the twenty years for which he had been involved in the government, all his works and efforts had been to its honour and glory. . . . Lastly [he pleaded that] his being held in the 'strong' prison for seven months, with irons on his legs for a good part of the time, was sufficient penance to move the minds of his judges, even if he had been at fault in some matters. Then, having come to an end, he threw himself on his knees in front of the Signoria, together with his sons, asking for mercy and commendation. . . .

On Friday 12 June the Great Council was called in the morning, which was the twentieth meeting, to judge Messer Antonio Grimani. . . . They decided to count the Council and make sure that every member of the Council voted, and they sent four urns through the Council with four Chancellors of the Council of Ten going before them, so that everyone should place his ballot and be seen to do so. And 1212 ballots were cast, in total silence. Then, following the same order with these Chancellors, the motion to proceed to judgement was passed and this was the first vote:

Uncertain, 95; against, 435; to proceed, 682

and the motion was carried. D. C.

(d) The crime and punishment of Gabriel Emo, 1584–5
Alvise Michiel, *Memorie pubbliche della Repubblica di Venezia*: BMV ms. Ital., cl. VII, 811 (7299), ff. 321r–322r, 334r–v, 346r–347v.

[*November 1584 to April 1585*]

The Senate received a letter containing the dreadful news that Ser Gabriel Emo, Commander of the Galleys of the Condemned, had encountered two Berber galleys on his return from Cefalonia (whither he had carried the new Provveditore, Ser Alessandro Zorzi, and whence he was bearing his predecessor, Ser Gerolemo Tiepolo, back to Venice). One of these galleys took flight, ran for Zante, and was well treated by the governor of that island. The other put out a flag of truce, and lifted its oars out of the water, but the Commander [Emo] attacked it with two Cretan galleys, set free 290 Christian slaves, and butchered all [the rest]. Aboard this great galley [*galera bastarda*] of twenty-six benches was the son of the late Pasha of Tripoli, with his mother, wife and children, who were bound for Constantinople with a vast treasure to have him appointed in his father's place. Others said he was the son of the King of Fez, even as they called the woman the Queen. They were flung into the water and died; of the others, some drowned, and others were hacked to pieces. The treasure consisted of eight chests of gold and silver, pearls and jewels, and thirty chests of precious materials, cloth of gold, carpets, velvets, sarcenet of high and low quality, and other such things to a total value of almost a million in gold. Most of these were presents intended for the Sultan and the grandees of the Porte.

This terrible news filled every heart with a profound bitterness. Since the Provveditore [dell'Armata] had sent Ser Lorenzo Priuli and his galley specially to deliver the news, everyone understood the great danger to all the Venetian merchants and their goods in the land of Turkey and the danger to the person of the Bailo. Greater still, however, was the fear that this incident might disrupt the peace with the Sultan.

Instructions were sent to the Provveditore that he must seek out Emo, take him prisoner, clap him in irons, and send him back to Venice under close guard.

95

The same applied to his nephew, to the secretary Fedel Fedeli, and to one other; all energy, zeal and authority must be used to recover as much of these goods as possible, to make an inventory, and to keep them in a safe place until further orders were issued by the Senate. . . .

The Provveditore dell'Armata sent to Venice Ser Gabriel Emo, a prisoner in irons, with the two galleys of Ser Antonio Zustignan, son of Benetto, and Ser Lorenzo Priuli, son of Constantin. With Emo there were fourteen prisoners, i.e. Fedel Fedeli, Zuanne Emo and other functionaries of the galley who had received money and goods from the plunder, and information was given that some articles had arrived in Venice on board a ship, and were directed towards a soldier of Signor Silvio da Portia, who held a command in Verona. All the culprits were cast into the prisons of the Heads [of the Ten], and Emo had become so corpulent that he could no longer walk, and was taken to prison by lamplight on his own. The Avogador Lando arraigned him, and then it was determined by decree of the Senate that the tribunal [*Collegio*] should consist of one [Ducal] Councillor, one of the Censors, one of the Heads of the Forty, and one Avogador, to be chosen by lot. Letters were sent to Verona, ordering the arrest of the soldier. . . .

The reading of the dossier [*processo*] of Emo's trial was completed, and when the Senate had been counted and sworn there were 199 votes.

The Avogadori came to the Collegio and moved a motion to determine whether the witnesses named by Ser Zuanne Emo, by Giulio Avogaro and by certain others in their defence ought to be examined, and it was resolved by a large majority that they should not, because they were not [our] subjects and were of no account. Then the tribunal had a resolution read to the effect that they were now done with six men, i.e. Gabriel Emo, Galazzo Avogadro, Stamati Paro, Zuanne Emo, Marco Ceseda, and Fedel Fedeli.

It was proposed to proceed against Gabriel Emo, and the verdict went as follows:

to proceed, 180; not to proceed, 6; uncertain, 13.

All the Collegio – i.e. the [Ducal] Councillors, Heads of the Forty, Avogadori di Comun, Savi del Consiglio, Savi di Terra Ferma and Savi agli Ordini – then proposed that he be beheaded in public, but they disagreed about the day of execution. Some wanted this to be the next day, a Wednesday, and others the Monday of the following week, for Wednesday would be too soon – given that Thursday was the feast of St Mark, and that on Fridays no one is ever put to death. Saturday was the feast of the Madonna, so they would have to wait till the Monday. When these two proposals were announced, Ser Lunardo Donato went to the rostrum, and argued that Emo should be put to death in a secret place and not in public, on account of the respect that must be paid to the Venetian nobility. He spoke of many things, but they all led to this conclusion.

He was answered by Ser Ferigo Sanudo, Savio del Consiglio, and then by two Councillors and two Heads of the Forty: i.e. Agostino Barbarigo, Councillor; Francesco di Priuli, Head of the Forty; Ser Piero Marcello, Councillor; and Ser Alvise Pisani, Head of the Forty.

They put the proposal that on Monday he should be executed in the condemned cell [*giesiola*[8]], and the verdict went as follows:

for the first proposal, that he die in public on the Wednesday	125
[for the proposal that he die] in the condemned cell	11
uncertain	63
	199

And so, the following day, the 23rd [of April], he was put to death in the usual place. He said nothing, and his head was struck off by a single blow in the presence of over 40,000 persons, almost all of whom wept for pity. All of his property which was judged to belong to the captured galley was to be deposited in the Mint, pending further orders of the Senate.

Zuanne Emo, his nephew, was sentenced to twelve years' confinement in a prison of the Heads [of the Ten], and should he escape he would be banished on pain of death; but, if within eight days he revealed any stolen property, in such a way that it could be realized, the Senate would then be entitled to reduce, commute and revoke the sentence of imprisonment.

Galasso Avogaro was sentenced to six years' imprisonment on the same conditions, Marco Ceseda to four [years' imprisonment] on the same conditions, Stamati Paro to two years' galley service on the same conditions, and Fedel Fedeli to eighteen months' [exile] in Capo d'Istria.

Many others were then released on condition that if they revealed [stolen property] they should have 10 per cent of anything realized from it.

This was a most noteworthy case, and there were fifty consecutive sessions of the Senate, lasting until the fifth hour of the night.

On St Mark's Day a Council was held, and there they published the sentence upon Ser Zuanne Emo.   B. P.

3   OPINIONS ABOUT JUDICIAL AND PENAL ADMINISTRATION

(a) Imprisonment and execution in the 1480s
From the Latin. Faber ed. Hassler 1843–9, III, 409–11 [for Faber see below, V.6].

[The Venetians] show pity not only towards those who deserve it, but also to those who incur the rigours of the law, for the criminal prisons are situated

---

[8] According to Boerio 1867, *chiesola* or *giesola* was sometimes used to refer to the chapel in which condemned persons were lodged for a time before execution.

beneath the walkway of the Palace, looking out towards the public square, and are lit by open windows barred by iron grilles, through which the prisoners can look out, stretch forth their hands, and hold converse with bystanders. If they are poor, they can beg alms from passers-by. In one prison I saw more than forty poor creatures going about and crying out for charity; in another I saw poor women calling for alms. In a third I saw imprisoned artisans sitting and working with their hands at their trades and earning money. In a fourth prison I saw rich men of business confined, but dicing and playing chess, and their wives with maids and servants stood talking to them through the bars. In another enclosure, set apart, I saw an aged Jew, confined for debt, who had strangled himself in prison, and the gaolers had placed his dead body on the public walkway of the Palace and posted certain persons to stand around him for many hours and see if anyone would come to incriminate or exonerate the dead Jew, showing that all the evidence clearly pointed to his self-destruction. Since nobody came, except to testify to his suicide, they dragged the corpse onto the square and cremated it by the seashore.

They deliberately guard many prisoners with less care and allow them the chance of flight, especially where they think the opposing party has been unduly harsh, and so they mind little when such people break out of prison and make off – as a few years ago a merchant of Ulm broke through the vaulting and escaped from custody. Those charged with heinous crimes, facing sentence of death, are kept in closer, but not unbearable, prisons. Among the many brutalities of the Germans is the fact that their criminal prisons are fearful, dark and cruel, damp, cold, and in deep dungeons, sometimes infested by snakes and toads, set far apart from men, and no one comes to console these poor wretches save those most cruel tormentors who frighten, threaten and torture them.

The Venetians also show pity even to the condemned, in that they kill them by means of swift punishments. For a man in a noose is not just left to hang, but the executioner lowers himself by the rope onto the victim's neck and tightens the noose with his feet, and so by great force he wrenches the life out of him and prises the soul apart from its adhesion to the body. Among our own hanged men the soul lingers on, to their indescribable agony, even after all movement has ceased. As I have often observed, [the Venetians] inflict these and other expeditious punishments upon the dying, and in Venice one never hears of the brutal practice of leaving a man to jerk upon a rope or to suffer still longer upon the wheel, as is the custom among us Germans.

In Venice fugitive criminals have one chance before they are taken. For, if the culprit presents himself for capture, and then runs to some canal where boats are waiting, and throws a ducat into a boat and jumps into it, the boatman is bound to carry him to whatever shore he asks for, and would be even if the servants of the Doge and all the Senate were after him, and even had he burned down the city or stolen the treasure of St Mark or assassinated the Doge himself. The boatman is not punished for bearing off the malefactor, but he would be if he deliberately ignored the criminal who fled to him.   B. P.

(b) A Welsh visitor's comments, 1549
Thomas, William, 1549, pp. 81–2.

Theyr advocates (as we shoulde saie our men of law) studie principally the civile lawes, and besydes that the statutes and customes of the citee, whiche are so many, that in maner they suffice of theimselfes. But he that substancially considereth the maner of theyr procedynges, shall plainly see, that all mattiers are determined by the iudges consciences, and not by the civile, nor yet by theyr owne lawes. For in every office there be dyvers judges, and that parte that hath most ballottes, prevaileth ever: be it in mattier of debt, of title of lande, upon life and death, or otherwise. And in every triall of thefte, murder, or suche other, the partie hym selfe is never suffered to speake. But there be certeine advocates waged at the common revenewe, whiche with no lesse studie pleade in their defence, than the Avogadori, in the contrarie. One daie the avogador cometh into the courte, and laieth against the fellon that, either by examinacion, by torture, or by witnesse hath been proved: And an other daie cometh in th'advocate, and defendeth the felon with the best aunsweare he can devise: so that many tymes the prisoner tarieth ii, iii and sometyme iiii yeres er ever he come unto his triall of life and death.

. . . this is cleere, there can be no better ordre of Justice in a commonwealth than theirs, if it were duely observed. How be it corrupcion (by the advocates meanes) is so crept amongest the judges, that poore men many times can want no delaies in the processe of theyr mattiers.   D. C.

(c) The case for convict oarsmen, c.1553–4
Canale[9] ed. Nani-Mocenigo 1930, pp. 172–4.

[It is sometimes argued that] all the prisoners in all the possessions of the Venetian Republic would scarcely be enough to man one single galley. This is

---

[9] Cristoforo Canale, or Da Canal (1510–62), was a galléy captain who made proposals to the Senate in 1542 for a new squadron manned by convict oarsmen. At first rejected, these suggestions were adopted in 1545, and he himself served as Commander of the Condemned from 1545 to 1548. The treatise from which this extract is taken was probably polished up by Ludovico Dolce; dated by its editor, Nani-Mocenigo, in 1540, it was in fact written in 1553–4 (Tenenti 1962, pp. 3–9, 17–19, 81–8). By 1569 there were a dozen galleys manned by convicts.

utter nonsense, because in Venice alone, almost as a matter of course, 300 men would be condemned to the oar every year (as we have taken pains to inform ourselves, from those who deal with them). These would suffice to supply two galleys. Think of what could be done with all the prisoners who are sentenced each year in the dominions, both to seaward and to landward. There is no doubt at all that, if the Venetian government so acted it could, in a very short time and at very slight expense, build up a very strong and well-chosen navy – not to mention the fact that this would certainly make many of our governors more prompt and eager to sentence criminals. At present they are reluctant to deprive these poor wretches of any of their limbs, and they would act more resolutely if they had to condemn them harmlessly to the chain instead. This would make the prisoners very happy, and would further the public interest without impeding justice.

Would we not do better to make slaves of the Uskoks and the people of Cimara,[10] who so often seize our small craft, and so make use of so many of these people, rather than kill them as soon as captured, with no benefit to ourselves? We undoubtedly would, and, just as a smith uses one hammer to make another, so should we employ the thefts and lawlessness of these creatures in order to capture others of their kind. In a short time our Gulf of Venice would then be free of their piracy. Perhaps, too, certain neighbouring princes, for their own advantage or other reasons, might send to us those convicts of theirs that they now despatch to other galleys, such as those of the Emperor or the Pope. However, I do not wish to base any plans upon the aid of foreigners, for I maintain that we could rely solely upon our own, and could easily equip at least two galleys a year from the resources of this Republic. Hence, as already stated, we could in a short time become masters of a numerous force.

The fourth and last argument of our opponents is founded upon religion, for they say that it ill becomes our Republic, which has always been a model of godly conduct and of holy and pious customs, to enslave baptized Christians and keep free men in servitude. They say that for 1100 years and more she has been able to vanquish all her foes with volunteer navies, and so acquire a great empire, and has the more truly succeeded in repelling the attacks of the kings and emperors of the west. If, then at the time of her first expansion, when her enemies were more powerful, Venice never wished to employ slave labour, all the less should she contemplate doing so now that her possessions are so great.

This fine argument may have its attractions, but it can easily be answered. As for her power, the Republic of Venice has never had a smaller supply of

---

[10] These were pirate peoples of the Adriatic. The robber economy of the Uskoks or 'fugitives' expelled from other regions was eventually based at Segna (modern Senj) in the area of the Vinadol to the east of the island of Veglia (modern Krk).

galleymen than she has today, for all that she owns more territory. For in past times those parts of Dalmatia and Greece of which she was mistress were all thronged with people who could very well meet the needs we then had. But now, as everyone can see, those countries do not retain one fifth or even one tenth part of their citizens. On the one hand, the continual invasions of the Turks deprive those provinces of their population; and so those who remain, thinking to protect themselves and live in peace, seek new countries. On the other, the desire for riches inspires them to leave their homelands or come to live in Venice. Hence those regions lie deserted and barren, so that for every ten men they gave us a century or two ago they can now scarcely give us five. In those days, however, the dominion did not draw men for the fleet only from its subject territories, but also from the city of Venice itself – indeed, Venice alone created huge navies on many occasions, as we read in our ancient histories. This certainly could not be done today, although the people are just as loyal and united as they then were. For there is now such an abundance of good things that only the most pressing need would ever make them volunteer for the galleys. In proof of this, do we not see that the galleys which recruit from this city are the worst ones of all, because they are manned solely by the beggars and destitute men who live among the people, and the good men shun the galleys? As for religion, I cannot see why we should be forbidden to do what is permitted to the Order of the Knights of St John, to the Most Christian King [of France], to the King of Spain (who calls himself 'the Catholic'), and finally to the Pope, who is Christ's Vicar on Earth. Contrary [to criticism], this is a pious act, and one pleasing to God, who desires not that a sinner should die, but rather that he should repent and live – that certain scoundrels should be condemned to this punishment, either for life or for a term of years, that they may recognize their faults and return to Christ, rather than be deprived of a limb, and so made desperate and of no use. In this way, too, the cities come to be cleansed of thieves and other evildoers who offend them and corrupt good customs, while such people, in that they bring benefits to us, become good as it were by force. For blasphemy, gambling, theft, lechery, drunkenness and other vices (if any remain) are strictly forbidden to them. Little by little they are introduced to the virtuous and Christian conduct they are compelled to observe on the galley, and there they are taught the trades most necessary to life, at their own choice, in such a way that on their release from slavery they may be able to earn a living. And all become well versed in nautical affairs. One may conclude, then, that a work so pleasing to God, so advantageous to princes and so beneficial to the prisoners themselves can only be of boundless profit.   B. P.

(d) Judges and advocates: a Florentine opinion c.1569

Relatione di Venetia divisa in tre parti, c.1569: Bodleian Library, Oxford, Bodley ms. 911, f. 413r–v.

The lords of Venice are accustomed to judge both civil and criminal cases according to their own laws, and they scorn those of the Empire; if any advocate pleading a case cites a Roman law, they make fun of him, which is a very clear sign of their great arrogance and ignorance. Nor are their laws very constant and stable, for they are often altered and fundamentally changed – hence the truth of the saying,

> Seven days suffice before
> Time obscures a Venetian law.
> [*Parte venetiana dura una settimana.*]

There are few people, indeed they are very rare, who have any knowledge of the humanities, let alone of the civil laws, which they never make their children study, and so they use the vernacular language for almost all their public acts. Some of them can barely read, and yet they think to judge cases. Everyone can understand what kind of judgements may be made by such people. But they are so haughty and arrogant as to believe that their decisions are more just, correct and godly then those of anybody else. They are not moved to judge by reason, but only by a kind of probity [*per una certa honestà*]. This is not, as it ought to be, governed by rational principles, but simply follows their own inclination, whatever this may be. However, the Councils are the best of all the tribunals, because so many people take part in them and the cases are minutely discussed, and so they arrive at good and praiseworthy judgements. This is a very rigorous procedure, and differs from anything found in their [subject] cities.

They never determine either criminal or civil cases of any kind until the advocates on both sides have presented their arguments verbally, and these men are in the habit of expostulating dreadfully, of shouting loudly, and of frequently repeating the same remark and the same point, and the man who shouts loudest is the one who most excels among them.   J. B., B. P.

(e) A papal nuncio's comments on the judicial administration of Venice, c.1580

From the report of Alberto Bolognetti, papal nuncio in Venice 1578–81 (Aldo Stella 1964, pp. 158–64).

Knowing the inclination of such people, and knowing that many of them take part in government, it is easy to understand how the magistrates of the Republic permit themselves to interfere in disputes which are the proper business of Church courts, especially when they are invited to do so by the clergy themselves. Their failure to arrive at any true and just decision arises not only from the practice in Venice of entrusting the task of judging to committees filled with large numbers of persons who may be amateurs and of any kind of calling so long as they are noblemen, but also from the time-honoured method and procedure used in arriving at judgements. For the judges are for the most part very little experienced in this occupation, and they do no homework and take no information concerning their cases other than what is publicly conveyed to them by the advocates, who therefore have great scope for deceiving and for demonstrating, as the saying is, that black is white. Hence they have no deep desire to explore the true and well-grounded arguments, and instead propound anything that seems plausible to them, and they attempt to win over their hearers with flights of rhetoric better suited to the stage than to the dignity of the most eminent magistracies and committees. In other places, as we read, the use of such tactics in the more solemn Councils has been expressly forbidden by law. Anyone knowing nothing of this manner of judging in Venice could have discovered the facts simply by observing what happened in the suit of His Eminence the Cardinal of Como against the tenants of the Follina. For the opposing advocates, on the day the case was to be argued, assembled the largest possible crowd of peasants who happened to be in Venice at the time, even if they had no stake in the region of Follina, and made them go in rags to the committee, ordering them to fall down on their knees in the doorway and beg for mercy. While the hearts of those gentlemen were so softened by the sight, the lawyers began to dilate on the poverty of the peasants, on the privation and hardship they suffered in feeding their poor children, and on their goodness and loyalty towards the Republic. On the other hand, they spoke of the privileges, power and wealth enjoyed by the Cardinal, and of the malice and lack of charity of the monks of Camaldoli, who were defending their case. They suggested, indeed, that in order to win honours and dignities for themselves the monks had persuaded the Cardinal Protector of their order to increase the income of the abbey by giving notice to the tenants. The lawyers turned frequently to one of the fathers who was present in court and asked him, 'What did you write to the Cardinal? Pray tell us, is this not true? Why did you not write that to give the poor notice would be to bleed them white, to deprive them of the fruits of so much labour, and to disperse their poor families?'

Because this way of dealing with lawsuits is so ancient, and because this is the way that Venice is governed, it seems impossible to change it, and virtually impossible to reform it. Otherwise I cannot imagine why so many senators, whose wisdom, goodness and ability I have recognized, should fail to cry out and to open the eyes of the others, causing them to reflect that, where you always side with the one who weeps most copiously, justice itself has good reason to shed tears, for it is easy for anyone to weep or lament, but especially so for one whose object is to deceive. To prove the poverty of the defendant and the wealth of his adversary is not a good-enough way to decide all lawsuits, for there is perhaps nothing more detrimental to general peace and quiet, or more capable of banishing true industry from the world and endangering not only the property of the Church but also that which any private person has acquired by his own worthy labours and those of his ancestors. Finally, it is wrong that in a free city, and in one such as Venice, which is not only free but also makes a great show of preserving the liberty of everyone, including exiles from almost every other place, the liberty of the Church should be so much interfered with on the pretext of favouring the poor, and, worse still, in the very act of judging. Hence the decisions of courts, although they were established with most holy intent to forbid injuries and usurpations, now serve as an invitation to the people to seize the property of the Church and then obtain judgements to confirm their usurpations. . . .

. . . there is the further fact that the Venetians make extensive use of discretion [*arbitrio*], for they are bound by no laws but their own, which are very general, and, compared with others, few in number. In their judgements and conjectures on criminal cases they go by the light of nature, and, even though they allow so much room to presumption, they are none the less accustomed to punish crime on the strength of conjecture alone in the same way as if the defendants had been fully convicted. Hence it happens that, if, as a result of any disputes over jurisdiction, the defendant is left to the Church courts, the Venetians almost always complain that the crimes are not adequately punished. This happened particularly in the case of the Veronese canon Migli, who was charged with having caused an arquebus to be fired (though without result) at another citizen. After much argument this case was, thanks to the efforts of my predecessor the Archbishop of Naples, referred to our courts. As I was to be the judge, they applied the spurs to me many times, both before and after the case, and one day the Doge himself said to me resolutely 'We want peace in our dominions; otherwise we will take action ourselves.' For all that, I would not depart from our laws, and, since the crime could not be proved conclusively, but only presumed, and therefore the defendant could not be condemned to the ordinary punishment, I exiled him for seven years. The Venetians remonstrated bitterly with me, asserting that in a less serious case, less deserving of punishment, the Signoria had recently condemned a convict to the galleys. But they were pleased with me when they heard that the same canon, on appeal from my sentence, had been totally absolved in Rome.   B. P.

THE REGULATION OF SOCIETY

*T*HIS SECTION *attempts to identify some of the most essential tasks of government and to suggest how these were performed. It also explores some of the motives which lay behind the attempts of Venetian councillors and magistrates to regulate, sometimes in minute detail, the social and economic life of the people of Venice; for, as Sir Dudley Carleton remarked [I.4], 'The le[a]st thing hath his superintendent.' Legal texts are used extensively here. No one can assume that these laws were successfully enforced; indeed, some evidence has been included to suggest that they were not. But the laws do provide evidence of the abuses that they were designed to correct, and they do record the intentions of the Senate and Council of Ten, if not their achievements.* B. P.

4   FOOD FOR THE CITY

Giovanni Botero found the principal causes of 'the magnificence and greatness of a city' in 'justice, peace and plenty' (Botero tr. Peterson 1956, p. 280). Venetian patricians and citizen secretaries might well have argued that, in addition to guaranteeing these things to their subjects, they must also protect their large and dense population (the greatest treasure of a powerful state) against famine, pestilence and the vengeance of God. These three scourges, potentially more terrible than the assaults of any human foe, were intimately connected. For plague, in the opinion of those who saw and feared it, could well be caused by bad food [document (a)(ii)] or spread by the wanderings and panic migrations to the towns that occurred in times of dearth; and plagues, like earthquakes and even military defeats, were not to be regarded just as natural phenomena or man-made disasters, but also as divine penalties for sinfulness and disorder in the community. A frugal, moral and orderly society, free of extravagance and unnatural vice, was good in itself, and it was also likely to be a prosperous one, for it would earn the favour of God, or at least avoid provoking his wrath.

The documents in this subsection deal with the government's essential duty to guarantee supplies of good and nutritious food. Alvise Cornaro [document (b)] was a strong and persistent advocate of the reclamation of land within Venice's mainland possessions, for he believed that the problems created by a marked increase of population in the Venetian Republic, as in other Mediterranean countries, could only be solved by attaining a much greater degree of self-sufficiency. At a conservative estimate, the population of Venice itself may well have risen by over 50 per cent between 1509 and 1563, from approximately 110,000 to about 175,000. The dire consequences of a severe food shortage are graphically described in document (c), which illustrates the whole range of measures employed by the Venetian government during a famine: the actions it took in the late 1520s and in the early 1590s were not very different. Here the chronicler is unusually frank about the threat of disorder and the extent of black-marketeering. Particularly striking are his accounts of popular resentment against a government – personified by the Doge, as principal scapegoat [cf. II.14(e) on the fate of Doge Alvise Mocenigo a few years later] – which had failed to provide a large white loaf at a reasonable price, and had resorted to inferior substitutes for wheaten bread. An English traveller was later to find the ordinary Venetians a frugal people, but still very much attached to fine white bread (Moryson 1907 edn, IV, 95–6).

BIBLIOGRAPHY *In general: Brunetti 1956; Aymard 1966; Pullan 1971, pp. 240–5, 287–96, 355–60; Mattozzi 1983. On the famines of the 1590s: Braudel 1972, I, 599–602; Davidson 1985; Pullan 1985. On population: Beloch 1899, 1902; Contento 1900; Beltrami 1954. On agriculture: Beltrami 1955, 1961; Aldo Stella 1956; Woolf 1968.*   B. P.

(a) Against bad flour, 1484, 1494

(i) From the Latin. Faber ed. Hassler 1843–9, III, 396–7.

16 January 1484

About the hour of Vespers on that day there was a great crowd of people coming together and rushing across the bridge to Rialto to see the burning of adulterated flour. For a certain man had imported sacks full of flour in a ship to sell them, and it was discovered that the flour was mixed with ash and chalk and other kinds of white dust to make it seem more plentiful; for there was then a severe famine in Venice and flour and corn were very costly in the market place. When the fraud was detected the authorities brought the sellers of the flour under arrest to Venice and they ordered all the purchasers to return it, and they lit a fire in the middle of Rialto and threw all the flour upon it and burned it in the sight of an enormous crowd.   B. P.

(ii) Decree of the Provveditori alla Sanità, 12 June 1494 (*Venezia* 1979, p. 366).

By order of the Signori, etc.

There have been many complaints to our office that rotten and stinking flour is being sold in the flour warehouse, a thing that could easily infect this city with pestilential disease on account of the poor people who buy it because it costs them less.

To avoid any unhappy consequences that might arise from this [abuse], we give orders that from henceforth no shopkeeper who has or holds a shop in the warehouse may sell or keep in his shop any rotten or stinking flour, but must keep and sell good flour that can [properly] be sold. If there is anyone, no matter who, that presumes to keep and sell in his shop rotten and stinking flour of this kind he shall at once be liable to a fine of 50 lire and shall forfeit this rotten flour, which shall be burnt or else flung into the water, and, if there is an accuser and through his accusation the truth is discovered, he shall have the said 50 lire and his name shall be kept secret.

Proclaimed by Pietro di Riccardo, herald.   B. P.

(b) Growth of population and shortages of food, 1540

From a memorandum of Alvise Cornaro, 15 December 1540: ASV Provveditori sopra i Beni Inculti, reg. 299 (Beltrami 1955, pp. 32–3, with some minor inaccuracies).

In past times this city has had good cause to fear a failure of supplies or at least a shortage of food for its people, and we should still be afraid of such things, for the reasons that I will now state. The population of Venice has increased so far that, whereas 30,000 staia of corn would once have supplied it for a month, 45,000 are now not enough.[11] This increase stems from the wars which have broken out in all parts of Italy and have forced many foreigners to come and live in Venice. Furthermore, those deadly outbreaks of plague which used to carry off one fifth of the population every eight to ten years have ceased on account of the measures adopted by your lordships. Hence the survivors increase the population by their own presence, and double their numbers by means of their children, so it is possible that in a hundred years' time the population of Venice will have doubled. The cessation of the plagues is responsible for the same increase in nearby foreign countries. Hence there is more need for grain in

[11] According to Aymard 1966, p. 17, in the second half of the sixteenth century between 3 and 4 staia of crops per head of the population were needed each year in order to feed the people of Venice (1 staio = 83 litres or 62 kilograms). In 1540 the population of Venice may well have been nearing 150,000.

every place, and still its price rises. Another cause of the growth in population is the new way of making war, whereby they no longer fight the pitched battles that used to carry off 25,000–30,000 persons at a stroke. We must, then, believe that in future, on account of this increase of the people, this city will have need for more crops.

Moreover, Venice used to have forty great roundships, by means of which she obtained much grain; but now there are no more than eighteen, and the cost of hire has increased so much on account of the shortages that the grain trade cannot bear the expense, or, if it does, the prices must increase twofold. Venice once possessed Cervia and Ravenna and many towns in Apulia,[12] which used to ship a great quantity of grain, but now they have been lost to us, and, knowing this city's need, they increase their duties and charges and play the merchant themselves. This they did not do until the states became concentrated into the hands of only three rulers,[13] for then there were many petty lords from whom grain could be obtained for this city easily and on good terms, as from the despots in the Morea, and from the lords of Rimini and Pesaro in the March [of Ancona]. Cyprus used to give plenty of grain, but now it yields us little or nothing, because they have given the land over to barley and cotton and sugar cane, on account of the locusts which damaged the corn. The population of the rural districts has also increased, whilst the land has been reduced. Flooding has ruined a great many fields in the Venetian dominion, and they cannot now be sown save, in some years, with millet and sorghum. Hence it is necessary to force the good lands and impose on them greater burdens than they can support, and not to allow them to lie fallow for two or three years, as is done in Rome and the Marches and indeed in all the other places where they have a great plenty of land. Hence the fields suffer from exhaustion and can barely yield five for one, where they once used to give a good ten.   B. P.

(c) Famine and tumult in Venice, 1569–70
Cronaca Agostini: BCV ms. Cicogna 2853, ff. 164r–168r, 183r, 187r–188r.

On 4 October there was in Venice the worst shortage of bread and flour ever seen within the memories even of aged men. For six days on end there was no bread in the bakers' shops and no flour in the warehouses, so that the poor

---

[12] Venice acquired Ravenna in 1441 and Cervia in 1463, but was compelled to surrender claims to the Romagna as a condition of peace with Pope Julius II in 1510, after the War of the League of Cambrai. Monopoli and other Apulian cities were acquired (officially as pledges for a loan to King Ferrante of Naples) in 1495 and 1496, but the Venetians abandoned them during the War of the League of Cambrai.

[13] Probably the Pope, as lord of the Romagna; the Habsburg Emperor, as lord of the Kingdom of Naples; and the Turkish Sultan, as overlord of the Morea (i.e. the Peloponnese).

could not buy victuals in any part of the city. In the morning and the evening over 400 poor persons were seen around the bakers' and in the breadshops in search of bread, and they could not spend so much as a marchetto on it, although many came to blows in their attempts to get their hands on the stuff. These wretched conditions, with the poor running so frantically to the breadshops, lasted about four days. And, to be sure, if the hardship had lasted even a little longer disturbances would have been seen throughout Venice. But measures were taken immediately, for the government found it advisable to make in each of the warehouses a deposit of 50 staia of flour every day. Hereupon the people became even more agitated, and they said many strange and dishonourable things about the government, remarking that the last thing of all was death and they ought to be cut to pieces. Certainly the city was in dire need, and there was much whispering.

The Heads of the Council of Ten exercised all their usual care and diligence in taking every possible measure, and they issued a proclamation to the effect that everyone who wanted to make bread should be permitted to do so, and that the confectioners were no longer to make or sell ring cakes, but must make bread instead. In fact the confectioners did not stop making these cakes, but great relief was afforded when the Council of Ten ordered sacks full of biscuits from the munitions to be sent every day to the bakeries at San Marco and Rialto at a charge of 3½ soldi per pound. This was a great help to the city of Venice, and they did not cease to make provision by this means, and as I have already said they sent 50 or even 100 staia of state flour to the warehouses every day, and there was a great tumult on account of the great crowd of people who wanted to buy flour. By decree of the Signoria the Heads of the Council of Ten had to station themselves with men at the doors of the warehouses, and there was one nobleman for each place to act as guard, so that no unseemly behaviour and no disturbance should break out, for the city was already beginning to riot. These small quantities of flour were discharged into the stores by night, on account of the people, i.e. 50 staia only at San Marco and the same at Rialto, and they would give only 1 quart of flour to each person and no more, and the crowd of people who wanted it was so great that no more could be given. The doors of the warehouses had to be kept shut, and only a few people were admitted at a time; otherwise many would have been suffocated, because of the great crush of people coming together to get flour.

On 26 October, on account of the great famine in Venice, quantities of flour made from millet were deposited in the stores by the Signoria at 12 lire per staio, together with its own wheaten flour (there was no other) at 17 lire 12 soldi per staio, and flour made from rye at 12 lire 16 soldi per staio, and flour made from beans at 14 lire. Those who wanted flour could not have more than a quart each, half of it of wheat and the other half of millet, or else one quarter of beans, and it was sorry stuff. The frenzy was so great that people were killing each other to get flour, and this [measure] got the people complaining bitterly (indeed, one heard nothing else in the streets) that they could not eat such horrible food, but in spite of themselves they had to buy what they could get, and not what they wanted, if they wished to remain alive. If anyone wanted flour of good quality it had to be bought from the houses of noblemen and citizens at 30 lire and more per staio. Bean flour had never before within living memory been sold at the warehouses. The shortage lasted like this for some time and even grew worse, for deliveries to the warehouses began to be made no more than once a week, i.e. 50 staia a time at San Marco and 100 staia at Rialto.

The Signoria then had flour given out to the bakers in the parishes, and they made bread with it, and two deputies in each parish, i.e. one noble and one citizen, were ordered to be present at the distributions of bread. These persons made a description of the people, and gave them tickets entitling them to the amount of bread specified on them, at the rate of two loaves per head per day, one half of wheat and one of millet, paying 1 marchetto each for them. After this ordinance things became very calm, whereas before it was passed many people had been smothered on account of the crowds demanding bread from the bakers, and many poor women had been unable to get anything because the crush was so great.

Permission was given to everyone to make and sell bread throughout the city, so that great quantities of bread were seen and sold. Some of it came from nearby places around Venice, and some was made in the city itself, and all of it was called Lonigo bread, for Lonigo is a fortress in the province of Vicenza which has the reputation of making the best bread in Italy. Everyone said they wanted this Lonigo bread, and called it that even when it was made in Venice, and it was very white and good, but the loaves were so tiny that you got less than 1 ounce per soldo: indeed, a row of four loaves joined together turned the scales at 7 ounces and cost 9 soldi. It was reported that much of this Lonigo bread was sold at 10 or 11 ducats per staio, or even more, because everyone could bake it in his own way, and in all the streets there were chests and coffers full of this so-called Lonigo bread.

At this time certain Arsenal workers, perhaps a dozen of them, attacked and robbed a number of persons who were selling bread in the city, and forcibly deprived them of some 5 ducats' worth without paying. On account of this abuse the Council of Ten and the Zonta passed a decree that, if anyone in future should dare to use violence and snatch bread by force from anyone, he should be hanged by the neck, and the person who arrested him, be he an official or be he some other person, should have a reward of 600 lire. A number of bakeries were attacked by night, in Cannaregio and at the Due Ponti,[14] and the bakers were wounded when their bread was stolen.

[14] In the parish of San Marcuola (otherwise Santi Ermagora e Fortunato) in the *sestier* of Cannaregio.

The Signori sopra le Biave decreed that a bounty of 1 ducat per staio should be given to anyone who brought corn from foreign lands, and that it should be sold here at the rate of 15 lire per staio. Throughout Venice one heard talk of nothing but this terrible famine, and in truth it struck the greatest imaginable terror into the hearts of men.

On 11 October the Council of Ten and the Zonta, wishing to alleviate the great dearth of grain which had occurred in Venice, decreed that everyone, within eight days of the publication of the decree, must declare all the grain and flour in the country possessions of noblemen, citizens, prelates, friaries, monasteries and convents, hospitals and Scuole of the city of Venice. They were to bring all this grain to Venice by the end of the month of October, and they were also obliged to declare all the grain which is here in Venice and sell it here, and likewise to declare all the mouths in each household. . . . Furthermore, all persons who, after the proclamation of this decree, sold abroad any corn or flour which belonged to anyone other than the bodies listed above were to be banished for ever from Venice and its district and from the places where they were. . . . All persons who had grain in Venice were obliged, within eight days of the publication of the decree, to declare it to the Ufficio delle Biave. . . .

It should further be remarked that on Easter Sunday, 26 March 1570, quite apart from the dearth of other things, eggs (and they were not newly laid) were sold at five a grosso, lamb at 6 soldi a pound, and red cheese [*formaggio della creta rossa*] at 10 soldi a pound. At the end of June newly sieved flour and fresh bran began to arrive at the warehouses in Venice and was sold at 18–24 lire per staio, because it did not come in great quantities, and it was sold little by little as it came in, with much turmoil among the people on account of the recent famine. Everyone was free to sell flour at any price, because the usual decree limiting the price of flour to 13 lire per staio had been suspended in the hope of attracting large quantities of flour to Venice. The harvest of corn and other crops was abundant, although it came late.

Such was this terrible famine in 1569 and 1570 that great numbers of peasants who were dying of hunger came into Venice from the villages, and at home one could do nothing but answer the door to these peasants who hammered on the doors in the town for two months on end throughout April and May; and such poverty and wretchedness were truly pitiful sights. . . .

On 7 April 1570 the Senate resolved that the warehouses must be closed and that no more flour should be placed in them, because it was all being removed by noblemen who by using the poor as a pretext [*sotto colore de poveri*] were buying it themselves at the rate of 17 lire 12 soldi per staio, and then selling it in bread at more than 36–40 lire per staio. Hence it was decided that all the flour should be given to the bakers of the city, who were to make it into bread and give it to the poor; but even the bakers did the same thing, by giving away the flour, and they did not make the bread. Hence it was decided to summon all the heads of the parishes, both noblemen and citizens, who had been appointed at the time of the Arsenal fire.[15] They went to the Collegio, and there were instructed to attend at the bakers' shops at specified hours in the mornings and evenings, to ensure that all the bread that had been made was given to the poor in exchange for tickets, at so much per head. And this was an excellent measure. . . .

[After the death of Doge Pietro Loredan on 3 May 1570] for some time they postponed the announcement of his death to the people. For the Doge had a most evil reputation, since he was held responsible for the famine, for the many deaths, for the war, and for the dreadful fire at the Arsenal; and there was a kind of pestilence then in Venice, with many dying of the spotted fever. On the day that his death was proclaimed the gates of the palace were shut, and guards composed of men from the Arsenal were posted there in the customary fashion. After the mid-day meal on the following Sunday, 7 May, his funeral was held in the church of St Mark's and attended by all the clergy of Venice and by the Scuole Grandi. It was decreed that all the awnings that had been erected in the Piazza for the stalls for the Ascension-tide fair should be removed to allow the procession to pass through the Piazza with the torches. Note that the funeral, as I said, was held at St Mark's and not in Santi Giovanni e Paolo, where the canopy had already been set up, and where the Scuole Grandi and Piccole and some of the clergy had already started to go. But, because rain was falling, the Signoria was impeded by the weather, and it was decided that the funeral should after all be held at St Mark's, where the customary ceremonies were enacted and the funeral oration was delivered by Missier Antonio Zeno, son of Missier Francesco.

Because the Doge was hated by the people, when his corpse was raised on the bier in the middle of the great doorway of St Mark's, all the people shouted at the tops of their voices,

> Rejoice, rejoice! The Doge is dead,
> Who gave us millet in our bread!'

---

[15] The great fire in the Arsenal in 1569 was widely believed to have encouraged the Turks to attack Cyprus. By a decree issued by the Council of Ten on 22 September 1569, fire-fighting squads of seventy-five men in each parish (fifty armed men and twenty-five *guastatori* or demolition workers) were to be established, and each parish force was to be placed under the command of two deputies, one nobleman and one citizen (BCV ms. Cicogna 2853, ff. 159v–163r).

[*Et otto,*
L'è morto il Dose
Del meiotto!]

It was said that had his body been carried to Santi Giovanni e Paolo there would have been some 400 men waiting there, equipped with millet loaves, and ready to drag him along on his bier. And there was a great outcry among the people, who went on shouting throughout the day and night, 'The millet Doge, who had the bakers sell the millet loaf, the millet Doge is dead!' And the little boys went about by day and night singing,

> Long live our saint and lords of noble birth;
> Dead is the Doge who brought upon us dearth!

[*Viva San Marco, con la Signoria,*
Che è morto il Dose della carestia!]

and other songs, such as

> Let bells ring out, for Loredan's dead,
> Who fed us tickets with our bread!

[*L'è morto il Dose Loredan, campanin,*
Che ne faceva mangiar il pan con il bollettin!]   B. P.

5   THE STRUGGLE AGAINST PLAGUE

Outbreaks of bubonic plague were the most merciless killers and the greatest inspirers of terror encountered by the inhabitants of early modern cities, although typhus and syphilis presented new and formidable problems in the sixteenth century. One of Venice's most powerful administrative organs was designed to fend off plague and to control it when, despite all precautions, it invaded the city. The Health Office, ruled by the Provveditori alla Sanità, had a continuous existence from 1490 onwards, and its powers were subsequently, in the late 1520s and late 1530, extended to include the co-ordination of poor relief, the suppression of vagrancy, and the control of prostitution [VII.3, III.6(d)]. There were fourteen outbreaks of plague in Venice between 1456 and 1528 [cf. VII.8]. After that time the visitations of the disease became much less frequent, but the mortality rose to far higher levels, sweeping away some 25 per cent of the population in 1575–7 and over 30 per cent in 1630–1. The documents in this subsection deal with the struggles of physicians and administrators against plague. The resolution in 1630 to build the church of the Salute [X.5(d) – selected as an example of state patronage, but also relevant here] shows how the

Venetians put their faith not only in natural remedies, but also in penitential rituals and votive offerings intended to placate the wrath of God.

BIBLIOGRAPHY *Casoni 1830; Rodenwaldt 1953; Pullan 1971, pp. 249–51, 314–24; Rapp 1976, pp. 34–41; Palmer 1978, 1982; Preto 1978; Venezia 1979; Ulvioni 1989.*   B. P.

(a) The plague and the pesthouses, 1464–1468

(i) From the Latin. Senate decree of 17 April 1464 (*Venezia* 1979, p. 365).

Every possible measure must be taken against the plague, and the first of such remedies is to beg for the grace and mercy of our God and saviour Jesus Christ.

BE IS THEREFORE DETERMINED that our most reverend Lord Patriarch be requested to have prayers recited unceasingly in all convents and religious houses for the deliverance of this our city from the sudden assaults of such a dangerous disease. Furthermore, two suitable and competent citizens not of noble rank [*cives populares*] shall be chosen for each sestier of this our city, and each of them shall have a monthly stipend of at most 4 ducats from our Salt Office, as can best be arranged, and they shall conduct a careful and thorough investigation throughout their sestieri, and provide for persons to be conveyed immediately to the Nazareth[16] in a manner appropriate to their status. That this may be done promptly, two additional boats shall be hired by our Provveditori al Sal, and there shall be two boats at the Terra Nova and another two at Rialto. They [the citizens] shall also arrange for the houses of infected persons to be evacuated, and do everything they can to persuade their inhabitants to leave the city; and to enable them to do so more easily they shall offer them suitable sums of money. On this matter they shall confer with Don Fulgenzio, who has offered to visit the aforesaid infected persons, and to seek to put this important plan into execution by all honourable methods and arguments, for the sake of the city's health. And the Collegio shall be entitled to make further provisions and adjustments from time to time in this matter, as the situation shall demand.

                                                                        B. P.

[16] The island of Santa Maria di Nazareth, within the Lagoon and off the Lido, was the site of the earliest permanent hospital for plague victims, established by decree of the Senate of 28 August 1423 (see *Venezia* 1979, pp. 104, 165, 365; and below, VII.2). The older hospital of 1423 later became known as the Lazzaretto Vecchio, the convalescent establishment of 1468 as the Lazzaretto Nuovo.

(ii) From the Latin. Senate decreee of 18 July 1468 (*Venezia* 1979, p. 366).

The institution called Nazareth, as everybody knows, has been and is of extra-ordinary assistance in preserving this city from the plague; but it cannot be wholly effective because those who leave Nazareth after being cured return immediately to Venice and infect and corrupt those persons with whom they associate. Measures must be taken to set matters right.

BE IT THEREFORE DETERMINED that our Provveditori al Sal shall by the authority of this Council cause a hospital [*locum*] to be built on the Vigna Murata,[17] as they see fit, and those who have left Nazareth after being cured must go to this hospital and remain there for forty days before they return to Venice. The expenses incurred in building this hospital shall be met from the proceeds of renting out the shops and quays which are government property. And, since the Vigna Murata belongs to the monks of San Giorgio, be it resolved that the Provveditori [al Sal] shall pay these monks an annual rent of 50 ducats. The Provveditori shall be fully entitled to incur any expense, both in building the aforesaid place and in other matters, as they are with Nazareth.

B. P.

(b) The plague orders of 1541
From the records of the Health Office: ASV Provveditori alla Sanità, reg. 2, ff. 103r–104v.

Ordinances to be observed when plague is discovered in the city, that steps may be taken to ensure that, by God's grace, it does not spread further.

When the [Health] Office has been notified that a death has occurred in the city within a few days or hours [of the onset of illness], the doctor of the Office must be sent to view the body, and examine it thoroughly to see if there is an abscess, carbuncle or other symptom [*apostema, carbon over altro segno*]. If plague is found, the whole house must immediately be placed under a ban, with all its inhabitants and others too who have had contact with it. Then the notary and an attendant at the Office must be sent to examine the inhabitants on oath and under threat of punishment. The master of the house must first be examined, and then the others separately, to establish the likely provenance of this disease. The notary must take special care to ask if the sick or dead person has been in any house where anyone has died; whether foreigners have lodged with him;

---

[17] On the island of Sant'Erasmo.

whether goods have been brought to him from foreign parts; for how many days he has been ill; how many times the doctor has visited him; from which pharmacy he obtained the medicines; whether the patient was bled from a vein or by cupping-glasses; whether the parish priest or [other] priests and friars have been to the house to hear confession and give the rites of the Church; whether any relative or friend has been there to visit and how many times; whether they have been at the bedside or merely in the house; whether any of the neighbours has come in to help around the house, as often happens; whether any goods have been taken out of the house, and where, and to whom. This examination, which must be performed thoroughly and shall exact other information as seems appropriate to those responsible, shall be carried out in the presence of the parish priest or sacristan of the parish church, together with two residents of the parish. The last-named must sign [the record of] the examination, which must then be presented to the Provveditori alla Sanità, who will issue such orders as they see fit.

If the doctor has made only one visit to the sick person, no matter whether he has taken his pulse or merely stayed at the door and examined the urine, he shall be placed under a ban for twenty-two days. . . .

[Further regulations for the banning of plague contacts]

Those inhabitants who live beneath the dwelling of the sick or dead person shall be banned for twenty-two days; but, if they have been all together in a single rented unit with one kitchen, they too shall be under a ban for forty days.

If by chance plague should be found in a religious house, the said house and its church must be put under a ban, and remain under it for forty days. The sick or the dead must immediately be sent to the Lazzaretto Vecchio with all the goods from their rooms, and then all healthy persons who have nursed them must be sent with their goods to the Lazzaretto Nuovo. Concerning doctors and barbers, the rule shall be followed as above.

To avoid all possible dangers, it must be noted that, when someone has recovered in the Lazzaretto Vecchio (his abscess having been lanced and healed), he shall be sent to the Lazzaretto Nuovo, taking no goods with him. There he shall stay for thirty days – that is, fifteen in [the part of the Lazzaretto called] *prà* and fifteen in [the part called] *sanità* – and then he shall be sent home, there to be under a ban for ten days. But, if someone has an abscess which has not been lanced but has resolved itself, he shall stay in the Lazzaretto Nuovo for forty days – that is, twenty in the *prà* and twenty in the *sanità*. Then he shall be sent home, where he shall stay under a ban for ten days.

The doctor at the Lazzaretto Vecchio shall send a note to the [Health] Office and another to the Prior of the [Lazzaretto] Nuovo, giving these and similar details about the sick person, so that the aforesaid rules may be observed. The doctor of the Lazzaretto Vecchio shall take care to clean the abscesses and to purge the patients well so that they do not relapse. And he must warn those who recover not to be disorderly, so that they do not relapse.

And it is to be noted above all that one of the reasons why plague persists in the city is as follows. In time of plague, when measures have immediately been taken and the people from [a stricken] house sent to the pesthouses (that is, the sick and dead to the Lazzaretto Vecchio, and the healthy to the Lazzaretto Nuovo with their goods), those in the *prà* at the Lazzaretto Nuovo begin to air their goods. Each takes care of his own and thinks when he does so that these goods are aired, but in fact they are more infected than ever. And therefore steps must be taken to ensure that, when families are sent to the Lazzaretto Nuovo they are kept apart from each other, both persons and goods, and [the goods] must be aired separately. Note that, when newcomers are sent to the Lazzaretto, they are not to mingle with those who are already there, but each shall serve his time separately. And the Prior must act responsibly and diligently in this matter, with all those punishments which can be given at the discretion of the Provveditori alla Sanità.

In time of suspicion [of plague] all parish priests must be instructed to announce in their churches that everyone must report to the sacristan those members of his family who have fallen ill. The sacristan must bring these reports to the Office every day, or at least every Saturday, as the Provveditori see fit to order. No parish priest, no other priest and no one else may remove a corpse from a house and bury it without a licence from the Office. This order about licensing burials must be observed throughout the year, even when there is no suspicion [of plague].   R. P.

(c) The plague of 1575-7
From an account of the epidemic by a Venetian notary, Rocco Benedetti: Benedetti 1630.

The plague continued, killing more people with every hour that passed, and every day inspiring greater terror and deeper compassion for its poor infected victims. Onlookers wept as these people were carried down to their doors by their sons, fathers and mothers, and there in the public eye their bodies were stripped naked and shown to the doctors to be assessed. The same had to be done for the dead, and I myself had to carry down three whom I had lost: my mother, my brother, and a nephew. Neither in life nor in death had they shown any symptom of plague, but they were assessed by the parish doctor as 'of concern' [*di rispetto*], and, since there was an order that [two] cases 'of concern' were equivalent to one 'of suspicion' [*di sospetto*], I was compelled to spend forty days confined at home.

The fate of those who lived alone was wretched, for, if they happened to fall ill, there was no one to lend them any assistance, and they died in misery. And, when two or three days had passed without their appearing and giving an account of themselves, their deaths were suspected. And then the corpse-bearers [*pizzicamorti*], entering the houses by breaking down the doors or climbing through the windows, found them dead in their beds or on the floors or in other places to which the frenzy of the disease had carried them.

It was a fearful sight to see the thousands of houses around the city with doors crossed with wooden planks as a sign of plague. But even more horrifying was the spectacle of so many boats plying continuously back and forth: some being towed by other boats to quarantine at the Lazzaretto Nuovo; some heading out to certain appointed places, loaded up with the mortal remains of the wretched and luckless victims; some returning to the city laden with poor unfortunate widows and orphans who had completed their quarantine. Thinking it a miracle that they had been restored to life, they did not cease to offer up to Heaven praise and thanks to the Lord God. All these things represented a sad and sorrowful triumph of death. It seemed all the more horrible and cruel in that it appeared that Divine Justice had sent it deliberately as the other side of the coin to the splendid and sumptuous celebrations held previously (as I have said) to welcome the Most Christian King of France [see II.11(b)].

But, to leave the city and turn to the pesthouses, I say truly that on the one hand the Lazzaretto Vecchio seemed like Hell itself. From every side there came foul odours, indeed a stench that none could endure; groans and sighs were heard without ceasing; and at all hours clouds of smoke from the burning of corpses were seen to rise far into the air. Some who miraculously returned from that place alive reported, among other things, that at the height of that great influx of infected people there were three and four of them to a bed. Since a great number of servants had died and there was no one to take care of them, they had to get themselves up to take food and attend to other things. Nobody did anything but lift the dead from the beds and throw them into the pits. It often happened that those who were close to death or senseless, without speech or movement, were lifted up by the corpse-bearers as though they had expired, and thrown onto the heap of bodies. Should one of them then be seen to move hand or foot, or signal for help, it was truly good fortune if some corpse-bearer, moved to pity, took the trouble to go and rescue him. And many, driven to frenzy by the disease, especially at night, leapt from their beds, and, shouting with the fearful voices of damned souls, went here and there, colliding with one another, and suddenly falling to the ground dead. Some who rushed in frenzy out of the wards threw themselves into the water, or ran madly through the gardens, and were then found dead among the thornbushes, all covered with blood.

On the other hand, the Lazzaretto Nuovo seemed a mere Purgatory, where unfortunate people, in a poor state, suffered and lamented the death of relatives, their own wretched plight and the break-up of their homes. Sometimes at the height of the plague 7000–8000 sick persons languished at the Lazzaretto Vecchio. Pray consider, Your Excellency, how many medicines, syrups, plasters, ointments and cloths were required to treat them, and how much broth and pap and how many distillations and other things were required to restore them. It was truly impossible to provide for so great a need, there being so few to serve so many. We should not be surprised if scarcely one in ten survived, and if hundreds died every day upon those beds, stinking and blackened with smoke as they were.

At the Lazzaretto Nuovo, counting those within and without, and those in the boats (which resembled an armada), there were sometimes a good 10,000 persons. Their numbers increased beyond this to such a point that the pesthouses could not contain them, and two hospitals for the sick were established, one at San Lazzaro and the other at San Clemente, and for the healthy 500 wooden houses were erected at the Vignole, and others in the Lagoon. Certain individuals, hoping to make a profit, endeavoured to build on stakes, so that their constructions looked like huts for bird-catchers. In addition to this, many vessels called *burchielli* were brought from the Arsenal to house the poor, and on the old hulls of great galleys shelters were run up for the quarantine of those who had emerged from the Lazzaretto Vecchio after recovering.

When the bodies could no longer be burned because of the great stench, a cemetery was established a little way off on the Lido, at a place called Cavanella, and there very deep pits were dug. Following the practice at the Lazzaretto, a layer of corpses was placed in them, and then a layer of lime, and then a layer of earth, and so on from layer to layer until they were full, in such a way that from one day to the next all bodies were buried. The dead from the city who had been assessed as 'of concern' were taken for burial in their coffins at Sant'Avario di Torcello. And, because neither the Certosa nor any of the other places assigned for airing goods was big enough, and because goods had to be aired for as long as forty days, so that most were ruined by exposure to air, wind and rain by day and by night, permission was given to those with spacious houses to air [their goods] themselves at home or in other suitable places.

To sum it all up, in maintaining so many people and bearing such expense the Doge spent a huge sum of money. Administration became chaotic, so that all the Savi were bewildered, not seeing how to provide for so great a need, nor which course to take to protect us from such a hail of arrows, showered down in all directions by the plague.   R. P.

6   THE DEFENCE OF MORALITY

All the texts here deal with various forms of loose living, from fornication and unnatural vice to gambling and swearing. Documents (a), (d) and (e) show that, rather than attempt the impossible task of suppressing prostitution, the Venetian government preferred to isolate and control it, as a necessary evil which had to be condoned in the hope of escaping worse disorders. Official attempts to confine it to Rialto did not succeed for long. The castelletto *regulated in document (a) was designed to replace another fortified brothel, founded a century earlier, and now beyond repair. To judge by document (e), a major concern of legislators by the 1540s was not the common prostitute but the prosperous courtesan. Sexual ambivalence [document (b)] and homosexual practices were vehemently condemned and threatened with savage punishments; but the diarist Girolamo Priuli [document (c)] gives reasons why the law was not rigorously enforced. He was describing the mood of self-accusation which overtook the Venetians in June 1509, when they explained the catastrophic defeat of their armies at Agnadello partly as punishment for their own failure to put down luxurious, lascivious and perverted behaviour. The jurisdiction of the Council of Ten [documents (f)–(g)] extended to blasphemy as well as sodomy, and such disrespect for heavenly beings came to be treated as an equal or even greater danger to the state. A subcommission of the Ten, the* Esecutori contro la Bestemmia, *was established in 1537, and the increasingly wide range of its concerns is suggested by document (g).*

BIBLIOGRAPHY   *In general: Pullan 1971, pp. 375–94; Pavan 1980; Scarabello 1980; Labalme 1984; Ruggiero 1985; Olivieri 1985; Martini 1986;* Il gioco dell'amore *1990. On the* Esecutori contro la Bestemmia: *Grendler 1977; Derosas 1980; Pullan 1983, pp. 79–85.*   B. P.

(a) The Rialto brothel and the regulation of prostitution, 1460

From the Latin. Extracts from regulations proposed in the Collegio by the Heads of the Sestieri and approved by the Doge and his six Councillors on 4 September 1460 (Orford 1870–2, pp. 56–9).

By command of the most illustrious Signoria the Lord Heads of the Sestieri have been entrusted with the task of finding a suitable and proper place where the whores [*meretrices*] must abide, and of making fitting arrangements for these sinful women [*peccatricibus*]. Hence the noble and wise Lords and Heads of Sestieri, Francesco Contarini, Marino Coco, Pietro Lombardo, Antonio Coppo and Natalin Nadal, together with Ser Andrea Gradenigo of the Criminal Court of the Forty (in place of the Head of the sestier of San Polo), faithfully executing the orders issued to them by the most illustrious Signoria, have examined all places on the island of Rialto, and have agreed that the best solution and the least harmful to that island would be for these sinful women to abide in the houses of the noble Priamo Malipiero. They are situated in a street behind the inn called the Ox, and Don Priamo has granted them to the Heads of the Sestieri on the same terms and conditions, and at the same rent, as when the first fortified brothel [*castelletus*], which is now to be demolished, was built.

First, the Lord Heads of the Sestieri, having looked into the matter thoroughly and taken information, have determined that every sinful woman who resides in the said alley or street shall be bound to pay 6 lire per month by way of rent for each room, and other sinful women who do not reside in that common place but do occupy vaults [*voltas*][18] on the island of Rialto shall be obliged to contribute to the common place or fortified brothel the sum of 3 lire per month apiece, that being the sum they used to pay towards the fortified brothel which is now to be destroyed. And the said Don Priamo shall be bound to build and provide a sufficient number of vaults or booths [*apotecas*].

That the said Don Priamo shall now and in the future be obliged to keep the said houses or booths in a good state of repair at his own expense, and shall further be bound to provide suitable and necessary accommodation for these sinful women.

That two castellans shall be appointed to remain on guard in the said fortified brothel from the twenty-fourth hour [sunset] to the second hour of the night, lest the sinful women be molested or injured. Each castellan shall receive 3 litre per month from public funds, and shall observe all the other rules which used to apply in the fortified brothel that is now to be destroyed.

That from henceforth no one may enter the fortified brothel bearing a knife or other weapons, upon a fine of 25 lire and one month's imprisonment, notwithstanding any licence or permission he may have to bear arms.

Item. The said Lords have ordained that from henceforth all whores of the island of Rialto must repair to the public place and to the vaults assigned to them, upon a fine of 10 lire and twenty-five lashes each.

Item. They have decreed that no sinful or other woman may have herself touched or have carnal knowledge of any man in the daytime in any inn, tavern

---

[18] *Voltae* or *volte* were literally vaults or storerooms to house merchandise; in this context the word suggests a bleak, utilitarian room without windows, and perhaps expresses the notion that prostitutes were merchandise.

or bath-house, on pain of ten lashes and a fine of 5 lire for each offence; and any keeper of an inn, tavern or bath-house who permits a woman to have herself touched on his premises during the day shall be fined 10 lire for each woman.

And, since the said whores, who make a living from their wretched condition, have been dragged by keepers of inns, taverns and bath-houses, with much confusion and inconvenience and with excessive expense, before magistrates to whom they are not subject, [the Heads of the Sestieri] have decreed that no one may constrain or compel a whore, or cause her to be so treated, save by the authority of the Heads of the Sestieri, to whom whores are and always have been subject.

Item. They have ordained that no keeper of an inn, bath-house or tavern may henceforth charge any sinful woman more than 2 ducats per month for food, wine and the rent of her room, upon a fine of 50 lire to the keeper of the inn, bath-house or tavern, who shall also forfeit the extra charge he has made, and shall have no right to claim it. . . .

Item. The said Lords have decreed that these whores may not leave the island of Rialto by day or by night without the permission of the Heads of the Sestieri, save on Saturday mornings; they must not wrap themselves in cloaks, but must display the usual sign, on pain of 10 lire and ten lashes for each offence, for which they shall also forfeit the cloak.

Item. They have ordained that the said whores may not remain in their place or in their vaults after the second hour of the night, in order to avoid many scandals, upon the penalties specified above.

Item. They have determined that from henceforth no keeper of an inn, tavern or bath-house, or any other person, may have, hold or receive any sinful woman as a pledge, nor may he give, supply, lend or pay anything on her behalf to any person upon [the security of] the said sinful woman or whore, upon pain of six months' imprisonment and a fine of 100 lire each, with the forfeiture of all money or goods given, lent or supplied upon [the security of] the said whores. Liable to a similar penalty shall be anyone who receives, has, holds or has had a pledge upon a whore, and has pledged her, and he shall also be banned from Venice and district for a year. These fines shall accrue to the Lord Heads of the Sestieri and also to the accuser, who shall be kept secret.

Item. They have ordained that no sinful or other woman may presume to enter the fortified brothel or to live above the vaults unless she has first presented herself to the Lord Heads of the Sestieri and to their office, on pain of 10 lire and fifteen lashes. . . .

Item. They have ordained that no whore or sinful woman may dare to enter or to live in any house, vault or room on the site where the Scuola di San Gottardo once stood, or in any other place opposite to the church of San Matteo di Rialto. If there is any vault or room close to the door of the church, then out of reverence for God and the Virgin Mary it must be walled up so that no sinful woman may occupy it, on pain of 10 lire and fifteen lashes, and of 100 lire for the proprietor who allows them to live and remain there. . . .

Since in this holy and just city there are many pimps and procurers [*lenones et ruffiani*] and other undisciplined young men who do not care to live by their own toil and labour, but prefer to pursue the said whores and make a living from their wretched and lamentable state, [the Heads of the Sestieri] have ordained and decreed that such pimps and procurers shall not only suffer the penalties prescribed in the decree of 1423,[19] which must now be observed in all respects, but shall also be banished from Venice and district for a period of two years.

B. P.

(b) Sexual dissimulation condemned, 1480
From the Latin. Decree of the Council of Ten, 15 March 1480 (Orford 1870–2, p. 233).

The coiffure [*habitus capitis*] which Venetian women have recently taken to wearing could not be more indecent in the sight of God and men, since by means of this coiffure women conceal their sex and strive to please men by pretending to be men, which is a form of sodomy; and·therefore

BE IT DETERMINED that by the authority of this Council the Heads of the Ten or at least two of them shall go to our Lord Patriarch and persuade him, by means of the confessors and also through an edict to be published in all the parishes, to prohibit the hairstyle [*gestamen capillorum*] which women adopt, and which they call a 'mushroom' [*fungus*], and which hides the forehead; and to order the hair to be drawn and tied back behind the head, and the forehead and face to be made free of it, that they may be seen to be women, just as God made them, and as was their custom before the present corrupted age: all this upon pain of excommunication. Once this commandment has been published in the churches, be it resolved, so that it may also be obeyed through the fear of temporal penalties, that if any woman is seen wearing this indecent coiffure and hairstyle, her husband shall be compelled by the Heads of this Council to pay a fine of 100 ducats, which shall be given to the accuser, and both the husband and wife shall be immediately proclaimed upon the steps, as many times as may be necessary, as fearing neither God nor our own laws.

If the woman concerned is unmarried, then her father or brother or any other person in whose power she lies shall be punished as well as herself. The

[19] The decree prescribed for pimps and procurers a fine of 25 lire and one month's imprisonment, followed by one year's banishment from the island of Rialto (Orford 1870–2, p. 39).

enforcement of this decree shall be entrusted to the Heads and Inquisitors of this Council, or to another Council, upon their oath.

The Lords of the Night and the Heads of the Sestieri shall be instructed that, once these edicts have been published, all whores found wearing this arrangement [*sixam*] of hair shall first be whipped and then have their whole heads shaved. Having been so shorn, they shall be led to the steps and there proclaimed, and their accuser shall have 25 lire from the goods of each woman, and after being whipped, shorn and proclaimed they shall not be released from prison until they have paid over this money.   B. P.

(c) Homosexual practices unpunished, 1509
Priuli ed. Cessi 1938, IV, 35–6.

I have yet to speak of another wicked and pernicious vice, which was widely practised and highly esteemed in this city, and this was the unnatural vice called sodomy, for which, as we read in ancient writings, the great God sent down fire upon the two cities so notorious to all.[20] This vice was openly practised in Venice without shame; indeed, it had become so habitual that it was more highly regarded than having to do with one's own wife. Young Venetian nobles and citizens tricked themselves out with so many ornaments, and with garments that opened to show the chest, and with so many perfumes, that there was no indecency in the world to compare with the frippery and finery of Venetian youth and their provocative acts of luxury and venery. Truly they may be called not youths, but women. They were tolerated by their fathers and relatives although they deserved punishment; had [their elders] taken action, and forbidden this indecent clothing, this lascivious and dishonourable behaviour, this effeminacy on the part of their sons and relatives, perhaps things would have gone differently and the heavens would not have allowed such a catastrophe to fall upon us. But such was the love of fathers for their children that they were blind to their ruin, sunk and drowning as they were in this accursed vice, and they neither saw nor realized it. By the power of money these [young people] turned from men into women, and now that after this disaster money must needs be in shorter supply they will do far worse things in their desire to obtain it, for they have been brought up to expect these lascivious refinements which one cannot have without money, and they cannot resist such things.

What must I say and write, wise readers, about the Venetian patricians and senators, white-bearded, advanced in years and full of wisdom, who were so

[20] Genesis 19:24–25.

sunk and drowning in this vice of Gomorrah that at their age they became passive homosexuals [*patientes*], and paid the young men money to satisfy them in this perversion, their own fathers and senators becoming, as has been said, the ones who submit [*patientes*]? Surely this is a wicked and abominable thing, unheard of in our own times, especially among old men. It was said that this vice on the part of the aged had come from Rome, for the prelates and other old people were given to it, and there were passive homosexuals in the papal court. Be this as it may, it was a most shameful and detestable excess, and greatly to be condemned in persons of all ages, but especially in old men, and a dreadful sin which was not to be tolerated by the heavens, much less by human courts of law. In the city of Venice there were so many decrees, laws and ordinances for the punishment of this execrable perversion that the books were full of them, and they imposed the penalty of burning on persons who committed such crimes.[21] But these laws, ordinances and decrees were neither respected nor enforced, and that was because the persons responsible for their execution were themselves involved in these offences and had no heart to carry out the punishment, for they feared that the same penalty might fall upon themselves or their own children. For these reasons the thing was suppressed, and the fire which these criminals deserved was quenched and doused with water. It was true that, as it is written (I think) in earlier books, the punishment of this vice of sodomy was entrusted to the Council of Ten to arouse fear and trembling, for in the Venetian Republic nothing had greater authority, wisdom and judgement than the Council of Ten. However, the vice had now become so much a habit and so familiar to everyone, and it was so openly discussed throughout the city, that there came a time when it was so commonplace that no one said anything about it any more, and it neither deserved nor received any punishment – except for some poor wretch who had no money, no favours, no friends and no relations: justice was done on people like that, and not on those who had power and money and reputation, and yet committed far worse crimes. But I do not wish to leave this subject without assuring my most worthy readers that what I have said above, about Venetian patricians and senators implicated in this vice of Gomorrah, does not apply to everyone; for truly there are many good, pious, and righteous fathers and senators. I say it only of some of them, and I think there are very few involved in this bestial practice – which is no wonder, for even among the twelve apostles there was one bad one.   B. P.

---

[21] See, for example, the Ten's decree of 25 August 1464 (Orford 1870–2, p. 63). In the course of debate two Heads of the Ten proposed that convicted sodomites should be burned alive, but the Council decided to continue the more merciful custom of beheading them first and then burning the body.

(d) The regulation of prostitution, 1539
Decree of the Council of Ten and Zonta, 12 September 1539 (Orford 1870–2, pp. 101–2).

In the last few days orders were given by the Collegio and by the Heads of this Council to the Provveditori sopra la Sanità to bar from this city many poor persons suspected of carrying the plague, who, as we had heard by letters from Milan, had been expelled from the Milanese state and from Piedmont, and it was thought that they were certain to come here. Not only did the Provveditori carry out these orders both wisely and thoroughly, but they also expelled from Venice some 4000–5000 beggars and other kinds of person who had recently come to live in this city. Many of these were sent to serve as oarsmen on the galleys, and the Provveditori gave sound instructions that no one was to beg in the city without their permission, and the beggars have now been reduced to much smaller numbers. The Provveditori have also lodged in the hospitals many children who have found shelter there.

Since all these good and praiseworthy acts had been performed by the aforesaid Provveditori, they were given further orders to apply themselves to regulating the many abuses committed by the public whores who walk the streets of Venice. But, appearing before the Heads of this Council, they stated that their commission and authority did not extend to matters concerning prostitution. Now, on several occasions a number of good, fruitful, and necessary measures, to the praise of God and the honour of the city, have been suggested in this matter, to wit

1 that all whores that have come to live here in the past two years shall be expelled;
2 that whores shall not be permitted to live near churches;
3 that they shall not be allowed to go to churches at the times when these are frequented by women of good and respectable standing;
4 that they may not keep in their service girls or serving-women aged thirty years or less;
5 that travelling female servants, until they find a place to live, may lodge only in the house of some woman of good reputation, and one such person shall be appointed in every parish, as shall seem best.

When these things are done, they will not only preserve the honour of God, but will be of no little benefit to this city; and, since steps must be taken to deal with all these matters,

BE IT DETERMINED that, by authority of this Council, the execution of the proposals and of the five articles listed above shall be entrusted to the aforesaid Provveditori alla Sanità, who shall be entitled to take any steps that they judge necessary and appropriate in order to put them into effect, with the same authority as if they were taken by this Council.   B. P.

(e) Prostitution and ostentation; the whore defined, 1543
From a Senate decree of 21 February 1542 Venetian style (Orford 1870–2, pp. 108–9).

There are now excessive numbers of whores in this our city; they have put aside all modesty and shame, and go about openly in the streets and churches, and furthermore are so well dressed and adorned that on many occasions our noble and citizen women have been confused with them, the good with the bad, and not only by foreigners but also by those who live here, because there is no difference of dress. They set a bad example to women who enter and see their dwellings, and they cause no little discontent and scandal to everyone. Seeking to please the everlasting God, we must take steps to prevent these bad examples and scandals, and to curb the excessive expenditure of whores upon their own garments and upon the decoration of their houses.

BE IT [THEREFORE] DETERMINED that, whilst in all respects the decrees already adopted concerning the clothing of women and the adornment of houses shall be confirmed, no whore living in Venice may dress in, or wear on any part of her person, gold, silver or silk, except for her coif, which may be of pure silk; and such women may not wear necklaces [*cadenelle*], pearls, or rings with or without stones, either in their ears or in any other imaginable place, so that gold and silver and silk and the use of jewels of any kind shall be forbidden to them, whether at home or outside, and even outside this city.

They may not keep in their houses any furnishings forbidden by law, and furthermore they may not have any furnishings of silk, or arrases, or upholstery, or bench-covers, or leathers of any kind, but only cloths of Bergamo or Brescia, and these must be plain and have no patterns [*destagi*] cut upon them. Those who break this rule in any respect shall forfeit the goods and pay 100 ducats for each offence. . . .

The term 'whore' [*meretrice*] shall be understood to refer to those women who, being unmarried, have dealings and intercourse [*comertio et praticha*] with one man or more. It shall also apply to those who have husbands and do not live with them, but are separated from them and have dealings [*comercio*] with one man or more.   B. P.

(f) Blasphemy: the *Ave maris stella* case, 1593

From the records of the Collegio, series Esposizioni Roma (De Leva 1887, II, 149–50).

[On 26 November 1593 the papal nuncio reported to the Collegio] that a night or two ago six young men went about a Venetian parish, loudly singing, so that all could hear, the hymn *Ave maris stella*, in such a manner that they added to the opening verse the most vile and shameful insults that anyone could imagine heaping on the lewdest and basest of harlots. Then, having recited the second verse of the hymn, they followed it up with the same epithets, and so on from verse to verse until the end. After that they chanted the litanies too, and one would begin to recite 'Sancte Petre', and the others would respond with most infamous words in contempt and slander of St Peter's name. The Doge and all members of the Collegio at once, in word and deed, expressed great disbelief and horror at this appalling crime. The nuncio then said that for his part he would not fail to do whatever might be necessary; but he also begged the Doge to assist him with the authority of his lay magistrates in ensuring that justice should be done in so detestable and monstrous a case – and, indeed, it seemed to him that such an excess was worse than the attacks of Lutherans and Huguenots. Asked in what parish this occurred, and whether the guilty men were known, the nuncio answered that everything was very well known, and would be revealed when and to whom it should prove necessary, although for the present it ought to remain a secret. However, the facts had been clearly established by unimpeachable witnesses, and the persons identified too; as would be shown, they were inhabitants of Venice. He added that one of the Doge's servants, who had himself heard these impious words with great horror and pain, had wept copiously and fallen to his knees with all his family, begging the Lord God to temper his most righteous anger with his infinite mercy. The Doge again showed great agitation of spirit, and said that he too would certainly take the most severe and drastic action, for there could be nothing more distasteful to him,. and to their most excellent lordships, and more contrary to the modest Christian life of the city, than was this affair.[22]   B. P.

(g) Good order and morality, 1612

From a proclamation of the Esecutori contro la Bestemmia, 8 November 1612: ASV Esecutori contro la Bestemmia, b.57, notatorio IV, f. 274r–v.

Those who, in this city of Venice and its district, or upon any boat, barge, roundship or other vessel belonging to subjects of the most serene Signoria,

---

[22] Suspected of these offences, Francesco di Federico Vendramin, a nobleman, with Angelo, a

even if these are in foreign parts, blaspheme against the most holy name of God, or of the most blessed Virgin Mary, or of any male or female saint, or of any other heavenly being, not only in clear and explicit terms but also under any other conceivable form of words that may vilify and offend the majesty of God, the Virgin and the saints as above, shall without fail be punished by servitude in the galleys, imprisonment, banishment or mutilation, and may even be condemned to death as the nature of this heinous and detestable crime may demand, with a payment of 400 lire to the accuser, who shall be kept secret.

Those who draw weapons in any churches, convents, or other sacred places, and in the Scuole of this city, or who in some other way behave scandalously in word or deed, by resorting to fisticuffs, blows or other unseemly behaviour in these places, shall be punished by banishment, imprisonment and galley service, and by other yet harsher penalties, according to the gravity of the offences.

Likewise, if anyone ravishes and has his way with women, deceiving them by a promise of marriage, he shall be severely punished.

If anyone keeps a saloon [*ridutto*], or serves in one, and contravenes the law in the matter of gaming, taverns and saloons, he shall incur the penalties specified in the laws of the aforesaid excellent Council of Ten, and other penalties at discretion.

And, if anyone publishes any book, song, prophecy, letter or other such matter without proper permission, or falsely makes it appear that it was published in some other place, he and any persons who sell such things shall be condemned to prison, the galleys or banishment, as the offence shall require.

[The remaining clauses of the proclamation are concerned with the licensing of lodging-houses for foreigners.]   B. P.

---

dealer in second-hand goods, and Alvise, a goldsmith, were arrested and tortured by the Council of Ten; having refused to confess, they were released on 5 January 1594.

Part IV
Public and Private Wealth

*T*HE THEMES *of part IV are the material wealth of Venice and the methods employed by the Venetian state for transferring a proportion of these riches to the public coffers. In 1469 just over a million ducats reached the treasuries in Venice itself; during the years of rising prices at the close of the sixteenth century the corresponding figure was about 2.5 million ducats. In IV.1–10, the wealth of Venice, held in the form of buildings, land, merchandise, bullion, shipping, food, wine, salt, and so forth, by both laymen and clerics, is seen chiefly through the eyes of the state officials and legislators attempting to register, evaluate and tax it. Accounts of taxation and public spending help to establish the functions of the Venetian state, and the extent of its concern with defence and preparation for war. In IV.11–13, on public borrowing, emphasis falls on the ways in which the state, through its public loan funds, served as a source of profit and loss for private persons, but become fearful of incurring excessive obligations to its creditors – perhaps even of allowing a parallel state to develop, as happened with the Banco di San Giorgio in Genoa. Hence in the late sixteenth century the Venetian government made strenuous and surprisingly effective attempts to rid itself of the burden of debt accumulated during the War of Cyprus. IV.14–20 are concerned with the rise and fall of private fortunes: with the processes, both dramatic and prosaic, by which money was made and lost through commerce and manufacturing, in family partnerships or other ventures. Finally, IV.21–5 illustrate some of the private uses of wealth, and contrast luxurious, comfortable and shabby lifestyles, using as sources both sumptuary legislation and literary accounts. Luxury and ostentation, however, were never matters of indifference to the state, and the fines imposed on the violators of sumptuary laws could well be regarded as equivalent to a tax on luxuries, a means of transforming private into public wealth, that does not show in the financial statements.*

PUBLIC REVENUE AND EXPENDITURE

*T*HESE DOCUMENTS *introduce the complicated subject of the raising of revenue by direct and indirect taxation levied in Venice itself, by forced loans, by the sale of salt, and by sums of money sent to Venice by its mainland and overseas possessions. IV.3 contains a comprehensive statement of the principal sources of Venetian revenue in 1469; attempts have been made to explain some of its allusions with the aid of information scattered through Fabio Besta's large, invaluable but unindexed volume on the* Bilanci generali, *although some mysteries remain unsolved. In the second half of the fifteenth century the state levied direct taxes on private wealth with increasing regularity, and assessed them not through personal declarations, but through a huge fiscal register or* catasto *recording income from various sources, especially house property and land. IV.1 shows how houses were to be valued for the purposes of taxation intended to improve the amenities of the city of Venice itself. The Senate decree of 1463 [IV.2] establishes the procedure for levying the tenth on various kinds of income, and gives details of other taxes, of 1 per cent only, which were imposed at the same time. Several tenths could be demanded in the same year; indeed nearly forty tenths, each of them raising 75,000–80,000 ducats, were imposed and paid between 1463 and 1479 (Cozzi and Knapton 1986, p. 327). As the financial statement in IV.3 indicates, special levies were also imposed on official salaries. Of some 620,000 ducats collected in the capital, 310,000 were raised through excise duties, 135,000 by the sale of salt, 155,000 through direct imposts, and 20,000 through lesser sources of revenue (ibid., p. 315).*

In time of war the Venetian government set out to raise additional funds by treating a wide range of minor offices of profit as a form of property, both salable and inheritable [IV.4]. At times during the sixteenth century the position of senator (held for a year) and the honorific office of Procurator of St Mark's (retained for life) were sold to raise funds (E. Besta 1899, pp. 71–2; Cozzi 1961, p. 191). However, the elective magisterial offices reserved to and rotated among the Venetian nobility escaped such treatment. Sale of office was to be much more freely employed as a fiscal measure during the seventeenth century.

IV.5 provides a small illustration of the ways in which customs revenues were farmed out and offered a small investment to private speculators, to whom the state transferred some of the risks attendant on fluctuations in its income — sometimes with unhappy results for the innocent or foolhardy.

As IV.6 and 7 imply, the state's freedom to tax the property of those who enjoyed its protection was limited by the claims of the clergy to form a privileged order that could be taxed only with the Pope's permission. For this and other reasons the Venetian state looked askance at the enrichment of religious institutions, especially if this process involved the transfer of houses and land (the most easily traceable of taxable assets) from lay to clerical ownership. When the law of 1536 [IV.6] was extended to the mainland provinces in 1605, it helped to provoke the interdict pronounced on Venice by Pope Paul V [V.17].

At its inception the tenth was accompanied by taxes which fell not only on property and rents, but also on other sources of income, and were sometimes called tenths themselves, as the statement at IV.3 implies. From the end of the fifteenth century these taxes were usually called tanse, *and more clearly distinguished from the tenth, which fell upon houses and lands. In 1548 the* tansa, *sometimes known as the* tansa universal, *became a normal impost, and all inhabitants of Venice and all lay religious organizations were ordered to present to the tax-assessors declarations concerning all kinds of asset held 'from Corfu to Venice', including merchandise, shares in the state debt, credits with government magistracies, 'offices purchased' and letters of exchange. Those who had property subject to the tenth were to pay half the* tansa *every year; those who had not were liable to the full* tansa *(F. Besta 1912, pp. clvii–clx). IV.8 provides an example of a tax return, made in 1554 by two mercers who claimed to have no landed property at all.*

IV.9 and 10 provide a comprehensive statement of the revenues and expenditure of the Republic at the close of the sixteenth century, its main concerns being naval and military defences, the servicing of state debt, the payment of official salaries, and the accumulation of reserves against future emergencies. As in IV.3, the statement includes both taxation levied in Venice itself and sums sent to Venice by provincial treasuries on the Italian mainland, together with small contributions from a few administrations in Dalmatia. These documents have their limitations; much money would be spent on the spot by the local governments in the Venetian dominions to seaward and to landward and not be sent to Venice, so the statements, comprehensive though they may seem, cannot be said to include all public revenue exacted in all parts of the dominions. Nor do the documents convey any idea of the kind of emergency expenditure the state would incur in, for example, times of pestilence [see above, III.5].

Towards 1620 the ambassador Bedmar reported to the King of Spain that 'within a few years the public wealth of the state of Venice has increased to 3½ million ducats of ordinary revenue, truly a very remarkable sum because many years ago, even when the Venetians possessed the Kingdom of Cyprus and many other states to seaward and to landward, they had no more than 2¹/₂ million ducats of income or perhaps a little more, and we find that in 1578 they drew only 2,230,170 scudi' (F. Besta 1912, pp. 464–5).

BIBLIOGRAPHY   *In general: Canal 1908; Luzzatto 1961, pp. 207–8, and 1963, pp. 259–65; Lane 1973, pp. 237–8; Cozzi and Knapton 1986, pp. 275–346; Concina 1989. On sale of office: Antonio Stella n.d.; Mousnier 1952. On revenue from salt: Hocquet 1978–9. On clerical taxation: Cecchetti 1874, I, 130–1, 153–8. For the 1580s: Aldo Stella 1955. For the Arsenal and military forces: Forsellini 1930; Lane 1965, pp. 125–201; Romano 1968; Mallett and Hale 1984.*   B. P.

1   THE VALUATION OF HOUSES AND LAND, 1459
Senate decree of 31 May 1459 (F. Besta 1912, pp. 133–4).

Moneys are now collected in this city for the digging of canals and for the repair of bridges, quays, paved ways and the like by the magistracy of the Piovego and by that of the Commissioners for Wells. These are not exacted in an equitable manner, nor are they properly apportioned as the city requires. On the contrary, many persons are forced to pay large sums when they ought by rights to pay little or nothing, and some pay nothing when they ought to be meeting much of the expense. These errors and injustices arise because no survey of this city has been compiled for over twenty-three years. Within that period, as everybody knows, there have been many changes in property and houses: for some have grown old and dilapidated, some have been transferred to other persons by legacies and sales, and a great many have been reconstructed or newly built, whilst waters and marshes, orchards and wastelands have been transformed into most desirable estates, with spacious dwellings upon them. It is only right that everyone should take a proper share of these burdens, and so
BE IT ENACTED that, for the effective enforcement of the decree passed by the Senate on 13 August 1457, in the name of Jesus Christ, this Council shall elect by scrutiny eight officials [*savii*], four from the near side of the Grand Canal and four from beyond it. Each must be at least thirty years of age, and each shall receive a fee of 100 gold ducats, tax free, on completing this valuation. No one may refuse to serve, on pain of a fine of 100 lire each. They shall be assigned two rooms at Rialto, and those from the near side shall meet in one, and those from the far side in the other. Each of these two bodies shall have a capable clerk, house agent [*sanser de chaxe*], house carpenter and mason of its own, and the clerks shall receive a payment of 50 ducats apiece, and the house agents, masons and carpenters one of 40 ducats apiece, to cover the whole time it takes them to complete the valuation. These officials, clerks, agents, masons and

carpenters shall swear before the Signoria to make these valuations in a true and faithful manner. The Signoria shall determine by lottery which of them shall draw up the valuation for the near side and which for the far side of the Grand Canal.

The said officials must value the sestieri to which they are assigned by looking over the properties and houses in question, always hearing the opinions of the above agents, masons and carpenters who accompany them. They shall not fail to value any house or land. They must note the size and quality of the houses, both of landlords and of tenants [*si de stacio como de sergenti*], and of the lands in those sestieri. They may value neither their own houses nor those of their relatives; but the houses on the near side of the Canal shall be valued by those assigned to the sestieri on the near side, and whatever is done and determined by the majority of them shall be accepted as final.

Where a person has deeds or other papers or titles to a property, it shall be registered in his or her name; but if not it shall be listed as in the last survey, so that this new survey shall not appear to confer rights or take them away from anyone.

Once a sestier has been valued and its properties listed, the officials responsible must appear before the Signoria and have their assessments read out before them; and this shall be done for every sestier in turn, once the assessment has been completed.

To pay for this labour and to meet the fees, the office of the Provveditori di Comun must, as soon as this assessment has been completed, levy a general tax on all the sestieri in accordance with the new survey, and collect enough money to cover the expenses mentioned above, upon the terms customarily observed in such cases.

For the decree, 128; against, 11; uncertain, 14.   B. P.

2 LEVYING THE TENTH, 1463
From the Latin. Senate decree of 15 June 1463 (F. Besta 1912, pp. 135–9).

For the sake of all measures taken or to be taken for the preservation of our state, it is vital to establish methods and procedures whereby additional supplies of money may be efficiently obtained in the fairest possible manner to meet all the needs that may arise from time to time. Therefore

BE IT DETERMINED that, in the name of Jesus Christ, for whose honour and glory such sums are to be spent, the following arrangements shall be made and applied when the need arises, so as to raise whatever sums of money may be judged necessary in the circumstances by this Council.

1   All annual rents of houses, fisheries, mills and other properties (however described) that lie between Grado and Cavarzere shall be recorded in a book, sestier by sestier, in a series of entries, by nine nobles listed below, who shall be assigned to the task. That the burden may fall equitably upon everyone and the expenses be shared by all, the said nobles must estimate how much each house in owner occupation [*domus a stacio*] would yield if it were rented out, and register each item in the book, as above.

2   They shall likewise note all the annual income that Venetian citizens receive from estates, mills, fields, houses, rent charges, and other properties and assets which they possess in any part of the mainland, either within our own territory or under foreign rule.

3   Likewise all the income from bishoprics, abbeys, canonries, parishes, and any benefices whatsoever enjoyed by the people of Venice.

4   They shall likewise note all income received by any prelates, religious, parish priests, canons, and clergy of any rank and status, in any of our cities, territories, castles and other possessions, both to landward and to seaward, allowing no exceptions whatsoever.

5   Our ambassador in Rome shall be instructed, in whatever form of words the Collegio shall see fit, to petition the Pope in our name to grant one tenth of these benefits to ourselves, in view of the present state of affairs.

6   The nine nobles shall also record the 4 per cent interest payments received from loans to the state, and a full tenth shall be paid upon them. And because the annual interest is divided into two payments, of which one is actually made during the year and the other carried forward to the next, be it declared that an instalment of the tenth shall be paid in cash to the government on the first payment when it falls due, and the balance shall be debited against the other payment, to make up the full tenth due to our government.

7   All sums paid for the hire of ships, galleys and other vessels of ours must likewise be recorded from time to time as they set sail, and whenever a tenth is imposed a tax of 1 per cent shall be paid upon them (as upon merchandise, as will be stated below). Ships departing for Flanders shall be liable to the same tax.

8   [The nine nobles shall also record] all income from the hire of necklaces or jewellery.

9   All merchandise of Venetians, be it in or out of Venice, shall be taxed at the rate of 1 per cent whenever a tenth is imposed on all the assets mentioned above, and the officers shall exact it, as they exact the other dues.

10   The nine shall also determine how much is to be paid on account of any profits and revenues derived from shops situated in Venice, or from shops outside Venice but kept by Venetian citizens, whenever a tenth is imposed by this Council, so long as these shops are of some importance.

11   Let it now be resolved that nine Venetian noblemen shall be elected by scrutiny in this Council, and that they must perform the tasks described above and any others that shall be assigned to them by this Council. When we need to raise money from the aforesaid revenues, it must be collected by means of tenths, or half tenths, or several tenths, as this Council shall judge best.

12   Let it now be declared that, after all the points contained in this decree have been noted and acted upon, the books must be sent to our Governatori delle Entrate, who shall be obliged to exact the tenth or tenths, or whatsoever other taxes this Council shall impose. From those who fail to pay they may and indeed must exact a penalty of 2 soldi per lira, which shall be shared between the Governatori. They may not levy this penalty unless they also collect the principal which is owed, on pain of being fined twice the sum they exacted, and the Avogadori di Comun shall collect the moneys and have them credited to the account of those who would have paid these fines without also paying the principal. This measure shall apply for at least two years, and shall continue until rescinded by this Council.

13   The Jews of the mainland must pay an annual tax of 3000 ducats to our government, and the Jews of the seaward possessions a sum of 2000 ducats in addition to what they now pay.

14   Oil and salt money shall be subject to the tenth, in that when those who supply oil to the Ternaria, and those who are creditors of the Salt Office, demand an instalment of the money due to them, they must pay a tax of 1 per cent upon it to our government.

15   A tax of 1 per cent shall be paid upon gold imported from Barbary, whether on ships or on galleys, as it is upon merchandise. And the Governatori responsible for collecting this tax shall be bound to make diligent inquiry both of the masters of the galleys and ships and of the pursers and others, as they shall judge best. Should any fraud be detected the guilty parties shall pay a forefeit of 20 per cent, which the aforesaid Governatori shall exact. They shall receive one third of it, one third shall go to our government, and one third to the accuser, and he shall be kept secret.   B. P.

3   REVENUES OF THE VENETIAN GOVERNMENT IN 1469
F. Besta 1912, pp. 148–50, based on several manuscripts in BMV and BCV, but chiefly on BMV ms. Ital., cl. VII, 90.

In the name of Christ, Amen. Venice, 1469

These are all the revenues of the government of Venice, and first:

Ducats

The Governatori delle Entrate, for the 20, 30 and 40 per cent
   collected annually at their office[1]   40,000
The tenths upon houses, annually   20,000
The tenths upon estates, annually   6,000
The tenths upon [interest from] loans, annually   15,000
The tenths upon merchandise, annually   18,000
The tenths upon the hiring of ships and galleys   1,000
The tenths paid by the clergy   18,000
One third of the interest from loans[2]   27,000
The fixed taxes [*tanse limitade*][3]   6,000
Taxed debts   3,000

Annual total   154,000

The Salt Office, from the profits from salt which are transferred
   every month to the Camerlenghi [di Comun], 8,000 ducats a
   month, which annually amounts to   96,000
And from the rent of shops, traders' pitches [*statij*], storehouses
   and wharves, [the Salt Office] collects each year and dispenses
   at its office   54,000
And from the levy of one third upon the notaries of the High
   Court, the said offices collect   5,000

Annual total   155,000

Eight [revenue] offices[4] yield in all as follows:

The duty upon wine   77,000
The duty upon the taverns   12,000

[1] This refers to a levy on the salaries and profits of all public officials and magistrates in Venice
and its possessions. By a Senate decree of 26 February 1464 (1463 Venetian style), those with
salaries of less than 100 ducats per annum were generally to pay at the rate of 20 per cent, and those
with more than 100 ducats at the rate of either 30 or 40 per cent – for which see F. Besta 1912,
pp. 143–5. For earlier examples of levies on official salaries and other income from offices see ibid.,
pp. 104–5 (1434), 129–30 (1455).
   [2] See below, IV.11, n. 41.
   [3] Taxes or duties were exacted *in limitazione* when the Senate allowed a guild, a commune or
some larger entity to settle, either temporarily or permanently, for a fixed sum of money, itself
taking over the responsibility for apportioning payments to individuals. See F. Besta 1912,
introduction, p. xliii.
   [4] By decree of the Great Council of 17 November 1381, the income received from eight major
revenue offices – described as 'the revenues from the wine excise in any form, from the "three
tables", from the Giustizia Nuova, from brokerage, and from meat; and the income from Chioggia'

	Ducats
The duty upon goods entering Venice	34,000
The duty upon goods leaving Venice	15,000
The duty upon brokerage [*mesetaria*][5]	36,000
The duty upon meat	22,000
The duty levied at the oil store[6]	28,000
The duty upon delicacies[7]	9,000
The salt-pans of Chioggia	500
Annual total	**233,500**

Twenty-five offices which contribute to the fund from which stipends are paid:

[On the written authority of] the Palace, annually	65,000
Wells, waters and rafts contribute annually	750
The office for extraordinary revenues, the quarter assigned to the Arsenal	7,500
Annual total	**73,250**

The revenues of nine cities of the mainland:

The Patria di Friuli: 7500 ducats, expenses 6400, remainder	1,150
Treviso: 49,850 ducats, expenses 11,320, remainder	37,730
Padua: 65,500 ducats, expenses 14,600, remainder	50,900
Vicenza: 34,600 ducats, expenses 7450, remainder	27,150
Verona: 52,800 ducats, expenses 1800,[8] remainder	34,500
Brescia: 75,000 ducats, expenses 16,000, remainder	59,000
Bergamo: 25,400 ducats, expenses 9500, remainder	16,000

– were assigned to the payment of interest upon the public loan funds. The 'three tables' mentioned were presumably the Ternaria (see below, n. 6), and the offices which levied duties on goods entering and leaving Venice. The Giustizia Nuova was responsible for the supervision of inns and taverns. For the text see F. Besta 1912, pp. 78–80.

[5] A tax on business transactions and transfers of property: a small proportion of the value of the goods involved was paid to a broker, and a rather larger proportion to the state. The tax can be traced back to 1258. See F. Besta 1912, p. 43.

[6] *Datio della ternaria de l'oio*. The magistrates known as the Visdomini della Ternaria were concerned with levying duties on a very wide range of imported goods. At least from 1437 a proportion of the oil imported to Venice had to be deposited at the Ternaria at a price determined by the government, and it was then sold by the Ternaria at a very modest profit. See F. Besta 1912, pp. 44–5, 60–2, and introduction, pp. cviii–cxii.

[7] *Datio della grassa*. Cheeses and salted meats were prominent among these goods for fiscal purposes in Venice. In the late sixteenth century, sardines and caviare were also included among them. See F. Besta 1912, introduction, p. cxv, and pp. 607, 620.

[8] Presumably an error for 18,000.

	Ducats
Crema: 7400 ducats, expenses 3900, remainder	3,500
Ravenna: 9140 ducats, expenditure 2850, remainder	6,290
Total revenue, deducting expenditure	236,220
The revenues of the commune of Venice, annual total	615,750
The nine cities of the mainland, total	236,220
The overseas possessions	180,000
Grand total, i.e. the annual revenues of Venice, of the nine cities of the mainland, and of the overseas possessions	1,031,970

The valuation of the houses.[9]

These are the valuations made of the estates of Venice, and first:

	Lire
The sestier of San Marco is valued at	117,028
The sestier of Cannaregio	82,684
The sestier of Castello	85,771
The sestier of Dorsoduro	55,046
The sestier of Santa Croce	47,549
The sestier of San Polo	67,771
Total	454,849

Cash account [*Conto di cassa*].

	Ducats
Our most serene Lordship of Venice must give, by way of paying interest upon loans, each year	154,000
And in government stipends, which are paid on a note from the Palace, normally each year	26,000
And to the most serene Lordship of Venice, on account of revenues, after deducting the charges made upon them in the city	281,000
Total	462,000 [*sic*]

---

[9] Very likely the lire used in these valuations are lire *di grossi*: one lira *di grossi* is equivalent to 10 ducats.

Ducats

Our most serene Lordship of Venice must receive, in moneys
collected on account of the eight offices allocated to the Camera
degli Imprestiti in 1467 — 193,650

Through the income of the fund allocated to the payment of
government stipends, by authorization in 1467 — 45,600

Through the moneys of the deposit allocated to the war, and likewise collected by arrangements made in 1467 — 222,300

By way of revenue from wells, canals and the post, and from
water and rafts — 700

Total — 462,250

The most serene Lordship of Venice must receive, on account of
the excess of revenue over expenditure, the sum which remains
of — 281,750

And from the revenues of the treasuries of the mainland, meaning
the cities and their districts, e.g. Padua and the Padovano,
deducting the expenses — 236,220

Annual total — 517,970

B. P.

4   THE SALE OF MINOR OFFICES, 1510

From a decree of the Senate and Great Council, 8–10 March 1510 (F. Besta 1912,
pp. 192–4).

Our state has now come to such a pass that, as everybody knows, it is necessary
to raise a substantial sum of money for its preservation and increase, and
without this money it is impossible to achieve any good result. And, because it is
the duty of everyone in the government to make every effort to raise money,
whilst imposing the smallest possible fiscal burden on our noblemen and
citizens, although it is also right and proper that our government should draw
on its own resources to help itself,

BE IT DETERMINED by the authority of this Council that, notwithstanding any
other decree to the contrary, [the following resolution shall apply to] each and
every post of clerk, notary, collector, steward, broker in the German exchange
house, warehouseman, weighman, superintendent, valuer or servant in
government offices, and to every other kind of post, by whatsoever name it may
be called, whether held for life or for a fixed term, with the exception of
positions in our Chancery and those of bailiff [*gastaldi*] and others in the offices

of the Procurators [of St Mark's]. Persons who hold these posts for life, and have sons or nephews or brothers, if they give to our government 100 [ducats] for every 10 which they receive in stipend and net profits, according to their rating at the office of the Governatori delle Entrate, may reserve their posts for their sons after their death; or, if they have no sons, they may do so for their nephews or brothers. These sons, nephews or brothers shall, however, be entitled to hold those posts for their own lifetime only. Those who have the aforesaid posts for a fixed term may give 80 ducats for every 10 that they receive in stipend and net profits, according to their tax rating as above, and they shall then retain their offices for life. B. P.

5 THE HAZARDS OF SPECULATING ON CUSTOMS DUTIES, 1528–9
From a petition of Bernardo Arian, considered by the Senate on 23 September 1535: ASV Senato, Terra, reg. 1534–5, f. 175.

In 1528, when I was fifteen years of age, Ser Antonio Butazo, contractor for the 3 per cent duty on [imports] by sea, approached me and had me take one share in that duty, although I had no understanding either of shares or of duties. Hence, on account of my share, I owe the office of the Rason Nove 800 ducats for the loss sustained by that duty. I incurred this debt because the galleys of Beirut and Alexandria were due to leave Venice at the end of July 1528 according to the terms on which they were auctioned, but for various pertinent reasons they departed in October, and so did not return within the period of the said duty, because this ran from March 1528 to February 1529; and because they failed to leave at the proper time they did not return within that period; and since they are the mainstay of that duty they caused a loss of over 12,000 ducats. Furthermore, because of the famines at that time, the ships which should have gone to pick up merchandise went instead to lade corn by order of Your Serenity, for the benefit of the public but to the great loss of that duty, which heaped ill upon ill. B. P.

6 RESTRICTIONS ON THE TRANSFER OF PROPERTY TO RELIGIOUS USES, 1536
Senate decree of 22 December 1536: ASV Dieci Savii sopra le Decime in Rialto, cap. I, f. 43r–v. See also Senato, Terra, reg. 1536–7, ff. 83v–84r.

We must not allow all landed property to pass to churchmen by way of legacies or donations to religious uses [ad pias causas], as a large portion of it has already passed. Our ancestors took sound measures against this [disorder] by decreeing that no one could bequeathe or otherwise dispose of any landed property in this city to religious uses in perpetuity or indeed for any period exceeding ten years. But this law has not been observed, doubtless because too much time was allowed in which to sell property, and new measures must now be adopted, as such an important matter requires, for the sake of the public and the private interest.

BE IT DETERMINED that, having due respect to other laws adopted in this matter, in so far as they relate to past infringements, and confirming them in all matters which do not conflict with the present law, it shall henceforth be ordained that no one may bequeathe, or convey by donation between living persons, or otherwise commit any piece of landed property to religious uses in perpetuity or for any period longer than two years. And the notaries who are called upon to draw up any will that bequeathes, donates or otherwise commits any of the aforesaid property to the said religious uses for any longer period must, on pain of deprivation for ever of the right to exercise their profession in Venice, go to the office of the Dieci Savii sopra le Decime within fifteen days of receiving the request, and there register the [relevant] clause of the will. Here the clauses shall be recorded in a special book, and when the two years have elapsed the Dieci Savii shall be bound upon oath to cause to be sold by public auction the property which has been, as above, bequeathed, donated or otherwise committed to religious uses, and the proceeds shall be sent to the offices of our Procurators [of St Mark's], in accordance with their instructions. Then the Procurators, with the assistance of the trustees [*commissarij*] or of any other executors there may be of the [testator's] orders, must use the proceeds to carry out the instructions of those who have bequeathed, donated or otherwise committed the property to religious uses, i.e. by giving all the proceeds to the one who ought to have them if the property has been freely bequeathed or given by donation between living persons, or else by distributing them at the times, and in the quantities of money or other things which were specified in the [testator's] instructions. If landed property is dedicated to religious uses for a period of more than two years through testamentary schedules or by some means other than the hand of a notary, these instructions may only be carried out by following the method and procedure described above. We further declare that the Dieci Savii shall receive from the purchaser 2 per cent of [the proceeds of] the sales which they conduct as above, to be divided between them and the notaries and other servants of theirs, as is done with such profits at the Giudice di Esaminador. In all such sales the rights of close kin and collateral relatives shall always be respected, in accordance with our laws.   B. P.

7   CLERICAL TAXATION: THE GRANT BY POPE PAUL III, 1544
Instructions of the Senate to the Venetian ambassador in Rome, 5 July 1544: ASV
Senato, Secreta, Deliberazioni 1543–4, ff. 156v–157r.

To the ambassador at the Curia

We have been informed by your letters of 28th of last month of the grant of
clerical tenths which His Holiness has made to us, and of the stipulation he has
told you he intends to make, to the effect that one tenth is to fall upon the
revenues of this year and the other tenth upon the revenues of the next year,
with the exemptions specified by His Holiness and by the reverend Treasurer.
This [proposal] has greatly troubled us, for should the brief be issued in this
form His Holiness would have granted nothing that would meet any of our
needs. Hence we and the Senate instruct you to betake yourself to His Holiness
and first thank him warmly in our name for granting the said tenths. You must
then beg him that, since the heavy expenses we incur are not solely for the
benefit of laymen, but also for that of the clergy who receive income from within
our state, and for all the rest of Christendom, he may be pleased to declare in
the brief that both the tenths shall be collected this year, and cause everyone to
pay in the manner authorized by His Holiness himself and by his predecessors
on other occasions. For the exemptions, especially those of bishoprics and rich
benefices and well-endowed religious houses, would amount to so much as to
leave at our disposal only a tiny sum of money, paid only by poor and destitute
persons. For the rich benefices are all in the hands of cardinals and curialists,
and we would not have made any request to His Holiness for a grant as small as
this. You will entreat him that, for the reasons which persuaded him to grant us
the tenths, he may now see fit to allow us to take full advantage of them, for if
our right to collect them be delayed and reduced we shall ourselves have to
delay and reduce the measures which are vital to the preservation of our
overseas possessions and of our fleet, and essential to protecting the interests
both of the clergy and of the laity. Laymen, as you know, are incomparably more
heavily burdened on account of our needs than are ecclesiastics. You will
therefore make every possible effort to obtain His Holiness's permission to
collect the two tenths this year without exempting anyone, and will prove to him
that if he does otherwise the favour that His Holiness is granting us will be of
little value and of no help to us. We are sure that, given your great wisdom and
ability, you will know how to do this; and you will inform us when these
instructions have been carried out.   B. P.

8 TWO MERCERS MAKE A TAX RETURN, 1554

From an unbound document in ASV Miscellanea di Carte non Appartenenti ad Alcun Archivio, bb. 18–19.

Praise be to God. 1554

In obedience to the decree enacted in the most excellent council of the Senate, we, Gabriel and Andrea Cusini, mercers at the sign of St Andrew, who live in the parish of San Giuliano in a house and shop belonging to the Lord Procurators [of St Mark's] di Supra, make our return to you, our honourable and most noble lords the Sixteen Savi in charge of the *tansa*. We inform your most excellent lordships that we keep our little shop going in a small way with mercers' wares – that is to say, braids or ribbons [*cordele*], veils, a little serge, and other stuff [*bonichalli*] – some of which we obtain on credit at the warehouse and at Bergamo, as could easily be demonstrated to your most excellent lordships.

Item. We do not have revenues of any sort whatsoever, from houses or land or bonds of any kind, nor do we have any money; but merely that small hope of profit from mercery, as explained above, which counts for very little when set against the very heavy expenses we have, as we shall explain below.

Item. We find ourselves paying 45 ducats a year to the Lord Procurators for rent of the house and shop.

Item. We are fifteen mouths, including wife and children and one apprentice. We have seven children, all little ones, and the eldest is thirteen years of age and of the others none is older than nine, so that your most excellent lordships may well consider the grave and excessive expenditure needed for the sustenance of all these mouths when we have only that little profit from the shop. And, with the state of things at the moment, there is very little business and very little income.

Item. We do not have silk of any kind made, and we know no trade but buying and selling, so that at the year's end we have a great struggle to meet such heavy expenses. Your most excellent lordships can well imagine how things may go with so many children and such little income, bearing in mind the many other tribulations which have occurred in recent times, as could easily be demonstrated to your most excellent lordships.

Without further ado, we commend ourselves to your most excellent lordships, kneeling humbly before you.   R. M.

9 REVENUE OF THE VENETIAN REPUBLIC IN 1587, 1594 AND 1602

From a manuscript in BCV Cicogna collection (F. Besta, 1912, pp. 365–8). All amounts in ducats.

	1587	1594	1602
The duty upon			
Wine	291,157	280,133	293,665
Goods at 6 per cent	27,481[10]	91,637	118,658
Goods leaving[11] Weighing such goods	208,532	227,265	264,724
Goods entering from the land[12]	81,255	80,235	91,353
Meat	45,032	omitted	12,000
Places to sell wine[13]	33,562	37,111	47,949
Imports at the corn office	86,000	89,000	90,080
Oil	61,978	79,500	106,148
Brokerage	8,645	9,666	11,500
Iron	7,831	8,925	8,244
Delicacies	13,982	14,005	20,785
Wine from the cask	12,516	12,083	13,290
Fish of the Padovano, Treviso, Lombardy	13,772	10,848	14,309
Fish 'at the post'[14]	3,6 . .	3,654	5,126
Places to sell malmsey[15]	. . .	484	391

[10] Some of these figures can be checked against those given in the Regolazione Generale delle Casse (General Regulation of the Money Chests) proposed in 1587 by three Commissioners of the Mint and three Revisors of the Public Revenues, printed in F. Besta 1912, pp. 341–4. At p. 343 this figure is given as 77,481, and the duty is described more explicitly as 'the duty of 6 per cent levied at the customs house of the sea and of the Levant' [*datio delle 6 per cento a doana da mar et Levante*]. It was imposed on goods arriving in Venice by sea from either the eastern or the western side of the Adriatic and from the Levant, and was the result of attempts made between 1577 and 1579 to rationalize and simplify a very complex system of payments – although there were many specified exceptions to the rule that goods should be charged at 6 per cent (ibid., pp. 602–9).

[11] The general rule laid down in 1563 was that goods exported from Venice by Venetians and Venetian citizens should be charged at the rate of 5 per cent, and those exported by foreigners at 7 per cent (F. Besta 1912, pp. 597–9).

[12] In 1579 the duty on goods entering Venice from the land was merged with the duty on goods entering by sea from the west [Ponente] – i.e. goods coming from Western Europe and originating outside the Adriatic (F. Besta 1912, pp. 609–11).

[13] In 1579 there were 'forty-one places where wine is sold' in the six sestieri of Venice; thirty are mentioned in 1582–3, and only six in 1595 (F. Besta, 1912, pp. 265, 290–1, 381).

[14] That is, the duty paid at the post to which the boat was moored when fish from outside the Lagoon, e.g. from Istria and Dalmatia, was brought into Venice to be sold (F. Besta 1912, p. xcv).

[15] There were twenty of these in 1579 (F. Besta 1912, p. 278).

	1587	*1594*	*1602*
Stones and lime	1,16 .	1,251	863
Firewood gathered from the forest,			
less expenses	2,677	2,531	2,328
Wood, 1 soldo per load	1,551	1,324	702
Woollen cloths	32,254	33,039	32,605
Timber	11,790	9,309	13,717
The impost on the silk-workers	3,000	3,000	3,000

The consular dues

From the *bailo*'s offices in			
Constantinople	3,399	4,390	5,601
In Cyprus, 2 per cent	1,552	1,351	3,655
On the silk and spices of			
Constantinople	667	712	418
The duty on hostelries	. . . .	1,052	1,049
The impost on notaries for instru-			
ments and wills	. . . .	1,426	1,972

The duty on

Condemnations and contraband,			
3 soldi per lira			
Contraband, one quarter	2,2 . .	1,889	2,288
Velvets and stitched hides	875	1,484	1,186
Fruits	2,391	2,503	9,104
Various revenues of the Ufficio alle			
Acque			
Corporation of Chioggia, for duty on			
delicacies	10,3 . 2	7,070	11,476
Community of Chioggia, for			
sandbanks	2,000	2,000	2,000
The same corporation, instead			
of the tenth	600	600	600
The same corporation, to repay a			
loan	500	500	500
Duty and revenues of the German			
exchange house	45,998	49,940	63,168

Contribution [limitacion] due to the Council of Ten

From Venice			
From the Dogado	12,030	8,086	8,104
From the mainland			

	1587	1594	1602
From the court officials of Istria and Dalmatia	7,443	9,630	7,475
The tenth upon the interest paid by the Camera degli Imprestiti	21,705	21,705	
Office of the Beni Inculti, for waters	815	1,646	788
Remission e penderi[16] of the Avogadori	1,165	1,447	1,382
Fishing-grounds leased by the Rason Vecchie			
Various revenues of the Rason Vecchie	1,868	2,724	2,593
The duty upon the hemp at the rope factory			
The anchorage duty			
Goods sold by the office of the Arsenal	10,198	11,107	11,483
The office of the Procurators di Supra, for their dues [*censo*][17]	1,000	1,000	1,000
Transit dues on fish		2,416	13,863
Revenues of the Salt Office, less expenses	190,982	252,074	200,000
The treasury of			
Padua	80,2 . .	78,382	73,509
Vicenza	53, 2 . .	55,143	59,845
Verona	117,808	132,318	130,406
Brescia	99,805	106,075	112,693
Salò	4,631	4,921	5,016
Bergamo	40,775	42,167	43,651
Crema	12,403	13,939	14,134
Rovigo	7,728	7,529	7,860
The administration [*Rezimento*] of Cologna	2,745	2,206	1,619
The administration of Treviso	55,347	53,095	52,133
The treasury of Udine	18,822	17,589	13,587
The administration of			
Conegliano	4,635	4,248	3,964
Feltre	1,618	1,570	1,574

[16] Possibly fees paid for 'pardons and stays of execution'.
[17] Payable to the Council of Ten.

	1587	*1594*	*1602*
Cividale di Friuli	1,567	887	780
Pordenone	54	44	102
Mestre	170	170	170
The taxes on the territories for men-at-arms	23,165	22,576	22,576
The contribution paid by the territories for buildings	7,885	7,886	7,884
The tenth on stipends and profits [from public offices][18]	27,932	26,767	26,766
The subsidy paid by the mainland state[19]	78,966	82,739	80,000
The administration of Cividale di Belluno	2,153	2,490	2,204
The administration of Sacile	340	463	463
Proceeds of half hire		4,687	2,644
From various offices and administrations, from [the addition of] 2 soldi per lira to fines, and similar things		2,695	2,700
From the reduction of superfluous expenditure [*scansation*][20]		3,099	5,100
The administration of			
Cadore	318	318	318
Cherso and Ossero	620	620	620
Veggia	1,440	1,440	1,440
Spalato	1,200	1,200	1,200
Curzola	185	185	185
Sebenico	1,500	1,500	1,500
Liesena	1,786	1,786	1,786
Trau	2,700	2,700	2,700
Zara	2,013	2,013	2,013
The office of the Governatori, for old debts	25,000	20,000	15,000

[18] On 13 January 1573 (1572 Venetian style), during the war of Cyprus and Lepanto, the Great Council had imposed a 10 per cent tax on all stipends and profits from magistracies and minor public offices in Venice and its dominions. This measure was intended to last, initially, for twenty years. For the text see F. Besta 1912, pp. 243–5.

[19] For this direct tax, originally imposed as a wartime measure and later transformed into a regular tax, see F. Besta 1912, pp. clxxx, 218–9.

[20] There is a reference in the regulations for 1595 to moneys being collected into a *deposito de scansation* at an average rate of 3099 ducats per annum.

	1587	1594	1602
The duty			
On millet at Crema		966	
On iron at Brescia		3,774	
On leases and fiefs		197	
Of the citadel of Padua		1,577	
Called the *muda*, at Seravalle and Treviso[21]		1,086[22]	
On corn exports			7,614
Spirits [*Acqua de vitta*]			1,772
The tenths upon the clergy			40,000
Tenths and *tanse*[23]			80,000
Raisins			3,155
Entry fees [*ben intrade*] of offices			70
2 per cent of brokerage from outside			305
Brokerage of the Turks			1,576
Revenues due to the Provveditori di Comun			993
The soldo per lira of the Levant			6,000
The Governatori delle Entrate, for debtors without penalty			10,000
The Rason Nuove			6,000
The soldo per lira on account of Palma[24]			70,000
The fifth of oil[25]			17,345
Total			2,444,064
			B. P.

---

[21] The total up to this point is given as 1,998, ...

[22] The total up to this point is given as 2,098,315.

[23] See above, IV.2 and 8.

[24] The great fortress in Friuli.

[25] Oil-importers now had an obligation to sell one fifth of the oil which they brought into Venice to the Ternaria Vecchia, which then sold the oil to 'the poor [*la povertà*]' at a modest profit (F. Besta 1912, introduction, pp. cviii–cx). In 1595 it was stipulated that oil should be distributed both through the sestieri and through the organization for the care of the *poveri vergognosi* or 'shamefaced poor' (ibid., pp. 391–2, and below, VII.10).

10   EXPENDITURE OF THE VENETIAN REPUBLIC IN 1587, 1594 AND 1602

From a manuscript in BCV Cicogna collection (F. Besta 1912, pp. 368–9). All amounts in ducats.

	1587	1594	1602
The Arsenal			
For workmen	102,864	119, . .6	120,000
For materials	58,261	81,434	81,836
For saltpetre and artillery	30,000	30,000	30,000
Payments to the navy and materials for the contractor [*conduttor*]	126,195	122,918	260,767
The office of the fortresses, for various expenses	22,326	22,1 . .	54,978
Expenditure of the keeper of the chest of the Collegio	199,090	258,.49	142,015
The militia of Crete and Corfu	117,809	132, . .8	187,695
Men-at-arms[26]	63,799	62,0.0	59,845

The Offitio sopra le Camere[27]
Important persons, colonels,
  commandants (22,648)[28]
Infantry of the mainland (44,716)

[26] By the General Regulation of 1587 [see above, IV.9, n. 10] specified revenues to the value of approximately 1,450,000 ducats were to flow into seven deposits, and most sources of income were carefully earmarked for a particular deposit or for some other use. The seven deposits were (1) the 'public deposit of the Mint, of 501,450 ducats', also known as the 'great deposit' (see below, n. 36); (2) the 'deposit for the Arsenal, for purchasing materials, and for saltpetre'; (3) the 'deposit for sending payments to the fleet, and for purchasing materials for clothing the condemned', i.e. the convict oarsmen who manned a large part of the fleet in peacetime [see above, III.3(c)]; (4) the 'deposit for the quartering of men-at-arms'; (5) the 'deposit for the militia of Crete and Corfu'; (6) the 'deposit for special needs' (*occorrentie*), which was the responsibility of the keeper of the money chest of the Collegio (*cassier*) and appears here under his name (money could lawfully be taken from this deposit only by resolution of the Senate, and 'only to meet those expenses for which we do not at present make any other assignment of revenue, because they are uncertain'); (7) the 'deposit for the fortresses'. See F. Besta 1912, pp. 343–50.

[27] By the General Regulation of 1587, this office was to be assigned revenues amounting to 130,924 ducats from the treasury of Brescia and from the administrations (*reggimenti*) of Salò, Cividale di Friuli, Pordenone, Mestre, Sacile, Cadore, Raspo, Capodistria and Montona, together with 'all the moneys which the territories pay on account of men-at-arms and military contractors', for the purpose of paying troops and their commanders. The *personaggi* or 'important persons' of this document are perhaps related to the 'war chiefs' (*capi da guerra*) mentioned in 1587 (F. Besta 1912, pp. 354–5).

[28] It was calculated in 1587 that payments to such people would amount to 29,776 ducats (F. Besta 1912, p. 354).

	1587	*1594*	*1602*
Infantry of Dalmatia and Albania (28,748)			
Cavalry of Dalmatia and Albania (22,228)	142,351	152,156	360,592[29]
Gunners in various places			
Castellans in various places			
Hirings [*nolli*] and other expenses			
The office of the Camerlenghi di Comun for stipends[30]	59,552	62,833	73,001
The chest of the Council of Ten[31]	75,828	35,0.3	34,541
The Camera degli Imprestiti for the Sussidio, [Monte] Nuovissimo and Monte Vecchio[32]	225,421	225,6.4	197,501
The office of the Rason Vecchie, for expenses[33]	8,743	7,466	8,188
The Ufficio alle Acque, for expenses[34]	25,429	22,541	24,552
The interest on the 14 per cent [loan funds][35]	16,706	9,215	6,000

[29] In this year the number of items of revenue allocated to the office had greatly increased; its assets now included the meat duty, tenths and *tanse*, and the duties on corn (F. Besta 1912, pp. 371–2).

[30] Some salaries and allowances were paid by the Camerlenghi di Comun and others by the money chest of the Council of Ten. The Camerlenghi had a general responsibility for the salaries and allowances of the Doge and Dogaressa, and for those of the Councils (including the Councils of Forty), magistrates, and provincial governors and administrators (F. Besta 1912, pp. 268–9, 351–2).

[31] The responsibilities of the money chest of the Council of Ten included the payment of ambassadors and secretaries resident at foreign courts, the stipends of members of the Ducal Chancery, the support of a police force, and the payment of the rewards offered for the capture of criminals (F. Besta 1912, pp. 269–70).

[32] That is, for the payment of interest upon these loan funds. In 1579 the interest payments due were estimated at 56,660 ducats on the Monte di Sussidio, 64,450 on the Monte Nuovissimo, and 96,000 on the Monte Vecchio (F. Besta 1912, p. 266).

[33] The Rason Vecchie were responsible for the entertainment of important foreign visitors, but expenditure for this purpose does not feature clearly in the fiscal documents published by Besta, which show that they contributed to the expenses of the Ducal Chancery, spent something on wax (presumably for ceremonial uses), provided ballots for the Great Council, and supplied the 'bread of prisoners' (F. Besta 1912, pp. 278, 360).

[34] On 'the lagoon, sand-banks and rivers' (F. Besta 1912, p. 359).

[35] Life annuities at 14 per cent were introduced by a Senate decree of 11 April 1538: it enabled investors to lend money to the state and receive a very high rate of interest on the understanding that on the investor's death all claim to either capital or interest would cease. On 14 January 1573

	1587	*1594*	*1602*
Biscuits for the navy	102,000	204,000	160,000
To make the great deposit[36]	501,451	501,451	501,451
To give to the most reverend Patriarch of Aquileia and Missier Celio Magno,[37] from the treasury of Udine	3,225	3,225	3,225
To a Procurator, by way of restitution[38]	1,000	1,000	1,000
Totals[39]	1,882,030	2,051,539	2,307,186
Required also for Crete		10,000	
Required also for the Offitio sopra le Camere		4,000	
	1,882,030	2,065,539	

Po (200,000)
Great galleys (70,000)
Extra workmen (40,000)
Extra captains (20,000)

(1572 Venetian style) the Council of Ten invited investors to lend to the state at a similar rate for a period of seventeen years, after which all claim on the state would likewise cease. In the General Regulation of 1587 there was much concern with servicing the 14 per cent life loans (F. Besta 1912, pp. 216–18, 245, 344).

[36] The 'great deposit', of just over half a million ducats, was established in 1584 when the government had succeeded in freeing itself of the obligation to pay interest to the extent of half a million ducats to its creditors [see below, IV.13]. Revenues to the extent of half a million ducats a year, instead of disappearing into the pockets of private persons, would now be assigned to a new reserve fund, which would be drawn upon only in times of 'open war' (Senate decree of 15 June 1584: F. Besta 1912, pp. 339–40). According to detailed regulations drawn up in 1587, the duty upon wine, the 6 per cent duty, the duty on goods leaving, and the net revenues of the Salt Office (these four items then amounted to 767,408 ducats) were to be assigned to the 'great deposit'. Once its needs had been met, the remaining quarter-million ducats or so would be devoted to other uses: biscuit for the fleet, artillery, gunpowder, the payment of the Arsenal labour force and the servicing of the 14 per cent life-loan funds (ibid., pp. 343–4).

[37] Elsewhere (F. Besta 1912, pp. 270, 346) Celio Magno is described as a secretary.

[38] From 1579 onwards there are references in the documents to the obligation to restore a loan made by one of the Procurators; in 1595 he is identified as 'the noble Ser Polo Nani' (F. Besta 1912, pp. 270, 379).

[39] So in the original document.

	1587	*1594*	*1602*
The rest of the *scansation*	2,000		
All revenues not applied to the present regulation			
The rest of the revenues from the prisons, which by resolution of the Council of Ten must go to the Senate			

B.P.

PUBLIC BORROWING: THE MONTI

*V*ENETIAN PUBLIC FINANCE, *especially in wartime, depended on raising large sums through forced loans rather than outright taxation; as the financial statements [above, IV.3 and 10] indicate, a sizable proportion of the state's income was assigned to servicing the public debt, which was secured upon certain earmarked taxes. In 1262 outstanding loans to the state had been consolidated into the loan fund which became known as the Monte Vecchio, paying interest at 5 per cent of the face value of the holdings. IV.11 records the proposal of 1482 to create another such fund, soon to be dubbed the Monte Nuovo, at the time of the War of Ferrara [cf. below, V.14]; as IV.12 mentions, it had by 1509 expanded far beyond its original limit of 550,000 ducats, and as much as 3 million were now invested in it. Taken from Girolamo Priuli's lively if verbose account of the crisis that followed Venice's military defeat at Agnadello in 1509 by the invading forces of the League of Cambrai, IV.12 shows how holdings in the Monti had become for many Venetians a supposedly safe and trouble-free security preferable to landed estates. Himself smarting from the experience, Priuli tells how the value of state bonds could plummet when war broke out and the state lost its capacity to pay interest. IV.13 describes an operation designed to shed the massive burden of debt incurred by the Venetian state during the War of Cyprus and Lepanto in 1571–3. Between 1596 and 1620 further arrangements were made for the liquidation of the older consolidated loan funds. As IV.10 has shown, interest on the ancient Monte Vecchio, and on the Monte Nuovissimo and Sussidio (more recent legacies of the Italian wars of the early sixteenth century), consumed nearly 10 per cent of the revenues flowing into Venice towards the year 1600. The text of IV.13 is taken from an official history of Venice by an eminent statesman, Nicolò Contarini, who was eventually elected Doge in 1630; after his death the Council of Ten decided that his work contained so much secret material that it could not safely be published, for experts had opined that 'It contains maxims of government so intimate that in truth we do not know if it would be good to divulge them' (Cozzi 1958, pp. 197–227).*

BIBLIOGRAPHY   In general: Luzzatto 1961, pp. 205–11, and 1963; Lane 1966, pp. 87–98; Pullan 1971, pp. 138–40; Cozzi and Knapton 1986, pp. 323–8. On the operations set in motion by Priuli in the 1570s: Corti 1894; Beltrami 1957.   B. P.

11   THE ESTABLISHMENT OF A STATE LOAN FUND, 1482

Decree of the Great Council establishing the Monte Nuovo during the War of Ferrara, 23 April 1482 (F. Besta 1912, pp. 154–6).

No longer can we postpone measures to raise money for the present War of Ferrara. The two tenths which are imposed upon every taxpayer every year, and are given outright to our government, are not enough to meet even a tiny fraction of our needs; and when imposing other burdens we need to consider those who are so placed that their scanty resources would not be able to bear them. Efforts must be made to raise moneys by borrowing, in addition to the two ordinary tenths which are imposed annually according to need, and we must borrow from those who can most easily pay the money, with some profit to themselves, so that, as well as being compelled to lend, they may be all the more ready to do so.

BE IT DETERMINED, then, that all who pay a total of 8 ducats or more per annum for each tenth, on account of all their income from houses, estates, loan interest and merchandise, in the period from mid-June 1481 to mid-June 1482 and subsequent years, and those who pay taxes [*tanse*] upon the storehouses of merchants which are not artisans' workshops, upon soapworks, etc.,[40] and upon exchange transactions – those who, we say, pay 8 ducats or more on account of each tenth upon all the above things, must lend to our government a sum equivalent to [up to] three of the tenths they pay to our Camera degli Imprestiti on account of all the things listed above. They shall pay either one tenth, or two, or three, as our government shall see fit, within the time limit laid down by this Council. When this time has elapsed, the loans may not be collected by the aforesaid officials [of the Camera degli Imprestiti], on pain of a fine of 1000 ducats; nor, upon the same penalty, may any proposal be made to extend the time limit. Rather, the books shall be sent to the Uffiziali delle Cazude, who shall exact the sum owed together with the penalties due to their office. These moneys shall be collected on their own account, separately from the other

---

[40] Legislation proposed in 1453 had distinguished between premises on which 'industrial and mercantile activity' (*industria et mercatura*) was carried on, and those devoted only to *artes mecanice*, or places where barbers or others earned a living 'by the work of their hands alone' (*de simplice labore manuum*). 'Soapworks' are probably mentioned here as one example of industrial and mercantile premises; others, mentioned in 1453, were dye-works, nail-works, timber-stores, furnaces, wharves and shipyards (for the text see F. Besta 1912, p. 121).

tenths which are given outright. None of the above-mentioned moneys, collected by either of the said offices, may be spent upon anything other than the war.

That everyone may be the readier to pay, be it resolved that everyone who has lent the aforesaid tenths shall at once be individually credited with his principal, in a book kept at our Camera degli Imprestiti. When the War of Ferrara is over, the principal shall be restored proportionately to every creditor from every kind of government money. While they are creditors, they shall receive interest of 5 per cent per annum in two payments, which shall be made to them from the 27,200 ducats which are received from the Camera degli Imprestiti on account of the 1 per cent which is paid by those who do not themselves make loans.[41] The same condition shall apply to those who make payments to the Cazude, with penalties [as above], for whatever sum they have paid. This procedure shall be followed from time to time in imposing 'loaned tenths' [*decime ad imprestido*] according to the city's needs, in restoring loans, and in paying interest in the aforesaid manner, quite apart from the two ordinary tenths which are imposed in advance every year and are to be paid by all taxpayers without exception, and are to be given outright to our government, as has been done up to the present time. Unless he has first paid these two 'given tenths' [*decime donade a la nostra Signoria*], a person shall not be entitled to any profit from paying the 'loaned tenths'. Should it happen that the present war continues, and it becomes necessary to seek large sums of money through borrowing by the method described above, be it resolved that this loan fund [*monte*] may not be extended to more than a total of 550,000 ducats, to be lent by the method previously described, upon which the interest at 5 per cent will amount to 27,500 ducats. No kind of impost may be laid, by this or by any other measure that may be adopted, upon either the principal or the interest. The creditors shall be at liberty to transfer their principal and interest to anyone they choose, so long as they pay 4 soldi for the entry on the books [*partida*], and there shall be no other charge.

The present decree may not be revoked, suspended, glossed or otherwise interpreted, either with regard to the 27,200 ducats which are pledged to the interest payments, or with regard to the payment of imposts, nor may there be

[41] Some persons had holdings in the Venetian state debt, acquired by purchase or other means, but were not themselves obliged to contribute to forced loans, because they were foreigners, or perhaps recent immigrants or persons counted as 'citizens' but not yet placed on the tax registers. On 26 September 1391 a Senate decree (see F. Besta 1912, pp. 87–90 for the text) clearly spelt out the principle that those who themselves made loans to the government should receive interest of 4 per cent on their holdings, while those who did not make such loans (*illi qui habent imprestita et non faciunt de imprestitis*) would have 3 per cent only. In the 1430s all holders of state bonds had been compelled to pay a tax amounting to one third of their interest, but in 1439 this requirement was modified, and retained only for 'those who do not make any loans' (ibid., pp. 107–10, 111–12).

any talk of suspending interest payments, upon all the penalties and conditions which are contained in all the regulations of the Camera degli Imprestiti. The present decree shall not be valid unless it is adopted by the Great Council and in other essential places, as in the Camera; and the Collegio must take action concerning the method of keeping the said accounts, by the clerks who are now at the Camera, or by others who may be assigned to the task.

Anyone who has first paid the two tenths which are given outright to our government, and has then lent whatever sums shall be determined by this Council, and any other person who is not obliged to pay the tenths mentioned above, may then lend whatever further sum he chooses, and may, on account of such a loan, receive the same profit, and have the principal restored in the same way, free of any impost, as if he had lent on account of the tenths.

For the decree, 992; against, 147; uncertain, 72.   B. P.

12 INVESTMENT IN PUBLIC LOAN FUNDS AND IN LAND, 1509
Priuli ed. Cessi 1938, IV, 15–17.

By this collapse of the Venetian state, [holdings] in the loan funds of the Monte Vecchio and Monte Nuovo were depressed to a very low level, and there were no buyers and no money [for the bonds], for in the face of these catastrophes all were thinking of their own interests and wanting to preserve their money, so that in case of disaster they could save themselves and escape from all danger, holding on to the money, for otherwise they would be ruined and undone. This loan fund of the Monte Nuovo used to enjoy the highest reputation in the city of Venice, because the holdings were valued at 102½ per cent before the present war, and I, the present writer, bought myself some 4000 ducats' worth, as can be seen from our account books. This happened because the nobles, citizens and people of Venice were so flush with money that they knew not what to do with it, and so they purchased these bonds, because they collected their payments every six months in good money and cared about nothing else. It did not occur to them that, should war break out, the Camera [degli Imprestiti] would have to be closed. To tell the truth, as I am bound to do, no one would ever have imagined that the Venetian mainland state could be lost and destroyed within fifteen days, as we have now seen. The holdings of the Monte Nuovo were now worth 40 per cent at most, and I myself, as stated above, had spent that great sum of money on buying them at 102½ per cent, and have received but one interest payment, so you can imagine how terrible is my loss. We must be patient, for these are 'goods of fortune' [*quia sunt bona fortunae*], and the fund of the Monte Nuovo was done for, because the moneys allocated to it, which paid its interest every six months, were to a large extent secured upon the treasuries of the mainland cities subject to Venice, using the deposits from the salt revenues. These had been granted to the cities and their people in accordance with the custom of Lombardy, whereby all the lords of Lombardy and Italy gave the impost on salt to their cities. So, when the cities of Lombardy and the mainland state were lost, it became impossible to continue the customary interest payments, with the result that the holdings of the Monte Nuovo were now worth less than 40 per cent. It was impossible to estimate how much loss the closure of the fund inflicted upon the noble citizens and people of Venice – how many poor trust funds, widows, wards, religious houses, hospitals, mass-benefices, crafts, rich, middling and poor men, nobles, citizens and ordinary people had invested their slender fortunes in this fund for the support of themselves and of their children and households in accordance with their station. . . .

The same was true of the Monte Vecchio: there was no one willing to pay for these holdings, and at first they were sold at 25 per cent, and then at less than 15 per cent. Although all the revenues of the city of Venice were pledged to the payment of interest upon the Monte Vecchio, none the less, in this great need, for the sake of preserving the city of Venice, there was to be no regard for decrees and laws but the money was to be taken from wherever it could be found. There was already a saying that when the Venetian army was broken so too were the laws and decrees, and everything possible had to be done to maintain this city and Republic and to keep alive this most sickly, indeed moribund, body, because, if the city of Venice fell, the interest from loan funds and indeed all things would fail with it. But, if the city were preserved, they would in time be paid. So nothing should be heeded but the preservation of the Republic and city of Venice, and all else should be put aside, and all due and necessary measures be taken as the times and events required.

How many citizens and nobles and people there were who could have put their money into land and other goods, but did not want to do so, to spare themselves the trouble of going to the mainland! Many, too, wanted to avoid the expense of horses and carriages, for the mainland calls for luxuries, such as estates and great houses, with other expenditure, and much of the income is consumed in such pleasures. Some, again, were anxious not to turn their sons into country bumpkins, for ever attending to their estates, and to give them no such pretext they were reluctant to buy land and wanted their heirs to apply themselves to commerce and become merchants instead, following the most ancient custom of the city of Venice, and so have no reason to go in pursuit of pleasures, which cannot be done without incurring enormous and unceasing expenditure. By the same token they preferred to invest their money in the Monte Nuovo rather than in estates. So, when they witnessed the ruin of the Venetian state and the closure of the Monte Nuovo, they were very ill content and wished that they had bought landed estates – for, although, as they perceived, these were now lost and had fallen into enemy hands, they still hoped for their recovery in future. Moreover, these properties had a firm foundation, which the enemy could not remove, and if their revenues could not be collected in one year they could be gathered in another, for things could not go on as they now were, and in time they would be turned to good account. But these Monti Vecchi and Monti Nuovi were just castles in the air; they were nothing but books, made of paper and ink. Many who had loudly praised the Camera degli Imprestiti were left in no doubt that they had been deceived, knowing that land and property were better [than government bonds]. The Monte Nuovo owed some 3 million ducats, a vast sum of money, and the interest due upon this was 150,000 ducats, in two payments each year of approximately 75,000 ducats at six-monthly intervals. And in truth all this money had been spent on the wars of Lombardy and the defence of the mainland, but now all was seen to be lost, and the debt had been passed on to the poor nobles and citizens of Venice.   B. P.

13   THE REPAYMENT OF PUBLIC DEBT, 1577–84
From Nicolò Contarini, *Historie Venetiane*, I (extracts Cozzi 1958, appendix, pp. 312–17).

The Republic had contracted a huge debt to private persons in the three years of that all-consuming war with the Turks in 1570 and the two years which followed. It amounted to more than 6 million ducats in the Mint alone, with some bonds paying 10 or 14 per cent for the lifetime of the creditors, and others yielding 7 or 7½, but for the most part 8 per cent, until such time as the principal should be repaid; and there was also the interest on certain loan funds, as will be stated later. Hence the Republic was bound to make heavy annual interest payments, so that its revenues were to a large extent pledged. Hence anyone who thought carefully about the public welfare had good reason to wonder how we could meet the expense if there should be another sudden outbreak of war. There would be great danger if the state were deprived of its revenues and all its income were allowed to pass into the hands of private persons, for what could happen in other regimes was well known – where there was no longer a public exchequer, and everything was administered in accordance with sectional interests, and there was no control on the freedom from which only the private individual could benefit. In these circumstances every public-spirited person racked his brains to think of a remedy; but most people, as often happens when ordinary intelligences approach difficult undertakings, gave it up as an insoluble problem. Others might have brought themselves to do more, but did not want to make a proposal, for they knew not how it would be received, and reflected that if it had an unfortunate outcome this would be blamed neither on those who had resolved upon the measure, nor on unforeseen circumstances, but rather on the person who had urged it. And they reflected that to get excited about public affairs is often harmful to one's personal ambition and to one's own peace and quiet. But there was a third group of a few able men who did not wish to get lost in the difficulties, since the worst of all evils is to lose hope. It is true that not all were equal to such an enterprise, for everyone expected to encounter a great many obstacles in his path.

A few years after these controversial matters had begun to be aired, there came forward Giovanni Francesco di Priuli, an aged senator, with much experience in the matter of public finance and fiscal accounting, and he presented a remarkable calculation, in which he showed how with only a small sum of money we could easily achieve in a short space of time everything we desired and everything vital to the safety of the public. Some time before, in order to deposit certain savings in the treasury, that it might not be totally empty when the need arose, it had been decreed that the yield of the tenths and *tanse*[42] imposed every year upon the inhabitants of the city should be set aside and treated as sacrosanct, and should never be drawn upon unless there were a declaration of war. From these moneys Priuli proposed to remove a mere 200,000 ducats, and he showed that by adding the interest payments which would cease as a result of the liquidation[43] we could go forward by degrees, slowly at first and then more rapidly, until within the space of some twenty years we had freed our revenues from the interest payments and from the heavy burden which was laid upon them. This calculation or demonstration was a very artful one. Hence many did not fully understand it, and others rejected it, perhaps out of envy, for they had not thought of it themselves, and it would bring glory to Priuli. Others opposed the scheme – calling it foolish and certain to fail – because of the benefits accruing to their private fortunes from substantial interest payments. Indeed, it seemed that some people wanted to blame Priuli for publicly revealing mysteries which perhaps ought to have stayed hidden for the sake of the public good, and so at first the proposal was rejected.

However, Priuli was not discouraged by opposition. Indeed, he redoubled his efforts, for he well knew that nothing can do more to reveal the worth of a man and his enterprise than to experience vigorous opposition, for this ought to stimulate great minds rather than restrain them. To smooth his pathway, Priuli

---

[42] See above, IV.2 and 8.

[43] The 200,000 ducats would be used to repay a small part (between 3 and 4 per cent) of the state's debt; the money previously used to pay interest on the 200,000 ducats would then be applied to making further repayments, so that the interest could be further reduced.

had his accounts verified and clarified by people of the highest intelligence and by those best qualified to make such calculations, and he again put forward the rejected proposal, this time with greater clarity and with the greatest effect, although his authority counted for more than his rhetoric. Once the proposal was better understood, it triumphed over envy and discomfited private interest. Hence, on 20 June 1577, it was adopted by almost all the votes of the Council of Ten with the Zonta, in which body it was then customary to deal with these matters. Two months later, when all the material had been prepared with astonishing diligence, the names of creditors were drawn by lot in the Collegio, in the presence of the Heads of the Council of Ten, that they might be repaid systematically, starting with the 14 per cent bonds, and then going on to the others. When it was observed that in practice the work proved to be much easier than had at first been thought possible, and that incalculable benefits to the Republic would follow, the idea that it was impossible was forgotten, there was greater understanding on the part of those who had failed to grasp it at first, and feelings hostile to the public good were quelled. Then all men began to strive and contend without hindrance to assist the enterprise. Even those who had not at first supported the measure now attempted to bring it at the earliest possible moment to the desired end, either out of patriotism, or lest they be charged with failing in their duty. Hence all the moneys exacted from old debtors were, with universal consent and amazing diligence, applied to the liquidation [of the public debt]. Many estates and other properties which belonged to the fisc and yielded little income were now publicly auctioned and the proceeds assigned to the repayment of the debt.

A special magistracy was established for this purpose, and to it were elected three very scrupulous senators, Giovanni da Molino, Bernardo Zane and Giacomo Contarini, who spared no pains whatever in carrying out their tasks.

Furthermore, in the year 1579 a very thorough examination of the public revenues was also undertaken, and these were entrusted to the care of Zaccaria Contarini, Lorenzo Bernardo and Gierolamo Barbarigo. They considered the extent of public expenditure and of the annual receipts from public imposts, assigning determinate sums for the payment of the navy and of the land forces, for the garrisons and other needs of the eastern islands, for the repair of fortresses, for weapons, artillery and military supplies, for expenditure on men and materials for the Arsenal, for the salaries of magistrates and persons who have deserved well of the state, and for all other public needs, either ordinary or extraordinary. They also deducted a sum which they determined to keep in the most secret place and under the most strict conditions. They then discovered a considerable surplus of money, which was consigned to a special chest and subsequently used for the liquidation of the state debt. Hence the operation which would, in Priuli's estimate, have taken twenty years was actually rounded off to the full within less than seven – thus exceeding expectations, a thing which seldom happens. So by 15 June 1584 the 14 per cent, 10 per cent, 8 per cent and 7 per cent bonds had all been redeemed, and an annual surplus of 550,000 ducats had been set free, in addition to what had previously been accumulating in the special reserve. And it was agreed that this should all be set on one side and added to the funds which were being amassed as a result of earlier decrees. The strictest regulations and the severest penalties were laid down to prevent these funds from being drawn upon save in the event of war.

B. P.

COMMERCE: FORTUNES MADE AND LOST

E^{NTREPOT TRADE} *in a huge variety of goods was the mainspring of Venetian prosperity, although throughout the period from 1450 to 1630 there was a strong and perhaps an increasing tendency to invest heavily in mainland estates if not in agricultural enterprise [cf. I.4; III.4(b); IV.12; VI.1(a), (d), (f), (g)], and Venice's own textile industries flourished in the sixteenth century as never before. IV.14 offers two enthusiastic accounts of Venetian commerce, one composed at the end of the fifteenth century, the other at the start of the seventeenth: the first was written by a Jerusalem pilgrim from Milan, the second by a famous political commentator, Giovanni Botero (1544–1617), then tutor to the sons of Carlo Emanuele, Duke of Savoy. Within a few years of each account, shadows were to fall upon Venetian prosperity. IV.15, the foundation decree of the Venetian board of trade, the Cinque Savi alla Mercanzia, reflects the pessimism consequent upon the Portuguese sailings to Calicut, for their discovery of the route round the Cape of Good Hope to the Indian Ocean threatened to exclude Venice from trade in the highly profitable goods originating in the Far East. For the early seventeenth century compare Sir Dudley Carleton's account of Venice's declining shipping and manufacturing [above, I.4], written seven years after the publication of Botero's comprehensive account of Venice.*

Other documents describe some of the perils of commerce and banking. As IV.16–17 and 19 bear witness, misfortune is often more vividly described than prosperity in the petitions and other records that survive in archives and libraries. Contrasting with these sombre pictures of disaster and failure are two documents, IV.18 and 20, that record in more neutral and matter-of-fact terms the ordinary transactions of businessmen, both in Venice itself and abroad.

BIBLIOGRAPHY For general accounts of the Venetian economy between the late fifteenth and the early seventeenth centuries: Luzzatto 1961; Lane 1966, 1973, 1987; Pullan 1968; Rapp 1976. For merchants' letters and for the activity of individuals: Tucci 1957, 1973, 1981; Pullan 1965, 1973; Mackenney 1990. B. P.

14   THE ABUNDANCE OF GOOD THINGS IN VENICE

(a) In the late fifteenth century
Casola ed. Newett 1907, pp. 128–9.

Something may be said about the quantity of merchandise in the said city, although not nearly the whole truth, because it is inestimable. Indeed it seems as if all the world flocks there, and that human beings have concentrated there all their force for trading. I was taken to see various warehouses, beginning with that of the Germans – which it appears to me would by itself suffice to supply all Italy with the goods that come and go – and so many others that it may be said that they are innumerable. I see that the special products for which other cities are famous are all to be found there, and that what is sold elsewhere by the pound and the ounce is sold there by canthari and sacks of a moggio each. And who could count the many shops so well furnished that they also seem warehouses, with so many cloths of every make – tapestry, brocades and hangings of every design, carpets of every sort, camlets of every colour and texture, silks of every kind; and so many warehouses full of spices, groceries and drugs, and so much beautiful white wax! These things stupefy the beholder, and cannot be fully described to those who have not seen them. Though I wished to see everything, I saw only a part, and even that by forcing myself to see all I could.   B. P.

(b) In the early seventeenth century
Botero, Giovanni, 1605, pp. 74–5.

Not only is there bread in abundance; there is also an incalculable wealth of all goods and delicacies, which are brought hither, not only by the rivers and canals of the mainland, but also by the sea, from as far afield as Egypt, Syria, the Archipelago, Constantinople and the Black Sea. To Venice come the oils of Apulia, the saffrons of the Abruzzo, the malmseys of Crete, the raisins of Zante, the cinnamon and pepper of the Indies, the carpets of Alexandria, the sugar of Cyprus, the dates of Palestine, the silk, wax and ashes of Syria, the cordovans of the Morea, the leathers, *moronelle*[44] and caviare of Caffa. There is such a variety of things here, pertaining both to man's well-being and to his pleasure, that, just as Italy is a compendium of all Europe, because all the things that are scattered through the other parts are happily concentrated in her, even so Venice may be

[44] Florio 1611 defines *Moronella* as 'a kind of meate-like Caviare made of the fish *Morone*', i.e. a variety of sturgeon; he also defines *Morone* as 'a kind of fish like flesh, that is eaten in Lent'.

167

called a summary of the universe, because there is nothing originating in any far-off country but it is found in abundance in this city. The Arabs say that, if the world were a ring, then Ormuz, by reason of the immeasurable wealth that is brought thither from every quarter, would be the jewel in it. The same can be said of Venice, but with much greater truth, for she not only equals Ormuz in the variety of all merchandise and the plenty of all goods, but surpasses her in the splendour of her buildings, in the extent of her empire, and, indeed, in everything else that derives from the industry and providence of men.   B. P.

15   THE ESTABLISHMENT OF A BOARD OF TRADE, 1507
From Capitolare no. 1 of the Cinque Savi alla Mercanzia (Borgherini-Scarabellin 1925, pp. 16–17).

15 January 1506 [Venetian style], in the Senate

Everyone is surely aware of the prestige, profit and benefit which trade imparts to this city, for it is through such commerce that our state has not only established and maintained itself, but has also expanded and, with God's help, attained the position which it enjoys today. Since, as everybody knows, this commerce has now been reduced to the worst possible condition, it is essential to take some action, and to provide our citizens with every facility for sailing the seas. And, because our Collegio, on account of the business which arises incessantly from all quarters, cannot itself make these vital arrangements for the restoration of health,

BE IT DETERMINED that by scrutiny of this Council five prominent gentlemen of Venice, experienced both in commerce and in navigation, shall be elected from among members of the Senate. They shall be assigned an office and staff at Rialto, and a notary from our Chancery as may prove to be appropriate. They shall be obliged, acting together or separately as they see fit, to send for those merchants whom they deem to be knowledgeable and experienced in both commerce and navigation, and shall inform themselves of and thoroughly investigate every disorder and unseemly occurrence, and shall adopt every possible counter-measure for the benefit and increase of the commerce and revenue of our government. Each one of them may convey his opinions to the Senate and make any proposal he chooses to the end described above, but he must first consult with our Collegio, which shall retain its freedom to propose, either with them or separately, those decrees which seem good for the benefit of our state. They may not refuse [this office] on pain of [a fine of] 500 gold ducats, which shall be collected by the Avogadori di Comun, without any further session of the Senate. They shall serve for two years, and no member of our Collegio may be elected, for fear of impeding affairs of state; but those elected [to this office] may be elected to the Collegio and to any other position, office or governorship.   B. P., R. C. M.

16   INDEBTEDNESS AND BUSINESS FAILURE, c.1500

(a) Nicolò Baron, Venetian citizen

From the Latin. Decree of the Great Council, 18 September 1500: ASV Compilazione delle Leggi, b.309, f. 150r–v.

Our government has been accustomed to intervene and show clemency, having regard to the circumstances, in cases involving Venetian citizens oppressed by misfortune, and to bring charitable assistance to those wretched and unlucky persons. Among them now is our poor and loyal Venetian citizen, Nicolò Baron, who, having lost his assets through no fault of his own, has been kept in prison for sixteen months and more, in violation both of Christian charity and of Venetian humanity. All the thorough investigations conducted by his creditors have established that Nicolò has nothing left but hope and diligence [spem et industriam], which as a poor prisoner he can put to no use on account of the harshness of some of his creditors, whom neither prayers nor kindness and charity have been able to sway or bring to an honourable agreement. Hence it is proper that our merciful government should act as it has done before in similar cases.

BE IT [THEREFORE] DETERMINED that by the authority of this Council Nicolò shall be, and shall be understood to be, included among those covered by the decree previously moved in this Council by the noble Ser Ermolao Donà, concerning those who fail or are burdened with debts. The Sopraconsoli shall conduct a thorough inquiry into his assets and shall, together with the Council of the Forty, agree upon terms with his creditors as they judge best in conscience, that he may not be forced in such a cruel and godless fashion to die in prison for so trifling a reason; and in that Council the said Nicolò may assert and declare his rights, that by virtue of such an agreement he may be freed from prison.   B. P.

(b) Heinrich Stamler and brothers, German merchants

From the Latin and Italian. Senate decrees (Simonsfeld 1887, I, 330–2).

4 July 1499

That to Heinrich Stamler and Brothers, German merchants, who have failed for the sum of 12,000 ducats, being assets of our noblemen and citizens, a safe-conduct be issued on the authority of this Council, extending only to their persons, that they may have the opportunity to come to our city and reach agreement with their creditors, within the next two months only.

For the decree, 134; against 11; uncertain 1.

30 August 1499

Heinrich Stamler and Brothers, German merchants, have absented themselves from this our city, being in debt to several of our nobles and citizens; and wishing to satisfy their creditors they have proposed an agreement on the terms set out below. The majority, indeed three quarters [of the creditors], have been content with this agreement and have put their names to it; but a few, out of stubbornness rather than any other motive, have refused their assent. Now it is a godly act to assist the said Germans, especially as they cannot apply to our magistracy of the Sopraconsoli, since they are aliens and not subject to its jurisdiction; and we must also save all these our noblemen and citizens from losing their credits; and this has been done for other foreigners in similar cases.

BE IT [THEREFORE] DETERMINED that by the authority of this Council the agreement and accord shall be confirmed and approved, both for those who have put their names to it and for those who have refused to do so, and it shall be binding upon all as if it had been signed by all, as has been granted in other such cases.

The agreement is as follows:

[In the name of] Jesus Christ.

Gentlemen creditors, we, Heinrich Stamler and Brothers, on account of the hard times, the fluctuations of trade, the collapse of many of our schemes and projects, and the failure of many of our debtors outside this city, and for many other reasons, find ourselves burdened with debts which we cannot pay at the present time. But we are eager, so long as we are granted reasonable time, to satisfy all of you, gentlemen creditors, in full, even as good merchants should. Hence we, Heinrich Stamler and Brothers, do pray and beseech you, by subscribing to the agreement set forth below, to allow us to pay you in full and in good money in four payments, of which the first shall be made in mid-May 1501, and [the others] in mid-May of the years following, until the whole debt has been discharged. And we implore you to put your names to this agreement.

I, Alberto da Ca Venier, am content with the above proposal. . . .

[Twenty-eight similar declarations follow; some creditors sign on behalf of brothers and fathers as well as themselves.]

For the decree, 101; against, 30; uncertain, 2.[45]   B. P.

[45] None of these decrees finally settled the matter with which it was concerned: another such decree was issued on behalf of Nicolò Baron on 6 April 1501, and Stamler and brothers were

17   THE ACTIVITIES AND MISFORTUNES OF A MERCHANT FAMILY, THE ZANE, 1524–50
From a petition of Zuane di Andrea Zane and brothers, 31 July 1550: ASV Senato, Terra, filza 11.

We will not count among our losses the damage inflicted by the Rialto fire, nor what the sea took from us at that time, nor yet the large sums borne away by debtors, nor yet the marriage portions of our three sisters and a natural daughter of the late Missier Maphio our brother – although these things amount to a great deal of money. We will speak only of the disasters which have overtaken us since the year 1524. In April of that year we sent a ship of 1300 butts to England, and our brother Beneto was aboard it, armed with the most ample safe-conduct from the Most Christian King [of France]. On its return voyage from England in May this ship was attacked off Cádiz by a French captain named Gioan Fiorin and captured after a lengthy fight. In defending himself our brother received seventeen wounds, and, being so dreadfully torn and mutilated, he was taken prisoner. It was not God's will that he should die then, but ill fortune kept a far worse fate in store for him. Upon that ship were our wools, kerseys, cloths and tin, and a large sum in cash to buy salt at Ibiza if other business should be lacking – so that, taking account of the ship itself, equipped as it was with guns and with everything else necessary to sailing such seas and encountering so many different peoples, and taking account too of our own merchandise and money, the loss amounted to over 22,000 ducats. We say nothing of the cargo of sugar we were due to take on in Cádiz and the profit expected from the merchandise and from various freight charges of more than 8000 ducats, and there was a clear loss of another 11,000 ducats and more – a thing one shudders even to hear about, let alone suffer oneself, and all the worse because at that time we were debtors on Rialto for more than 7000 ducats.

A year later, our brother Beneto escaped from the captain's clutches. He then went to the Most Christian King to recover what he could, and he engaged in prolonged dispute with the captain and his men for eight months and more at a stretch. At last his case was brought before His Royal Majesty by Your Serenity's ambassador, Don Sebastiano Justiniano, the King was shown his own safe-conduct, and on hearing everything he promised him a prompt and fair judgement. After this was known, when our brother, accompanied by the secretary Don Hieronimo da Canal, was returning from a visit to the Grand Chancellor's secretary concerning the lawsuit, at about the first hour of the

---

forced to renegotiate the deal with their creditors in order to gain more time to pay (see ASV Compilazione delle Leggi, b.309, f. 152; and Simonsfeld 1887, II, 335–8).

night, he found armed men waiting for him at the Venetian ambassador's door, and was wounded many times and killed. So we lost our beloved brother and everything with him, and all the disasters overtook us, so that we suffered inestimable losses, were impoverished at the instance of our creditors, and were deprived of all hope. But, since we deserve justice, because we suffered such terrible violence despite that very full safe-conduct which we had and still have from that Most Christian King, we have asked and we continue to ask of the most serene Prince and Your Serenity that we be granted the reprisal which we truly deserve in compensation for such savage robbery and violence and for the cruel death which our brother suffered, although we have always been denied this remedy for political reasons [*per li rispetti delle cose publiche*], and were it not for these considerations we would ask for it again. But if we cannot have it, and we are worthy of justice and pity, we hope that through your boundless goodness and mercy this just reprisal may be converted into some other form of redress and that this may be offered to us.

Never ceasing to trade in order to live and earn our living, we kept in the Morea our brother Missier Alvise as our man of business in the whole of that region, and he sent to Venice great quantities of corn (in some years more than 30,000 stara), and many oak-galls [*valonie*], which greatly swelled the customs revenue, and various other goods which proved to be of great profit and benefit to this city. In these activities we sustained several very severe losses. It happened that Prince Doria[46] went with the imperial fleet to take Coron, and on his return he took great plunder at Patras in the Gulf of Lepanto, and it fell to us to have our marine warehouses pillaged. In these we had great quantities of raisins, not yet stored in sacks or barrels, and we also had wrought copper and quantities of soap, and they robbed us of almost everything. And, because we saved our house at Patras by a gift of 400 gold ducats to a captain of foot soldiers, the Turks began to suspect us of being in league with Prince Doria. Fearful of the danger, our brother went off by himself to Zante, leaving our merchandise and credits in the hands of agents. One of these, Marco Cucholino, entered the Gulf to lade a ship of ours with corn, and on account of this suspicion he was taken from our ship and for no good reason beheaded by Huctu Bey, commander of the [Turkish] fleet which was then at Lepanto, and they robbed him of a hoard of 350 gold ducats belonging to us, which he had taken with him to provide for his release, and many other things as well, and they sent the ship back empty, to our own great loss.

War with the Turks then followed. Before this happened we sent Missier Piero Marcello, our nephew, to take charge of our affairs, and from the very start he suffered great trouble and loss. On the outbreak of war, his house and

---

[46] Andrea Doria (1466–1560), first citizen of Genoa, Prince of Melfi, and admiral in the service of the Emperor Charles V. Venice and the Emperor were allies against the Turk in 1538–40.

stores were pillaged and everything removed, including the books and documents which recorded our great credits with many persons in that land, and we were despoiled and deprived of everything, and our nephew enslaved and clapped in irons, and he spent almost four years in that harsh servitude between Patras and Constantinople. Hence our brother [Alvise], seeing that he and all of us were ruined and without the means of recovery, and in debt to the extent of 5000 ducats and more, was overcome by grief and melancholy and so died, as everybody knows, and as the Twenty Savi in charge of the *tansa* acknowledged; for they, having seen the evidence which we produced, exempted us from the *tanse*, from number 18 onwards, as persons who had been ruined, and plunged into the deepest misfortune. Our need is all the more pressing because, in so far as in us lies, we have had to pay a large part of our debts at the expense of our own daily needs. Now, having lost our brothers and everything we had in the world, both our own assets and other people's, we can no longer either pay our creditors or support ourselves, and being now old and feeble we have no remedy but the just judgement of your most excellent lordships and your most illustrious and merciful Council, and we throw ourselves at your feet and beg you to grant us the means to support what remains of our wretched lives, whilst paying our creditors everything that we can allow them. We ask that, out of your inherent mercy and charity, as an act of justice, and in exchange for the reprisal which for political reasons we could not be allowed, you will grant to us one of the first two offices of bailiff in Crete [*gastaldie di Candia*] which may fall vacant, for a guaranteed period of fifteen administrations [*rezimenti*], and longer if we live longer, thus benefiting from the decree concerning reprisals passed in the Great Council on 17 September 1456, which empowers the most excellent Senate to grant a reprisal to subjects and citizens who have suffered losses, just as if the resolution had been adopted by the Great Council itself. We will say no more, but only remind Your Highness of our fallen state, in that we are now poor persons, indeed reduced to beggary, and we humbly commend ourselves to your favour upon our bended knees.[47]   B. P.

---

[47] The Senate decided to grant Zuane Zane and his brothers a pension of 10 ducats a month each, in lieu of the reprisal, for a guaranteed period of six years and for as long as they should live after that. Should any brother die within the six-year period, his pension would be transferred to the others.

18   LETTER OF A MERCHANT IN ALEPPO, 1551
From ASV Miscellanea di Carte Non Appartenenti ad Alcun Archivio, b.20, Registro
Lettere Private.

Aleppo, 7 December 1551

I, Giovanni Alvise Taiapiera, hereby send you, Messer Marchio de Gasparo
Grando, a memorandum for your visit to Tripoli (I pray the Divine Majesty may
take you there and bring you home again safely, and may you be able to set your
affairs to rights as you desire).

As I told you, then, at the end of October I made a sale and consigned 36
pieces of kersey – that is, thirty-six – to a Jew named Prospero Romano, whose
home is in Damascus, and the price of the said goods was 9 Venetian [ducats]
the piece, and I have received on account 154 Venetian [ducats], and have given
him two months (that is, until the end of December) to pay the remainder,
which amounts to 170 Venetian [ducats]. And, since the aforesaid [Jew] lives in
Damascus, and I have no plans for the time being to go there, he has given me
as guarantor and principal payer Rabbi Samuel Alegre, who resides in Tripoli
and has a shop almost opposite Ca' Novo; and he has given me a written record
of his debt in the hand of his notary, signed by several witnesses and also by the
said Prospero. And knowing no one who would do me such a service more
readily than you, I have decided to take advantage of this arrangement and to
beg you to receive the money, for I would do as much for you if you thought me
fit to serve you. Hence I beg you, when you have reached Tripoli, to find the
above-named Samuel Alegre at once, telling him to make ready to pay the bill
when it falls due, and saying that you will return him his note in exchange.
When you have put this to him and he has accepted it, I beg you not to delay
and to spare no expense, for the sooner I receive this money the more I shall
value this service, for you know very well what money is worth at the moment;
and once you have collected, if it turns out that you have to linger, may it please
you to send me the money, either by the first of our countrymen who is coming
over here, or else with the first consignment of accumulated cash. . . .   R. M.

19   FAILURE OF A BANK, 1584
Francesco da Molin, *Compendio . . . delle cose che reputerò degni di venerne particolar
memoria*: BMV ms. Ital., cl. VII, 153 (8812), pp. 123–4.

The following year, 1584, I heard of the failure of the Pisani and Tiepolo bank
for a very large sum of money. This was caused chiefly by the bankruptcy of one

Andrea da l'Osta, a Tuscan, a Pisan, and a very rich merchant, who had lived in our city for many years. He had built up much credit by his many business transactions, but in truth it was based on his reputation alone and not upon his capital, for this market and the city of Venice are naturally very much inclined to love and trust in appearances. Hence, heaping business upon business, his reach exceeding his grasp [*abbracciando molti ne esso tutto stringendo*], he suffered the fate of almost all those who want to be bigger than other men. With his fall came the fall of the bank, because its creditors believed that he owed it more than he really did, because he could call upon it at will, and so they all wanted to be satisfied at the same time. The bank kept going for a few days, paying them off as best it could, but in the end the crowd of creditors increased and the bank collapsed and failed, to the detriment of numberless people and great damage to this market, which was without a bank for four years, so that business shrank to an unbelievable extent. The Republic felt the effects of this, and took very extensive measures, but to no avail.   B. P.

20   AN AGREEMENT TO ESTABLISH A MERCHANT PARTNERSHIP, 1596
From the acts of the notary Besciani: ASV Archivio Notarile, b.559, ff. 69v–71v, 29 August 1596.

The most noble Francesco Tiepolo, son of the most illustrious and worthy Alvise, Procurator of St Mark's, on the one hand, and the honourable Zuane di Negri, son of Messer Agustin, merchant, on the other, have formed the present partnership in the name of the Holy Spirit in good fortune and to their common benefit. . . .

The said Signori Tiepolo and Negri have invested 21,000 ducats at 6 lire 4 soldi per ducat as capital in favour of this partnership, 15,000 from the said Francesco and the other 6000 from the said Zuanne, part in cash, part in merchandise, and part in credits, *oratii* [?] and trading voyages, as shall be set out clearly in the account book of this partnership . . . and these 21,000 ducats shall be placed in the hands and control of the said Zuanne.

The said Zuanne di Negri shall be bound to use his own best endeavours, in good faith and with all possible diligence and care, to apply this capital to the manufacture of cloth from Spanish wool of 60 and 70 grade, both in his house and outside it, according to the laws and customs of this city.

The said Zuanne may also buy ready-made cloth, both dyed and undyed, wool, cochineal and other merchandise as opportunity arises, both for cash and upon credit. He may trade in this cloth and cash and in other kinds of merchandise as they become available and he judges them to be good business.

The said Zuanne shall keep double-entry accounts of all his daily business.

The most noble Tiepolo shall also have a similar book drawn up, that both may see how the business is going at any time. Similarly the said Zuanne shall be obliged to draw up a balance sheet of the business of the present partnership at the pleasure and request of the said Tiepolo.

In addition to the capital he has invested in the above partnership, the said Zuanne may also trade with other capital of his own, and do business with it for his own use and advantage, in order to buy and have made cloths, silks, camlets and anything else which he chooses.

The present partnership, which shall trade in the name of Alvise Tiepolo, son of the said most noble Zanfrancesco [sic], and the said Zuanne Negri, shall last for the next five years, beginning on the first day of next September.

Should the said Tiepolo desire to end the present partnership before the said five years have elapsed, then the said Zuane shall, if requested by the said Tiepolo, begin to wind up the business. And, should the said Zuane also wish to bring this partnership to an end, he may do so on condition that he puts through the loom all the wool that he has purchased and that it is possible to put through (i.e. the cloths that have their weft yarn), and that he draws the profit from all woollen cloths which are ready, finished and dyed. The present partnership shall then be brought to an end.

At the end of the present partnership, having first discharged debts of every kind, paid the agents and other employees, the rents of houses, shops, warehouses and vaults, and met the other costs arising from the operation of this partnership, the investments made by each partner, i.e. 15,000 ducats by the most noble Tiepolo and 6000 by the said Zuane di Negri, shall be withdrawn, in cash if this be possible, and otherwise in the best assets remaining in the partnership. And what remains shall be divided into two parts, one for the most noble Francesco and the other for the said Sier Zuane, and, if there should be losses, which the Lord God prevent, then each partner shall bear one half of these losses. . . .

And because the said most noble Tiepolo and the honourable Negri have worked together in a partnership on similar business, as may be seen in the records of Messer Pietro Patternio, public notary of this city, for 4 January 1592, and have ended and finished that partnership with the establishment of the present one, each partner has declared and declares that he has received the capital he invested in the partnership and one half of the profit from it. Neither party owes anything to the other from the account of that partnership.   A.C.

CONSPICUOUS CONSUMPTION AND STYLES OF LIVING

*H*ERE *the emphasis shifts from getting to spending, and from commercial disaster to the wilful dissipation of fortunes. Legal texts such as IV.21–3 are often valuable not as evidence of effective law enforcement, but as testimony to the practices that they condemn. Laws intended to restrain ostentation and lavish spending had been issued by Venetian councils at least since 1299, but only in the late fifteenth century was their enforcement entrusted to a specialized magistracy, and only in the early sixteenth to a permanent one [IV.21]. Motives for the legislation were not always clearly stated, but these laws were almost certainly designed to encourage profitable investment rather than reckless expenditure; to save the fortunes of the ruling orders from erosion by ruinous competition between their members; to preserve the appearance of unity among nobles and citizens by forbidding the display of individual wealth; and, on occasion, to prevent confusion between respectable and dishonourable women [see above, III.6(e)]. Like much other social legislation, they were also designed to prevent the community from angering God by luxurious living. There are two selections here [IV.22–3] from the code of sumptuary laws issued by the Senate in 1562; some of them repeated measures passed earlier in the sixteenth century.*

IV.24 and 25 are designed to contrast two styles of life in the artistic and literary circles of sixteenth-century Venice: that of a flourishing painter, Titian, and that of a struggling hack writer, as Anton Francesco Doni, a renegade priest from Florence, liked to portray himself.

English travellers were impressed by the tendency of Venetian, as of other Italian, nobles to go in for conspicuous investment in building or parks, in things that lasted and could be kept in families, rather than for conspicuous consumption on clothing, feasting and large retinues of servants (Coryat 1905 edn, I, 397–8, 415; Moryson 1907 edn, III, 492–3, and IV, 94). Perhaps, therefore, the sumptuary laws were not completely ineffectual, and not wholly at odds with social custom.

BIBLIOGRAPHY In general: Newett 1902; Bistort 1912; Hughes 1983. On dress: Newton 1988. On Titian's style of life: Padoan, 1980. On Doni: Grendler 1969.

B. P.

21   A MAGISTRACY TO ADMINISTER SUMPTUARY LAWS, 1515
Senate decree establishing the Provveditori sopra le Pompe, 8 February 1514 Venetian
style (Bistort 1912, pp. 54–5).

It can be plainly seen, and it has come to our attention, that in the city of Venice
there is much gross and unncessary expenditure on meals and banquets, on the
adornment of women, and on the decoration of houses, so that fortunes are
squandered and a bad example is set to those who seek to live modestly. It is
proper, therefore, especially in these hard times, to make every effort to put
these matters right, and so do honour to the majesty of God.

BE IT DETERMINED, therefore, that by scrutiny of this Council there shall be
chosen three commissioners to deal with all ostentatious acts and immoderate
expenditure which contravene our regulations [*tre proveditori nostri sopra le
pompe et spese immoderate che se fano contra la forma de li ordeni nostri*]. They must
be members of the Senate, shall serve for two years, and may not refuse
[election] upon a penalty of 500 gold ducats apiece, unless they are members of
the Collegio. After two years the Councillors shall be obliged upon their oath to
appoint others in their place, on the express condition that those currently in
office may not relinquish it until their successors have been appointed; and, if
during this period there should be a need to replace anyone, this must be done
immediately, so that there are always three persons in office.

They shall be empowered to reach decisions by the vote of two of them
through the ballot box [*per do de loro a bossoli et ballote*], and appeals from them
shall lie to the Collegio dei Venti Savi in Rialto, according to the resolution
reached in our Great Council, observing at all times the decree concerning
pledges.

Of the fines which they impose, two thirds shall be divided between them and
the office, and the remaining third shall go to the Arsenal.

The present decree may not be revoked, suspended or altered unless the
proposal is made by all the [Ducal] Councillors, by the Heads of the Forty, and
by all the Savi of both orders, and unless it obtains five sixths of the votes of the
Senate, assembled to the number of 150 persons or more.   B. P.

22   THE REGULATION OF BANQUETS, 1562
From a Senate decree of 8 October 1562 (Bistort 1912, pp. 378–81).

Since acts of ostentation must be controlled in accordance with the most recent
resolution of this Council, it is necessary to set out the regulations as briefly and
succinctly as possible, that everyone may understand them better.

BE IT THEREFORE DETERMINED that, at nuptial feasts, at banquets for public and private parties, and indeed at any meal of meat, not more than one course of roast and one of boiled meat may be provided. This may not include more than three kinds of meat or poultry, which must consist of the things which are permitted at nuptial feasts. Wild birds and animals, Indian cocks and hens, and doves shall be strictly forbidden. At meals of fish there may be two kinds of roast, two kinds of fried and two kinds of boiled fish, accompanied by *antipasti*, salads, dairy produce and other ordinary things, with a serving of the usual cake, marzipan and common sweetmeats. Banned from all banquets shall be trout from any place whatsoever, sturgeon, fish from the lake, pasties, confections and all other things made of sugar, and anything else that has not been expressly mentioned above. It is strictly forbidden to include both meat and fish or any other sea food in the same meal. Oysters may be served only at private meals for twenty persons or less, and not at larger banquets or feasts; collations must be provided in the rooms, on the tables, and not otherwise, and they must consist of modest confections, of the ordinary products of pastry cooks, and of simple fruits of any kind, according to the time of year. No other kind of confection or seasoning may be served, upon a penalty of 10 ducats for anything provided in contravention of the present regulations at gatherings of twenty-five persons or less, and a penalty of 25 ducats for any prohibited dish served at gatherings of more than twenty-five persons.   B. P.

23   REGULATION OF THE WEARING OF PEARLS, 1562
From a Senate decree of 15 October 1562 (Bistort 1912, pp. 403–5).

We must ensure that the number of pearls in this city does not increase, but rather diminishes as painlessly as possible, and so

BE IT RESOLVED that all who have pearls and wish to make use of them in Venice shall be obliged within the next eight days to go to the Provveditori sopra le Pompe, and declare the number, weight and quality of those pearls. They shall have them registered in their name, and within the next twenty days after that they must have them sealed with the seal which the Sopraprovveditori and Provveditori shall approve and which shall be kept in the office, so that if from time to time the strings should get broken they can be resealed with the same seal after first making sure that they are [registered] in the same name, and are of the same number and weight. Once this period of twenty-eight days has passed, no more pearls may be registered or sealed.

When these pearls have been registered and sealed, they may be transferred from one name to another, as is done at the Dieci Savi [sopra le Decime]. If anyone commits a fraud in the matter of these pearls, he shall be deprived of the

179

privilege of using them in future, as well as suffer the penalty stated below, and whatever punishment he may deserve in accordance with the gravity of the fraud.

These pearls, duly registered and sealed, may be worn round the neck on a tight string only by the wives of those in whose names they are registered, for a period of ten years and no more, which shall be reckoned from the day of their marriage. B. P.

24 LIVING WELL: SUPPER AND CONVERSATION IN TITIAN'S HOUSE
From Priscianese 1540. Extract from appended letter following the sixth book.

To the Very Reverend Missier Ludovico Becci and his [friend,] Missier Luigi del Riccio

On 1 August I was invited to celebrate the kind of Bacchanal which, I know not why, is called *ferrare agosto*, so that for most of the evening I argued about it in a delightful garden belonging to Missier Titiano Vecellio, the excellent Venetian painter (as everyone knows), a person truly suited to spice every worthy feast with his pleasantries. There were gathered together with the said Missier Titiano (because birds of a feather flock together) some of the most rare intellects that are found today in this city, and from our set principally Missier Pietro Aretino, the new miracle of nature, and beside him Missier Jacopo Tatti, who is as great an imitator of nature with his chisel as is our host with his brush, and there was Missier Jacomo Nardi and myself, so that I was the fourth amongst so much wisdom.[48] Here, before the tables were set out, because the sun despite the shade was still making his heat much felt, we spent the time looking at the lifelike figures in the excellent pictures which fill the house and in discussing the real beauty and charm of the garden, which everyone marvelled at with singular pleasure. The house is situated on the far end of Venice by the edge of the sea, and from it one sees the pretty little island of Murano and other lovely places. As soon as the sun set, this part of the sea teemed with gondolas adorned with beautiful women and resounded with the varied harmony of voice and musical instruments which accompanied our delightful supper until midnight. But, to return to the garden, it was so well laid out and so beautiful and as a result was so much praised that it called to my mind the most pleasant gardens [*Horti*] at Sant'Agata [in Rome] belonging to our revered patron, Monsignor Ridolfi. J. F.

[48] On Titian, Aretino and Jacopo Tatti [Sansovino] see below, X.1 and preceding headnote. Giacomo Nardi (1476–1563) was a Florentine republican who after 1530 lived in exile, mainly in Venice, where he wrote his Florentine history. Priscianese himself was another Florentine exile, a cleric and a grammar-teacher born at Pieve di Presciano, near Arezzo.

25   LIVING POORLY: THE SQUALID LODGINGS OF ANTON FRANCESCO DONI,
1550
From a letter, possibly fictitious, to Girolamo Fava, New Year's Day (i.e. 1 March) 1550:
Doni 1550, pp. 86–8.

Let us now talk about my home comforts. . . . There are four people lodging
here: i.e. Prester John, who is in the back room, a superabundant man, of many
skills. With his hand he plays the lute, with his foot the harp, with his mouth the
flute and with slop-pail the bagpipes. I deeply regret that I cannot at one go
describe for you all the details of his room, because the jewels that he keeps
there cause him to keep it locked. Apart from him, we consist – from head to
tail – of myself, my uncle in the middle, and my pseudo-wife. Then I have other
rabble, such as footmen, household servants, stepmothers and others whom I
hold in small account. We have one bed between the lot of us, and each has his
own (O beautiful secret!) chamberpot, because the privies are common to all.
So I make this distinction in order that you properly understand my comfort.
To express in a word my state of ease, at one and the same time I can be
writing, at table, in bed, or sitting in front of the fire, not to mention in the shit-
house. Then I am in every country [at once] and see all mankind if I stand at the
window; it looks out onto a place where I can behold Slavs, Greeks, Turks,
Moors, Spaniards, Frenchmen, Germans and Italians: different faces, a variety
of clothing and weird ways of behaving. Then, if I cast my eyes around the
room, I have there the Emperor with the King of France portrayed from life,
Michelangelo Buonarotti, Bembo and (not to prolong the list) the portraits from
life of my friends and enemies [he lists other items – presumably prints:
mythological stories, views of towns, antiquities, etc.]. . . . Whoever reads this
letter would think I was the most well-off man in the world, and that such a
place costs me some tens of florins a month. . . . I came to Venice in those days
to practise printing, and to be quit of various lodgings I have had which are
unworthy to expose beside this place where I am now. I have the most wretched
room (if you can call it that) in the whole town, and the worst company, and I
suffer the worst discomfort in the world. For the consolation of sleep, I have a
solid mattress, a good, soundly made hard bed, an empty pillow, coarse sheets
and a blue counterpane of the type used in hospitals; at night, in the manner of
a cruel doctor, an army of huge bedbugs, as large as Mocenigos,[49] and a mob of
fat fleas, test my pulse and bleed me; above my head, in an old loft, I think there
is a college of mice and a consistory of cobwebs; below, there is a street where
all night long wretches who waste the daytime pass up and down singing
strambotti [lewd songs] noisily and certain erotic little madrigals; not to mention

[49] Silver coin of the time of Doge Giovanni Mocenigo (1478–85).

Prester John I told you about, who is next door to me, separated by a board partition. Afflicted by a canker, he energetically struggles, hour after hour, with pills, plasters, embrocations, cupping-glasses, sticky plasters, cauteries, adhesives, wads and enemas; he shouts at the top of his voice and shits with great difficulty. His tabernacle being locked up all day, I swear to God that no corrupted grave gives off such a stench when it is opened. On the other side of me I have an old woman and a tailor who, what with the noise of the scissors and the coughing of the toothless crone, pass away two thirds of the night for me with pleasures of the most wretched sort to be found in all the world. No sooner is it daybreak than the boats, barges and gondolas appear in a stinking, fetid, vile canal, with people shouting and braying with coarse and disjointed voices, competing with each other, one with Brenta water, another onions and fresh garlic and mouldy melons, rotten grapes, stale fish and green kindling wood, enough to drive crazy everyone of sound mind. D. C., D. T.

Part V
'The Present Face of Religion Here'

*A*S FORCEFULLY *as any European state, the Venetian Republic presented itself as a defender of the faith. In its own eyes at least, it was a holy community, enjoying the special favour of a Gospel-writing saint; it ardently collected holy relics for its own protection, and was a prominent defender of all Christendom against the infidel Turk. Its prosperity was believed to depend on its piety, on its capacity for pleasing and propitiating God, and so earning his favour. One of the Doge's duties was to pursue heresy, and the Council of Ten, the redoubtable committee of public safety, was charged with the repression of blasphemy and unnatural vice [see above, III.6(c), (f)]. On the other hand the Venetian government feared some of the claims of the Catholic hierarchy to temporal power and to special privileges and immunities that reduced the state's authority, both fiscal and judicial, over the clergy. In general, Catholic teaching insisted on obedience to superiors, but it could on occasion claim for the Church an authority higher than that of the state.*

The texts presented here describe some of the religious institutions most characteristic of Venice, point out their social and political as well as their religious significance, and help to analyse the problems associated with them – particularly in the half-century before and after the issue in the 1560s of the decrees of the Council of Trent for the reform of the Church. These texts will convey some idea of the elements of tension and collaboration, of conflict and compromise, which contributed to the relationship between Venice and the Catholic Church. If the Venetian nobility needed the Church to legitimate and sanctify their authority, the Church needed the sanctions applied by the Venetian government to ensure that religion was respected and wrong belief suppressed.

B. P.

THE CLERGY AND THE PEOPLE

*A*CCORDING TO *the censuses of 1586 and 1593, about 3 per cent of the population of Venice could be classified as secular or regular clergy or as nuns: in 1586 there were 536 priests, 1238 monks and friars, and 2403 nuns in a total population estimated at 148,640 (Beloch 1902, pp. 13–14, 27). Had account been taken of tertiaries and of persons in minor orders, the numbers might well have been appreciably higher. The texts which follow are chiefly concerned with the pastoral work of the Patriarch and the parochial clergy and with the friars' sermons to the people.*

V.2, written in the wake of the great earthquake of 1511, a disaster attributed to the sins of the city, demonstrates the importance attached to religious ceremony as a means of placating the wrath of God, and baldly describes the topics chosen by Lenten preachers, especially Franciscan observants, when they exhorted the people to repentance. Other texts [V.1, 3 and 4] convey essential information about the organization of the diocese, ranging from the elections of parish clergy to the special status and privileges of St Mark's as the Doge's chapel, famous for its music. Various definitions are given of the body of persons entitled to elect parish priests. V.4 describes long-established structures and organizations such as the congregations of parish priests, and conveys some idea of the impact of the Tridentine reform of the Church, especially in the account of the provisions made for the formal education of the clergy through seminaries. The Ad Limina reports were drawn up in response to the requirement renewed by Pope Sixtus V and his successors that diocesan bishops or their representatives should visit Rome and make a report to the Holy See at regular intervals: Italian bishops were required to do so every three years. Contrasted with their bland though informative statements are the acid comments of William Bedell [V.5], then chaplain to the English embassy. An enthusiastic missionary, he was assessing the possibility of converting influential Venetians to the Protestant faith in the aftermath of the famous interdict of 1606–7 [V.17–18].

BIBLIOGRAPHY *In general: Niero 1961; Benzoni 1961, 1973; Logan 1967; Prodi 1973; Davidson 1984. On the musicians of St Mark's: Glixon 1983.* B. P.

I   ELECTIONS OF PARISH CLERGY, *c*.1460, 1517
(i) Constitution of the Patriarch Andrea Bondumier, early 1460s, in *Constitutiones et privilegia patriarchatus et cleri veneti*: BMV ms. Marciana 84d, 138, f. 28.

We decree that on the death of a parish priest, or of any other holder of a clerical title, or of any benefice-holder in the city and diocese, after the funeral all members of the chapter of the church concerned who are in holy orders shall be called to the election [of his successor], provided they are present and personally resident. If they are absent, they shall be awaited for no more than twenty-four hours after the death has occurred. After the Mass of the Holy Spirit and recitation of the hymn *Veni Creator Spiritus*, these persons shall immediately proceed to the election by scrutiny, or by ballot, or by general agreement, as God inspires.[1] If they do otherwise, the election shall be invalid. Further, we decree that no one shall be elected to the beneficiary title of a priest unless he is an ordained priest; and no one to the title of deacon unless he belongs to the order of deacon; and the same rule shall apply to a subdeacon, except by dispensation.

We further decree that, when any election is made, candidates shall always be chosen from the chapter of the church, promoting them by one step, i.e. a deacon to the title of priest, a subdeacon to the title of deacon, and so on, provided they are fit by virtue of life, morals and age. Otherwise, a better candidate may be chosen from any church.   O. L.

(ii) From the Latin. Extracts from a brief of Pope Leo X, 4 February 1517, in Stefano Cosmi, *Origine della Clementina* . . . : BCV, ms. Gradenigo 46, ff. 1–3.

Our beloved son Marino Zorzi, patrician of Venice, ambassador of your nobility and of our beloved sons in the Venetian dominions to ourselves and to the Apostolic See, has recently made representations to us in view of the fact that in your city persons of sound morals, prudence and exemplary life have by custom been nominated and presented to churches subject to patriarchal jurisdiction, otherwise called parishes or cures, by the parishioners of the same, summoned to and assembled in a specifically designated place. . . .

We decree and ordain that henceforth in perpetuity, whenever a vacancy occurs of the churches or cures subject to this right of patronage, those having

---

[1] A synodal decree of the Patriarch Lorenzo Giustinian, in 1438, had stipulated that 'all those resident in the city' should 'proceed to election by scrutiny or by general agreement, unless it is long-established custom that they elect by ballot or by acclamation, which custom we permit' (in the same manuscript, ff. 27v–28r).

the right of presentation [*patroni*] cannot give their assent except when they are assembled in the customary place, and following the summons of those who should participate in the presentation, and after due discussion.   O. L.

2   THE EARTHQUAKE OF 1511 AND THE PURGING OF SIN AND MISBELIEF

DMS, xii, cols 79–80, 84–5, 98–9, 114, 121, 122.

On 26 March, a Wednesday, at the hour of 20¾ [about three hours before sunset], the weather being somewhat unsettled, a mighty earthquake came suddenly upon this city of Venice. It seemed as though the houses were collapsing, the chimneys swaying, the walls bursting open, the bell-towers bending, objects in high places falling, water boiling, even in the Grand Canal, as though it had been put on a fire. They say that, although it was high tide, when the earthquake came some canals dried up as though there had been a tremendous drought. The earthquake lasted as long as a *Miserere*; all felt the sheer horror of it, in view of the great danger to the people of Venice, who are not used to such earthquakes and have suffered none for many years. The bells in their towers rang by themselves in many places, especially at St Mark's, a terrifying thing to happen. It chanced that the Senate had just assembled to deal with affairs of state, and they had scarcely entered and begun to have a letter read when they heard the noise and felt the trembling of the chamber; then everyone jumped up, the doors were flung wide, and they descended as best they could by the wooden staircase, so quickly that some were carried from top to bottom, their feet touching none of the steps, so fierce was the stampede.

Notable things happened in the midst of all this, and the first was that at St Mark's the marble statues of four kings fell. They were on the façade, in front of which they stood upright, and no other damage occurred, except to certain columns in the church. On the San Basso side, however, there fell the marble statue of a woman, the figure of Prudence, who stood up straight in the midst of other Virtues. At the Ducal Palace, the high ridge of the roof above the great balcony of the Great Council chamber fell, with a figure of Justice which was set upon it; but the marble St Mark stood firm and did not fall. Let me say, too, that one of the battlements above the Great Council chamber, in the middle, fell down; or rather one half of it, made of marble with lilies carved upon it, landed in the courtyard at the foot of the stone staircase on a hard stone [*pietra viva*]² with the head of the lily downwards. Many took it for a good omen that the lily, the heraldic emblem of France, should fall and be destroyed – for

---

² The material 'brought from Rovigno and Brioni, a citadel on the Dalmatian coast' [see above, I.3].

they believed this to be God's will, for the good of Italy, which is flayed by these barbarians. Some took it as an omen that Prudence had fallen, and thought that if the auguries were taken now they would say, 'Venice, beware, and learn to be wise in these times, which are days of evil; take no false step as you did two years ago, for if you fail to rule yourselves with prudence this commonwealth may suffer great loss; and just as St Mark stayed intact above the Palace, even so will this city remain faithful to Jesus Christ, and be the preserver of the Catholic faith and the defender of the Church. You used to love justice; if it has fallen, restore it.' Many say that there was no figure of Justice above the balcony, but I maintain that there was. . . .

27 March 1511

Then our Patriarch, Don Antonio Contarini, came [to the Collegio], saying that the earthquake is a sign from God, and that misfortunes occur on account of sins. Venice is full of these, especially of sodomy, which is recklessly practised everywhere. The female whores have sent to him to say that they cannot make a living because no one now goes to them, so rampant is sodomy: even the old men are getting down to it. He has heard from confessors that fathers are interfering with daughters, brothers with sisters, and so forth. And the city is becoming irreligious. The preachers have told him that it is wrong not to preach the word of God this Lent, for Venice is free of sickness, and it was a mistake to stop the sermons. We are now halfway through Lent. In other years the confessors would have heard the confessions of half the Venetians by this time; but now they have heard no one but the female tertiaries and a tiny number of others. The Patriarch then said that he wished to order processions at St Mark's for three days, and processions in the parishes in the evenings, and three days fasting on bread and water to appease the wrath of God. And he said other things too. The Doge and other members of the Collegio supported him; they were taking measures against blasphemy, and making sure to dispense justice, etc. Today, in the Council of Ten, they would take action against sodomy.

Hence all the preachers appointed to the churches were ordered to preach, with effect from tomorrow morning, and the Patriarch ordered a three-day fast on bread and water and a procession around the public squares in the evenings, singing the litanies, with one at St Mark's in the mornings. I applaud these things as an aid to piety and good conduct; but as a remedy for earthquakes, which are a natural phenomenon, this was no good at all. . . .

2 April 1511

It became known that at this time Fra Rufin Lovato, who is preaching on Campo San Polo, had attacked the Jews, saying it would be good to deprive them of everything they owned and put them to the sack, because this city is full of Jews who have fled to it. Yesterday he preached at length. Fearing a disturbance against them, the bankers Anselmo and Vivian[3] went this morning to the Heads of the Ten and made a complaint. The Heads of the Ten in turn approached the Signoria, and they resolved to admonish this preacher, together with those of the Frari and San Cassiano, who are also preaching such things, to ensure that there is no attack upon the Jews. . . .

13 April 1511 (Palm Sunday)

After dinner there was a sermon at St Mark's by the preacher of Santo Stefano, Fra [. . .], and he blamed three vices: blasphemy, sacrilege and sodomy. Note: at this time the Patriarch issued orders that, upon pain of excommunication, no one whatsoever who [improperly] entered a religious house might be absolved by anyone other than the Patriarch himself. . . .

18 April 1511 (Good Friday)

After dinner Fra Rufin Lovato, of the order of Franciscan Observants, who preaches on Campo San Polo, gave the sermon in St Mark's. He spoke of the blessedness of contemplating Christ and the Cross; then he talked briefly of the Passion, and greatly blamed the Jews, saying that you could with a clear conscience take everything they have and drive them away; and he wishes to hold to this conviction. The same man preached at St Mark's this day two years ago.

B. P.

3 THE CLERGY AND MUSICIANS OF ST MARK'S, 1581, 1626
(i) Sansovino 1581, ff. 39r–40r (ed. Martinioni 1663, pp. 103–4).

Attached to this famous church, which has been privileged, favoured and exalted by various Popes, are several other sacred places, because the convent of the Vergini recognizes the Doge and the church of St Mark's as its head, and so do the hospitals of San Marco and the Casa di Dio, the church of Santa Maria in Broglio, the church of San Felice d'Aimano (otherwise Santi Filippo e Giacomo), the abbey of Santo Egidio di Fontanela, the priory of San Giacomo di Pontida, and the church of San Giovanni Nuovo at Rialto.

The leading figure in this church, after the Doge, is the chief priest

---

[3] Asher Meshullam of Mestre and his brother Chaim, known in Italian as Anselmo del Banco and as Vita or Vivian (Pullan 1971, pp. 479–86).

[*Primocerio*], who was appointed to hold office of the Doge when St Mark's was first built. He is chosen and invested by the Doge and provided with a generous income commensurate with his position. By laws of 1471 and 1478 he must be a Venetian nobleman, at least twenty-five years of age. When he celebrates he dresses as a bishop, with mitre, ring and crozier, by virtue of a grant from Pope Innocent IV in 1252. He has a rochet, by a brief of Pope Alexander V. By a bull of Pope John XXIII he gives his blessing to the people. He grants an indulgence of forty days, after himself celebrating Mass, by authority of the same Pope Alexander, by whom he is also authorized to consecrate the priests of St Mark's.

After the chief priest comes the Vicar, who is selected from among the most honourable and reputable priests in the city, and this title was transferred from the church of San Teodoro to that of St Mark. The third is the *maestro di Coro*, the fourth are two sacristans, and the fifth are two *basilicani*, who are in charge of the revenues [*preventi*] of the clergy. Then there are twenty-four canons, appointed from ancient times to be chaplains to the Doge, and twelve of them are priests who belong to St Mark's, while the other twelve are parish priests from the city, in accordance with a rule laid down in 1434 (at which time there were six canons and eighteen parish priests). Should a vacancy arise through the death of one of the canons [of St Mark's] he is succeeded by one of the six subcanons, and if one of the parish priests dies he is succeeded by another parish priest. Then there are four deacons and four subdeacons, and other orders too, appropriate to the honourable clergy of such a famous and renowned church. These canons received from Pope Martin V the right to wear the *mozzetta* or amice, made of the skins of various animals. The order of service in this sacred place follows the usage of the church of Constantinople, but it is not very different from the Roman, and it is performed with such zeal that nothing surpasses it.

As for the things necessary to these activities, the annual expenditure is over 12,000 ducats, since they employ two organists from among the best in Italy, at a very generous salary, and there are also the *maestro di cappella* with a large number of singers, the canons and subcanons, the masters of mosaics, the architects, the vergers, and various other functionaries, to say nothing of the wax, incense, oils and other materials essential to such a great church.

Apart from these things the church has, by grant of Pope Alexander III, in recognition of the favours he received from the Republic, a perpetual indulgence which begins on the eve of Ascension Day and lasts for the whole of the day itself, while the fair is held in the Piazza. Not only do all the people of the city and of the surrounding areas flock to this out of devotion, but foreigners come too, even from distant countries.   B. P.

(ii) From the preface to Rovetta 1626.

For many years now it has been my profession to play every sort of instrument, and while I have worked quite hard at this I have not neglected the study of composition. Since I wanted to employ my talents in this field, I got the most illustrious and excellent Procurators to appoint me to a musical post in St Mark's. Moreover, I hoped to be able to fill the post of *vice-maestro* in the absence of the *maestro di cappella,* and my hope did not prove groundless; for, since this need arose shortly after I took up my position, I was honoured by the most illustrious Procurators, my patrons, who asked that I serve until they could make a new appointment. Although certain people have found it amazing that I should have passed so quickly from the profession of instrumentalist to that of composer and director of music on different feast days, they have been wrong to judge that I could not compose sacred music. Since I realize that such opposition could very quickly make a bad impression on those who do not know me, I have adopted the expedient of printing these sacred songs so that the most illustrious and excellent Procurators may see that, although they were kind to me, I do possess the same grounding [in musical skills] as anyone else who has been appointed in the past. And let it be known, moreover, that these really are my compositions and not those of others, and I am prepared to prove this with every sort of evidence to anyone who believes otherwise. And let no one wonder that I was first a player and then set myself to be a composer, for Striggio, Priuli, Valentini, and almost all the best school of composers have worked in such a manner. In fact, because of this experience, I am truly qualified for the position of *vice-maestro di cappella* of St Mark's, since in this most serene service there are not only more than thirty singers, but also over twenty instrumentalists, both strings and winds. Therefore, virtuous gentlemen, if you should find in these compositions of mine something not entirely pleasing to your taste, you will excuse me from blame, since I have told you why I had to have them printed, and I shall not fail to prepare something else which will please you.[4]   I. F.

---

[4] Giovanni Rovetta's father had been employed as a violinist in the *cappella* at St Mark's, which had been systematically expanded and strengthened by the Procurators since the appointment of Adrian Willaert as *maestro di cappella* in 1527. Giovanni himself had begun his career as a singer and instrumentalist at the basilica. Whether or not the Procurators were impressed by the *Salmi concertati,* on 22 November 1627 they did appoint Rovetta permanently to the post of *vice-maestro* which he coveted, at a salary of 120 ducats a year.

4   THE CHURCHES OF VENICE AND THE EDUCATION OF THE CLERGY, 1604,
1612

(i) From the Latin. Extract from the Ad Limina report of the Patriarch Matteo Zane,
20 December 1604, pp. 1–3: ASVat. Archivio della Sacra Congregazione del Concilio,
Relazioni dei vescovi dopo le visite Ad Limina, Venezia.

Almost all the parish churches are collegiate, each with a parish priest (who is
head of the clergy, and chiefly responsible for the cure of souls), at least two
other priests, and a deacon and subdeacon. All these together make up the
chapter. They, and especially the priests, are to aid and support the parish
priests in caring for souls. It may be that in earlier times they failed to perform
these duties without quarrelling and complaining; but they are now so willing to
give assistance, and so prompt to administer the sacraments, that on my
visitation I found no one to reprove for failing to assist parish priests or failing to
tender the sacraments, especially to the poor and sick – even though there are
almost 200,000 souls distributed among the parishes. The election of parish
priests is the business of those who own houses in each parish.[5] That of the
clergy who hold beneficiary titles is the business of the chapter. But the
installation of all these persons is the responsibility of the Patriarch. I strive with
all the energy I can muster to ensure that when a vacancy occurs in any of these
titles the chapter may always elect a person whose knowledge, way of life and
morals have already been approved by a thorough examination, that he may be
the better equipped to assist in the care of souls.

The regular revenues of the parish churches and the beneficiary titles are
almost all very scanty, so that the priests would be short of food and clothing if
they were not assisted by the offerings of the faithful, which are unpredictable.
Parish priests and holders of titles earn these things for themselves by their
readiness to provide services and by the alms bestowed upon them by the
faithful for celebrating Masses for the dead, either as perpetual endowments or
for a limited period of time.

As for church buildings, their interior decoration and the state of all things
needed for divine worship, I found them all to be splendidly and generously
appointed, so that it seems that nothing can be added to them and there is no
more to be desired. The fraternities, especially those of the Holy Sacrament
which are established in every parish, must be given credit for the splendour
and magnificence of the churches, for it is their labours and expenditure that
have brought the churches such fame, and they strive every day to adorn them

[5] Cf. Sansovino ed. Martinioni, 1663, p. 290: 'parish priests are elected by the vote of those
citizens and plebeians who own property in the parish, and they are approved and confirmed by
the Patriarch'.

still further, since the revenues assigned to the fabric of churches are so slender
and inadequate.   B. P.

(ii) Extracts from the Ad Limina report in the name of the Patriarch Francesco
Vendramin, 1612, ff. 15, 15v, 17: in the same archive as (i). The report was written and
presented on behalf of the Patriarch by 'Ioannes Andrea de Salicibus, doctor in
philosophy and sacred theology, his specially appointed agent for this purpose'.

. . . lest the clergy suffer damage, there are masters of grammar and theology in
each sestier of the city. They are recruited from the religious orders and chosen
for the purpose of teaching the clergy Latin and cases of conscience, and, above
all, those things that pertain to the cure of souls. This scheme is being put into
effect, with the greatest benefit to the clerical office. . . .

In every church there are many mass-benefices [*mansionariae*]. Some are
bestowed by laymen, others by parish priests, and some by other persons. They
were endowed by the charity of the faithful for the salvation of souls. When the
most serene Republic, by liquidating the loan funds which financed religious
activities [*montium pietatis extinctione*],[6] shed the burden of paying for a large
number of these foundations, the Patriarch when conducting his visitation of
churches came to realize the need, and he himself established several mass-
benefices both for the sake of the living and of the dead, with his own money, in
those churches where it appeared most advisable to do so. From this charity the
greatest possible number of poor priests receive support.

The Venetian clergy are divided into nine congregations of priests, and at
funerals or public processions each priest follows the cross of his own
congregation, and the parish priests and the holders of titles of the churches are
admitted to these bodies. They have regular revenues, which are distributed
among the brothers. They often gather to sing Masses or hold funeral services.
Of the brothers, some have full shares and some have half shares, and those
who are full participants receive the sum of 25 or 30 Venetian ducats from the
congregation. Each congregation elects an archpriest and two officials, and
when all [these representatives] are assembled together they make a college of
twenty-seven, and they transact the business of the nine congregations. . . .

There is a Patriarchal Seminary, in which eighteen clerics are maintained
under the rule of the excellent fathers of the Somaschian order, and the
Somaschians are diligently protected by the most reverend Patriarch, for when

6 He refers to the liquidation, from 1596 onwards, of government loan funds, which had
previously provided a fairly safe and blameless source of income, at modest rates of interest, for
ecclesiastical institutions and lay confraternities (see Pullan 1971, pp. 139–40).

they were expelled from the Seminary of St Mark they were all received into his own church of the most holy Trinity. In the Patriarchal Seminary they also educate a great many young noblemen, from whom the Somaschians receive numerous benefits, which are important because the seminary is endowed with little revenue. It is governed by a congregation headed by the most reverend Patriarch himself. Of his own generosity he continually bestows many good things on those clerics and upon the Somaschian fathers.

There is another seminary, called the Seminary of St Mark, which is governed by the most reverend chief priest of that church, for it is under the patronage of the Doge himself. Since this church of St Mark's is the Ducal chapel as well as being a collegiate church in which the cure of souls is exercised, it is exempt from the jurisdiction of the reverend ordinary, and so are the churches attached to it, i.e. the parish churches of San Giovanni Elemosinario and of San Giacomo in Rialto, and the convents of Santi Filippo e Giacomo and of Santa Maria delle Vergini.   B. P.

5   AN ENGLISH PROTESTANT LOOKS AT VENETIAN RELIGIOUS LIFE, 1608
From a letter of William Bedell, chaplain to the English ambassador in Venice, to Adam Newton, Dean of Durham, 1 January 1608 (Shuckburgh 1902, pp. 228–9).

Next are the ordinary Priests and Curates of the severall churches of the Citty. In the choice of whom (not here onely, but as I've been told by those, that have reason to know, throughout Italy) it is aimed at that they be such, as they are sure to be either noe sticklers (for which they take a good order by choosing noe great Clerks) or else sound for the present state: whereunto they are allso obliged by dispensations for many benefices and church-dignities. And generally these, if they needs will be preaching (which is but supererogation) must be licens'd soe to doe, and are enjoyn'd for the rule and square of their doctrine the Catechism of the Council of Trent, which is by the Patriarchs commandment enjoyn'd to be taught allso in Schools, and by all means made familiar to the people, being set forth in the Italian tongue, with large indulgence to those that teach and learne it.

Thus is the office of preaching wholly in a manner devolved to the Fryars, and when they were here to the Jesuits. Of which last I can say nothing, since 'twas not my ill-fortune to meet them here at my coming. . . . As for the Fryars, which I have heard here, their whole intentions seem to be either to delight or to move: as for teaching, they know not what it means. But to hear their strange wresting of the holy Scripture, to see the fooleries of their Idolatry to the little crucifix that stands at their elbow, the anticks of their gesture more than player or fencer-like, their vehemency of which a man may well use that of the poet, *magno conatu magnas nugas.*[7] It is (I assure you, Sir) matter of great patience: and for my part I have found myself better satisfied (at least wise less cloy'd) with the sermons of the Jews, than with theirs. And in one thing the very Jews contemne them, and not undeservedly, as merchants of Gods word. For in the middest of their sermons still the preacher makes some pretty occasion or other to fall into the common place of moveing them to alms; and 3, or 4 with long canes, and a bag at the end skims over the whole auditory; and the people generally not undevout, being taken in a good mood, while the impression is yet new, are not unliberall. Out of this the preacher hath his share: the rest goes to the collectors, or Guardians of the fraternity, or other school that heard him.

And because I am fallen in to the mention of the people, that you may at once understand the present face of Religion here; If ever there were any Citty, to which the Epithets would agree, which St Luke gives to Athens, (which he calls *kateidolon*)[8] this is it. Such a multitude of idolatrous statues, pictures, reliques in every corner, not of their churches onely, but houses, chambers, shopps, yea the very streets, and in the country the high wayes and hedges swarme with them. The sea it self is not free; they are in the shipps, boats, and water-marks. And as for their slavery and subjection to them, it is such, as that of paganisme came not to the half of it. Whereof to give you such a taste as may be allso for some cause of it; noe sooner doe their Children almost creep out of their Cradles, but they are taught to be Idolators. They have certain childish processions, wherein are carried about certain puppets, made for their Lady, and some boy that is better Clerke than his fellows goes before them with the words of the Popish Litany; where the rest of the fry following make up the quire. A great tyrant is custome and a great advantage hath that discipline which is suck'd in with the mothers milke. But to convey superstition into the minds of that tender age under the forme of sport, and play, which it esteemeth more than meat and drinke, is a deeper point of policy, and such as wise men perhaps would profitably suck somewhat out of it for imitation to a right end.

But one thing certainly they goe beyond us in: and that is their liberality and cost in the solemn setting forth of their service and adorneing their churches; and especially at their feast-days. Wherein if they pass measure allso, as possibly they doe, yet is that extreme less exceptionable, and allways more curable, than our beggary, the scorne of our religion. Not only popular conceits, but the most part of men of whatsoever quality are led much more by shews than substance. And what a disproportion it is, to come from ours soe unhonestly kept (for in Buildings we generally goe beyond them) to the glittering churches and monasteries of Italy, you may easily discerne. Truly, Sir, I have heard some wise men account this as noe small cause of the perversion of soe many of our young Gentlemen that come into these parts. B. P.

---

[7] 'Saying very trivial things with much effort' – Terence, *Heauton Timorumenos (The Self-Avenger)*, 621.   [8] Acts 17:16.

RELIGIOUS HOUSES AND REFORM

*L*ONG BEFORE *the general reform of ecclesiastical discipline demanded in the mid sixteenth century by the decrees of Trent, and long before the coming of strict and dedicated new orders such as the Jesuits, Capuchins and Theatines, attempts were made to recall lax and opulent religious houses, both male and female, to strict observance of their founders' rules. Contrasts between the austerity of the reformed Dominicans and the classical splendours of an unreformed house find expression in the censures of the scandalized Felix Faber as he gazes on the wonders of Santi Giovanni e Paolo, the Doges' mausoleum, in the last quarter of the fifteenth century [V.6]. Far greater bitterness could be aroused among nuns. For much of the sixteenth century slack discipline in Venetian nunneries, permitting free and easy contacts with the male admirers sometimes known as* munegini, *was a cause of grave concern to moralists, and the roles of the more exclusive convents as religious and as social institutions were often in conflict. As early as 1420 a Senate decree had complained that, because of the high cost to persons of standing of providing dowries to enable their daughters to obtain husbands of suitable rank, fathers were improperly compelling many of their girls to enter convents instead (Bistort 1912, p. 107). Nunneries, therefore, acted as conservatories for large numbers of women with no strong sense of religious vocation, and there may have been a tacit agreement, among all parties to these transactions, that the rules of the order would not be rigorously enforced. At intervals, however, and particularly at times of trial when it seemed especially important for the state to win divine favour by virtuous conduct, there was a call to restore discipline in the more aristocratic convents, such as the Vergini (which was attached to St Mark's and under the Doge's patronage) and San Zaccaria. Reforms were bitterly resented, both by the nuns themselves and by their relatives. V.7–10 describe the perennial problem and some of the attempts made to deal with it in the earlier and later years of the sixteenth century. They begin with the brave and unpopular endeavours of the Patriarch Antonio Contarini in 1519–21 to reform certain convents by forcibly introducing communities of nuns vowed to strict observance of their rules. V.10 is a comprehensive discussion by a papal nuncio of the problems of the traditional* *male and female religious orders, such as Benedictines and conventual Franciscans, and it describes an interminable struggle on the part of would-be reformers.to separate monks, friars and nuns from the intrigues of their Venetian kinsfolk and patrons. Not all unmarried women of high status, however, were bound to enter convents. They could also become* pizzocare *(i.e. tertiaries or members of the Third Orders of St Francis and St Dominic), who took vows of chastity, followed a rule and did good works, but lived outside the cloister. The will of Francesco Tiepolo, dated 1611 [below, VI.5], shows that a nobleman of the early seventeenth century could at least conceive of the possibility of a daughter living as a spinster in the household of her brothers, although he thought it inadvisable for her to do so.*

BIBLIOGRAPHY *Paschini 1958; Zanette 1960; Giuliani 1961; Pullan 1965, pp. 135–43; Logan 1967.* B. P.

6 SPLENDOUR AND WORLDLINESS: SANTI GIOVANNI E PAOLO IN THE 1480S
From the Latin. Faber[9] ed. Hassler 1843–9, III, 425–6.

Here [at Santi Giovanni e Paolo] there are always over 100 friars and many doctors. But the rule is poorly observed there and the place has not yet been reformed, and the friars live in some worldly pomp and splendour, and on festival days they sing Mass and Vespers and Compline with figured music and worldly ceremonial. Hence a great crowd of young men and women flock to these services, not to hear the divine office, but rather to listen to the music and the singing. They have two organs, and the sacristy is extensively and elaborately decorated. Several Doges of Venice are buried in the church. I have never seen more opulent tombs or more ostentatious monuments; even those of the Popes in Rome cannot equal the tombs of the Doges of Venice. For these are raised above the ground and let into the walls, and the whole surface of the wall is bedecked with different marbles and carvings and gold and silver, and decorated to excess. The images of Christ, the Blessed Virgin, the apostles and martyrs and other saints whom everybody loves are placed in the middle of the tombs, as the most important figures; but around the edge are the images of

---

[9] Felix Faber (otherwise Fabri) was a pilgrim from Ulm who embarked from Venice on journeys to the Holy Land in 1480 and 1483, the first trip proving abortive and the second successful. A member of the order of strict, reformed or 'observant' Dominicans, he was highly critical of the splendours of the unreformed convent of Santi Giovanni e Paolo, of its church, of its role in the Corpus Christi procession of 1483, and of its lavish hospitality to the Dominican Chapter General which he attended in 1487 (Faber ed. Hassler 1843–9, I, 105–6, and III, 434–5). By contrast, the small observant convent of San Domenico di Castello earned his respect and admiration.

pagans, of Saturn, Janus, Jupiter, Juno, Minerva, Mars and Hercules, with emblems of their fables. I saw there in our church, on the rich tomb of a certain Doge to the right of the entrance,[10] a carving of Hercules which showed him clad in the skin of the lion which he killed, and not in a cloak, and closing in combat with the Hydra, a terrible monster which had seven heads, and when one of these was cut off another seven grew at once in its place. There are naked gladiators with swords and spears in their hands and shields about their necks, but without cuirass or breastplate or helmet, and these really are idols. There are naked boys with wings on, holding the emblems of victory, or else wrestling together, and many such symbols of paganism are inserted among those of our redemption. Simple people think these are images of saints, and they honour Hercules, thinking him Samson, and Venus, mistaking her for the Magdalen, and so forth. [The Venetians] also carve upon tombs sea monsters, and the arms of the deceased, and verses recounting his achievements.

B. P.

7   LAXITY AND STRICT OBSERVANCE: THE REFORM OF NUNNERIES, 1519–21
DMS, xxviii, cols 321, 402, 407, 409; xxxi, cols 276–7.

23 May 1519

Certain relatives of nuns of [Santa Maria delle] Vergini came into the Collegio to plead that these nuns did not want others to be placed there; it was enough that they be strictly enclosed and brought over to the observance. The Doge [Leonardo Loredan] dismissed them, saying that he did not want to hear them, and that the decrees of the Council of Ten should be obeyed. . . .

Note that the nunnery of Sant'Anna has been divided, and after seven nuns had come from San Giovanni Laterano and had been given possession of half of it, this morning the remaining nuns, [. . .] in number, all arrived, so that all will be living in Sant'Anna. The abbess of Sant'Anna, of the noble house of [. . .], together with four other nuns, wanted to join those of San Giovanni Laterano and become observants. They were accepted by the nuns of San Giovanni Laterano, who said they would have her as abbess. . . .

20 June 1519

This morning the Avogadori di Comun, by order of the Collegio and the Heads of the Ten, in obedience to the wishes of the Patriarch, to whom the Doge had granted all his own authority over the nunnery of the Vergini that it might be

---

[10] The tomb of Doge Pietro Mocenigo (1474–6), by Pietro Lombardo.

2 Pietro Lombardo, The Tomb of Doge Pietro Mocenigo (1474–6; monument
completed in 1481) in Santi Giovanni e Paolo, Venice.
(Photograph copyright the Conway Library, Courtauld Institute of Art)

reformed, went with constables, officials and masons to that nunnery, which is the second to be enclosed. There they made a forcible entry, breaking down doors, and by walling up doorways and so on they partitioned off a section of it, i.e. the new part of the building which looks towards the Patriarch's palace. This part they intend to give to the observant nuns of Santa Giustina, who will move into it. The nuns of the Vergini protested that they had been the victims of violence and had been cast out from their own hearths and so on, but they have to resign themselves to it. The Doge and Signoria charged Sier Alvise Barbaro, son of Sier Zaccaria, Cavalier and Procurator and Provveditor al Sal, with walling and dividing off the part of the nunnery in which the observant nuns were to be installed. . . .

25 June 1519

This morning . . . since the Doge and Signoria had heard that yesterday the nuns of the Vergini had knocked down the wall built to partition them off and permit the introduction of nuns from Santa Giustina into part of the convent, the Signoria and the Heads of the Ten sent all three Avogadori, clad in their silken robes, to that convent. Seeing what the nuns had done, they delivered a stern reprimand and sent for the Patriarch, who was at San Biagio Catoldo, intending to inspect the convent, reform it and then leave. He came and joined the Avogadori in the chapter house. There they summoned the nuns, upbraiding them for their actions. The nuns asked for pardon, saying that it was hard to be cast out from their home, and although the Patriarch was threatening to punish them he was not their superior. They left without further ado, and the builders continued the work of dividing the convent. . . .

28 June 1519

This morning the Patriarch came into the Collegio and had audience there with the Heads of the Ten, the Avogadori and the Collegio, all other persons being sent outside. He complained that the nuns of the Vergini had, yesterday and throughout the night, rung bells to celebrate the arrival of a brief from the Pope addressed to his legate, to the effect that the nuns were to be reformed but that no others were to be introduced into their convent. There was much discussion as to what was to be done about the matter. They noted that there was an earlier papal brief which gave faculties to the Patriarch to reform the said conventual nunneries and bring them to observance, taking what measures he chose, and it seemed to the Doge and Patriarch and to all the Collegio and the Heads of the Ten that they should not obey this second brief. . . .

21 August 1521

Four conventual abbesses came [to the Collegio], i.e. the abbess of the Vergini, of the noble house of Donado, the abbess of San Zaccaria, of the noble house of Michiel, the abbess of the Celestia, of the noble house of [. . .], and the abbess of Santa Marta, of the noble house of [. . .], with many kinsfolk. The reverend Patriarch was also present. . . . These ladies fell to their knees before the Doge [Antonio Grimani] and the abbess of the Vergini talked Latin and made quite a speech. Then Sier Nicolò Michiel, son of Sier Francesco, who had sisters and daughters in San Zaccaria and had sat down among the Savii agli Ordini, spoke eloquently of the cruelty shown to noble persons. Our own gentlewomen had been ruined and dispersed, and all on account of a certain Vicar General to the Patriarch, a Romagnol who had been banished from Rome with a price on his head; he had made great difficulties for these nuns, that he might rob them or have his wicked way with anyone he pleased. [Sier Nicolò] added that at San Zaccaria, where all used to be noble, there were now installed nuns of another order, following a different rule and wearing a different habit – base-born women, Greeks and plebeians to boot. What had stood for 760 years had now been taken from them, when they had spent 46,000 ducats on the church, the convent and the magnificent refectory. Santa Marta had been assigned a mere 11 stara of wheat and would have no wine because of the storms. He made further points so that the whole Collegio was aroused; and he concluded that, while all the nuns wished to obey the Pope's command, the execution had gone awry, and he begged the Doge that the matter should be referred to the legate or some other prelate. The Heads of the Ten were there, and the Collegio felt very strongly, and three Savi del Consiglio vigorously supported [Sier Nicolò], i.e. the Procurator Antonio Trun, Sier Francesco Foscari and the Cavalier Polo Tiepolo. So did Sier Zorzi Pisani, who said that he was procurator of Santa Croce on the Giudecca: he did not want anyone to invade these convents, and all should stay as they were, in their own places. All the kinsfolk of nuns let loose at the Vicar General, Don Octaviano of Pesaro, who was there in person, and they heaped insults upon him.

Then the Patriarch spoke, saying first that, if his Vicar had misconducted himself, he should be examined and punished, and he begged the Doge and Collegio to see to it. He went on to say that, to avoid offending God by the vices practised in nunneries dedicated to God, even during Lent, or so he had heard, he had appeared in the Collegio before the late Doge, who took appropriate action in the Council of Ten with the Zonta. [The Patriarch] then caused to be read a decree of the same Council of Ten, of 4 March 1519, to the effect that nuns of San Giovanni Laterano were to be put into Sant'Anna, and so on, and that the conventual nunneries were to be reformed. The business was to be entrusted to the Patriarch and requests were to be made to Rome for papal briefs and bulls; he himself had acted accordingly and had done nothing without the permission of the Collegio with the Heads of the Ten. So no blame attached to him.

He regretted that the nuns, who are forbidden to leave their convents on pain of excommunication, should have come here to the Collegio. Of the Vergini he said that the silver would have been sent away if he had not prevented it, and he had given 25 ducats to the accuser by orders of the Council of Ten, and had made the money over with his own hand. Then he said that the women of San Zaccaria were not the nuns they once were: on a visitation he had been shown a paper to the effect that a century before they had been observants. It was then their custom, one feast day, i.e. [. . .], to go veiled in a barge to San Raffaele, and somebody then set fire to the convent. When they returned they saw the flames, tried to enter the church, and were burnt. For the last century the nuns have been conventuals, and their misdeeds are notorious, and complaints laid against their admirers and followers [*munegini*] have been proved before the Avogadori and proceedings taken against two reprobates. But no action was taken against the others, who were leading figures, and these abuses have brought divine displeasure upon us. As for Santa Chiara, the most reverend Cardinal Grimani, son of the Doge and protector of the order, had granted him authority over it, and things had been done quite correctly and in execution of the papal bulls and briefs.

The Savi strongly criticized the Patriarch, speaking ill of his Vicar. Then Sier Michiel Trevisan, formerly Avogador, spoke, saying that his sister was abbess of San Zaccaria, and he spoke strongly against the Vicar General, asking for the bulls to be examined, so that one could see whether right had been done and the papal bull executed. After that Sier Piero Tron, a Head of the Ten, rose to say that they were plainly in agreement, for the conventuals wished to be reformed and the reverend Cardinal had undertaken to do this, though how it would be done remained to be seen. The bulls and briefs should be taken in hand and the Council of Ten with the Zonta be called one day to discuss the matter, since it was there that the business started. He was applauded by all, but when the Vicar tried to speak he was put down by the members of the Collegio.

O. L., S. C. W.

8   FOUNDATION OF A MAGISTRACY RESPONSIBLE FOR CONVENTS, 1521
Decree of the Council of Ten and Zonta, 17 September 1521: ACPV Archivio Segreto, 32, Monasteri visite, 1452–1730.

BE IT DETERMINED that by the authority of this Council three most honourable gentlemen, from among the most eminent in the city, shall be chosen by scrutiny of this Council that, with the reverend Patriarch, they may hear and take note of the grievances and complaints of the conventual nuns concerning their livelihood [*viver*]. Where proper resources have not been allocated to the nuns for their livelihood, [these gentlemen] shall be free by majority vote to make provision that shall enable the said conventual nuns to stay in the convents and live there in a manner befitting their status and quality. They shall do the same for the observants. They shall give each of the parties, whether conventual or observant, that portion which seems suitable and honourable. All matters concerning the nuns' livelihood shall be determined and resolved by a majority [of these gentlemen], and their decisions shall be as firmly established as if they were acts of this Council.

No person, of any status or degree, may open his mouth to discuss these allocations once they have been made; nor may he attempt in any way to work against such allocations and decisions, or to oppose anything else in the bulls and papal briefs issued upon this matter, on pain of the displeasure of this Council and of the other more severe punishments contained in its most stringent decrees. Neither fathers nor brothers nor blood relations nor paternal nor maternal uncles either of conventual or of observant nuns, nor persons that have leases or rents of these convents, nor persons that act as their procurators, may be elected to this office.

Those that are elected [to this office] are bound and obliged to examine with diligence the leases and rents made by the conventuals and observants of the convents after their reform, or even before, if they so choose. If they find that anything has been done to the detriment or prejudice of these convents, they shall have the freedom and authority to revoke or annul [these agreements] as they see fit for the benefit of the convents.

Furthermore they may not rent or lease any property of the convents on behalf of conventual or observant nuns to persons who are related to those nuns, not to mention their immediate family [*a persone che ad esse fossero coniuncte de parentella che se caza de capello, non intendendo pero la casada*].[11]

V. P.

9 ABUSES IN THE CONVENT OF SAN ZACCARIA, 1528, 1585

(a) The misconduct of nuns' servants, 1528
From a letter of the Patriarch Hieronimo Querini to the abbess of San Zaccaria, 12 March 1528: BCV ms. Cicogna 2583, f. 48v.

It has come to our ears that four servants of your convent are very bad characters, namely bawds. Two of them are now pregnant; one of these is away

---

[11] For the meaning of *casada/casata* in an official document of 1533, see below, V.15.

from the convent to give birth; and the others are still there. It is very disturbing that this matter was brought to our notice by outsiders. You, who ought to look to it, have not done your duty by warning us of this, for we wish to do everything we can to cleanse your convent of this disease. For the present we charge and command you, on pain of immediate suspension from your office of abbess if you disobey our orders, to hasten to conduct prudent inquiries and to discover the truth about the said servants: their names are Antonia, who is with Madonna Isabella Michiel; Caterina, with Madonna Orsa Onoradi; Nicolosa, with Madonna Christina Bollani; and Helena, with Madonna Marieta Diedo. On finding this to be true, as we believe it must be, you shall within three days expel and banish from the convent those three who are still in it, and you shall not allow the said Antonia to return. If you do otherwise we will not only suspend you from your present office, but will also proceed to heavier penalties against you.   V. P.

(b) An illicit liaison between a nobleman and a nun, 1585

Alvise Michiel, *Memorie pubbliche della Repubblica di Venezia*: BMV ms. Ital., cl. VII, 811 (7299), f. 350, 17 February 1584 Venetian style.

There was published in the Great Council a sentence pronounced by the Provveditori sopra i Monasteri upon Ser Zuanne Dolfin, who had broken the laws concerning nuns by visiting at forbidden times and on several occasions a nun in one of the convents of this city, although he was not within the degrees of relationship permitted by the law.[12]

He was to be banned from the Council for six months, and to pay a fine of 300 ducats, to be distributed in accordance with the decree of the Council of Ten; and the period of his ban was to begin only when he had paid the fine of 300 ducats.

The Great Council thought the sentence a very light one, since it was notorious that this gentleman had had dealings with this nun for the last twelve years and had been reproved on many occasions. She was in the convent of San Zaccaria and belonged to the noble house of Da Mula, being the daughter of Ser Nicolò; she was not a handsome woman, and her age was some thirty-six to forty years. This sentence, light thought it was, pleased everybody, given the stake that the city had in the nunneries, for people spoke very ill of their honour, and everyone wanted to see them reformed.   B. P.

---

[12] On 29 January of the same year the Great Council had published a decree of the Council of Ten to the effect that nuns were to receive visits only from their fathers, brothers, and paternal or maternal uncles; even cousins and other kinsmen were now to be excluded, although the previous regulations had admitted them (Michiel, *Memorie*, f. 345v).

10   MONKS, FRIARS AND NUNS, *c.*1580
From the report of Alberto Bolognetti, papal nuncio in Venice 1578–81 (Aldo Stella 1964, pp. 116–18, 191–2).

The practice of harassing certain clerics is highly detrimental to the liberty of the Church. Perhaps equally pernicious, however, are certain kinds of favour conferred upon other clergy by persons who have no business to meddle with their affairs. I refer to the protection extended by the most eminent noblemen, not just to religious houses in general, but to individuals within the cloisters, both monks and nuns. These people then begin to disobey their superiors and scorn to observe their rules, so that scandal, discord and confusion continually arise.

To take the men first: it is impossible to satisfy everybody at the chapters or diets or distributions of office made by their generals, because the number of candidates exceeds the number of offices and dignities distributed by each order, and a single dissatisfied person can throw all the monasteries of a province into confusion by having prompt recourse to his supporters. They would think their honour cheapened and their reputation lost if the monk they favour failed to get what he wanted. If they cannot help him by other methods, they apply to the Collegio through friends and relatives and make a public issue of it, complaining that religious who are subjects of the Venetian state are suffering from the envy of foreigners, and that the Venetian government is not accorded as much respect as other princes. Hence, unless the nuncio were always on his guard, the measures taken by general chapters and by their distinguished protectors for the regulation of religious orders would frequently be impeded by this means.

The same thing happens with nuns. Most of them are noblewomen, and they enjoy such favour and support that they make bold to oppose the wishes of their prelates. The rulers of Venice are moved to favour them, not only by ties of kinship, but perhaps also by the assistance they receive from them in pursuing the honours of the Republic. For these women, by calling upon their fathers, brothers and other close relatives, and by begging them to favour one man or another, can well help or harm them in their political dealings. So it would be very difficult to prevent the transactions made with nuns in Venice. I would like to think this business legitimate and respectable, but it surely gives rise to a freedom and licence which may have most undesirable consequences.

Furthermore, the favours of these noblemen have been extended to far less deserving persons, in the shape of renegade monks and friars [*sfratati*], and others who were living apart from their orders without permission although they kept the habit, and who, shameless as they now were, did not mind being excommunicates and irregulars. The whole state was full of these people, especially the city of Venice itself: it was deeply shocking to see a great crowd of them walking every morning and evening upon the Piazza di San Marco. When, by order of His Holiness, I tried to take measures against this abuse, it turned out that they enjoyed innumerable, far-reaching favours from various noblemen and senators whom they served, as tutors or in other capacities, before I published an edict against them. It is likely that, to win themselves a sure asylum and immunity in Venice (these are appropriate terms), they wrote with much more care and gave greater satisfaction than did other kinds of person who might have found places elsewhere. They had advanced so far as to gain control, as it were, of the city's spiritual life, for almost all the mass-benefices [*mansionerie*] were in their hands, and children were learning their letters and manners from them, together with the first elements of divine worship, thus receiving to their detriment at a tender age a secret dose of that deeply polluted milk. Worst of all, although they were excommunicate and disobedient to their rules, they still administered the most holy sacrament. Some of them celebrated in the morning, and then later in the day went off to draw magic circles and conjure up spirits to find treasure; in my time very lengthy proceedings were taken against them.[13] It is true that after many entreaties, and even conflicts, we have by the grace of God overcome all the difficulties raised by the government, which at last investigated the need for this reform, agreed to it, and granted assistance against them in just the way that was required.

However, the execution of this reform is still being hindered by the officers and prelates of religious orders, who on various pretexts refuse to take them in. Some of them plead poverty, others the great number of monks they have to support already; and yet others object that those whom they are asked to admit are not sons of their monasteries. Others invoke the strict and blameless life appropriate to religious, saying that these people would be a great nuisance to them, for they are besmirched by many vices and accustomed to live in freedom. Finally, others point out another danger – how grave it is I know not – by saying that these people, if readmitted to their orders, would soon take over the highest positions and become like tyrants in their monasteries, for they are bolder and more assertive and enjoy more favours than do others who have always lived a pure life in their cloisters. These arguments, however, are outweighed by the thought of the scandal which would spread from day to day if they were left in their accustomed freedom. And, incidentally, it would also be good to deal in some way with those who have been expelled from their orders

---

[13] Bolognetti is almost certainly referring to Antonio Saldagna or Saldanha, a renegade Franciscan observant from Lisbon, described by one of his employers in Venice as 'a splendid writer and a most elegant humanist'. Saldagna was tried and sentenced to life imprisonment in 1579 by the Inquisition for his involvement in magical practices, and himself denounced a number of persons for secret Judaism. See Ioly Zorattini 1980–, IV (1571–80), 133–362, and V (1579–86), *passim*. See also Pullan 1983; R. Martin 1989; and below, V.22.

for misconduct. For they cause just as much scandal, and it seems hard that they should profit by their faults and live in peace and escape punishment while others are being reformed. . . .

I think we can truly say that the surest way of reforming the nunneries would be the one I have mentioned twice above, when I spoke of priests taking orders and friars taking the habit: the closest attention should be paid to the inclinations of the girls who are received into convents. Someone should first ascertain whether they are inspired to immure themselves for ever out of pure devotion and the desire to be better placed to serve God, or whether they are being forced to become nuns by the fear of their fathers, who have used threats to make them consent to do so with their tongues, but not with their hearts. For their fathers cannot marry them to their equals because they are not rich enough to do so, and will not marry them to lesser men for fear of tarnishing the prestige of their families. From this root spring all the disorders in convents. For a time the malaise and suffering which the poor girls undergo on being thus imprisoned are tempered by their enjoyment of a new experience; but in the end they are made worse by the passage of time, by the burdensome duty of obedience, and, very often, by the many discomforts they suffer, which can well drive them to despair. It is hard for them to find consolation, for on the one hand their sufferings can end only with death, and on the other they are condemned for ever to this wretched existence (as they think it), through no fault of their own, and not by the malice of enemies, but rather by an impious and wicked sentence pronounced by their own fathers. For, in order to make a larger portion for other daughters, who may well be inferior in spirit although more handsome in body, their fathers have chosen to deprive them, not only of that share in their property which is due to them by the law of nature and by reason of kinship, but also of any kind of comfortable and elegant life, and even of liberty itself. So they can truly say, 'Our darkness makes another's dawn.' It would be most advisable, as I have said, to find a remedy for these abuses, for in them lie the origins of almost all the scandals and disorders that occur in nunneries. But it is not within the nuncio's power to do it, or to take any other of the necessary measures. This is a most delicate matter, because the Doge has appointed three senators to take charge of the business of nuns, and they oppose all measures which could conceivably be held to conflict with the government's wishes.   B. P.

FRATERNITIES OF THE LAITY:
THE SCUOLE GRANDI AND PICCOLE

*R**ELIGIOUS FRATERNITIES*, generally called Scuole, shaped the devotional lives and moral conduct of many ordinary Venetians. These organizations needed clerics to serve as chaplains and celebrate Mass on their behalf, but they were officered by laymen, and their supervision was the responsibility of magistrates and government councils rather than of the Patriarch. By the early sixteenth century the rules of these associations were highly standardized. Extracts from the statutes of one small brotherhood are given in V.11; the claim that it was the first Scuola in Venice dedicated to the Rosary is open to dispute (Meersseman 1977, III, 1206–14; Niero 1974). The task of such associations was to pursue salvation collectively by doing good and avoiding evil; the charitable activities of the Scuole, a major part of their good works, are described elsewhere [below, VII.1, 8 and 9]. Election to the governing-body of one of the greater brotherhoods or Scuole Grandi conferred prestige on non-noble citizens of Venice, and the more opulent Scuole were inclined to spend lavishly on building, decoration and pageantry: so much so that puritans began to suspect that their officers were building memorials for themselves rather than glorifying God or honouring their patron saints. Alessandro Caravia, the goldsmith poet, attacked all the Scuole Grandi and compared them unfavourably with the parish fraternities of the Holy Sacrament [above, V.4]. His criticisms of the Scuola Grande di San Rocco and the Scuola Grande della Misericordia are given as V.12. When the Scuole Grandi amassed great wealth, a division arose between brothers of the bench and brothers of the discipline: between those who administered the charities of the Scuola, and those who joined in the hope of receiving charity and were therefore obliged to turn out for funerals and perform other onerous ceremonial tasks as a condition of retaining their benefits. V.13, recording an internal inquiry conducted in 1555, describes the rebellion of one brother of the Scuola Grande di San Rocco, resentful and weary at being distracted from earning his living.

BIBLIOGRAPHY *Barbiero 1941, pp. 135–41, 187–214; Niero 1961b, 1974; Sbriziolo 1970; Pullan 1971, pp. 33–193, and 1990; Mueller 1972; Howard 1975, pp. 98–112;*

Wurthmann 1975; Meersseman 1977, III, 1170–232; Pignatti 1981; Mackenney 1986, 1987; P. F. Brown, 1987, 1988; Black 1989. B. P.

11 THE RULE OF A LAY FRATERNITY, 1535

From the Mariegola or mother rule of the Scuola di San Chiereghino e del Rosario, established in the church of San Simeone Profeta on 12 September 1535 (Niero 1961b, pp. 329–36).

[I] *Prologue* Clearly and manifestly do we see how brief, how fleeting and how transitory is the present life amidst the frailty of humankind, for wretched beings in this world are for ever spurred and driven by their greed and care for temporal goods, which will themselves only pass away, and they are oppressed and engulfed in sin, and so each man lives all his days in sin. If we claim to be sinless we deceive ourselves. St John says, 'If we say that we have no sin, we deceive ourselves'.[14] Hence while man lives in this world he must think of his end and reflect that each one will receive the reward of the good and evil things he has done in this present life. And because Our Lord Jesus Christ teaches and admonishes us, saying in the Holy Gospel, 'Watch therefore, for ye know neither the day nor the hour wherein ye shall pass from this life',[15] we, being inspired by his divine grace and mercy, have thought and conceived of gaining the salvation of our souls through the love of brotherhood and the aid of prayer, and have thought fit to appoint to be our advocate in Heaven the glorious Mother of God, Our Lady Mary, the refuge of us miserable sinners. The apostle says that we must pray and call upon God continually and unceasingly,[16] if we would be saved, for prayer without ceasing does much to help the salvation of our souls. So do all of us, whose names are and shall come to be inscribed below, with a joyful heart and mind, and a determined will, and a united spirit, for the honour of almighty God, and his glorious and unblemished mother Mary, and of St Mark the Evangelist, and of all the saints of God, whom we devotedly serve. And we have now established this blessed Scuola and fraternity of our reverend and holy Lady Mary and of the glorious martyr San Chiereghino,[17] that through his support and aid we may be saved by that Scuola, and that, by drawing on the merits of all the saints of God, both male and female, we may attain the glory of eternal life. Amen.

[14] 1 John 1:8.
[15] Cf. Matthew 25:13.
[16] 1 Thessalonians 5:17.
[17] Otherwise St Cyricus, Quiricus or Cyr, a three-year-old child martyred with his mother Julitta at Tarsus in the reign of the Emperor Diocletian, about 304; a patron saint of children (Farmer 1978, p. 99).

II   First, it is our wish and command that for the honour and veneration of Our Lady, an oil lamp shall always be burning by day and by night before the altar of Mary, our holy lady of grace, and that it shall be kept alight by drawing on the funds of this our blessed Scuola and fraternity.

III   Further, it has been ordained and decreed that everyone enrolled as a brother in this our Scuola of the Rosary must have a little board [*tolela*] inscribed with his name and his mark beneath to identify it. . . .

IV   It is likewise our wish and command that every [first?] Sunday of every month throughout the year shall be regarded as our appointed day for transacting the business of the Scuola, as shall all the festivals of Our Lady Mary. On all the appointed days of Our Lady Mary every brother of the Scuola shall be obliged to come and hear the Mass which shall be said on behalf of the Scuola. Each brother must have and hold in his hand one of the Scuola's candles, which shall be alight, both at the procession which must be held on the appointed days, and at the Mass for the Scuola. Throughout the said Mass there shall be set forth six lighted tapers, with two large wax candles beside them; and when the Mass is finished they shall be extinguished. . . .

V   Furthermore, it is our wish and command, for the support of our poor but pleasant Scuola, and lest anyone be burdened and discouraged from good works, that each brother shall be obliged, when he picks up his board on all the appointed days, to pay 3 tiny coins [*pizoli*] to the officers for the aid and assistance of the poor of our Scuola, and also, as we say, to keep it supplied with wax and to meet other needs. . . . Likewise each brother of the Scuola must pay the same sum of 3 tiny coins [*pizoli*] for each brother who passes from this life to the next. . . .

VI   . . . We decree and ordain that from all the brothers one shall be elected to serve as our bailiff [*gastaldo*] and two others to be deans [*degani*], and they shall be men of good life and reputation and experience, and they shall be sure to transact the business and manage the affairs of our Scuola and fraternity with all possible zeal and devotion to duty. Every year these officers must give a full account of their administration and hand over the property of the Scuola, in accordance with the inventory, to the new bailiff and his colleagues who shall come to replace them, so that all is done in good order, for the preservation and increase of this blessed Scuola and fraternity.

VII   Furthermore, it has been decreed and resolved, to ensure that each of us brothers takes his share in the honours, responsibilities and labours of this our Scuola and fraternity and in its government and upkeep, that every year after the festival,[18] on the first Sunday in the month, a chapter general of our Scuola

---

[18]   The feast day of St Cyricus is 16 June; this clause seems to be referring to another festival or holiday in March, possibly to the New Year (1 March).

must be held. All brothers are obliged to attend this chapter on being notified by the bailiff or by the deans or by the verger [*nonciolo*] and others of the Scuola. In this chapter we must always elect the new bailiff and the two deans by majority vote. The old deans shall serve with the new bailiff for half a year until the next chapter, which shall be held on the first Sunday in September. Each brother shall be bound to attend this chapter as well as the other, as an act of charity and obedience. The new deans, elected at the preceding chapter, shall then take up office and the change shall be made; and this procedure shall be followed every year. . . .

VIII Furthermore, because it is a pious act and one of the seven works of spiritual mercy to visit the sick, especially if they are our own brothers, it has been decreed and ordained, and is our firm desire, that, if any of our brothers falls ill and is in such poverty that he needs aid and support, our bailiff and deans shall be bound to pay him frequent visits and to assist him in his needs by drawing on the funds of the Scuola. If, as could well happen, these funds are not sufficient to maintain the sick man in his needs, then, that the poor sufferer may be assisted and maintained, our bailiff and the deans shall be fully entitled to summon certain worthy men of our Scuola and commend the patient to them, that they may out of charity draw on their purses and give alms to their poor, sick brother; and [the bailiff and deans] shall also have him commended at our Mass, where the priest shall call upon all our other brothers if it seems the right and necessary thing to do, because the man's sickness and affliction are prolonged. And this shall be done as an act of pity and charity, that God may restore him to health and grant us his grace even unto eternal life. Amen.

IX Furthermore, because the burial of the dead is a work of mercy and charity, and is enjoined upon us by our holy Mother Church, it is our wish and command that, as an act of obedience and of pity, to say nothing of the duty of brotherly love to which we are all bound, when one of our brothers passes from this life to the next (and all of us will one day make this journey, one after the other), we should all go to him and wash his body and pityingly accompany it to burial, bearing the cross, the banner, and our great candles and tapers. And we will give him honourable burial within the city of Venice, taking all due and proper care. Should he be so poor that his estate will not pay for his funeral, we must not fail to show true charity towards our poor brother: for by our wish and command his burial shall be paid for from the funds of our Scuola, and he shall have as much honour as our other dearest brothers, that there may be no discrimination between us brothers of the Scuola. For this brother we shall say the Our Fathers which we are all accustomed to recite for the good of his soul, that the Lord God may pardon his sins and bring him to enjoy the blessings of eternal life.

X . . . it is our wish, and it shall be firmly ordained, that no one who publicly blasphemes against God and Our Lady may be enrolled and received into this blessed and devoted Scuola, called that of the Rosary. And the bailiff and deans shall be obliged to make thorough inquiries as to whether any brother is blaspheming against God and Our Lady, and if so the bailiff shall be obliged to admonish him once and even twice both gently and charitably; and, if by the third time he has not corrected this vice and failing, he shall then be deprived of and expelled from this our fraternity and Scuola as an enemy of God and Our Lady and a servant of Satan, deserving no pardon in the world.

XI   The same rule shall apply to those evil livers who publicly keep whores or concubines or take the wives and women of their neighbours, in defiance of God's commandment, thus living continually in mortal sin and in the disfavour of God and of the people of the world. If this is tolerated, quite apart from the shame that will descend upon the officers who accept them, they will be the cause of the downfall and confusion of this most devout and pious Scuola and fraternity. . . .

XII   Furthermore, that this our Scuola and brotherhood may maintain itself and increase in charity and brotherly love, and that no discontents or quarrels may arise within it, it is our wish and command that, if some dispute arises between one brother and another, for any reason whatsoever, our bailiff and his deans shall be obliged to make every effort to bring them to peace and harmony, for the honour and glory of God and Our Lady, and for the perpetual and peaceful preservation of this brotherhood, ever world without end. Amen.

B. P.

Caravia, Alessandro, 1541, ff. D v–Dii r.

An account of grave errors to you I shall render
Concerning some people who dress up in splendour;
And, though I may not list their names, they would tender
The saint of the plague[19] as their common defender.
They've had at the Scuola such mighty works done:
Festoons and harpies, fine beards by the ton,
Columns all carved with fresh leaves in a cluster
To show that as bosses their work passes muster.

[19] 'The saint of the plague': St Roch or San Rocco.

To tell you the truth, each new board's intention's
To show itself ever so full of inventions:
By moving the stairs and changing dimensions,
They make the doors useless; and so interventions
Breed more interventions, with quarrels incontinent:
'So-and-so's schemes are all highly incompetent,
And as for old what's-his-name' – huffing and puffing,
They claim to know all, when in fact they know nothing.

Then often they choose to devise celebrations,
All dishing out orders to gain reputations,
And free with advice and with denunciations,
As, all in the service of more complications,
First one interrupts, then the next, and the rest;
Though each keeps *his* money locked safe in its chest.
They never allow their spending to soar
When what is in question is funds for the poor.

Four-score thousand ducats they happily spend
Where no more than six would achieve the same end.
The rest they hang on to: it's pointless to send
Cash for the shoeless, the naked, befriend
All those groaning with hunger, for whom life is rough.
One word I would say to them, one – that's 'Enough!'
For, as charity goes, it's clear theirs is the cause
That fills up the coffers – but never withdraws.

As all of us know, we are only life's guests,
As witness your pieties, pardons, bequests,
But it's time to put paid, if you heed my requests,
To this feast of what we may call 'All Treasure Chests'.
There are many who stand in real need of a hand-out,
There's nothing for paupers that might keep the wind out.
In Venice their numbers seem close to infinity –
Starving and barefoot, and all needing charity.

What's due to the poor is splashed out in vast oceans
On building, but certainly not on devotions.
With sideshows in squares they make such commotions,
And every year brings a fresh influx of notions.
On trivial projects they've money to burn,
When their care and affection to Christ they should turn,
And for love of him use all their badly spent money
On clothes for the naked, on bread for the hungry.

Then, when they march off in their mighty processions
At St John, Corpus Christi, they make no professions
Of faith, as they should, with contrite intercessions,
But are drawn up like foes and vent their aggressions
To ensure that their banner is always the first;
And often the heads of the columns will burst
Into fighting, as torches are used in attacks
In which some poor soul's face gets a dose of hot wax.

'Have mercy, have pity!' I'm bound to shout out,
Considering what the Scuola's about,
And, now that you've heard me, you'd better take note
And quickly grab six down-and-outs by the throat.
You'll just have to throttle these paupers so miserable,
So that they breathe never a word, not a syllable.
I say to whoever built all of those rooms, they
Will not reach completion, not this side of Doomsday.

They've made such a vigorous start with their schemes
That the walls are already much bigger, it seems,
Than the towering walls of the Castle of Dreams;
And Sir Warden, in charge of the edifice, deems
That fame and repute will be his as of right
If he drives away paupers with all of his might
Without their receiving some 'misericordia',
Creating instead a great house of discordia.

Rather than 'Mercy' its title should be
'The Scuola Administered Mercilessly
Of the Sweet Virgin of the Green Valley.'[20]
These men have caused ruin, it's easy to see,
Merely to satisfy whims on condition
Of giving San Rocco some stiff competition;
It would have been better if money so dead
Had offered some comfort to paupers instead.

Pride, envy and things which to others belong
Create in this world a great measure of wrong.
To the regions of darkness will go before long
Those unhappy souls in a criminal throng
Who in vices like these have been sinking their energy;
They've no love of God and no feelings of charity,

[20] The Scuola Grande della Misericordia was dedicated to Santa Maria della Valverde (St Mary of the Green Valley).

For, if God and if charity had any hold,
They wouldn't set store by pride, envy and gold.

There by the canal is what little remains
Of all the money that's gone down the drain,
But it isn't permitted to audit – that's plain –
To reckon the losses and who stood to gain.
It would be impossible clearly to tally
Inflow and outflow with no shilly-shally.
Suffice it to say that the Scuola's shelled out –
A bit more or less let's not argue about.

It's not that they don't keep a proper account
Of debits and credits, amount by amount:
It's just that sometimes it is too dark to count,
And so there is always a bit to discount.
Good weather and money make nature grow fat;
Days and months fly – so do years, come to that.
In the end the great die and so do the small.
Each goes with his sack to the mill, one and all.

How many orphans and how many widows,
And how many others need help, d'you suppose?
There must be some poor little damsels you know
On whom they ought some of this wealth to bestow,
Thus keeping their honour and saving their skin.
But it seems that now everyone takes a pride in
Pursuing caprices and selfish ambition,
Not thinking he's sending the poor to perdition.

R. M.

---

13   A SMITH'S REBELLION AGAINST THE SCUOLA GRANDE DI SAN ROCCO, 1555
From the register of the decisions of the officers of the Scuola: Archivio della Scuola
Grande di San Rocco, Registro della Terminazioni 2, ff. 158v–159v.

29 December 1555

Ser Battista di Francesco Tordetti, our brother, took the stand, and on being
asked what he knew of Ser Francesco di Mattio, smith, he testified upon his
oath as follows.

'I came with our Scuola for the funeral of the most reverend Monsignor
Patriarch [Francesco Contarini], and when the Scuola had entered the church I

stayed outside on the square of San Pietro di Castello, and the said Francesco di Mattio, smith, approached me, saying things about the bosses of the Scuola, and I asked him what he meant by not coming to do his duty, which was to carry the canopy [*ombrella*] with me, and he answered, "What have I got to do with this Scuola?" I answered him, "Take care, the master of ceremonies [*Vardian da Mattin*] has marked you absent", whereupon he turned to face the church door and made a rude sign with both hands and said, "What silly buggers they are. I don't lick San Rocco's boots as they do, and I'd say that to their faces if they were here." Then he turned and saw Missier Zuan Antonio dei Garofoli and two other men (I don't know who they were, but they gave evidence against him this morning in the great hall). I said, "Francesco, be quiet, they're all our bosses, you've got to take your hat off and do what they say", but he bade me be hanged and quartered, and told me to shut my mouth, for I was just an idiot, and he said, "I'm shouting it loud, because I know there are these people from the Scuola in front, and I want them to hear me, and for 2 pence I'll resign from it. What good comes of those clothes they give you? They can stuff all their gowns and their houses!" I said, "If you don't want to be in the Scuola, say so in a friendly way, and don't get into a row", and he bellowed in reply that he'd do no such thing, no, not he, he wouldn't be nice about it. Again I begged him to be quiet, but again he began to insult me, and I left him there, and he went into the church, and he said much else which I don't remember, and this is what I have to say of the words spoken in Castello yesterday.

'As for St John's Day, the 27th [of December], the master of ceremonies had told all the brothers downstairs in the Scuola, before they went off to St John's, that by command of the government they must all assemble on the following day at the sixteenth hour for the funeral of the most reverend Monsignor Patriarch, on pain of losing the benefits of the almshouses, and the monthly alms, and the property of the Scuola. Then the said Francesco di Mattio, smith, told the master of ceremonies that he would not come, and would go and earn a crust instead, and the master of ceremonies told him that of all the brothers he was the only one to answer back, and he must do as he pleased, but they would do something about it. Francesco had a long argument with him, and then he came to pick up the canopy with me, and on the way he kept on insulting the master of ceremonies and saying that away from the Scuola he was nothing but a fucked-up old billy-goat, and he'd have liked to rip his beard off, and many other insults which I don't remember, although my other two comrades on the canopy, Meneghin, girdle-maker, and Agustin de Hyeronimo, were shocked to hear what he said.'

The witness said he could remember no more, and when his deposition had been read over to him he confirmed it all, upon his oath, just as it stands.

[On 25 January 1556 Francesco di Mattio, smith, was expelled from the Scuola Grande di San Rocco.]   B. P.

CONFLICT AND COMPROMISE WITH THE HOLY SEE

*A*T ALL TIMES *Venice claimed to be a devoutly Catholic republic, but the proximity of its dominions to those of the Papacy helped to bring it, at long intervals, into collision with the Holy See. Venetian territorial ambitions in the regions of Ferrara and the Romagna, and the papal determination to consolidate and centralize the States of the Church and to develop the port of Ancona, made Venice and the Papacy uneasy and sometimes quarrelsome neighbours. Equally offensive to some of the Popes was the determination of the Venetian government to control or at least strongly influence the distribution of ecclesiastical patronage [V.15] and to prevent the limitless expansion of ecclesiastical property through gifts and bequests of land [V.17]. Two papal attempts to bring the Venetians to heel by the use of interdict and excommunication, in 1482 and 1606, are recorded here in V.14 and 17. Some of the devices used in 1482 for resisting papal censures were applied in the face of later interdicts, including that imposed by Julius II during the War of the League of Cambrai in 1509–10. V.18 illustrates the persistent government hostility, in the early seventeenth century, towards the Society of Jesus, making it clear, at the same time, that the Jesuits had rich and influential supporters within Venice. As the most determined upholders of papal authority, the Jesuits had observed Paul V's interdict in 1606, in defiance of the state's orders that church services should continue as usual. Their withdrawal from the Venetian state was soon transformed into a collective expulsion and followed by charges of fomenting rebellion; individual Jesuits, as V.18 shows, were known to return from time to time. The order returned to Venice only in 1657.*

Prolonged hostility and mutual suspicion between the Venetian Republic and the Holy See followed the interdict of 1606–7 and the ban on the Society of Jesus, and contributed heavily to Venice's reputation as an anti-clerical state. Many other disputes, however, were settled by compromise, each party realizing how much it needed the other's support and co-operation. V.15 and 16 provide examples. A permanent feature of the distribution of wealth and power within the Venetian nobility, as V.15 implies, was the emergence of a small group of families who were disproportionately successful in engrossing valuable ecclesiastical patronage, and were suspected by their enemies of achieving this by virtue of special favours enjoyed at the papal court. Anti-clericalism was not a sentiment shared by the whole of Venice's ruling order.

BIBLIOGRAPHY In general: Cecchetti 1874. On the interdict of 1482: Dalla Santa 1899; Pastor 1891–, IV, 372–88; Cozzi and Knapton 1986, pp. 65–70, 238–9. On that of 1606–7: Ranke 1908, II, 114–45; Pastor 1891–, XXV, 111–216; Brodrick 1928, II, 113–43; Bouwsma 1969, pp. 232–628; Benzoni 1970; Wright 1974; Pullapilly 1975, pp. 118–32; Wootton 1983, pp. 45–76. Printed sources include Sarpi 1626; Cornet 1859; Cappelletti 1873; Smith 1907; Pirri 1959. On bishoprics, their distribution, and pro- and anti-papal families and factions: Gallo 1944, pp. 83–6; Cozzi 1958; Pullan 1965, pp. 125–34, and 1973, pp. 397–400; Logan 1967, p. 178ff, and 1978; Cairns 1976. On the visitation of 1581: Tramontin 1967.

B. P.

14   THE INTERDICT OF POPE SIXTUS IV, 1482
Malipiero, Domenico, ed. Longo, ed. Sagredo 1843–4, pp. 281–3.

On 23 June [1482] Pope Sixtus decreed in consistory that the divine offices should be suspended, in Venice itself and throughout the Venetian state, unless the siege of Ferrara was abandoned within fifteen days.

Francesco Diedo [ambassador to the Pope], when he departed from Rome to return to Venice, left an agent behind him. The Pope asked this man if he had written to the Venetian government about the Interdict; the agent answered that he had not, because it was not his business. After a few days the Interdict was posted on the doors of St Peter's, and it included the following words.

> Since, for fear of the Venetian authorities, there is no one who dares to report our interdict at Venice or to post it there in public places, we decree by virtue of our apostolic authority that an interdict attached to the doors of the church of St Peter shall have the same effect as if it had been attached to the palace of the Doge of Venice.

Within a few days the Pope sent a mace-bearer with a letter to Don Maffio Ghirardo, Patriarch of Venice, ordering him to convey the Interdict to the Doge and Signoria, 'upon pain of excommunication, malediction, suspension, and interdict'. The Patriarch feigned illness, and informed the Doge and the Heads of the Ten. He was told to keep everything secret, and in no way to act upon the orders.

The words of the Interdict were as follows.

> If within fifteen days the lords of Venice fail to raise the siege of Ferrara, they themselves and their subjects, supporters, advisers and adherents, together with

other specified cities, lands and places subject to their rule, not to mention all persons both lay and clerical dwelling therein, shall, if they fail to obey the prescribed admonitions, orders and commandments, be accursed and excommunicate in their persons, while their possessions shall be laid open to plunder by all nations.

The Interdict was considered, and with the Senate's concurrence it was resolved to evade it by any reasonable method.

Before the Senate disbanded, Missier Geronimo Lando, Patriarch of Constantinople, approached the Signoria. On being admitted to the Collegio, he suggested that an appeal be made, observing the proper forms, to a future Council. On his proposal they determined to appoint five presidents, all prelates of good reputation and well known to the court of Rome. These were: Missier Antonio Saraco, Archbishop of Corinth; Missier Nicolò Franco, Bishop of Parenzo; Missier Piero da Monte, Bishop of Croja; Missier Leon Garaton, Bishop of Sitia; and Missier Francesco Contarini, Bishop of Negroponte. They also appointed certain noblemen to represent the Dominion: Missier Bernardo Zustignan; the Cavalier Sebastian Badoer; Missier Domenego Moresini, and Missier Francesco Venier. These men were to submit the appeal to the presidents. The legal advisers on the appeal were Missier Girolamo Perleon of Rimini, Missier Daniele Zucuol and Missier Cristofolo Reghini, all of them doctors in civil and in canon law. Five other doctors also wrote opinions on this matter, independently of one another. The notaries were Aloise Zanberti, Andrea di Pase and Francesco Morando, notaries to the Avogadori di Comun; Filippo Morando, notary to the Patriarch; and Aurelio Bacineti. In the appeal they adduced and expounded all the arguments of the Venetian government against the Interdict. The appeal was allowed by the presidents, as having been correctly presented. This business was all transacted in the chamber of the Criminal Court of the Forty, in the presence of all the persons named above, and of the entire Collegio, and of Zuane Dedo the Grand Chancellor, and of Alvise Manenti, Secretary to the Council of Ten. Three copies of the appeal were drawn up for publication and then presented to the Doge and Signoria. They sent it to Rome by the hand of Traversin of Bergamo, a most loyal courier, with orders to post a copy on the door of the church of San Gelso. The courier departed, and carried out his instructions to the letter. On 9 July he returned.

On the morning of 3 July the Pope was told of the Venetian government's appeal, which had been posted the previous night, and heard that the whole city of Rome was in uproar. However hard they tried, they failed, until much later, to discover how it had happened. As recompense for his trouble the courier was given a place at the warehouse, where he was appointed measurer of flour.

B. P.

(i) From a letter of the papal nuncio Gerolamo Aleandro to Jacopo Salviati, 29 July 1533 (*NV*, I, 88).

The vacancy of the bishopric of Concordia has been a seed-bed of contention here since, as the most reverend Grimani and the most reverend Cornaro have been competing before the Signoria for the grant of temporalities, they have upset the granting of temporalities for Treviso and Corfu, which should by all accounts have been dealt with on one of these days. Now feelings are running so high that they cannot easily be calmed down, not on account of His Holiness but on that of the reverend cardinals, who are said to have appropriated between the three of them all the churches in the Venetian dominions.[21] So, when the honourable Messer Vittore Grimani, the Cardinal's brother, entered the Collegio, the Doge [Andrea Gritti]·told him to his face that he would abdicate rather than allow them the grant of temporalities. For the reverend gentleman [Cardinal Marino Grimani], if he obtained this, would be lord of the whole of the state from the north and east of it to the west which borders on Germany, and down to the threshold of Venice itself, all in one piece: for he would have, in addition to Concordia, the patriarchate of Aquileia and the bishopric of Ceneda, not to mention certain abbacies which have temporal as well as spiritual lordship. [The Venetians] say they will write to His Holiness entreating him with all due reverence to nominate anyone he chooses, provided he does not, by giving everything to a few, inflict great harm upon the commonwealth and stir up contention within it. They will complain, too, that not only do these three families hold almost all the churches of their dominions, but, worse still, there is no hope of anyone other than these people's kinsmen having so much as a small benefice. . . . I think it would be all to the good if His Holiness proceeded without undue haste, so as to give time for the kinsmen of the reverend cardinals to placate their opponents.   O. L.

[21] The three Venetian cardinals complained of were (1) Francesco Pisani, promoted cardinal 1517, Bishop of Padua 1524–55, administrator of Cittanuova 1526–35, administrator of Treviso 1528–38 in face of the objections of the Venetian Senate, d. 1570; (2) Marino Grimani, promoted cardinal 1527, Bishop of Ceneda 1508–17 and administrator of the see 1531–40 and 1545–7, Patriarch of Aquileia 1517–29, 1535–45 (in 1529 he resigned the see to his brother Marco, resuming it on Marco's resignation in 1535), administrator of Concordia 1533–7, d. 1546; (3) Francesco Cornaro, promoted cardinal 1527, administrator of Brescia 1531–2 (in 1532 he resigned the see to his brother Andrea, who held it until his death in 1551), d. 1543. See *HC*, III, 17, 19, 20, with many cross-references.

(ii) From a letter of Aleandro to Pietro Carnesecchi, 5 November 1533 (*NV*, I, 130–1).

I must tell you that it is a basic condition of most private business negotiated with the lords of Venice that, since this nobility is large, it includes both rich and poor, but has more of the latter, and that the rich give these every favour, for no one nominated by His Holiness can challenge any of these poor nobles who have taken possession of benefices; even when they know that they do not have right on their side, the rich still delay the resolution of the matter, simply in order to give the poor the means of subsistence, and to dissuade them from plotting unrest and the like in the state because of dire need. My conclusion is that the difficulties the Venetians are making to ensure that no more than one [cathedral] church is given to any one of their citizens are not really prompted by regard for divine worship, on the grounds that such people cannot reside in person in all of them, but rather by the desire to avoid envy and discontent among [the nobles] and give everyone a livelihood. Hence, being well provided for, they will not entertain evil thoughts, as persons in straitened circumstances are prone to do: 'the people cannot face hunger.' Sometimes, because of the strong case their adversaries have against the said nobles, they get their way in the end and favours are of no avail; but the lords of Venice think, by such a show of favour, albeit unjust, to keep their poor nobles quiet. However, if there is a question of giving one of their [cathedral] churches to an outsider or even to a subject who is not a Venetian noble, then, if there is no alternative, they would prefer one of their nobles to have three or four bishoprics rather than permit a non-noble to have a single one. This is the real point at issue. Sometimes, however, an outsider has so many points in his favour that they will give their consent out of respect for him, as they did for the Bishop of Verona.[22]   O. L.

(iii) From a letter of Aleandro to Carnesecchi, 24 December 1533 (*NV*, I, 147).

The Doge told me of his intention to propose a decree concerning the reform of the clergy and the better distribution of the ecclesiastical revenues of the Venetian dominion. Among the main points in this proposal were the stipulations that henceforth no one should hold more than one bishopric and no family [*casata*] should have revenues of more than 3000 ducats; nor should any cardinal enjoy revenues of more than 8000 ducats. He then asked me for my opinion and advice. I replied that everything they might do with the authority of the Holy See would be right and holy; and so they appended to the decree a

[22] The papal datary Gian Matteo Giberti, subsequently famous as a reforming bishop.

clause that everything should be done with the authority and favour of the Pope, which they directed their ambassador to seek. The proposal was made by the Doge at the last Senate and adopted by a large majority, to the great satisfaction and even delight of the whole city. They say that it will be put to the Great Council and, if, as is hoped, they adopt it there, they will send it to be one of the next pieces of business negotiated by the ambassador Suriano. I certainly thought that it contained many things which would be good for divine worship as well as promoting good order in the Venetian Republic, and I think it will bring considerable profit to the Holy See.[23]   O. L.

16   THE APOSTOLIC VISITATION, 1580–1

(i) From the report of Alberto Bolognetti, papal nuncio in Venice 1578–81 (Aldo Stella 1964, pp. 249–51).

The Venetians pronounced the visitation unnecessary because none had ever been conducted in the entire history of the Republic, which was Christian and Catholic at its birth more than 1100 years ago, and had always kept itself so without help from any visitation. They also argued that there was less need for it than ever in the past, because, or so they said, the dress and conduct of the clergy were now more seemly than ever before. Since this improvement had begun without the aid of a visitation, progress could reasonably be expected to continue in the absence of any such novelty (to use their word). They said there was no need for it because it would not produce the desired effect. For, once the ignorance and immorality of the priests, especially the parish priests, had been exposed (thus scandalizing the entire neighbourhood, and indeed the whole of the city), they would still have to put up with these people because there was no one better available, and because it would be impossible to deprive those who were already in possession by virtue of their election by the nobles of each parish, according to the ancient custom of Venice.[24] Finally, they thought it superfluous because the Patriarch had never failed to carry out a continuous visitation of exemplary thoroughness, as his office required. They added that, where his powers were insufficient, and could not touch regular clergy and

---

[23] The decree, cast in the form of a resolution to send certain instructions to the ambassador in Rome, was passed by the Great Council on 28 December 1533 by 1026 votes in favour to 288 against, with 57 uncertain: ASV Maggior Consiglio, Liber Diana (1522–36), ff. 186r–187v. For the purposes of the decree the family was to consist of 'fathers, sons, grandsons, brothers, and sons of brothers'.

[24] According to other sources the right to elect parish priests lay rather with the owners of houses or land in the parish [see above, V.4].

other exempted persons, these could be extended by giving him new commissions and more ample authority.

The Venetians likewise opposed this visitation by calling it prejudicial and damaging, and striving to demonstrate that it could affect the honour, interests and freedom of the Republic. The state's honour would be impugned because, they asserted, it was not usual for the Holy See to send visitors to royal capitals: Milan had been visited, but Madrid had not. True, the Venetians had allowed the visitation of Brescia and of Istria; but these are not, as Venice is, the seat of the most serene Signoria, which is assuredly to be numbered among the crowned heads. The visitation could well conflict with the city's interests on account of many disorders which, as I have already pointed out in another context, were anticipated in the matter of the nuns – for some of these were already threatening to leave their convents and had refused, at the mere rumour of the visitation, to take the veil; and some had refused to enter them at all. Since marriage portions are becoming excessively large, rising to 20,000–22,000 ducats and even more, this would prove all the more damaging to the interests of the city. And, if the failings of the convents were made public, through visitations and proceedings, the good name and even the peace of the city could be harmed. They feared that the visitation might threaten the freedom of the Republic because they said that the visitors would not only collect detailed information concerning the benefices attached to poor convents, in order to compel them to pay tenths and fifteenths, but would also lay hands on the hospitals which were, or so they said, subject to the Senate; on the trust funds which are managed by the Procurators of St Mark's; and on the Scuole. They maintained that responsibility for these brotherhoods had lain with the Council of Ten from its earliest days, even before it became such an important body on account of those incidents which gave it supreme authority in affairs of state. They also argued that matters would not stop here; once the ice was broken and the way cleared, other Popes would want to intrude still further. So they thought it best to prevent them by opposing this procedure at the start.   B. P.

(ii) Alvise Michiel, *Memorie pubbliche della Repubblica di Venezia*: BMV ms. Ital., cl. VII, 811 (7299), ff. 100r–101r.

The Pope [Gregory XIII] stood firm and said that he was ordering the visitation out of his duty to God and for the benefit of our clergy, who were sorely in need of one. It seemed strange to be Pope in every place but Venice, and he was determined to have it.

In this difficult situation the nuncio [Bolognetti] began the visitation after a fashion in San Francesco, acting alone and without a colleague, and he wanted to mend matters here and effect a settlement with the Pope, but he pleased neither side and acted in such a way as to ruin himself, for on observing these proceedings the Pope at once recalled him to Rome, and he left Venice within two days. He came to the Collegio and conveyed this news, begging them not to write to Rome in his support, for such a commendation would be fatal to his career, and so he left; and, although he had not behaved very well towards the Republic, the sight of his ignominious departure moved many to pity. He was a sound doctor of laws, and a man of letters too. He was Bishop of Massa, and held that diocese while he was nuncio here, a man forty-two years of age. He left, and in his place came Lorenzo Campeggio, Referendarius utriusque Signaturae [a papal official responsible for dealing with petitions], a nobleman of distinguished lineage and well disposed to the Venetian government. He and the Bishop of Verona [Agostino Valier], who was the government's choice, the Bishop of Padua [Federico Cornaro] being excluded, then carried out the visitation of priests and monks, but not that of nuns. Their visitation was very mild, and they drew up some regulations for them which were subsequently little observed. The Patriarch of Venice [Giovanni Trevisan] then carried out the visitation of the nuns with great tact and skill, and with this the year 1580 [*sic*] ended.   B. P.

17   THE INTERDICT OF POPE PAUL V, 1606
From the Latin. Extracts from the pronouncement of Pope Paul V before the cardinals, 17 April 1606 (De Magistris 1941, pp. 32–5).

His Holiness pronounced as follows.

We are reluctantly compelled to take further action against the lords of Venice. We have repeatedly urged them, both through letters and through our nuncio, to withdraw certain decrees which they have issued to the great detriment and prejudice of the liberty and jurisdiction of the Church, and to hand over to our nuncio two clergymen whom they are holding in prison in the city of Venice: to wit, a certain canon of Vicenza [Scipione Saraceno] and the Abbot Brandolino. We have awaited for several months the ambassador whom they sent to us upon this matter, and have listened to him with care, and since he has adduced no argument of importance, and has held out no hope of their amending, and they seem to become more obstinate as a result of our patience, it appears that there is nothing left to us but to employ the spiritual weapons which belong to the Church. On other occasions, in this sacred place, we have explained that these decrees prescribe that landed property which has been granted by churchmen to laymen upon emphyteutic leases may not, at any time, or for any reason (even the extinction of the line of heirs) return to the churches. The right to enjoy the property cannot be restored to the owners, but must always remain with the laity, a thing which undoubtedly seems most unjust. In no part of the Venetians' dominion may churches, hospitals and religious institutions be built without their permission, on pain of losing the churches. Landed property may not be transferred to churchmen, and if it is left to them for religious purposes it must within a specified period be sold by a certain Venetian magistracy.[25] These decrees, and especially the law that landed property may not be transferred to churchmen, and that bequests for religious uses must be sold, are contrary to the prescriptions of common, civil and canon law, contrary to the accepted opinions of your lordships, and contrary to the liberty of the Church; in one way they deprive the faithful of Christ of the opportunity to redeem their sins by almsgiving, and they take away the pious endowments and foundations of churches. Hence they have always been condemned and rejected both in the ancient general Councils and in the modern Councils [of the Church]. . . .

The privileges which the Venetians have of proceeding against clergymen in criminal cases are four in number. Two were granted by Sixtus IV; the originals have not been produced, but only copies, and these are limited to three crimes, i.e. treason, false coining and wicked vice. There are two other privileges which speak of heinous crimes, issued by Innocent VIII and Paul III, and these apply only to the city and diocese of Venice. But the Venetians, going beyond the terms of these privileges, proceed against churchmen in every part of their dominion without the presence and assistance of the Patriarch of Venice and his Vicar, as is required by the text of these privileges. Still more regrettable is the fact that they even proceed against persons who hold ecclesiastical offices, and sometimes against bishops, and they encroach upon the jurisdiction and liberty of the Church in other ways which it would be tedious to relate.

We therefore propose, with your lordships' agreement, by way of dealing with the Venetians as leniently and kindly as possible, to pronounce excommunicate the Doge and members of the Senate and their supporters and accomplices, taking their names as read, unless within twenty-four days, to run from the day of publication of our letters, they have obeyed us and offered us full satisfaction

---

[25] For the offending legislation and decisions of the Senate see ASV Senato, Terra, filza 162, 23 May 1602 (a decision in a case involving an emphyteutic or perpetual lease of land owned by the monastery of Praglia); filza 169, 10 January 1603 Venetian style (extending to the Venetian dominion on the mainland of Italy a law approved for the city of Venice only by the Great Council on 27 December 1561: the new version stated that nobody, lay or clerical, and no religious confraternity, was to erect 'convents, churches, hospitals or other places of shelter for regular or secular clergy in the cities, towns or territories subject to the Senate's jurisdiction without the permission of the Senate'); filza 174, 26 March 1605 [a law extending to the Venetian mainland an earlier law of 1536, for which see above, IV.6].

– thus allowing eight days for the first Catholic admonition, eight for the second, and eight for the third, which shall be final and decisive. But, if the said twenty-four days have elapsed, and they have incurred the sentence of excommunication three days later, then the city of Venice and all its dominion shall be subject to an interdict of the Church. In imposing this excommunication and interdict, as of now and as of then, we reserve to ourselves the power of proceeding to other, more drastic remedies in accordance with the sacred canons, if the need arise. God knows that we are moved by no private interests, but only by zeal for the honour of the Holy See, the defence of ecclesiastical liberty and jurisdiction, and the salvation of the souls of those who are in the greatest danger on this account, for in other respects we love them in the Lord.

B. P.

18   THE JESUITS, 1619

Gian Carlo Sivos, *Libro Quarto delli Dosi di Venetia*: BMV ms. Ital., cl. VII, 122 (8863), f. 172r–v.

In November 1619 a certain Venetian gentlewoman died and gave instructions in her will that her body be preserved in a coffer until the Jesuit fathers returned to live in this city, and that a tomb should then be built for her in their church and her body laid to rest in it; and she left the fathers a large income. For these reasons her will was declared invalid and the woman was buried, and notaries were forbidden under heavy penalties to draw up any will in which the Jesuits were named as beneficiaries. Any such will would be null and void, for [the lords of Venice] want no one to be able to leave any income to the Jesuits. And the Jesuits themselves were banned from the whole of the Venetian Dominion on pain of death, and so were former Jesuits who had left the order, unless they produced evidence of the time at which they had left the order and of their reasons for leaving. This was because there had come a Jesuit of Vicenza, of the family of Valmarana, who pretended to have left the order, and he claimed an inheritance, attempting to displace some of his nephews, who were the children of his deceased brother. He sent all the money he could lay hands on to the Jesuit fathers at Parma. This man was banished. And Cardinal Vendramin, when he died, left by his will 600 ducats income to the Jesuits, from the time they returned to Venice.[26] For this reason [the lords of Venice] do not want any more legacies to be made to the Jesuits, and they do not wish them to do business in this city in the dress of a priest.

B. P.

---

[26] Francesco Vendramin, Patriarch of Venice from 1608, became a cardinal in 1615 and died in Venice on 7 October 1619 (*HC*, IV, 362).

HERESY AND SUPERSTITION

*D*ESPITE *the toleration that they extended to non-Christians and to non-Catholics born abroad (particularly if such people's presence was useful to commerce, and if they caused no scandal), the Venetian authorities were often deeply suspicious of heretical acts and opinions on the part of their own subjects and of other Italians. For them, as for other governments, a native-born heretic was a dangerous creature liable to question all authority, and not merely that of the Church; hence repression and censorship were matters of equal concern to Venice and Rome, especially in the period between the late 1540s and the 1580s. V.19 shows how the Roman Inquisition in Venice was composed and how it was strengthened by the collaboration of representatives of Rome, of the diocese, and of the Venetian government. V.20 describes the meeting in Venice in 1550, to settle disputed points of doctrine, of supporters of one of the most radical heresies the Inquisition had to encounter. Pietro Manelfi, a prominent figure at this gathering, had suddenly returned to the Catholic faith and surrendered to the Inquisition at Bologna; his case was transferred to Rome, where he gave information that enabled the Inquisition to act decisively against the Anabaptists. The famous encounter between Veronese and the Inquisition, over his painting of the Last Supper for the Dominicans of Santi Giovanni e Paolo, is given here [V.21] as a concise example of some of the Inquisition's concerns and of its methods of interrogation. Very likely the Inquisition was acting on the recent decree of the Council of Trent (session 25, 3–4 December 1563) to the effect that 'No image shall be set up which is suggestive of false doctrine or which may furnish an occasion of dangerous error to the uneducated.' V.22 hints at the change of direction in the preoccupations of the Inquisition which occurred about 1580, when there was less danger from systematic challenges to Catholic doctrine in the form of Anabaptism or of what was loosely described as Lutheranism. For the real problems now seemed to lie in the supposedly foolish and un-Christian beliefs not only of ordinary people, but – as the case of the treasure-seekers suggests – of some friars, noblemen, and intellectuals as well.*

BIBLIOGRAPHY In general: Benrath 1887; Paschini 1959; Pommier 1959; Santosuosso 1973, 1978; Grendler 1977; Pullan 1983; Davidson 1982, 1987, 1988 and forthcoming;

Mackenney 1987, pp. 166–214; J. Martin 1987; Rossato 1987; R. Martin 1989. On Anabaptism: Aldo Stella 1967, 1969; Williams 1972. On Veronese: Fehl 1961; Pignatti 1976.   B. P.

19   THE APPOINTMENT OF THREE NOBLEMEN TO ATTEND THE INQUISITION, 1547, 1551
(i) Ducal decree of 22 April 1547 (Albizzi *c.*1680, pp. 42–3; Sforza 1935, pp. 195–6).

We, Francesco Donà, Doge of Venice, know that nothing is worthier of a Christian prince than concern for religion and the defence of the Catholic faith, a duty entrusted to us by our Ducal commission and always provided for by our ancestors. Hence, for the honour of our holy Mother Church, we with our smaller Council have chosen you, our most beloved noblemen, Nicolò Tiepolo, Francesco Contarini, doctor, and Marco Antonio Venier, doctor, as upright, prudent and Catholic men who are diligent in all your actions, especially where you know that the honour of God is at issue. We adjure you to make diligent inquiries concerning the heretics in this city and to receive any complaints which may be laid against any of them, and to join with the most reverend Legate and his servants, and with our reverend Patriarch and his servants, and with the venerable Inquisitor into heresy, urging each one of them to take proceedings whenever and wherever it may be appropriate, and at these proceedings you shall be present [*sarete assistenti*], and you shall ensure that appropriate sentences are passed upon those that are found guilty. And from time to time you shall inform us of everything that happens, that we may not fail to offer every kind of aid and support, in accordance with our promise.

Given on 22 April 1547.   B. P.

(ii) From a letter of Ludovico Beccadelli, papal nuncio in Venice, to Cardinal Bernardino Maffei in Rome, 5 September 1551 (*NV*, V, 279–80).

Having seen from the instructions [from Rome] that the intention of His Holiness is that these gentlemen concerned with heresy shall attend only as executors, without having cognizance of the case or any part in the sentence, in accordance with the ancient canons, I wish in this matter to satisfy my conscience and to do my duty, although I will always give way to anyone who knows more than I do. Your Reverend Lordship ought to know that here we have to distinguish between the city of Venice and the Dominion. In the city, which, being the populous capital, was deeply infected by its transactions with

Germans and other foreigners, a tribunal was established to deal with this problem in Monsignor Della Casa's time [as nuncio] and with the authority and approval of Pope Paul [III] of happy memory. This measure was accomplished by the effort and goodwill of the present Doge [Francesco Donà], who was a warm friend to it, for otherwise nothing would have been achieved, on account of the variety of humours which exist in the Republic.

The tribunal is made up as follows. An auditor of my own, and the ordinary inquisitor, and our fiscal and notary, sit every other day in a private chapel [that of San Teodoro] at St Mark's, and they hear and act upon complaints and evidence and take proceedings as the need arises. Three noblemen, from among the oldest and most highly regarded in the city, go to sit with them, and these noblemen are chosen by the Doge himself as he sees fit. They attend, and hear the things which are said, and give their opinion, although they always defer to the auditor and inquisitor, and the sentences are pronounced and the trials conducted in the name of the auditor and inquisitor, and a constable of the Council of Ten is charged with carrying out the tribunal's orders. Hence, the Holy Office is made to inspire fear in all men, and has put into effect some excellent measures, and is still doing so. These successes are due, above all, to the presence of these three gentlemen, whose authority is more respected than our own. Now, if this were to be called into question, and if it were to be said that they ought to have no part in the trials and sentences, I think they would certainly stay at home, and I am quite convinced that the arrangement would be spoiled, and that the wicked would rear their heads again and form their sects and conventicles, as is their wont. And, if Venice should retreat in this matter, Your Reverence may be certain that no good will be done in its Dominion, for all things are ruled by the head. So great care must be taken in handling this business, which, as I have said, has made a promising start, and all prelates who have been in Venice will know how difficult it is for us to get anything done by our own unaided efforts.   B. P.

20   AN ANABAPTIST SYNOD IN VENICE, 1550

(i) From the interrogation of Don Pietro Manelfi by the Master of the Sacred Palace, acting on behalf of the Holy Office in Rome, 13 November 1551: ASV Santo Uffizio, b.9 (Manelfi ed. Ginzburg 1970, pp. 65–6).

[Manelfi deposed,] 'As for our lodgings, we stayed in rented rooms in various palaces, in groups of three or four, and if I had with me a list that I keep in Padua I would be able to tell you who the landlords were, because it was my responsibility to pay them; but they knew nothing of our meetings, save that a landlady asked me one day, "What have all these people come here for?" I told her she was being paid, and that was enough.'

Asked who had summoned so many Anabaptists, especially from Basel and the Grisons, he replied, 'It was Ticiano, who knew those places well, and so did his companion, Joseph of Asolo.'

Asked who had given them the money for the gathering, and their travelling expenses, and so forth, he replied, 'In the state of Venice we spent only 27 crowns, because we fasted every day and ate frugally. The money was collected from the Anabaptists of Vicenza, Padua, Treviso and Cittadella; and I collected it at these churches and then disbursed it myself. On the journey, everyone spent the allowance made to him by his own church.'

Asked which books were studied during the synod, he replied, 'We studied only the Old and New Testaments, in the vernacular, since we allow no Latin in church.'

Asked who was the first to open discussion, or teach, or make decisions at the synod, he replied, 'Virtually every day we would meet in a different lodging, in order to avoid discovery. First of all we prayed together, saying the "Our Father" in the vernacular, then one of us would say, "Brothers, let him who has the gift of the word open the discussion and seek to illuminate us and to resolve those questions which we have assembled to consider." And so, day by day, we gathered together all the opinions which I included in my confession, holding to all the established opinions of the Anabaptists, and particularly to that about the [temporal] magistrates which is stated above.[27] In fact, the first time that we met I spoke after the prayer, suggesting that we should discuss the doubts [that had arisen] concerning the incarnation of Our Lord Jesus Christ. I said that we had assembled in that place not to walk in blind ignorance of our master Christ, but to determine whether he was just a man, born of the seed of man, or God, conceived of the Holy Ghost. In time we reached the resolutions which I have confessed, and after forty days we gathered together all the teaching and agreed to proclaim it in all the churches. So we all dispersed, with the doctrine defined. And in Venice during the said council we celebrated the Supper together in the manner described above,[28] about three times. And all of us who met there were bishops of the said church: their duty is to preach the Word, and to install ministers in the churches as they visit them in turn, and they are called "apostle

[27] In a previous interrogation in Bologna, Manelfi had reported the Anabaptist belief that secular magistrates cannot be Christians (Manelfi ed. Ginzburg 1970, p. 33).
[28] Manelfi described the Anabaptist method of celebrating the Supper in a deposition on 12 November 1551 (Manelfi ed. Ginzburg 1970, p. 63): after an exhortation on the origins of the celebration, the minister would take the bread and confess his belief in Christ as Lord, and in his own status as a member of Christ's body, before swallowing a mouthful and passing what remained around the room. Each person present would copy the minister, and the same procedure was then followed with the wine, which was held in a glass.

bishops", among whom I was one, as were also Nicola of Treviso, Ticiano, and Joseph, who all went on tour after the said council.' N. D.

(ii) From the draft abjuration of Paolo Beltramino of Asolo, who had been at the synod (Beltramino abjured on 16 June 1552): ASV Santo Uffizio, b.9.

On many occasions I assembled with various members of the said sect and church, in different places, and while we were together we spoke about matters of religion. And I attended the election of the ministers of our church, who are called bishops, apostles and deacons, and I too was elected an apostle, whose office was to go about preaching the word and the doctrine of the Church. And on one occasion I attended one of our meetings [*una nostra congregatione*] held here in Venice, when it was stated that painters, sculptors, sword-makers and similar craftsmen should not be accepted in our church, and that, as for the birth of our Lord Jesus Christ, it was enough to believe that he had been born as it had been foretold. . . . I also held and believed, along with the other members of our church, that no temporal magistrate or judge or minister of justice should be admitted to our church, for we wished that all should be equal, and that there should be neither superiority nor pre-eminence among us. N. D.

21 VERONESE BEFORE THE INQUISITION, 1573

From the Latin and Italian. Text as given in Fogolari 1935, pp. 384–6. (Other texts of the trial, with small variations, appear in Fehl 1961, pp. 348–54; and Pignatti 1976, I, 255–6.)

Saturday 18 July 1573

Master Paulo Caliari, painter, dwelling in the parish of San Samuele, was arraigned in the Holy Office before the sacred tribunal.

Asked his name and surname, he answered as above.

Asked his occupation he answered, 'I paint and make figures.'

Said to him, 'Do you know why you are brought before us?'

He answered, 'No, my lords.'

Said to him, 'Can you imagine why?'

He answered, 'I can well imagine why.'

Said to him, 'Say what you imagine.'

He answered, 'On account of what was said to me by the reverend fathers, or rather by the Prior of Santi Giovanni e Paolo,[29] whose name I do not know, for he told me that he had been here, and your lordships had instructed him to have the figure of the Magdalen inserted in the place where there is now a dog.[30] I answered him that I would willingly have done that and more for my own honour and that of the picture. But I did not think that the Magdalen would be suitable, for many reasons which I will state whenever I am given the opportunity.'

Said to him, 'To what picture do you refer?'

He answered, 'To a painting of the Last Supper that Jesus Christ took with his apostles in the house of Simeon.'

Said to him, 'Where is this painting?'

He answered, 'In the refectory of the friars of Santi Giovanni e Paolo.'

Said to him, 'Is it on the wall, or on wood, or on canvas?'

He answered, 'On canvas.'

Said to him, 'How high is it?'

He answered, 'Perhaps 17 feet.'

Said to him, 'How wide is it?'

He answered, 'Some 39 feet.'

Said to him, 'On this Lord's Supper, did you depict any servants?'

He answered, 'Yes, my lord.'

Said to him, 'Say how many servants there are, and tell us what each of them is doing.'

He answered, 'There is the master of the house, Simon [sic], and below this figure I have also put a steward, and have made it look as though he has come for his own entertainment to see how the feast is going.'

He then added, 'There are many figures which I cannot recall, for it is a long time since I put up the picture.'

Said to him, 'Have you painted any Suppers other than this one?'

He answered, 'Yes, my lords.'

Said to him, 'How many have you painted, and in what places?'

He answered, 'I did one in Verona, for the reverend monks of San Lazzaro; it is in their refectory.'[31]

He said, 'I did one in the refectory of the reverend fathers of San Giorgio, here in Venice.'

It was said to him, 'That is no Supper, and it is not called "The Lord's Supper".'[32]

[29] Adriano Alviani.

[30] As though to establish that the subject of the picture was the Supper of the Magdalen in the house of Simon the Pharisee (Luke 7:36–50), where the 'woman in the city, which was a sinner' was traditionally identified with Mary Magdalen.

[31] For the monastery of Santi Nazaro e Celso in Verona. For this Supper of the Magdalen see Pignatti 1976, I, 117; II, figs 188–90.

[32] It was in fact a Marriage of Cana (Pignatti 1976, I, 126; II, figs 375–6). See X.5(c).

He answered, 'I did one in the refectory of the Servites in Venice, and another in the refectory of San Sebastiano, here in Venice.[33] And I did one in Padua, for the fathers of the Maddalena. I do not recall having painted any others.'

Said to him, 'In this Supper which you painted in Santi Giovanni e Paolo, what is the meaning of the painting of the man with a bleeding nose?'

He answered, 'I meant him to be a servant whose nose is bleeding on account of some mishap.'

Said to him, 'What is the meaning of those armed men, dressed in the German style, each with a halberd in his hand?'

He answered, 'I must say a few words here.'

He was told to say them.

He answered, 'We painters take[34] the same licence as do poets and madmen, and so I made those two halberdiers, one of them drinking and the other eating,

3   Paolo Veronese, *The Feast in the House of Levi*, detail showing two German halberdiers.
(Reproduction by kind permission of the Accademia, Venice)

[33] Both were Suppers of the Magdalen (Pignatti 1976, I, 132, 135; II, figs 431, 454).
[34] In the trial transcript the word 'have' (*havemo*) is crossed out and 'take' (*pigliamo*) has been substituted.

234

next to a blind staircase, and they were put there to be ready to perform some task, for I thought it fitting that the owner of the house (who, as I have been told, was a great and rich man) should have such servants.'

Said to him, 'And that man dressed as a clown, with a parrot on his fist, for what purpose did you paint him on the canvas?'

He answered, 'For ornament, as one does.'

Said to him, 'Who are at the Lord's table?'

He answered, 'The twelve apostles.'[35]

Said to him, 'What is St Peter, the first of them, doing?'

He answered, 'Dividing the lamb, to give it to the other head of the table.'

Said to him, 'What is the one next to him doing?'

He answered, 'He has a plate, ready to receive what St Peter is about to give him.'

Said to him, 'Explain what the next one is doing.'

He answered, 'There is a man who has a fork and is attending to his teeth.'

Said to him, 'Who do you think was really present at that supper?'

He answered, 'I believe that Christ and his apostles were present. But if there is space left over in the picture I decorate it with figures[36] of my own invention.'

Said to him, 'Did anyone commission you to paint Germans and clowns and the like in that picture?'

He answered, 'No, my lords; my commission was to adorn that picture as I saw fit, for it is large and can include many figures, or so I thought.'

It was said to him, 'When you, the painter, add these decorations to your pictures, is it your habit to make them appropriate to the subject and to proportion them to the principal figures, or do you really do as the fancy takes you, without using any discretion or judgement?'

He answered, 'I make the pictures after proper reflection, within the limits of my understanding.'

He was asked, 'Did he think it proper to depict at the Lord's last supper clowns, drunkards, Germans,[37] dwarfs, and other lewd things?'

He answered, 'No, my lords.'

He was asked, 'Why, then, did you paint them?'

He answered, 'I did them on the understanding that they are not within the place where the supper is being held.'

He was asked, 'Do you not know that in Germany and other places infected with heresy they are accustomed, by means of outlandish paintings full of indecencies and similar devices, to abuse, mock and pour scorn on the things of

[35] Following this in the transcript are these words, deleted: 'Said to him' "Do you know St Peter, who is the first to carve up the lamb?" '

[36] Following this in the transcript are these words, deleted: 'as I am instructed [*si come mi vien comesso*], and'.

[37] Following this in the transcript is the word 'weapons' (*arma*), deleted.

the Holy Catholic Church, in order to teach false doctrine to foolish and ignorant people?'

He answered, 'I agree, my lord, that it is bad; but I must say again that I am obliged to follow the example of my predecessors.'

Said to him, 'What did your predecessors do? Did they do anything like this?'

He answered, 'In Rome Michelangelo, in the papal chapel, depicted Our Lord Jesus Christ, his mother and St John, St Peter and the heavenly court, all of them (after the Virgin Mary) naked, in various attitudes, and with little reverence.'

Said to him, 'Surely you know that it is not to be supposed that there will be clothes or such things at the Last Judgement, and so there was no call to paint clothing, and in that painting everything is of the spirit – there are no jesters, no dogs, no weapons, no frivolities of that nature. On the strength of this or any other example, do you think that you did well to paint this picture as it now stands, and do you wish to maintain that it is seemly and in good order?'

He answered, 'Most noble lord, no, I do not wish to defend it. But I did think I was doing right. And I did not think of such important things. I thought I was doing nothing wrong, especially because those figures of jesters are not in the place where Our Lord is.'

After which their lordships determined that the said Master Paolo should be compelled to correct and amend the picture considered at this session,[38] as the Holy Office sees fit, within the space of three months, this correction to be carried out at the discretion of the Holy Office, at his expense, and under threat of penalties to be imposed by the Holy Office. And so they decreed with all due propriety.   B. P.

22   MAGIC AND SUPERSTITION, c.1580
From the report of Alberto Bolognetti, papal nuncio in Venice 1578–81 (Aldo Stella 1964, pp. 286–7).

. . . the Venetian tribunal of the Holy Office has been continually employed upon various matters related to heresy. The commonest of these, or those which have taken up most time, are the superstitious use of incantations, and the infidelity of Christians who turn to Judaism.

---

[38] Following this in the transcript are these words, deleted: 'so that it becomes suitable for the Lord's last supper' (*ita, ut conveniat ultimae cenae Domini*). In fact the title of the picture was changed, so that it became the Feast in the House of Levi (Luke 5:29: 'And Levi made him a great feast in his own house: and there was a great company of publicans and of others that sat down with them').

It is true that the incantations were generally accompanied by activities which made them matters for the Inquisition, i.e. the adoration of demons, the recitation of prayers, the burning for magical purposes of styrax gum, incense, sulphur, asafoetida, and other substances which give off sweet or foul odours. But the incantations did not arise from any inclination towards heresy. Rather, they were directed towards two ends, love and gain, which wield great power over empty-headed people. Sometimes, indeed, love was directed towards gain, for it seemed that incantations might be placed under the threshold of a door to instil love into creditors and make them refrain from exacting debts. These incantations produced truly diabolical results, as with those who, being at first unable to consummate their marriages, freed themselves from impotence by urinating in the immediate surroundings of a tomb or the door of a church. It also happened that a whore (who was subsequently accused of similar acts) long kept a young gentleman prisoner in durance vile, as in those romances one reads about the imprisonment of knights, and on the orders of Rome measures had to be taken to prevent the marriage, by instructing the parish priests to take no part in it. In my time something similar happened to another rich young noble, who was brought by these spells to such a pass that he could not wait even a day to join himself in wedlock at Padua to a low-born woman almost broken by age, of extreme ugliness and dire poverty. His affliction came to light because, being overcome with anxiety and distress, he pestered the bishop all day about the matter.

Let me pass over many other superstitions, such as the practice of showing, in vessels full of liquid, how thefts were committed, or of revealing in the stones of rings things still to come, and making the sibyls appear within them. Especially noteworthy, however, was a conspiracy discovered among a small group of persons who were both foolish and impious.[39] Hoping to find treasure, they began to seek out books of necromancy, such as *The Key of Solomon*, *The Book of a Hundred Kings*, and other such works. Having found them, they set to work to consecrate them by performing the acts of worship and igniting the substances mentioned above, within a circle which they had made according to all the rules and regulations of necromancy. This treasure they believed to be among the mountains of the region of Verona, where (they had heard) there was a vast mass of gold in a cavern, although it was guarded by spirits in such a way that if anyone took it he would never find his way out unless he returned the treasure to the place from which it came. They went to great pains to consecrate the books in order to induce the spirits to abandon their vigilance.   B. P.

---

[39] Bolognetti is referring to the case of Cesare Lanza, Gregorio Giordano, Antonio Saldagna, Francesco Oglies, Giulio Francesco Morosini and Giovanni de Schioffi, whose trial by the Inquisition in 1579–80 is printed in Ioly Zorattini 1980–, IV (1571–80), 133–362. See also above, V.10.

Part VI
Social Orders

*C*ENSUSES *compiled in 1563, 1586 and 1593 categorized between 4 and 4.5 per cent of the population of Venice as noblemen, noblewomen and noble children. Between 5 and 8 per cent were classified as citizens and their families, and 76–9 per cent were reckoned to be artisans or shopkeepers and their families (Beloch 1902, pp. 13–14). Noblemen (also called 'gentlemen' or 'patricians'),* cives populares *or non-noble citizens, and artisans enrolled in the* Arti *or crafts formed, according to Sanudo [I.1], the 'three classes of inhabitants'. Strictly speaking, they were not classes, if classes are defined by economic criteria and held to consist of persons who share similar life-chances, or have a similar relationship to the means of production, or prove themselves capable of engaging in conflict with other classes over the pursuit of material interests. Rather, these three bodies formed estates, or legally defined status groups. Each of these three estates consisted of persons who, despite differences of wealth and varied occupations, shared specific privileges and performed certain functions in society and the state; people within each of these orders were acknowledged to be of the same 'quality' or 'condition' (terms regularly used in official Venetian documents). The texts presented here deal with the definition of status and the criteria for entry to these privileged bodies; with the social institutions which they officered and manned; with their obligations to the state and to the community; with their family life; with the rituals and ceremonies of the life cycle; and with the disposal of property at times of transition from one phase to another – from the single to the married state, from maturity to old age, and from old age to death.*

THE NOBILITY

*T*HROUGHOUT *the period 1450–1630 the nobility were essentially an 'estate of birth': male children acquired by legitimate birth into a noble family the right of entry to the sovereign Great Council on reaching political adulthood (between the ages of twenty and twenty-five), and hence the right to participate in governing the city and its dominions. Procedures for establishing noble status through the registration of such births are set forth in VI.1(b), which explains the origins of the famous golden books or* libri d'oro. *As VI.1(a) suggests, baptisms were not just religious ceremonies or family occasions: they also provided, through the institution of godfatherhood and spiritual kindred, opportunities to form alliances and factions within the patriciate.*

VI.1(c)–(f) will serve as reminder that each noble family was in part an association for managing property and pursuing or at least preserving wealth. These notarial documents record arrangements for the transfer, distribution and control of assets, especially in the form of landed property. They give useful examples of the nature and location of the land and houses owned by typical noble families, and of the relationship between the value of the properties and the rent they were expected to yield. VI.1(c) describes the dowry brought by a noble bride to her marriage; should she survive her husband, and choose to return to her own family (as many brides did), a large proportion of it would be detached from his estate and used for her support; VI.1(d) captures some of the complications which could well be associated with the fraterna, *a consortium of brothers administering their inheritance as a single unit, as though in obedience to the exhortations of a father such as Francesco Tiepolo [VI.1(e)], to remain together and collaborate 'to maintain the reputation of our family'. Provisions for and advice to daughters appear in the two successive versions of Francesco's will, and there are various indications – especially in VI.1(f) – of the extent to which married women and widows could claim and dispose of property on their own account. VI.1(g) returns to the first quarter of the sixteenth century and presents Sanudo's account of the death and funeral of the most princely patrician of his day; to judge by Sansovino (Sansovino ed. Martinioni 1663, pp. 403–4) the ceremonies which marked his passing had changed very little by the 1580s.*

VI.2 shifts attention from private to public life. The most far-reaching privilege of the Venetian nobility lay in its monopoly of the magisterial offices to which the Great Council elected only its own members; and in the opportunities which noblemen therefore enjoyed of shaping the policies of the state to their own interests. They could draw stipends, legitimate profits called utilità, *and illicit gains from the posts to which members of the Great Council were appointed for periods not normally expected to exceed two years. However, the cost of certain forms of state service could prove inordinately high, and they could well act as a form of super-tax which descended on many of the richer families. These documents offer illustrations of the burdens which could be imposed by service to the state upon members of the elite, although elsewhere in this book there is some countervailing evidence of corruption, peculation and profiteering both from the exercise of office and from the privilege of voting in the Great Council [see especially II,12–17].*

VI.3 presents an unflattering portrait of the Venetian nobility by the Marquis of Bedmar [see I, headnote], whose account, which stresses the tensions rather than the equilibrium within Venetian society, leads into the question of the nobility's relations with its social inferiors, and can again be contrasted with the jottings of the English ambassador, Sir Dudley Carleton, in 1612 [I.4].

BIBLIOGRAPHY   *For the social and economic history of the Venetian nobility: Davis 1962, 1975; Pullan 1965, 1973; Burke 1974; Georgelin 1978, pp. 619–66; Cowan 1982, 1986; Cozzi and Knapton 1986, pp. 117–31. On the nobility and landed property: Beltrami 1961; Woolf 1968. On the Corner: Arbel 1988.*   B. P.

I   THE LIFE CYCLE AND FAMILY ARRANGEMENTS

(a) The regulation of baptismal ceremonies, 1505
From a decree of the Council of Ten, 12 August 1505 (Bistort 1912, pp. 201–2).

It is the duty of this Council to extirpate anything that might result in disorder and impropriety, as could easily happen in consequence of an unseemly and insufferable practice recently introduced by the gentry of Venice, who in baptizing their sons and daughters have begun to invite large numbers of other Venetian gentlemen to act as godfathers, feasting them, and also making them handsome and expensive presents, for the sole purpose of creating obligations and making use of these people, a thing which must surely be severely reproved; and there is also the fact that such spiritual ties act as a bar to intermarriage.

BE IT [THEREFORE] DETERMINED that from henceforth no gentleman of ours may take any other gentleman for godfather either at baptisms or at christenings, on pain of being deprived of all offices, benefits and governorships, and of [the

243

right to sit in] councils, for a period of five years, and on pain also of a fine of 200 ducats, which shall go to the accuser, who is to be kept secret; and no pardon, relief or remission may be granted save by all seventeen votes of this Council.   B. P.

(b) The Registration of Noble Births, 1506

From a decree of the Council of Ten, 31 August 1506: ASV Compilazione delle Leggi, b.294.

BE IT DETERMINED (and this law shall be strictly obeyed) that, whenever a son is born in lawful wedlock to any Venetian gentleman and to any woman permitted by Venetian law, the father of the boy, if he is alive and in Venice, and otherwise the mother or two of the closest relatives of the newborn child, shall be obliged within eight days at most of the birth to come and notify the birth to the office of the Avogadori di Comun, and to declare this fact upon a solemn oath in the presence of all three Avogadori (or, if any of these are relatives, of one or more of the Councillors, who shall take their places). They must give the date of the child's birth, and state that he was born in wedlock, and give the first and second names of the child and his mother, and they must also declare the nationality and surname of the mother, in order to establish whether the child was born of a woman permitted by our laws as above, and they must also provide guarantors both of his legitimacy and of his age, as is now the practice, upon all the penalties laid down by our laws.

When sons are born outside Venice to Venetian gentlemen, their father, or their mother if she is alive, or their two closest relatives shall be bound to come and perform this duty, following all the procedures described above, within eight days of their return to Venice.

That the registration and proving of the said gentlemen may proceed with all due propriety, and any kind of fraud be eliminated, all parish priests or others having the cure of souls in the parishes who have baptized male children shall be obliged within three days of the baptism to come and notify the office of the Avogadori di Comun of the children they have baptized, upon pain of perpetual banishment from Venice and its district if they fail to observe this order.

If these children are born outside Venice, notification must be given to the governors of the place, either by the parish priests or by other curates of the [local] church, or else by the father or mother, and the governors must at once communicate the information by letter to the Avogadori di Comun, and when they [i.e. the parents or relatives] come to Venice they shall still be obliged to carry out all the procedures specified above for children born in Venice, and a record shall be kept of all the acts so performed on two books kept in the office of the Avogadori.

When any of the aforesaid gentlemen who has duly been registered and proved in accordance with the above procedures attains the age of twenty years, his name shall, with a certificate authenticated by the signatures of all three Avogadori di Comun, be included in the box for the lottery to be drawn on the Festival of St Barbara.[1] Alternatively, when he reaches the age of twenty-five, it shall be sent with a certificate (as above) to the Forty that he may become a member of the Great Council. In either case, to eliminate fraud, the father or mother or the close relatives (as above) must swear upon oath that this is the son who was registered, upon all the aforesaid penalties if the truth is found to be otherwise. This proof, made at the time of birth, shall be used in all the proofs that may have to be made for all public offices, magistracies, governorships, castellanships, lordships [Patronie] and seats in our Councils, always respecting, however, the authority enjoyed by our Avogadori di Comun to challenge and investigate any proof which seems to them to have been made improperly and not according to our regulations, and which relates to persons whom they regard as unworthy of admission to the nobility; and respecting, too, [their authority to deal with] any fraud or misconduct that may have been committed.

We further declare that no one may be enrolled or proved in the manner described above unless his father has been approved for the Great Council; but anyone who wishes to prove himself to be of the Great Council shall be entitled to put himself to the proof, and to be brought before the Council and Collegio, according to our laws.[2]

The decree of 26 May 1422,[3] which concerns gentlemen who contract marriages with women of low degree, and prescribes how these gentlemen must

[1] Lots were drawn by the Doge every year on 4 December, as a result of which one fifth of the young noblemen aged between twenty and twenty-five became eligible to sit and vote in the Great Council. Those who did not succeed in the lottery had to wait till the age of twenty-five: 'every gentleman comming to that age hath presently the right of a citizen, and is made pertaker of the publike authoritie' (Contarini tr. Lewkenor 1599, pp. 19–20).

[2] Cf. Contarini tr. Lewkenor 1599, p. 20: 'If it so happen that the father or grandfather of any gentleman . . . had never used this publique right, nor his name never been registred in the common booke . . . it is provided by a lawe, that they should prove their nobilitie by witnesses and publike writings, and that the advocators [Avogadori di Comun] should make report over to the forty men, and so . . . it is at length iudged whether the party pretending is to be admitted for noble or no.'

[3] This stipulates that, 'If any member of the Great Council marries a slave woman of any race or status whom he bought for money or for any other consideration, the children he has by such women or slaves shall be barred from the Great Council and may by no means be part of it. Furthermore, should it happen that any Venetian nobleman has carnal intercourse with any female servant of his or any other woman of low degree, and that he says that he has married her, then the children born of such women may not attend or be part of the Great Council unless the bridegroom proves the matter in person on the day of the wedding to the Avogadori di Comun by the testimony of reliable witnesses, who have themselves been present at the ceremony.'

245

come and give notice of the marriage to the office of the Avogadori di Comun at the time of the contract, shall be confirmed, and its stipulations duly observed.

· If any Venetian gentleman fails to notify [the births of] sons within the prescribed period, then after this time has elapsed registration at the office of the Avogadori di Comun will not suffice; they must be brought before the Council, as was resolved in the Council itself on the 19th day of this month.

B. P.

(c) A marriage contract, 1583
From ASV Avogaria di Comun, 113/3, no. 306.

In the name of the Holy Spirit, 3 October 1583, Venice

I, Bernardo Sagredo, son of the most noble Zuan Francesco, have drawn up and contracted this marriage agreement after the order of our Lord God and of holy Mother Church between the honourable Zuanne Francesco Sagredo, son of the most noble Hierolamo, and the honourable Orsetta Moro, daughter of the most noble Marin, and widow of the honourable Vicenzo Bragadin, son of the most noble Zuanne. This has been drawn up with the agreement of her most noble brothers, Bortolamio, Agostin, Santo and Daniel Moro, the sons of the most noble Marin, who promise to give the honourable Madonna Orsetta, their sister to the aforesaid the honourable Zuan Francesco, with a dowry of 11,023 ducats at 6 lire 4 soldi per ducat, in the manner which shall be stated below.

The honourable Zuanne Francesco promises to take the said honourable Madonna Orsetta as his wife with the aforesaid dowry. To guarantee this dowry the said Zuanne Francesco pledges all his goods, both present and future, on the understanding that, if the aforesaid dowry has to be handed back (may His Majesty the Lord God grant a long and happy life to bride and groom), the houses in this city, the quayside and house at Bassano and the estate at Villarazzo shall be returned at the prices at which they were given to him (Zuan Francesco). All the costs of maintaining the houses in Venice and on the estate at Villarazzo shall be made good to Zuan Francesco or to his heirs. The aforesaid dowry comprises, first:

An estate of some 52 campi in Villa Villarazzo, near Castelfranco, of which the house and land are at present rented by Zuan Domenego Ongaran, as recorded in the rental contract made by Messer Francesco Ricato, notary. The total value amounts to 4500 ducats.

A house at San Giacomo dell'Orio, rented out in three apartments for [a total of] 84 ducats, i.e. to Antonio da Schio, called the Lame Man, for 28 ducats, to the mercer [at the sign] of the Ox for 40 ducats, and to the spinners from Conegliano for 16 ducats. Valued by agreement at 2100 ducats.

Part of the house at San Giovanni Nuovo, shared with the honourable brothers Daniel, Hierolamo and Piero Pasqualigo, sons of the most noble Vettor, which brings an annual income of 15 ducats, and is valued by agreement at 375 ducats.

A quayside at Bassano, at the Porta di Margnan, and a house at the Porta di Brenta, which are rented out at 23 ducats a year, and whose agreed value is 575 ducats.

Furniture to be valued to the benefit or disadvantage of the honourable Madonna Orsetta, which may be worth some 300 ducats.

A string of pearls to be valued to the benefit or disadvantage of the honourable Madonna Orsetta, which may be worth 900 ducats.

Produce and wine which shall be sold from the estate at Villarazzo, to the benefit or disadvantage of the honourable Orsetta, at a probable value of 200 ducats.

1000 ducats, on which the honourable Gasparo and Alvise Bragadin, sons of the most noble Zuanne, pay [interest] to the honourable Madonna Orsetta every six months at the rate of 6 per cent, as recorded in the agreement drawn up by Messer Luca Cabrieli, notary, on 22 January 1583.

Dr Gensa, timber merchant on the Zattere, is to pay 200 ducats, the remainder of his debt.

The honourable Madonna Orsetta shall receive from her brothers 273 ducats.

555 ducats, owed by the aforesaid Gasparo and Alvise Bragadin in capital and interest in addition to the aforesaid 1000 ducats, shall be paid in cash.

47 ducats to make up the total to 11,025 ducats.

The total value of the said dowry, as stated above, is 11,025 ducats.

In addition to this dowry, the honourable Madonna Orsetta shall bring as her *dimissoria*[4] a further 580 ducats, which she may dispose of freely as she wishes and chooses. This *dimissoria* comprises the rents of the houses in this city, and likewise of the quayside and house at Bassano, which have not yet been collected. The aforesaid honourable Orsetta and her most noble brothers and the honourable Zuan Francesco Sagredo shall signify below their agreement to the matters declared above. May God's Majesty in his mercy give them long life in his holy grace, amid the love and peace proper to husband and wife.

A. C.

---

[4] The *dimissoria* was the share of her dowry brought by a widow into a new marriage.

(d) Partial division of a *fraterna*, 1593
From the acts of the notary Vettor Maffei: ASV Archivio Notarile 8220, ff. 171r–175r.

10 May 1593

The most noble lords Marc'Antonio Foscarini, son of the late most noble
Battista, and Sier Andrea his brother, have previously agreed that Marc'Antonio
shall remove the dowry of his consort, a total of 14,000 ducats, from the assets
of the *fraterna* in order to trade for his own gain or loss, and that the income
from the other property shall be divided in two equal halves between the
brothers. . . . In execution of this agreement, the aforesaid dowry has been
removed and the income from the above property which remains in the *fraterna*
has been divided. The said brothers are desirous that the property now
belonging to the *fraterna*, houses, land, *livelli* and other goods, shall remain
undivided. In future, however, each of the brothers shall trade for his own gain
or loss, so that the one shall not profit or lose by any agreement negotiated or
put into operation by the other, and in future it shall be understood that all
trade has been carried out on the separate account of each brother. Furthermore, since the said Andrea wishes to live with his brother without taking any
responsibility for managing the household or administering his property, the
following agreements and declarations have been drawn up to be strictly
observed and endorsed by each party.

The said Andrea, in ratifying and approving the removal of the dowry, and
seeking to live in peace and without care, gives, cedes and renounces freely to
his brother, the aforesaid most noble Marc'Antonio Foscarini (binding his heirs
and successors to do the same), one half of the rents and income from all the
property in the undivided *fraterna* for a period of eight years commencing on
1 June next. . . . Andrea has made this cession so that his brother Marc'Antonio
shall be ready and bind himself to gratify him and shall observe the following
conditions. . . .

First, the most noble Marc'Antonio promises and undertakes to give and pay
to Andrea (binding his heirs and successors to do the same) 700 ducats a year. . . .

A.C.

(e) Clauses from the wills of a nobleman, 1606, 1611
(i) From the first will of Francesco, son of Alvise Tiepolo, 25 January 1605 Venetian
style: ASV Archivio Tiepolo, b.99, no. 1488.

I leave 800 ducats to Marinetta, my natural daughter, that she may take the veil
as a nun in any convent which may be chosen by my trustees. . . .

248

I leave to Madonna Lucretia, my dearest wife, the whole of her dowry, which is 22,000 ducats, i.e. 19,000 which I have received up to now from her brothers, my brothers-in-law, and 3000 which remain to be handed over. . . .

I leave my son Marchetto my diamond on condition that he keeps it for the love he bears me. It shall never be demanded from him, or added to an account, or given by him to others, but he may leave it upon his death to whomever he thinks fit. . . .

. . . and because I have four daughters born of Madonna Lucretia my wife, and wish to provide for them in the best possible way without touching buildings and lands which shall be subject to entail, as shall be set out below . . . I wish that all my chattels, movables, merchandise, cash, jewels, pearls, gold, silver, tapestries, wall hangings, carpets, boxes of velvet, pieces of velvet, and my linings, and everything else which is clearly marked in my great account book, shall be sold at once, and all my credits exacted. . . . I wish that all the rents from my houses in Venice, except for my own house, which shall remain the family residence, shall be collected from time to time by my trustees and invested from year to year with the other capital to provide all my daughters with dowries or to pay for them to become nuns. . . .

The remainder of all my goods, movables, immovables and lands, both present and future . . . I leave equally to all my legitimate and natural sons, both those who are already alive, and those yet to be born . . . on condition that my sons do not divide up my property, but administer and profit from it as one, remaining together . . . and collaborating to maintain the reputation and honour of our family.   A. C.

(ii) From the second will of Francesco Tiepolo, 10 May 1611: in the same place as (i).

Since I do not have enough movables, silver, jewels and other property at present to fulfil my wish that my trustees should provide for my daughters as set out in my first will . . . , finding that I have so many sons, I ask my daughters to be content to become nuns and to give me this pleasure because I am certain that they will always be happier and believe themselves to be more content [as nuns] when they consider the trials which must be undergone by those who marry. Should any of them resolve not to become a nun, but live at home as a single woman [disghetata] with her brothers (a thing I do not advise), I wish her to be given 200 ducats a year during her lifetime, and a female servant. She may not live away from her brothers; but, in case my sons decide to make a division among themselves (which I hope they will not do, because I wish them to maintain their reputation and that of our family), then she shall live with whichever of her brothers she prefers, and the other brothers who do not live with her shall be obliged to contribute to her maintenance and that of her servant. I exhort my sons to use the 200 ducats a year to maintain their sister in honour and sufficiency, and to be good companions to her. After her death, these 200 ducats shall return to my residuary estate. I leave 60 ducats a year for life to each of those who become nuns.   A. C.

(f) A widow hands over her estate to her sons, 1613

From the acts of the notary Besciani: ASV Archivio Notarile, b.590, ff. 353v–355r.

23 January 1612 [Venetian style]

The most noble Cecilia, daughter of the most noble Ferigo Gradenigo, son of Cattarin, and widow of the most noble Pietro Paulo Contarini, son of Alessandro, being now come to old age and wishing to live in serenity for such space of time as the Lord God shall allow to her, far from all the care and trouble of running a household, has decided to assign to her sons, the most noble Alessandro and Fantin Contarini, those goods which the Divine Grace has deigned to pass to her and which she owns and may therefore freely dispose of, so that each of them (knowing what is his share) may apply himself to the careful administration and increase of this property with greater love, diligence and promptitude, now that they are [both] of age to do so.

She has acquainted these most noble lords her sons with her decision and with the ways in which she intends to make this disposition, and they accede to the just wishes of their mother and are content to accept the property which the most noble Cecilia intends to assign to each of them as his portion of *beni materni*.[5]

All this has been enacted by the said most noble Cecilia in the presence of the notary and of the witnesses named below, and has been freely given for the aforesaid reasons and because of the love which she bears her sons, and as best she can she has assigned these things to them by way of a pure, true, valid and irrevocable gift.

To the most noble Alessandro she has given and gives all the property of every kind which she owns at present in Villa Nova and Morgana, territory of Treviso, except for the two fields in Villa Nova which are subject to the entail of Giacomo Valentino, although Alessandro may profit from those fields during the lifetime of his mother. And, since the most noble Fantin, her son, has obtained Alessandro's share of a house in the parish of San Giovanni Mattio in Padua by a judgement obtained at the Procurator's office on 27 November

[5] *Beni materni* were the property which passed to a widow from her dowry after her husband's death.

1607, the most noble Fantin is content that his own share of the house shall be assigned to Alessandro as part of the present distribution, and gives up all rights which he might expect from it.

And to the said most noble Signor Fantin, her elder son, she gives all the property of every kind which she has and owns in Villa di Piombino, territory of Castelfranco, with the specific obligation to pay to the illustrious Alvise Duodo the capital of a *livello* of [...] s and the annual interest, which shall be ra[...] [...]rmore, after Cecilia's death, he shall be ob[...] andro in place of the rent of the two fields wl[...] tino.   A. C.

(g[...]
D[...]

[handwritten annotation: Secretary, Citizen, most important past. Marin Saundo's diary*]*

27 July 1527

This morning, when the Cavalier Procurator Zorzi Corner[6] had been ill for some days, he wished to receive Communion from the hand of his son, the Archbishop of Spalato, and this he did most devoutly, giving his blessing to his sons and daughters, and he said, 'Apart from the will which I have made, I wish 500 ducats to be given to the Archbishop.' He is in a bad way, and the doctors fear greatly for him. . . .

31 July 1527

After dinner. Be it known that today at the fourteenth hour died, at the age of seventy-four, the Cavalier Procurator Zorzi Corner, who had been sick of a fever for many days. He was with the Doge [Andrea Gritti] in the same Company of the Hose.[7] They wanted to keep his death secret, and his sons-in-law and cousins attended the Great Council to vote on a proposal – i.e. Sier Piero Trivixan, Sier Zuan Antonio Malipiero, Sier Jacomo Contarini, and Sier Zuan Francesco Loredan, who are of the great house, and Sier Nicolò di Prioli, his cousin-german. They said he was just ill, but everyone knew he had died. . . .

[6] Zorzi, son of Marco Corner, widely believed to be the richest man in Venice, was the brother of Caterina Corner, wife and later widow of Jacques II, the last of the Lusignan kings of Cyprus. Hence this branch of the family was known as the Corner della Regina. Zorzi had been instrumental in persuading Caterina to resign her crown into the hands of the Venetian Republic in 1489; he was knighted for this service, and after holding high office became a Procurator of St Mark's in 1509. Zorzi Corner had used his great personal wealth to have his son Marco promoted cardinal in 1500, at the age of seventeen. Caterina had died in 1510, Marco in 1523 or 1524.

[7] See below, IX.15, 16.

1 August 1527

This morning after Terce they sounded the bells, two strokes at a time, to mark the death yesterday of the Cavalier Procurator Zorzi Corner, as the custom is, and the Cavalier Marco Dandolo the doctor, his brother-in-law, and Sier Piero Soranzo, the son of one of his daughters, appeared before the Doge in the Collegio to invite him to attend the funeral tomorrow. [The deceased's] wish was to be buried in his chapel at the Santi Apostoli, where his father lies, and where he built him on one side [of the church] a tomb of polished marble; he has left instructions that his own tomb should be placed on the other side. At ground level is the tomb of his mother, in a sarcophagus [*casson*]. Furthermore he has left orders that two tombs be built at San Salvatore, one for the Queen [of Cyprus] and the other for the Cardinal, his son, on which 1000 ducats a year shall be spent until they are completed. Again, he has made many legacies for religious purposes. A chapel shall be built at San Maurizio and a Mass shall be said there in perpetuity, and on this 500 ducats shall be spent. Marriage portions of 25 ducats each shall be given to ten maidens every year for ten years. He has left all his parks and country estates [*parchi et parche*] free [of ties], but the great palace is entailed upon his sons and must always remain in the Corner family; Il Barco[8] shall pass from eldest son to eldest son. He leaves his wife her dowry, which was very small, indeed [. . .], and, should she not wish to remain in the house, a dwelling-place, and a certain quantity of corn, wine and money, and four furnished rooms, and other things. Again, to all his daughters 100 ducats each at the rate of 10 ducats a year; to Sier Nicolò di Prioli his cousin a basin of silver which was used in the house, etc., as in the will. He leaves the rest to all his four sons, upon condition that Sier Hironimo, who is in Crete, comes back to live in Venice: otherwise he will lose his share. Again, he leaves his natural son the Archbishop of Spalato 2000 ducats: these are to be invested in an estate; he is to enjoy the revenue; and after his death it will go to [the Procurator's] sons. In addition to this, he left [the Archbishop] 500 ducats by word of mouth when he gave him Communion by his own hand. To conclude, a very rich citizen has died; he is thought to have left [. . .] thousand ducats in cash, and landed property and other goods to the value of [. . .]. Again, he has left instructions that 60 stera of flour be distributed every year, one half at the Santi Apostoli and the other at San Maurizio, not more than half a stero to be given to any one person.

That night the body was carried to the church of San Maurizio, dressed in the habit of the Scuola, with a golden mantle and spurs and the sword of a knight; on his head was a black velvet cap, round and flat [*in taier*].

---

[8] The summer residence built for Caterina Corner at Altivole outside Asolo, the town in the province of Treviso to which she had retired after abdicating from the throne of Cyprus.

2 August 1527

In the morning betimes many relatives and other gentlemen who had been invited, wearing mantles, assembled at Ca Corner to join the family mourners [*corozosi*], and I, Marin Sanudo, was among them. Nine Procurators came. . . .

The service was held as usual, with our most reverend Patriarch, Don Hironimo Querini, in attendance, and the procession began with the parish of San Maurizio, the nine congregations,[9] the chapters of [the cathedral in] Castello and of St Mark's, the most reverend Patriarch in his robes, fifty Jesuati[10] with torches weighing [. . .] pounds each, twenty-four monks of San Sebastiano, fifty mariners with torches weighing [. . .], and then the Scuola della Misericordia with 200 torches, 100 of their own and 100 from the deceased, and there was a great number of these flagellants, because he left them [. . .] soldi each. Then came twelve of his servants, wearing long mantles and cloth upon their heads, in front. The corpse was beginning to decompose. Then they came down, two by two, family by family, and followed the body through the city to the Piazza San Marco, where it was raised three times, as is the custom with Procurators, and the bells of St Mark's were tolling, two strokes at a time. Meanwhile the Doge, and the ambassadors of the Pope, England, Milan, Florence and Ferrara (he of Mantua has returned to Mantua), the Bishop of Scardona, Sier Domenego Trevixan and the Procurator Lunardo Mozenigo came down from the Palace to the church, where they met with the family mourners, and the Doge took the first one to himself, and in the same way each of the ambassadors, Ducal Councillors and Procurators took a partner, and they went off through the Merceria and through the city to the Santi Apostoli, where a high platform [*pulpito*] had been made ready in the church. There they placed the litter, with the Jesuati and the mariners round about it. This platform was bedecked with torches [*dopieri*] and great candles and black cloths, and the dead man's coat of arms was placed in the middle, together with those of the Queen of Cyprus and of the Scuola della Misericordia. All round the church were fine black cloths and coats of arms. Then the Doge took his seat, together with the ambassadors and family mourners and anyone else who wished to stay, and I myself was among them. The funeral oration was delivered by Sier Carlo Capello of the Civil Court of

---

[9] See above, V.4.

[10] Half a century later, 'A funeral is held to be more honourable, or less, according to the number of Jesuati who take part' (Sansovino 1581, f. 154v.; ed. Martinioni 1663, p. 403). The Jesuati were members of a congregation founded in Siena in 1366 by Giovanni Colombini and devoted to spiritual good works; they were so called because of their habit of crying out the name of Jesus. They were suppressed in 1668. The church called the Gesuati on the Zattere was actually built in the eighteenth century by the Dominicans, who succeeded the Jesuati in possession of the site.

the Forty, son of the Cavalier Francesco. He had on a pleated mantle, and someone was reading [his speech] to him from behind. The oration won no praise. It was very long, but said little about the dead man's father, the Cavalier Marco. When this was done, the Doge and everyone else departed, and the Patriarch in his robes went to perform the service over the body, which was buried in the tomb at the foot of the altar in his chapel; and the ceremony finished at the [...] hour. The Doge returned with the barges to St Mark's, and the family mourners returned home by boat, and so this most sumptuous funeral came to an end. It was followed by a great number of poor females, who were given [...] soldi each. The shops were closed from the dead man's house all the way to the Santi Apostoli. The Doge wore a scarlet mantle with golden bells and a scarlet cap; he was in the same Company of the Hose. . . .

And the Doge was his dear friend. B. P.

2 SERVICE TO THE STATE

(a) An embassy to Spain, 1561
From a petition of Benetto Tiepolo and brothers, considered by the Senate on 29 September 1561: ASV Senato, Terra, filza 34.

Most Serene Prince [Doge Hieronimo Priuli], would that the energy and resources of Benetto Tiepolo and brothers, sons of the late Missier Stefano, Procurator [of St Mark's], allowed us to continue assisting Missier Paolo our brother, who is now your ambassador to His Majesty the Catholic King [of Spain], and to help him to meet the heavy expenditure he is forced to incur on this mission – given the widespread and constant shortage of all things that prevails in that kingdom, as Your Serenity is very well aware. If our brother could expect to complete his mission within the next three or four months, we would not trouble you on this account. But we are in such dire straits that we cannot ourselves provide for his needs, and his successor (the fifth person to be chosen since the resolution to replace him) is unlikely to leave Venice for some time to come, so that a year will have to pass before our brother's return to this city. Hence we can only throw ourselves at Your Serenity's feet, and humbly beg you that, since our brother has used up a large part of the portions destined for two poor daughters, whom he has still to marry off, and since we have assisted him with the greatest imaginable trouble to our own family, you may now be pleased to aid him out of your own great charity and generosity. Since you have judged it necessary to provide a subsidy of 1000 ducats to your ambassadors on their departure from this city, with another 1000 after they have spent two years at court, you will no doubt bear it in mind that our brother has served four years in this embassy. The last two ambassadors to return from Spain will assure you that this is the most expensive embassy of all, because everything costs two or three times as much in Spain as it does anywhere else. We say nothing of the heavy expenditure forced upon him by so many marriages and deaths, since for this reason Your Serenity twice sent extraordinary ambassadors; nor will we dwell on his misfortunes on the journey from Flanders to Spain, when he travelled overland and sent some of his household and the Secretary by sea. We will not mention the prolonged illness of the Secretary, and of all the household, and the losses of the best horses and mules that he could have. But, if, as we feel confident, you are prepared to consider all these matters carefully, we are sure of being heard and of being assisted in our needs by virtue of your generosity and favour, through your allowing our brother the 1000 ducats Your Serenity grants to your ambassadors when they have served two years abroad, although he has served four, or through any other measures that you in your wisdom may choose, that he may keep up his standards for the time that remains to him. This cannot be less than a year, and must force him to spend at least 2000 ducats over and above the stipend which Your Serenity gives him.[11]   B. P.

(b) Equipping a galley during the War of Cyprus, 1570–1
From a petition of Marco di Geronimo Morosini, finally dealt with by the Senate on 17 December 1588: ASV Senato, Terra, filza 109.

On 14 January 1570, at the height of the war with the Turks, Your Serenity [the Doge was then Alvise Mocenigo] and the most excellent Senate were pleased to elect me one of your thirty governors [of galleys]. Immediately after that election, the need being most pressing, we were all summoned before you in the most excellent Collegio, where we were ordered to prepare ourselves to arm as swiftly as possible. Being a most obedient son and servant of this most excellent Republic, I did not refuse to perform this task, as several others did on account of the many troubles and difficulties of that time. Rather I began with great

---

[11] On 31 May 1561 the Senate had already made Paolo Tiepolo a special grant of 400 ducats (ASV Senato, Terra, reg. 1560–1, f. 77v–78r). He was now granted a further 600 ducats. Tiepolo eventually returned to Venice at the end of 1562. According to Albèri, the nineteenth-century editor of the Venetian ambassadorial reports on foreign countries, Tiepolo was appointed ambassador to Philip II (then in the Low Countries) on 6 June 1558, which would mean that he had only served three years on that particular embassy at the time of his brothers' petition. Previously, however, he had been ambassador to Ferdinand of Habsburg, King of the Romans, his mission ending before 12 October 1557, when he reported on it to the Senate; furthermore, he claimed at the end of his account to have served in 1549 on a costly embassy to Mantua. For Tiepolo's reports see Albèri 1839–63, I.iii, 145–74, and I.v, 3–76.

promptitude that very day to engage officers, freemen [*scapoli*] and galleymen, whom I retained for over four months, making them loans and gifts at my own expense until the first twenty galleys departed. After they left, the remaining ten of us were released, and, although I was promised that the expenditure and loss I had incurred on this occasion would be made good, I never received and never asked for anything, and was left to bear the cost of all the gifts and loans I had made to the men whom I had engaged.

The following year, when news came that the enemy's navy had invaded the Gulf, I was ordered to make ready [*metter a banco*] together with the most excellent Provveditor General Bragadino of happy memory and with seven other governors, and I was given a subsidy of 500 ducats. I spent this, and much other money which I had to raise at interest (I still feel the effects of it), in the service of Your Serenity, in hiring a new batch of sailors, freemen and others. How much one had to spend in those disastrous times is very well known to Your Serenity [Doge Pasquale Cicogna], whose distinguished family took so great a share of the toil, loss and danger of that war. Apart from the expenditure just mentioned, much else had to go on repairs to the oars, the bow and stern sheets [*pizzuol*], the paintings, and the other fittings and ornaments essential to the galley. Once I had put the ship in perfect order and taken it to San Marco, the crew was assigned to me; but as soon as they had begun to pay the officers I was ordered to disarm, without being able to recover a penny, because I had been allocated boatmen of the ferry stations [*gente di traghetto*].[12]   B. P.

(c) The office of Bailo in Constantinople, 1598
From a despatch of the papal nuncio Gratiani, Bishop of Amelia, late August 1598: ASVat. DN, filza 33, ff. 117v–118r.

A day or two ago Signor Alvigi Priuli, the Cardinal's brother,[13] a gentleman of good name and reputation, was appointed to be the new Bailo in Constantinople. In earlier times this post was a desirable one, because [the Bailo] handled large sums of money belonging to the Republic and gave no account of them, or at least did so in such a way that one had to trust him and take his word for what he had spent, because he had to keep all the ministers sweet with presents, and to penetrate into the councils of the Turks by means of secret bribery and

[12] Government officials, the Tre Savi sopra i Conti, a Public Accounts Committee, were now, some seventeen years later, trying to recover the subsidy from Marco Morosini. He was eventually exempted from the obligation to restore 300 ducats of this, on condition that he paid the remaining 200 ducats within the next eight days.

[13] Lorenzo Priuli, Patriarch of Venice from 1590 to 1600, was created Cardinal in 1596 (Niero 1961a, pp. 99–106).

corruption. Now that this need has ceased, and the fear of the Turks has passed away, these expenses have for the most part ended, although the perils of a long voyage and other possible mishaps are still attached to the post; and, since opportunities for gain are lacking, men not only do not want the job, but actively avoid it. Cardinal Priuli is deeply displeased at his brother's election, and told me yesterday that his people are thinking of trying to excuse him, on the grounds that as the brother of a cardinal he would command no confidence at Constantinople. For the Pope's name is held in awe there by the Turks, on account of the aid he has given to the Emperor, and the belief they have that he is for ever contriving leagues and alliances of Christians against them.   B. P.

3   NOBLES, CITIZENS AND PEOPLE IN VENICE, *c.*1618
From a report on Venice attributed to the former Spanish ambassador, Don Alonso della Cueva, Marquis of Bedmar: BL Additional ms. 5471, ff. 147–53.

The noble families of Venice enjoy great wealth. They equal, if indeed they do not surpass, the other nobilities of Europe, for there are some families whose incomes amount to 20,000–25,000 ducats, and large numbers who have 4000–8000, for these noblemen show more skill in amassing money and acquiring great possessions than do any others in the world. In the first place, they are not forbidden to engage in commerce, not is it thought unseemly for them to do so, although, being rulers and not subjects, they might well be ashamed of it. On the contrary, such activity adds to their reputation, and does not diminish it.

They make huge profits from this occupation, and their gains are all the greater because the authority and superiority over other people which they have acquired for themselves free them from the dangers that beset other merchants. It may happen, as it often does, that someone ceases trading because he thinks he cannot pay his debts. Should he owe anything to noblemen, he would be well advised to satisfy these creditors or leave the country, because the nobles not only induce the law courts to exceed their powers but also resort to private violence and intimidation, which frighten those poor debtors more than do any legal actions. Hence, as I say, they make large fortunes; indeed, I am told that pretty much the greater part of the business on the Rialto market is transacted on account of noblemen, whether they are openly involved or engaging in commerce under other people's names. Apart from this, their wealth derives from the time-honoured custom of going out to snare birds [*d'andare uccillando*] – that is, to ravish girls who are nubile if not noble, and sometimes not even of citizen rank, just so long as they bring with them an ample dowry or inheritance. The nobles are so good at this game that seldom do they let these rich morsels escape. It brings in immeasurable wealth and has been the making of many families that without such assistance could never have aspired to high honours and positions within the Republic. No wonder, then, that such opulence should prevail among the nobility, for these skills would be enough to enrich a whole kingdom, let alone a narrow circle of six or seven hundred families.

Furthermore, they do not have to spend profusely, as do the gentry of the mainland; and this, again, is a very good reason for their prosperity, for their dress is sensible and does not call for lavish expenditure, nor do they have many servants, for they only need enough to perform the essential household duties without engaging others just for show, as is commonly done elsewhere. They are free of the expenditure on horses that impoverishes their own and other people's subjects, and, although some nobles do keep them, they are not extravagant in the matter, for they are people who, on account of the property they possess, can maintain horses easily enough, and indeed have to do so for the purpose of visiting their estates. Since little spending and much heaping-up of treasure come together in the Venetian nobility, it is easy to imagine the extent of their wealth. Let me add, too, that much of their gain arises because those who administer public moneys (and there are large numbers of such people, who are for ever changing, in accordance with the constitution of the Republic) do not in practice show as much loyalty to their prince as they profess in words and speeches. This failing is no worse in Venice than it is in all the other great principates, including our own, for, as the proverb says, it is difficult to protect yourself from servants. I know that in the present war leading servants of the state, in positions of the highest trust, have helped themselves and taken stipends far in excess of the rewards due to them for their efforts. This was not merely suspected by the Senate: they actually got wind of it, and sent a commission of inquiry into the field to seek out the truth, and, although proceedings were instigated against the criminals, very little could be discovered, for these are crimes which are hard to expose unless the culprits are caught red-handed. Nor could they find senators eager to challenge the leading figures in the Republic by inquiring into so uncertain a matter, for these people could on some pretext impede their advancement or even ruin them on grounds of suspicion alone.

From these enormous riches let me pass to the other extreme – that of an unspeakable poverty, which none the less reigns among these same noblemen and indeed beggars belief. When they are old or have big families they are forced to apply to the preachers and through them seek aid and support. If they are young noblemen they often get involved in disreputable activities and misdeeds and come to a bad end. On this subject I remember being told by a charitable man who had been charged with visiting these unfortunates and helping them at Easter that he had been taken to hovels where he had found five or six girls of noble birth lying on mats covered with filthy rags, where they had to stay all day because they had nothing to cover their bodies if they stood up.

That good man wept as he told me, and I was much moved to hear him, and although these people enjoy the privilege of noble rank they are ashamed to appear before others, and there are no public funds to relieve this dreadful poverty and provide them with the means to live passably well. If nobility could be sold, you would find poor men ready to give up their rank for a hundred maravedis.

Then there is another class of noblemen placed between the moderately rich and the exceedingly poor. They do have means of their own, but these are not enough to maintain the honourable style of life appropriate to their status. They are not so down on their luck, but help themselves by any means they can find, respectable or not. This is the most unpleasant of all the nobles' characteristics, for they oppress poor artisans both when they buy and when they sell, and make them do things which often drive them to desperation, and provoke the artisans into forgetting the respect which they owe the nobles as their masters. These people use threats and reproofs to frighten simpletons, who hear at their backs the curses and threats of a nobleman, and very frequently agree to do everything demanded of them. In short these noblemen trade wholesale upon their own authority and rank, through which they pursue those additional benefits which fortune has denied them. . . .

After the nobles the citizens hold the most honourable position, so that they are accustomed to say that the nobles are princes and they themselves are gentlemen. They dress in the same fashion as the patricians. They want to be addressed as noblemen are, and they too enjoy great riches, which they have acquired and enhanced in similar ways. Almost all of them are employed in honourable posts, such as those of secretary, notary, chancellor or superintendent, and in other such offices, from which they derive considerable benefit. They learn and cultivate their skills with greater application than do the noblemen, for they cannot be sure of advancement unless they show themselves to be intelligent, sharp-witted and endowed with good qualities. However, there prevails among them a certain hauteur not far removed from insolence, which in many of them seems almost more insufferable than in the nobility (perhaps the Venetian climate made them that way, or perhaps it is induced by impudence and by the fact that their dress is the same as the nobles'). Hence they permit themselves many things that would not be so readily tolerated if they were recognized for what they are. So anyone who intends to stay in Venice contrives to distinguish between noblemen and citizens, that he may know how to conduct himself, and not be overawed by the borrowed plumage of persons who want their gowns to serve both as robes and as swords. The citizens are not well disposed towards the nobility, for many of their families think themselves just as ancient and honourable as the noble houses, and some of them are actually richer and better dressed than noblemen. Hence they realize with distaste that they are mere servants and functionaries who, apart from one or two public occasions, are not called upon to give aid and counsel but only to provide services, with no hope of rising above their rank, which can only be called servile, through their own industry or merit.

Since so much merchandise converges upon Venice from all parts of the world, a large proportion of the population is employed in commerce and making more money than it would in any other place. Furthermore, in such a populous city there are plenty of opportunities for poor people who are willing to bestir themselves in the pursuit of honest gain. Hence, since under the Venetian Republic the people are so treated that they can live passably well and are persuaded that they would not do so in other places, they are inclined to love their prince and to show their affection for him. The more other regimes are depicted as tyrannical and insufferable, and the more the Venetian government is represented as mild, good, pious and charitable, the more the love of the people grows, and hence they are willing to contribute some of the proceeds of their labours to the state, for they are given to understand that these will be used for the defence of their prince, and hence of themselves as well. For the rest, the people are very simple-minded, and will readily believe anything they are told, however absurd it is. But they are also impatient and seditious, and I believe it would be hard to keep them calm in the event of famine. They have violent quarrels among themselves, and because these are ignored by the prince they often give rise to still more scandal, and men are killed almost every day for the most trivial of causes. The city is divided into two factions, which are said to be tolerated for a good reason. There is no doubt that many abuses could be avoided if justice were enforced a shade more rigorously; but the lords of Venice believe that if they allow these people free rein they will gain more goodwill. Rather than waste time on discourses little to the point, I leave it to the wise to consider whether this policy is likely to succeed.   B. P.

THE CITIZENRY

*I*N ONE SENSE *noblemen admitted to the Great Council were the only true citizens of Venice, in that they alone enjoyed full political rights, and they alone were entitled to become members of the councils which made policy, to hold offices that ranked as magistracies, and to elect peers to such positions. Sanudo refers to Zorzi Corner [VI.1(g)] as 'a very rich citizen', and Gasparo Contarini, in his classic treatise on Venetian government, calls noblemen* cives *or* citizens. *However, Venetians also used the term* cittadino, *or* civis popularis, *to refer to persons not of noble birth who none the less enjoyed certain legally defined privileges of considerable importance, administrative or economic or both. From 1478, native-born citizens [*cittadini originari*] were entitled to be considered for posts of great trust in the permanent civil service or Ducal Chancery, which gave support to the elected magistrates and diplomats and ensured continuity in administration. This secondary elite gradually evolved into a form of secondary nobility; by 1622 it was firmly established that to achieve this status a man had to be capable of proving that his father and grandfather as well as himself had been born in Venice, and that for three generations the family had abstained from manual labour. VI.4–6 are chiefly concerned with those who were 'citizens' in this sense, with their style of life, their family concerns and their public duties.*

VI.4(a), a Venetian counter to the famous Florentine Ricordanze *or family histories, is taken from the earliest and most detailed known account of a family of secretaries in government service, the Freschi. It was begun by Tomaso de'Freschi (1453–1534) or by Zaccaria de'Freschi (1456–1510) and continued by Zaccaria's son Agostino. The extract from this chronicle concentrates chiefly on an alliance by marriage concluded in 1506 between two secretarial families. The child hero of VI.4(b), taken from letters written by his father Martino and his uncle Giovanni Battista, grew up to be a Chancery secretary, but one of no great interest as an adult. VI.4(c) offers a modest 'citizen' equivalent to Sanudo's account of a great nobleman's death and lavish funeral [VI.1(g)].*

Luigi Da Porto (1485–1529), the author of VI.5(a), came of a noble family in the Venetian subject city of Vicenza. He was not in Venice in the month of October 1509, to which this text relates, but in his native place, which was then under the control of the imperial forces that had invaded the Veneto during the War of the League of Cambrai. He had probably learnt of the situation in Venice through rumours of discontent, inspired and magnified by the wishful thinking of imperial partisans. Loredan's oration presented in VI.5(a) is a literary composition for Da Porto's History, *written in the form of letters a decade or so after the events it describes. None the less, the speech introduces two influential and recurrent themes in the analysis of Venetian politics and society: the belief of critics and enemies that the citizens must surely be deeply frustrated by having no prospects of joining the ranks of the nobility [cf. Bedmar's remarks in VI.3]; and the assertion of apologists for Venice that the citizens enjoyed ample compensation for their exclusion from the patriciate. VI.5(b) shows how Maximilian of Habsburg, Emperor elect, endeavoured to appeal to the* cives populares *of Venice against the nobles who allegedly tyrannized over them, although the Venetian* popolo *appear to have consistently supported their masters against Maximilian's claims.*

VI.6 deals further with the public responsibilities of secretaries, including [see also VI.4(c) on this point] the hopes and frustrations that surrounded elections to the post of Grand Chancellor, Da Porto's 'Doge of the popolo'. Pietro Bressano, who describes his own career in VI.6(a), was the son of an arsenal foreman; his brothers were shipwrights. He had entered the Chancery in 1498 and became a secretary of the Senate in 1522; in response to his petition he was awarded the right to hold the chancellorship of the small town of Montagnana for five annual terms. Ten years later the post was to be worth 150–180 ducats a year. The failure of Antonio Milledonne to gain the Grand Chancellorship in 1581 [VI.6(c)] was attributed by some observers to his unpopular zeal in promoting and extending the authority of the Council of Ten.

VI.7 deals with the type of citizenship which carried economic privileges and was awarded to persons born outside Venice who had shown their worthiness to become naturalized Venetians by long residence in the city and punctilious taxpaying. Citizenship de intus *entitled its holder to be admitted to any of the guilds, to trade within the city, and to hold minor public offices; citizenship* de intus et de extra *allowed the citizen to ship goods and trade between Venice and the Levant, and [see IV.9, n. 11] to pay customs duties at a lower rate than foreigners. In the late Middle Ages and the sixteenth century the requirements for citizenship were adjusted from time to time in accordance with the demand for desirable immigrants and settlers; the rules laid down in 1552 [VI.7(a)] were, as VI.7(b) demonstrates, still strictly enforced in 1630.*

BIBLIOGRAPHY   On the Ducal Chancery and cittadini originari: Trebbi 1980, 1986; Neff 1981, 1985; Cozzi and Knapton 1986, pp. 141–6. On citizenship de intus et de extra: Pullan 1971, pp. 99–112; Tucci 1973, pp. 362–4; Cozzi and Knapton 1986, pp. 133–40.

4   THE LIFE CYCLE AND FAMILY ARRANGEMENTS

(a) Pages from a family chronicle, 1456–1506

From the Latin (except for the marriage contract). Extracts from *Memorie dell'illustre Famiglia de' Freschi Cittadini Originarij Veneti*: BMV ms. Ital., cl. VII, 165 (8867), ff. 31v, 35r–v, 43v–44v, 112r–v. (The account of the wedding festivities is included in Morelli 1820, pp. 155–8.)

A son was born to Giovanni Davide de'Freschi of his wife Elisabetta [Pencin], on Thursday 14 October 1456, at sunrise, in the parish of San Martino, in the Dogeship of Francesco Foscari.

Baptism at the sacred font in the same San Martino, by the parish priest. Godfather: Evangelista Pergulano, Doctor of Arts and Medicine. Names given: Zaccaria and Beda. . . .

On Sunday 8 January 1485 [Venetian style], Zaccaria de'Freschi entered into a contract of marriage with Dorotea Zaccaria, legitimate and natural daughter of the late worthy Antonio Zaccaria, Venetian citizen and admiral at the Arsenal. In the Dogeship of Marco Barbarigo.

On Wednesday 5 April 1486, on the great square, in the parish of San Basso, occurred the public espousal of Zaccaria de'Freschi and his betrothed wife Dorotea, in a style befitting the honour of the occasion. Present were many noteworthy men and women of the family of the girl's mother, Signora Lucia de'Angelis. The best man was Alvise Basso, brother of Pietro.

On the same fifth day of April [Zaccaria] brought his new wife home, to his house in the parish of San Giovanni Nuovo, not far from the church of Santi Filippo e Giacomo on the Rio di Palazzo.

On Sunday 16 April 1486, Zaccaria de'Freschi celebrated his marriage with a feast more sumptuous than all other banquets. Besides relations by both blood and marriage there were present a large number of eminent men, all opulently dressed; nor was anything omitted which is customary at the most elegant wedding entertainments. . . .

A little girl was born to Zaccaria de'Freschi of his wife Dorotea on the morning of Monday 19 May 1488, at midday, in the parish of San Giovanni Nuovo by the Bridge of Santi Filippo e Giacomo, in the Dogeship of Agostino Barbarigo.

Baptism in the church of San Giovanni Nuovo, on 31 May 1488, by the parish priest, Marco Gallipoleo. Godfather: Pietro Giustinian, citizen of Treviso. Names given: Giustina and Bernardina. . . .

As his sacred duty Zaccaria de'Freschi arranged the marriage of Giustina, his second daughter by his wife Dorotea Zaccaria, to the worthy young man Lodovico Bianco, son of the late esteemed Ducal Secretary Pietro Bianco, with a dowry of 1200 gold ducats; as is noted in the marriage compact recorded at the Avogaria di Comun according to the new law on dowries. [Giovanni] Davide de'Freschi [Zaccaria's brother] negotiated the settlement. In the reign of Doge Leonardo Loredan, on Thursday 17 September 1506 at the first hour of the night.

Saturday 25 September 1506. With the bride's house adorned with garlands of flowers, tapestries, and the arms of family and kinsmen, a solemn assembly was held and the marriage was announced. The fifes and trumpets of the Doge sounded forth, with other kinds of instrument. Innumerable eminent patricians, relatives by blood and marriage, and worthy citizens came to pay their respects and to see the bride. Then the bride herself came forth, regally attired, dancing several times with great style, and following her her sister Samaritana, likewise resplendent, who danced with her to great acclaim. Both wore crimson velvet, adorned with chains and necklaces, and golden chaplets set with gems and pearls. Among the distinguished senators present were Pietro Balbi, Alvise da Molin and Alvise Venier, Heads of the Senate; Francesco Foscari, knight, Ducal Councillor; Giorgio Pisani, knight and doctor, and Francesco Bragadin, Savi del Collegio; and Giorgio Emo of the Ten. Welcoming them at the open door of the house were [Giovanni] Davide de'Freschi, [the bride's] uncle; Melchiorre della Nave, Samaritana's husband; and Giovanni Antonio de'Freschi, brother of the bride, dressed in purple with a black velvet sash as is the wont of eminent citizens; but first came the bridegroom, dressed in black for the death of his brother. At the top of the stairs, at the entrance to the hall, Tommaso de'Freschi, uncle [to the bride], likewise dressed in purple, received those who entered. And in the place of honour the father, Zaccaria de'Freschi, remained seated, also dressed in purple, amongst the senators. The gathering continued all day, with greetings, congratulations and embraces exchanged by all.

On Sunday, the following day, was celebrated a gathering of the maids and matrons of the family, including four new brides, dressed in splendid clothes, and they stood in a line of forty to receive the young people, the brides and the matrons who assembled to the tune of fifes and trumpets. For the entire day and much of the night the master of the feast called for ceaseless games and dances, while crowds of nobles, men of note in all fields, kinsmen and in-laws called endlessly to pay their respects. Masked players in various forms and figures performed: mimes, dancers and actors. After a lavish and generous breakfast of sweetmeats there followed a most magnificent banquet, with a succession of dishes served upon silver.

On Wednesday night, which preceded 30 [September], the Feast of St Jerome, the best man Sebastiano Bonamico arranged a concert: at dawn, trumpets, fifes,

horns and other instruments performed numerous and varied melodies in
honour of the bride. As the sun rose, with all in order, at the sixth hour, fifes,
trumpets and other instruments preceded the bride Giustina and her troop of
attendants, both matrons and brides, to Santa Maria Formosa. The bride and
her sister Samaritana wore velvet with wide purple sleeves and an underskirt
likewise of crimson velvet, trimmed with gold and jewels.

At the church was the Doge's son; on his left stood Zaccaria de'Freschi with
Giorgio Corner, knight, brother of the Queen of Cyprus and senator of the first
rank; and the place was thronged with other patricians, and with kinsmen, in-
laws and a whole multitude of plebeians. After a solemn Mass and the blessing
of the ring, the bridegroom took her to wife, attended by the best man
Bonamico. They then returned home in the order in which they had come.
Some of the matrons had stayed at home, for fear of infringing the [sumptuary]
law.

All the family silver was brought out for an excellent, elegant meal. The hall
and the chambers, and even the upper storeys of the house, were filled with the
splendour of our guests. The whole day, until nightfall, was spent in singing and
dancing, and in mimes, music and spectacle. At the second hour of the night,
the bride was led by her kinswomen to the home of her husband, where, after
the usual *bons mots*, a lavish dinner was served, although it was attended by few
from either family.

At daybreak on 1 October, the best man Bonamico offered the bride
sweetmeats of sugar and pine nuts surrounded by gold; hens' eggs; a nymph
moulded in sugar with a flag; a small oblong silver basket, skilfully made; a
needle case, likewise of silver, filled with needles from Damascus; and silver
tongs and a thimble covered in fine filigree work. A party was then held at the
home of the bridegroom, with all the ladies who had attended the day before
and their husbands, and all kinsmen, and relatives by marriage, with a great
many nobles come to see the bride. Luncheon was served to the sound of
trumpets, fifes and other types of instrument, in a most sumptuous and elegant
style, displaying all the silver. Then there was dancing and jests and songs, and
actors performed a comedy, and a large crowd came to see it, and the day was
spent in these amusements, until night came. And gifts were given to the Doge
and friends and relatives: sugar figures and almond cakes infused with sugar
and rose water, sprinkled with gold. . . .

The marriage contract

17 September 1506

In the name of the Holy and Indivisible Trinity, of the Father, the Son and the
Holy Spirit, of the most glorious Mary ever-virgin Mother of God, of the
Blessed Mark, Apostle and Evangelist, and the entire celestial court triumphant.

265

Be it noted that the respected Misser Zacharia di Freschi, secretary of the most illustrious Council of Ten, promises to give his legitimate daughter Madonna Justina as wife to the worthy Misser Lodovico Biancho, legitimate son of the late worthy Misser Piero Biancho, secretary of our most illustrious Signoria: the aforesaid Misser Lodovico Biancho likewise promises to take the aforesaid Madonna Justina as his lawful spouse and wife, as God and Holy Church command. And the two parties have agreed as follows: i.e. that Misser Zacharia di Freschi shall give him in dower and by way of dowry of the aforesaid Madonna Justina 1200 ducats, in this wise: that is, a house built of masonry, with an upper storey, and with an orchard and fields, and a barn built of stone, with a yard, in the village of Sant'Andrà in the district of Treviso, with all of its appurtenances and surroundings, valued at 450 ducats, hitherto owned by the aforesaid [Misser Zacharia]. Item: jewels and pearls to the value of 200 ducats. Item: clothes and other adornments and possessions of the aforesaid lady to the value of 350 ducats. Item: [moneys] in cash or in the bank, 200 ducats. And Misser Lodovico pledges that, having received the dowry, he will draw up a document promising to repay the said sum of 1200 ducats. And thus shall both parties subscribe to the present contract, and I pray Misser Jesus Christ to let them live in happiness, prosperity and joy, and grant them sight of their descendants even unto the third and fourth generation, and at the end the paradise of life eternal. Amen.

I, Zacharia dei Freschi, am content with what is written above, declaring that the estate at Sant'Andrà includes the house built of masonry and the barn and land, fit for occupation, beyond the road, and all lands whatsoever that I possess in the village of Sant'Andrà, which may well amount to 12–13 campi.

I, Lodovico Bianco, son of the late Piero, am content with what is written above.

[An inventory follows, of all items included in the dowry.]   M. N. S.

(b) A merchant's child and his progress, 1509–11
Dalla Santa 1916–17, II, 1574, 1575–6, 1570. The letters are taken from a collection of 'Lettere Commerciali' in the ASV, not further identified.

4 March 1509 [Zuan Francescho's father, Martino Merlini, writes to the boy's uncle Zuan Batista]

Zuan Francescho salutes you heartily. He remembers you, and often at table he says, 'When will my uncle, Meser Zuan Batista, come?' He can say anything, loud and clear, and says, at the correct time, the 'Our Father' and the 'Hail Mary'; it's a pleasure to hear him. He comes out with so many other stories and jokes that it keeps the whole household amused. He's visibly growing: if he lives, please God, he'll be a fine figure of a man. He'll be big and broad, may God make him good! I want to send him to school soon, please God, and I believe he'll learn quickly and well, and have a good mind and a ready tongue.

29 December 1509 [probably from Zuan Batista to Martino]

Zuan Francescho writes to you every day; he has made his cousin Piero prepare for him an inkhorn, complete with ink and pens and paper, and I will send you some of his letters, together with Piero's.

He has become the sweetest and most beautiful little boy you could ever hope to see, and is marvellously intelligent; he picks things up by ear incredibly quickly: he knows the 'Our Father' and the 'Hail Mary', the Creed, the *Salve Regina*, the *Qui abitat* and many other prayers which his mother has already taught him. Come Lent, please God, he will begin to learn to read; he knows the entire alphabet by heart, and so many songs and stories that I can't begin to tell you. He is a champion dancer. Every day as he gets dressed and every evening as he takes off his clothes, as soon as he's down to his doublet he wants to dance; if you could see him, nothing would give you greater pleasure than his dancing and capering; if it weren't for this cursed war and one dared to spend a bit of money, we'd send him for some proper dancing-lessons. He looks so good with his straight little body and his trim, shapely legs that it's a pleasure to see him. Every day he says he wants to come and visit you with Piero, but he wants to bring his nurse with him, as you should know; he tells me he's writing to you to have a robe and doublet of camlet made for him, as you'll see from his letter.

9 March 1511 [Zuan Batista to Martino]

Zuan Francescho has chosen for himself a poor fellow to whom he gives alms every Friday for your sake, and every day he says a lovely prayer to Our Lady for you, and the prayer to St Sebastian to protect you from the plague; and he asks me to tell you this. . . .

[From about the same period; Zuan Batista to Martino]

Could you give me some news as to how you are getting on with your ships? Your son Zuan Francescho prays to God for you every day and gives alms to all the poor that come to the door, and he asks me to write to you about all his doings. He commends his ship to you, and other childish prattle. M. N. S.

(c) The death and burial of a Secretary of the Council of Ten, 1524
DMS, xxxvi, cols 154, 158.

4 April 1524

Note. During the night occurred the death of Gasparo di la Vedoa, Secretary of the Council of Ten. He had a salary of 200 ducats a year and held by official grant eight stalls in the meat market, which he rented out for [. . .]; he also held a tied house near the Ducal Palace. He had been ill and, when he heard that his sons were coming to blows on Easter morning, it was more than he could bear. The great distress of failing of election to the Grand Chancellorship had also brought him low, especially as he had often served as acting Chancellor. He was honourably buried the next day in the church of San Zaccaria in his tomb behind the altar.

5 April 1524

Gasparo di la Vedoa, First Secretary of the Council of Ten, was buried this morning at the ninth hour, in the habit of his Scuola Grande. He was carried from San Giovanni Nuovo through the Piazza San Marco, accompanied by the chapter of his parish, two congregations [of clergy], the two chapters of St Mark's and Castello, and the Jesuati and the mariners, carrying torches weighing [. . .] pounds apiece; and the canopy set up at San Zaccaria was likewise surrounded by huge candles. He was buried at this church in his tomb. He had neither made his confession nor received Holy Communion; nor had he made a will. He left a considerable estate: 14,000 ducats in cash, it is said, and revenue of [. . .]; his annual salary was 200 ducats. He leaves five sons. One, Hironimo, was at the Chancery until he became a priest, whereupon Gasparo kicked him out of the house. It was he who threatened to kill his brother Francesco on Easter morning. Francesco works at the [court of the Giudici di] Proprio; another son [Giovanni], at [the Rason Nuove], offices bought for them by their father. Another son, Jacomo, is secretary to the ambassador at Constantinople, and [Marc'Antonio], the fifth, is also in Constantinople.   M. N. S.

5   THE CITIZENS, THE *POPOLO* AND THE STATE

(a) Nobles and citizens in Venice, 1509
From a letter of Luigi Da Porto, 1 October 1509 (Da Porto ed. Clough 1961, II, 139–46).

It was said that in past days there had been some murmuring by the *popolani*[14] against the nobles, the former complaining that very soon, for reason of war, it would be needful for them to pay many taxes, tenths and other imposts, without participating to any degree in the governing of the state; and so they were saying that these nobles, receiving from the war all the honour and the benefit, should sustain all its expenses. This, however, is not true, while in Venice, as you know, there is no *popolo*[15] as such; apart from a few with long-established citizenship, who indeed hate the nobles, but dare very little, all the rest are such new people [*gente si nuova*] that there are very few of them whose fathers were born in Venice; and they are Slavs, Greeks, Albanians, come in other times to be sailors, or to earn money from the various trades pursued there, the profits of which have been able to keep them [in Venice]. These people are so obsequious towards the nobles that they almost worship them. There are also many people who have come from diverse places for dealing and warehousing, as from Germany and all of Italy, and have thereafter stayed on to make money and been residents a long time; but the majority also have families in their own countries, and many after a little while leave for home, and in their place send others, who care for nothing except making money; and so from them can come no disturbance whatever. And therefore, as the *popolo* referred to is composed of so many elements, I do not think it can ever, no matter how, start a tumult, even though it is large enough to fill or occupy a city as large [as Venice]. It is surely true that, being alarmed by certain murmuring which meant nothing, the terrified nobles were on the verge of conceding nobility to some citizens; but before they came to grant such a thing (which they esteem beyond measure) they wanted to test the mettle of those whom they feared so vainly; and this is the way they did it.

[Informal soundings of public opinion were taken, and eventually Antonio Loredan, a Savio Grande, delivered a harangue to a large number of *popolani* in the Hall of the Great Council, seeking to persuade them that they had a stake in the government and a privileged position in the economy and society of Venice. His speech included the following observations.]

And to start first of all with the benefits: are there not in this city a great many offices yielding most substantial incomes, which through our favour and the disposition of the city pass among you from one heir to the next; whereas among the nobles not one is to be found, however insignificant, which they hold

---

[14] In this text the term *popolani* or *popolari* (literally, 'men of the people') refers to Venetian citizens, or at least to relatively well-to-do persons who might aspire to citizenship, rather than to artisans and lesser people.

[15] That is, no *popolo* in the sense in which the word was used in Da Porto's own city of Vicenza and in other mainland cities of the Venetian dominion. There it meant a body of guild-members that once had had a share in political power, at least during the thirteenth and fourteenth centuries.

beyond the year? Your citizens with these offices very often not only keep themselves and support a great number of children and servants, but also grow rich thereby. We, however, through those which we share among ourselves, more often than not become poor because of the expense of clothes, of grand furniture, of banquet, of games arranged for the populace, of ceremonies and other excessive expenditure, which is presently the practice, and which we, because it is the custom, have to incur. None of these expenses do you have to incur for yourselves, nor is there any evident need for them; instead you simply enjoy your undiminished gains in peace. And so if I should ask you, Venetians, how many are these offices, how much benefit comes from them, how many among you have been enriched by them, I am sure that because there are so many you would not know how to answer without long and mature consideration. For, leaving aside the offices where there is no judicial element, from which you make great gains without care or effort, are there not many others held by clerks who are *popolari* and who stay secure in office as long as they live, while the nobles are changed from year to year? And when the latter have to give judgements and sentences in disputed cases they do not decide otherwise than according to the opinion of the clerks and secretaries, in whose great experience they trust firmly: hence not the nobles but the *popolani* can usually be deemed the effective judges. How many offices of secretary, clerk and notary come to be enjoyed by you, which are better and more profitable than any office in this city granted to us, and to which it would not be unseemly for someone of noble birth to be appointed? Such is the benefit you derive from them! And how many positions are there outside the city, such as that of Grand Chancellor in Cyprus, and others most fitting for any noble to hold, which we leave entirely to you? But, coming to honours, do you not have a Grand Chancellor, who, comparably to our most serene Prince among the nobles, is called 'Doge of the *popolo*', with generous allowances and most ample liberty to enter into any of our councils, to consult, to admonish and to propose, as I and the other nobles have, and almost as the Doge himself has? Are there not, in our most excellent and secret Council of Ten, six secretaries who are *popolari*, whom every man of noble birth acknowledges, whom all respect, and whose high rank all envy? For as the Council changes among the nobles every year, and the secretaries stay for life, it is necessary for the new Council, and for the Heads especially, to acquire from them full information about past events; hence our most secret occurrences are known to them, better than to any noble. How many secretaries with equally solid and secure provision, and with very considerable authority, are there with our exalted Senate, who remain as long as they live, whereas nobles change every year? And the former know the Senate's past and present affairs so much better than even the Senate itself. And, although I pass over a great number of the honours and gains flowing from the state, will you not admit to possessing honours which are very great, and to your surpassing by far all the profit the nobles may derive from the state? Surely you cannot deny this, unless you perhaps want to make yourselves enemies of truth. Will you not rather admit that you have enjoyed all these many benefits without any effort or risk? For they do not interrupt your calm and refreshing sleep, these prickly cares of the state, the need to protect it in one place with the strength of soldiery or walls, in another through simulation or rewards; to quell this enemy by mildness and that one by menaces; to search out the secrets of the world, sending one's mind in an instant to every single part of it. For you, there is never any occasion to fear for your own lives in war, since we alone carry the cares of war, the harvest labours, the bitter captivities, the most cruel deaths, and the endless terrible losses that are the usual lot of the defeated.

G. B., C. H. C.

(b) Maximilian of Habsburg's appeal to the people of Venice, 1511
Bonardi 1915, p. 142.

Maximilian, by the grace of God Emperor elect of the Romans . . .

To each and every one of you, the *populari* of Venice, you alone, our grace and goodwill. Considering the ancient servitude in which you, the Venetian *Populo*, have lived for so long, owing to the insatiable cupidity and avarice of the so-called gentlemen and rulers [*signorezanti*] of the said city of Venice, we have declared that in accordance with our imperial clemency and natural inclination we are prepared to take up arms against the aforesaid rulers in order to free you from this unbearable oppression. Nor will we abandon this resolve until, to your benefit, comfort and profit, we have cast down their excessive pride. Therefore, it seems reasonable that you, the aforesaid *Populo*, recognizing this undertaking of ours as a special favour, should demonstrate your wish that we should set you free, and find ways and means to show that you are truly loyal to us and well deserve what we can bestow. You should bear in mind that, should you not be liberated, their pride and conceit will be such that you and your fortunes will soon be utterly destroyed and ruined by them. But, if you take care to do what we hope you will do, and if the cities, castles and villages now in the possession of those rulers are handed over to us, we promise by this deed to leave you free and unmolested to enjoy, possess and dispose of at your pleasure the houses, palaces, tenths, estates, properties and goods of every kind which in the past you have owned on the mainland. Moreover, we promise to you all the offices, privileges and other benefits, according to our most generous custom, and we promise that in future you will share the government of the city of Venice with the others, and that they will not exclude you from it as they have in the past. As

271

a pledge of this we have had the present letters drawn up, and we send you them sealed with our seal.

Issued at our town of Innsbruck, 1 August 1511. . . .   D. C.

6   SERVICE TO THE STATE

(a) A secretary's career, c.1496–1516

From a petition of Piero Bressan: ASV Consiglio dei Dieci, Parti miste, filza 38 (1516), f. 229r. Undated, but considered by the Ten on 10 January 1517 (ibid., filza 40, f. 159r).

In the name of Jesus Christ. To the most illustrious and most excellent Council of Ten

How excellent and ample are the gratitude and generosity of this well-ordered and vigilant Republic to those who deserve well of her!

All the greater, therefore, most illustrious lords, are the faith and hope extended to this poor, afflicted and loyal supplicant that he may find pity and mercy in his desperate and wretched plight! For, while on state business, he was imprisoned and held to ransom, and since the siege of Brescia he has been sorely vexed and oppressed.

It was, then, the year of Our Lord 1511. The city of Brescia had been breached and entered by the French captain, Monsieur di Foes [de Foix]. The unfortunate Piero Bressan, notary of the Chancery, and faithful servant of the most illustrious Signoria, who was then secretary of the most noble Procurator General[16] [Andrea] Gritti, was imprisoned, robbed, stripped down to his doublet and, in the month of February, thrown into a dungeon, to live on bread and water. Then it happened that the most illustrious Lord Zuan Jacobo Triultio, and the said most noble Gritti, sent the supplicant, whom they had freed upon a bond of 500 crowns, to come before this most illustrious Council to impart the proposal of the late Louis, the Most Christian King of France, for a meeting with the Venetian government; he was then sent back to Milan with the response. They [Gritti and Triultio] dispatched him from Milan to Venice again, as two depositions in his hand in the minutes of this Council of Ten attest. Fate, or possibly the needs of the Republic, ordained – it was never publicly stated – that the said Piero was to return again to Milan. It was at the time when an alliance was being negotiated with the Swiss to drive the French out of Italy. After the French had been forced back beyond the Alps and the most noble Gritti had returned to his homeland, your supplicant was constrained to pay 250 ducats – in other words, to pledge his entire salary for seven years – to the aforesaid Gritti, to his total ruin. As this unhappy man

---

[16] Bressan uses this term again later, but the office is usually called Provveditore Generale.

incurred imprisonment and misfortune in the service of this most illustrious Signoria, at whose behest he was sent to the field, and as the bond of 500 crowns was negotiated in order to send his person to propose the aforesaid meeting, in the interests of the public service, he is confident that the magnanimity of the most illustrious lords will not allow them to abandon him; and all the more because, had he not been set free from the hands of his gaolers and sent back and forth on affairs of state of the utmost importance, in great peril of his life, the government would have lost the great boon of the peace and alliance with the Most Christian King – on account of which all Venetian prisoners were set free without ransom.[17] And, as the poor supplicant has spent his entire youth traversing the farthest parts of the world, in various princely courts, and elsewhere, [attending] several most noble servants of this glorious State, it can well be said that he has been away from this city to one place or another, on the public service, for more than ten years, and has spent another ten years working here in the Chancery – with what diligence is well known, for he has been working day and night, although deprived of any salary whatsoever, for the past two years. Worse still, he is compelled to wait another five years for it, making in all seven years' privation of his means of support, so that, what with the pledge of 250 ducats and the interest on what he will have to borrow to maintain himself, he will incur a loss of well over 400 ducats, an intolerable burden for a man of his limited means. With all humility and due reverence, casting himself at the feet of your illustrious Signoria, he begs you to deign to recall his labours of twenty years, and to provide for his support, granting him for seven terms the first of the following chancellorships to fall vacant – namely, Montagnana, Este or Rovigo – so that I [sic] may rent it out, and with this subvention make good my losses and maintain myself and my poor little family, which has suffered and still suffers in the service of the serene State of your illustrious lordships, without whose gracious clemency there is no hope of relief.

Below is a list of all the places where the aforesaid supplicant has served, and of the most noble representatives of this most serene State whom he has accompanied in the public interest, and first:

> with the fleet at the time of the Turkish War with the most noble commander-in-chief, Don Antonio Grimani, Procurator of St Mark's, as assistant secretary [coadiutor];
>
> in Germany at the court of his Imperial Majesty with the late most noble ambassador, Don Francesco Capello, knight, as secretary;
>
> in Spain at the court of the Catholic King Ferdinand with the most noble ambassador Don Francesco Corner dalla Piscopia, as secretary;

[17] In other words, he now owes Gritti, who posted the bond, a debt that was waived for all the other Venetians imprisoned by the French.

    in Ferrara at the court of the late Duke Ercole with the famous
    ambassadors Don Cabriel Moro, knight, and Don Andrea Foscolo, as
    secretary;

    in the field with the most noble Procurator General Don Domenico
    Contarini, as secretary;

    at Rhodes as envoy to the most reverend Grand Master [of the Knights of
    St John], Fra Fabricio dal Carento;

    in the Ferrarese, sent by the exalted lord Heads of this most illustrious
    Council on matters of state, as a deposition in my hand addressed to this
    Council attests;

    in the field with the most noble Savio di Terra Ferma, Don Giustiniano
    Morosini, as secretary.

Have I not suffered trials, dangers and expense in these services, particularly at
the siege of Padua; at the battle of Brescia, where I was captured; and at three
investments of Verona, at all of which I was serving the state? This I leave to the
judgement of your most wise and illustrious lordships, to whose grace I most
humbly submit and commend myself.   M. N. S.

(b) Election of the Grand Chancellor, 1511

DMS, xii, col. 76.

23 March 1511

After dinner the Great Council assembled, ready for the election of the Grand
Chancellor, and on the stairs there were great numbers of noblemen and
commoners, canvassing for Faxuol. When we met, and those not entitled to stay
had been sent out, there were 1821 of us in Council . . . and the [Ducal]
Councillors chose only three candidates, and Zuam Piero Stella, who wanted to
be nominated, found no one willing to put him up. So the candidates were: first,
Faxuol; secondly, Zuam Jacomo di Michieli; thirdly, Zamberti. After drawing
their names [*butate le tessere*] they were voted upon in that order, and the
successful candidate was Faxuol, on account of his vigorous campaign and
because of the young nobles and the bad ones. But all the true senators and
patricians wanted Zuam Jacomo. Gasparo di la Vedoa deputized as Chancellor
throughout the session, because Zuam Jacomo was not there in person. And the
order of voting and the votes were as follows.

    [Number present] 1821
    Chosen Grand Chancellor of Venice in place of Sier Alvise di Dardani,
      whom God pardon:

	[*For*]	[*Against*]
Alvixe di Zamberti, first notary to the Avogadori di Comun	739	1100
† Dr Francesco Faxuol	1251	595
Zuam Jacomo di Michieli, Secretary to the Council of Ten, who has for many years performed the duties of first chancellor to the Great Council	1075	767

M. N. S.

(c) Losing the post of Grand Chancellor, 1581

From the despatches of Alberto Bolognetti, papal nuncio in Venice 1578–81, ASVat. DN, filza 22, ff. 13v, 30.

January 1581

The honourable Frizier, Grand Chancellor to the government, has passed to higher life, and on Thursday evening they held the funeral in the presence of the Signoria and of the ambassadors, with the customary ceremonial. At the next Great Council tomorrow they will appoint his successor, who, it is thought, must surely be the Secretary Milledonne, a person of great goodness and efficiency, although his rivals are heavily engaged in electioneering [*brogli*]. He too is being forced to take part in such activities, although, on account of a certain gravity and reticence in his character, he has always distanced himself from them – a thing that tells against him with the young men, for they do not see as natural to him his practice of neither greeting others nor returning greetings; rather, they think him haughty and overbearing.

14 January 1581

The result of the Grand Chancellor's election was quite remarkable, not only because Milledonne won fewer votes than did Signor Frumento,[18] and fell behind all but one of the other candidates, but also because the word went round these past few days among the nobility that Milledonne had been wronged. Since almost everybody thought so, he would have gained considerably by his exclusion had he not made a mistake which was judged to be very serious – for he would not go the following morning, as did the other disappointed

[18] According to Sansovino, Frumento – otherwise Giovanni Formento, Secretary to the Council of Ten – had 'carried out more than twenty missions for the Republic' (Sansovino ed. Martinioni 1663, p. 619).

275

candidates, to thank the nobility, according to the custom of the city. None the less, it is said today that the government has granted him an income of 600 ducats by way of consolation.

21 January 1581

After the appointment of the Grand Chancellor their illustrious lordships did not wish to leave unrewarded the many labours of the Secretary Milledonne, and so they decided to allow him to bequeathe to all his heirs [an income of] 500 ducats which he has, [and which is chargeable] to the chancery of Brescia.

In place of Signor Frumento the honourable Missier Francesco Ghirardi has been appointed Secretary to the Council of Ten.   B. P.

7   CITIZENSHIP BY PRIVILEGE

(a) Citizenship at home and abroad, 1552
Decree of the Great Council, 21 August 1552: ASV Maggior Consiglio, Deliberazioni, Liber Rocca (1552–65), ff. 4r–5r.

Our ancestors have always striven to take those measures which have seemed in the circumstances to be most necessary and vital to the well-being of this city, by proposing many deliberations and orders, and especially by giving the benefit of Venetian citizenship to various foreigners, as can clearly be seen by these laws. A reading of them makes it clear that the benefit and privilege of citizenship are extended to those persons who wish to remain in this city and be domiciled permanently herein, together with all their descendants, renouncing allegiance to every other city, with the firm intention of dying and living on through their descendants in this land. To such persons, indeed, should every grace and favour be extended.

However, for some time past many aliens, who do a great deal of business and have become citizens by living in this city for fifteen or sixteen years and making themselves liable to *tansa* for the paltry sum of 3 or 4 ducats, have obtained great tax advantages under this particular privilege. Furthermore, when they have stayed in the city for as long as they wish, and have done business here and enjoyed the aforesaid privileges and amenities and amassed huge sums, they leave Venice as wealthy men and go to live elsewhere, repaying with ingratitude our commonwealth which was so generous in granting them these privileges with the intention that they should establish themselves permanently in the city. Such abuses are quite contrary to the wishes of the Republic and of its well-conceived laws on this matter, which were designed both for these persons' benefit and for the interest and credit of our Republic. In 1534, wishing to curb this malpractice, the Senate resolved that all who desired privileges should be obliged as stated above to establish a permanent residence here. Moreover, such persons would be obliged to present themselves as Venetian citizens in every part of the world, on pain of a fine of 500 ducats to be awarded to the accuser (though no one has so far proved willing to make any such accusation). Since harsher and stricter measures are needed to counter these abuses,

BE IT DETERMINED that from henceforth persons who wish to become citizens of this city at home [de intus] only, by virtue of a privilege, shall not be entitled to do so unless they have first lived here for fifteen consecutive years with the whole of their families, and unless they have paid the city's taxes for fifteen years as do all our other citizens. Those who take a Venetian woman to wife shall not be accepted as citizens at home unless they have lived in Venice for eight consecutive years after their marriages and have for eight years paid the taxes as they should.

Those who wish to become citizens abroad [de extra] must have lived in Venice for twenty-five years and have paid the taxes, as stated above, throughout that period. Be it resolved, also, that they must present themselves as Venetian citizens in every part of the world where they trade, as stipulated in the aforesaid decree of 7 November 1534. When they ask for the aforesaid privileges, they shall be obliged to swear at the office of our Provveditori di Comun a solemn oath that they will observe this decree, and furthermore that at the end of five years they will bring to the said office a certificate from the places where they trade to the effect that they are presenting themselves as Venetian citizens. Should it be discovered and proved that they are doing otherwise, they shall at once forfeit their privilege, and shall be obliged to pay at the rate for foreigners all the duties on the business they have transacted since the privileges were granted [to them]; as is only proper, these duties shall be increased by one quarter, and this quarter shall be assigned to the accuser. Nor may they be granted any privilege at any other time. It is only right that those who want to enjoy this benefit of citizenship should be true and not false citizens. The same provisions shall apply to all who have enjoyed such privileges before the passage of this decree, so that they too shall be obliged to swear an oath at the office of the Provveditori di Comun to the effect that they will present themselves as Venetian citizens in every other place, and will then bring a certificate every five years – otherwise their privileges shall be null and void.

And because there are many persons who under cover of their privileges carry to and from the city various goods belonging to foreigners, passing them off as their own and evading the duties that would be payable on them if they were recognized as the property of foreigners, be it resolved that all persons who are our citizens by virtue of a privilege, and all those who present themselves as such in their business and commercial transactions, and indeed all Venetians, be they nobles or commoners, must, in moving goods in and out of the customs houses and the magistracies where they are cleared, swear an oath to the effect that these goods are truly theirs and on their account. The oath shall be in this form. They shall write with their own hand in a book kept for the purpose, stating, 'I swear on the holy gospels of God that these goods are mine and on my own account', so that by these procedures and measures of ours our government may not be defrauded of revenue. Any clerk who gives clearance without this oath shall lose his post and be banished for ever from this city. The enforcement of this decree shall be entrusted to the three Provveditori sopra i Conti, who must make inquiries and take proceedings against those who have offended against the order concerning the above-mentioned oath, on the understanding that offenders shall immediately forfeit the value of everything they have imported to or exported from this city. This forfeit shall be divided equally between the magistracy of the said Provveditori and the accuser, who shall be kept secret. In no way shall [this decree] detract from the authority of the Avogadori di Comun or of the Provveditori sopra i Datii. The present decree shall not be valid unless it is also passed by the Great Council.

For the decree, 1156; against, 77; uncertain, 24.

On 13 August this was put to the Senate.

For the decree, 174; against, 10; uncertain, 10.   M. C., B. P.

(b) Two citizens of Bergamo seek citizenship of Venice, 1629–30
(i) Petition of the brothers Asperti: from papers in ASV Senato, Terra, filza 312, under the date 9 March 1630.

We, Nicolò and Joseppe Asperti, sons of Simone, citizens of Bergamo, most earnestly desire to serve Your Serenity in all things becoming to loyal subjects, and to be equal to other merchants in this place of business both in our trade and in the profits that it brings, a thing which has not been wholly granted to us by law through the citizenship at home [de intus] only which we have as Bergamasques. We must therefore present ourselves at the feet of Your Serenity and humbly beg you to grant us the benefit of Venetian citizenship at home and abroad [de intus et extra], that we may enjoy all the privileges granted by law to the aforesaid citizens, especially in transacting business as merchants; and, since we have not in the past been unsuccessful in that activity, we hope that, in the future, if we are permitted to trade with the Levant, we shall make larger profits and so enhance the customs revenues and bring prosperity to our own families, and we will always be ready to place our very lives at the service of Your Serenity, to whom we make humble obeisance. We give you thanks.

B. P.

(ii) Report of the Savi alla Mercanzia: in the same place as (i).

We, the Savi alla Mercanzia, have examined the petition laid at the feet of Your Serenity by Nicolò and Gioseppe Asperti, citizens of Bergamo, in which they seek to be made citizens at home and abroad. Since you have instructed us to respond to this petition, we will respectfully remind Your Serenity that it has been established by decree of the most excellent Great Council that this privilege may be granted to those who live in Venice for a spell of twenty-five consecutive years and pay the city's taxes for the same period. As for the period of residence, we see by the testimony of witnesses taken upon oath in the office of the Provveditori di Comun that they know only the aforesaid Nicolò, who has indeed lived for twenty-five consecutive years in this city, although there is no evidence that he has paid any taxes, since no tax estimates have been prepared for this city since 1581. We feel, however, that since Nicolò has fulfilled the requirement of residence he may be granted the privilege which he seeks in the manner set out below, i.e. that their lordships the Dieci Savi sopra le Decime shall be instructed to assess the aforesaid Nicolò Asperti, and he shall make payment of whatever tax is now imposed upon him for each of the last twenty-five years, and he shall continue to pay that tax in future. In this way he shall also meet the obligation to pay the taxes; and this privilege shall not come into effect unless he has brought to our magistracy proof that he has been assessed and has paid everything in full, so that orders may be issued to the customs stations that he is to be treated as a citizen. We give you thanks.

From our office, 27 November 1629

[Signed by four of the five Savi alla Mercanzia, i.e. by Alvise Renier, Lorenzo Contarini, Benedetto Grimani and Zuane Morosini.][19]   B. P.

[19] The Provveditori di Comun concurred with this recommendation in a later report, dated 14 December 1629. On 9 March 1630 the Senate granted citizenship *de intus et de extra* to Nicolò Asperti only, on the conditions suggested by the Savi alla Mercanzia.

CRAFTSMEN, BOATMEN AND PORTERS

*C*RAFTSMEN *or* artigiani *formed the third estate of Venetian lay society. Virtually all of them were members of both an Arte and a Scuola: the Arte consisted of all persons legally entitled to exercise a particular trade, whilst the Scuola was, as always in Venice, a religious brotherhood consisting of persons who came together to honour saints, maintain altars and lights, and assist each other in times of distress. Almost any group of persons could form a Scuola, which helped to establish their identity and give them a focus, and it was natural that people exercising the same trade should do so and be encouraged to do so by the state. In the documents which follow 'Arte' is translated as 'craft' and 'Scuola' given as 'Scuola', although in practice Venetians often used the terms interchangeably. The distinction is particularly important in VI.11, which shows how a group of foreign workers had been allowed to form a separate Scuola of their own for devotional purposes, and how the Scuola was later accused of trespassing on the territory of the Arte, whose business was to regulate the baking-trade. Each Venetian guild was a combination of these two institutions, which, while distinct in principle, generally though not invariably contained the same people. Boatmen of a certain age would, if they were fortunate, belong to an organization known as a* traghetto *or ferry station, some of whose concerns are illustrated in VI.10.*

VI.8–11 record some of the concerns of the craft and the brotherhood: with enforcing their monopoly of the trade and resisting the competition of foreigners and other mavericks not registered on their books; with defining the trade itself; with the regulation of payments for services. Retailers, boatmen, victuallers and porters put in an appearance here. The lengthy description of all the items which the mercers claimed as their own in the mid-fifteenth century [VI.8] provides another demonstration of the variety of goods involved in Venetian commerce and lends authority to Sanudo's declaration [I.1] of the Merceria that 'Here is all the merchandise that one can think of, and whatever one asks for one finds.'

Both VI.11 and VI.12 provide evidence – from unsympathetic observers – of the tension and unrest that arose at intervals in various sectors of the labour force: among the foreign workers in the baking-trade, and among the privileged skilled workers of the great public shipyard, in a year when their standard of living was threatened by inflation and by the government's wish to retrench. At the time of the disturbances in 1581 the Arsenal was probably employing over 2500 workers, or some 2.4 per cent of the total population of Venice (Romano 1968, pp. 75–6). VI.13 affords a glimpse of the Arsenal's low-paid casual labour force, which an enterprising foreman was trying to transform into a body of more highly skilled men; the text shows how the ordinary porters of Venice were compelled to render labour services to the huge industrial concentration so vital to the defence of the Venetian state.

Venetian Arti were not, like those of many late medieval or early modern cities, a means of obtaining representation in the commune or entry to its principal councils. They were subordinated to government magistracies and part of their function was to transmit the state's commands to the labour force. Perhaps their most burdensome responsibility was to guarantee supplies of oarsmen for the reserve fleet of galleys. VI.14 shows how, at the close of the sixteenth century, the system of recruiting a reserve navy, to be called out in time of emergency, was intended to work.

BIBLIOGRAPHY For guilds in general: Lane 1973, pp. 312–20; Rapp 1976; Mackenney 1981, 1984, 1986, 1987. On builders and stonemasons: Sagredo 1856; Pullan 1964; Connell 1988. On shipwrights: Lane 1934, pp. 73–87, and 1965, pp. 67–79; Romano 1968. On boatmen: H. F. Brown 1904, pp. 85–112. On the baking-trade: Aymard 1966, pp. 72–82. On fishermen: Zago 1982. On the reserve fleet: Pullan 1971, pp. 140–56; Lane 1973, pp. 362–9.   B. P.

8 THE CRAFT AND WARES OF THE MERCERS, 1446
From the Mariegola or rule book of the mercers (1471–1787), ff. 1or–14r: ASV Arti, b.312.

XXIII The chapter which establishes the foundations of our trade, and is to be read at every meeting.

We are aware that for some time now many foreigners from various countries haye begun to stock and sell mercery, on the Rialto bridge, on the Piazza San Marco and throughout the city, on stalls, on stands, and on the ground, and from makeshift shops [*botege e postize*], both on holidays and on working days; and because of this our trade of mercery is being destroyed, although mercers pay high rents and heavy imposts, being burdened with large families and bearing the taxes allocated to the city. If no measures are taken, the said mercers, your most loyal citizens, will shortly be ruined.

Item. There has occurred, and continues to occur, the greatest damage to the commonweal because every day these offenders take a substantial amount of mercery from the German exchange house, a little at a time, without paying duty. They may not trade in these wares, because they are foreigners, and are therefore offending against our holy laws. Worse still, we have seen some Germans from the exchange house openly setting up makeshift shops, thus snatching the bread from the mouths of your most loyal citizens. It is necessary and most fitting to make provision against such things. Be it determined that from now on no person, male or female, citizen or foreigner, of any status whatsoever, may sell or cause to be sold any mercery or any item that pertains to it, in any part of Venice, from stands or from stalls, or from the ground, or from makeshift shops, or from the squares, or from the bridges, or from the balconies of closed shops, either on working-days or on holidays; they may do so only from the proper shops, and not from makeshift ones. . . . But we very much wish that, as an act of good faith, all those who keep these makeshift shops should have a period of one month after the confirmation of this decree, within which they may take shops in the Merceria or in other districts of the city, wherever they may please. They must manage these honestly and do what is right and proper in the eyes of God and the world, and we shall accept all of them and love them as brothers, and they may, like each mercer inscribed in our rule book, go to market on Wednesday at San Polo and on Saturday in the Piazza, and, as is customary, remain there until the ninth hour. . . .

Item. There are many tradesmen, such as fustian weavers, apothecaries, goldsmiths, and those in silk and other trades, and fruiterers, and dealers in second-hand clothes throughout the city, who through certain people buy violet silk and have many things made, such as silken and linen thread and cord and fringe and belts of silk and things for the house [soratilli],[20] and display them on balconies and sell them retail and wholesale. This they must not do. If such offenders wish to stock such items and other things which pertain to mercery they should come to our bailiff and his fellow officers and be enrolled. . . .

Mercery, which is understood to include goods which pay duty, and goods which do not, whether they pay more or whether they pay less, and whether they pay on import or on export, may not be stocked unless [the holder] enters the craft [arte], and whoever breaks this rule shall be liable to the said penalty.

Item. Scandals have occurred and continue to do so, and we are ridiculed and scorned by many because our rule book does not specify what is to be understood as mercery. Of these goods there are many types, of which some pay an export tax of 25 per cent, others one of 10 per cent, and yet others one of 5 per cent, whilst some pay nothing at all. No matter how large or small the tax imposed by the government, these are still mercers' wares and must be subject to our rule book.

---

[20] This may be Venetian for *suppeletili*, later defined by Florio 1611 as 'all things moveable in a house, all manner of houshould stuffe, goods or chattel or implements.'

Item. Many trades[men] stock basins and candlesticks and copperware and other articles in brass which pay 10 per cent on export, and the offenders say that these are not mercery, and they allege that mercers' wares pay 5 per cent on export, and this is a source of constant confusion to us.

Item. Many stock breastplates, gloves, harness, and weapons from abroad, such as crossbow strings, winches, wheels for loading crossbows, cord for winches, and many other things which pay 25 per cent on import. Many trades[men] stock such items for sale in their shops and are not members of the craft. These things are not permitted. They allege that they pay 25 per cent on import, whereas mercers' wares pay only 5 per cent; and in this way we are defrauded every day and are in great disarray.

Item. Many have in their possession mercers' wares made in Venice and outside it which pay nothing on export: for example, sickles, Flanders pewter which comes with the galleys, and many other items which pay high duty on import and on export absolutely nothing. Such offenders as these, with whom we struggle every day, offer the excuse that these are not mercers' wares, and do not pay export duty as such. Yet they are mercers' wares.

Item. For some time now many foreigners have been arriving, Flemings, Frenchmen, Germans, Italians, and men of other nations, and they are still arriving every day. They have settled here, and they make girdles, big bags, woollen and straw hats, wallets, playing-cards, caps, and dyed skins for girdles and bags. For these activities and many others they ought to join our Scuola. That all may be regulated and scandal be avoided, be it understood that all persons, Venetians or outsiders, male or female, of whatsoever status, who produce or cause to be produced, or sell or cause to be sold in their shops, articles which appertain to mercery shall be subject to our rule book and obliged to join the craft, and offenders shall be liable to the said penalty.

Item. Because in the Merceria, and at San Polo, and in many other parts of the city, there are men who employ their mothers or wives in their shops, and they themselves are there too, but do not pay dues to the Scuola, and because of this many men out of their own malice and meanness enrol [only] the said women and the women are held responsible for everything, be it understood that from now on no one may under such cover or fraud refuse to join the Scuola. These people must do so, and pay dues like everyone else, and those who offend are liable to the said penalty. Moreover, we ordain that, if the said women wish to join the Scuola for their devotions, we shall be obliged to accept and enrol them like the other women mercers who are established in the various districts of the city and who go to market at San Marco and San Polo and to the fairs. All these women shall be subject to our rule book and shall pay their dues as is customary.

Item. Be it understood that all mercers' wares which come into the German exchange house shall be subject to our trade, and that our mercers may freely stock and sell these goods, such as basins and other brassware, iron and tin, locks, mirrors, mirror glass, caps, gloves of wool or hide, cups, bales of cloth [*torselli*].[21] shears, scissors, jugs, Paternoster beads, hats, spectacles, *pexii da ducatio* [?], razors, axes, belts, combs of horn or wood, cushions, serges, coarse cloth, and every other kind of mercery, even though it be not named: everything shall be regarded as subject to our trade.

Item. All mercers' wares which come from Milan and other parts of Lombardy shall likewise be subject to our trade, whether they pay duty or not, and whether they pay much or little, either on import or on export. All these things shall be subject to our rule book. The same shall apply to all mercers' wares that come from Florence and other parts of Tuscany, such as tinsel, half-gilded bridal chests, bone mirrors, bone chests for brides, balls, finely wrought brushes [*sedole lavorade*], counting-tables, pruning-knives, and many other wares. None of these goods from Tuscany pays anything on import, save for a royalty of 9 grossi once a year; some pay 10 per cent on export, and some 5 per cent, some more and some less.

Item. Be it understood that all knives which come from Bologna, the Romagna, Modena, Ferrara, and any other place, are subject to our mercers' trade. Such cutlery pays no duty on entry, apart from a royalty of 9 grossi, as is the custom.

Item. It is our wish that all other mercers' wares made in Venice or outside Venice be subject to our craft, i.e. combs of ivory, felt caps of all kinds and felts for making caps, cotton and silk veils, spools, weaver's paste, handkerchiefs (whether worked in silk or not), fans, veils, coifs, vestments, gold from Cologne, pewter which comes with the Flanders galleys or into the German exchange house, cushions made of chequered cloth and of tapestry, and pouches. Be it understood that all the aforesaid items, whether mentioned specifically or not, being articles which mercers have been accustomed to stock, shall all be subject to our rule book. . . .

Item. We have at chapter XXI a decree to the effect that the lords of the Giustizia [Vecchia] are free to issue licences to pedlars who carry mercery, entitling them to sell in the city goods up to the value of 40 soldi. The said decree is to remain in force, with an additional clause to prevent trickery, because under cover of the said 40 soldi they carry – whether openly or secretly – goods of much greater value. This does much damage to the mercers, male and female, who keep shops throughout the city, and so the intention of the government's decree is not fulfilled. From henceforth all the officials of the Giustizia Vecchia, acting alone or in company, shall be charged with investigating offenders of this sort and searching all the mercery they have on

---

[21] Edler 1934 defines *torsello* as 'a long flat bale (something like the torso of a statue in shape, covered with felt, canvas, etc.; usually transported by a pack animal; used especially for shipping all kinds of cloth).'

them or in their sacks, whether openly displayed or hidden. Those found to have goods to a value of more than 40 soldi shall be liable to the said penalty. . . . The bailiff and his fellow officers, acting alone or in company, may likewise search and fine the said pedlars.

On 20 May 1446 the said decree was passed by the bailiff, Messer Nani di Piero dala Colona, and his fellow officers by vote and ballot, and all were in favour, and it was passed.

On 23 May 1446 the said decree was passed in our chapter, there being fifty-three persons present. Fifty-one voted in favour and two against, in the church of San Giuliano.   R. M.

9   CHARITY, RITUAL AND WORK: THE CHARCOAL-BEARERS, 1479
From the Mariegola or rule book of the charcoal-bearers (1479–1781): ASV Arti, Carboneri, b.61.

XVII   Item. We wish and ordain that, should any of our porters be ill and unable to work, the said porters shall be obliged to give him as alms 20 soldi every Saturday, the money to be taken from their earnings.

XVIII   Item. We decree and ordain that when we wish to receive a new member [*Compagno*] into the said Scuola the bailiff shall take our cross in his hand, and go before our altar with the man who wishes to join, and kneel with the new member and make him kiss the cross so that God may receive him into the benefits of eternal life.

XIX   Item. . . . . [that at a funeral of one of our members] the bailiff must go before all others, and all members shall be obliged to honour him, and when the said bailiff enters or goes into the church he shall be obliged when he is with the members [to take] some holy water, and if the said bailiff fails to observe the above order and to carry out his duties he must pay [a fine of] 4 soldi for each offence, and this money shall be placed in the Scuola's coffers for its benefit.

XX   Item. Be it enacted and ordained that no porter may carry any basket of charcoal to the smiths in the parishes of San Salvatore and San Luca for [a payment of] less than 16 denari per basket; and whoever carries [charcoal] from the Ponte delle Ancore up to the Ponte dei Dadi must be paid 2 soldi [per basket] by the smiths; and the same shall be paid by the smiths at San Giuliano, San Lio and Santa Maria Formosa, on this side of the bridge of Calle Garufa; and whoever carries [charcoal] beyond the said bridge must be paid 3 soldi per basket on each occasion; and whoever goes beyond the stone Ponte dei Fuseri down to the Ponte di San Moisè must be paid 2 soldi per basket; and whoever goes beyond the stone bridges of San Fantin and San Moisè must be paid 3 soldi for each basket, which, as everybody knows, has always been the custom. If anyone takes more he shall pay a penalty of 10 soldi to our Scuola.   R. M.

10   THE BOATMEN OF SAN TOMÀ

From the statutes of the ferry station at San Tomà on the Grand Canal, fifteenth century to 1539: Sydney Jones University Library of Liverpool, Mayer ms. 20.9.83.37.

[From the first statutes, which seem to be prior to 1487]

First of all, no one seeking to join our ferry [*trageto*] may be received into it unless he is at least forty years of age, according to the law made for this station [*postegio*]. Each entrant must pay an entry fee of 1½ ducats, together with a yearly subscription [*luminarie*, literally 'light-moneys'] of 36 soldi. This must be collected [in instalments] every four months, and the bailiff and his fellow officers may not receive anyone into the Scuola in violation of this order, and if they do admit anyone below the age of forty they shall themselves be expelled from the ferry. . . .

III   Furthermore, it is our wish that no boatman of our ferry who undertakes to teach a boy to row a boat may charge a fee of more than 1 ducat, and that he who teaches the boy must give our Scuola the sum of 40 soldi, as is the custom. . . .

V   The boatman of the ferry stations of this city are guilty of a grave abuse, in that they are so presumptuous and evil-minded as to keep people in their boats for longer than they ought, and out of their greed for more passengers they make trouble for everyone. Measures must be taken to prevent this. It is our will that from henceforth, as soon as one of the boatmen of our ferry has two people in his boat, he must immediately cross over to the other side; if in the meantime other persons have arrived, he may take up to six passengers, but he must not delay in such a way as to cause inconvenience. . . .

[From enactments approved by the Provveditori di Comun in 1507]

XVIII   Furthermore, be it declared that from henceforth the boatmen of the ferry station shall not be permitted to take more than four passengers when it is their turn at the ferry, and if they have accepted more than four they must immediately surrender the additional passengers to the boatman whose turn comes next. . . .

XXVI   *23 August 1511*   Since we ought to do something for our poor brothers who fall sick and suffer greatly because they cannot work and cannot row their boats, and we ought to provide for their needs,

BE IT DETERMINED, as proposed by Agustin Zenovese, bailiff of the ferry of San Tomà, and by Zuane of Bergamo and Simon of Brescia, his fellow officers, that from henceforth, when any of our brothers falls ill and cannot row his boat, the sick man shall, after four days of not being able to come and row, be entitled to send a man with his boat to the ferry until such time as he is cured of his illness, so that he can continue to work at the ferry. . . .

XXIX   *2 July 1519*   In view of what St Matthew says in his tenth chapter, 'Love your brothers that you may be saved',[22] and that love, charity and freedom may, with the help of Jesus Christ, remain among us brothers, not only in life but also at our passing and after death,

BE IT DETERMINED that, as I, Philippo of Legnago and my fellow officers propose, from henceforth each one of us, when we come to the end of our lives, may have freedom to give up his [place in] the ferry to another person, on condition that he who surrenders his place must leave half a ducat if he wishes to be buried by our Scuola; otherwise we shall have no obligation to bury him.

And the vote was as follows:

Those in favour, 21; those against, 3

and it was accepted.

4 March 1536   Simon of Brescia, boatman at the ferry of San Tomà, appeared in the office before the lords Marco Basadona and Piero Bollani, honourable Provveditori di Comun, in the absence of their third colleague, the Lord Dolphin, and begged their lordships that he, being aged and feeble, might rent out his place, as has been permitted to others by their lordships in similar circumstances. They have been informed, also, that the said Simon has promised in the chapter of the boatmen not to work any longer at the ferry, and that the said chapter voted by ballot to accept his undertaking and promise, as witness the paper now produced in the office by Ser Filipo of Legnago, bailiff of the ferry. Hence their lordships . . . have granted permission to the said Simon to rent out his place [*libertà*] in the ferry to some person who shall be skilful and competent.   C. H. C., B. P.

I I   THE CRAFT AND THE BROTHERHOOD: MASTER BAKERS AND GERMAN ASSISTANTS, 1543

From the Mariegola or rule book of the bakers (Simonsfeld 1887, II, 338–40).

19 September 1543. Against the evil-doers

On 13 July 1422 their honourable lordships the Heads of the Council of Ten granted to the German assistants authority to form a brotherhood for the sole

---

[22] This may in fact be an allusion to 1 John 2:10 or 1 Peter 2:17.

purposes of looking after their souls and of correcting the errors to which they are prone. But they have arrogantly presumed to take over the brotherhood and Scuola of the craft of bakers. Imitating the Lutherans, and rejoicing in having thrown into confusion what used to be the most Christian country of Germany and converted it to their own superior faith, they are now striving to ruin the craft of bakers [in Venice] – although the grant was made by the Heads to the bakers with an express declaration from the Council of Ten to the effect that these assistants were not to impede the bakers' craft, but rather to obey its bailiff.

So presumptuous are these scoundrels that they pay no heed either to this document or to the regulations issued at various times by the Provveditori alle Biave, as the representatives of this august state, upon stringent penalties. They have gone so far as to elect their own bailiff, with assistants and other functionaries, to assemble and conspire together. Hence, when the bailiffs of the bakers have to assemble on the orders of the Provveditori to take the necessary steps for the nourishment of the city by making bread for the people, and to make regulations for their trade, these rogues flock to their own officers and violently disturb the brotherhood of bakers assembled to benefit and regulate their trade. They condemn those masters who have reproved them for not working as they should, although they have made agreements with them according to the regulations of the craft approved by its officers. You may see these presumptuous creatures wearing weapons to work, as if they were going to do battle in their masters' houses to make themselves feared. They have attacked their masters in their own homes and bakeries, and at San Barnabà they have even murdered them and caused their deaths, and they have beaten and injured the poor widows who are mistresses of bakeries, even in their own homes, as witness the complaints to the Provveditori alle Biave and other magistracies. Your worships may obtain further information from Messer Giacomo Ronco, baker in Cannaregio, who was attacked by these knaves. They abandon their work, leaving the flour and paste in the kneading-troughs, and they loiter as long as they like at inns and saloons and other places, and they get together in various parts of Venice to the utter undoing of the bakers, and they distribute the assistants among the shops after their own fashion, assigning them whatever numbers they choose – otherwise they will not work, and threaten the bakers.

Finally, they have met in the Scuola of the bakers, and have arrogantly elected their own body of officers in violation of the orders that they may not hold a meeting without the permission of the bailiffs of the bakers or upon some other authority. Fearful of these things, Master Zuanne de Battista, baker at San Luca and bailiff of the bakers, together with the whole company of the bakers' craft, has applied to the Heads of the Ten, begging their excellencies to take measures against this appalling and misguided behaviour, which could well inflict further damage upon the bakers and the city, and to give the bailiff permission to assemble the ordinary chapter of the craft, to take measures in accordance with the regulations approved by the Heads of the Ten and by the Provveditori alle Biave. . . .

BE IT [THEREFORE] DETERMINED that the officers of the Scuola of assistants, together with the persons named below, shall each be fined 100 ducats and deprived for ever of any titles they may have and of their positions as officers, and they shall be expelled from the bakers' craft of Venice as trouble-makers and leaders of a conspiracy [*seduttori et capi setta*]. . . . The assistants shall never again be permitted to assemble in the said Scuola or in any other place to conspire in such a manner; but, like all others who wish to be bakers' journeymen [*lavoranti*], they must henceforth enrol in the Scuola of the bakers, and obey the said bailiff in all matters concerning the trade, and also concerning the care of souls, according to the decree of the Heads of the Ten in favour of the bakers (which has now been confirmed), so that it shall still be regarded as one single Scuola and all others shall be dissolved, upon the orders of the Heads of the Ten, with special provisions against these other offenders.

On 19 September 1543 the above proposal was put to the vote in the presence of me, Agostino Sanson [clerk to the Provveditori alle Biave]; there were fourteen votes in its favour and one against, and the decree was passed.

[There follows a list of sixteen names of persons who are to be expelled in accordance with the decree.] B. P.

12 THE PROTEST OF THE ARSENAL CRAFTSMEN, 1581

(i) Alvise Michiel, *Memorie pubbliche della Repubblica di Venezia*: BMV ms. Ital., cl. VII, 811 (7299), f. 175v, 27 November 1581.

There was a strange incident, in that the Council of Ten had given orders that the Arsenal craftsmen should not be registered that day, and all the said mariners went to protest to the Collegio and complain at the news, for they said that amid this terrible dearth they had no way to earn a living, and their situation seemed most hard. The Doge [Nicolò da Ponte] answered them with scant courtesy, so when they left the Collegio one of them, whose name was Bongerolamo, shouted, 'There is nothing for it, brothers, but to go and plunder the public granary.' At these words they all made for the storehouse at St Mark's and began to rob it of flour with great force and fury, shouting down those who tried to dissuade them, so that some 120 staia of flour were borne away to Castello. The Heads of the Ten and the Avogadori [di Comun] sent at once to arrest them and began to prepare charges. Bongerolamo was arrested, and another man escaped from the hands of Tibio, the constable of the Heads of the Ten, whom the Heads afterwards deprived of his post. Two boatmen and two others were also seized, and other persons were proclaimed, and every effort was made to take them. The Avogador Miani and Ser Luca Michiel, one of the Heads of the Ten, then went to the Arsenal itself, for there were reports of disturbances there. But in fact they found nothing.

On Wednesday morning Bongerolamo was hanged. That evening the sailors' brotherhood [*Scuola delli Marineri*] wanted to come and give him honourable burial. But they were forbidden to do so by the Heads of the Council of Ten, on pain of the gallows. The following day they hanged a caulker and condemned five people to the galleys, sentencing the boatmen to ten years therein.   B. P.

(ii) From a despatch of the papal nuncio Lorenzo Campeggio, 2 December 1581: ASVat. DN, filza 22, f. 349r–v.

This week there was some turmoil among the Arsenal craftsmen on account of the present dearth, and the consequences might have been serious had not severe punishments been promptly imposed. This was what happened. The government was once accustomed to employ all the craftsmen of the Arsenal for the entire week. But then, in order to cut down the high expenditure, they reduced the work to a mere four days in every week – although the pay was so good that the workmen could live off it in years of plenty without having to take other jobs as well. But they cannot do this now that because of shortages the price of flour has risen to 3 golden crowns per staio. On Monday morning more than 200 of them assembled and went to the Collegio, where they urged the Doge to provide for their needs, using haughty and disrespectful language, better suited to a protest than a petition. Furthermore, as soon as they emerged from the Collegio some of them went straight to the public flour stores, from which they forcibly removed some 20 staia of flour which were kept there in sacks. The Senate at once gave orders that the ringleaders should be arrested, and that evening their spokesman in the Collegio was taken, and during the night another of their leaders was brought in. This man was hanged the following morning, and the speaker on Wednesday. Others who had been proclaimed came and presented themselves, but it is thought that now the frenzy has passed they will not proceed against them so harshly. . . .

On Thursday members of the Collegio went together to visit the Arsenal, and were said to be doing so by order of the Senate on account of certain sites which had to be prepared for the construction of new galleys. Some, however, said that the visit was on account of the incident described above, reasoning that, since the Arsenal was in the hands of its craftsmen, the Collegio had thought it necessary to take a good look at certain things, and also to pacify those people by putting on this show.   B. P.

13   THE PORTERS AT THE ARSENAL, 1586-8

(i) From a petition of Gasparo di Lorenzo, one of the *capi di bastasi* or foremen porters of the Arsenal, on behalf of Zuanne Vernazza and Antonio di Maffio dall'Oglio as well as himself: ASV Senato, Terra, filza 96, 23 January 1585 Venetian style.

I, Gasparo, foreman of the porters of your house [of the Arsenal], have proposed in my petition to Your Serenity that I should supply the Arsenal with porters, on the understanding that I receive from each porter the sum of 1 lira per month. This will enable me and my colleagues to rectify the disorders and improve the poor services from which the Arsenal is now suffering. Where force is used, goodwill cannot prevail; and, without goodwill, good work comes to an end.

Every porter is now ordered to serve at the Arsenal for two weeks in every month, or at least for three weeks in every two months, except for those who happen to be passed over, as the world pleases and their own good fortune decrees. This obligation bears little relation to the pay they receive from the Arsenal, and is exacted in a great many different ways, as you in your wisdom may reflect, though modesty forbids me to mention them all. Men are now pressed into service at the cost of much time and personal effort, since the transmission of orders involves so many foremen and so many bits of paper. But if my proposals were adopted the porters would be ready and eager to serve you in response to one single command, and there would be no loss of time or money or both together, as now befalls those who are ordered on Monday to serve for the whole of the week. For, if the Arsenal needs 100 men, they allow for some defaulters, and to be sure of getting the quota they summon 130 men and later dismiss those who are superfluous, so that, as it were, these men lose the day. But with my method there would be an end to those stresses and losses which porters at present suffer in several ways, for they vie with one another to be among those who are dismissed, preferring to lose a day and incur some other expense rather than to serve a whole week for so small a wage.[23]

At present the porters are raw and inexperienced; they waste much time and treat the materials badly, being clumsy and unwilling in the way they handle them. But if my offer is accepted they will all be strong, skilful and willing men,

---

[23] At this time the 'summer' wage (from March to August) paid by the Arsenal to those classified as porters [*fachini*] was 13 soldi a day, while those called labourers [*manoali*] received 10 soldi a day. In 'winter', from September to February, the rates were 10 soldi for porters and 8 for labourers. These compared poorly with, say, the daily wages of builders' journeymen [*lavoranti*], who averaged about 27 soldi for each day worked over the whole year during the 1580s (Pullan, 1964).

picked and trained in a very short time through constant practice at these jobs. There is no doubt that some show greater strength and skill in lifting oil or stone, whilst others are used only to handling planks or boards, and are best at working with timber. Where men are used to working in the Arsenal, a few can take the place of many, with a saving, I believe, of at least a third. Expenditure will be reduced, materials will be conserved, the hemp will be used sparingly, the tools will be kept in order, and at least twenty-four carpenters, who now have to hang about waiting for the porters, will be put to work. These porters will get to know the names of places and the properties of the woods used, and how best to turn, pull, carry and erect them. The same will apply to the gun foundries, and to many other such jobs that have to be done in the Arsenal. The city will be better served, because, since people are now burdened in so many ways, they have to help themselves somehow, and if there are plenty of porters available in the public squares they will have to serve in competition with each other for a bargain price. This measure will please them greatly, and since it will eliminate the trickery of those who make such gains [from the present arrangements] everyone, as they will tell you in the public places, will pray to God for it, with the exception of more than eighty bosses, and those who are now exempt and who came to the Collegio. And, indeed, it seems only reasonable.

We shall not call on the services of or require anything from those who are too young or too feeble to work in the Arsenal, and the paymaster [*patrone che sera alla. cassa*] shall identify such people. [We shall call on] others only when they are in Venice, and not during the months of the year when they are staying at home (for that time, and that alone, they shall be free). My colleagues and I are happy that they should either pay the lira per month, or (if they do not wish to pay it) work in the Arsenal for one week a month only at the ordinary rate of pay. These regulations can easily be issued by the most noble Provveditori and Patroni of the Arsenal, who are very experienced in this business, and all the troubles will cease.

May God inspire you to do what is best for this most serene Dominion, to which I make humble obeisance.[24]   B. P.

(ii) From a petition by Antonio dall'Oglio, one of Gasparo's associates: ASV Senato, Terra, filza 106, 28 April 1588.

[The arrangement proposed by Gasparo had worked satisfactorily during the year 1586] but in this year that followed, 1587, things went quite the other way,

[24] On 23 January 1586 the Senate accepted Gasparo's proposal for a trial period of two years, to begin on 1 March next.

because Gasparo failed to observe that excellent rule of retaining only experienced porters who understood the principles of the work, so that the craftsmen would find on returning from dinner that the ribs and other timbers had already been positioned by the porters, and none of the carpenters had to waste time giving the porters instructions. As soon as Gasparo, overcome by greed, broke this excellent rule, and took on raw and useless men (such as wool-workers and silk-spinners) in order to hire them more cheaply, those directing the work had to assign a carpenter to give orders to these untrained men, with the result that twenty-eight to thirty carpenters, who ought to have been doing their proper jobs, were instead being delayed by inexperienced porters. He also took on large numbers of boys to serve as porters.[25]   B. P.

14   CRAFTSMEN AS OARSMEN: MANNING THE RESERVE FLEET, 1595
From a Senate decree of 25 November 1595: ASV Senato, Mar, reg. 55, ff. 203r–205r; a printed copy may be found in ASV Arti, b.314 (Marzeri, Capitoli e Parti 1508–1608).

So great were the expenses incurred by the crafts of this city last year when some galleys were made ready for service, and so serious were the problems, that the prompt action which was necessary to obtaining galleymen was impeded. So, to set such important matters right in future, three Presidents of the Collegio della Militia da Mare were, by a decree of this Council of 20 October 1594, charged with compiling a roll of the men aged eighteen and above in every craft, trade and ferry station of every sort, and in all the fraternities and Scuole, in the city and in the Dogado, upon those conditions and with those powers which are set out in detail in that decree. The Presidents have now compiled this new roll in full, acting personally and with great speed, and taking note of 23,000 persons – a thing which had not been done since 1539, with notable disservice to the public weal. . . .

BE IT THEREFORE DETERMINED that, since we must have 160 galleymen from the people of the city and Dogado ready for each of the fifty galleys as soon as possible, a total of 8000 men (for all that number is necessary), and, since we must have a further 1000 in reserve, so that those to be enrolled rise to the number of 9000, the Presidents of the Collegio della Militia da Mare shall be empowered to include each and every craft and trade, and all ferrymen and watermen, and all fraternities and all the Scuole Grandi and Scuole Piccole.

[25] On 28 April 1588 the Senate, on the recommendation of the Provveditori and Patroni all'Arsenal, determined that the contract to provide Arsenal porters should be put up for auction, and awarded to the man who offered to impose the lowest monthly tax on the porters of Venice who would not be working at the Arsenal. The contractor was to draw exclusively on a picked labour force of 300 men, to be chosen by the Arsenal administration.

They must then take account of the number of persons in each craft, and of the nature of the trades, and of the obligations which each craft has hitherto had in this matter, and must divide and allocate the number of 9000 men at the rate of so many per Scuola, craft and ferry station, in such a way that each bailiff knows how many men have been apportioned to him. Once this has been determined, in the shortest possible time, let the Presidents summon before them individually each bailiff or head of each craft or Scuola (whatever his title may be), and give him a note of the exact number of men which his Scuola or craft is due to send to the fleet. They must explain to him that, if the craftsmen themselves wish to choose men by lottery, or wish in some other way (for example, by offering the reward of a mastership) to find volunteers who are enrolled in the craft, and then maintain that number even in the event of death or other accident, they must within the next month present them to be enrolled by the clerk to the said magistracy. He shall note down their names, surnames, fathers and places of origin, and their complexions and distinguishing marks, in a special book, of which the craft itself must have a copy, so that whenever the need arises they may be found ready without any difficulty, and so that substitutes may be found for those who, as has been said, are removed by death or other unavoidable accident. After the month has passed, if they do not wish or cannot of themselves make the aforementioned contribution, it shall then be for the Presidents, with the bailiffs or otherwise designated heads present, to have lots drawn without further delay amongst all members of the craft who are between the ages of eighteen and forty-five and therefore fit for galley service. They shall follow the same procedure in each Scuola, taking each one separately. Those whose names are drawn shall be enrolled by the clerk of the Militia, as stated above, in a special book, a copy of which shall likewise be kept by the Scuola or craft; and [the names of] those who remain after lots are drawn shall be kept in a special purse under two keys, one of which shall be given to one of the Provveditori sopra l'Armare, while the other remains with one of the Presidents of the aforesaid Collegio della Militia, and they must make diligent inquiries concerning those who drop out at any time; and when the truth has been established other names shall be drawn, one by one, from that purse and enrolled as stated above. The bailiffs or otherwise designated heads of the craft, fraternity or Scuola must notify the same magistracy of any case of death or absence, so that within eight days another name may be drawn to replace whoever has died or fled. They must likewise go and add to the purse the name of any new member of the Scuola, whenever it is necessary, on pain of 10 ducats for each offence, to be added to the fund for galleymen.   R. M.

Part VII
Charity and the Poor

*I*N ALL PROBABILITY *at least two thirds of the population of Venice lacked reserves or savings and risked becoming, at some point in their lives, dependent on charity – on the tiny donations of casual almsgivers, on the ampler bounty of institutions, or on parish relief. Densely populated by widows and young children, the ranks of the poor were swelled by unfortunate persons from every social order. VII.1 and 2 are factual descriptions by foreign observers of the more systematic charities that served the Venetians about 1500, especially religious brotherhoods and hospitals – a term that included places of shelter and elementary education as well as establishments for the care of the sick. The varied functions of the great fraternities called the Scuole Grandi, and the tensions created by the rival demands of charity, ceremony and display, have already been described [V.12 and 13]; here Battista Sfondrato, the Milanese envoy, concentrates on their methods of relieving the poverty of their less fortunate members. VII.3 gives the text of the comprehensive poor law of 1529, the Venetian contribution to the many schemes that were being devised between about 1520 and 1560, in most parts of Western Europe and especially by cities, to assist the deserving poor and expel or punish the fraudulent. This law established, in broad outline, the state's official approach to poor relief and its official classifications of the poor for the remainder of the sixteenth century; it attempted to establish a system of 'voluntary' parochial relief to supplement the efforts of charitable brotherhoods and hospitals, and to introduce one of forced labour for the idle and fraudulent poor.*

VII.4–7 record details of the aims, educational activities, administration, fund-raising devices and financial problems of some of Venice's principal hospitals. VII.7, in particular, attempts to establish the division of labour between them. All the great hospitals, other than the Pietà, were sixteenth-century foundations, established in response to particular crises: the Incurabili to the syphilis epidemic of the Italian wars, Santi Giovanni e Paolo to the great famines of the late 1520s, the Mendicanti to those of the early 1590s. These documents reflect, especially, the problems of the chronically sick and infectious, of the very young, and of the aged, the homeless and the feeble-minded. Concerned both with the care of sickness and with the protection and education of children, hospitals were managed by congregations of governors, laymen of high social standing [VII.5(b)], to whom their officials were made responsible. There was a

297

difference in principle between the foundlings of the Pietà (whether bastards or not), who had been abandoned by a living parent or parents out of shame or poverty, and the orphans of Santi Giovanni e Paolo, who were in principle children of legitimate birth, separated from parents by death. By the eighteenth century the children of the Pietà, the Incurabili, Santi Giovanni e Paolo and the Mendicanti were all more famous for their splendid choirs and orchestras than for the more mundane forms of manual labour for which [VII.6] most of their children had been trained. VII.6(c), from the 1570s, offers a small early hint of the importance of singing.

VII.8–10 are concerned not with the inmates of institutions, but with the much larger body of the house poor of Venice: those who clung precariously to their own lodgings in imminent danger of eviction for arrears of rent, or in hopeless embarrassment when called upon to produce a lump sum to endow a nubile daughter who might otherwise go to the bad. These were the 'shamefaced poor' or poveri vergognosi *of Venice, ranging from the abject decayed nobles described above by Bedmar [VI.3] to respectable shopkeepers or craftsmen fallen on hard times and to their widows and children. They shrank from openly begging on bridges or in churches, but were often found [VII.9] pleading for assistance from the officers of their religious brotherhoods in the formal language of a petitioner – doubtless with assistance from a clerk or notary who knew the form. All the Scuole Grandi [VII.8 and 9] assisted the 'shamefaced poor' among their own members, but a society which concentrated on outsiders, the Fraternity of Sant'Antonino, was established in 1537. Unlike the Scuole Grandi, it was solely concerned with poor relief, upholding the laws against begging by seeking to make begging unnecessary. Its activities at the close of the sixteenth century are described in VII.10.*

BIBLIOGRAPHY   In general: Pullan 1971, 1978, 1988b; Mueller 1972; Semi 1983; Vanzan-Marchini 1985; Aikema and Meijers 1989. On the Pietà: Cecchetti 1885. On orphans: Arte 1978; Constable 1988. On almshouses and the housing of the poor, Pavanini 1981; Gianighian and Pavanini 1984; Concina 1989, pp. 73–104. For studies of religious brotherhoods see the bibliography preceding V.11.   B. P.

THE GENERAL SITUATION

I   THE CHARITIES OF VENICE, 1497

Letter of Battista Sfondrato, Milanese ambassador in Venice, to Ludovico Sforza, Duke of Milan, 23 March 1497: Archivio di Stato Milan, Archivio ducale Visconteo-Sforzesco, Carteggio, Potenze Estere, Venezia, cart. 1062, ff. 89–92 (letter as sent), 188–9 (rough draft).

My Most Illustrious and Excellent Lord,

You wrote to me recently, asking me to inform you whether in this city [of Venice] there are charitable institutions such as hospitals, confraternities [*schole*] and the like, as there are in Milan, and to write to you concerning their quantity and quality and how they spend their incomes. I have applied myself diligently to meeting your request; although it is difficult to understand the situation in detail, I shall not fail to describe it in those general terms which are really almost all that we can know and understand.

In this city there is no famous hospital like that of Milan, but only a few years ago a hospital was begun whose founder was Fra Michele da Carcano. This will be quite beautiful when it is finished; but so far only one section has been furnished, and the rest is incomplete. It has as yet no income whatsoever, and hence it is not used except to provide a room to the occasional person of status who falls upon hard times. I believe, however, that, with the alms they will collect annually as a result of the indulgence which has been granted them, the institution can be turned into an honourable one.[1]

The best things that Venice has, then, are four famous Scuole Grandi belonging to confraternities or companies of flagellants, such as there are in Milan. In Venice they go in procession, clad in a gown of white wool and with a hood in the manner of a friar; on their breasts is a red symbol which distinguishes one Scuola from another, while each Scuola, especially of the four principal ones, also carries candles of a different colour.[2] They are entitled as

---

[1] The hospital of Gesù Cristo di Sant'Antonio.

[2] This sentence appears only in the draft reply, and not in the final version.

4   Gentile Bellini, *The Miraculous Cure of Pietro de'Ludovisi*, in the Accademia, Venice, detail showing a woman seeking alms from officers of a Scuola Grande.
(Photograph: the Witt Library; copyright John Bernasconi)

follows. First is the Carità, with an income of about 4000 ducats; the second is the Misericordia, with some 3000 ducats; the third is San Giovanni [Evangelista], with over 2000 ducats; the fourth is San Marco, with little more than 800 ducats. There is another, San Rocco, which so far has no income whatsoever, even though it is nearly of the same size as the other four, and in time will surely not be inferior to the others. Each of these five Scuole has 700 members, most of whom are non-noble citizens [*popolari*], artisans and boatmen; there are also nobles, but they hold no rank in them. The revenues are spent in part on decorating the Scuole, all of which have elaborate and gilded ceilings, and are now becoming more imposing than ever: their buildings are being embellished with façades of marble and stone of great value. Some of the revenues are spent on the many religious services that they perform continuously, where they dispense innumerable candles; and the balance is spent on helping members of each Scuola. Each one has a regular membership of 700. There are always many infirm among them, who are cared for, fed and clothed, along with their families, until they get well or die. After the death of a member, another person is chosen in his place and is similarly cared for.

On the other hand, the Scuola recognizes no obligation toward the survivors of the dead man, who are treated as though they had never been connected with the Scuola, with a single exception: marriageable daughters of the deceased are provided for in the same manner, year in and year out, as the daughters of living members who marry. Otherwise, the survivors of the deceased receive no aid, even if they are in great need. Since the revenues of the Scuole are insufficient to meet their obligations towards the poor, the sick, and the girls in need of dowries, it is a custom that those members who are healthy and successful in their occupations should give alms each month. This practice brings considerable returns, and permits the Scuola to meet most of the obligations mentioned above. Besides almsgiving, many people make bequests by leaving all or part of their patrimony to the Scuole, and make the Scuole trustees for the distribution of these legacies. Connected with each Scuola Grande and attached to it is a house rather like a special hospital, where sick members are brought and cared for when they are not better off in their own homes. These hospitals have no revenues of their own, but are just branches and receptacles of the Scuole. So much for the four Scuole Grandi.

The fifth Scuola [San Rocco], which I have called Grande as much as the others but which has no income, meets the same obligations as the other Scuole, as much as it can, solely with the alms given by members and with a few bequests; however, for lack of regular income, it cannot match the others, so that it does not spend in all more than 1000 ducats a year.

Besides the Scuole Grandi there are many small private Scuole which have little or no revenue, but which, by drawing on the alms they collect, spend annually some 600, 500 or 300 ducats, more or less. Each provides solely for its own members, who never complain about giving alms, and do so generously many times each year, since they know that the aid provided by the Scuola is mutual, and it is as though each were helping himself. For each member who helps a needy brother knows that he too will be aided when he can no longer care for himself and falls on hard times.

Apart from these Scuole, which have names such as La Trinità, La Divinità, and the like, there are also private Scuole for each nation, which have some secure incomes, and Scuole for each craft and trade, all of which support some poor. In other words, the Scuola of each nation aids the poor of that nation (albeit not all of them), within the limits of its revenues; similarly, the Scuole of the crafts sustain their own artisans. Even though these Scuole do not relieve the misery of all the poor who can be found here, they do assist a great many of them.

There are some other special hospitals, situated in certain parishes of this city, at a considerable distance one from the other, which have very little income, if any; but they too are attached to some ancient church and they lend assistance to the very poor of that parish. There is one institution, called the

Pietà, which supports little base-born children [*li puti picoli bastardi*]; it has no income except for what is provided by alms and by the Procurators of St Mark's.

There is a hospital which resembles the others in being connected with a church, in this case San Pietro.[3] Here they bring those who have lost one or more limbs by judicial mutilation and who therefore cannot help themselves or earn a living; such cases are cared for until death.

This is as much as I can relate to Your Excellency concerning these charitable institutions. Although there are many of them, the number of the poor of all conditions who are found here is much greater, and they still seem not to be well provided for, despite all the opportunties that exist. The reason for this seems to be that none of the Scuole, and especially not the Scuole Grandi, which give more in aid than the others, admit members without an entrance fee of 10 or 12 ducats, or something similar. Thus he who cannot help himself finds himself without help.

Many alms are given, and many goods are distributed regularly for charitable causes, by the Procuracy of St Mark's, according to the wishes of deceased persons who name the office of the Procurators of St Mark's as trustees and executors of their testaments.

I commend myself humbly, as always, to Your Excellency.

Venice, 23 March 1497

Your most loyal servant, Battista Sfondrato

[Addressed on reverse] To the Most Illustrious Prince and Most Excellent Lord, the Lord Duke of Milan, with my respects.   R. C. M.

2 THE HOSPITALS OF VENICE, *c.* 1500

From the French. Extracts from Anon., *Description ou traictié du gouvernment ou régime de la cité et seigneurie de Venise*, ch. IV: BN Fonds Français 5599, ff. 14v–16r.

First of all, in Venice there is a hospital [*maison*] called the Pietà, which accepts children not born of legal marriage whose parents do not wish to rear them. These small children are fed and provided for from the revenues and alms of this hospital until they are able to learn a trade or become servants – that is, the boys; the girls are cared for until they find husbands or secure some other honest livelihood [*manière de vivre*].

Item. There is another large hospital outside the city, at a league's distance from it, called Nazareth,[4] which receives all those who are stricken with the

---

[3] The hospital of San Pietro e San Paolo in Castello; see Semi 1983, pp. 78–82.

[4] The Lazzaretto Vecchio, founded in 1423. Its name derived from the convent of Santa Maria di Nazareth, which it took over.

plague [*malade d'epydimye*], and they remain there until they recover or die. There is an administrator in charge of these sick persons, of expenditure, and of other necessary matters. There are also chaplains, physicians and surgeons, apothecaries and other staff and servants necessary for caring for the bodies and souls of these sick persons, both in death and in life.

There is another hospital, distant about a league and a half from the former, which is large and beautiful and in a pleasant spot, and is called New Nazareth.[5] There they bring those who have recovered from the said illness, so that they do not return directly to the city and infect others; and they remain there for two months, or [at least] for the course of two moons. All those, moreover, who have come into contact with these sick persons are sent to this place, where they reside for the same period of two moons. If any of them should fall sick of the plague during this period, they are sent to the first Nazareth, called Old Nazareth. And for this purpose many boats and boatmen [*gens propres*] are provided to transport them; these men are hired to take the healthy, the sick and the dead back and forth where necessary. Should anyone die of plague in the city, he is brought for burial to Old Nazareth. At New Nazareth, too, there is an administrator in charge of making expenditure for those who are brought to this place, who own nothing at all from which to provide for themselves; and there are also other officers necessary to it. . . . Nearly all the said expenditure is of government money, since the hospitals themselves have very little revenue.

Item. In Venice there are many other hospitals, both for men and for women, to the number of about forty; and the poor who live in them are amply provided with food and clothing from the revenues of these hospitals, some of which are middle-sized and others small. But another hospital has been begun which will be perfect: it will be so beautiful and grand that in all Italy there will be none or few to surpass it.[6]   R. C. M.

3   THE GENERAL SCHEME FOR POOR RELIEF, 1529
Senate decree of 3 April 1529: ASV Senato, Terra, reg. for 1529, ff. 125v–127r. (*Documenti* 1879, p. cccxiii).

Charity is, without any doubt, to be considered the most important form of good work, and it must always be practised towards our neighbours. As is everyone's duty, we must look to the interests of the poor and the health of the sick and offer food to the hungry; and never should we fail to extend our aid and favour to those who can earn their bread in the sweat of their brow. These

[5] The Lazzaretto Nuovo, founded in 1468 [see above, III.5(a)(ii)].
[6] The hospital of Gesù Cristo di Sant'Antonio.

things we must do in order to please our supreme and almighty God, who will bring to perfection every well-conceived and well-intentioned undertaking; in order to root out a wicked custom and an evil way of life, in the form of begging and cheating, to which so many people resort in this noble city, bringing some notoriety to Venice; and in order to enhance the good name of this well-ordered Republic. We must neglect no method of promoting such an important enterprise. Therefore, that the poor of the city may be able to get their living both by their own efforts and by the means made available to them, and that the sick may be cared for and fed, and that those who wish to practise the trades of the beggar and the cheat may be expelled from this city, let us adopt the following measures, which shall be arranged below under headings and specified in detail.

First, the beggars from outside who daily enter the city shall be sent back to their own territories with letters of commendation exhorting the governors of those places to provide for their support, and not to allow them to return to Venice. Each of these people must be cared for in his own part of the country [*patria*], by the methods which seem to those responsible to be most appropriate to this task.

The poor people of Venice who are driven by want, and who cannot live by their own industry or manual labour on account of infirmity, shall be placed in and distributed among the hospitals or wherever it seems they can best get support. This measure shall be applied to those persons of either sex who have no fixed abode.

Those persons who are feeble [*impotenti*] and yet have a dwelling-place may on no account seek alms in the city. They must go or send to the priests in their parishes, who shall provide for their support by the methods described below.

And, because there is another kind of men, who are robust and hardy and could well live by their own efforts, but instead devote themselves to the shameful and forbidden trade of fraudulent begging [*furfantaria*] and cannot be dissuaded from it, we do not wish them to be treated in this way. Rather, the masters of all vessels shall be invited to take on board whatever number of poor they choose, and they shall pay their expenses, as they do those of other sailors, and they shall give them half the normal pay. Likewise, the Provveditori sopra l'Armar and the paymasters shall be obliged to place on the light galleys and the *fuste* whatever number of poor persons may seem appropriate to them.

As for the other poor who remain in this city and are not taken on board the ships (for perhaps they will be very numerous), measures shall be taken as follows to prevent them from going begging. All the bailiffs [*gastaldi*] and their colleagues and other officers of the brotherhoods of all the crafts shall be obliged to take them on, at the rate of three or four for each craft, causing them to learn the trade and providing them with victuals and wages according to need and as they judge best.

[handwritten: employment program for able bodied beggars]

There are also many women, widows and persons of other status, who have young children and cannot engage in the activities mentioned above, but who seek to make a living for themselves and their families by other kinds of labour. The parish priests and deputies must ensure that they have materials on which to exercise whatever skills they possess, and if they cannot live by this work they must be given alms to meet their needs, and this regulation shall apply to those who have no choice but to go begging or send others to beg for them.

That this good work may progress more smoothly to a good end, and that the poor may be assisted, the most reverend Monsignor Patriarch and the Provveditori alla Sanità shall charge each parish priest that, together with the named and appointed deputies of the parish, he shall go throughout his district seeking alms from the well-to-do [*potenti*], and the money and the goods so given for the love of God shall be distributed with care and diligence to the aforesaid poor of Christ who dwell in their parishes.

The poor of the city must be divided and distributed among the parishes in such a way that each parish has a number of poor appropriate to its wealth and standing.

Members of the brotherhoods of Corpus Domini shall be bound to perform the duty of assiduously commending the poor and exhorting all men to give alms, until this arrangement concerning the parishes has been placed on a firmer footing.

Religious houses, hospitals, religious brotherhoods, prelates, procurators and others who have ample resources shall be urged and invited, either by the Provveditori alla Sanità or by other suitable persons, to assist the aforesaid poor, who are distributed among the parishes. They shall give such alms as they see fit to those appointed to deal with this matter.

The preachers appointed to preach for the time being shall be charged warmly to urge the people and earnestly to exhort the well-to-do [*potenti*] to help the poor, and to encourage all suitable and proper persons to exert themselves and to promote the present ordinance concerning the poor.

The parish priests and deputies shall present themselves once a month either to the most reverend Monsignor Patriarch or to the Provveditori alla Sanità, as they judge best, and there they shall report in detail on the progress of the business of Christ, so that they may be given any help they need. They must speak of the poor on every festival day in their churches and move and inspire the inhabitants of their parishes to assist them and give them alms.

Every year the parish priests must assemble their parishioners, and then they shall elect by ballot two nobles, one citizen and one artisan, who shall be responsible for promoting the well-being of the poor, and, as far as may be, for preventing any offence to God in their parishes. They shall ensure that every year a voluntary tax is requested in their parish, and this tax shall be applied to the use of the poor, and accounts shall be kept both of its collection and of its dispensation, and it shall be distributed according to the needs of the poor in the parish.

The parish priests and the elected deputies shall see that the poor of their parishes are employed in those trades and crafts to which they are best suited and in which they are most skilled, and those who will not work at them as above shall be banished forever from Venice.

No poor person may depart from one parish to go and reside in another without a certificate from his parish priest, which must be presented to the priest of his new parish, so that such action may be taken concerning these persons who change places as the priest and deputies may judge best.

In each parish there shall be placed a box for the support of the poor, and the keys to it shall be kept by the parish priest and deputies, and the alms which are found in the poor box must be spent solely upon the assistance of the poor. The priest and deputies shall be obliged to give a true and precise account of these alms and of any other collection of moneys which may be taken up for this purpose, and of their distribution (and these accounts must be reviewed annually by the Judges of the Palace, each one of whom shall be allocated the accounts of one sestier, as the Provveditori alla Sanità shall judge best).

The most reverend Monsignor Patriarch shall be requested to commend and recommend this godly ordinance for the assistance of the poor to the faithful of Christ when he goes on his visitation of the parishes, so that, having been well begun, this ordinance may produce good results.

Every parish priest, on pain of a fine of 10 ducats to be distributed to the poor, must on every festival day at the time of the Gospel during High Mass remember to commend this new scheme. The Provveditori alla Sanità shall have in administering this ordinance the same authority as they have in matters concerning diseases, so that if new measures are required from day to day they may take whatever steps are needed.

All the abbesses of nunneries shall be exhorted to receive into their convents, if they have need of these girls, those poor and needy maidens of good and honourable life whom the parish deputies shall hand over to them, although the choice must be made by the said abbesses.

The parish deputies shall scrutinize the accounts of the brotherhoods of Corpus Christi and other small religious companies and shall examine the administration of the moneys of the said brotherhoods, and if there is found to be a surplus then their bailiffs and their colleagues [li gastaldi et compagni] shall be exhorted to apply whatever sum they see fit to the use and maintenance of the parish poor.

For the decree, 116; against, 34; uncertain, 49.   B. P.

THE POOR IN HOSPITAL

4 AN INDULGENCE FOR A VENETIAN HOSPITAL, 1487
From a letter issued by Pope Innocent VIII from Rome on 22 July 1487, in favour of the hospital of Gesù Cristo at Sant'Antonio: ASV Procuratori di San Marco de Supra, Chiesa, b.107, processo 255.

Some time ago our predecessor of happy memory, Pope Sixtus IV, heard that the late Doge Pietro Mocenigo and our beloved sons the senators of Venice, fired with devotional fervour, were proposing, God willing, to erect and construct in the city of Venice, with those material means bestowed by God, a certain notable hospital, with a church or chapel in it or adjoining it, for the kindly reception and charitable treatment of the poor and other wretched persons who came to that hospital from every place, and for the performance of other pious and charitable works. Hence the said Sixtus our predecessor graciously granted and bountifully enjoined that the said hospital should be built in a style worthy of it and, once erected, should be maintained and preserved and be visited and held in due veneration by the faithful in Christ. That the aforesaid faithful might the more willingly flock to the hospital out of devotion and might the more readily stretch out helping hands to pay for the fabric, and for the sustenance and nourishment of the poor and of those who from time to time might have recourse to the hospital, besides showing concern for other necessities of this kind, and so that the faithful might be seen to benefit more abundantly in the hospital by this gift of heavenly grace, he [Pope Sixtus IV] granted and bestowed a plenary remission and indulgence for all their sins upon all faithful persons who had truly repented of and confessed their sins and who should visit it each year on the fifth and sixth days of Holy Week [i.e. Maundy Thursday and Good Friday] after the hospital's foundation and should offer assistance in the building of the hospital and the said church or chapel as well as in the sustenance and nourishment of the aforesaid poor persons, or should suckle infants abandoned there, or should nurture them after weaning, or should carry out work in the same building at some time in accordance with the instructions of the prior [*presidens*] of the hospital then in office, or should make a bequest to the same building consonant with their status and their means; [and he granted the same remission and indulgence] to those responsible at the time for the rule and administration of the same hospital. [This he did] by virtue of his apostolic authority through a brief which, according to his wishes, was not to remain in force for more than twenty years from that day. But, since, or so we have heard, the aforesaid hospital was soon afterwards begun, and housed in a great, sumptuous and distinguished building, and in it poor and otherwise wretched persons with all kinds of infirmities are being sheltered, and abandoned infants are being taken in and the necessary food provided for them until they are restored to their former state of health, and nurses are provided for the aforesaid abandoned infants, [the Pope agrees to extend the indulgences granted by Sixtus IV eleven years earlier for another twenty years after their expiry, as the hospital has no fixed revenues other than the offerings of the faithful].

And, that every faithful Christian may be able to partake of this indulgence, we grant licence and faculty to the procurators of the said hospital now and at any given time to appoint twenty suitable secular priests, to be presented by them to the Patriarch of Venice then in office and to be approved by the same Pariarch, to hear the confessions of the faithful in Christ who come to this church or chapel to obtain this indulgence during eight days before and eight days after the time of this indulgence and to absolve them after confession from sentences of excommunication, suspension and interdict and other ecclesiastical censures and penalties, and of all and each of the sins and trespasses which they have confessed, and of those which they have not confessed because they are not aware of them. [Certain exceptions are then made, and the indulgence is also extended to persons who send donations, but who are prevented by good reasons from going to the hospital chapel at the appointed time].

M. C., WITH ASSISTANCE FROM MEMBERS OF THE
TEACHING-STAFF OF EXETER UNIVERSITY

5 THE HOSPITAL OF THE INCURABILI, 1522, 1539

(a) Chronically sick beggars are compelled to enter the hospital

From a decree of the Provveditori alla Sanità, 22 February 1521 Venetian style (Orford 1870–2, pp. 97–8).

The most reverend Monsignor Patriarch informs us that many gentlemen and gentlewomen and others have been moved to take pity on numerous persons sick and sore of the French pox [*mal franzoso*] and other ills. Some of these persons in their bodily weakness [*impotentia*] languish in the streets and the doorways of churches and public places both at San Marco and at Rialto to beg for a living; and some, being inured to this profession of begging [*gagioffaria*], have no wish to seek a cure, and loiter in these same places, giving forth a terrible stench and infecting their neighbours and those with whom they live. This [abuse] gives rise to the most vociferous complaints, not only from our own people, but from all who come to our city, at its failure to provide for such wretchedness, as is done in all other parts of Italy, both in our own possessions and in foreign states – especially as we are told that the stench may breed infection and disease, to the universal damage and destruction of this our city.

Now, because the aforesaid charitable persons are making every possible effort to care for these sick people – who are plunged into the deepest destitution and misfortune – in a hospital of theirs [*uno suo locho*] at the Spirito Santo, very well adapted to this good work which deserves the praise of everybody; and because there are some sufferers who, being accustomed to the wretched state of beggary, are reluctant to receive medical help and care, so that even upon request they refuse to go and be looked after, nursed, physicked and healed; we, Francesco Ruzini, Sebastian Contarini and Zacharia Valaresso, Provveditori sopra la Sanità, being informed of the facts stated above and wishing to give every encouragement to such a good work, which is most pleasing to God and beneficial to this city, decree, by the authority which pertains to this office, that, if from henceforth any men or women sore of the French pox or other ill are called upon by the agents of the aforesaid hospital to go and enter the place to be nursed and looked after, and yet refuse and will not go, even in response to a further summons from the constable or servants of our office, they shall be, and shall be known to be, banished from this our city.

B. P.

(b) The governing-body of the hospital
Decree of the Great Council, 7 January 1538 Venetian style: ASV Maggior Consiglio, Deliberazioni, Liber Novus, f. 39.

Everybody knows that the preservation of our religious institutions is of the greatest credit, benefit, and advantage to this our city. Since the hospital of the Incurabili, because it is well governed and redounds to the praise of God, brings the greatest honour to Venice, and since it needs to be preserved by means of sound regulations, through which it began and grew to the praise of the Lord God,

BE IT DETERMINED that by the authority of this Council this hospital of the Incurabili shall always have between twelve and twenty-four governors, both nobles and citizens of this city, as shall seem appropriate. Nobody, no matter who he is, may ask to be given it *in commendam*,[7] by becoming its prior or by assuming any other title. Anyone who does so shall be exiled for ever from this city and district and from all other parts of our dominion, and all his possessions shall be confiscated, to ensure that the hospital shall always be subject to the government and care of several persons, as it is at present, to its own marked benefit. The enforcement of the present decree shall be the responsibility of our Avogadori di Comun. And the Doge shall take particular care to have it strictly observed.

For the decree, 1313; against, 192; uncertain, 75. M. C., B. P.

6 FOUNDLINGS AND ORPHANS

(a) Adoption of a child from the foundling-hospital
From the will of Antonio, son of Leonardo Capello dal Banco, of San Samuele, 17 June 1539: IRE, Derelitti E62, fasc. 10.

In 1526 I took a child of the Pietà as my adopted son [*fio de anima*] and named him Bonaventura, and the child lives in the home of Sier Zorzi ... agent of Sier Filippo[?] Capello. [Zorzi's] sons have taken the child into the goldsmith's shop which they have on Rialto, to teach him the trade. I give Sier Zorzi and sons, for the maintenance of the child, what is agreed in the contract between us. I wish my trustees to give the aforesaid Sier Zorzi what is agreed in the contract, and ask my trustees to provide for him until the age of eighteen years, after which he shall be given his clothing and money from my trust, and gain his independence. I beg my trustees and relatives most fervently to regard him as entrusted to them. M. C.

(b) Wages of orphans working outside the hospital of the Derelitti at Santi Giovanni e Paolo
From a sixteenth-century copy of the resolutions of the governors of the hospital of Santi Giovanni e Paolo: ASV Ospedali e Luoghi Pii, b. 910, fasc. 2, ff. 1v, 2v; also in IRE Derelitti A2.

[7] The phrase *in commendam* referred to a benefice which was 'commended', i.e. given in charge to a clerk or layman to hold, with enjoyment of the revenues, in the absence of a regular incumbent. The Venetian government feared that the hospital might, with the connivance of the ecclesiastical authorities, be taken over by one person who would use it purely as a source of income and offer no hospitality to the poor.

18 December 1565

It is a thing of the greatest importance, appropriate to the pity and charity which must be exercised in this holy place, that we should above all else have a care of the poor orphan boys and girls entrusted to us and placed in our charge, and that we should always watch over the health of souls and the well-being of the body. We should not therefore permit that, when children are given out to masters and agreements are made on their behalf and signed by those masters, each of those persons, showing little respect for the Lord God and even less for the laws of man, after keeping these boys and girls for months and sometimes even for years, should then feel at liberty to return them, saying that they are unsuitable. The masters often withhold the children's wages, even for the period they have actually served, without showing any good cause why these proper and valid agreements should be broken. Since these agreements cannot be broken by the poor orphans without good cause, they should not be broken by their masters either. Since action must be taken against this abuse, Missier Piero Loredan and Missier Gabriel Boldu, Presidents, propose

That in the agreements henceforth made by this hospital, when the masters have had these poor orphans on approval for a period of one month, or a little more or less as they please, it shall be stated that the masters must keep these boys and girls for the period for which they are given them, both in health and in sickness, and must feed and clothe them and at the end of their time pay them what has been agreed. Once the contract has been made, and signed by these masters or by others on their behalf, it shall no longer be in their power to withdraw from it, save for some good cause which shall be shown to these governors and recognized by the laws of this well-ordered Republic. If they wish to withdraw without such cause, the masters must pay the children all their wages for the whole period covered by the agreement and give them all the clothes they have hitherto obtained for them; and it shall likewise not be lawful for those orphan boys and girls to leave without good cause, and if they do so they shall lose all their wages and restore all the clothing hitherto obtained for them by their masters. In this way the bargains shall be fair and balanced, and this instruction shall be strictly observed; it shall be read to the masters by the governor who records the agreement, before the master signs or has others sign the document on his behalf; and the governor concerned shall be informed that if he fails to do so he will have to account to God for any damage that this orphan boy or girl may suffer for this reason.

9 February 1567 [Venetian style]

Because it often happens that the poor boys and girls who are sent out to live with others are unable to obtain the wages promised to them by their masters, either because of their own weakness or for some other reason,

BE IT DETERMINED that from henceforth it shall be stated in the agreements that are made that every year these masters must bring to the hospital the wages that have been agreed with them, and these shall be entered upon the account books of our hospital. M. C., J. B., B. P.

(c) Raising money by singing
ASV Ospedali e Luoghi Pii, b. 910, fasc. 2, f. 2v; also in IRE Derelitti A2.

4 April 1575

It was determined by fifteen brothers, who were all in agreement, that of the moneys found and in future to be found in the collection boxes which are circulated in the places where our girls sing, one half shall be used to help the girls to marry or to take the veil. A special account must be kept of them, and the girls shall be credited with the money, and the money shall be given out from time to time to assist the girls to marry or become nuns. The other half shall go into the current account, for the benefit of the institution.

M. C., J. B., B. P.

(d) Making sails for the Arsenal
From a copy of the Chatastico dei Testamenti de l'Ospedal di San Zuane Pollo: IRE Derelitti C4, p. 105.

Praise be to the Lord. 2 June 1584

The most illustrious Provveditori and Patroni all' Arsenal, with the approval of our government, have reached agreement with the governors of the Hospital of Santi Giovanni e Paolo to have made up to a good standard of workmanship [*de tuto poncto*] mainsails, reefs and foresails to equip the 100 light galleys, at the prices quoted below, on the understanding that the material shall be delivered ready cut, with the thread, to the hospital, as has hitherto been the practice with the other sails made up by the hospital. These must likewise be paid for at the same price, as follows:

Mainsails	45 lire each
Reefs	65 lire each
Foresails	8 lire each

Payment must be made in cash, both for work completed and for any future work undertaken. M. C.

(e) Child abandonment and the hospital of the Pietà

(i) From a petition of the governors of the Pietà: ASV Senato, Terra, filza 165, 15 February 1602 Venetian style.

The expenditure of the hospital is perpetually increasing on account of the multitude of children who are being abandoned in far greater numbers than they used to be, so that no day passes without four or five babies being brought here and left in the niche [*scaffetta*]. Hence the nurses, too, multiply, and every Friday we have to pay them more than 150 ducats in wages, and we cannot meet the other regular and unavoidable expenses, which amount to a total of 24,000 ducats per annum, while our regular income does not exceed 8000. Even this includes the interest from the Monte Nuovissimo and the Sussidio, and, on account of their liquidation,[8] [our money] has been lying idle for a year because of the many difficulties we encounter in finding safe investments. We have been able to invest only a part of these, about a month ago, and so have suffered a loss of income.[9]

B. P.

(ii) From a further petition of the governors: ASV Senato, Terra, filza 182, 5 April 1607.

Now we, the representatives of the deeply impoverished hospital of the Pietà, are spurred on by the most pressing needs of this hospital, because, as must be well known to you, its expenses have almost doubled within the past few years, both on account of the terrible shortages and because of the enormous increase in the number of children being abandoned and for ever being brought to this institution. They come both from this city and from other places in much greater numbers than they did a few years ago, to such an extent that both on the premises and outside them we have to feed more than 1500 mouths (one shudders even to hear that number mentioned). There are also the wages of the nurses, which we have had to raise in response to the nature and demands of the present times, and we have also been compelled to increase their numbers in view of the number of children being abandoned. Hence, neither the scanty revenues of this institution, nor the slender profits derived from the labours in which the girls in the hospital continually engage (although many of them are

----

[8] These state loan funds, in which both churches and charities had extensive holdings, were liquidated (as was the Monte Vecchio) between 1596 and 1620. See Pullan 1971, pp. 138–40; and above, IV.11–13.

[9] The Senate granted the hospital 100 staia of corn to replace 200 staia of flour which had been lost with the barge which was bringing it to Venice.

ill), nor the legacies, nor the alms given both by the state and by private persons, can meet the immense demands which are made upon the hospital. We have therefore had to incur many debts, and these are constantly growing, because the artisans have no work, and they cannot maintain their families. So they resolve to send even legitimate children to the hospital, as we see by the results, because in this current year approximately 100 more children were abandoned than in the previous one, and that means expenditure of a further 2000 ducats. At the same time we received 720 ducats less in alms, so that, while the children are multiplying and the expenses growing, the alms are greatly diminishing. We are threatened with another very severe loss, in that annual revenue of 842 ducats from the Monte Vecchio will soon be wiped out, and this income is one of the mainstays, of this poor institution. So, unless vigorous and timely help arrives through the mercy of God and the singular charity of Your Serenity, who is always a zealous protector of this charitable institution, we shall soon be overwhelmed and unable to recover, and that would mean the loss not only of the lives of many most innocent children, but also of their souls, through our losing the resources which enable us to take them in.[10]   B. P.

7   RESPONSIBILITIES OF THE MENDICANTI AND OTHER HOSPITALS, 1619
From the instructions to the 'Governors of the Poor' in the printed statutes of the hospital of the Mendicanti: *Capitoli* 1619, pp. 48–9.

[The types of poor who may be admitted to the hospital of the Mendicanti are as follows.]

First, those suffering from the sickness of St Lazarus, otherwise called leprosy.

Secondly, poor and indigent persons suffering from the scabious itch [*Rogna*], in such a way that they need help to be rid of it, until such time as they have been sufficiently physicked and anointed for this illness.

Thirdly, all those indigent inhabitants of the city of either sex and any age who have no fixed abode and are forced to beg throughout the city, and are not capable of earning enough to support themselves, either because of their youth, or because they know no trade, or because of personal incapacity, or because of old age and decrepitude.

Now, the other great hospitals and religious institutions have also prepared aid and assistance for various kinds of poor and needy persons, and each of these hospitals and institutions has its own responsibility, and it is entirely

---

[10] The hospital was granted the sum of 2 soldi per lira on the proceeds of all contraband goods dealt with by any Venetian magistracy, with effect from 1 May 1607.

reasonable that each of them should discharge its task, so that the burdens may be distributed in an orderly manner. Hence, it is well to know which poor people and what kinds of person are destined for the other institutions, as follows.

> To the hospital of Santi Giovanni e Paolo, the orphans, the derelict, the feverish, and those who suffer from ringworm [*tegna*].
> To the Incurabili, the sick and sore [*impiagati*], orphans, and persons afflicted by other incurable ills and venereal diseases [*mali gallici*], and by other such sicknesses, to take the waters at the normal times when the hospital administers this benefit to the poor.
> To the Pietà, abandoned babies of either sex; and to the many other religious institutions, such as the [Fraternity for] thé Shamefaced Poor, the Zitelle, the Soccorso[11] and others, those kinds of person who are properly their concern, as is very well known.   B. P.

---

[11] For the Fraternity of Sant'Antonino for the shamefaced poor see below, VII.10. The Zitelle, on the Giudecca, was intended for young girls in danger of being betrayed into prostitution, and the Soccorso, in Dorsoduro, was designed to provide a refuge for women already involved in prostitution but wishing to escape from it. See Pullan 1971, pp. 385–94; Aikema and Meijers 1989, pp. 225–48.

8   THE POOR BROTHERS OF THE SCUOLA GRANDE DELLA MISERICORDIA, 1478
From the case stated by the Guardian and officers of the Scuola Grande della
Misericordia, in litigation with four trustees of the estate of Jacopo di Bernabò, who had
made his will in 1438: ASV Giudici di Petizion, Sentenze a giustizia, reg. 168, ff. 38r–
39v, 19 November 1478.

Ser Jacopo [di Bernabò] bequeathed to our Scuola 800 lire [*di grossi*], face
value, in state loan funds [*imprestidi*] earning 3 per cent, which yields 24 lire *di
grossi* per annum, and he left instructions in his will that the Guardian Grande
and his fellow officers of the Scuola, together with Ser Jacopo's trustees, should
choose twelve poor and needy men, and that from the annual income in interest
each of these should be given one cloak, one hood and one pair of shoes of dark
cloth. Another twelve poor men were to be chosen in a similar fashion, and each
to be given 1 staro of flour and 1 quart of wine; and yet another twelve poor men
were to be given 1 ducat each for wood, and the rest of the 24 lire was to be
distributed by ourselves alone, by the Guardian and his colleagues, as stated in
the will. With time, however, abuses crept in, and out of gross and woeful
ignorance men began to distribute the goods purchased and the alms derived
from our 24 lire interest not to our own poor, to whom they were left and to
whom they pertain, but to quite different people, of all kinds and of other
Scuole without distinction. Hence the rightful beneficiaries have only the
smallest share in the bequest and what it yields, although it was made over to us
on the books of the Camera degli Imprestiti, in accordance with the instructions
of the deceased. These abuses have arisen on the pretext that freedom was
given to dispense the benefits according to conscience; but the parties
concerned do not realize that freedom and conscience cannot and must not
extend to giving other people things that are not due to them.
   Now our Scuola, to which the capital and interest were left, is not just a thing
made of stones, or tiles, or mortar: there are 616 men subject to the discipline,
and over 400 nobles of the Council. Of all the brothers there are more than 400

who are poor, needy and fallen on bad times, some on account of the city's taxes, some through misfortune, sickness and other accidents, being of the most distinguished families, of nobles and citizens and other good stock; and they serve the needs of our Scuola by day and by night, as can be seen at first hand in the present year of the pestilence. We have already conducted perhaps 100 burials of persons dead of the plague, and each funeral has been attended by from seventy to 150 mourners, running such grave risks that many of them, because they bear and handle and come close to these corpses, have themselves died of the plague. As poor men, these people expected, and still do expect, to receive alms and assistance from their loan funds and from their Scuola, in accordance with the legacy of Ser Jacopo de Bernabo, who was their good father and our own.[12]   R. C. M.

9   REQUESTS FOR AID FROM THE SCUOLE GRANDI, 1558–93

(a) Antonio, shoemaker of Rio Marin
From the minute-books of the Scuola Grande di San Marco: ASV Scuola Grande di San Marco, 21, ff. 158r–v, 203v.

10 August 1558

Most honourable Lord Guardian, honourable and most wise lords, the goodness and godliness of your lordships has been at all times such that not only have the poor members of this blessed union consoled themselves by their hopes of your generosity, but when they have actually fallen into need they have felt the benefits of the Christian dispositions of your lordships. If any such person deserves assistance, I, Antonio, shoemaker of Rio Marin, believe myself to do so (by your favour) far more than many others, for I am in great decrepitude and no longer able to support myself by the work that used to earn me a pittance. I am in all respects most feeble, with an aged wife and four children who are quite without possessions, and to increase my wretchedness I am in debt for rent of my dwelling for the sum of about 12 ducats. So long as my old landlord, Signor Ambroxo Spa, was alive, I was allowed to let this run on, but now his heirs, who are themselves poor men, are demanding payment. They would send me to prison and take my little house away, and this would be to bury me alive and strike the final blow to my family and expose my children to an evil fate – among them a poor girl who failed two years ago to obtain even a

[12] The Giudici di Petizion upheld the argument of the Scuola that the charity should be dispensed only to brothers of the Scuola itself, and the defendants signed statements accepting the judgement of the court.

single grant of assistance from this holy institution. In the midst of my trouble and misfortune I see no hope of aid from any quarter other than the love and favour of your lordships. I cast myself at your most merciful feet and beg you by your most generous charity and by the bowels of Jesus Christ to make me worthy of some alms on this occasion in my so numerous needs, to save me from imprisonment in my extreme old age, and my children from being driven from that tiny shelter and reduced to beggary and desolation. With this work of charity, not only will you do things pleasing to God, who so lovingly commends to you his poor; you will also do things entirely worthy and to be expected of your own great goodness, for which reason also may the Lord preserve and prosper you and yours and grant you all good fortune.

The Honourable Missier Hieronimo Bonaldi, Guardian Grande, asked whether or not this petition should be accepted.

Those in favour, 24; those against, 2

and it was accepted.

BE IT DETERMINED that, as the Honourable Missier Hieronimo Bonaldi, Guardian Grande, proposes, the said petitioner, Ser Antonio, shoemaker, shall be given from the resources of our Scuola the sum of 6 ducats.

For the decree, 21; against, 5

and it was accepted.

10 August 1560

Honourable Lord Guardian Grande and members of the Bench, I, Antonio, shoemaker dwelling on Rio Marin, beg you by the love of God to put a proposal on behalf of my daughter Laura, because I now have an excellent prospect of marriage for her, and if I could only provide a bed and bedding the man would take her. She has been put up for a dowry several times and has not succeeded, and so, not having the means to perform this work, I throw myself at your feet, begging you all to assist me in getting my daughter wed; and I trust that you will not fail me, and commend myself to your favour.

According to the decree on this matter, the Honourable Missier Cesare Ziliol, Guardian Grande, asked whether or not this petition should be accepted.

Those in favour, 22; those against, 3

and it was accepted.

BE IT DETERMINED that, as the Honourable Guardian Grande proposes, the Guardian Grande for the time being shall spend 8 ducats on a bed and bedding for the aforesaid petitioner, when she brings the certificate of her marriage, according to the custom of our Scuola.

For the decree, 25; against, o.

Passed.   B. P.

(b) Filomena Stella, widow of Paulo d'Anna, formerly Guardian Grande of the Scuola Grande di San Rocco

Archivio della Scuola Grande di San Rocco, Registro delle Terminazioni 3, f. 230v.

2 June 1593

Most honourable Lord Guardian Grande, honourable lords of this most venerable Scuola di San Rocco,

If ever there was a case deserving of the Christian charity of yourselves, honourable governors of the Scuola, it is mine, that of the wretched and unhappy Filomena Stella, widow of the late honourable Missier Paulo d'Anna, and all Christian hearts must surely go out to me, for I am reduced to such a parlous state by the misfortunes I have suffered, in which the late Ser Paulo left me. For it is well known that nothing remains to me but the hopes I have of God and of Catholic Christians, who must consider the rank to which I was born, the parents of whom I was born, and the husband to whom I was married, for your worships know all these things, and are aware that I am brought to such destitution that I have to beg for a living from those who will pity me. Worse still, I have no means of getting shelter or of paying rent, for nothing remains to me in the world save pain, tears, sighs and trouble, and I am left desolate and utterly without hope; and were I not aided and relieved by the hand of God, for those who trust in him are not forsaken, I would know not what to do but beg my bread in a public place. My further misfortune is that I am burdened with a crippled son. But for him, I would have arranged to go as a servant to others, for so my harsh and sorry fate decrees, but with this impediment I cannot do as I wish.

Now, however, I have been inspired by God's providence to have recourse to the aid, assistance and favour of yourselves, the honourable governors of this Christian Scuola, that you may deign to make me a small gift which will afford me some relief. Your worships have on the Giudecca and also in Venice itself a number of small and lowly houses let at paltry rents of 4, 5 or at most 6 ducats a year, and even these cannot easily be collected, because only very poor and wretched persons live in them. I beg you to let me have one of these houses free of rent [*per l'amor di Dio*] for as long as I shall live; and, if you cannot do so, at

319

least to allow me to live in it for one half of the present rent, so that by this means, poor and destitute as I am, I, formerly the wife of one who in his time was Guardian Grande of this blessed Scuola, may have some relief after so many troubles. I offer to pray the Lord God to exalt your worships and to preserve you and your descendants from such painful and lamentable obscurity as I have experienced myself; and to pray that you may be saved by his hand from the trials and tribulations of this world and be granted grace and glory in the next. Amen.

And so, humbly kneeling, I commend myself to you as did Mary Magdalen at the feet of Our Lord Jesus Christ.

[*Response to the petition*]

BE IT DETERMINED that, as the Guardian Grande proposes, on the first vacancy of one of the houses in Venice belonging to our Scuola or the trusts at a rent of 15 ducats or less, this house shall be rented to the said Madonna Filomena. If it belongs to the Scuola itself the honourable Guardian Grande shall determine the rent, and if to the trusts it shall be leased at the rent which Signor Bortolamio, [mercer at the sign] of the Chalice, offers and binds himself to pay for her, according to the arrangements which shall have been made for settling the rent, as above.

In favour of the proposal, 21; against, 0

and it was accepted.   B. P.

↦ Homesitting poor

10   THE SHAMEFACED POOR, 1596
From a petition of the governors of the Fraternity of Sant'Antonino: ASV Senato, Terra, filza 139, 9 April 1596.

[The Fraternity] visits the poor families of noblemen, citizens and merchants who have fallen into destitution on account of worldly misfortunes and accidents, and have retreated into their houses out of poverty and shame, not daring to ask for alms. It provides in all charity and secrecy for such persons in their want and misfortune; it helps widows and women in childbirth, assists wards and aids orphans, consoles the afflicted and troubled, and takes care of sick persons of every status. Each day it dispenses medicines, and for this purpose it maintains on its own premises a pharmacy stocked with the choicest materials, and it spends heavily on these, and upon workers, bread, wine, meat and money, and at the proper times it spends upon wood, charcoal, clothing and all other necessities according to the needs of the poor. In short it seizes, promptly and willingly, every opportunity of helping neighbours, both in their bodies and in their souls. Various noblemen, citizens and merchants administer and apply themselves to this Christian work. Out of pure zeal for God's honour they assemble every morning at the sound of the *marangona*, at the house assigned for the purpose in the parish of Sant'Antonino, to read the notes sent to them by the parish priests concerning the cases which occur in their districts, and when these notes have been read the governors go out, two to each sestier, to see the people concerned, and neither bitter cold nor blazing heat deters the governors from going to visit these persons, even in the most distant parts of the city, as the sick may require. On being well informed of their wants, the governors report on their condition the following morning, and they are given immediate assistance in accordance with their needs. All are reminded to give thanks to God; to pray for their benefactors (especially this most serene Dominion); to bear their troubles with patience; to ensure that their children go to learn Christian doctrine and the older girls live as Christians and do not fall into error; to perform frequent acts of piety; and to apply themselves to some virtuous activity in accordance with their character, raising themselves to the best of their ability above the base condition into which the misfortunes of the world have plunged them. For these reasons, above all, there are great numbers of poor persons and of families burdened with children who are dying of hunger, cold and all kinds of want, and in particular there are many in distress at the present time through the failure of work in the wool and silk trades, which generally support great numbers of children.[13]   B. P.

---

[13] By way of assistance the Senate exempted the Fraternity of Sant'Antonino from the tax of 5 per cent payable on all legacies other than to close relatives. This tax, instituted in 1565, was designed to finance the engineering-works or 'excavations' (*cavamenti*) of the Magistrato alle Acque in the Lagoon. See F. Besta 1912, pp. 232–3.

Part VIII
'Most of their People are Foreigners'

*A*T THE CLOSE *of the fifteenth century Philippe de Commynes, the French envoy, said of the Venetians that 'most of their people are foreigners' (Commynes ed. Kinser 1969–73, II, 493). It was indeed true that the population of Venice, subject like that of other great cities to high infant mortality and savage outbreaks of pestilence, could only be sustained by heavy immigration both from mainland Italy and from further afield. Some came as artisans, casual labourers or traders, others as soldiers or sailors. Foreign merchants were constantly being attracted to Venice from regions of Europe and the Levant which had not been penetrated by Venetian merchants, or in which the interest of Venetian merchants was beginning to wane. Some immigrants acquired a domicile and took out citizenship; others, as temporary residents or regular visitors maintaining ties with their native countries, or as persons set apart from Venetians by their religion and culture, formed distinctive foreign communities regulated by Venetian law. They were generally both privileged and restricted. Privileges might well include the granting of special tariffs on goods imported and exported from Venice, a monopoly of particular forms of economic activity, or the guaranteed right to practise their religion openly. Restrictions were generally aimed at reducing competition between Venetian craftsmen and their foreign counterparts, and – especially in order to safeguard the dominant Catholic religion – at preventing completely free association on equal terms between Venetians and foreigners. Places of public worship (other than embassy chapels) and burial grounds of their own were not permitted to Protestants, but they were conceded both to Greek Orthodox Christians and to Jews.* — did get burial & worship [faith scare]*

This section is concerned with five legally recognized foreign communities, with the institutions on which they focused, with their occupations, and with their relationship with Venetian society and the state. VIII.1–4 deal with the German community, laying some emphasis on the collegial exchange house or Fondaco dei Tedeschi at Rialto, and on the neighbouring church and inns at San Bartolomeo. A place of compulsory residence for German merchants, many of whom hailed from the important cities of Nuremberg, Ratisbon (otherwise Regensburg) and Augsburg, the Fondaco was destroyed by fire in 1505 and subsequently rebuilt. As is clear, however, from the papal nuncio's account [VIII.3], the German population was never confined to the rich merchants or humble pedlars of the exchange house [see also VI.11, for the role of German assistants in the bakers' shops]. The spread of Lutheranism among the German population near the heart of the city's central business district was a perpetual source of concern to the papal representatives in the second half of the sixteenth century; but the Venetian government was too jealous of its traditional commercial interests to contemplate closing the Fondaco.

VIII.5–7 reflect the uncertain relationship between the Venetian government, the Catholic clergy, and the large Greek Orthodox population of Venice, many of them immigrants from Venetian colonies in the eastern Mediterranean. It was possible for them to claim convincingly [VIII.6 and 7] to be good Catholics following the Greek rite, and not heretics or schismatics, on account of the formula of union (unity of faith and diversity of rite) arrived at in 1439 by the Council of Florence – though this had never won the acceptance of all Greek Orthodox Christians. Over the period as a whole, the degree of understanding displayed towards members of other faiths fluctuated in accordance with the attitudes, sometimes conflicting, of the Papacy, the Patriarch and the Venetian government. It also reflected the state of dialogue on the subject of a closer and more effective union of churches.

The corporation of Jews or Università degli Ebrei consisted of three 'nations'. Of these the first was composed of the so-called Germanic or Ashkenazic Jews ('Ebrei Tedeschi'), although many were really of Italian origin. Such people gathered in large numbers in Venice itself after the invasion of the Veneto in 1509, and from 1516 were compelled [VIII.8] to live in the quarter known as the Geto, the site of a disused foundry: hence the term 'ghetto', which appears in documents of a somewhat later date such as VIII.9 and VIII.12–14. This was employed not only in Venice but generally, to mean a separated place reserved by law for the accommodation of Jews. The Jewish presence in Venice was officially justified not merely by the services rendered by Jews as moneylenders to the poor, but also by the possibility of converting them to the Christian faith; the experience of one such convert is described in his own words in VIII.9. VIII.10 and 11 record some of the activities for which the Ebrei Tedeschi were well known. VIII.11 is taken from one of the very lengthy condotte *or contracts concluded between the Venetian government and the Germanic Jewish nation. These documents specified, in minute detail, the terms on which the Jews would be allowed to reside in Venice for the next few years, until the* condotta *came up for renewal.*

While the Germanic Jews were associated chiefly with moneylending and with the trade in second-hand clothing and used articles, Sephardic Jews from Spain, Portugal and the Levant were welcomed chiefly as traders. New Christians from Spain, Portugal and the Low Countries, converts to Christianity suspected of returning secretly to Judaism, were stigmatized by the abusive term 'Marrano' and officially banned from Venice as heretics, in 1497 and again [VIII.12] in 1550. In practice many were able to live and trade in Venice if, discarding their

Christian past, they went promptly to the Ghetto and declared themselves to be Jews. The government officially recognized a category of Levantine Jews who were subjects of the Ottoman Sultan, and in 1541 the Jewish quarter was expanded to accommodate them [VIII.13]. In 1589 the government was persuaded by a Sephardic Jew, Daniel Rodriga, to make special concessions to Sephardic merchants, some of them undoubtedly of New Christian origin, in order to attract them to Venice under secure conditions and develop trade with the Dalmatian port of Spalato or Split [VIII.14].

'Turkish' merchants, non-Jewish subjects of the Sultan from the Balkans and Asia Minor, had been present in Venice at least from the early sixteenth century, and from the 1570s onwards their critics began to urge that they and their merchandise should be concentrated in a central place, which would have something in common with both the German exchange house and the Ghetto. The idea found some support among the merchants themselves, who were eager for greater security and convenience, while the Venetian authorities were anxious to prevent scandals caused by the loose association of Christians with persons of other faiths. Premises capable of accommodating all and not just part of the Turkish mercantile body (or bodies) were provided only in 1621, and VIII.15 presents some of the regulations for the new exchange house for the Turks.

BIBLIOGRAPHY   On the Germans: Simonsfeld 1887; Braunstein 1977. On the Greeks: Geanakoplos 1962; Fedalto 1967; Beck et al. 1977; Ball 1982, 1985; Mavroidi 1989. On the Jews: Roth 1975 edn; Pullan 1971, pp. 431–578, 1983, 1988a; Ravid 1976, 1978, 1979, 1982, 1983a and b, 1987a and b; Jacoby 1977; Ioly Zorattini 1980–; Finlay 1982; Adelman 1985; Calimani 1985; Cozzi 1987; Modena ed. Cohen 1988. On the Turks: Preto 1975; Vercellin 1979, 1980.   B. P.

THE GERMANS

1 GERMAN MERCHANTS AND THE EXCHANGE HOUSE, 1475
From regulations approved by a Senate committee on customs duties, 31 August 1475
(G. M. Thomas 1874, pp. 223–32).

10   No Venetian citizen or subject may go to Germany, or to any part of Germany, or to anywhere to the south of Germany, to the port of Trieste or any other place, to buy or sell merchandise from any German, on pain of losing all the goods bought or sold, and paying as much again by way of penalty. The accuser shall have one third, the governor another third, and our own government the remaining third. This rule shall not, however, apply to horses or to weapons or to provisions, and notice of the fact shall be given to our governors in those regions, and an exception shall be made for all ordinary fairs.[1] . . .

13   To remove all possible causes of doubt and dispute, it shall be declared that all Germans, whether from Upper or Lower Germany, and whether they are subjects of the Emperor or of any other German ruler, and likewise Poles, Hungarians and Bohemians, shall be liable with all their merchandise to pay the duties at our exchange house in the usual manner, and, if any excisemen or others acting on their behalf attempt to remove or actually do remove the aforesaid goods from the exchange house to subject them to other duties, they shall incur a penalty of 100 ducats for each offence, to be divided into three parts, and the duty shall still be payable to our exchange house. . . .

17   As has been decreed on other occasions, no German merchant may on any pretext take lodgings in any place outside the exchange house, upon a penalty of 50 ducats, and the same penalty shall fall upon anyone who has lodged or has received into lodgings such a person. The steward of the exchange house shall

---

[1] The principle stated in clause 10 had first been established by a law of 1363 (G. M. Thomas 1874, p. 63). The words 'an exception shall be made for all ordinary fairs' were deleted by a Senate decree of 2 June 1494, because they had given rise to many fraudulent claims (ibid., pp. 273–4).

be obliged to inquire thoroughly into the matter and to report to our administrators [*Visdomini*] of the exchange house, and they must proceed against the offenders.   B. P.

2   HOUSE RULES FOR THE NEW FONDACO DEI TEDESCHI, 1508
From the Capitulary of the German Nation (Simonsfeld 1887, I, 363–4).

12 May 1508

To prevent bitter quarrels between merchants, and for the benefit and good appearance of the new exchange house, [it is decreed,] most serene Prince and most excellent Signoria, that no one may presume to place in the corridor outside his room more than one chest per person, and this chest must be no longer than the distance between doors [*ne piu longa che passa da portta*]. That is because in the old exchange house the passages were so sorely impeded by chests, counters and barrels that often you could not get past or look down into the courtyard. This rule must be observed both by merchants and by others, on penalty of 100 ducats each time they are detected, and this fine shall be distributed by the administrators [*visdomini*] of the exchange house as follows: one third to St Mark, one third to the accuser, and one third to the administrators themselves.

No one may break through the walls on either side, unless he wishes to make a door from one room to another. Otherwise no one may make holes in the wall, or make stovepipes, or chimneys for stoves, or anything else that branches off the main chimneys. No one is to break or alter anything on penalty of 100 ducats for each offence, to be distributed in the manner described above.

All merchants who wish to have iron grilles placed over the windows of their rooms shall be obliged to pay for them out of their own money, and they shall make all the grilles in the same fashion for the sake of good order, and they must be of the same size, so that none projects further from the walls than another.

The rooms on the first and second floors shall be rented at 12 ducats a year each, and those on the third floor at 8 ducats, to be paid in full to St Mark, on the understanding that all the merchants shall pay in addition to this rent all the other royalties and expenses which they have been accustomed to pay, and shall similarly make the customary payments to the steward [*masser*] of the exchange house.

Six rooms on the third floor shall not be assigned to particular merchants, but shall be reserved for the accommodation of travellers and vendors of cheap cloth [*Viandanti et Grissolletti*],[2] to prevent them from lodging at the inns outside

---

[2] *Grisi*, or coarse grey cloths, were to be considered suitable wear for convicts in the galleys in the late sixteenth century; see F. Besta 1912, pp. 272, 273, 347, etc.

the exchange house, for they cause great loss to our most illustrious government.

On account of the storehouses and vaults in the exchange house, payment shall be made in full to St Mark of the sums specified in the present document, which allots and leases them to merchants and has been drawn up by the hand of Antonio Falascho, clerk to the exchange house.[3]   B. P.

3   HERESY AND IRRELIGION AMONG THE GERMANS OF VENICE, *c.*1580
From the report of Alberto Bolognetti, papal nuncio in Venice 1578–81 (Aldo Stella 1964, pp. 278–80).

[Father Jacob the Jesuit] told me that there were in all some 900 Germans living in Venice, including those in the exchange house, and that in his opinion all were heretics, with scarcely 200 exceptions. The Germans may be divided into three categories. Some are servants in private houses, and to outward appearances they live as they ought to do, but it is hard to make any judgement about their private lives, because in view of the perpetual to-ing and fro-ing of peoples which one sees in Venice it must happen that they come both from Catholic and from heretical regions. Some are artificers, bakers, goldsmiths, tailors and the like, and they, being intent on earning a living, seldom discuss matters of faith. But they do live very loosely, and, although there are some who confess and communicate at Easter, most of them are heretics who either omit to do so or else go to the German border in Holy Week to sup and receive their Communion in the manner of the heretics. The remainder are merchants, richer and more prosperous folk, or their agents and correspondents, and there are not many of them. Apart from those who have wives, most of them dwell in the exchange house. There were more before the plague, but when that broke out many directed their trade elsewhere, left Venice and have never returned. So scarcely more than 100 remain, although, if you count officials and servants as well, there are nearly 200 living in that great building. They live as in a college, having everything in common, and they eat in the same place at a set hour, which proves very convenient for their business. I used to hear that they lived in a more disreputable fashion than any of the others, for they kept heretical books, ate meat and other foods of every kind at will on forbidden days, and conversed as they pleased of matters of the faith. And, if anyone arrived who showed by his diet or speech or in any other way that he clung to

[3] A list of these allocations follows. Twenty-five such storehouses and vaults were assigned to merchants, for a total annual rent of 276 ducats. For the allocation of rooms to merchants on 19 January 1508 see Simonsfeld 1887, I, 359–61: sixty-eight rooms were allocated and eight left vacant, of which six were reserved for *viandanti*.

the rites of the Holy Roman Catholic Church, he would be scorned and ridiculed by the others. Although Father Jacob would often go among the lowly craftsmen and do some good among them, exhorting them to prayers and other sound practices, it was in vain that he tried to do the same for the inhabitants of the exchange house. Several times did he go to expound the Gospel to them while they sat at table, on account of the friendship he at first had with some of them; but in the end they forbade him to return, for they would not submit to the authority of an outsider, and knew very well how to read the Gospel by themselves. I hear, too, that they lived with the same licence in two Venetian inns, the Black Eagle at San Bartolomeo and the White Lion, where it once happened that, when a German Catholic from Vienna was praising the Emperor for expelling that heretical preacher, many at once contradicted him in an insulting manner. Hence that German complained and said he found it strange that in the Catholic city of Venice he could not safely mention what the Emperor in Germany was doing to assist the Catholics. . . .

Would that these improper occurrences were confined to the inns and the exchange house, for there were tales of still more outrageous things happening in public places. Hence the Venetian government ought to realize that to allow so much freedom to Germans in the middle of the city is to nurture a viper in their own bosom. I thought it a very serious matter when I was told that in the church of San Bartolomeo, where they preach in German, it was customary to preach heretical doctrine in public, and that a preacher had caused songs abusing the Catholic faith (which they call 'popery' [*fede papistical*]) to be sung publicly in church, while he himself acted the drunkard in the pulpit to the laughter of the people. In my time there occurred a scandal of no less gravity, and this . . . was that in the church of the Carmini in Venice they posted up a number of propositions which were not merely heretical but truly monstrous and horrendous, in that they denied Purgatory, Hell, the Trinity and the divinity of Christ, and in short went so far beyond impiety as to verge upon atheism; and the author included in his writings a number of arguments in support of his opinions, and challenged the preacher to reply from the pulpit the following Sunday.   B. P.

4   AUCTIONING THE BLACK EAGLE INN, 1630
Senate decree of 20 April 1630: ASV Senato, Terra, reg. 103 (March–September 1630), f. 89.

For many years the state has been accustomed to grant and concede the land-lordship of the Black Eagle Inn [*l'inviamento et insegna dell'Hostaria all'Aquila Negra*] in this city to various subjects, and on the last occasion it was bestowed upon Thomaso Mathais. With his death this position has now fallen vacant, and, since the public interest requires that the matter be resolved in the most appropriate and advantageous manner possible,

BE IT DETERMINED that this position of landlord shall be sold by public auction to the highest bidder by the Governatori delle Entrate, upon the conditions that those magistrates shall deem most useful to the public and most likely to promote the sale. It shall be stipulated, however, that the host must be a German and that on no account may he lodge Italians. The concession must, however, be approved by two thirds of the votes of members of the Collegio, and before making the concession the Governatori must appear before the Collegio to report the offer made to them. B. P.

5 | THE CHURCH AND THE SCUOLA AT SAN BIAGIO IN CASTELLO, 1470, 1498
(i) Decree of the Council of Ten and Zonta, 28 March 1470: ASV Consiglio dei Dieci, Parti miste, reg. 17 (1466–72), f. 138.

BE IT DETERMINED that orders shall be issued that in the city of Venice no services may be held according to the Greek rite in any place other than San Biagio, as has been resolved on other occasions, upon a penalty of 100 lire to any priest and of 50 lire to any layman who attends such services. This law shall be made known to the Greeks, that no one may plead ignorance, and the Lords of the Night and the Heads of the Sestieri shall exact these fines and give all the money to the accusers.   J. G. B.

(ii) Petition of the Greek community, c.1498: ASGG C.13.219, f. 27; ASV Consultori in Jure, vol. 427.

Most Serene Prince, most illustrious Signoria, most glorious and exalted Council of Ten,

In all sincerity, submission and reverence, this petition is made in the name of the community [Università] of Greeks who live in this most holy and nourishing city, and especially in the names of the most loyal and warm-hearted servants, Zuan of Sancta Maura, carpenter, and Master Alesio of Corfu, spicer, who have the duty of asking this favour of Your Serenity. For the Greeks have at all times been good and most loyal servants of this most holy State, and have striven at every opportunity to meet the needs of Your Serenity, both on land and on sea, especially in the conquest of Dalmatia, where they thought it a glorious thing to spill their blood for the expansion of your state and exposed themselves to certain death, because at that time most of the galleys of your

333

illustrious government were manned by the people of the Levant. The said
Greeks, knowing the most merciful disposition of Your Most Excellent
Serenity, and trusting in their past service and unfailing loyalty, beg and petition
Your Serenity and the most illustrious and excellent Council of Ten that as a
matter of grace they may in their infinite mercy permit the Greeks to found a
Scuola at the church of San Biagio in the sestier of Castello, as the Slavs,
Albanians and other nations have already done;[4] and the Greeks ask this on the
grounds of their devotion. The Scuola shall be dedicated to St Nicholas, and
the greatest good will result from it, especially through giving maintenance to
sick and feeble persons, through giving burial to those who from time to time
die in great poverty, and through helping widows and orphans who have lost
their husbands and fathers in the service of Your Serenity and are sunk in
misfortune and intolerable want.

[Your petitioners] commend themselves to your favour, humbly and upon
bended knees.

28 November 1498. In the Council of Ten

By the authority of this Council the humble request of the above petitioners
shall be granted, that they may establish a Scuola in the church of San Biagio in
Venice in the name and title of St Nicholas. They may not receive more than 250
males, but they may admit as many females as may wish to enter the Scuola. . . .

J. G. B.

6 THE CHURCH OF SAN GIORGIO DEI GRECI, 1511
Petition of the Greek soldiers to the Council of Ten, 4 October 1511: ASGG C.13.219,
f. 32.

Every good Christian must set the holy faith above all other things, and must
pursue it with all energy and diligence as the be-all and end-all of his actions
and as the thing which will lead him to the blessed state he desires.

We have been brought to this land by your excellencies to serve as your
soldiers and as defenders of your glorious State, and most of us have brought
with us our families – that is, our wives and children – with the intention of
living and dying under your protection. We have no church in which to give the
thanks due to Our Lord God by celebrating divine service according to the

---

[4] The Scuola di San Maurizio e di San Gallo degli Albanesi (founded 1442, established at San
Maurizio from 1447); and the Scuola di San Giorgio e di San Trifone e di San Gerolamo (founded
1451, at first in the church of San Giovanni del Tempio and later established independently as San
Giorgio degli Schiavoni in Castello). See Pignatti 1981, pp. 89–118.

334

Greek rite, since the chapel of San Biagio, previously granted by your lordships to our nation for this purpose, no longer suffices, for the place is too small and our people have increased to such an extent that they cannot be accommodated either inside or outside it. In that chapel, too, there is such a mixture of people, tongues, voices and services, both Greek and Latin, at the same time that it creates a confusion worse than that of Babylon, when God, enraged at Nimrod for his rebellion, confounded the human race by the division of languages.[5] They do not understand us, nor we them: indeed, it might be said that neither they nor we can understand each other, and even, dared we say it, that God himself cannot understand our prayers or theirs for the confusion that arises from such variety and miscellany. Worse still, there is no place to bury the dead, as in all [other] churches. They mingle our bones with those of galleymen, porters and other low creatures; even this would be more tolerable if the graves were not upon the public way, and those poor bodies and bones were not dug up and thrown into the water within a few days of burial. This is done to clear the place, that others may be buried, for burials are the greatest source of gain for the parish priest of San Biagio, since the church is very poor and has no other income. It is fine for that priest, but most cruel and evil for us. At the Last Judgement the fishes of the sea will be hard put to it to yield up our bones and organs that our bodies may be completely restored.

Impelled, therefore, by these hardships, discomforts and grievances, and having nowhere else to turn, we apply to your lordships, knowing you to be most Christian, devout and merciful, and beg you humbly upon our knees to permit us to purchase a site in this city and there at our own expense to build a church in praise of Our Lord and in the name of our most holy leader [*Confaloner*] St George, so that with God's help and St George's favour we may be more warmly inspired to dedicate our lives to the service, honour and benefit of your lordships. We ask this not out of cowardice or meanness of spirit, or from any lack of loyalty and love towards you, but solely to make it known that we have no place of burial, an abuse which will not recur when we have a cemetery of our own. This we beg as a special favour, being confident that your lordships will grant it, both because you are men of honour and devotion, and to show us that in your eyes we are no worse than the Armenian heretics and the Jewish infidels who here and in other parts of your lordships' dominions have synagogues and mosques for worshipping God in their own misguided way. On the contrary, we believe that your lordships regard us as true and Catholic Christians, and will treat us as such by granting us this most holy favour. Otherwise we shall know that your lordships treat us worse than the Turks and Moors do their Christian subjects, for they let them have churches and conduct their ceremonies and services in public, and we, who are such loyal servants of your lordships and

---

[5] See Genesis 10:8–10 and 11:1–9.

Christians to boot, cannot believe that you will refuse us this most honourable request, but rather hope that you will grant us even more than we ask.

And to your lordships we commend ourselves for ever.[6]   J. G. B., B. P.

7   A PREACHER CENSURED FOR ATTACKING THE GREEKS, 1596
From a letter of Monsignor Gratiani, Bishop of Amelia, papal nuncio in Venice, to the Cardinal Secretary of State, 13 April 1596: ASVat. DN, filza 32, ff. 251r–252v.

The other day one of the Dominicans, who is preaching in the church of the order at Santi Giovanni e Paolo, expounded the views of Luther on Purgatory and then refuted them, or so he says, by citing eighty passages. In the course of this he mixed up the Greeks with Luther and ended by launching into a tirade in which he proclaimed his wish to have all the Greeks of Venice listening to his sermon, that they might be confounded and might come to know the Catholic truth in the matter of Purgatory. Certain Greeks who were present began to protest among themselves at the end of the sermon, and there was some whispering in the audience, but the commotion among the Greeks grew to the point at which large numbers of them rushed off excitedly to the Collegio to lodge a serious complaint with the Doge and the Signoria concerning those words which the preacher had uttered against them. On hearing of the fuss they were making, the preacher offended them still further the following day when from his pulpit he begged God to convert them. The lords of Venice, who have for many reasons of their own a great interest in keeping the Greeks content, showed great displeasure at the preacher's behaviour, and after calming the Greeks down they sent to ask the father what he had said against them. He replied that he had said he would have wished to have all the Greeks at his sermon, in order to strengthen their belief in Purgatory. My lords, on being told that he had said this to confound the Greeks, and had named them together with the heretics, ordered him to abstain from preaching because they wanted him to withdraw the words that had offended the Greeks, and they desired him to say the following words from the pulpit:

> Preaching the sermon on Purgatory, I said 'O God, would that I had before me all the Greeks in Venice, to strengthen their belief in Purgatory'. Gentlemen, I declare publicly that I meant no disrespect to this *Catholic* nation, and I have

---

[6] On 30 April 1514 Doge Leonardo Loredan referred to the permission granted by the Council of Ten on 4 October 1513 to 'our loyal and active stradiots [light cavalry]' to buy a site on which to build a church dedicated to St George. He approved their purchase of land in the parish of San Canciano, stipulating that papal permission must be sought for the building of the church. Although this was quickly forthcoming, the foundation stone was laid only in 1539 and the building (at Sant' Antonio, not San Canciano) completed only in 1573. See Fedalto 1967, pp. 42–5, 76, 126.

always most firmly held that they believe in Purgatory *even as we do ourselves*, and I said these words in all innocence. Since I now know that these remarks have given scandal to the Greek nation, as I never wished or intended, I would happily shed my blood if only I could undo it, and if the Greek nation has been offended I beg pardon of God and of every single one of them.

The father reported that he had said these words in the pulpit, except for those underlined, which he admitted to having withheld. They had promised him that after this he might continue to preach, and indeed he said that on Easter Sunday he was to preach in St Mark's before the Doge and the Signoria; and so the matter has been smoothed over.

Because the Collegio does not meet on these holy days and the usual audiences are not given, I have complained to many people in private (and I know that my remarks have been reported to their lordships) of their readiness to interfere with the authority of the Church. I shall complain to the Collegio too, although the father Inquisitor and others acquainted with local custom tell me that this is the way the Venetians do things, and repeat many stories of preachers who, because they spoke of the Greeks or commented on matters of state, have been forced to withdraw their words, or to give up preaching and themselves withdraw from Venice. One of those who had to retract on account of the Greeks was Panicarola,[7] when he gave sermons in this city. Furthermore, the conduct of this Dominican father deserves rebuke because, the father Inquisitor tells me, they summon all the preachers before Lent and one of the admonitions they give them is an order not to speak of the Greeks, and this the father ought to have obeyed, because everybody knows the interests which the lords of Venice have in the Greek nation.

The preacher also deserves reproof because he never informed me of these goings-on, so that I did not know of them in time to give Your Most Illustrious Lordship an account of them last week, and could only make a brief mention of them. I humbly commend myself to your favour.   B. P., N. D.

Interests over faith when it comes to the Greeks

---

[7] Francesco Panigarola (1548–94), Franciscan observant, correspondent of Carlo Borromeo, ardent foe of the Protestant reformers and supporter of the Catholic League in France, Bishop of Asti, 1587–94. He is known to have preached the Lenten sermons to huge audiences in the Venetian convent of San Francesco della Vigna in 1579.

'EBREI TEDESCHI': THE GERMANIC AND ITALIAN JEWS

8 THE 'GETO AT SAN HIERONIMO', 1516
From a Senate decree of 29 March 1516 (Ravid 1987b, pp. 248–50).

Several laws of the Senate and Great Council have prescribed that Jews shall not be permitted to stay in Venice save for a total of fifteen days in any one year. Other godly and necessary ordinances have been issued for the purpose of frustrating the treachery of the Jews, and since these measures are well known to everyone it is pointless to recall them. However, given the urgent needs of the present times, the said Jews have been permitted to come and live in Venice, and the main purpose of this concession was to preserve the property of Christians which was in their hands. But no godfearing subject of our state would have wished them, after their arrival, to disperse throughout the city, sharing houses with Christians and going wherever they choose by day and night, perpetrating all those misdemeanours and detestable and abominable acts which are generally known and shameful to describe, with grave offence to the Majesty of God and uncommon notoriety on the part of this well-ordered Republic. Since it is most necessary to take appropriate and effective action,

BE IT DETERMINED that, to prevent such grave disorders and unseemly occurrences, the following measures shall be adopted, i.e. that all the Jews who are at present living in different parishes within our city, and all others who may come here, until the law is changed as the times may demand and as shall be deemed expedient, shall be obliged to go at once to dwell together in the houses in the court within the Geto at San Hieronimo, where there is plenty of room for them to live. That they may obey this order, and not evade it, arrangements shall be made for the immediate evacuation of all these houses, and the Jews must pay a rent which will be higher by one third than that received at present by the landlords of the aforesaid houses. The Jews may not keep an inn in any part of the city, save in the Geto. That the landlords may the more readily grant them the houses, be it resolved that they are not to pay tenths on the increment of one third added to the rents for such time as the Jews are occupying these

338

houses. To prevent the Jews from going about all night, provoking the greatest discontent and the deepest displeasure on the part of Jesus Christ, be it determined that, on the side towards the old Geto, where there is a little bridge, and likewise on the other side of the bridge, two doors shall be made, one for each of these two places. These doors must be opened in the morning at the sound of the *marangona*, and in the evening they shall be shut at the twenty-fourth hour [sunset] by four Christian guards, who shall be appointed for this purpose and paid by the Jews, at whatever rate shall seem appropriate to the Collegio. Furthermore, two high walls shall be built to close off the other two sides, which rise above the canals, and all the quays attached to the said houses shall be walled in. These guards shall be obliged to live in the place, day and night, alone and without their families, in order to keep a close watch on it, with such orders as may be issued by the Collegio. Furthermore, the Collegio must assign two boats to patrol around the place by day and by night, and they too shall be paid for by the money of the Jews. All orders, however, shall be balloted by the Collegio, and those that obtain more than half the votes shall have as much force and permanence as if this Council had determined upon them.

If by chance any Jew is found by officials or public servants outside the Geto after the hours specified above, they shall be bound to arrest him at once for his disobedience.   B. P.

9   THE CONVERSION OF A JEW TO CHRISTIANITY, *c.*1569

From the testimony of Marc'Antonio degli Eletti, formerly Isaac, son of Mira and Mandolino Pugliese, to the Inquisition in Venice, 15 November 1569 (Ioly Zorattini 1980–, II (1561–70), 104–6).

I will tell you that I came into contact with Christians through the craft I had to work at on Murano, and I had a licence from the Cattaveri to stay outside the Ghetto to work at night upon my trade, for I have a privilege from the government to make glass globes, and the honourable Messer Antonio Boldu got me the licence from the Cattaveri. Many times, over three or four months, did we talk and argue over matters of faith, and since I would not understand what he said about Christianity he took me to a sermon at Santi Giovanni e Paolo, where there was a preacher very learned in the Hebrew language, possibly from Ferrara. Messer Pietro Loredan, who was Savio del Consiglio,[8] was there in front of me, and, as the most reverend preacher spoke in the Hebrew language about the faith, he, Messer Pietro Loredan, would say to me, 'Mark this passage', and so on several times. This most noble lord invited me to

---

[8] Pietro di Lorenzo Loredan (1505–68).

see him from day to day, and on one occasion I went in person to talk to the aforesaid preacher and to the honourable Messer Antonio Boldu together. Messer Antonio made me buy a Hebrew book entitled *Galatinus*, which has been translated from Hebrew into Latin.[9] I used to read that book every day with Messer Antonio, and he explained to me some passages of the greatest importance concerning the advent of the Messiah. On encountering some difficult passage I would visit the Jews in the Ghetto and get them to expound it to me, and so I asked certain learned Levantine Jews whether it was true that the blessed Jesus Christ came as the Messiah. They answered, 'Yes, but one cannot see it.' And so, arguing and talking and thinking continually for more than a year, and resorting to various methods such as prayer and fasting, I besought God to give me the light and grace to understand these difficulties in the Scripture, and hence the Majesty of God inspired and summoned me to the holy Catholic faith by means of holy baptism. I have been baptized for no purpose other than the saving of my soul, and so I wish to persevere to the end, and I will accept death for the faith as readily as any other good fortune, and I hope to be the means of bringing other Jews to the light of the holy Christian faith.   B. P.

10   LICENCE FOR A JEWISH PHYSICIAN, 1589
(i) From a despatch of the papal nuncio, Archbishop Matteucci, 4 February 1589: ASVat. DN, filza 26, f. 477.

When I went to pay my respects to the Doge on the Festival of the Purification, many leading senators of the Collegio urged me to grant a licence to two Jewish physicians to exercise their profession. When I explained that I had no authority to do so, they pressed me, in a way that brooked no refusal, to obtain one for them from the Pope himself, asserting that these doctors were men of long-tried worth, and that they had full knowledge of the constitutions [*complessioni*] of the senators and of their families. Should His Holiness prove unwilling to grant a licence in general terms, they would still beg him to allow the doctors to attend them and their families. Of these physicians I know one, David de Pomis by name, who is a doctor by papal authority, has published several books, and last year, I believe, dedicated some work to the Doge. He has the reputation of being, although a Jew, a good man, and is said to have effected some

---

[9] The work of Pietro Colonna, otherwise Galatinus, *Opus de arcanis catholicae veritatis* (Orthonae Maris, 1518). This was designed to convert the Jews by invoking their own writings against them, including the kabbalah.

remarkable cures at the time of the plague. Should Your Illustrious Lordship see fit to raise the matter with His Holiness, I will appeal to his wisdom.

B. P.

(ii) Petition of the Jew David de Pomis to Pope Sixtus V, 1 July 1589: ASVat. DN, filza 28, f. 282.

Most blessed father,

Need compels me, the Christian duty of charity persuades me, and the supreme goodness of Your Holiness emboldens me, unworthy as I am, to write you these few lines. I beg you with clasped hands and mouth to the ground to send the licence to attend Christians, for myself alone, to one of your servants who resides here in Venice. He will find me now decrepit and burdened with a family. I have held doctorates in medicine and philosophy for more than forty years, with the papal licence, and after the Council of Trent this favour was granted me by Pope Pius IV, of happy memory, by the hands of the [Cardinal of] San Clemente, who was then head of the Inquisition. It will likewise be attested that during the plague which broke out here I performed immense services to the state in visiting and caring for the afflicted without any reward. This man will know, too, that I have no occupation other than that of letters, accompanied by the practice of medicine, and, apart from the lexicon which I dedicated to Your Holiness and gave to you by the hands of Missier Benedetto da Segni, a Jew and your loyal servant, I have written eight other works, most of which have been published by the printing-press. Recently I have composed a discourse on [the Book of] Daniel, in which I have demonstrated things not previously noted by other commentators – especially what is meant by the fourth monarchy, and what it tells of the Church of St Peter and the alliance which must be made, the war of the Turk against the Persian, and other remarkable things. And, if I were worthy to meet with Your Holiness, I know you would not be dissatisfied with me, your most humble servant, and I pray God to keep you long in health and happiness.

Venice, 1 July 1589.

Your Holiness's most devoted and humble slave.

David de Pomis, Jew.
B. P.

11 MONEYLENDING AND THE SECOND-HAND TRADE, 1624
From the *condotta* or agreement with the Germanic Jews (Ebrei Tedeschi) authorized by the Senate on 16 November 1624 (Ravid 1978, pp. 106–23).

2   For the greater convenience of the poor, the Jews shall be bound to provide them with loans of 3 ducats or less on each pawn ticket, upon interest of 1 bagattino per lira per month[10] and no more. The three bankers who are at present serving the poor must until the end of December next continue to do so on the same terms as they have had in the past from the corporation [*Università*] of the Jews, so that within that time this corporation can either make a further agreement with the same banks or else provide three others equipped to meet this need. These must, by the end of October next, or by such earlier time as they can be ready, begin to serve and lend to the poor in the manner described above, and as laid down in the last contract [*condotta*]. The leases of the premises on which the banks store their pledges shall be continued, and the bankers shall share between them the rents which are due to the landlords of these properties. Let it be clear that the Jews are not obliged to lend upon gold, silver, pearls, jewels, tapestries and silken cloths, with the exception of bracelets, silver plates, gold rings, and other rings set with false stones or no stones at all, on which they must provide loans, and they may not refuse, excuse themselves or delay making these loans on any account in dealing with any person whatsoever, on pain of a fine of 20 ducats for every time they fail. This fine must be exacted from them in full by the Sopraconsoli, and one half of it shall go to the accuser, who shall be kept secret, and the other half to the magistracy which enforces this decree. The Jews are not to issue more than one ticket upon any one pledge. . . .

12   The Jews may engage in the second-hand trade, but they may not sell new materials of any kind, either by piece or by length, nor may they make or cause others to make clothing or other goods of new cloth or other new material. Should they break this rule and the report be proved, they shall forfeit the material and pay 50 ducats for each offence, of which sum one half shall go to the accuser, who shall be kept secret, and the other half to the office of the Sopraconsoli, which shall be charged with the enforcement of this law. They may not work as furriers, nor may they keep, sell or work upon any kind of new hides, but only keep things which pertain to the second-hand trade. They may, however, engage in the manufacture of veils and coifs. Let it be clear that coats and sleeves and other articles of chain mail are not to be regarded as second hand goods, upon pain of forfeiting these articles and paying a fine of 50 ducats

[10] Since there were 12 bagattini to the soldo and 20 soldi to the lira, the rate of interest was equivalent to 5 per cent per annum. It had remained at this level since the *condotta* of 1573.

342

for every infraction of this rule. In accordance with the agreement reached between the Jews and the Craft of the Tailors of Venice before the Savii of the Collegio in the last contract, no Jew may work as a tailor for himself or for others, nor may he cut or stitch even in the Ghetto on pain of a fine of 50 ducats for each occasion on which he is found working, and of forfeiture of the material. This penalty shall apply both to the Jew who does the cutting and to anyone who gives him sewing or other work to do. No Jew may import to this city any new clothing of any kind, on pain of a fine of 100 ducats and forfeiture of any material discovered. He may not give tailor's work, either in the Ghetto or outside it, to anyone who is not a qualified master of the Craft of the Tailors, whether male or female, on pain of a fine of 50 ducats for each offence, the same sum to be paid by any unqualified person who accepts work.   B. P.

12 LEVANTINE JEWS AND THE GHETTO VECCHIO, 1541
From a Senate decree of 2 June 1541 (Ravid 1987b, pp. 250–1).

As can be seen, most of the merchandise which arrives from Upper and Lower Romania[11] is brought here by travelling Levantine Jewish merchants and is in their hands. They have petitioned our Cinque Savi alla Mercanzia, saying that because the Ghetto is so cramped they can find nowhere to stay in it (as our Cinque Savi alla Mercanzia have seen for themselves), and so they want a place to be provided for their lodging.

BE IT THEREFORE DETERMINED, that they may have better reason to bring their merchandise here, to Venice's advantage, and that they may have a place in which to lodge, that the Collegio may license any magistracy they choose[12] to attempt to accommodate the said travelling Levantine Jewish merchants in the Ghetto, and, should there be no room for them there, let them have authority to lodge them in the Ghetto Vecchio, as they judge best, in such a way and upon such orders as the Collegio may give to that magistracy. However, the said travelling Levantine Jews must always be enclosed and guarded in the same way as those of the Ghetto Nuovo, and they may not engage in banking or the second-hand trades or in any employment other than pure mercantile activity. Everything done by the magistracy charged with this responsibility shall have the same force and permanence as if it had been done by this Council.

B. P.

[11] The Balkan peninsula.
[12] They chose the Cinque Savi alla Mercanzia.

13   MOTIVES FOR EXPELLING THE MARRANOS, 1550

From two letters of Hieronymo Feruffino, ambassador of the Duke of Ferrara (Kaufmann 1890, pp. 304–5).

23 July 1550

From Messer Giovan Francesco, salaried secretary to the ambassodor of Urbino, I have had further information about the reasons for the banishment of the Marranos, in addition to what I gathered from M. de Morvilliers[13] and wrote to you before. There are several motives for this act, and the first is that the lords of Venice have been advised that the Marranos are worse than Jews, because they are neither Christians nor Jews. All the Jews live together in the Ghetto, separated from Christians, but the Marranos have to do with Christians and live in several parts of the city. The lords of Venice have been informed of this, and have been shown that such association is the cause of many errors, especially in making many Christians transgress. Furthermore, the Marranos lend money upon usury, and they may by their familiarity persuade our own people to do the same thing. And they are a malevolent, faithless people, up to no good, and they might suffice to infect not only the souls of Christians but also their bodies with some pestilential disease. The secretary added that he had it on good authority that the lords of Venice had issued this ban at the exhortation of the Emperor, who had asked how this Christian dominion, which professed to be Catholic, could allow a people so wicked, perverted and filthy to live in Venice and its territories. If things are as he says, I hold that the decree of banishment will be fully enforced, and not modified in the way in which the French ambassador told me he was inclined to believe.

24 July 1550

Concerning the renewal of the decree against the Marranos, which was issued on 9 July, I have spoken to the ambassador and have heard from him that the principal reason for the decree and the banishment was that it had been demonstrated to the lords of Venice that, if the Marranos continued to associate as they now do with Christians, they would corrupt many and sow among them a wicked and evil doctrine. And, because the Marranos lived three or four families to a house, and dwelt in squalor and kept their lodgings very poorly, there arose the fear and suspicion of illness and indeed of some pestilence on account of their conduct and way of life. Although the said Marranos have tried to contrive that up to 300 of them should be allowed to remain, by showing that they bring and will continue to bring profit to the city, the ambassador none the

---

[13] The French ambassador.

345

less thinks that, being reviled and in dire straits as they are, they will not
succeed – indeed, that the lords of Venice will wish this renewed decree to be
fully enforced.   B. P.

14   THE CHARTER OF THE JEWISH MERCHANTS, 1589
Petition of Daniel Rodriga, consul of the Sephardic Jewish merchants (Ravid 1976,
pp. 214–17).

Most Serene Prince and most illustrious lords,
    The desire which I, Daniel Rodriga, your most humble and ardent slave,
have always had to serve you (as you may clearly understand from many of my
previous activities) has already inspired me to bring it about that my brother
Jacob with his son-in-law and ten other families of our relatives and friends
should come to live in this most illustrious city. The same desire still burns
within me more fiercely than ever, and has now caused me to come to your feet
and humbly beg you that, since I plan to bring more families hither and so
increase your customs and excise duties both in Venice and in Spalato
[otherwise Split], you may do me the favour of granting me the privileges and
concessions that I present with this my petition, both to those [Jewish
merchants] that are here already and to those whom I shall in future bring to
live in this city and in Spalato. In Spalato I would wish Your Serenity to
construct a ghetto for their dwelling-place according to the plan which I
likewise present to you, with rents to be paid as shall be deemed appropriate.
Since the Jews of Spalato are correspondents of the Jews of Venice, it will make
it easier to stay there and bring great benefit to Your Serenity, and they will help
me pursue my wishes. I will take these concessions as a notable sign of your
benevolence and generosity and also as some recognition of my merits. I
humbly and respectfully commend myself to you.

The articles of the privileges presented at the feet of the Doge by Daniel
Rodriga in the name of the Levantine, Spanish and other Jewish merchants
living in Venice with their families.

1   That all the above merchants may live in security in person, and with their
families, merchandise and property, without any danger or molestation, in this
city of Venice and in any other city and possession of this most serene
Dominion, to seaward and to landward, where they may come, remain and
depart as they please without hindrance, and that they may sail the seas freely
both to windward and to leeward, as Venetian citizens do; and, as the travelling

Levantine Jews do at present, they shall pay duties at the same rate as Venetian citizens.[14]

2 That the aforesaid merchants of Jewish descent, whatever their nation, may live in security according to their religion, without being subject to inquisition by any office or magistracy, either clerical or lay, even if in other places they have worn some other dress and followed some other religion. Once arrived in this state, they may freely live as Jews and always practise their rites, precepts and ceremonies and hold their synagogues according to the law of Moses and the custom of the Jewish faith. If for any reason this most serene Dominion should decide that they are no longer to live in the state, these merchants and their families, merchandise and property may leave freely and without hindrance, and ships, boats, wagons and horses and other necessary things shall be made available to them at the normal and lawful rates of payment to enable them to go wherever they please. There may be no reprisals against their persons, merchandise or property upon any claim or accusation made against them; and should they be dismissed as aforesaid they must be given eighteen months' notice before departure, and they shall first be paid by all who owe them money.[15]

3 That whenever war breaks out, either with the Sultan of Turkey or with any other prince, none of the aforesaid nations of merchants dwelling here may be detained or any reprisal be taken against their goods, nor may their families be disturbed in other ways, nor may they be dismissed on account of the war. Rather, they must continue to enjoy security, and may buy, sell and make contracts, conveying any goods or merchandise without danger or loss, both by sea and by land, so long as they pay the normal duties. They shall not be protected from dismissal for some reason of state, in which case the guilty parties shall not only be dismissed but most severely punished, while the innocent persons continue to enjoy the same security and freedom, without being troubled in time of war with the billeting of troops or obligations of personal service. In time of pestilence they shall have the same opportunities to save themselves as have other subjects of this most serene Dominion.[16]

[14] By its decree of 27 July 1589 (Ravid 1976 pp. 219–22) the Senate agreed in general to Rodriga's proposals and made them the foundation of a *condotta* or agreement which was to run for ten years, with some significant modifications. For example, the suggestion in Rodriga's first article that Jews should be in the same position as Venetian citizens was omitted on the advice of the Cinque Savi alla Mercanzia.

[15] In the matter of persecutions for religious offences the Senate decree was much less explicit than the Rodriga proposals, and protected the Jews only against molestation by 'any magistracy on account of religion'. In practice, however, the Inquisition in Venice did not proceed on charges of heresy against Sephardic Jews.

[16] These proposals were accepted by the Senate.

347

4 That the aforesaid merchants shall not by this agreement have any obligation to contribute to any tax or impost to support the loans made by the Germanic Jews through the banks. They shall only be obliged to pay the normal duties and shall remain free of any other burden in that they have no other craft but that of a merchant, and merely trade with their capital for the benefit of the customs and of the artisans. They shall be permitted to elect their own officials, persons appointed to various tasks, duties and other employments, as they wish, with authority to impose taxes among themselves, assign everyone his proper portion and compel him to make any payment that may be required, and they may proceed without opposition against the persons and goods of the disobedient immediately at any summons issued by the deputies. Should the need arise, they may also issue excommunications, according to their rite. Because it is not the intention of the aforesaid Jews that anyone other than civilized and respected men should be admitted to this nation, lest in a manner contrary to their honourable purpose some disreputable person should be brought in and disturb the security of these merchants by fraud or robbery or other malpractices, and depart from the good and honourable conduct which these merchants intend to follow, no one may live here, and no house may be given to anyone, without a certificate from the deputies countersigned by the consul, upon such penalties as shall seem appropriate to the most noble Cinque Savi sopra la Mercanzia. By virtue of the decree adopted by the most excellent Senate on 10 May 1586 these magistrates have been appointed summary judges, without possibility of appeal, of all disputes which may arise between Jewish and Turkish merchants. They shall also be made judges over the aforesaid merchants, and shall be responsible for ensuring that they are given houses and a burial ground and provided with all things necessary to living according to their rites and customs at the normal prices, as they have hitherto done for the travelling Levantine merchants.[17]

5 That the aforesaid merchants in Venice and its state may enjoy the above privileges, and that those who wish to live in or pass through Spalato, in addition to enjoying the aforesaid privileges, may keep shops of any kind of merchandise or craft, and act as brokers, and indeed do anything else that is permitted to the citizens of that city. There they shall be granted houses, and a place to live in with their families, and a burial ground, and every other facility, and permission to keep a bank for the benefit both of the inhabitants and of passing merchants, upon those terms and conditions which shall be agreed with

[17] The exemption from any obligation to contribute to the banks was resented and contested by the Germanic Jews, and the obligation was introduced in 1598. Only Venetian magistrates were allowed to proceed against defaulting taxpayers. Newcomers seeking to join the community of resident Jewish merchants were to be approved not by the deputies and the consul, but by the whole body, subject to their winning the approval of four of the five Savi alla Mercanzia. Anyone not approved by the Jews could appeal to the Cinque Savi.

that honourable community by Daniel, our consul. For fear of evildoers they may outside Spalato wear the black hat in all parts of Dalmatia, and all the aforesaid persons, both in Venice and in Spalato, who enjoy the above privileges, shall be obliged to pay to the aforesaid Daniel our consul such sums as shall be allocated to him by the Heads of the Congregation of Venice and Spalato as a reward for his many merits, and for his trouble and expense.[18]

B. P.

[18] The decree makes no mention of Spalato.

In the Senate decree, penalties were introduced for lending one's name to persons who were not privileged and trading with their goods, and the Senate stipulated that the Jews concerned must wear the yellow cap and live in the Ghetto Nuovo with other Jews.

THE TURKS

15   HOUSE RULES FOR THE NEW FONDACO DEI TURCHI, 1621
From the regulations drawn up by the Cinque Savi alla Mercanzia, 27 May 1621, for
the new Turkish exchange or Fondaco, which was to be established in a house on the
Grand Canal formerly belonging to the Duke of Ferrara, in the parish of San Giacomo
dell'Orio: ASV Cinque Savi alla Mercanzia, nuova serie, b. 187, fasc. II.

1   . . . No Turks may be introduced into this dwelling-place until all the
following conditions have been met and approved by our own magistracy.

2   All the doors on the landward side shall be walled up, both those which give
onto the paved way [*sallizada*] and those which give onto the Rio del Megio.
The only doors to be left shall be the main door which gives onto the paved way,
and the door halfway along the Rio del Megio, which shall serve only as the
entrance to the residence of the guardian [*custode*].

3 · On the Grand Canal, the existing landing-stage shall remain. Two others
shall be added, one on either side, to enable the Turks to unload their
merchandise more easily; these two new landing-stages shall normally be
closed, and shall be opened only when merchandise needs to be unloaded.

4   It shall be made impossible to see into the courtyard of the house from the
landward side: either a wall shall be erected to block the view, or else all the
windows and openings shall be stopped up, so that the Turks cannot be seen by
their neighbours. For the same reason the old wall between the court and the
two houses which overlook it shall be raised to the [word illegible] of the lower
of those houses.

5   The wall on the Grand Canal overlooking the landing-stage shall be raised
by another 4 feet.

6   The storerooms now on the ground floor shall be brought to a total of
twenty-six. The three above the Grand Canal on the Rio del Megio side shall
be joined with the guardian's residence, and shall be separated from the rest,
access to them being only through the guardian's residence. The other rooms,

twenty-three in number, shall be at the disposal of all the Turks, Bosnians and Albanians. Each of these storerooms shall have a large balcony with iron railings, to be built underneath the timbers of the first floor, in order to give more light. This shall apply not only to the storerooms above the paved way, but also to those àbove the Rio. Balconies facing into the house shall be altered as may seem necessary and appropriate.

7   The balconies of the storerooms which are now above the Grand Canal shall be walled up.

8   The offices [*mezadi*][19] which are now in the house shall be brought to a total of twenty-five. The seven which are on the Rio del Megio side, above the Grand Canal, shall become part of the guardian's residence, and there shall be no access from them to the Turks' quarters, and no balconies, openings, or other ways of looking onto the Turks, and the wall of the guardian's terrace, which looks towards the courtyard, shall be raised to a greater height than the wall which is to be made for the purpose of shutting off the balcony above the colonnades. The other eighteen offices shall be divided, so that the eight on the side of the Rio del Megio shall be available for occupation by the Turks of Asia [Minor] and Constantinople, and the other ten, on the side of the paved way, shall be for the Turks of Bosnia and Albania. . . .

12   On the side of the Rio del Megio there shall be thirteen chambers and six upper chambers [*sopracamere*], with a wash-house and common room, which shall lead to the offices below, and shall be for the use of the Turks of Asia and Constantinople. . . .

13   On the side of the paved way, there shall be nine chambers, including the two which are to be made out of the kitchen, with seven upper chambers, and the existing corridor, and a wash-house, and a common room, which shall also lead to the offices below. These chambers shall have only one door, and all these rooms shall be for the Turks of Bosnia and Albania. . . .

21   Above the door of each storeroom, office, chamber and upper chamber shall be placed a number, to regulate the rents that the Turks will have to pay, according to the tariff which is indicated below, and which, for the information of all Turks residing in this exchange house, must be posted up in a prominent place.

22   Here is the tariff of the rents that the Turks will have to pay for the storerooms, offices, chambers, and upper chambers listed below. . . .

23   The guardian shall keep twenty-five lamps burning throughout the night.

---

[19] Boerio 1856 explains that, as merchants and lawyers in Venice were accustomed to use mezzanines as places for transacting business, the word *meza* (*mezado* in this document) had come to refer to their offices.

351

24 He shall be obliged to keep the wells full of water, so that there shall be enough to satisfy even those Turks who use a large quantity.

25 He shall sweep out the exchange house several times a day, as often as is necessary, and shall have all rubbish and other impurities removed.

26 He shall be obliged to lock the doors, both to landward and to seaward, at dusk, and to open them again at sunrise, from the outside, with good and effective keys, which he must keep.

27 He must keep two men on the doors, one on the landward and the other on the seaward door, and they must always be there to man those doors. These men must first be approved by our magistracy.

28 The said doorkeepers shall not allow either women or beardless persons who may be Christians to enter the exchange house at any time, on pain of fitting punishment.

29 The said doorkeepers shall not allow anyone in the exchange house to carry weapons of steel or iron, or arms of any kind, or arquebuses, or sulphur, or gunpowder, or other things forbidden by law, on pain of fitting punishment. Should any such weapon be found, the guardian must report this immediately to our magistracy.

30 The said doorkeepers shall not allow anyone bearing arms of any kind to enter the exchange house, lest scandal arise within it, upon such penalties as the court shall determine.

31 Turks who are now in this city, and those who shall in future come to it, must go to live in the exchange house in full conformity with the decrees of the Senate and with that of the Collegio of 2 March last. Nobody, therefore, even if he is a broker [to the Turks], may give lodgings to Turks in contravention of the said legislation on any pretext whatsoever, on pain of those fines or corporal punishments that may be deemed appropriate by the magistrates. If any brokers infringe these regulations, they shall be immediately deprived of their posts.

32 The guardian shall undertake to observe all the aforesaid regulations, on pain of fines and corporal punishments as the magistracy shall deem appropriate, and on pain, also, of forfeiting his post.

33 Because, from day to day, for the purpose of directing and regulating this exchange house, some points may require modification, clarification or regulation, we reserve to ourselves and our successors the right to make additions or deletions to these regulations, and to clarify or adjust them as we deem it necessary.   S. G. D.

Part IX
Cultural Life: Learning and Literature, Book-Publishing, Entertainment

THE PROMOTION OF LEARNING AND LITERATURE

S CHOLARSHIP *and literature had traditionally been less favoured by Venice's utilitarian, profit-minded elite (allowing a few exceptions) than in many other Italian cities. Nor did the Venetian government make any provision for elementary education, although private masters, teaching not only the abacus and other merchant skills but also grammar, flourished. By the mid fifteenth century, however, there was a growing acceptance in Venice of the usefulness and prestige attached to learning, including the varieties of it promoted by humanistic luminaries in Florence, nearby Padua and elsewhere; already, since 1407, the Senate had assumed some responsibility for the financial support of the Studium of Padua, and Venetians were obliged to go there, and nowhere else, for higher education. By the 1450s the Senate was making its own nominations to academic posts, and, as a result of Paduan disloyalty (1509), after the War of the League of Cambrai the governing magistracy of the three Riformatori dello Studio passed to Venetian patricians elected by the Senate, an arrangement made permanent in 1528. Meanwhile, since the late fourteenth century a bequest had endowed public lectures and disputations on learned topics (mainly Aristotelian) to be held at Rialto [IX.4], and from the 1440s there was also a school for Chancery trainees, and public lectures at St Mark's on rhetoric and other subjects. Other cultural initiatives included the founding of St Mark's Library. This is illustrated by the moving letter [IX.1] from the Greek cardinal Bessarion (1403–72) which accompanied the donation of his private book collection (about 1000 titles, over half of them Greek) to Venice. Bessarion, who had visited the city in 1460–1 as Pius II's legate to promote the Crusade and been made an honorary member of the Great Council, now professed to see in Venice the main hope for the survival of Hellenic culture in the face of Turkish conquests. His panegyric of the Republic was no doubt contrived to flatter the Senate with what he knew they would like to hear, but, in spite of the unanimous acceptance of his gift and the commitment to provide secure premises where the books could be consulted, the philistinism of the Venetian nobility still seems to have prevailed. Bessarion's books were stored in the hall where the courts of the Forty met; some crates were opened, and some books stolen or even sold.*

355

Admittedly, a few privileged borrowers were allowed, such as the scholarly printer Aldus Manutius. Aldus affected to complain in 1514 [IX.3] that he was too much in demand from intellectual and other distinguished visitors (Erasmus had been among them in 1508–9); in other words that he, a pedagogue turned artisan, had entered high society on equal terms. Nevertheless only in 1515, by Senate decree, was the government obliged to build a library near San Mark's 'as an eternal monument to our descendants and an example for the whole of Italy'; and, even so, it was not until after the patrician literary scholar Pietro Bembo (1470–1547) had been appointed librarian, in 1532, that a proper adminis- tration was set up, during the boom period for public building initiatives under Doge Andrea Gritti (1523–38). In 1537 construction of the library at last began; designed by Jacopo Tatti (Sansovino), it was eventually finished some time between 1554 and 1565. Meanwhile, at the end of the fifteenth century, late by the standards of other leading cities, government support had been mustered for the writing of a history of Venice in Latin, on the Ciceronian model, underlining moral examples learnt from the past. Sabellicus, a non-Venetian, wrote the first such work [IX.2, 10] and received a pension for it, but the appointment of his continuator, Venice's first official historian, still lay in the future (1516). It may have worried some Venetians that they could claim few if any major contributions to vernacular literature; one of the few exceptions, Pietro Bembo (who spent much of his life away from Venice), conceded in his masterly essay on the Italian language that the Tuscan form was superior to the Venetian [IX.5]. The growing fervour to identify education with Catholic duty led eventually, in 1551, to proposals to establish free elementary schools in each sestier [IX.6], though insufficient funds delayed the scheme until 1567, when four – not six – grammar schools were founded. Their success seems to have been limited, given the competition from private schools and those of the new religious orders, particularly the Jesuits, whose schools, established at about the same time, continued until the order's expulsion in 1606. But the most ambitious scheme to relate the acquisition of knowledge to Venetian political and religious ideals and mythology was the Academy founded in 1557 by Federigo Badoer (1519–93). This institution was in some ways similar to other academies of the later sixteenth century, but it was unique in respect of the extensive cultural, moral and spiritual benefits it promised, the government support it received, its highly bureaucratic organization and its involvement with salaried lecturing and book- publishing on a grand scale. Some of its programme is expressed in the letter addressed to the Procurators by Badoer himself [IX.7]; the combination of patriotic and commercial enterprise seems peculiarly Venetian, and its financial collapse together with Badoer's disgrace in 1560 underline this too. The experiment was not repeated, and Padua remained much more congenial than Venice for scientific and literary academies; nevertheless more informal discussion groups continued to flourish. During the 1580s radically minded and morally

356

committed 'Giovani' looked to the ridotto *of Andrea and Nicolò Morosini; this group included the Servite friar Paolo Sarpi (1552–1623), according to his biographer, who mentions Sarpi's presence in later, quasi-Protestant, gatherings too [IX.8]: evidence of the vitality of Venetian intellectual life round the turn of the century.*

BIBLIOGRAPHY   In general: Arnaldi and Stocchi 1981–3. On Bessarion and St Mark's library: Labowsky 1979; Zorzi 1987. On early printing and Manutius: Fulin 1882; Lowry 1979. On Sabellicus and official historiography: Pertusi 1970, esp. pp. 321–31; Gilbert 1971; Chavasse 1986. On institutions of learning: Nardi 1971 (also in Arnaldi and Stocchi, 1981–3, III); Ross 1976; Baldo 1977; Grendler 1989. On Pietro Bembo: Dionisotti 1960; and in DBI. On the Venetian Academy: Rose 1969; Pagan 1973–4. On Sarpi and intellectual life c.1580–1620: Micanzio tr. anon. 1651; A. Favaro 1893; Smith 1907; Cozzi 1958; Seneca 1959; Wootton 1983.   D. C.

I   THE ORIGINS OF ST MARK'S LIBRARY: CARDINAL BESSARION'S GIFT, 1468
From the Latin. Letter accompanying the deed of donation (Mohler 1942, III, 541–3).

From almost the earliest years of my boyhood I strove with all my might, main, effort and concentration to assemble as many books as I could on every sort of subject. Not only did I copy many in my own hand when I was a boy or youth, but I spent what I could set aside from my small savings on buying books. For I could think of no more noble or splendid possession, no treasure more useful or valuable, that I could possibly gather for myself. Books ring with the voices of the wise. They are full of the lessons of history, full of life, law and piety. They live, speak and debate with us; they teach, advise and comfort us; they reveal matters which are furthest from our memories, and set them, as it were, before our eyes. Such is their power, worth and splendour, such their inspiration, that we should all be uneducated brutes if there were no books. We should have hardly any record of the past, no example to guide us, no knowledge whatever of the affairs of this world or the next. The tomb would cover the names of men, just as it covers their bodies.

This aim, then, has always occupied my whole mind; but my sense of urgency became the greater after the destruction of Greece and the pitiful enslavement of Byzantium. Since then, all my strength, my effort, my time, my capacity and my concentration has been devoted to seeking out Greek books. For I feared – indeed I was consumed with terror – lest all those wonderful books, the product of so much toil and study by the greatest human minds, those very beacons to the earth, should be brought to danger and destruction in an instant. Plutarch speaks of 200,000 volumes in the library of Apamea,[1] of which barely 1000 have survived to our time. But I tried, to the best of my ability, to collect books for their quality rather than their quantity, and to find single volumes of single works; and so I assembled almost all the works of the wise men of Greece, especially those which were rare and difficult to find. Finally, I reflected that my dream would not have been fully realized if I failed to make sure that the books which I had assembled with such care and effort were so disposed in my lifetime that they could not be dispersed and scattered after my death. They must be preserved in a place that is both safe and accessible, for the general good of all readers, be they Greek or Latin.

As I considered this problem and thought of many cities in Italy, your glorious and most splendid state at last presented itself to me as the only one on which I could settle with complete peace of mind. First, I did not see how I could choose anywhere safer than one where justice rules, the laws are upheld, wisdom and honesty are at the helm, and where virtue, restraint, morality, justice and good faith have their dwelling; where power has the most formidable resources at its disposal, but is exercised only in just measure; where minds are free to think as they wish, without fear of any hostile passion or violence; where the levers of power are in the hands of the wise; where the good are preferred to the wicked, and all forget their private advantage in the single-minded, honest service of the commonweal. All this makes us hope that your state will expand its might and prestige with every passing day, and we pray that it will do so.

Next, I came to understand that I could not select a place more suitable and convenient to men of my own Greek background. Though nations from almost all over the earth flock in vast numbers to your city, the Greeks are most numerous of all: as they sail in from their own regions they make their first landfall in Venice, and have such a tie with you that when they put into your city they feel they are entering another Byzantium. After all this, how could I better dispose of this gift than amongst those to whom I was myself most tightly bound by their many gifts to me: than in the city which I had chosen as my new home when Greece was enslaved and where I had been welcomed and acclaimed by you with such honour? Age weighs me down ever more, while the various ills which afflict me and the others which could follow make me well aware of my own mortality. So I have given and granted all my books, both in Latin and Greek, to the most holy shrine of the Blessed Mark in your glorious city, sure in the knowledge that this is a duty owed to your generosity, to my gratitude, and to the country which you wanted me to share.   M. L.

[1] A Hellenistic city on the Orontes.

2 HUMANIST HISTORIOGRAPHY FOR VENICE: A JUSTIFICATION, 1487
From the Latin. Extracts from the preface to Sabellicus ed. Zeno 1718, pp. 6–7.

As I embark upon the history of Venice from the founding of the city, I can claim both truly and honestly something that several other historians – not without a trace of ambition – have claimed; I begin a history that is not just colourful, and thereby of the greatest interest, but also very much to the public good; thus it should delight the reader through the very originality of its content, and also teach every civic virtue through a host of most worthy examples.

Almost every kind of new reading enables the reader to finish better educated than when he started; this will be especially true of the study of Venetian history, to the extent that it will be able to stand out more easily and more completely than any other study.

Who can deny the great and glorious deeds of certain nations that have at some point attained imperial status – at the forefront of whom are the Romans? Before the magnificence and scope of their foreign conquests, we should perhaps yield, but, in the inviolability of its laws, the impartiality of its justice, its integrity and the sanctity of its constitution, Venice shall be not inferior, but indeed far superior. No wonder: unless you think the tales of the poets are to be trusted, the origins of these other nations are thought to be altogether base and indeed almost squalid. . . .

In contrast, they were noble men, deeply pious, who founded the city of Venice; and they established a state whose justice was impartial to all and whose constitution was most sacred, since they wished to guarantee for ever the freedom in which the city was born. All future generations from the very founding of the city onwards were so zealous in pursuing this pure aim, that it is clear to one and all that the Venetian Empire, which today spreads far and wide over land and sea, has grown more through these virtues than through zeal in warfare; and for this reason it is right to judge that, if anything can escape mortal death, Venice shall never perish.

As this is agreed to be the case, I have begun to wonder greatly why it is that from so many educated men, amongst whom the study of rhetoric has flourished in recent years, not one to my knowledge has yet written anything on the history of Venice. For there are several people who by reason of their singular intellect and pre-eminent learning would have been well prepared to undertake this vast subject, whatever its size, and to handle this undertaking in a worthy manner. Yet, as to exactly why other men have shunned this task – nay, rather honour – it is difficult to tell.

Since I was to venture something in full public view, and could see that my subject had been so totally butchered, as it were, lying scattered limb [hacked] from limb, in various sketches, utterly clumsy,[2] I thought I would at least do something useful in, so to speak, venturing upon a desert never before inhabited by anyone. This is to hand on a work that, whatever its value, has been so carefully, so virtuously prepared that whoever writes on Venice after me will, having once read my work, have confidence that, now so great a subject has been broached, it can more easily be carried to completion.   R. AND P. C.

3   THE IMPACT OF PRINTING: ALDUS'S WORKSHOP AS AN INTELLECTUAL CENTRE
From the Latin. Aldus's introduction (1514) to Pseudo-Cicero, *Rhetorica ad Herennium* (Orlandi 1976, I, 129–30).

There are two things in particular, apart from the other 600, which continually break in to interrupt my work: first, the frequent letters of learned colleagues, which are sent to me from every part of Europe, and which would need whole days and nights of writing if I were to reply to them all; second, the visitors who come to see me, partly to say 'Hello', partly to find out what new scheme I have in hand, partly – and this is by far the largest crowd – because they have nothing better to do. That's the moment for them to say, 'Let's drop in on Aldus!' So they come in droves and sit around gawping 'like leaches which will not let go of the skin until they have a bellyful of blood.'[3] I shall not even bother to tell you about those who come to recite their poem, or something they have written in prose and now want to have published in my types. For the most part the works are crude and unpolished, because the authors cannot be bothered with the time and trouble needed to polish them; but they cannot see what is wrong with their poem, just because it has not had 'many days and many blots to force it into shape, or smooth it down ten times so that a nail would not catch on it.'[4] I have begun at last to protect myself from these thoroughly tedious interlopers. I do not reply to those who write to me if it is not a matter of much importance, or, if it is, I reply in a few words, like a Spartan. I must ask everyone not to treat this as arrogance or contempt on my part, or to take it in any other spirit than I do – as a way of keeping what time I have for producing good books. And I have taken care to greet those who come to see me with a warning epigram which will stop their constant and infuriating interruption of my reading and research. Above the door of my study stands written like an edict 'Whoever you are,

---

[2] Perhaps an allusion to the various chronicle traditions (see Baron 1968). Sabellicus might also have been aware and critical of the *History of the Origin of Venice* by Bernardo Giustinian (1408–89), though it was not printed until 1492 (see Labalme 1969, esp. pp. 247–304).

[3] Horace, *Ars Poetica* l. 476.

[4] Ibid., ll. 293 – 94.

Aldus asks you again and again to say whatever it is you want of him in a few words and then be on your way, unless like Hercules you have come to take the world on your shoulders and give weary Atlas a rest. There will always be something for you to do, and for all others who turn their feet this way.' I am putting the notice in here too, so that more will get to hear of it.   M. L.

4   THE RIALTO SCHOOL OF PHILOSOPHY IN SESSION, 1524
DMS, xxxvii, cols 150–1.

5 November 1524

Today at San Bartolomeo the school of philosophy was opened. The church had been specially prepared, and everyone assembled in it, among them the papal legate (the Bishop of Feltre); the Procurators Sier Alvise Pasqualigo, Sier Lorenzo Loredan and Sier Alvise Pisani; the knights Sier Gabriel Moro [and five others]; Sier Sebastian Foscarini, doctor and lecturer [and five other nobles described as doctors]; and others from the Senate, among them me, Marin Sanudo. . . . In the pulpit [*cariega*] was the *domino* and doctor [. . .] Marin from Treviso, who lectures on philosophy at Rialto after dinner, in place of Foscarini, who gives the morning lecture and pays him. And the chair-holder [*catedrante*] for the disputation in logic was Sier Jacomo Foscarini, son of Sier Michiel, aged eighteen. And first the lecturer gave a short oration, then the said Sier Jacomo did likewise, and six of his fellow logicians held an argument. Among them there was only one nobleman, Sier Nicolò Michiel, son of Sier Hironimo de la Meduna, aged sixteen. After the disputation it was twenty-three hours and a half [half an hour before sunset]; then Sier Zuan Morexini, son of Sier Michiel, a young man aged [. . .], came forward and delivered an oration in praise of philosophy; it was truly excellent, long and well pronounced, as though by a wholly expert orator, so that it was praised by all and brought him great honour. It lasted until after the first hour of night, to everyone's satisfaction. I have noted this to his eternal praise and memory. He is a pupil of Master Stefanin, [who] lectures at San Lio.   D. C.

5   BEMBO'S ACKNOWLEDGEMENT OF TUSCAN SUPERIORITY IN LANGUAGE
From Bembo 1525, ff. xiii r–xiiii v (Bembo ed. Dionisotti 1960, pp. 111–13).

Tuscan words sound better than Venetian ones; their sound is sweeter and more pleasing, lively and fluent. They are not truncated and do not appear to lack any parts, as we can see that [a great] many of ours do, which also have no double consonants. In addition, Tuscan words have a more proper beginning, a more orderly middle and a more delicate end. They are not so loose and languid; they have more regard for rules, tenses, numbers, articles and persons. Tuscans use many modes of expression which are full of judgement and beauty, and many sweet and pleasing figures [of speech] which we do not use; and how much these adorn [any speech] need not be doubted. But all I want to say now is the following: that our language has no writer in prose whose work we should keep close at hand and should use as a model of order; verse-writers, without a doubt, are very few. One of them was highly valued in his times, or even in our own, but not so much for the style of his poems, as for the manner in which he issued them as songs. Indeed the songs are still called 'Giustiniane' after his surname.[5]

That poverty and scarcity of writers is due to the fact that, when a language is put on paper in the same way in which it is used by the populace in reasoning and talking, it does not satisfy; and [on the other hand] examples cannot be taken from writings because, as I said, we do not have any worthy and accepted writers. Whereas the Tuscan language is both pleasant when it is spoken and most orderly when it is written, because, directed from time to time by many of its writers, it is now so noble [*gentile*] and well regulated that there is little more to be wished for.

L. D. S.

6 THE ESTABLISHMENT OF SCHOOLS IN THE SESTIERI, 1551
Senate decree of 23 March 1551: ASV Senato, Terra, reg. 37, f. 105 (F. Besta 1912, pp. 219–21; Baldo 1977, pp. 102–3).

In every well-ordered city, as is this city of ours by the grace of God and the prudence of our ancestors, every effort must be made [to ensure] that the youth of the city are worthily occupied, so that they do not waste in idleness but serve and bring credit to the Republic while growing up in a well-disciplined manner to their own honour and that of persons close to them. For this reason, since there is in this city a flourishing and numerous body of young people, we must ensure that the young be given an opportunity to engage in the study of letters, so that the desired end is attained. Since there is only one public professor of the humanities, who teaches at St Mark's, those who live some distance away are unable to attend his lessons at the appointed hour, and, a matter of great importance, there are no masters of grammar, the foundation and beginning of the whole study of literature. Such a need must be met, so that, encouraged by

---

[5] The humanist and poet Leonardo Giustinian (1338–1446).

easy access, all our youth may be encouraged to learn. Therefore . . . be it determined that the Riformatori dello Studio di Padova shall provide as soon as possible four able and meritorious teachers of literature, in addition to the most excellent Robertello and Giovita,[6] already appointed and in receipt of salary, who continue to teach. To each of the four up to 200 ducats a year may be paid, with the proviso that they may be removed from office should they be found wanting; and, since Robertello teaches at St Mark's, the other five teachers should be allocated one to each sestier, as appropriate, and shall be assigned to the most convenient places, and given the most suitable times for lecturing. The Riformatori must themselves endeavour to seek out six other good teachers of grammar to be placed in each of the six sestieri, to assist the principal teachers, and to teach grammar as the need arises. These may be paid up to 60 ducats a year.

In order to raise funds for the salaries of the four teachers of literature [*humanisti*] and the six grammar-teachers (the other two literature teachers being already provided for, as stated) let all those persons who take out letters entitling them to hold benefices of any kind, pay half of 1 per cent of the income from their benefices to the treasurer of the Chancery, in the same way as they pay 1 per cent to the Pietà.[7] Moreover, whenever magistracies sell by auction either movable goods or real property, no exceptions being allowed, let 1 soldo per ducat be collected from the purchasers; and let money collected for the aforesaid purpose be deposited every month by the treasurers with the Procuracy di Citra, on pain of [being proclaimed] *furanti*;[8] and let the treasurer of the Chancery be bound to proceed likewise.

And, because six masters are paid, one in each sestier, by the clergy of this city to teach those who wish to take orders and those who serve the churches, it is to be hoped that, through the good offices of the authorities concerned, they will agree to transfer the money to our six masters, from whom they will assuredly obtain better results. Such moneys will thus be applied to a purpose common to both clergy and laity. The total sum of money will easily meet the need. The present resolution is to come into effect immediately after its adoption. That it may produce the desired effect more promptly, and that such an important matter may be managed with the attention it requires, the aforesaid Riformatori, together with our Censors,[9] shall appoint by ballot [*a bossole e ballotte*], after all necessary investigations, two qualified noblemen and

[6] On Francesco Robertello (1516–67) and Giovita Ravizza (1476–1553), both experienced humanist teachers – Ravizza had for years been urging upon the government its responsibility for education – and a full discussion of these schools, see Grendler 1989, pp. 63–70.

[7] For the foundling-hospital of the Pietà see above, VII.1, 2, 6 and 7.

[8] Persons convicted of malversation of public money; their names were read out in the Great Council on the first Sunday of March, as an additional lifelong disgrace (Cozzi 1973, p. 322).

[9] See above, II.8(a).

one citizen for each parish. Their duty will be to encourage the young in [their respective] parishes to attend the schools, and to visit the schools and report on the diligence of each [pupil] and whatever promise he shows, and to inform the Riformatori and the Censors of what is going on. In this way, everyone will be stimulated to do well and to live virtuously, and good [pupils] will be praised and their ability recognized, while the negligent and the indolent will remain without praise.

For the resolution 133; against 34; uncertain 30.   M. C., D. C.

7   THE VENETIAN ACADEMY AND ITS PROGRAMME OF UNIVERSAL KNOWLEDGE, 1560
From the petition of Federigo Badoer to the Procurators of St Mark's; ASV Procuratia di San Marco de Supra, Atti, reg. 129, ff. 34–7; (Rose 1969, pp. 228–33, with abbreviated translation on pp. 210–11).

Since that day when God inspired me to try holding in my house meetings of professors of the sciences, the [liberal] arts and faculties, such as are customarily held all over the world, embracing matters of both public and private interest, by persons who apply themselves to both good and bad ends, I resolved to dedicate this thought of mine and my efforts to the public benefit, just as I have for twenty-four years devoted my labours, faculties and life itself to my native country.

Thus, guided by experience, I drew up procedural rules for meetings, seating-arrangements and the holding of discussions and debates, seeking professors from every branch of knowledge. It has so happened by the grace of God that the rules and activities [operationi] of this assembly have been acknowledged everywhere to bring most virtuous entertainment to the whole city and to have conferred benefit upon all who profess literature not only in this city but in different provinces, by means of the many works that have been printed.[10] And that this meeting of so many professors of virtuous ability brings profit, delight and great prestige [ornamento] to the city all good souls and lovers of virtue in this city and abroad bear witness, through the praises which they have bestowed. These meetings of learned professors have been tried out many times, allowing many nobles and citizens and others free access to their discussions and debates. A supplication was presented to the Collegio by these virtuous learned men [virtuosi] to offer their service to the public in that loving and prudent manner which your illustrious lordships will appreciate from the

[10] Printing and bookselling were a major commercial activity of the Academy, which also aimed to exploit the German market (see Pagan 1973–4).

enclosed copy, and such honour, praise and gracious favour was bestowed upon the Academy by the most illustrious Senate, as your lordships can see from their decree. And, moreover, it pleased the exalted Council of Ten to appoint this Academy, and no other body, to have the charge of printing all the laws and other ordinances of whatsoever council and magistracy of this city, with authority in other matters to do with printing. . . . Your lordships may know that, in accordance with the will of the most serene Prince, the most eminent overseers of the Palace building-works [*Provveditori supra le fabriche del Palazzo*] made a decision, set down in writing, that a scheme [*uno aparato*] should be drawn up by the Academy for the 'inventions' [i.e. subjects] of paintings to be set up in the place between the doors of the most illustrious Collegio and Senate, the Council of Ten and the Chancery,[11] and equally they have responsibility of choosing the painter. Accordingly [the Academy] has drawn up in writing a most beautiful 'invention' illustrating the way [*la prova*] to rule a state in a Christian manner – virtuously, in security and splendour; as an ornament to this most serene State it will outdo anything of the kind that has previously been executed, not merely in this city but in any other [city] in the world.

These most virtuous minds [*spiriti*] are directed therefore to the glory of the Procuracies and of your most illustrious lordships, who, as they have said in their supplication, represent the origin of what with truly divine inspiration their most wise ancestors founded, aided by the grace of God, who with eyes of infinite wisdom penetrates into your religious minds, intent upon the conservation of divine works and offices . . . especially in the sacred temple of the most glorious protector of this city [the Basilica of St Mark], where each external ornament denotes the inner reverence which everyone tenders to our Creator and Saviour. And thus, as they have said they will bring about, the lecturers will deliver lectures in the room near to the library[12] and will gain a larger audience, more comfortable arrangements for themselves and their listeners, and will feel a continuous, ardent compulsion to apply themselves to their duties. The magnificent [nobleman Pietro] Loredan, who is keeper of the library, will be aided in maintaining and expanding it by the help he will continually be given, so that the aims which the Academicians express in their supplication to your most excellent lordships will be achieved. Not only will he attend to the conservation of the books in the library, but he will also strive to add new acquisitions in such quantity as will in [the Academicians'] judgements suffice to increase its beauty, and enhance the dignity [*ornamento*] of your lordships; with which is combined the usual benefit that, if any book no longer in print comes to light, it will not fail to be added. Nor, likewise, will [the

---

[11] The Sala delle Quattro Porte [see below, X.2(e)].

[12] The vestibule, decorated by Titian, of Jacopo Sansovino's new library of St Mark's. Formerly lectures were held in Badoer's own house.

Academicians] fail, having once received the order to proceed, to apply themselves to devising a system of arrangement of the books, in such a way that things which are known only through the intellect can also be understood visibly, so that people may know by written instructions [*brevi*] that on one side all the sciences and arts are put together in their true order, and on the other [side] languages, according to whatever distinctions they seem to reveal on their own account. And subjects worthy of praise, together with those in some way defective but which could be improved upon, should be arranged on this side in accordance with the wishes of the said Messer Loredan, a nobleman of rare goodness and deep learning, and a very great lover of this virtuous undertaking. And, furthermore, they shall not fail to elect persons to relieve Loredan on certain days, when he wants to do no less than show the library, and all the Academy's rules, to important persons and foreign lords, so that, instructed by these rules, they may be moved to admire this glorious city in literary matters in just proportion to their admiration of its armoury in the Arsenal and the Council of Ten, and the treasure which is guarded and preserved by your most excellent lordships. Thus, in addition to your three principal charges, concerning God's temple [St Mark's], the Piazza and the Palace, you have this one too: to be the overseers of virtue in its entirety. Thus you may glory in being the guardians of those four bulwarks necessary to all cities and states, but in no other part of the world given into the charge of a single authority.

In short, the whole nobility, and anyone else of whatsoever condition, who comes to listen to the matters under discussion in the Academy every day, both morning and evening, will obtain two precious and delicious forms of nourishment. One of these is the taste of true virtue, the left hand of God on earth and empress of the world, served by the twenty queens who are the sciences and faculties. What I mean to say is that not only will everything which the whole of mankind needs to know for necessity, profit, contentment and self-enhancement [*ornamento*] become attainable, but, as I can readily affirm, everything concerning all the virtues will be attained easily by listening to the discussions and their resolutions. The other benefit, which the nobility in particular will receive, is this: to get instruction concerning the provinces and states of the world – not just this most serene State, but also every other power, both Christian and infidel – whence they will come to know all the internal and external characteristics of every prince and lord who rules at present, all types of governments and courts, and everything dependent upon them. . . .

This, most illustrious lords, is a treasure of such qualities, a single benefit so clearly illuminating the intellect, fitting it to operate in safety both within and without this state, that it can be called an inestimable treasure, because from knowledge the means of gaining all treasures and goods is born. . . .

Federico Badoer, founder of the Venetian Academy.

D. C.

8   SARPI'S PRESENCE IN INTELLECTUAL CIRCLES, c. 1600
From Fra Fulgenzio's life of Sarpi: Micanzio tr. anon. 1651, pp. 49–51.

The father [Sarpi] being come back to *Venice*, resumed the course of his former studies, and of his retirednesse from businesse; frequenting his accustomed vertuous conversations, and the resort that was to the house of signor *Andrea Moresin*[13] . . . being growne very numerous, and frequent because there came thither a great part of such as profest learning, and not onely of the nobility whereof some subjects are since risen to be great Senators, and like starres in the firmament of the most serene Common-wealth for goodnesse, Religion, learning and civill prudence: but there were likewise admitted into that meeting, all sorts of *virtuosi*, as well seculars as religious, beside the most eminent persons of learning that were then met at *Venice*, or in *Italy* or of any other nation that did not faile to be present in that place, as in one of the most celebrated conventions that had ever beene consecrate to the *Muses*. In my life I have not seene more vertuous exercises and I wish it had pleased God that as the vertues of those two Andria and Nicolo the uncles (which discended by inheritance unto their nephews) so there might have beene in Venice such another meeting, where there were met sometimes five and twentie or thirtie men of rare endowments. At this meeting the ceremony (which is a thing so much affected in our times and so superfluous) had no countenance which tries the braines of the wiser sort, & vainelye spends so much time in an artificiall kind of lying, that signifies nothing because it signifies so much, but a civill and free confidence was onely there in use. It was allowed every man to make his discourse of whatsoever pleased him best, without restriction of passing from one subject to another, provided it were alwaies of new matter, and the end of their disputation was for nothing else but to finde out truth. But the felicie of our father was rare, who upon any subject that was propounded did not onely discourse without premeditation; but made no diference of sustaining or impugning any proposition in a scholastique way. All which he did with so much facilitie that it raised a wonder in all men. And afterwards in his riper age, when he was put in minde of those exercises, he would smile at them as at puerilities. At this time the civil warrs in France flam'd out, and the father was pleas'd to heare such as could discourse of them. And that pleasure continued with him to his lives end, to hear and understand any thing of the state of the world, and how things were carried. This was a general Idea with him, wherein he seldome failed in his judgment, if any newes that were spread abroad, was either true or false, that upon things present he would settle a judgement with so much prudence in relation to what succeeded, that it made men wonder and seeke

---

[13] On the *ridotto* of Andrea Morosini in the 1580s see A. Favaro 1893; Cozzi 1958, pp. 46–52.

after his opinion as if it had been a prognostication. And for as much as at 'The Golden Ship' in the merchants street [Merceria] there used to meete a sort of gallant and vertuous gentlemen to recount their Intelligences, one with another; among which the good Perrot a frenchman . . . thither also came Merchants that were strangers, and such as had not onely beene over all *Europe*, but in the east and west Indies, and the father among others found meanes to be among them. And as in that minde of his every little thing tooke impression, so he had likewise an admirable dexterity to make other men enter into discourse.

B. P., D. C.

THE BUSINESS ORGANIZATION OF EARLY
PRINTING AND PUBLISHING

*A*S *ALDUS MANUTIUS'S own testimony [IX.3] suggests, the introduction of printing and development of publishing in Venice had a profound effect upon cultural life there. When, in the 1470s, printing began to turn the spread of knowledge into big business, Venetian entrepreneurs were fairly swift to move in and take a part in what had begun as mainly a foreign enterprise. Aspects of the early business organization behind this cultural revolution are illustrated in this section. Venice produced roughly a sixth of all the books printed in Europe before 1500, and through investment agents such as Nicholas of Frankfurt soon obtained half the market for academic books in Germany. The documents selected here show that this was not accomplished without some ruthless business methods; production quality and ethical standards sometimes suffered, and piracy was a danger, as the legislation granting Sabellicus copyright of his* History of Venice *demonstrates [IX.10]. Profits could be huge: for example, Nicholas of Frankfurt was all set to double his investment from the sale of his working-partner's Bibles [IX.9]. On the other hand, a partnership – claiming to represent the highest standards – which tried to break into Greek printing [IX.11] just after the government had granted Aldus Manutius a monopoly of the printing of Greek texts (25 February 1496) subsequently lost a lawsuit and had to move out of Venice. The partnership of Aldus (a non-Venetian) and Andrea Toresani, set up in 1495, is the best-known early printing-operation in Venice. Greek texts represented only a part of the partners' extraordinary output [IX.13], which earned them a pre-eminent position for twenty years. But Venice was a centre not only for the printing of books and pamphlets: it also led Italy in the expert production of woodcuts and engravings, both as book illustrations and as independent works. One of the most ambitious prints, the enormous* View of Venice *by Jacopo de'Barbari, was the subject of a petition for exclusive rights of sale by its German sponsor [IX.12]. Likewise, Venice excelled in the printing of music: this is shown by the letter a Venetian composer wrote to his patron, a prominent republican exile from Florence, hoping to get his liturgical settings printed for high profit [IX.14].*

369

BIBLIOGRAPHY   In general: Arnaldi and Stocchi 1981–3, III. On the earliest printers: Fulin 1882; Scholderer 1966. On early copyright, Chavasse 1986. On the Aldine press: Pastorello 1965; Orlandi 1976; Lowry 1979. On the View of Venice by Jacopo de'Barbari: Schulz 1970, 1978. On mid-sixteenth-century printing: Grendler 1977.   D. C.

9   A CONTRACT BETWEEN TWO GERMANS TO PRINT BIBLES, 1478
From the Latin. Fulin 1882, pp. 100–1.

Master Leonardus [Wild, of Ratisbon otherwise Regensburg],[14] son of Ser Gerard . . . printer of the parish of San Benedetto in Venice, on the one hand, and the excellent Lord Nicholaus,[15] son of the Lord Henry of Frankfurt, a German, on the other, came each of his own will and accord to the following agreement, contract, investment and transaction, and do solemnly undertake the same on their own part and on that of their heirs and successors.

In the first place, the above-mentioned Lord Nicholaus for his part has promised to give and to pay to the said Master Leonardus, for his labour and for the printing of the aforesaid books,[16] the sum of 243 gold ducats and all the paper needed to print them. Of the 930 books, the aforesaid Lord Nicholaus should have just 910; the others, up to the said total, should be for Master Leonardus.

The said Lord Nicholaus is required and obliged to disburse and pay these funds to the said Master Leonardus in the following manner: as often as the said Master Leonardus has delivered and consigned to the said Lord Nicholaus one complete gathering of all the copies, then the said Lord Nicholaus is bound to pay 5 ducats, and so he must continue to pay 5 ducats for each successive gathering until the full sum of 243 ducats has been paid. There must be no exceptions.

The said Lord Nicholaus is also obliged to give the same Master Leonardus paper for the printing of the books, at Lord Nicholaus's expense, and at the good pleasure of Master Leonardus. Furthermore, should there be any pages in the printed copies which have not been clearly printed and stamped and are not to the liking of the said Lord Nicholaus, in that case the aforesaid Master Leonardus is obliged to reprint them at his expense though with Lord

---

[14] Leonardus printed thirteen editions between 1478 and 1481, but evidently needed capital to meet his outlay on paper and wages.

[15] This German merchant (the title 'Lord' seems merely formal), attached to the Fondaco, had already invested in printing in 1473. By 1481 he is recorded publishing and selling on his own.

[16] That is, Bibles. This printed text of the Bible, sold for 1 ducat in the 1480s, has been identified (Hain 1826–38, n. 3067).

Nicholaus supplying the paper as above. This is the agreement which they have solemnly negotiated and reached.

14 March 1478.   M. L.

10   COPYRIGHT LEGISLATION TO PROTECT SABELLICUS'S HISTORY OF VENICE, 1486

From the Latin. ASV Collegio, Notatorio, reg. 13, ff. 118v, 145r.

1 September 1486

The history of our city, written by the very learned Marcus Antonius Sabellicus from Rome,[17] deserves for its eloquence and historical veracity to come into full public view. Therefore we, the undersigned noble Councillors, have debated and decreed that the aforementioned work by the aforenamed Marcus Antonius can be entrusted to some expert printer to print, at his own expense, and to publish the said work in such a manner as befits a polished history worthy of immortality; furthermore, we shall not permit anyone other than him to have the said work printed, under penalty of the displeasure of the most serene Signoria and [a fine] of 500 ducats, either in Venice or in any other city or region of the most serene Signoria.

(Councillors) Ser Lucas Navagero; Ser Fantinus de Cha de Pesaro; Ser Zacharius Barbaro, knight; Ser Sebastianus Baduario, knight; Ser Benedictus Trevisano.

18 May 1487

We, the undersigned noble Councillors, representing a majority of the most illustrious Signoria, for the purpose of removing any possible dispute, real or imagined, about the decree passed on the first day of September last, have confirmed that the work written by the very learned Marcus Antonius Sabellicus from Rome may be printed by a leading printer and that we shall not permit anyone other than him to have it printed etc. as in that decree; furthermore we have also decreed that no one except Marcus Antonius himself may authorize the aforesaid work to be printed either in Latin or the vernacular, either now or in the future; nor, even if the said work was printed in other regions, including those not subject to the aforementioned Venetian Signoria, may it be sold by anyone. However, it shall be permissible to sell those copies

---

[17] See above, IX.2.

which the aforenamed Marcus Antonius has authorized to be printed; this also is subject to the abovementioned penalty imposed by the decree of 1 September.

(Councillors) Ser Nicolaus Mocenigo; Ser Franciscus Marcello; Ser Joannes Mauro; Ser Hieronymus Contareno. R. AND P. C.

11 TWO PARTNERS PETITION FOR COPYRIGHT TO PRINT CLASSICAL GREEK AUTHORS, 1497
From the Latin. Fulin 1882, p. 131.

The ruinous ignorance and neglect of printers is corrupting books more and more every day, to the public disadvantage and the shame of this most glorious city. For this reason your most truly faithful subject Gabriel of Brasichella [*sic* for ?Brisighella] and his partners, being most eager to do what is best for the general good, honour and reputation of our most splendid Republic, have determined to begin printing in Greek and Latin in this illustrious town, using their new and most beautiful technique with the highest care and precision. The aforementioned Gabriel and his partners have spent a great deal of money in this admirable and most useful enterprise,[18] and, because the debt is heavier than their own resources can bear, they hope to receive some sign of Your Most Merciful Serenity's kind favour. Furthermore, there may be many who, through hatred or jealousy, will use any means to injure the said company or crush it entirely. For these reasons the above-named Gabriel and his partners, being most faithful subjects of this truly glorious State, throw themselves with all possible reverence and humility at the feet of Your Serenity, beseeching you to show your usual kindness and mercy by granting them the special favour of a monopoly allowing no other person to use their new technique in the lands and territories of Your Most Illustrious Highness for the next ten years, nor to sell the following four Greek works – *The Letters of Brutus and Phalaris*, Pollux, Philostratus [*Imagines*], and the *Fables* of Aesop – on pain of forfeiting all copies and paying a fine of 1 ducat per volume. In this way your said most faithful subjects will be able to free themselves from the great debts which they have incurred in bringing their scheme, which is of such paramount use to all, to its perfect form. They would also gain some advantage from their labour and experiment, and would not be ruined for having made the attempt. That would certainly be against the will of Your Serenity, to whose favour they most humbly commend themselves.

7 March 1497 M. L.

[18] Gabriel had begun printing in Greek with the editorial help of the Cretan Zacharias Callierges and investment from a banker called Vlastos, the source of the debt here mentioned.

12 JACOPO DE'BARBARI'S PANORAMIC VIEW OF VENICE: PETITION FOR
COPYRIGHT, 1500
ASV, Collegio, Notatorio, reg. 15, f. 28r (Cicogna 1824–52, IV, 647, with minor errors).

To the Most Serene Prince and excellent Signoria.

Antonio Cholb, German merchant, supplicates Your Sublimity that, because
it is he who three years ago had [to ensure that] that work, principally
[redounding] to the fame of this most excellent city of Venice, was accurately
and properly drawn and printed, and because many details from it are copied in
other works, and because of the almost unattainable and incredible skill
required to make such an accurate drawing both on account of its size and [the
size] of the paper, the like of which was never made before, and also because of
the new art of printing a form of such large dimensions and the difficulty of the
overall composition, which matters people have not appreciated, considering
the mental subtlety involved, and given that printed copies cannot be produced
[economically] to sell for less than about 3 florins each, so that he does not in
general hope to recoup the moneys invested: he therefore supplicates Your
Sublimity that grace may be conceded for the said work to be exported and sold
in all your lands and cities without payment of any duties and without any
restriction.

(30 October 1500. Copyright granted for four years, but exemption from duty
was not granted.)   D. C.

13 BUSINESS RECORDS OF ALDUS MANUTIUS AND ANDREA DI ASOLA, 1500–1
Extracts from the accounts of the trust (*commissaria*) of the Procurator Pietro Barbarigo
(Pastorello 1965, pp. 189–90).

8 January 1500

Ser Andrea de Toresani of Asola deposited in the company's account with the
bank of Ser Mafio Agostini[19] one half of the 62 ducats collected from a German
for books, the sum of 31 ducats.

7 March 1501

Tadeo Contarini credits the account of Messers Aldo Romano and Andrea of
Asola at the bank of Mafio Agostini and his brothers with the sum of 30 ducats
collected from Ser Jordan of Dinslaken, now deposited in the said bank.

19 This banking-establishment, one of the largest in Venice, had invested in printing since 1473.

20 April 1501

Paid into the said bank for printed books, to the credit of the company of Messers Aldo Romano and Andrea of Asola, the sum of 152 ducats collected from Messer Tadeo Contarini.

25 May 1501

Ser Piero Benzoni,[20] bookseller on the bridge of the Merceria, pays into the company's account with the said bank the sum of 4½ ducats for copies of the *Cornucopia* sold by him.

20 November 1501

Ser Jordan of Dinslaken,[21] German, pays the company 40 ducats for 101 copies of *Cornucopia*.[22] He takes delivery of them in two batches, the first immediately, the second in a few days.   M. L.

14   THE PRINTING OF MUSIC: A COMPOSER IN SEARCH OF AN AGENT, 1536
Letter of Costanzo Festa to Filippo di Filippo Strozzi: ASF Carte Strozziane, serie V, 1209.I.84 (printed and translated in Agee 1985, pp. 232–4: some variations below).

Magnificent Sir, comrade:[23]

For the present I am sending the madrigal that you bid me [set to music]. If it is not as worthy as it might be, pardon me because, in truth, I feel quite bothered by gout, although if it does not please Your Lordship, let me know so that I may do it in a different way. I would like a service of Your Lordship that would make me most grateful: that one of your agents search in Venice for someone who prints music (although I have been asked I do not know the name). Have him [the printer] understand that, if he wants my works – that is, the hymns [and] the Magnificats – that I do not want less than 150 *scudi*, and, if

---

[20] Manager of a bookshop for the French printer Nicholas Jenson during the 1470s.

[21] Jordan's father was probably Gaspar von Dinslaken, who had been a member of John of Cologne's company in the 1470s. Jordan was still trading in the 1520s.

[22] A large and popular grammatical work compiled by Niccolò Perrotti, Bishop of Siponto (d. 1480).

[23] Costanzo Festa (*c*.1490–1545), composer and singer, is writing to the Florentine patrician Filippo di Filippo Strozzi (1488–1538), who was then in Venice; Filippo and his family were prominent connoisseurs of music, able to acquire new and unpublished music through widespread business contacts.

he wants the *basse*, 200 in all. If he wants to print them, he can place the hymns and Magnificats in a large book [i.e. a choirbook] like that of the Fifteen Masses,[24] so that all choirs would be able to make use of them. The *basse* are good for learning to sing, to [write] counterpoint, to compose, and to play all instruments. Hence, [I would be pleased if] Your Lordship does me this favour. And to your good health I recommend myself, from Rome, 5 September 1536.

Your servant and comrade, Costantio Festa.   I. F.

[24] A reference to the *Liber . . . quindecim missarum* (Rome 1516) of Andrea Antico (before 1480 – after 1539) who had moved to Venice *c*.1518–20.

ENTERTAINMENT

*E*NTERTAINMENT *of themselves and – on behalf of the Republic – of foreign rulers and other dignitaries visiting Venice was one of the main purposes of the Companies of the Hose (Compagnie della Calza), which youthful patricians organized. IX.15, with its ponderous preamble full of political overtones, sets out the earliest recorded statutes of such a group, the Modesti, and dates from 1487; but these aristocratic youth clubs existed long before that. Some Companies of the Hose also played an important part in sponsoring public entertainment, a function that developed out of performances at private banquets and at secular and religious festivals, such as the Carnival period before Lent. This, traditionally a time when moral taboos were relaxed and it was even permitted to mock the establishment [IX.18], seems by the 1520s to have included a brief theatre season. In the absence of a princely court, patricians – both as individuals and within the framework of the Companies of the Hose – took the initiative in staging plays, and it became normal to charge for admission. IX.16–17 show that, alongside ancient Roman comedies, vernacular dramas drawing on contemporary themes and ridiculing social behaviour were staged. Particularly popular in the 1520s – even if some spectators claimed to be shocked by their lewdness – were the down-to-earth comedies of peasant life by the Paduan playwright Ruzzante [IX.16]. Theatrical performances were suppressed in the early 1580s as a result of Jesuit pressures upon patrician opinion, but the vitality of Venetian comedy was soon reawakened in 1607 after the Interdict [IX.21]. Music, dance and song were essential to these dramatic entertainments, and music also played a vital role on grand religious occasions; but it was, too, a source of private pleasure, as illustrated by a letter of 1534 [IX.20] concerning a secular commission to the celebrated Flemish composer Adrian Willaert (c.1490–1562). In 1527 Willaert had become choirmaster of St Mark's, and he did much to make the Basilica an unequalled centre for polyphonic music. Venetians also had a taste for sheer spectacle, and a letter of 1530 [IX.19] describes an elaborate mock battle performed on the water before the Doge's Palace. The writer's only complaint was that it was all over too quickly.*

376

BIBLIOGRAPHY   On Companies of the Hose: Venturi 1909. On performances of masques and comedies: Cozzi 1959; Padoan 1978, 1982 and in Arnaldi and Stocchi 1981–3, III.iii, IV.i. On the choir of St Mark's and music in the Scuole: Glixon 1983. On carnival events and spectacle in general: Molmenti 1927–9; Muir 1981.   D.C.

15   THE STATUTES OF THE MODESTI, A COMPANY OF THE HOSE, 1487

From BCV ms. Cicogna 3278, n. 24, ff. 25r–29r (Venturi 1909, pp. 196–200). Preamble from the Latin.

In the Name of Eternal God, Amen

The following most notable patrician youths [list of names] . . . recognize that nothing is more pleasant, or binds us more closely together, than sharing good morals with those who have the same aims and the same intentions, so that everyone loves his neighbour as himself and it happens – as Pythagoras wished concerning friendship – that one person arises out of many. A great community is one which comes about through benefits given and received reciprocally, which are mutually appreciated. For the binding force in society is reasoning and speech, which, by means of teaching, learning, communicating, debating and judging, reconcile men with each other and join them together in a certain natural society. But, of all societies, none is more excellent, none more stable, than one where men sharing good morals are joined together in close friendship. As a result of this follow marriages, the relationships based on them, and many kinsmen. This propagation and supplying of offspring is the origin of republics, as may be seen in this most excellent Republic, in which the patricians are like so many brothers, and in this way [society] arises out of many [persons].

Therefore, the foresaid lords, desiring to follow in the steps of their ancestors, have formed and wish to be a single and equal society and fraternity to the praise and honour of Our Lord Jesus Christ, of His Glorious Mother the Virgin Mary, and of the Lord Mark the Evangelist, Protector of this most famous city and most illustrious Republic. To give greater force to their promises, and for the future record, they have asked me, the below-named notary, to register among my authentic acts the articles of agreement made by the same noble youths, and written in the vernacular style, and to draw them up in public form. Which articles of agreement are as follows.

In the Name of Christ, Amen. 1486 [Venetian style], on 20 February, in Venice, at Rialto

In these below-written items of the agreement [*capitoli*] is set down for all who shall hear or read it, the solemn and binding promise to be observed by all who

377

5 Vittorio Carpaccio, *The Miracle of the True Cross*, detail showing a member of a
Company of the Hose.
(Reproduced by kind permission of the Accademia, Venice)

subscribe below as our companions and brothers of the Fraternity and
Company here entitled [blank for 'Modesti']. The companions, who henceforth
shall be incorporated into the fraternal company, must subscribe with their own
signatures, and then those who have subscribed must one after another take the
oath to observe the items of agreement written below, with an undertaking to
act together in future as loving and good brothers, to be most prompt
reciprocally for the honour and well-being of each other. This is likewise to be
understood by those who in the future wish to be admitted. The admission of
companions is to be made from time to time by ballot, not by word of mouth or
by writing. Every companion who is balloted shall be elected when he has three
quarters of the ballots, which balloting, in the admission [procedure] below
written, must be secret and not open, under penalty of 25 gold ducats for each
person whenever this is contravened. . . . For the election of the Lord or Head
of the Room at our feasts or revels [*zogi*] we wish lots to be drawn among those
who have first been selected by ballot, and all the companions are to be balloted
in order . . . it being understood, however, that anyone who has once been Head
of the Room cannot be re-elected. . . . Once the Lord has accepted office, all

the companions are obliged to deposit a pledge of 50 ducats, because the said Lord has the liberty of condemning anyone who fails in his duty, and whoever disobeys his precepts will fail. He has this liberty for three days: the day before the feast or revel, the feast day, and the day following it. His precepts are to be understood as only concerning matter to do with the feast of which he is the Lord, and those condemned by the said Lord cannot receive his grace except by the payment of 40 gold ducats. It is declared that this liberty of the Lord will begin from the time we put on the hose until we have taken it off. . . .

Item. That the hose of old rose colour must be worn for eight years, and in 1489, before the Carnival, a feast must be held at the house of the Marquis [of Mantua?] or elsewhere as the Company shall decide, and all the companions shall be obliged to wear the embroidered hose of the Company and be clothed in silk of the same colour and in whatever manner our companions shall decide, everyone being obliged to observe all the foregoing under penalty of 100 ducats for a contravention. And, because it might happen that in holding dinners some of our companions might want to lay on something superfluous, our will is that, the only sweet confections may be pancake twists, ring biscuits, pastries [*storti, Buzoladi, Ochieti*] . . . and at supper, nothing but green salads, tripe with boiled meat, roast meat, oysters, pears matured in wine[25] and fruit may be served.

Item. That in the portico not more than six torches can be placed, and the said companions wish there to be only two in the room.

Item. Outside in the street, the companions may not be escorted by more than four torches.

Item. That each of the said companions is obliged at his dinners to retain two pipers and one bagpipe [*piva*], and, if the said companions contravene this, they will be fined 20 ducats to be spent as the majority of the companions shall decide.

Item. That each of the companions shall be obliged when he gets married to hold two dinners for all the companions, one at his own house, and one at the house of the bride.

Item. Should it happen that one of the companions dies, the rest are obliged to take off the hose and wear a gown for eight days, on penalty of 10 ducats fine, as above.

Signed and sealed by the notary Antonius de la Ecclesia, son of Sier Jacobo, citizen of Cremona.

[Names of fifteen signatories, signifying their agreement.]   D. C.

---

[25] *Pere vaste*, i.e. the ancient concoction known as *pere guaste*, over-ripe pears matured in wine.

16   COMEDIES SPONSORED BY A COMPANY OF THE HOSE DURING CARNIVAL,
1525
DMS, xxxvii, cols 559–60 (Padoan 1982, p. 88, provides some emendations).

9 February 1525

After dinner few members of the Collegio assembled, because some of the Savi
of the Council went to see a comedy rehearsed at Ca' Arian at San Raffaele. It
will be performed on Monday the 13th of this month, in the feast organized by
the Company of the 'Triumphanti'. The author is Zuan Manenti, the Lord of
the Feast is Sier Marin Capello. . . . He gave a supper for 300 [including
various Procurators of St Mark's, two Heads of the Ten, and more than forty
other senators], very well prepared and beautifully arranged with the written
device 'Dedicated to Concord'. . . . People went there in the rain, but the hall
was full in good time; thus neither the Senate nor the Council of Ten held
meetings. Two brothers of the Doge were present. . . . It began at the twenty-
fourth hour [sunset] and lasted until the sixth. There were nine intermezzi and
three comedies. First [there was] one in prose by Zuan Manenti, called
Philargio and Trebia and Fidel.[26] Then the Paduans Ruzante and Menato, as
rustics, did a comedy about peasant life, totally lascivious and full of filthy
words, so that everyone disapproved of it and cried 'Shame!' There were almost
sixty ladies present in the upper seats, wearing long gowns, the young ladies
wearing coifs, who were horrified at things being called by their names. The
whole conclusion was about fornicating and cuckolding husbands. But Zuan
Polo acted very well, and the intermezzi they did were very beautiful, with all
the skill in music and singing that one could wish for; they were dressed in
various costumes as Moors, Germans, Greeks, Hungarians, pilgrims and many
other costumes, but without masks.   D. C.

17   ENTERTAINMENT IN THE DOGE'S PALACE DURING CARNIVAL, 1526
DMS, xl, col. 785.

5 February 1526

And after the Council of Ten had come down, after the second hour of night
[i.e. about 7 p. m.] a very beautiful mummery took place in the courtyard of the
Palace, with six principal performers who danced, dressed very beautifully, with
twelve persons dressed as Saracens bearing torches; and they danced various

[26] Padoan 1978, p. 115.

new dances so that all who saw it took great pleasure, and there were many persons in the Palace courtyard, and the Doge was on the balcony of his Palace. There was also a comedy performed at Sant'Aponal in Ca' Morexini, put on by Zuan Francesco Benetier, a customs officer, and some of his friends; admission was by ticket and space was limited. Cherea acted, and it was a piece by Plautus, *The Two Brothers*, not very good. It ended at the fourth hour.   D. C.

18   ROLE REVERSAL: MASQUERADES DURING CARNIVAL, 1533
DMS, lvii, col. 548.

25 February 1533. Carnival Tuesday

The Savi did not meet after dinner, and there were many people masquerading in the city among whom were some wearing ducal sleeves in scarlet and silk and velvet hoods, and one had a gold collar upon his chest like the Grand Chancellor, and others were dressed up like Commanders and others were being led around by a company of trumpeters and pipers to show that the Signoria was passing in procession, which in my opinion was not well done.

D. C.

19   AQUATIC SPECTACLE: A MOCK NAVAL BATTLE, 1530
From a letter of the Mantuan ambassador, Benedetto Agnello, to Duke Federico Gonzaga, Venice, 23 October 1530: ASMn Archivio Gonzaga, b. 1464, ff. 202r–203v (Luzio 1888, pp. 133–4).

Today took place the naval battle about which I wanted to inform Your Excellency . . . opposite the entrance to the Palace of the Great Council [*sic*] a wooden castle was built upon some rafts in the middle of the Grand Canal. It looked very fine because it was all faked to look like marble, and also because it had the appearance of a very fine fortress with four big towers, one at each corner, and a great tower in the middle. The said castle was fortified with artillery both large and small, and various other things necessary for the defence of a city; the captain, Gattino, took on the role of guarding it with forty companions-at-arms, and thus, at dawn, they entered it. After a huge crowd had assembled to watch the festival, at about the nineteenth hour [probably about 1 p.m.] thirty armed brigantines[27] appeared from the direction of the

[27] *Bregantini* were 'simplifications of the light galley rowed by one or two men and oars to a bench' (Lane 1934, p. 13).

Arsenal. . . . Those within defended themselves very well, and hurled into the water those who tried to scale the ladders, so that it was a very good thing to watch, but it would have been a lot better if it had lasted longer, because within half an hour from the start of the battle the castle was taken, the men of the fleet gaining entry by means of the artificial fire they employed, and in spite of the fact that, after the outer walls had been taken, the tower in the middle was still defended; this also lasted only a short while, and within a moment all was lost. Once the castle was captured, an infinite number of rounds of artillery were discharged in the Piazza of the Palace. This was a signal for the collation to follow; it was borne out by 460 squires led by twenty-three nobles of the Hose,[28] each of them having twenty squires under his command. Each squire carried a silver plate or dish of sweetmeats made of sugar; some had a Cupid, others a Venus, many a Neptune or a Mercury, and others had a variety of different figures of gods, men or animals, so that it was a very delightful sight. This collation was delivered in part to the Signoria, and to the Dukes of Milan and Ferrara, who were watching the festival from above the portico of the Palace, and in part to 106 very beautiful ladies and many noblemen who were sitting on a stage built in front of the Palace. This stage, covered by deep blue cloth and decorated with very fine carpets, very beautiful silken upholstery [spalleri] and every other sort of adornment, was judged on this account and also because of the ladies, who had been invited because they exceeded in beauty all the others in the city, to have been the best thing in the whole festival. After the collation, dancing began on the stage. . . . The ball lasted until the third hour of the night [probably 9 p.m.], then everyone went home, and thus ended the festival, which was praised by many, but many also criticized it, saying that it could have been arranged a lot better than it was.   D. C.

20   COMMISSIONS FOR VERSE AND MUSIC, 1534
Letter of Ruberto Strozzi to Benedetto Varchi: copy of lost original in ASF Carte Strozziane, serie 1, cxxxii, f. 71r (original published in 'Smarrito' 1734, IV.i, pp. 125–6; copy printed and translated in Agee 1983, pp. 1–2: some variations below).

In the name of Jesus. On the 27th day of March 1534

My esteemed Messer Benedetto,[29]
    I received yours of the 10th, and with it eight sonnets and two epigrams, and in faith you could not do me a greater service in the world, and I ask you to

[28] See IX.14–15.
[29] Ruberto (d. 1566) was one of the seven legitimate sons of Filippo di Filippo Strozzi [see above, IX.14, n. 23]. Varchi (1503–65) became famous in Padua and Florence as a literary figure, Academician and historian.

continue to send me other such things when you do them, as they certainly give me a great deal of pleasure. You would like me to have one of those epigrams set to music by Adriano [Willaert]:[30] I will do everything I can, but will not promise you for certain, because it is a great trial of one's patience to get him to do anything; still, I will try with all my power, and if I get it, I will send it to you. As I told you, I received the madrigals that you sent me, and they were very pleasing. But having been asked to have another one made in praise of Madonna Pulisena,[31] and having no one else to turn to, I must come to you, and certainly I do it with that boldness with which I would ask one of the women I love [to let me screw her (*chiavarla*): crossed out in ms.] to make love. And therefore I ask you, since you served me so well the first time, not to fail me the second. Make it in praise of the said Pulisena (who sings very well both in improvising and in reading music), put her name in it, make the two final verses rhyme, and make then eleven syllables apiece, and she would like her name to be mentioned somewhere after the middle of the madrigal. I decided to mention each detail, so that you would not complain as you did last time that I had not explained it to you. So now you can see very well what the lady wants. I leave it to you, who would know better what to do than I what to say. I don't want to tell you not to speak to a soul on earth about this, because I would insult you, which certainly would not be right, because I have more faith in you than the Hungarians have in their swords. Let me have it, the sooner the better, and without further ado I recommend myself to you *per infinita saecula saeculorum amen.*   I. F.

21   REOPENING OF THEATRES AFTER THE INTERDICT, 1607
From the diary of Gerolamo Priuli: Österreichischer Nationalbibliothek, Vienna, Fondo ex-Foscarini ms. 6229, f. 307v (Cozzi 1959, p. 189).

23 May [1607]. The Eve of Ascension Day

A company of comedians began to perform publicly in the city comedies which had been banned for about thirty years on account of the 'Jesuits [selling tickets] at 6 and 8 soldi per person. And they performed first in Ca' Lipomano at Sant'Alvise, then in Rio Marin in the courtyard at San Basegio, hired by them for rent. Then[32] – the taste for this sort of thing increasing in the city –

---

[30] The implication that Adriaan Willaert, the most important composer then writing in Venice, and *maestro di cappella* at St Mark's, was a slow worker is confirmed by an anecdote in Zarlino 1588, p. 326.

[31] Probably Pulisena Pecorina, a prominent figure in Venetian musical life.

[32] Priuli (not to be confused with his namesake a century earlier) revised his diary in 1621; hence the additional information.

theatres were established at Ca' Tron at San Cassiano, Ca' Zustiniano at San Moisè, and at Ca' Tron at San Salvatore, so that sometimes there were three companies performing at the same time, and all of them had a following and audiences, and they customarily performed from Martinmas until Lent, and from the Ascension until the middle of July.   D. C.

Part X
The Visual Arts

*T*HE POWER *and mythology of the state pervaded the visual arts in Venice, and it is not always easy to separate the different sources of patronage. Just as the government controlled the guilds to which artists belonged, and ultimately controlled the Scuole and – to different degrees – many religious foundations, so in a sense it may have fostered (or sometimes hindered) private patronage, through economic policies and by providing individuals with experience in managing projects under its own patronage. For there was a vast area of direct and essentially secular state activity relating to the upkeep, decoration and improvement of public buildings and other facilities. The state maintained a structure of salaried posts attached to different departments, creating opportunities for specialists: hydraulic and military engineers, sculptors and painters, architects, metalworkers, mosaic workers, carpenters, cartographers, and so on. The Salt Office, with its monopoly profits, paid for the upkeep of the Ducal Palace and other government buildings; the Procurators of St Mark's maintained the Basilica and the Piazza; both appointed head architects called 'Proti' (protomaestri). The rewards in state service could be high: favoured painters such as the Bellini brothers might receive the lucrative sinecure of a brokership in the German exchange house; Jacopo Sansovino, who was 'Proto' to the Procurators from 1529, was congratulated on his advantages in a somewhat idealized account written by his friend Aretino [X.1(a)]. Art was an asset to the state, a source of collective pride used to impress both inhabitants and foreigners: this is obvious from many earlier passages in this anthology [e.g. I.1, 2] and is underlined here in an extract from the earlier of Francesco Sansovino's bestselling manuals for sightseers [X.1(b)].*

Selected texts illustrate some of the major government projects. One was the redecoration programme for the Hall of the Great Council, started in the 1470s but behind schedule by the 1490s, so that the Republic was prepared to pay heavily for the services of Perugino, a non-Venetian celebrity [X.2(a)]. Another example is the project for the clocktower on the Piazza, pursued in spite of successive war crises between 1495 and 1500 [X.2(b)]. This was perhaps a demonstration of the political use of art to bolster morale, as was a reported speech of Doge Loredan from the period of the War of the League of Cambrai, drawing attention to supposed political allegories in details of the fabric of St Mark's [X.2(c)]. More imaginative, but likewise political in slant, were Pietro Contarini's iconographical reading of the flagstaff bases in the Piazza [X.2(d)] and the hyper-sophisticated programme of moral allegories devised for a room in the Ducal Palace [X.2(e)]. This scheme was probably initiated by members of the Venetian Academy, and after the fire of 1577 it was applied to sculptures rather than wall paintings. The massive post-fire reconstruction programme involved, among many other items, a new ceiling for the Hall of the Senate, and X.2(f) focuses on the contract drawing and the designer's complaints that rival artists had been allowed to deviate from it, exploiting their corrupt relationship with the secretary to the Provveditori in charge of the Palace repairs. Finally, the competition for another major project of the 1580s, to design and build a durable stone bridge at Rialto, is represented by one candidate's proposals [X.2(g)] following the prescribed aesthetic, economic and structural criteria. His proposals were rejected in favour of the design (1588) of Antonio da Ponte, Proto of the Palace.

The diverse uses to which art might be put by the government included diplomacy. On the positive side, an artist might be recommended or even loaned to a foreign ruler [see above, I.1, n. 34, for the case of Gentile Bellini] or commissioned to produce a work of art to be presented as a gift [X.3(b)]. On the negative side, when the Marquis of Mantua sent painters to Venice to copy a map, Doge Loredan denied them access on the grounds that the Marquis had been making remarks hostile to Venice [X.3(a)]. Artists might often find or believe themselves to be not so much the beneficiaries as the victims of political and legal operations: the protests of the Venetian stonemasons and sculptors against their Lombard rivals is a case in point [X.4(a)]. The Lombards, working particularly on the Ducal Palace after the 1483 fire, outnumbered the Venetians and refused to take local apprentices. On the other hand, the painter Albrecht Dürer, on a working visit from Nuremberg, found himself heavily penalized for contravening Venetian laws protecting native craftsmen [X.4(b)]. And, although official portraiture was a lucrative area of Venetian state patronage (for instance, Doges had to be portrayed on the frieze of the Hall of the Great Council, and also featured on ex voto canvases), the Procurators of St Mark's were checked in their expenditure on portraits, particularly miniatures of themselves [X.4(c)]. The Venetian regime opposed the cult of individual fame, and the ideal of corporate unity resulted in endless pictures of elderly contemporaries identically clad. The well-known refusal to allow a monument to the military commander Colleone to be erected on the Piazza (Verrocchio's equestrian statue had to go to an obscurer site by the Scuola di San Marco) is matched over a century later by the order to melt down a bronze statue erected to honour a Venetian governor of Belluno [X.4(d)].

Turning to religious and quasi-religious institutions, the patronage of a Scuola is illustrated by a document about a large-scale painting for the boardroom [albergo] of the Carità [X.5(a)]. Such ambitious programmes illustrating the deeds of the patron saint were something of a Scuola speciality, financed from corporate funds and expressing the rivalry between the confraternities, and can sometimes be well documented from Scuola records. The example given here illustrates their competitive character, and the way a cycle might be divided amongst a group of painters, whose individual reputations were closely involved. It also reveals that the patrons were rather vague about the subject matter required, and this seems to have been fairly typical. The government, through the Council of Ten, backed such projects, and grants were occasionally made to advance them or help with repairs. On the other hand, the principal church of Venice, St Mark's, was subject to direct and political control. As the responsible magistracy, the Procurators di Supra investigated allegations that the artists working on a mosaic project had filled in details with paint; Titian's disingenuous evidence in their defence is quoted here [X.5(b)] and the extract, taken from the extraordinarily full record of these hearings, should serve to draw attention to an area of Venetian art which for this period has been little studied. Another way in which the state became directly involved with religious institutions was through its foundation of splendid churches to express collective thanksgiving for the cessation of plagues: the Redentore (1577) was followed after the 1630 plague by Longhena's Salute [X.5(d)], which, although Baroque in conception, owed aspects of its design to Palladio's San Giorgio (1561–2) and Redentore, as well as the cupolas of St Mark's. Even parish churches, while depending for their upkeep and embellishment upon the initiatives of clergy and private patrons, may quite often have been subject to government interference – through, for example, the intervention of the Procurators of St Mark's in their role as testamentary trustees. This is another theme that has been investigated. Religious houses were likewise formally independent of the state, and the major monastic foundations afforded much scope for artists' work, although Venice (unlike Florence) produced no in-house monastic painters; the chief demand was for acoustically suitable choir space and furnishings. In practice, however, the independence of these institutions could be compromised through patrician and patronal pressures, or the need to obtain government concessions; for instance, the Benedictines of San Giorgio Maggiore – Palladio's patrons – had to gain permission to fell oak (normally reserved for shipbuilding) on their estates near Treviso. However, the commission to Veronese (known to be a fast worker) to paint a huge scene in their refectory [X.5(c)], which Palladio had designed, seems to have been independently resolved, and set a fashion for Veronese's huge canvases of banquets which had only a dubious relevance to scriptural text. Nevertheless such profane interpretations of biblical scenes later got the artist into trouble with the authorities [see above, V.21].

389

BIBLIOGRAPHY   On Aretino: DBI; *and Aretino ed. Camesasca and Pertile 1957–60. On Jacopo Sansovino: Howard 1975; and, in relation to Doge Gritti, Tafuri 1985. On the relevant guilds: Sagredo 1856; E. Favaro 1975; Connell 1988. For miscellaneous documentation relating to state patronage of architects and sculptors: Paoletti 1893. On painters: Paoletti 1894; Ludwig 1903–5; von Bode et al. 1911. For documentation in general: DMS; Zorzi 1960–1. For an overview of patronage: Fletcher 1983. For projects in the Ducal Palace: Lorenzi 1868; Wolters 1965–6, 1983. On 'official' painting and allegory: Hope 1980; 1985. On narrative cycles of painting: P. F. Brown 1988. On some further examples of political allegory: Perry 1977. On the Rialto Bridge: Cessi and Alberti 1934; Calabi and Morachiello 1987. On portraiture of Doges: Romanelli 1982. For Tintoretto's portraits of Procurators: Rossi 1974. On sixteenth-century Venetian painting in general: Rosand 1982. On works for the Scuole: Wurthmann 1975; Pignatti 1981. On Veronese's work for monasteries: Pignatti 1976. On his* Marriage at Cana: *Fehl 1981. On St Mark's: Ongania 1886. On Titian and the mosaicists: Merkel 1980. On the Redentore and Salute churches: Niero 1979.*

J. F., D. C.

1   LITERARY PRAISE FOR ART AND ARTISTS

(a) The benefits to Jacopo Sansovino of working in Venice, 1537.
Aretino 1609, I, no. 237, f. 190v.

To Master Jacopo Sansovino

The execution of the works brought forth at the height of your genius now completes the splendour of the city which we, thanks to her liberal bounty, have chosen as our home;[1] and we have been fortunate because here a worthy foreigner not only equals the citizen, but ranks with a gentleman. Behold from the evil of the sack of Rome good has come forth, because you [now] make your sculpture and architecture in this godly place. I am not surprised that the magnanimous Giovanni Gaddi, apostolic cleric,[2] together with cardinals and popes, pester you with letters requesting your return to the [Papal] Court so that they can again commission work from you. It would seem strange to me, should you decide to leave the safe nest and put yourself in danger, leaving Venetian senators for courtier prelates. . . .

Moreover, a greeting from these noble Venetian sleeves is worth more than a gift from those ignoble mitres. Look at the house you occupy, a worthy prison for your art, which shows in what esteem the talented are held by this Republic,[3] which is able to marvel at all that you create daily with [the skill of]

[1] Aretino and Sansovino both came to Venice in 1527.
[2] A Florentine financial operator for whom Jacopo Sansovino built a palace in Rome.
[3] Sansovino had been granted an apartment in the Procuratie Vecchie on the Piazza. His first duty as Proto was to repair the cupolas of St Mark's.

your hands and intellect. Who does not not praise the continuous work of restoration which sustains the church of St Mark's? Who is not astonished by the Corinthian structure [*machina*] of the Misericordia?[4] Who is not overawed by the rustication and Doric order of the Mint?[5] Who is not overwhelmed on seeing the carved Doric order with the Ionic above, together with the appropriate decoration, begun opposite the Ducal Palace?[6] What a beautiful sight the building will be, with its combination of different stones and marble, which is to be built beside the said palace, the form of which is to be composed of all the beauties of architecture, and which will serve as a loggia under which will stroll the leading personalities from this large body of nobles.[7] What shall I say of the foundations which must support the proud roofs of the Corner family?[8] What of the Vigna?[9] What of Our Lady of the Arsenal?[10] What of the wonderful Mother of Christ[11] who proffers the crown to the protector [St Mark] of this unique fatherland, whose history you have shown to us in bronze on the singing-gallery in his dwelling-place [i.e. in the choir of St Mark's]? For this you deserve the regards and honour awarded to you by the generosity of the most serene spirit of his devoted followers. Now, God willing, let our days be many, so that you can go on serving them and I can continue to praise them.

From Venice, 20 November 1537.   J. F.

(b) Venetian art explained to foreign visitors, 1561
Dialogue in Sansovino 1561, ff. 16v–26v.

FOREIGNER   Certainly, signor, the paintings[12] in this room [the Hall of the Great Council] have given me much food for thought, because the variety of styles and their beauty and gracefulness, one finds most satisfying here.

---

[4] Sansovino's newly designed premises for this Scuola, begun in 1532, were never completed.

[5] Begun in 1536, Sansovino's design is heavily rusticated, as befitted its function and need of security.

[6] That is, the library of St Mark's [cf. IX.1].

[7] The Loggetta, begun in 1537 [see II.4].

[8] Their new palace at San Maurizio on the Grand Canal, built, with state help, to replace the palace burnt down in 1532.

[9] San Francesco della Vigna, for the observant Franciscans; Doge Gritti as their patron laid the foundation stone of the new church in 1534.

[10] A marble sculpture of the Virgin and Child (1534) at the Arsenal.

[11] Possibly Aretino had seen a preliminary, unexecuted design for the statue of the Virgin in the Chiesetta of the Ducal Palace.

[12] The narrative canvases by the Bellini, Carpaccio, Titian, and others, destroyed in 1577, and the fourteenth-century fresco of the 'Paradiso' by Guariento [see also above, I.1, n. 33].

VENETIAN   Do you take pleasure in painting perhaps?

FOREIGNER   A little. I also like sculpture and architecture a lot, but I don't know much about them.

VENETIAN   Have you seen what is going on in this city in the three professions that you mentioned?

FOREIGNER   No, I haven't seen much of what I wanted to see, but I have heard tell of wonders.

VENETIAN   Sir, you will also be satisfied on this count, now that I see you are interested in the subject. I will make it all clear to you, but I want us to begin with painting, because it was introduced earlier to this city than either sculpture or architecture.

FOREIGNER   As you please.

VENETIAN   We have had painting for a long time, as is proved by the portraits of the Doges which are in the lunettes of the ceiling in the Great Council Hall, and Gian Bellini and Gentile are no less alive in our memories.

FOREIGNER   I have heard tell of them.

VENETIAN   In their time they were much esteemed, so much so that the Great Turk asked our government for one of them, who went and accomplished what the Turk wanted, and returned here much honoured and rewarded.[13] Their style was very careful and almost like miniature painting. . . . Have you noticed that in Venice there are more paintings than in all the rest of Italy?

FOREIGNER   It is right and proper that you, being the richest men in Italy, should also have more beautiful things than the others, because craftsmen go where the money flows and where the people are soft-living and well fed. But talk a bit about sculpture.

VENETIAN   There is also a lot of sculpture, but there is less of it than painting, because it is less delightful; it does not have the same charm of colour, and it was discovered later than painting. . . . It is the custom in this city that the Doge during his term in office orders three things. His portrait taken from life, which is placed in the Hall of the Great Council beneath the ceiling in some lunettes, where Venier's is the last in the series to date,[14] and Titian[15] is paid to do this; a picture in the Collegio or in the Senate or in whatever other place where it seems best, in which is represented the Madonna and the Doge kneeling with other figures; lastly, a shield with the Doge's coat of

[13] See above, I.1, n. 34.

[14] Doge Francesco Venier (1554–56), whose portrait is not among the fragments from the frieze of paired Doges' portraits which survived the 1577 fire.

[15] Tiziano Vecellio (c.1480–1576).

arms which in his lifetime is hung on his ceremonial barge and on his death is placed in St Mark's to his eternal memory.   J. F.

2   SECULAR COMMISSIONS AND POLITICAL IMAGERY

(a) Perugino's contract to paint in the Hall of the Great Council, 1494

ASV Provveditori al Sal, b. 61 (Notatorio 3, 1493–1507), ff. 25v–26r (Lorenzi 1868, no. 237, p. 111).

9 August 1494

The magnificent lords, Missier Fantin Marcello and his colleagues, the most worthy Provveditori to the Salt Office, on the order of the most serene Prince, have fixed a price and are come to an agreement with Master Piero Peroxin the painter,[16] who has taken on the painting of a square space [*campo*] in the Hall of the Great Council[17] between one window and another facing San Giorgio. Between this section and the section with the story of the Carità there is another space or square area. He has agreed to paint the said space from one window to the other and there are three and a half vaulted sections completed in which he must paint as many Doges as there were,[18] and, below, the episode when the Pope flees from Rome and the ensuing battle.[19] He has to complete this painting from above the windows, beyond halfway. Item: the said Master Piero is immediately obliged to make a drawing of the work, and to give it to the aforesaid magnificent and noble Provveditori, and he is obliged to paint this story more quickly and to make it better rather than otherwise with respect to the other works painted in the said Hall, as is fitting for this worthy place. He is to make the said work more lavish [*richa*] than the first, and all at his expense, the gold, silver, ultramarine and pigments, and all the things that pertain to the art of the painter. The magnificent and noble Provveditori will have the canvas and the wooden support made for him, and the platform [i.e. scaffolding] and other devices that are needed for this picture. The said master will have as

[16] Pietro Perugino (1446–1523), famous for his frescoes in the Sistine Chapel, Rome. Although he never took up this contract, he was in Venice in 1497.

[17] Cf. I.1, n. 33; II.8(a).

[18] The Doges were arranged in chronological order according to the point already reached in the portrait sequence.

[19] The reference is to episodes in the legend of Pope Alexander III's quarrel with Emperor Frederick Barbarossa and their reconciliation thanks to Doge Ziani (1177). Cf. I.1, n. 33; see also Muir 1981, pp. 103–7. The Pope, having taken refuge in the monastery of Santa Maria della Carità in Venice, was recognized and subsequently protected by the Doge; the 'ensuing battle' is the destruction of Spoleto (an appropriate city for an Umbrian painter to represent), which Barbarossa attacked for its loyalty to Alexander.

payment for the said work, according to the conditions outlined above, four hundred gold ducats, that is 400 ducats, and he will paint from top to bottom above the [wood-panelling over the] Bench [*Banca*] all that work that to him looks best and in less time than that other, beginning at once. He will have his payment from the Salt Office from time to time as is necessary, and as the said master is doing the work.[20]

J. F.

(b) The clocktower on the Piazza, 1496–1500
(i) Malipiero ed. Longo, ed. Sagredo 1843–4, p. 699.

1496   And at the beginning of this month of June a beginning was made on the foundations of the Clock [tower] in the Piazza of St Mark on the Merceria and it will cost about 6000 ducats, and, although the building of the Palace has been somewhat interrupted because of the War of Naples, nevertheless, so that it should not seem that this city is completely without money, a beginning was made to this work.

R. G.

(ii) Valuation of the works up to November 1500: ASV Senato, Deliberazioni, reg. 13, f. 157 (Erizzo 1860, p. 153).

Since it was ordered by our most excellent Signoria that . . . we should appraise the cost of manufacture of all the works executed and caused to be executed for Master Zuan Carlo de Raniero da Reloi from Reggio [Emilia],[21] in the clock[tower] situated at the entrance [*in boca*] of the Merceria on the Piazza of St Mark's, we, the below-named, Master Piero Lombardo,[22] Master Spieraindio della Zecha,[23] and Master Tomaso dai Obisi and Master Pencino dai Relio,

---

[20] The Bellini were paid an annual salary together with lucrative brokerages, and so (understandably) prolonged the work. Following complaints, in December 1493 Bartolomeo Bon, architect to the Salt Office, was ordered to check daily that the painters were working (Lorenzi 1868, no. 235, p. 109). In 1515 Titian, when negotiating his own payment for the battle scene, referred to the high fee Perugino was offered (Lorenzi 1868, pp. 165–6; Chambers 1970b, pp. 83–4).

[21] An inscription records that Gian Carlo and his father Gianpaolo had been appointed to make the clock in 1493. Late in 1495 the decision was made to build the tower; on 1 February 1499 Sanudo praised the clock when it was first revealed to public view (*DMS*, ii, col. 396).

[22] Pietro Lombardo (*c.*1435–1515), Proto of the Palace 1498–1515.

[23] Presumably Sperandio Savelli (before 1431–1504), goldsmith and bronze medallist from Mantua, who worked in Venice 1496–1504. He had experience of the clocktower of San Petronio, Bologna.

declare on oath that we are all in agreement with this valuation, which includes [however] only those works[24] specifically described hereunder.

First, all the façade of Our Lady [facing towards the Piazza], with her throne completed with four angels and stars, and the friezes which decorate the balcony [*pozzuol*] . . . for its manufacture, valued at

122 ducats

Item. For the spherical clock face [*spiera*] towards the Piazza – that is, for the twelve celestial signs and planets, at top and bottom, with all of their graduated letters [the figures of the hours] and stars, all completed and decorated: for their manufacture, valued at

120 ducats

Item. For the four astrolabes with their mechanisms [*ordegni*] complete and decorated: for their manufacture, valued at

70 ducats

Item. For the friezes and cornices of copper [on the façade] towards the Piazza, which are [in length] about 125 feet in all, including both the large and the small: for their manufacture, valued at

70 ducats

Item. For making the small doorways with two angels positioned in the work: valued at

20 ducats

Item. For working the pictures of copper set into the façades of Our Lady and of St Mark, with their ties [*arpesi*], [which cost] 1200 lire, as can be seen in the accounts of the Arsenal: for their manufacture, valued at

33 ducats

Item. To set all of the pictures [i.e. the signs of the zodiac, etc.] and ornaments, with their ties, in the two façades . . . valued at

8 ducats

Item. For making all of the stars positioned in the said pictures, with the standard [*bandiera*] of the Prince with two crosses and two balls fixed above the large and small bells: valued at

15 ducats

Item. For the sun rays [*el razo*] on the Merceria [façade] fixed in the work, with a St Mark and a sun's head: for their manufacture, valued at

13 ducats

---

[24] It omits, for instance, the winged lion of St Mark, which originally had Doge Agostino Barbarigo in front of it, and the 'Moors', cast in bronze at the Arsenal by Ambrogio de le Anchore (1497).

Item. For gilding Our Lady and her throne, and four angels and the rays [of the sun] on the Merceria [façade], all *a mordente*:[25] valued at

13 ducats

Item. For the chamber [*caxamento*] and ornamentation of the clock, which is set within the tower, with its columns, cornices and friezes, and its plinth complete . . . for the manufacture, valued at

100 ducats

Item. For the clock positioned within the said chamber, all tinned [*stagnato*], together with all its necessary mechanisms positioned around it: for its manufacture, valued at

330 ducats

Item. For the movement of the clock face [*spiera*] with the motions of the twelve planets and epicycles, and the top and the base, with all of the cogs and necessary mechanisms [*ordegni pertinenti*]: valued at

800 ducats

Item. For the three Magi and an angel, with all of their movements and mechanisms complete . . . for their manufacture, valued at

132 ducats

Item. For gilding and enamelling [*per far dorar a fuogo*] the twelve signs and planets, and the stars and the housing [*caxamento*], gilded and silvered: for their manufacture, valued at

25 ducats

Item. For the mechanisms that provide the movement of the giants [*ziganti*, i.e. the 'Moors'] with the work of installing the counterbalances: for their manufacture, valued at

10 ducats

And this is the final sum here certified:

1848 ducats
R. G.

(c) Doge Loredan's perceptions of political imagery, 1509
Speech of Doge Loredan reported in a letter of Luigi Da Porto (Da Porto ed. Bressan 1857, pp. 92–5).

Luigi Da Porto to Messer Antonio Savorgnan,[26] *Udine: from Vicenza, 20 July 1509*

. . . We share the inland border of our state for a long stretch in one region with the Emperor, who is able to harm us very grievously at little cost; and in the

[25] An adhesive compound used to attach gold leaf or worked silver to a surface (Boerio 1856).
[26] Luigi Da Porto (1485–1529), writer and military nobleman of Vicenza, addresses the letter to

other direction we have the power of France, and, lower down, that of the Pope: each being more powerful and richer than we are, we are bound to act with them as subjected [people] if we do not wish always to remain under arms; and, if we do want to defend ourselves against them, we are obliged to furnish ourselves with armies at intolerable expense and be placed in the hands of foreign captains, who involve themselves with us more for gain than anything else, as many experiences have served to warn us. But this does not happen with affairs at sea, since there we are masters over all, and we conduct our own affairs alone, with true zeal. Nor does one know what stupidity ever drew us away from the sea and turned us to the land,[27] for navigation was, so to speak, an inheritance from our earliest ancestors and has left us with many reminders and warnings that we should remain intent on it alone. And for this we can find interpretations for ourselves from what we see in the very beautiful and rich floor of our church of St Mark's, where, as you know, there stand two lions,[28] one placed in water, which has the appearance of joy, fatness and happiness, the other one squarely on land, amidst fronds and flowers, but all mournful, consumed by hunger and discomforted. . . .

Now let us suppose that trust is to be placed in ancient divinations (and credence must be given to them, seeing that many things painted centuries long ago, in many places, or written, have come true in the present) and above all in those known in temples, as is seen in the stupendous church of Santa Sophia in Constantinople. There, a very long time ago, before the Turks had it, a mosaic was made [showing] eight clasped hands with a label [*breve*] above in Greek characters, meaning, in our language, 'they will hold sway'; and these hands showed to anyone wanting to fathom their significance that the Ottomans must destroy that empire and then occupy it, as they have done. If notice should be taken of such signs, I say we must exercise the greatest caution about going to war with the Germans; for we have seen that on the façade of our church facing the Rialto there is placed first of all in low relief a lion which, trying to gnaw an armed German, has been wounded by his sword; and, a little higher, the

---

his uncle. The original does not survive, and Bressan's text may be a collation of several versions; possibly, too, the letter was not written at all until *c*.1522 (see Clough 1963, pp. 5–15). It does not name the Doge as speaker, but other sources relate that Loredan did address the Great Council (e.g. *DMS*, viii, col. 497, 8 July) at this time of crisis in the war of the League of Cambria [cf. above, II.14(d)], when there were demands for action to regain Padua.

[27] The same point was reiterated by Priuli, who in his diary deplored the fact that capital investment on the mainland was increasing, while that in maritime trade was not (see Woolf 1968, p. 188).

[28] Only the 'fat' lion in the tesselated pavement survives (Stringa 1610, p. 232, repeats Da Porto's interpretation). Another section of the pavement subject to a political reading was the two cocks carrying a fox, thought to symbolize the French and Venetian destruction of Duke Ludovico Sforza's power in 1498–9 (Sansovino 1581, f. 34v; ed. Martinioni 1663, p. 98).

German is seen, flourishing one of his weapons of war, riding on the lion;[29] and above these two carvings, partly recessed and out of series with the other figures, is the head of a woman weeping and all dishevelled, who is interpreted by many as Venice. Since it is clear that this woman has been put there unnecessarily (for no architectural reason, nor any function of the building, requires her) she offers a bad augury to anyone pondering these matters, and imparts the utmost fear . . .   G. B., J. F.

(d) Political iconography of a flagstaff base in the Piazza c.1542.

Contarini[30] c.1542, IV, ff. E IIv–IIIv.

In front of the door [of St Mark's] there are three flags which blow in the gentle breeze. The lofty flagstaffs reach above the clouds. Their bases are made of Parian marble, their cases of bronze.[31] The one in the middle shows three ships coming from the high seas. On the stern of the first ship one sees the golden Virgin of the Pole [i.e. Astraea, goddess of justice], who, having been exiled by the wicked world, has fixed her abode in Venetian waters. In her right hand she has the honoured sword, but in the left she holds the head of a convicted traitor. A merman guides her golden vessel; the prow bears the balanced scales. An elephant carries the ship on his shoulders into the beautiful city. A robust triton helps her to tow it and goes along sounding a horn for pleasure. The other boat transports the Mother of the Granaries [i.e. the goddess Ceres], who in her bounteous hand holds ears of wheat above a dolphin's curved back. The heavy ship is borne along, which Cymothoe [a nereid], the pure wife, helps to tow, singing. Then in the third boat comes happy Victory in a white dress. In her right hand she holds up the palm branch; in the left, spoils of the enemy. In the middle, in the honoured vessel, the city of Venice is drawn along through the calm sea by snow-white horses. Portumnus, the god of ports, from whose chin hangs a green beard, assists her. Above this there are three lions [i.e. winged lions of St Mark] emitting a golden radiance. Nearby at all times are venal tradesmen in a kind of market.[32] Here you will find all kinds of fruit and grain,

[29] These so-called 'Germans' are just small figures in the surviving Romanesque roundels; the female head above them is no longer there.

[30] Pietro Contarini (1477–1543) held minor government posts in Istria and Dalmatia; in his eccentric – partly autobiographical – literary work *L'Argoa volgar* (1541, then translated) the hero, before leaving for a Greek city, celebrates the marvels of Venice (*DBI*).

[31] Erected in 1501–5. The original programme is lost; Sansovino's version of it is rather different (Sansovino 1581, p. 101; ed. Martinioni 1663, p. 293).

[32] The squalor of this market was notorious, and Jacopo Sansovino was commissioned to improve the Piazza (Howard 1975, pp. 11–14).

6   Base of Flagstaff on the Piazza San Marco.
(Photograph copyright the Conway Library, Courtauld Institute of Art)

and the good things that Mother Earth produces for the human race, all that nature has beneath the sea, and everything that flies through the air. . . . If some worthy man from ancient times could behold these sacred towers of the sea [i.e. the flagstaff bases] he would swear that they were the product of Phidias's genius, but he who has sculpted [them] is Alessandro Lionpardo,[33] the new glory of our age, who shines like a star upon the Venetian waters.   J. F.

[33] Alessandro Leopardi (active 1492; d. 1523), the expert bronze-caster, who cast and signed Verrocchio's monument to Bartolomeo Colleone.

399

(e) A programme for redecorating the Ducal Palace after the fire of 1577

BCV ms. Cicogna 585, 105, unpaginated (Wolters 1965–6, pp. 314–15, with some misreadings).

In the room[34] outside the Senate and Collegio there are four doors: one leads into the Hall of the Senate, one into the Collegio, and the third into the Heads of the Ten and the fourth into the Chancery. Above each should go three figures, with meanings appropriate to what goes on in the place which one enters through that door.

> Towards the Collegio: Vigilance, Eloquence, Facility of Audience.
> Towards the Senate: Peace, Pallas, nurse of the arts, and War.[35]
> Towards the Council of Ten: Supreme Authority, Religion and Justice.
> On the Chancery [door]: Secrecy, Diligence and Fidelity.

The above figures can be represented with the following symbols.

Eloquence should be placed on the right-hand side of the door. By the ancients she was represented wearing variegated colours, being a person who in her loquacity goes around telling stories and recounting different opinions and arguments; she makes up her mind and talks so colourfully that [her listeners] are converted to causes through the rapidity of her intellect, which by means of language swiftly moves both heart and mind with its promptness. They placed wings at the peak of her forehead; they made her clothing – that is, her cloak and tunic or skirt – ample with pleats and folds. In her right hand she holds a [sharp] file with a snake wound around it, for prudence and the cutting edge of ideas, and in the left hand she has Mercury's sceptre with two snakes or dragons on the top with wings, which stands for orations in treating of peace, concord and union, showing that by means of eloquence two armies may be pacified in war. With these sceptres Mercury and mercurial orators rise heavenwards and above the stars, and through the air over all the world and the abyss, so that ambassadors are called 'caduceus bearers', carriers of the sceptre of knowledge which is introduced even into games, judgements and marriages, like a Hercules in one of his guises, who with eloquence drew to himself [tiro a se][36] various peoples.

[34] The Sala delle Quattro Porte.

[35] The translation here depends on repunctuation of Wolters' transcription. The overall programme for redecoration after the Palace fire of 1577 was drawn up by two Venetian nobles and a monk (full text in Wolters, 1965–6, pp. 303–18). The twelve figures for the Sala delle Quattro Porte may have been adapted from proposals previously submitted by members of the Academy [cf. above, IX.7], and now to be realized in sculpture instead of by painting. Such pretentiously erudite fantasies reflected the availability of the works of iconography by Cartari (1556) and Valeriano (1556). See Hope 1985, pp. 401–4.

[36] Phrase omitted by Wolters. The reference here is to the 'Gallic' Hercules, described in, for example, Cartari 1556, f. 67r.

Facility of Audience is placed on the left-hand side of the door and will be portrayed as a beautiful woman, of healthy and beautiful aspect, with the symbol on her sceptre of a bird[37] called Hierazze or Sparrowhawk, which, because it is agile in rising from earth to heaven, swooping down from heaven without flexing its wings, and so able in combat and in fecundity, was venerated by the Egyptians as Venus and Mars and as Speed, as is found in hieroglyphs. This idea, therefore, is appropriately shown by an ascending staircase. And in one hand she has a cartwheel, and there are wings on her ankles, her head and her shoulders, [to represent] that [force] which moves the mind, body and intellect with ease in its sentiments, and nimbly raises every weight and oppressive thought, by means of that flexible faculty that can penetrate every action and feasible argument.

Vigilance, which goes in the middle between Eloquence and Facility of Audience, will be a woman who holds aloft the crowing cock in her hand, with two winged eyes, facing towards the sunrise, as she keeps watch at night and in the daytime awakens mortals, whether to their work, guard [duties] or all their other doings, or in every occasion of universal interest. These things signify most secure and profitable government, and equity in the outcome of affairs, helpful to all mankind, and it applies particularly to rulers and administrators. Beyond this [Vigilance] serves also in life, regulating the good health of mind, body and intellect. Vigilance was esteemed by the Socratics as the splendour of the sun, and because of this she was given as her attribute the Socratic cock, customarily sacrificed at sunrise. Afterwards Vigilance was given as her daytime work all the operations of the arts and sciences, whence the eyes on the sceptre with two wings, [signifying] the readiest listener and supremely perspicacious counsellor, the opponent of sleep and friend of security.

These three figures were given to the sculptor Girolamo Campagna.

20 December 1584. These figures were taken from Campagna and given to Messer Alessandro Vittoria.   D. C., C. H.

(f) The ceiling-framework for the hall of the Senate, 1578–82

(i) Contract drawing for the ceiling, 1578: Victoria and Albert Museum E509–1937, C. Sorte (Wolters 1961–3, pp. 137–45).

27 July 1578

I, Andrea of Faenza, am bound to make the ceiling according to the written

---

[37] The original reads *augello*, not (*pace* Wolters), *angello*.

7 Cristoforo Sorte, 'Design for the Ceiling of the Hall of the Senate.'
(By courtesy of the Board of Trustees of the Victoria and Albert Museum)

instructions and the present drawing, together with the profiles that will be provided by Master Cristoforo Sorte and the two architects [*Proti*] in charge.

I, Francesco,[38] woodcarver of the parish of San Moisè, promise that which is above-written.   J. F.

(ii) Cristoforo Sorte's complaint, 1582: BMV ms. Ital., cl. IV, 169 (5265), ff. 74–7 (Schulz 1961–3, p. 291).

I, Christoforo Sorte,[39] having appeared before your excellencies, Lords Provveditori for the restoration of the Palace, this morning 24 April 1582, with the petition recorded above, which has now been carefully read and considered, your excellencies have instructed me to tell you clearly what I have pleaded. . . . I respectfully declare that I am in conflict with Messer Lauro Zordan, secretary to the Provveditori, because he wants to favour Master Hieronimo the woodcarver,[40] his close friend, and likewise Master Antonio dal Ponte, the Proto in charge, who are both deeply opposed to my activities . . . which adversely affects my honour, as your excellent lordships will be able to determine from the facts. In the Hall of the Senate, this woodcarver has failed to abide by his obligation to make cartouches with a figure within them on the frieze between the little terms [*termineti*] according to the way he began it. Eight are missing, and this is a serious matter, and he has not made the foliage on the frieze according to the drawings, and in that part it is a shameful work. Nevertheless, Messer Lauro has favoured him and has paid. . . . Besides this the illustrious senators were very insistent that I should make vents in the ceiling, and I designed four which were highly praised, and the architect mentioned above never had them included in this work . . . but what is more, he has put in a truly disgraceful invention which he has made, consisting of certain vents which resemble funnels, like those they make in cellars for decanting wine, a most shameful thing. And, besides that, he has ruined the coping of the cornice of the frieze by making holes without due care. Thus your excellencies will recognize the deception worked upon your predecessors by these two men [who are now] exposed, as they gave their excellencies to understand that the Hall of the Great Council[41] was unfinished, and likewise the Hall of the Senate, which was untrue . . . and, because on their word these gentlemen had me

[38] Francesco, known as 'il Bello', frequently collaborated with Sorte: for example in 1577, on the seating in the Hall of the Senate.

[39] Cristoforo Sorte (*c.*1510–94), from Verona, cartographer, surveyor and writer about painting.

[40] An obscure Vicentine woodcarver who seems only to have worked on the frieze, not the central part of the ceiling.

[41] That is, the ceiling, also designed by Sorte.

discharged from the job given earlier to me, before work had been finished, . . .
I appeal to your discretion to cancel my dismissal because your predecessors
were deceived, and so that I may make an excellent end to the unfinished work;
otherwise my work will remain in my rivals' hands and things will end badly . . .
and the work will be shameful; but I will cry out against it to high heaven,
because I do not want the shame.[42]   J. F.

(g) A design for the new Rialto Bridge, 1587

ASV, Provveditori sopra la Fabbrica del Ponte di Rialto, Pareri, b. 3 (Cessi and Alberti
1934, pp. 349–51).

Guglielmo di Grande: presented on 23 December 1587

Most illustrious and excellent lords . . . ,

I, Guglielmo Grande, architect and engineer to the department of waterways
[*Officio sopra l'acque*] must state my opinion concerning the method to be used in
building the said bridge as is shown by drawings by my hand. I declare that such
a work must be made beautiful, magnificent, safe, useful and convenient, and in
making it the existing buildings will not be destroyed, especially in those areas
where they are very profitable.

As regards beauty and magnificence, on the top of this bridge I plan to make
a level area, 110 feet long by 8½ feet wide in the middle, along its length from
one end to the other. Aligned with the façade of the Drapparia, a thoroughfare
19½ feet wide, and on either side of this, 3 feet above, there will be a flat area
consisting of two rows of shops, each shop almost 10 feet square. One row will
overlook the street, the other the Canal, with a bit of balustrading; each side will
be protected from the rain by means of a portico on each side, which will serve
as a thoroughfare about 4 feet wide in addition to the one already mentioned;
and the portico above the Canal will help people to enjoy the view of the said
Canal from one end of the bridge to the other. . . .

As to soundness or safety, this work will be very safe, because I have planned
that the two piers which must support all the weight shall each have to be 20
feet thick and founded 31 feet below the normal water level, not counting the
piles which will be made beneath these piers according to necessity, and the
vault or arch will be 5 feet thick, and at the head of the steps in the middle
the joining will be such that it will not be possible for any knowledgeable
architect to judge it unsafe.

---

[42] The outcome of this petition is unknown. Some of the alterations to Sorte's design were
corrected, but the offensive funnel-shaped features are described in Sansovino ed. Martinioni
1663, p. 231.

As to profit, the work will be most profitable, because rents will be received from it for the shops and storage rooms [*volte*], which according to this design bring in 4560 ducats and more. The accounting is simple: above the level area of the bridge, twenty-eight shops will be constructed, twenty-four [of them] 9½ feet square ... all this adds up to 1560 ducats, which in all makes 4560 ducats as I said earlier, and when one adds the 1500 ducats which it yields at present, which has to be assigned to private individuals, the government will be left with 3060 ducats, and by spending 20,000 ducats on this work their investment will be repaid at about 4½ per cent.

As regards convenience, it will be very convenient both for the passage of shipping and of people. The shipping will have a channel 90 feet wide, covered by an arch 20 feet high, through which every large galley will be able to sail easily without its mast. The Doge's ceremonial barge and every large barge loaded with cargo will be able to pass there, and small boats and gondolas on meeting each other will be able to pass without changing course, and the current will be very little more than in the rest of the Canal. People will have easy access to the bridge from the main street by an ascent measuring 21 feet divided into 42 steps, each step being 1¼ feet wide in the beautiful style of a Roman stair, with its handrail most convenient for people of all kinds. On each head of the bridge there will be a stair on either side, 10 feet wide, which will have the same number of steps 1 foot wide, which will serve the people coming along the Canal side, who do not want to climb onto the bridge but to cut across it at the bottom. I have planned a vaulted area to be made at the foot of the first middle stairway on the public thoroughfare. . . . It will provide cover when it is wet for people to walk under, and the loggias in the middle will encourage many people to conduct their business dealings conveniently while enjoying the sight of everyone who passes by, whether by boat or on land.

This is the beautiful, magnificent, safe, useful and convenient work, worthy of the greatness of this most happy state, which will cause wonder not only to him who sees it, but also to him who hears about it.[43]   J. F.

(a) Mantuan artists refused permission to copy a map, 1506

From a letter of Isabella d'Este to her husband, Francesco Gonzaga, Marquis of Mantua, 10 November 1506: ASMn. Collezione Volta di Autografi, b. 1, fasc. 103 (D'Arco 1857, II, 72).

---

[43] Grandi's unsuccesful project was reconstructed in 1879–80; the drawings survive (Calabri and Morachiello 1987, figs 85–6).

My Illustrious Lord,

When Master Hieronimo the painter[44] and his companions went to Venice to copy 'the Italy',[45] I wrote to the magnificent nobleman Carlo Valerio[46] that I wanted him to help them, and he, being eager to serve Your Excellency, went to ask the most serene Prince [Doge Loredan] for his permission, because without that it would be impossible, since it is in his anteroom, and because on that other occasion those who allowed themselves to copy it without his permission nearly came to grief; but, from what Master Hieronimo has told me on behalf of the magnificent Carlo, the Doge does not want to listen, saying to him, 'Look at this letter which we have just received', by which they were informed that every day Your Excellency speaks words which are harmful to the government, not in public, where you speak honourably, but in private, and not only you yourself, but also certain of your Your Excellency's servants, a thing which is most damaging to that state, and which stirs up hatred in their hearts against Your Excellency, because every day they have similar reports.[47] The magnificent Carlo advises you to behave with circumspection, and is of the opinion that you should speak well [of Venice] with her ambassador to the Pope, so that he will have reason to make a favourable report, and not leave the Senate with such a bad impression of you. Whatever happens, he asks that you keep this to yourself, so that it is not known that this message comes from him. Concerning the copy of 'the Italy', he says that the matter must rest for a month or two, and then he will see about gratifying you.   J. F.

(b) A picture for the sister of the King of France, 1515–16

(i) Letter of the Heads of the Council of Ten to the Venetian ambassadors in France, 31 October 1515: ASV Capi del Consiglio dei Dieci, Lettere, filza 16, no. 383 (von Bode et al. 1911, p. 90).

The last day of October 1515. To our representatives with His Most Christian Majesty

We have carefully considered the matter about which we wrote to you a few days ago, concerning our decision to give to the most illustrious Madame d'Alençon[48] [*Madonna de Lanson*] a picture with the image of the Glorious

[44] Girolamo de'Corradi, active in Mantua from 1495; he may have been accompanied by Francesco Bonsignori or by his own brother Francesco.

[45] A famous map on canvas by Antonio di Leonardi, burnt in 1574 (see Gallo 1943, p. 47).

[46] Carlo Valier entertained Isabella d'Este in Venice in 1502 and later tried to obtain for her a painting by Giorgione (Luzio and Renier 1903, pp. 261–6).

[47] Since Francesco Gonzaga's dismissal as Captain General in 1497 Venetian relations with Mantua had deteriorated. He was currently serving Pope Julius II in the papal campaign to retake Perugia and Bologna.

[48] Marguerite de Valois, sister of François I and wife of Charles, Duke of Alençon. Venetian

Virgin, as excellent and perfect as possible. We have found in this city some very beautiful pictures, albeit old ones, but some people are opposed to our using one [of these], depending on the taste of those who have seen them. Because of this reaction – and wishing above all to satisfy Her Excellency, since this matter depends on the will and the wishes of the person who is to enjoy the picture – we have decided to have a new one made, completely beautiful and perfect. But we order you . . . to communicate this our desire and intention to the aforementioned illustrious lady, seeking to understand her will and pleasure concerning the size and quality of the said picture. As it is to represent the glorious Virgin with her Son, [find out] which figures she wishes to be placed beside the Madonna, and of what size, including all other details necessary. Concerning this you will use all possible diligence, so that we shall first understand everything and be able to carry out our decision.   J. F.

(ii) From a letter of Gaspare a Vidua to Giovanni Badoer, 15 January 1516: ASV Atti dei Procuratori di San Marco de Citra, Commissaria 57, fasc. XXIIB (von Bode et al. 1911, p. 90).

15 January 1515 [Venetian style]. To the magnificent and renowned Lord Giovanni Badoer, doctor and knight, Venetian ambassador to the Most Christian King of France at Piacenza

. . . I am urging the completion of the picture for the illustrious sister of the Christian King, which in truth will be a beautiful thing. The master is Zuan Bellin, and it will be completely finished very shortly.   J. F.

(iii) Letter of Giovanni Badoer, Venetian ambassador in France, to the Senate, 31 October 1516: *DMS*, xxiii, col. 204.

Today I had nothing to negotiate, because Her Illustrious Majesty the Queen Mother sent word that the perfumes and the picture for the Duchess of Alençon [*di Nason*] her daughter should be brought, and I went and showed her everything. There were a great number of fine perfumes, and the Queen Mother [Louise of Savoy] and the Duchess stayed there until evening. Her Excellency wanted to see everything. The Queen and her daughter[49] were present. She praised the picture a lot and Madame d'Alençon asked who had

relations with France had become courteous since the return of conquered territory at the Peace of Noyon (August 1516).
[49]   Claude, daughter of Louis XII, or possibly the infant Charlotte, who died aged eight.

painted it. The Ambassador told her that it is entirely by the hand of the first painter in Italy.[50]   J. F.

4 ART IN CONFLICT WITH GOVERNMENT

(a) Venetian sculptors and stonemasons object to foreign competition, 1491
From the Mariegola or rule book of the sculptors and stonemasons: BCV ms. Correr V, 150 (Sagredo 1856, p. 283).

On 25 October 1491 we of the Sculptors and Stonemasons Guild appear before you, magnificent sirs,[51] because many of our laws made by yourselves and recorded in our statute book are not being observed. This is solely because we do not control our [membership] elections [*no haver ordene de le nostre election*], as the non-Venetians, i.e. the Milanese and those from foreign parts, number 126, and at present they have about fifty apprentices who are from other places, and they do not want to teach your subjects. This is contrary to our statutes and the nature of our regulations, and opposed to the welfare of this city, and we Venetians, subjects of your magnificence, are no more than about forty, including those who lack the strength to work [*depossente*] and all who are inscribed in the book, and for this reason we demand the control of our elections, so that when we call a general meeting there will be present all our Venetian [members] and those from territory subject to your lordships, and not the Milanese or those from foreign parts, so that the leadership and other of our offices do not pass from hand to hand, and our laws and regulations do not fall into ruin.   J. F.

(b) Dürer is prosecuted by the Painters' Guild, 1506
From the German. Extract from a letter of Dürer, in Venice, to Willibald Pirkheimer, in Nuremberg, 2 April 1506: Stadtbibliothek Nuremberg, ms. Pirkheimer 394.2 (Rupprich 1956, p. 49; as translated in Conway 1889, p. 48).

The painters here, let me tell you, are very unfriendly to me. They have summoned me three times before the magistrates, and I have had to pay 4

---

[50] This autograph painting has not been traced, but the work of Bellini (who had in fact died two days earlier) was evidently welcome as a form of diplomatic gift. In March 1517 Odette de Foix, Governor of Milan, was presented with a *Dead Christ*, a painting by Bellini bought by the government from Cipriano Malipiero.

[51] That is, before the magistrates of the Giustizia Vecchia, who approved their petition. Hence its inclusion in this statute book of the guild.

florins to their Scuola.[52] You must also know that I might have gained a great deal of money if I had not undertaken to paint the German picture.[53] There is much work in it and I cannot get it quite finished before Whitsuntide. Yet they pay me only 85 ducats for it. Now you know how much it costs to live, and then I have bought some things and sent some money away, so that I do not have much with me now. But do not misunderstand me, I am determined not to go away till God enables me to pay you with thanks and to have 100 florins left over.[54] I should easily earn this if I had not got the German picture to paint, for all men except the painters wish me well. J. F.

(c) Control over expenditure by the Procurators of St Mark's on portraits, 1580
Decree of the Great Council, 11 September 1580: ASV Maggior Consiglio, Deliberazioni, reg. 31, ff. 71v–72r.

In the Procuracy di Citra, where previously they used to spend 5 ducats on the Procurators' commissions,[55] and then at the most 10 ducats for each one, as can be seen from the account books, 70 ducats were then spent on them. Now one discovers that this expenditure has increased so much that up until 1578, on fourteen admissions of fourteen Procurators, 696 ducats 9 grossi 18 pizzoli [tiny coins] have been spent, and besides this a goodly sum of the Procurators' money has been spent on pictures and portraits of the Procurators.[56] Whence, in order to prevent this kind of expenditure from increasing each year, which brings the said Procuracy into disrepute, it is ordered that, since the Procuracy di Ultra according to its regulations cannot spend more than 15 ducats on each Procurator's admission, the Procuracy di Supra and the Procuracy di Citra may likewise not spend more than 15 ducats on each Procurator's elevation, and they may not spend on paintings and other similar things even a fraction more than the other Procuracies. J. F.

[52] A heavy fine, but as a recently arrived foreigner Dürer was ineligible to join the guild and only allowed to sell pictures during the Ascension-tide fair; thus he had worked illegally for three months.
[53] *The Feast of the Rose Garlands* (National Gallery, Prague), an altarpiece ordered by the German merchants to decorate their altar at San Bartolomeo, near the exchange house.
[54] Dürer, who had been buying jewels and fashionable clothes, worked in Venice till early 1507 to pay off his debts (Conway 1889, pp. 55, 60).
[55] Manuscript copies of the statutes governing the Procurator's terms of holding office, equivalent to the Doge's *promissione* [see above, II.3(b)]. These often included miniature portraits.
[56] Procurators customarily commissioned individual and group portraits (often with the Virgin or patron saints) to commemorate themselves; these were hung in their premises on the Piazza. Tintoretto and his workshop specialized in such portraits.

(d) Order for the destruction of a statue at Belluno, 1623
ASV Pompe, b. 21 (Bistort 1912, p. 282).

In the Senate, 4 November 1623

The Council of Cividal di Belluno, acting against the public will and the orders published in recent months, has prepared a full-length [*intiera*] bronze statue in memory of our civil and military Governor,[57] which is to be erected on the piazza at Belluno, mounted on a conspicuous base which has already been made for that purpose. Since it is not fitting to allow such an improper abuse, which is contrary to the public will, it is proclaimed that it be handed over to the Superintendent of the artillery, who must immediately send for the master, if the said statue has already been cast, and make him transport it to our Arsenal to be melted down for cannon.

This Senate authorizes the Governor of Cividal di Belluno to raze to the ground the prepared base, as stated above, and in future the making of statues, coats of arms, banners and other similar things in memory of our representatives is to be banned in accordance with the relevant decrees issued by the said magistrates. Notice of the present deliberation will be given to all our representatives and their successors, whether on land or sea, with orders to register it in each chancery.   J. F.

5   ART FOR CONFRATERNITIES AND CHURCHES

(a) A commission from the Scuola della Carità, 1539
ASV Scuola Grande della Carità, reg. 256 (Notatorio 1531–43), ff. 103v–104v (Rosand 1982, p. 234).

6 March 1539

The excellent master, the painter Zuan Antonio from Pordenone,[58] is dead, to whom it was decided on 6 March 1538 to give the job of painting the canvas or compartment which was in our meeting-hall on the side where the twelve members of the Zonta used to sit, for the price entered in the book. The said master Zuan Antonio before he died came to the hall saying that he wanted to

---

[57] The roles of Podestà and Capitano were combined in one person at Belluno; in 1622–3 the Governors were successively Angelo Giustinian and Giovanni da Ponte (Tagliaferri 1974, p. lii).

[58] Giovanni Antonio Sacchiense (1484–1539), known as Pordenone, whose works in Venice included large ceiling paintings in the Ducal Palace and canvases in San Rocco.

begin the painting, and, upon his asking the opinion of these gentlemen as to
what story should be painted, he was asked whether when he received the
commission he had been obliged to paint any particular subject. He replied that
truly one of those gentlemen who was present at the time thought that the
Assumption of the Madonna should be painted. [He said,] 'I went away and
thought about this afterwards, and considered it would be unsuitable: first,
because of the location of the work; secondly, because that miracle does not
follow directly after the one already painted by the excellent master Titian,[59]
and because one sees such an Assumption painted in your assembly hall here,
near the door. Thus, having considered carefully, I do not find anything more
fitting than the Marriage of the Virgin, because it follows on that other canvas,
and because the place is big enough for such a subject.'

He was allowed, indeed ordered, to begin painting such a Marriage, because
it is also a rare subject, and this is true as one sees that the aforementioned
Pordenone has drawn it in chalk. Our omnipotent Creator having summoned
him to his own, the commission must of necessity be given to another painter,
capable of doing it. After the commission was announced, those listed below
came to make themselves known. They were first summoned into our
committee room and into the presence of our respected Guardian and sixteen
members of the Bench [*Bancha*] and nine members of the Zonta. They were all
heard, and their conditions concerning the painting of such a canvas. Then, one
by one, they were voted on as follows.

> Misser Paris Bordon:[60] 7 for; 18 against.
> Misser Bonifattio da Sant Alvise:[61] 13 for; 12 against.
> Misser Vettor Brunello:[62] 5 for; 20 against.
> Misser Zuan Piero Silvio: 19 for; 6 against.

This leaves the said Zuan Piero Silvio, who is obliged to sign a document drawn
up by us, which will state the price and the time within which the said canvas
must be finished, as shall appear in more detail in the document.[63]   J. F.

---

[59] Titian's *Presentation of the Virgin* remained in the Carità (now part of the Accademia, Venice).

[60] Paris Bordone (1500–70), from Treviso.

[61] Bonifacio Pitati (1487–1553), from Verona.

[62] An obscure artist (active 1529–45), probably related to Pitati, whose wife had the same
surname.

[63] Silvio (d. 1552) failed to meet the one-year deadline and in 1543 still had not completed his
undistinguished work (now the property of the Accademia, on loan to the parish church of Mason
Vicentino).

(b) Faked mosaic work at St Mark's: Titian's evidence, 1563

ASV Procuratia di San Marco de Supra, b. 78 (processo 182), fasc. 2, ff. 55r–56v (Ongania 1886, pp. 64–5, with some omissions).

22 May 1563

The above-mentioned Master Titian testified as follows: 'I tell you that, so far as work in mosaic is concerned, I don't see any better [examples than here], by which I mean all the works in the church [St Mark's] which were made in times gone by and which are exposed [to view], nor do I know of [any] defects [in them]. And, because I do not have much experience of the art of mosaic, I do not want to involve myself in talking about what I don't know, and I have seen that where the mosaic has been rubbed and washed down it seems to me that the images [*figure*] have come out more beautifully and clearly than otherwise.' . . . He said, on reading it over, 'According to my view, this is how it seems to be; of other things I can't say anything.'

He was asked, 'Does it appear to you that paint has been applied in some parts of these works, or not?'

He replied, 'Concerning this, I don't know, because if colours had been applied they would not have come out more beautifully and clearly after being wetted, and there is mosaic there underneath, it seems to me, where required.'

He was asked, 'Does it seem to you that in any place the surface of these mosaics has been painted with colour and with a brush?'

He replied, 'Yes, from what one sees, it seems to me that the surface of the mosaic has been painted; that is, the first and second *campanili* which are immediately above the steps at the entrance;[64] I have not seen it in other places, but here, as there is mosaic beneath, one cannot be in disagreement: but enough of this.'

He was asked, 'Supposing you are asked if those *campanili* could be made in mosaic in suitable colours, without brushes and paint?'

He replied, 'Reverend Sir, certainly they can be so made.' Continuing: 'If the churches had been done without *campanili*, it could be seen from the cartoons if the *campanili* had been designed before the work was begun, and it would be necessary to know whether the Zuccati themselves or others had painted the said *campanili*.'

He was asked, 'Who makes these cartoons?'

He replied, 'They have them made by different people.'

He was asked, 'Have you ever made them for these Zuchati?'

---

[64] The area in question was part of the vault of the nave above the main entrance, known as the *arcone* of the Apocalypse. The controversial *campanili* did not feature in the replacement.

He replied, 'Yes, Sir, and they [the Zuchati] also make them.'[65]

He was asked, 'Have you ever been up on the scaffolding?'

He replied, 'Yes, a few days ago, after Your Excellency[66] gave permission that everyone could go up on the scaffolding and return to work. When someone from the Procurators' office came to Valerio's workshop at Santi Filippo e Giacomo for drawings of things for women,[67] and to tell him other things, and finding me there in Master Valerio's workshop, he begged me to do him the favour of going to look, and so I came, and they pointed out to me the largest *campanile* which was rubbed out, and they showed me the gold mosaic beneath the place where the *campanile* had been.'

He was asked, 'Since this business began, have you talked about it with any painter?'

He replied, 'The other day, when Your Excellency summoned Tentoretto,[68] which was the Eve of the Feast of the Assumption, and then sent him away because Your Excellency was unable to go up the scaffolding because you were unwell, I talked with the said Tentoretto' – *he said on reading it over that he had talked with him twice* – '[about] how I thought that these worthy men, the Zuchati, had been wronged.'

On matters in general: 'I have been friendly with the Zuchati for very many years and Master Francesco stood as godfather when I had my little girl baptized, who died.'

He was asked, 'Have you had any business dealings with them, sureties, debts or credit?'

He replied, 'It is true that they said, "Look, what a calumny this is!" and so I said to them that justice would not be wanting, as they had done no wrong, and I eat and drink with Master Valerio for the sake of good company.' For the rest, it is correct, and after reading it over he said, 'Also, this morning I have spoken with Andrea Schiavon the painter,[69] and I said to him, "How is it that these poor fellows must redo such a beautiful work, seeing they are honourable men?" '

He was asked, 'When you were with the Zuchati on the scaffolding and saw the painted *campanile*, did you ask them who had done it?'

He replied, 'They said they didn't know but they had not made this *campanile*.'

He said that he knew no more, and after reading it over he swore that it was correct and to keep silent.   J. F.

[65] These cartoons would have been to scale, in colour and on paper. Later in the proceedings Valerio confirmed that Titian made cartoons for them. The vast St Mark above the main door, dated 1545 and signed by both Zuccati, has been attributed to him.

[66] He appears to be addressing Melchior Michiel, the Procurator in charge of the inquiry.

[67] Besides being accused of negligence in his duties at St Mark's, Valerio was denounced by one witness for drawing women's hats and clothes.

[68] Jacopo Robusti, 'il Tintoretto' (1518–94).

[69] Andrea Meldolla (*c*.1505–63), known as 'il Schiavone'.

(c) Contract of Veronese for the refectory of San Giorgio Maggiore, 1562
ASV Archivio San Giorgio Maggiore, processo no. 10 (Cicogna 1824–61, IV, 233–4; Pignatti 1976, pp. 253–4).

6 June 1562

The present document sets down how on this day Father Alessandro of Bergamo, procurator, and I, Father Mauritio of Bergamo, cellarer, are come to an agreement with the painter Master Paulo Caliari[70] of Verona, concerning the making of our painting in the new refectory.[71] It is to be as wide and high as the wall and is to cover it completely. He is to represent the story of the Supper of the Miracle worked by Christ at Cana in Galilee.[72] He is to paint that number of figures which will go into it comfortably, and which are necessary for the story. Master Paulo will paint the work and also provide all kinds of pigments at his own expense, and he will order the preparation of the canvas and bear the cost of anything else concerning it. The monastery will provide only the unprimed canvas, and it will have the support made for the painting, but the rest – including the canvas and anything else concerning it – he will pay for, and the said Master Paulo will be obliged to use the highest quality pigments in the work, of the kind that are approved by all experts. And for his payment for the work, we promise 324 ducats, at the rate of 6 lire 4 soldi, to be given him from day to day according to his need, and for earnest money we have given him 50 ducats. Master Paulo promises to finish the work[73] by the Feast of the Madonna in September 1563, and in addition to the fee we promise him a cask of wine, to be brought by us to Venice and consigned to him, and the monastery will pay for his food during the period that he is working on the said picture, and will bear the cost of the meals which he eats in the refectory. . . .   J. F.

(d) The resolution to build the church of Santa Maria della Salute, 1630
Senate decree of 22 October 1630: ASV Senato, Terra, reg. 104, ff. 363v–365r.

For ever increasing is the certainty that we have incurred the wrath of God for our sins, for the dreadful proof of this comes from the plague, and there is

[70] Paolo Caliari, 'il Veronese' (1528–88), had been resident in Venice from before 1555.

[71] The new refectory for the Benedictine monastery of San Giorgio Maggiore had been designed by Palladio, whose architecture influenced Veronese's composition and use of light.

[72] John 2:1–11. See above, V.21, for another biblical 'feast' scene, with similarly vague specifications.

[73] In spite of the huge dimensions (6.7 × 9.9 m), the painting (now in the Louvre) was completed in just over a year.

reason to fear worse evil unless God can be prevailed upon to show his great mercy instead, after he has exacted from us by blows the prompt recognition he would have of us for the sake of our salvation. Hence we must with our most sincere and humble petitions beg him once more to temper his anger, as is his most merciful and fatherly custom when he sees in princes and peoples, and in their public parades of respect, devotion and piety, the desire to submit to his justice and to render to his divine name all honour, reverence and obedience. The memory of the benefits received by our Republic in the year of the last contagion in 1576 from the vow to build the church dedicated to the Redeemer inspires in us the sure and certain hope of obtaining through a similar act of piety another such favour, especially by means of the powerful protection of the Most Holy Virgin, his mother and Our Lady, which we have always experienced and have always retained by our singular reverence for her since the birth of our Republic, for our city was founded on the day of the Annunciation to her, and under her auspices has kept itself for hundreds of years a virgin both in its faith and in its dominion, and has always demonstrated the supreme authority which derives from such happy and glorious tutelage.

BE IT THEREFORE DETERMINED that in honour of Our Lady, on each of the next fifteen Saturdays, there shall be a devout procession from our church of St Mark and around the Piazza. The Doge, the magistrates, the Senate and the nobility shall be present, wearing their ordinary robes and carrying, in all humbleness of heart and true contrition, the miraculous image of the Virgin which is preserved in that church, offering up their earnest prayers for the deliverance of this city and of our state from the present sickness, and these prayers shall be accompanied by a universal fast, which shall be an obligation on all these fifteen Saturdays.

On the first Saturday, after the procession, the Doge shall in the name of the commonwealth make a solemn vow to God to build a church in this city and to dedicate it to the most holy Virgin, calling it Santa Maria della Salute; and every year, on the day that this city shall be proclaimed free of the present sickness, the Doge and his successors shall pay a ceremonious visit to that church with the Senate, in perpetual memory of the gratitude of the commonwealth for this great benefit.

Be it further resolved that a sum of up to 50,000 ducats from the public coffers shall be spent on the building of this church, which shall be erected in a place to be chosen by this Council.

And the Senate shall elect by scrutiny from among its own members three honourable noblemen, who shall be responsible for proposing the site and for putting forward a model of the church for approval by the same Council, and for supervising the construction, and it must be a place of splendour which shall display our devotion, to help us to deserve such exalted and beneficial protection.

Decisions shall then be taken concerning the services to be held in the church.

For the decree, 106; against, 0; uncertain, 5.

Note that throughout the reading of the above proposal the Doge [Nicolò Contarini] remained standing with the horned bonnet in his hand, and the whole Senate also stood bareheaded in an act of singular devotion.   B. P.

PRIVATE COMMISSIONS

*P*RIVATE PATRONAGE *in Venice is generally difficult to document; though wills occasionally provide evidence, contracts are rare, and individuals might purchase works of art ready-made from stock, or order them by word of mouth or acquire them second-hand. X.6, in which a skilled gem-setter and trader who was evidently on familiar terms with leading Venetian painters places a mail order for the sort of small devotional panel typical of the Quattrocento workshop, contrasts with X.7, the clause in Doge Agostino Barbarigo's will concerning his large* ex voto *canvas by Giovanni Bellini. Here it is the iconography, not the artist, which most concerns the patron, whose main anxiety is about his own salvation. Portraiture is further illustrated in this section: during the sixteenth century not only patrician officials, but also an increasing number of citizens, ordered portraits. Here Lorenzo Lotto's account book [see also below, X.21–2] provides important evidence. His prices varied according to the work involved, but he often neglected to agree a fee in advance and sometimes his portraits were refused on completion, as is shown by one case when he turned the portrait into his best friend's patron saint [X.8]; meanwhile, his landlord, depicted with wife and children dipping into life's proverbial bowl of cherries, may have accepted this family portrait partly in lieu of rent [X.9]. At a more exalted level, correspondence between Titian and Philip II, King of Spain [X.10], illustrates the European reputation that Venetian painters had acquired for mythological pictures. These, conventionally described by the literary word* poesia, *centred upon erotically disposed reclining female nudes in episodes taken from Ovid's* Metamorphoses. *Finally, tomb monuments provided a lucrative form of private patronage for sculptors in a city where freestanding statuary was rare, particularly by comparison with Florence. Doges' tombs were obviously the most splendid, and because they were the responsibility of the individual Doge and his heirs, an extract relating to Marino Grimani's contract has been included here [X.11]. Doges of this period were not buried in St Mark's, and, while many chose to be interred in the great Gothic churches of the mendicant orders, where their state-orchestrated funerals were held, some, such as Grimani, preferred a tomb dominating a parish church previously embellished by their family. A*

417

lavish patron, he took a direct interest even in details of finish and the tools involved.

BIBLIOGRAPHY *For the Barbarigo altarpiece: Valcanover 1983. On portraits: Moretti 1983. On Lotto's social and cultural world: Fontana 1984. On painted allegories and* poesie: *Wethey 1975; Hope 1983. On Doges' tombs generally: da Mosto 1939. On Grimani's in particular: Timofiewitsch 1963.* J. F.

6 AN OVERSEAS ORDER FOR A DEVOTIONAL PICTURE, 1473
ASV Scuola Grande di Santa Maria della Misericordia, b. 23, Commissaria, Bartolomeo Gruato (Paoletti 1894–5, pp. 12–13).

18 April 1473. From Pera. To my brother-in-law Nicholò Gruatto[74]

... Then send me the Bible to read for [when] I have nothing to do; then go to Lazaro Bastian,[75] who lives on Campo San Polo, and have him make me a little picture as big as half a small sheet of paper with the figure of Lord Jesus Christ, which must be beautiful as I wrote to him, or, if by chance – God forbid – he should be dead, or does not want to do it, go to Ziane Bellino and show him my letter, and tell him I want it in the same style as the one with that gold frame fine and polished, and in this do not fail.... J. F.

7 DOGE AGOSTINO BARBARIGO'S ALTARPIECE, 1501
ASV Notarile (de Fiorini), Testamenta, b. 416, F. 6 (Nani-Mocenigo 1909, p. 246).

17 July 1501

... Item. We leave to the aforesaid convent [Santa Maria degli Angeli][76] four of our wall hangings and a large carpet divided into two pieces for the decoration of its church.

[74] The writer, Antonio Choradi, traded in jewels and other luxury goods in Pera, by Constantinople; the letter reveals that he also wanted to acquire relics of the True Cross. His brother-in-law, a building-contractor and sculptor, witnessed a legal document with Jacopo Bellini in 1470.

[75] Active 1449; d. 1512. In 1474 he was paid 6 grossi for the picture, which has not been traced.

[76] This aristocratic convent on Murano had long been associated with the Barbarigo family; Agostino [on whom see above, II.14(c)] had served as its procurator and two of his daughters were nuns there. In 1498 the chapter proclaimed him their father and patron and restorer of their church.

Item. We command that our large altarpiece which is in the *chrozolla*[77] of the [Ducal] Palace should be sent to the above-mentioned convent of Santa Maria degli Angeli because it is most suitable for placement on the high altar of the church.[78] The trustees [*chomissari*] must have it adorned above and below and on its side for our satisfaction and that of the venerable nuns, and the altarpiece should be put to use as quickly as possible so that we may live in greater hope that the Blessed Virgin Mary will be our advocate with God our omnipotent Creator, and that neither our sons-in-law nor our daughters nor our nephews will consider placing it in our [family] palace,[79] nor in another place, but only on the high altar of that most devout and holy convent, so that we may be reassured every time [the nuns] pray to God for our soul and the souls of members of our family who have departed this life.   J. F.

8 LOTTO ALTERS A PORTRAIT TO PLEASE A FRIEND, 1542

Lotto, *Il libro di spese diverse*. f. 16v, Archivio della Santa Casa, Loreto (Zampetti 1969, p. 20).

December . . . 1542

The above-mentioned Messer Bartolomeo Carpan owes me[80] for the portrait head of the Protonotary Messer Joan Maria Pizoni, painted in oils and remaining on my hands because of the disagreement between us.[81] And, as it is one of my good things, I want to give it to a dear friend, for which in return he must recompense me with something relating to his own profession – that is, some gemstone and its setting. I am obliged to provide the gold, and the value I leave to his discretion. And I have refurbished the said head and altered it to represent St Bartholomew the Apostle;[82] and between two dear friends it is worth 10 ducats [i.e. (in margin)] 62 lire.   J. F.

---

[77] A cross-shaped space (Boerio 1856, p. 210).

[78] Signed by Giovanni Bellini and dated 1488; after the deconsecration of this church in the nineteenth century, the painting was transferred to San Pietro Martire, Murano, where it hangs in the nave. The horizontal format made it unsuitable for a high altar; in view of this the Doge ordered the framing additions.

[79] The Chaxa Grande (now Palazzo Nani) at San Trovaso also features in Agostino's will. He ordered that adjoining properties should not be heightened lest they overlook it.

[80] Lorenzo Lotto (*c*.1480–1556) refers to a jeweller, his friend, with premises at Rialto.

[81] Pizoni had rejected the portrait in 1538.

[82] The (altered) portrait has not been traced.

9   LOTTO PAINTS HIS LANDLORD'S FAMILY, 1547
Lotto, *Il libro di spese diverse* [see X. 8], f. 61v (Zampetti 1969, p. 98).

23 September 1547

. . . Misser Zuan della Volta, my landlord,[83] must pay me for a picture which includes his portrait done from life, and his wife's [portrait] with his two children, altogether numbering four [portraits].[84] Because of its high quality and very fine pigments, with its cover on the *timpano*,[85] the said picture was valued at 50 ducats or more by skilled and disinterested experts, and therefore I agree to what he wants, and I am satisfied with 20 ducats . . . [i.e. (in margin)] 124 lire.   J. F.

8   Lorenzo Lotto, *Zuan della Volta, the painter's landlord, and his family, ca. 1547.*
(Reproduced by courtesy of the Trustees, The National Gallery, London)

---

[83] Della Volta had rented to Lotto for 20 ducats a year part of his house at San Matteo, Rialto; his wife helped the painter choose a housekeeper (Zampetti 1969, pp. 99, 127).
[84] National Gallery, London.
[85] This is obscure, but may refer to a cover on the upper part of the frame.

10   SACRED AND PROFANE PICTURES FOR THE KING OF SPAIN, 1554
(i) Letter from Titian to King Philip II of Spain, September 1554 (Dolce 1559, p. 231).

Sacred Majesty,

My spirit now rejoices with Your Majesty because of the new kingdom which God has bestowed on you[86] and my congratulations are accompanied by the painting of Venus and Adonis, which you will view with those approving eyes that are already accustomed to look at the works of your servant Titian; and, because in the *Danae* which I have already sent Your Majesty one sees everything from the front, I wanted in this other *poesia* to vary it and to show you the opposite side, so that the chamber where they have to hang will be more attractive. I shall be sending you immediately the *poesia* of *Perseus and Andromeda*,[87] which will have a different viewpoint, and likewise *Medea and Jason*, and besides these I hope with God's help to send you a most devout work[88] which I have had in hand these past ten years, wherein I hope that Your Serene Highness will see all the power of art that your servant Titian knows how to employ in painting. In the meantime, the great new King of England will deign to recall that his unworthy painter lives on the memory of being the servant of such a great and benign lord, and he hopes through him to have gained similarly the favour of his consort, the most Christian Queen. May the Blessed Lord God Almighty keep you happy and your kingdom content for many centuries, and keep likewise the peoples governed and guided by Your Majesties' holy and pious will.   J. F.

(ii) From the Spanish. Extract from Philip II's letter to Francisco Vargas, his ambassador in Venice, 6 September 1554: Simancas, Archivo General, Estado, leg. 1498, f. 17 (Cloulas 1967, p. 227).

The picture of Adonis that Titian has completed has arrived here and truly it seems to me to be as perfect as you told me; but it is disfigured by a crease[89] running across the middle in such a way that it now needs an extensive restoration. Concerning the other pictures that the painter is making for me, I desire that you take renewed care; and it would be most advisable if from now on you did not send them to me before informing me that they are finished and receiving my orders concerning their shipment.   J. F.

[86] Philip had married Mary Tudor on 25 August 1554; Titian sent his letter, and the *Venus and Adonis* (Prado, Madrid), to London.
[87] Wallace Collection, London.
[88] Perhaps the *Crucifixion* in the Escorial. The *Jason and Medea* was probably never begun.
[89] Still visible.

11 DOGE MARINO GRIMANI ORDERS MARBLE SCULPTURE FOR HIS TOMB, 1601
ASV Archivio Grimani, b. 25 (Spese Diverse, Sant'Iseppo), f. 95 (Timofiewitsch 1972, p. 269).

Agreement with Messer Hieronimo Campagna[90] for the statutes and figures for the tomb at San Giuseppe[91]

On 6 September 1601 it is stated in the present written agreement that Messer Hieronimo Campagna, the sculptor, at present living in the parish of Sant'Aponal, is obliged to make the figures mentioned below for the tomb of the serene Prince, the Lord Marino Grimani, in the church of San Giuseppe: that is, the three figures on the top of the frontispiece, 6 feet high, carved in the round and most beautiful in appearance, carved using a round hammer [*martello tondo*][92] as above; and in addition the scene with the Blessed Virgin with the Doge and his wife and two angels; and the perspective in half relief according to the form in the drawing, to be very well finished; and the six figures in half relief – two on either side of the inscription above the door, the other four below the sarcophagus – to be rasped to a high finish;[93] and the two figures on the pedestals and the two lions in half relief, to be most highly finished; and this for the sum of 670 ducats, at the rate of 6 lire 4 soldi per ducat. A further undertaking is that the Doge is obliged to have all the stone conveyed to the sculptor's house, except for the two lions which are at present to be found in the enclosure in the *campo* in front of San Giuseppe, and everything must be done according to the appearance and measurement in the drawing.[94] In addition it is established that, when the said Master Hieronimo wants money he must keep an account of the sum received, witnessed by the hand of Master Francesco de'Bernardi, the architect in charge, and, in case there should happen to be disagreement, the said architect, the Doge and the sculptor will freely and without recourse to law come to an agreement. Concerning which things I, Galeazzo Secco, the Doge's Chancellor, have drawn up the present lawful document in the presence of Sante Perande, the painter,[95] son of the late Master Nicolò, and Master Francesco Piston, the mason, son of the late Ser Jacomo. J. F.

[90] Girolamo Campagna (1549–c.1625), from Verona.
[91] Near the Arsenal. The vast tome survives.
[92] Probably a rounding-tool.
[93] According to the accounts, a polisher (*fregador*) did the specialized rasping and polishing.
[94] Probably the drawing by Francesco Smeraldi, architect to the Procurators, which is also preserved in ASV Archivio Grimani.
[95] Sante Peranda (1566–1638) made the cartoons for the mosaics behind the effigies of the Doge and his wife.

COLLECTIONS, CONNOISSEURS AND CRITICAL VALUES

*W*HEN *Dürer visited Venice, in 1505–6, he was impressed by the numerous experts there on painting, and private collecting was the corollary of this; one leading painter, Giorgione, seems to have worked almost exclusively for the private sector. Later, from the 1520 to 1530s, the patrician Marcantonio Michiel (1484–1552) kept descriptive notes about art in north-eastern Italy, including works displayed in private houses in Padua and Venice: his list of the very miscellaneous collection of the citizen Andrea Odoni [X.12] is particularly revealing, as it includes information about provenance, artist, subject matter and medium, even rudimentary hints about room setting. Correct attribution, too, was a problem which bothered Michiel [X.13]. The patrician Gabriel Vendramin was also among collectors listed by Michiel, but his own account (from his will) has been preferred here [X.14] because it is informative about his own motivations, values and preoccupations. His collection is unusual for its wealth of graphic art, including prints and several books of drawings.*

Critical evaluations of works of art are drawn from a variety of circumstances and sources. Opinions were regularly expressed by judges in state competitions and by official investigators sent to examine complaints. But they might also be articulated in direct response to an alien or innovative style, as with Duke Francesco Sforza's plan to build a huge Milanese type of palace on the Grand Canal [x.15], which his advisers discouraged on grounds of aesthetic and political prejudice in Venice, though his Florentine expert was equally scornful about Venetian building-designs. However, the prejudice against which Dürer laboured a few years later, that his work was not sufficiently in the antique style [see X.20], may point to an important recent shift in taste, and the extension to painting of the classical inspiration that formerly had been more evident in sculpture.

Only by the mid sixteenth century were Venetians, lagging far behind Florentine writers, beginning to publish books about art. Even then, some of the major exponents were Tuscans, such as Pietro Aretino, whose friendly or paternalistic relations with artists are expressed in letters intended for publication, and

423

combined praise with critical advice, as is shown by one to Tintoretto [X.17]. He may have been promoting here his Florentine preference for worked-up and finely drawn images, but Aretino often changed his opinions according to context, and he likened his own literary style to a boldly painted sketch (by analogy, suggesting the late technique of his friend Titian). Aretino is the protagonist in the important dialogue treatise on painting by Ludovico Dolce (d. 1568). The opening passage [X.16] echoes Aretino's letter in praise of Titian's Death of St Peter Martyr *as well as Vasari's views on progressive evolution in art; although fictional, the dialogue does seem to reflect real-life pronouncements made by connoisseurs when new works were unveiled. Finally, some of the sharper edges of criticism are conveyed by the dispute over a pay claim between Palladio and the Scuola dei Mercanti [X.18], which reveals the wheeling and dealing and the existence of factions favouring different artists within this Venetian confraternity. Whether or not Palladio's designs were as bad as alleged cannot be shown, but, as an outsider – albeit famous – from Vicenza, he may not have appreciated the custom whereby Venetian artists often offered their services to a Scuola for little or nothing.*

BIBLIOGRAPHY   *For collectors patronizing Giorgione: Battilotti and Franco 1978. On Venetian collectors in general: Levi 1900; Zorzi 1988. On Michiel: Morelli and Frizzoni 1884; Williamson 1903; Fletcher 1981. On Vendramin's collection: Ravà 1920; and, for its later history, Anderson 1979. On a major sculpture collection: Perry 1978. On Venetian historians of painting: Hope 1983. On Venetian art criticism in general: Pallucchini 1943. For Aretino's letters: Aretino ed. Camesasca and Pertile 1957–60. On Dolce: Cicogna 1862. On both Aretino and Dolce: Roskill 1968. For evaluation of Tintoretto's work: Momigliano-Lepschy 1983. On the 'Ca'del Duca': Beltrami 1900, Spencer 1970. On Palladio and Venice: Puppi 1982.*   J. F.

12   ANDREA ODONI'S COLLECTION, 1532

Marcantonio Michiel, *Notizie*: BMV ms. ital., cl. XI, 67 (7351), ff. 51r–53r (Morelli and Frizzoni 1884, pp. 155–64, with omissions).

In the house of A. Odoni,[96] *1532*

In the courtyard below. The marble head of Hercules larger than life, with an oak garland, was by the hand of Antonio Minello.[97]

The marble head of Cybele larger than life, crowned with turrets, was by the same Minello.

[96] Odoni, of Milanese origin, lived in a palace at Santa Croce, demolished in the nineteenth century. An inventory of his collection in 1555 appears in von Bode et al. 1911, p. 36ff.

[97] Active in Venice 1527–8. His last dated work, *Mercury* (Victoria and Albert Museum, London), was commissioned by Michiel.

The marble figure of a fully-clothed woman without the head and hands is antique, and used to be in Tullio Lombardo's[98] workshop, copied [*ritratta*] by him many times in his works.

The marble bust without head and hands seems to be taken from life; [it] is an antique work.

The many other mutilated and cracked marble heads and figures are antique.

The complete [*intiero*] marble foot mounted on a base was by the hand of Simon Bianco.[99]

The marble male nude without head and hands in the act of walking, which is beside the door, is an antique work.

In the little study above. The porphyry tazza was by the hand of Piero Maria Fiorentino[100] and it is the one that Francesco Zio[101] used to have.

The crystal tazza engraved by the hand of Cristoforo Roman[102] is that which used to belong to Francesco Zio.

The tazza made of petrified root was by the hand of Vetto di Arcanzeli.

The four frontispieces from the Book of Hours were by the hand of Jacometto,[103] and used to belong to Francesco Zio.

The David, and the beginning of the other Book of Hours, was by the hand of Benedetto Bordon.[104]

The five little vases made of semi-precious stones decorated with gold are modern and used to belong to Francesco Zio, as did the porcelain vases and bowls, the antique vases and medals and natural things, i.e. the crabs, fishes, petrified snakes, a dried chameleon, small rare seashells, crocodiles and strange fish.

The little wooden figure on horseback was by the hand of [. . .].

The small puppy in bronze was by the hand of [. . .].

In the bedroom above. The picture of two half figures of a young woman and an old woman behind [her], in oil, was by the hand of Jacomo Palma.[105]

The portrait of this Messer Andrea in oil, half-length, who contemplates the fragments of antique marble, was by the hand of Lorenzo Lotto.[106]

---

[98] Tullio Lombardo (*c.* 1455–1532), son of Pietro, collected classical sculpture and medals and based his style closely upon antique prototypes.

[99] Bianco, of Florentine origin, was active in Venice 1512–53.

[100] Pietro da Pescia, a specialist in gem-engraving and porphyry work.

[101] Odoni's uncle (d. 1530); Michiel also described his collection.

[102] This renowned sculptor and medallist had visited Venice in 1502. For the tazza, engraved with Old Testament scenes, see Morelli and Frizzoni 1884, p. 181.

[103] Jacometto Veneziano (active*c.*1472–97) also made small portraits.

[104] Benedetto Bordon (d. 1530) was a miniature-painter and printer who worked in Padua, then Venice.

[105] Palma Vecchio, from Bergamo (*c.*1480–1528).

[106] The portrait dated 1527 in the Royal Collection, Hampton Court.

The picture of Our Lady in a landscape, with the infant Christ and infant St John and the female saint[107] [. . .][108] was by the hand of Titian.

The chests in the same bedroom, the bedstead and doors were painted by Stefano, Titian's pupil.[109]

The large female nude stretched out behind [*da drietto*] the bed was by the hand of Jeronimo Savoldo of Brescia.[110]

The many little bronze figures are modern, by the hands of various masters.

In the *portego*.[111] The canvas of the young woman presented to Scipio [i.e. a *Continence of Scipio?*] was by the hand of Girolamo of Brescia.

The *Transfiguration* [*Conversion?*] *of St Paul* was by the hand of Bonifacio Veronese.[112]

The Hell [*Inferno*] with the cupid who holds the bow was by the hand of Zuan son of Zanin Comendador[113] and it is the canvas that Francesco Zio had.

The story of Trajan with the many figures with the ancient buildings was by the hand of the same Zuanne del Comendador, but the buildings were designed by Sebastiano Bolognese.[114]

The canvas with the monsters and Hell in the Flemish style [*alla ponentina*] was by the hand [. . .].[115]

The nude St Jerome who sits in a desert by the light of the moon was by the hand of [. . .], copied from a canvas by Zorzi de Castelfranco.[116]

The marble statue of the nude Mars who carries his helmet on his shoulder, 2 feet high, carved in the round, was by the hand of Simon Bianco.

In the bedroom above. The half-length portrait of Francesco Zio was by the hand of Vicenzo Cadena.[117]

The small portrait of the same Zio, armed, and represented down to the knee, was by the hand of the same Cadena.

The portrait of the little baby boy with a white beret in the French style,

---

[107] This work, which passed to the Reynst Collection, was similar to *The Holy Family with St Catherine* in the National Gallery, London.

[108] Michiel leaves a gap here, and elsewhere, when uncertain who the subject or artist was.

[109] Probably the Paduan painter Stefano dell'Arzere.

[110] Giovanni Girolamo Savoldo (*c*.1485 – after 1548). In Odoni's 1555 inventory it is described as 'un retratto de una nuda *nella callesella della lettiera*', i.e. in the space between the wall and the bed.

[111] The central reception room, usually extending from front to back on the first (upper) floor.

[112] Bonifacio Pitati (*c*.1487–1553).

[113] Better known as Cariani (*c*.1485 – after 1547).

[114] Sebastiano Serlio (1475–1554), the architect, a member of Michiel's circle.

[115] Perhaps by Hieronymus Bosch, whose work was represented in the contemporary Grimani collection (Morelli and Frizzoni 1884, p. 96).

[116] Giorgione (d. 1510). Both original and copy are lost. Connoisseurs so prized his work that they also owned copies (Morelli and Frizzoni 1884, pp. 51, 147).

[117] Vincenzo Catena (*c*.1470–1531). The portrait has not been identified.

[worn] on top of the coif, was by the hand of [. . .] and is a portrait of [. . .][118] acquired by our soldiers at the battle of Taro[119] amongst the royal booty.

The little panel pictures in tempera were by the hand of [. . .].

The Ceres on the door halfway up the stairs was by the hand of Jacopo Palma, and is the one that Francesco Zio had on the door of his bedroom.

In the portico. The portrait of Pollo Trevisan, painted and gilded, and many gilded figures all of terracotta.   J. F.

13   A PROBLEM OF ATTRIBUTION, 1529
Marcantonio Michiel, *Notizie*: BMV ms. Ital., cl. XI, 67 (7351), f. 60v (Morelli and Frizzoni 1880, pp. 88–9).

In the house of Messer Antonio Pasqualino,[120] *1529*

Some believe that the little picture of St Jerome dressed as a cardinal reading in the study is by the hand of Antonello da Messina,[121] but the majority with more justification attribute it to Giannes or to Membling, an old Flemish painter,[122] and so it shows that style, although the face is finished in the Italian way so that it seems to be by the hand of Jacometto.[123] The buildings are in the Flemish style [*alla ponentina*]. The little landscape is lifelike [*naturale*], minute and highly finished, and one sees it outside a window and beyond the study door, and then it fades out [*fugge*], and the whole work is perfect for its subtlety, colouring, drawing, strength and relief. In it a peacock, a quail and a barber's basin are all represented. A small open letter is attached to the desk, which seems to contain the master's name, but, notwithstanding, if one looks carefully at it from close up, it does not contain any letters but is all made up [*finta*]. Others believe that the figure has been repainted by Jacometto Veneziano.

                                                          J. F.

[118] Portrait on panel of the infant Dauphin by the Master of Moulins (Louvre).

[119] The battle of Fornovo on the river Taro (6 July 1495). The Venetian troops of the Italian League looted the baggage train of Charles VIII, King of France.

[120] The Pasqualini were Milanese silk merchants; in the fifteenth century they had built a palace at San Maurizio.

[121] Antonello (*c*.1430–79) worked in Venice in 1475; this painting, now firmly attributed, is in the National Gallery, London. Antonio also owned his father's portrait, dated 1475, by Antonello (noted by Michiel when he revisited the collection in 1532 and listed more paintings).

[122] Jan van Eyck (active 1422–40) and Hans Memling (active 1465–94). Michiel was familiar with the latter's work in Pietro Bembo's collection. See also Campbell 1981, pp. 467–73.

[123] Jacometto Veneziano (active *c*.1472–?97), an illuminator who painted small portraits. Pasqualino owned many of his drawings.

14 GABRIEL VENDRAMIN DESCRIBES AND JUSTIFIES HIS COLLECTION, 1548
From the acts of the notary A. Marsilio: ASV Archivio Notarile 1208, f. 403 (Battilotti and Franco 1978, p. 67).

3 January 1548
... *Item*: I have[124] in my small room [*chamerin*] and outside it many paintings in oil and tempera on panel and canvas, all of great worth, by the hands of most excellent men.

Item. Many drawings made by hand, part kept in some books, part framed, and part neither framed nor in books, also by the hands of excellent men and worth a lot of money.[125]

Item. Many prints on paper, engravings and woodcuts, the majority not put in these books.

Item. Many antiquities of stone and metal – that is heads, marble busts, and ancient sculptures made of metal – amongst which there are some whole [i.e. undamaged] pieces, all things of great value.[126]

Item. Large and small vases made of semi-precious stones, all things of great price.

Item. Many antique terracotta vases.

Item. Many gold and silver medals and many of copper, bronze, brass and Corinthian bronze, all antique and of great value.

Item. Many modern medals of gold and silver and other metals.[127]

Item. Many more works in metal, damascened.

Item. Animals' horns and diverse other things that are to be found in this little room of great value, like the skull carved in the round on a very small cameo, and other things that would take too long to relate.

However, I declare that all the things that are found in this small room, which are worth many hundreds of ducats, as distinct from everything that has been entered in our account books concerning the furnishings, would bring in much more than they cost, and that this expenditure has not deprived our family of a single ducat; rather I can say that it has brought it profit, and it remains for me to explain why. I cannot refrain from declaring that all these things, both for their high quality and because of the many years' hard work taken to acquire

---

[124] The palace of Gabriel Vendramin (1484–1552) at Santa Fosca was a meeting-place for connoisseurs. He appears in Titian's *Group Portrait* in the National Gallery, London.

[125] The collection, which included Giorgione's *Tempestà*, was unusually rich (for Venice) in graphic art. See for example the Raphael drawings and Jacopo Bellini's sketchbook, now in the British Museum.

[126] Many classical items came from Rhodes. An ancient bronze of Vendramin's is described in Doni 1552, p. 40.

[127] As a numismatist and antiquarian, Vendramin earned special mention in Vico 1555, p. 88.

them, and most of all because they have brought a little peace and quiet to my soul during the many labours of mind and body that I have endured in conducting the family business,[128] are so pleasing and dear to me that I must pray and beseech those who inherit them to treat them with such care that they shall not perish. And on this count I have no fear, because if they be virtuous men they cannot do otherwise, and, so as no longer to fail to make provision, I order that, if during my lifetime I have not assembled the things from both within and outside this little room, and in particular the paintings which decorate other parts of the house, they immediately be brought together after my death and an inventory be drawn up by a public notary and witnessed. I order that none of these things shall be sold, or pawned, or loaned, either in whole or in part or in any conceivable way, and that they should be subject to the same conditions under which I have bequeathed the house.   J. F.

15   ARCHITECTURAL STYLE FOR THE DUKE OF MILAN'S HOUSE IN VENICE, 1461
(i) From a letter of Benedetto Ferrini[129] to Giovanni Simonetta (the Duke's secretary), Venice, 26 January 1461: Archivio di Stato, Milan, Autografi, b. 82, f. 1 (Beltrami 1900, p. 30).

Magnificent, most distinguished and honoured Sir,

By the present bearer I am sending you the drawing showing how His Lordship's house has been begun [*fondata*]. If there is anything that you do not understand, tell me and I will make it clear. I advise you that I have already ordered two designs in relief from three masters. I do not believe that they will be finished in twenty days. I tell you, that in this place they pay masters very well, more than twice as much as they pay in Milan, and besides these three masters truly there are many other works to be done by painters and wood-turners. I believe that these two models will amount to 25 ducats or more; therefore I want you to send me the said sum so that I can pay the masters. Tell our illustrious Lord how well I have kept you informed concerning the work on the said house. It seems to me that Messer Andrea Corner[130] had a generous spirit because he started a magnificent and most stupendous work, just as he did not lack the will to make a most beautiful building; [but] as you can see from

---

[128] Mainly speculation in landed property and soap-manufacturing; however, in his will Vendramin urged his heirs to pursue navigation, learning (*lettere*) and the merchant's profession.

[129] Benedetto Ferrini (d. 1497), Florentine architect and military engineer, had entered the Duke's service *c*.1452–4.

[130] Andrea Corner (1419–73), who founded the Palace, lived in exile in Cyprus, having been convicted (1457) for corruptly seeking election to the Senate (*DBI*); his brother Marco sold the site.

429

the badly planned design [*el designo mal ordinato*] he was ill advised,[131] and this was the fault of his engineers.   J. F.

(ii) From a letter of Francesco Sforza, Duke of Milan, to Antonio Guidobono (his ambassador in Venice), Milan?, 7 March 1461: Archivio di Stato, Milan, Archivio Sforzesco, Potenze Estere, Venezia, cart. 348 (Beltrami 1900, pp. 32–3).

Antonio,

Yesterday Zohanne de Landriano arrived here; he has brought by boat the gifts sent by that illustrious Signoria. . . . He also brought the models of our house purchased from the honourable Messer Marco [Corner]; and while [we were] awaiting the said models, in order to understand and to see the appearance and state of the said house, we had no other means [*provisione*] to set the men to work. Now that we have them, we will have another one made of it in the style and form in which we want the said house to be built, which will be in the modern style and in the way in which they build here in our territory; and we do not doubt that our design will please everyone because it is a novelty in that city. This is to inform you, however, that the façade on the Grand Canal will be in the Venetian style.   J. F.

(iii) From a letter of Antonio Guidobono to Duke Francesco Sforza, Venice, 9 March 1461: Archivio di Stato, Milan, Archivio Sforzesco, Potenze Estere, Venezia, cart. 348 (Beltrami 1900, pp. 34–5).

Moreover Your Excellency writes that you are having a new model and design of the house made, and that you intend to do the façade in the Venetian manner and then the house in the modern and Lombard style. I do not doubt that Your Excellency will indeed give them a better form than the Venetian one; nevertheless the Venetians like their style and manner [*forma et modo*] better. I believe that it will cost more because some [of the] foundations will need to be extended and changed.[132] Nevertheless, that which pleases Your Highness will be done; it will be liked here, anyway, so long as they see that Your Excellency is having it built.   J. F.

---

[131] The previous architect, Bartolomeo Bon, had refused to hand over his designs to Ferrini.
[132] Cf. above, I.2.

16 A COMPARISON OF GIOVANNI BELLINI WITH LATER PAINTERS
Dialogue in Dolce 1557, f. 5r–v.

Aretino. Fabrini,[133] a fortnight ago finding myself in the most beautiful church of Santi Giovanni e Paolo, where I had met up with the learned Giulio Camillo[134] for the mass of St Peter Martyr, which is celebrated every day at the altar where that great painting is hung which illustrates the saint's story, by the skilled hand of my bosom friend Titian,[135] I thought that I saw you completely absorbed in looking at that other picture of St Thomas Aquinas, who, in company with other saints, was painted in tempera many years ago by Giovanni Bellini the Venetian painter.[136] If we had not both been sidetracked by Messer Antonio Anselmi,[137] who bore us off to Monsignor Bembo's house, we should then have made an unexpected attack on you, and kept you our prisoner all day long. Now that I recall having seen you completely absorbed in looking, I tell you that Bellini's picture is not unworthy of praise, because every figure is well done, and there are beautiful heads, and similarly the flesh tints and the draperies are no less lifelike. From which one easily recognizes that Bellini was for his period a good and painstaking master, but he has now been outdone by Giorgio da Castelfranco, and Giorgio has been left far behind by Titian, who imparts a heroic majesty to his figures and has found a way of colouring most softly, and whose colours are lifelike, so that one can truly say that they rival nature.

J. F.

17 ARETINO ENCOURAGES AND CRITICIZES TINTORETTO, 1548
Aretino 1609, IV, no. 420, f. 181r.

To Iacopo Tintoretto

Since the voice of public praise agrees with that which I myself have bestowed on your great narrative picture [*l'istoria*] consecrated in the Scuola di San Marco,[138] I am no less delighted with my earlier judgement of your art, which is

133 Giovanni Francesco Fabrini, a Florentine grammarian.

134 Giulio Camillo Delminio (d. 1544), from Friuli, was interested in the Kabbalah, astrology and memory systems. Dolce edited some of his works.

135 Titian's *Death of St Peter Martyr* was highly praised by Aretino in a letter to Tribolo (29 October 1537) and much copied in paintings and engravings; it was destroyed by fire in 1887.

136 Probably Bellini's *Madonna with Saints* (*c.*1475), including Aquinas; likewise destroyed.

137 Anselmi (*c.*1512–68), a Venetian writer, formerly secretary to Pietro Bembo, was painted by Titian (*DBI*).

138 St Mark freeing a slave who is about to be tortured for revering the Saint's relics, the first in

so outstanding. And, just as there is no nose so stuffed up with cold that it does not smell some of the smoke of the incense, so is there no man so little instructed in what constitutes good drawing and composition [*disegno*] that he is not astonished by the three-dimensionality [*relievo*] of the completely nude figure which lies on the ground, offered up to the cruelty of martyrdom. Its colours are flesh, its contours rounded, and the body is alive, so that I swear by the good that I wish you that the faces, airs and expressions of the crowd surrounding it are so lifelike that the spectacle seems real rather than simulated. But do not grow proud, lest you no longer desire to ascend to a higher degree of perfection, and blessed be your name if you can temper [your] haste to have done with patience in the doing [of it], although little by little the passing years alone will be enough to rein in the careless course so prevalent in swift and eager youth.

Venice, April 1548.   J. F.

18 PALLADIO CRITICIZED IN A DISPUTE WITH THE SCUOLA DEI MERCANTI,
1572
ASV Scuole Piccole, b. 417, fasc. e (Gallo 1955, pp. 37–41).

16 May 1572

Today the excellent Master Andrea Palladio, the Vicentine artist, affirmed that, having made the drawings for the building of this Scuola, and having been continuously involved for eight months with the building, ordering daily everything that was necessary, he has not been recompensed in any way. . . .
    [The Scuola replies that it has no contract with Palladio.]

20 November 1572

. . . The building does not need master architects [*Proti*] because it has to be constructed on top of the walls and above the corners of the old Scuola, which was first dedicated to St Christopher.[139] . . . The opinion of the late Giacomo de Grigis,[140] the architect, was sought concerning the strength of the old walls, and neither for this nor for other oral or written advice that he gave on different

the cycle of canvases of the saint's life which Tintoretto made for the meeting-hall of this Scuola Grande; now in the Accademia, Venice.
    [139] This Scuola had merged with the Misericordia in 1571. The Mercanti had moved from the Frari to rebuild on a site at the Madonna dell'Orto.
    [140] Giangiacomo dei Grigi (d. 1572), from Bergamo, who had competed unsuccessfully in 1554 to become Proto to the Salt Office.

occasions did he, being an honest man, ask for anything. . . . In this discussion [concerning the walls] the said Palladio took part, having come along with the above-mentioned late Zorzi Saler as his friend, because he designed the Celestia's building,[141] for which the said Saler was responsible [as the nuns' procurator]; and by what he said Saler encouraged the Guardian and his colleagues also to seek Palladio's opinion, which anyway would not cost anything. And in this way, after seeing the site, Palladio agreed with the view of the aforesaid late Iacopo [i.e. de Grigis] and provided a template for the door so disgraceful, deformed, over-elongated and badly designed that it has been necessary to incur other expense in correcting it, and the said Scuola has been continuously served free of charge by Master Salvador, an expert true architect, a pupil of Sansovin [Jacopo Sansovino] in anything that was needed.

1 December 1572

[Palladio gives the following reasons why he should be paid 25 ducats.]

First, that he, Master Andrea, from the beginning was requested by the later Messer Zorzi Saler, the procurator for the building, to go on the site of this Scuola dei Mercanti, to work and advise in his capacity as architect. Having gone there, he started to work, and continued for three months, being on site from day to day, as he was ordered . . . not only by the late Saler, but by the Scuola's other deputies responsible for the building.

Second, that at the end of the said three months he, Master Andrea, seeing that he was not paid the sum owed, ceased to go on working whereupon these commissioners for the building sent several times to his house, to ask him to go on working as architect in charge of this building, and so he carried on for about eight months in good faith, knowing that it is fitting and right that this Scuola should recognize his [right to] payment.[142]   J. F.

[141] Palladio (1508–80), who had worked in Venice since 1558, had redesigned the convent of Santa Maria della Celestia after the fire there in 1569.

[142] The Scuola accepted arbitration by two achitects (Giovanni Rusconi represented Palladio); the fee agreed was 15 ducats, which suggests that Palladio's role had been limited (see Puppi 1973, p. 398).

WORKING-PRACTICE, TECHNIQUE AND STYLE OF LIFE

OST WRITING about the 'social history' of Renaissance art has been over-dependent upon material from Florence – above all Vasari's anecdotal biographies of artists – and the princely courts. Unfortunately Vasari wrote only briefly about Venetian artists, and there was no local equivalent to him until Carlo Ridolfi's more specialized Lives of the Venetian Painters *(1648); meanwhile, artists' private records, such as letters, wills and account books, are scarce, though a few examples can be found. The will and inventory of Ercole del Fiore [X.19], the adopted son of a famous painter, contradicts the assumption that predecessors of the Bellini were humbler artisans, for Ercole possessed scholarly books and rich household furnishings. Another letter from Dürer [X.20], during his brief but productive stay in Venice in 1505–6, gives a vivid picture of the city teeming with traders, speculators, and jealous competitors of every sort; it reveals his contacts with dilettanti, musicians and others, and his respect for Giovanni Bellini. The book of memoranda and accounts of the eccentric Lorenzo Lotto is a unique survival. It provides, as an extract [X.21] shows, specific details about materials (Venice was a centre for the preparation and distribution of fine pigments), models, renting of premises, transport of works of art by water, exhibiting- and selling-techniques, and much else, including an apprenticeship contract, which was terminated mainly on account of the master's difficult temperament [X.22]. These mundane facts are counterbalanced by Palma Giovane's description (admittedly, at second hand, in a later literary source) of the techniques practised by Titian in his old age [X.23]; this portrait of a genius at work demonstrates just why and how the Venetian School of painting became indelibly associated with colour. Finally, an extract [X.24] from one of the eight wills of the celebrated sculptor Vittoria, who was a member of the Florentine Academy responsible for Michelangelo's funeral and monument, presents us with a specialist in commemorative sculpture who was a 'consumer' of his own work and (typical of his generation) much preoccupied with his own fame and its commemoration by works of art.*

BIBLIOGRAPHY *On the Venetian Painters' Guild: Favaro 1975. For miscellaneous records of commissions, payments, etc.: Paoletti 1894; Ludwig 1903, 1905; von Bode et al. 1911; DMS; Zorzi 1960–1. On the artist's condition: Puppalin 1976–7. On Dürer and Venice: Panofsky 1943. For Lotto's account book: Zampetti 1969; Muraro 1984. On Venetian painters' use of colour: in general, Lazzari 1983; on Titian in particular, Hetzer 1948. On Vittoria: Predelli 1908; Cessi 1961–2.*   J. F.

19   THE PROPERTY OF A PROSPEROUS AND LITERATE PAINTER, 1461

Extract from Ercole del Fiore's will and inventory: ASV Miscellanea Cancelleria Inferiore, b. 28 (Paoletti 1894, fasc. II, 9–11).

1 July 1461

I Hercules del Fior,[143] painter, of the parish of Sant'Agnese, not wishing to die intestate, write here with my own hand this my last will and testament. . . . I desire that my body be buried at Santa Maria della Carità. I leave half of the house in Padua situated in the quarter of Sant'Agostino that my father left me, to my dear friend master Jacomo da le Aste, the furrier, resident in Padua. . . .

Item. I leave all the books written in the vernacular that my father left me, to be given to the convent of Santa Maria degli Angeli on Murano.

Item. I leave my breviary to be sold, and the money made from the sale is to be used to release two prisoners from gaol and to be given to two novice nuns.

Item. I leave my prayer book to Don Bernardo, monk at the Carità, who used to be at San Clemente, and to whom I am bound like a brother.

Item. All the other books – that is a Psalter, the office of Our Lady and every other volume, numbering nine in all – and loose leaves of all kinds, are to go to Madonna Isabella (Nicola Zen's wife, my executrix) and all manner of things that she finds in my oratory and study.

Item. I leave all the drawings and everything else relating to the art of painting which are in the house or the workshop to the poor of the confraternity of the Carità, except for nine pieces of porphyry made from a piece that I bought and had sawn up by Master Zorzi, the Slav, glazier at San Fantin.

Item. All my clothes and every other thing noted down in my own hand in my inventory which is here included I want to be sold and from the proceeds first let my debts be paid, then the bequests made, and the money left over be distributed to the poor. . . .

[143] Ercole (d. 1484) was the adopted son of Jacobello del Fiore (for whose will see Paoletti 1894, p. 8).

Inventory

My Apocalypse.
Summa of Penitence.
The *De transitu* of St Jerome.
The Gospel and Epistle readings for all the year.
Life of the Holy Fathers.
The Dialectic of St Gregory.
Office of Our Lady.

> All these must be given to the nuns of Santa Maria degli Angeli on Murano

My breviary which cost me 40 ducats.
My prayer book to be given to Don Bernardo.
A book made of thick paper dealing with the Conscience of St Bernard, which is to be given to the white-hooded Gesuati who are at Sant'Agnese.
One volume which is part of a breviary – to be given to the Carità.
21 silver medals and 1 made of tin.
The Doge's *promissione*.[144]
The Statutes of Venice.
Trojan.[145]
A book made of parchment translated from the Latin dealing with Virtues and Vices that Don Agostino gave me.
And many other volumes and loose pieces of paper which must go to M[adonna] Isabella my executrix.
3 bench-covers made of dark green cloth – new.
A new bronze wash basin which holds the contents of 8 small bowls.
A new Psalter made of parchment.
An office of Our Lady – new.

> Not finished.

1 large damascened hanging lamp in my bedroom.
1 small damascened holy-water stoup in my bedroom.
1 damascened *fredaor* [cooler?].
1 damascened table fountain with 4 pieces which is in the hall.
3 German candlesticks.
1 tin candelabrum for 4 candles.
1 tin candelabrum for 6 candles.

> In the hall.

1 iron clock or alarm [*svegliador*].
1 wooden form for clothes.
1 pantry table folded up in a box.
1 rack for stockings painted green.
1 picture of Our Lady which I keep in my bedroom.

---

[144] See II.3(b) above. Possibly it was a copy of the *promissione* of Doge Pasquale Malipiero (1457–62), and Ercole had been commissioned to decorate it.

[145] Perhaps a romance of the Troy legend.

2 coffers covered with hide [*peloxa*] for heavy loads, 1 bound with iron.

1 small chest covered with hide.

1 old chest in the classical style.

2 old coffers which were made in Padua.

Item. 6 carved wooden panels for a bedroom. They are in the workshop. I
bought them to decorate. On one is carved the image of Our Lady. The
other 4 [*sic*] are crude works decorated with a print of the Madonna [*con
le madone relevado de carta*].   J. F.

20   DÜRER'S COMMENTS ON VENETIAN ARTISTS, 1506

From the German. Extract from a letter of Dürer, in Venice, to Willibald Pirkheimer, in
Nuremberg, 7 February 1506: Stadt Bibliothek, Nuremberg, ms. Pirkheimer 394.2
(Rupprich 1956, p. 43; as translated in Conway 1889, p. 48).

How I wish you were here in Venice! There are so many nice men among the
Italians who seek my company more and more every day – which is very
pleasing to one: men of sense and knowledge, good lute-players and pipers,
judges of painting, men of much noble sentiment and honest virtue; and they
show me much honour and friendship. On the other hand, there are also
amongst them some of the most false, lying, thievish rascals; I should never
have believed that such were living in the world. If one did not know them, one
would think them the nicest men the earth could show. For my own part I
cannot help laughing at them whenever they talk to me. They know that their
knavery is no secret, but they don't mind.

Amongst the Italians I have many good friends who warn me not to eat and
drink with their painters. Many of them are my enemies and they copy my work
in the churches and whenever they can find it, and then they revile it and say
that the style is not 'antique' and so not good. But Giovanni Bellini has highly
praised me before many nobles. He wanted to have something of mine, and
himself came to see me and asked me to paint him something and [said] he
would pay well for it. And all men tell me what an upright man he is, so that I
am really friendly with him. He is very old, but is still the best painter of them
all. And that which so well pleased me eleven years ago pleases me no longer; if
I had not seen it for myself I should not have believed anyone who told me. You
must know too that there are many better painters here than Master Jacob[146]
[*wider dawsen Meister J.*], yet Anton Kolb would swear an oath that no better
painter lives than Jacob. Others sneer at him, saying if he were good he would
stay here, and so forth.

[146] Jacopo de'Barbari [see above, IX.12].

I have only today begun to sketch in my picture [above, X.4(b)], for my hands were so scabby [*grindig*] that I could do no work with them, but I have got them cured.

J. F.

21   A PAINTER'S DAY-TO-DAY EXPENSES, 1541
Lotto, *Il libro di spese diverse* [see X.8], f. 303r–v (Zampetti 1969, pp. 235–7).

For Art

1541		Lire	Soldi
15 February	For nails and purified linseed oil		4
	Mastic 2 ozs		10
	Kermes[147] taken from Misser Sebastiano Serlio the Bolognese architect on account of certain credit that I have with him, 6 ozs at 6 ducats an oz	37	4
27 February	For transporting the pictures to decorate the house on Carnival Thursday [*zobia grassa*] and for returning them to the workshop – boat and porters		2
8 March	Purified linseed oil		
12 March	For an undamaged vessel for purifying linseed oil		3½
	1½ lbs of lead white		6
	Vitriol		1
	½ lb of cinnibar in powdered form		
[. . .] April	For transporting the painting[148] of the Graces and that of the Venus to the workshop and porters		9
	Linseed and walnut oil		5
2 September	For undressing a woman only to look[149]		12
	On several occasions oil for working	1	4
	Oil for the lamp and for washing brushes and cleaning the stones used for grinding pigments		16

[147] An expensive blood-red dye made from the blood of this insect.

[148] Probably *Venus Adorned by the Graces* (private collection, Bergamo), which Lotto gave in 1540 to his nephew Mario D'Armano (Zampetti 1969, p. 211).

[149] Lotto's nude models were usually poor people; on one occasion he first provided a bath (Zampetti 1969, pp. 236, 240–1).

		Lire	Soldi
	Brushes		8
	3 lbs of lead white		12
October	Gums 2 ozs		10
	Tin foil and ink		2½
	2 reams of thick blue paper for covering pictures		11
	Contribution to the Guild[150]		13
	And on 13 August last Master Gasparo da Molin, the landlord of the studio was given 5½ ducats worth	34	2
	Various pigments on several occasions		
	Drawing-paper, oils and nails	3	0
	To a woman for undressing	1	4
	On [. . .] November for walnuts to make oil		6
	For transporting the pictures to decorate the house for the delivery of Armana's second baby[151] – boat and porters		8

J. F.

22   LOTTO TAKES AN APPRENTICE, 1548

Lotto, *Il libro di spese diverse* [see X.8], f. 96v (Zampetti 1969, p. 154).

In Venice, 29 January 1547 [Venetian style]

I, Lorenzo Lotto, note how on this day I have taken to live with me for three years, as a pupil, Piero da Venezia, son of the widow Orsola, who lives in the courtyard behind the church of San Giovanni in Bragora. I will bear the cost of his food and faithfully teach him, and I will look after him like a son, and during this period I will give him 15 ducats, at the rate of 6 lire 4 soldi per ducat, as follows: for the first year 4 ducats, for the second 5, and for the third 6 ducats: as agreed in the office of the Giustizia Vecchia. Master Gregorio the dyer, who lives at San Giovanni in Bragora, and the said mother, Orsola, guaranteed that he would behave well and complete his term faithfully.

On 6 September 1548, I sent away the above-mentioned Piero notwithstanding that he is obliged to stay with me for one and a half years in order to complete his apprenticeship, because we could not get on with each other.[152] This was agreed amicably, and, because he has pocketed much more money than was his

---

[150] The *luminaria* to pay for candles and lamps on the Guild altar on feast days.
[151] Armana was the wife of Mario [see above, n. 148], who lived in Treviso.
[152] Lotto's accounts show that other of his apprentices failed to stay the course.

439

due, he remains in my debt for 58 ducats, which he will repay me in three years, as appears from the above statement. On my departure for Ancona,[153] I leave this, together with other matters, in the hands of Master Bartolomeo Carpan, the jeweller[154] in the Ruga in Venice, to negotiate.   J. F.

23   THE ELDERLY TITIAN AT WORK

From Palma Giovane's recollections recorded in Boschini 1674 (Boschini ed. Pallucchini 1966, p. 71).

Titian was truly the most excellent of all those who painted, because his brush-strokes always gave birth to expressions of life. Giacomo Palma il Giovane,[155] who himself also had the good fortune to benefit from Titian's learned precepts, used to tell me[156] that he sketched in his pictures with such a mass of colours that they served [so to speak] to make a bed or base for the composition [*espressione*], which he then had to build up; and I also have seen them painted with bold strokes, made with brushes loaded with pigments, sometimes consisting of a stripe of unadulterated red ochre [*terra rossa schietta*], and these served him for the middle tone. On other occasions, with a brush loaded with lead white and with the same brush tinged with red, black and yellow, he created the highlight and, using the same method, with four strokes he made the promise of an extraordinary figure appear. And, in every way, sketches such as these completely satisfied the most knowledgeable connoisseurs, with the result that many people wanted them, for they demonstrated the way to start off well in order to enter the Sea of Painting. After he had laid these precious foundations, he turned the pictures round to face the wall, and there he left them, sometimes for months, without looking at them, and, when he then wanted to reapply the brushes, he examined them with a rigorous scrutiny as if they had been his mortal enemies, in order to see whether he could find fault with them. And, on discovering something that did not agree with his refined intention, he [treated] them like an effective surgeon who, in curing a patient, will – if it is necessary – cut out some swelling or superfluous flesh, straighten an arm if the bone structure is not quite correct, and set right the position of a foot which has become dislocated, without pitying his patient's pain, and so on. Thus Titian, working and revising those figures, brought them to the most

---

[153] Lotto had been commissioned to paint the high altar at San Francesco, Ancona. He died as an oblate of the Holy House, Loreto.

[154] See above, X.8.

[155] Palma il Giovane (*c.*1548–1628), great-nephew of Palma Vecchio.

[156] Marco Boschini (1613–?after 1704) was an engraver as well as a writer about Venetian painting (*DBI*).

perfect symmetry that the beauty of Nature and Art can represent, and after this was done he put his hand to other works until these were dry, and he did the same again and from time to time; he then covered these quintessential extracts with living flesh, creating them layer by layer, so that they only lacked breath. Nor did he ever make a figure all in one go; and he used to say that he who improvises a song cannot provide learned or well-arranged verses. But the seasoning of the final retouching [consisted] in his going from time to time and rubbing with his fingers in the highlights, so as to bring them nearer to the middle tones and blending one colour with another. On other occasions, with a smear of the finger he also put a stroke of dark paint in some corner to strengthen it, and also some trail of red, almost like a drop of blood, which revitalized some superficial sentiment, and so he went on, bringing to perfection his lively figures; and Palma swore that in the last stages he painted more with the finger than with the brush.   J. F.

24   A SCULPTOR ORDERS HIS OWN TOMB, 1576

From a will of Alessandro Vittoria: ASV Testamenti (notaio Vittore Maffei), b. 657, no. 13 (Gerola 1924–5, p. 350).

It is my wish[157] that the small tomb consisting of the two little female figures that I made at my own expense, which is in my house near the door, should be finished, and that the top be made like that of the celebrated Signor Giulio Contarini's monument,[158] or like some drawings which will be found in the drawers of my writing-desk beneath the feet of the figures. A sketch in pen, rolled up together with another which I made for Contarini, will be found in the small drawers of the writing-desk, and the tomb shall be so high above the ground that it is out of arm's reach and placed in a good light, and, if it is possible to put it in the chapel of San Giovanni Elemosinario on the side towards the sacristy, I should dearly love to embellish it with my tomb and a slab on the ground for the grave.[159] The figures are to be placed as far apart as half the height of the monument, and the area between shall consist of a tablet with a short but good inscription, as shall please my executors. The figures shall be made to look at each other, as I know Master Francesco,[160] the worthy sculptor and architect and my very dear friend, will know how to arrange. . . .

[157] Alessandro Vittoria (1525–1608) became, after the deaths of Jacopo Sansovino and Titian, a dominant figure in Venetian artistic life. He wrote *memorie* and made eight wills (see Predelli 1908).

[158] Vittoria had made the Procurator Giulio Contarini's tomb at Santa Maria del Giglio.

[159] It was finally erected in San Zaccaria.

[160] Francesco di Bernardin Fossati (b. *c.*1550) from near Como.

Item. I leave my marble St John[161] to be placed every year on the high altar on the main feast days; and, because handling it is risky, it shall be deposited by the parish priest of the said church [San Giovanni in Bragora] in a little box with wadding; and, to make sure it does not get damaged, I want Monsignor the Patriarch out of courtesy from time to time to have a look and to take care of it.   J. F.

---

[161] This *St John*, one of Vittoria's earliest works, is mentioned in all his wills as bequeathed to the church currently selected for his tomb. It now adorns the right hand holy-water stoup in the nave of San Zaccaria.

References

This list is a key to the printed sources and studies used or cited in the present work under author's or editor's name (or, in the absence of such, a short title) and date of publication. It does not claim to be a comprehensive bibliography on Venice 1450–1630.

Adelman, H. E. 1985: Success and Failure in the Seventeenth-Century Ghetto of Venice: the life and thought of Leon Modena. PhD thesis, Brandeis University.

Agee, R. J. 1983: Ruberto Strozzi and the early madrigal. *Journal of the American Musicological Society*, 36: 1–17.

—— 1985: Filippo Strozzi and the early madrigal. *Journal of the American Musicological Society*, 38: 227–37.

Aikema, B. and Meijers, D. 1989: *Nel regno dei poveri: arte e storia dei grandi ospedali veneziani in età moderna 1474–1797*, Venice.

Albèri, E. (ed.) 1839–63: *Relazioni degli ambasciatori veneti al senato*, 15 vols, Florence.

Albizzi, F. *c.*1680: *Risposta all'historia della sacra Inquisizione composta gia dal R. P. Paolo Servita*, Rome.

Anderson, J. 1979: A further inventory of Gabriel Vendramin's collection. *Burlington Magazine*, 121: 639–48.

Arbel, B. 1988: A royal family in republican Venice: the Cypriot legacy of the Corner della Regina. *Studi Veneziani*, n.s., 15: 131–52.

Aretino, P., 1609: *Lettere*, Paris.

—— ed. E. Camesasca and F. Pertile 1957–60: *Lettere sull'arte di Pietro Aretino*, Milan.

Aricò (ed.): see Sanudo.

Arnaldi, G. and Stocchi, M. (eds) 1981–3: *Storia della cultura veneta*, III.i–iii: *Dal Primo Quattrocento al Concilio di Trento*; IV.i: *Dalla Controriforma alla fine della Repubblica*, Vicenza.

Arte 1978: *Arte e musica all'Ospedaletto. Schede d'archivio sull'attività musicale degli ospedali dei Derelitti e dei Mendicanti di Venezia*, Venice.

Aymard, M. 1966: *Venise, Raguse et le commerce du blé pendant la seconde moitié du XVIe siècle*, Paris.

Baldo, V. 1977: *Alunni, maestri e scuole in Venezia alla fine del XVI secolo*, Como.

Ball, J. G. 1982: Poverty, charity and the Greek community. *Studi Veneziani*, n.s., 6: 129–46.

—— 1985: The Greek Community in Venice 1470–1620. PhD thesis, University of London.

Barasch, M. and Sandler, L. F. (eds) 1981: *Art the Ape of Nature: studies in honour of H. W. Janson*, New York.

Barbiero, G. 1941: *Le confraternite del Santissimo Sacramento*, Treviso.

Baron, H. 1968: Early Renaissance Venetian chronicles: their history and a manuscript in the Newberry Library. *From Petrarch to Leonardo Bruni*, Chicago and London, 172–95.

Battilotti, D. and Franco, M. 1978: Regesto di committenti e dei primi collezionisti di Giorgione. *Antichità viva*, 17: 58–86.

Beck, H. G., Manoussacas, M. and Pertusi, A. 1977: *Venezia centro di mediazione tra oriente e occidente (secoli xv e xvi): aspetti e problemi*, 2 vols, Florence.

Beloch, G. 1902: La popolazione di Venezia nei secoli XVI e XVII. *Nuovo archivio veneto*, n.s., 3: 1–49. Repr. 1961 in Beloch, *Bevölkerungsgeschichte Italiens*, III, Berlin.

Beltrami, D. 1954: *Storia della popolazione di Venezia dalla fine del secolo XVI alla caduta della Repubblica*, Padua.

—— 1955: *Saggio di storia dell'agricoltura nella Repubblica di Venezia durante l'età moderna*, Venice and Rome.

—— 1957: Un ricordo del Priuli intorno al problema dell'ammortamento dei depositi in Zecca del 1574. *Studi in onore di Armando Sapori*, Milan, II, 1071–87.

—— 1961: *La penetrazione economica dei veneziani in terraferma. Forze di lavoro e proprietà fondiaria nelle campagne venete dei secoli XVII e XVIII*, Venice and Rome.

Beltrami, L. 1900: *La Cà de Duca sul Canal Grande*, Milan.

Bembo, P., 1525: *Prose di Messer Pietro Bembo nelle quali si ragiona della volgar lingua*, Venice.

—— ed. C. Dionisotti 1960: *Prose e rime*, Turin.

Benedetti, R. 1630: *Relatione d'alcuni casi occorsi in Venetia al tempo della peste l'anno 1576 e 1577*, Bologna.

Benrath, K. 1887: *Geschichte der Reformation in Venedig*, Halle.

Benzoni, G. 1961: Una controversia tra Roma e Venezia all'inizio de '600: la conferma del Patriarca. *Bollettino dell'Istituto di Storia della Società e dello Stato Veneziano*, 3: 121–38.

—— 1970: I teologi minori dell'Interdetto. *Archivio veneto*, ser. V, 91: 31–108.

—— 1973: *Venezia nell'età della controriforma*, Milan.

—— 1980: *I Dogi*, Milan.

Benzoni, G. and Zanato, T. (eds), 1982: *Storici e politici veneti del Cinquecento e del Seicento*, Milan and Naples.

Besta, E. 1899: *Il Senato Veneziano*, Venice.

Besta, F. 1912: *Documenti finanziari della Repubblica di Venezia*, ser. II, I.i: *Bilanci generali*, Venice.

Bistort, G. 1912: *Il magistrato alle pompe nella Repubblica di Venezia: studio storico*, Venice.

Black, C. F. 1989: *Italian Confraternities in the Sixteenth Century*, Cambridge.

Bode, W. von, et al. 1911: Archivalische Beiträge zur Geschichte der venezianischen Kunst aus dem Nachlass Gustav Ludwigs. *Italienische Forschungen*, ed. W. von Bode, G. Gronau and D. von Hadeln, IV, Berlin.

Boerio, G. 1856: *Dizionario di dialetto veneziano*, Venice, repr. 1971, Milan.

Bolognetti: see Stella, Aldo.

Bonardi, A. 1915: Venezia città libera dell'Impero nell'immaginazione di Massimiliano di Absburgo. *Atti e memorie della Reale Accademia di Scienze in Padova*, 31: 127–47.

Borgherini-Scarabellin, M. 1925: *Il Magistrato dei Cinque Savi alla Mercanzia dalla istituzione alla caduta della Repubblica*, Venice.

Boschini, M., 1674: *Le breve istruzione premesse a le ricche minere della pittura veneziana*, Venice. Ed. A. Pallucchini 1966 in *La carta del navegar pitoresco*, Venice.

Bossy, J. (ed.) 1983: *Disputes and Settlements: law and human relations in the West*, Cambridge.

Botero, G. 1605: *Della relatione della Republica Venetiana*, Venice.

—— tr. R. Peterson 1956: *The Greatness of Cities* (translation first published 1606), with *The Reason of State*, tr. P. J. and D. P. Waley, London.

Bouwsma, W. J. 1980: *Venice and the Defense of Republican Liberty: Renaissance values in the age of the Counter-Reformation*, Berkeley, Calif., and Los Angeles. (First published 1968).

Brasca, S., ed. A. L. Momigliano-Lepschy 1966: *Viaggio in Terrasanta*, Milan.

Braudel, F. 1975: *The Mediterranean and the Mediterranean World in the Age of Philip II*, tr. S. Reynolds, 2 vols, London.

Braunstein, P. 1977: Remarques sur la population allemande de Venise à la fin du moyen âge. In Beck et al. 1977, I, 233–43.

Brodrick, J. 1928: *The Life and Work of Blessed Robert Francis, Cardinal Bellarmine, S. J. (1542–1621)*, 2 vols, London.

Brown, H. F. 1904: *Life on the Lagoons*, 4th edn, London.

Brown, P. Fortini 1987: Honor and necessity: the dynamics of patronage in the confraternities of Renaissance Venice. *Studi veneziani*, n.s., 14: 179–212.

—— 1988: *Venetian Narrative Painting in the Age of Carpaccio*, New Haven, Conn., and London.

Brunetti, M. 1925: Due dogi sotto inchiesta. Agostino Barbarigo e Leonardo Loredan. *Archivio veneto-tridentino*, 7: 278–329.

—— 1956: Tre ambasciate annonarie veneziane. *Archivio veneto*, ser. V, 58: 88–115.

Burke, P. 1974: *Venice and Amsterdam: a study of seventeenth-century elites*, London.

Burns, H. (ed.) 1975: *Andrea Palladio 1508–1580* (exhibition catalogue), London.

Cairns, C. 1976: *Domenico Bollani, Bishop of Brescia: devotion to Church and state in the Republic of Venice in the sixteenth century*, Nieuwkoop.

Calabi, D. and Morachiello, P. 1987: *Rialto: le fabbriche e il ponte, 1514–92*, Turin.

Calimani, R. 1985: *Storia del Ghetto di Venezia*, Milan.

Campbell, L. 1981: Notes on Netherlandish pictures in the Veneto in the fifteenth and sixteenth centuries. *Burlington Magazine*, 123: 467–73.

Canal, B. 1908: Il collegio, l'officio e l'archivio dei Dieci Savi alle Decime in Rialto. *Nuovo archivio veneto*, 16: 115–50; 279–310.

Canale, C., ed. M. Nani-Mocenigo 1930: *Della milizia marittima libri quattro*, Venice.

Capitoli 1619: *Capitoli della veneranda Congregatione dell'Hospitale di Santo Lazaro et Mendicanti della città di Venetia*, Venice.

Cappelletti, G. 1873: *I Gesuiti e la Repubblica di Venezia*, Venice.

Caravia, A. 1541: *Il sogno dil Caravia*, Venice.

Cartari, V. 1556: *Le imagini con la spositione de i dei degli antichi . . .* , Venice.

Casola, P., ed. M. M. Newett 1907: *Canon Pietro Casola's Pilgrimage to Jerusalem in the Year 1494*, Manchester.

Casoni, G. 1830: *La peste di Venezia nel MDCXXX: origine della erezione del tempio a Santa Maria della Salute*, Venice.

445

REFERENCES

Cecchetti, B. 1874: *La Repubblica di Venezia e la Corte di Roma nei rapporti della religione*, 2 vols, Venice.

—— 1885: Documenti riguardanti Fra' Pietruccio di Assisi e lo Spedale della Pietà. *Archivio veneto*, 30.i: 141–7.

Cessi, F. 1961–2: *Alessandro Vittoria, scultore (1525–1608)*, Trento.

Cessi, R. and Alberti A. 1934: *Rialto: l'isola, il ponte, il mercato*, Bologna.

Chamberlain, J., ed. N. E. McClure 1939: *The Letters of John Chamberlain*, 2 vols, Philadelphia.

Chambers, D. S. 1970a: *The Imperial Age of Venice*, London.

—— 1970b: *Patrons and Artists in the Italian Renaissance*, London.

—— 1977: Marin Sanudo, Camerlengo of Verona. *Archivio veneto*, 109: 37–66.

Chavasse, R. 1986: The first known author's copyright. *Bulletin of the John Rylands Library*, 49.i: 11–37.

Chiarelli, L. 1925: Il marchese di Bedmar e i suoi confidenti. *Archivio veneto-tridentino*, 8: 144–73.

Cicogna, E. A. 1824–61: *Delle inscrizioni veneziane*, 6 vols, Venice.

—— 1862: Memorie intorno le vite e le scritte di Messer Ludovico Dolce. *Memorie dell' Istituto Veneto di Scienze, Lettere ed Arti*, 11: 95–113.

Clark, P. (ed.) 1985: *The European Crisis of the 1590s: essays in comparative history*, London.

Clough, C. H. 1963: Le lettere storiche di Luigi da Porto, fonti della *Istoria veneziana* di Pietro Bembo. *Archivio veneto*, ser. V, 73: 5–15.

Cloulas, A. 1967: Documents concernant Titien conservés aux Archives de Simancas. *Mélanges de la casa de Velasquez*, III, Madrid.

Commynes, P. de, ed. S. Kinser, tr. I. Cazeaux 1969–73: *The Memoirs*, 2 vols, New York.

Concina, E. 1989: *Venezia nell'età moderna. Struttura e funzioni*, Venice.

Coniglio, G. 1953: Il duca d'Ossuna e Venezia dal 1616 al 1620. *Archivio veneto*, ser. V, 52–3: 42–70.

Connell, S. M. 1988: *The Employment of Sculptors and Stone-Masons in Venice in the 15th Century*, New York and London.

Constable, M. V. 1988: The education of the Venetian orphans from the sixteenth to the eighteenth century: an expression of Guillaume Postel's judgement of Venice as a public welfare state. In Kuntz 1988, 179–202.

Contarini, G. 1543: *De Magistratibus et Republica Venetorum* (Latin original), Paris.

—— tr. L. Lewkenor 1599: *The Commonwealth and Government of Venice. Written by the Cardinall Gasper Contareno, and translated out of Italian into English*, London.

Contarini, P. *c.*1542: *L'Argoa volgar*, Venice.

Contento, A. 1900: Il censimento della popolazione sotto la Repubblica Veneta. *Nuovo archivio veneto*, 19: 1–42, 179–240; 20: 1–96, 171–235.

Conway, W. M. 1889: *Literary Remains of Albrecht Dürer*, Cambridge.

Cornet, E. 1859: *Paolo V e la Republica Veneta: giornale dal 22 ottobre 1605 – 9 giugno 1607*, Vienna.

Corti, U. 1894: La francazione del debito pubblico della Repubblica di Venezia proposta da Gian Francesco Priuli. *Nuovo archivio veneto*, 7: 331–64.

Coryat, T. 1611: *Coryat's Crudities*, London. Repr. in 2 vols, Glasgow, 1905.

446

Cowan, A. F. 1982: Rich and poor among the patriciate in early modern Venice. *Studi veneziani*, n.s., 6: 147–60.

—— 1986: *The Urban Patriciate. Lübeck and Venice, 1580–1700*, Cologne and Vienna.

Cozzi, G. 1958: *Il Doge Nicolò Contarini. Ricerche sul patriziato veneziano agli inizi del Seicento*, Venice.

—— 1959: Appunti sul teatro e i teatri a Venezia agli inizi del Seicento. *Bollettino dell'Istituto di Storia della Società e dello Stato Veneziano*, 1: 187–92.

—— 1961: Federico Contarini: un antiquario veneziano tra Rinascimento e Controriforma. *Bollettino dell'Istituto di Storia della Società e dello Stato Veneziano*, 3: 190–220.

—— 1970a: Domenico Morosini e il *De bene instituta republica. Studi veneziani*, 12: 405–58.

—— 1970b: Marin Sanudo il Giovane: dalla cronaca alla storia. In Pertusi 1970, pp. 333–58.

—— 1973: Authority and the law in Renaissance Venice. In Hale 1973, pp. 293–345.

—— (ed.) 1980–5: *Stato, società a giustizia nella Repubblica Veneta (sec. XV–XVIII)*, 2 vols, Rome.

—— 1982: *Repubblica di Venezia e stati italiani: politica e giustizia dal secolo XV al secolo XVIII*, Turin.

—— (ed.) 1987: *Gli ebrei e venezia (secoli XIV–XVIII)*, Milan.

Cozzi, G. and Knapton, M. 1986: *La Repubblica di Venezia nell'età moderna: dalla guerra di Chioggia al 1517 (Storia d'Italia*, ed. G. Galasso, XII), Turin.

Dalla Santa, G. 1895: Nuovi appunti sul processo di Giorgio Valla e di Placido Amerino in Venezia nel 1496. *Nuovo archivio veneto*, 10: 13–23.

—— 1899: Le appellazioni della Repubblica di Venezia dalle scomuniche di Sisto IV e Giulio II. *Nuovo archivio veneto*, 17: 216–42.

—— 1916–17: Commerci, vita privata e notizie politiche dei giorni della lega di Cambrai (da lettere del mercante veneziano Martino Merlini). *Atti del Reale Istituto Veneto di Scienze, Lettere ed Arti*, 76: 1547–1605.

Da Mosto, A. 1939: *I Dogi di Venezia con particolare riguardo alle loro tombe*, Venice.

Da Porto, L., ed. B. Bressan 1857: *Lettere storiche*, Florence; ed. C. H. Clough, 1961: A Critical Edition of the *Lettere Storiche* 1509–1513, 3 vols (DPhil thesis, University of Oxford).

D'Arco, C. 1857: *Dalle arti e artifici di Mantova*, II, Mantua.

Davidson, N. 1982: Il Sant'Uffizio e la tutela del culto a Venezia nel '500. *Studi veneziani*, n.s., 6: 87–101.

—— 1984: The clergy of Venice in the sixteenth century. *Bulletin of the Society for Renaissance Studies*, 2.ii: 19–31.

—— 1985: Northern Italy in the 1590s. In Clark 1985, pp. 157–76.

—— 1987: The Inquisition and the Italian Jews. In Haliczer 1987, pp. 19–46.

—— 1988: Rome and the Venetian Inquisition in the sixteenth century. *Journal of Ecclesiastical History*, 39: 16–36.

—— forthcoming: An Inquisition and its documents: some problems of method and analysis. In A. Del Col (ed.), *Gli archivi dell'Inquisizione in Italia.*

Davis, J. C. 1962: *The Decline of the Venetian Nobility as a Ruling Class*, Baltimore.

—— 1975: *A Venetian Family and its Fortunes, 1500–1900: the Donà and the conservation of their wealth*. Memoirs of the American Philosophical Society, 106, Philadelphia.

DBI: *Dizionario biografico degli italiani*, Rome 1960– (in progress).

Degli Azzi, G. 1952: Un frammento inedito della cronaca di Benedetto Dei. *Archivio storico italiano*, 110: 99–113.

De Leva, G. 1887: *La legazione di Roma di Paolo Paruta (1592–1595)*, 3 vols, Venice.

Della Croce, M. 1574: *L'historia della publica et famosa entrata in Vinegia del serenissimo Henrico III Re di Francia et Polonia*, Venice.

De Magistris, C. P. 1941: *Per la storia del componimento della contesa tra la Repubblica Veneta e Paolo V (1605–1607): documenti*, Turin.

Derosas, R. 1980: moralità e giustizia a Venezia nel '500–600: gli Esecutori contra la Bestemmia. In Cozzi 1980–5, I, 431–528.

Dionisotti (ed.): see Bembo.

DMS: see Sanudo.

Documenti 1879: *Documenti per la storia della beneficenza in Venezia*, Venice.

Dolce, L., 1557: *Dialogo della pittura intitolato l'Aretino*, Venice.

—— 1559: *Lettere di diversi eccelentissimi huomini*, Venice.

Doni, A. F., 1550: *La Libraria*, Venice.

—— 1552: *I Marmi*, Venice.

Edler, F. 1934: *Glossary of Medieval Terms of Business . . .*, Cambridge, Mass.

Erizzo, N. 1860: *Relazione storica-critica della Torre dell'Orologio*, Venice.

Eubel, C. 1901–11: *Hierarchia Catholica medii et recentioris aevi*, II–III, Münster (*HC*).

Faber, F., ed. C. D. Hassler 1843–9: *Evagatorium in Terrae Sanctae, Arabiae et Egypti peregrinationem*, 3 vols, Stuttgart.

Farmer, D. H. 1978: *The Oxford Dictionary of Saints*, Oxford.

Favaro, A. 1893: Un ridotto scientifico in Venezia al tempo di Galileo Galilei. *Nuovo archivio veneto* 55: 199ff.

Favaro, E. 1975: *L'Arte dei Pittori in Venezia e i suoi Statuti*, Florence.

Fedalto, G. 1967: *Ricerche storiche sulla posizione giuridica ed ecclesiastica dei greci a Venezia nei secoli XV e XVI*, Venice.

Fehl, P. 1961: Veronese and the Inquisition: a study of the subject matter of the so-called *Feast in the House of Levi*. *Gazette des Beaux-Arts*, ser. VI, 58: 325–54.

—— 1981: Veronese's Decorum: Notes on the *Marriage at Cana*. In Barasch and Sandler 1981, pp. 341–65.

Finlay, R. 1976: Venice, the Po expedition and the end of the League of Cambrai. *Studies in Modern European History and Culture*, 2: 37–52.

—— 1978: Politics and the family in Renaissance Venice: the election of Doge Andrea Gritti. *Studi veneziani*, n.s., 2: 97–117.

—— 1980: *Politics in Renaissance Venice*, London.

—— 1982: The foundation of the Ghetto: Venice, the Jews, and the War of the League of Cambrai. *Proceedings of the American Philosophical Society*, 126: 140–54.

Fletcher, J. 1981: Marcantonio Michiel: his friends and his collection, *Burlington Magazine*, 123: 453–67. Marcantonio Michiel: 'che ha veduto assai', ibid., 602–8.

—— 1983: Patronage in Venice. In Martineau and Hope 1983, pp. 16–20.

Florio, J. 1611: *Queen Anne's New World of Words*, London. Facsimile repr. Menston, Yorks, 1968.

Fogolari, G. 1935: Il processo dell'Inquisizione a Paolo Veronese. *Archivio veneto*, ser. V, 17: 352–86.

Fontana, R. 1984: Aspetti sociali e orrizzonti mentali dell'ambiente Lottesco. In Rosand 1984, pp. 359–62.

Forsellini, M. 1930: L'organizzazione economica dell'Arsenale di Venezia nella prima metà del Seicento. *Archivio veneto*, ser. V. 7: 54–117.

Fulin, R. 1865: *Relazione della republica di Venezia scritta da Raffaele de'Medici nel MDLXXXIX*, Venice.

—— (ed.): see Sanudo.

—— 1882: Documenti per servire alla storia della stampa veneziana. *Archivio veneto*, 23: 84–212.

Gabotto, F. 1891: Giorgio Valla e il suo processo in Venezia nel 1496. *Nuovo archivio veneto*, 1: 201–20.

Gaeta, F. et al. (eds) 1958– : *Nunziature di Venezia*, Rome (*NV*).

Gallo, R. 1943: Le mappe geografiche del Palazzo Ducale di Venezia. *Archivio veneto*, ser. V, 32–3: 47–113.

—— 1944: Una famiglia patrizia: i Pisani ed i palazzi di Santo Stefano e di Stra. *Archivio veneto*, ser. V, 34–5: 65–228.

—— 1955: Palladio a Venezia. *Rivista di Venezia*, 1: 37–41.

Geanakoplos, D. J. 1962: *Greek Scholars in Venice: Studies in the Dissemination of Greek Learning from Byzanitum to Western Europe*, Cambridge, Mass.

Georgelin, J. 1978: *Venise au siècle des lumières*, Paris and The Hague.

Gianighian, G. and Pavanini, P. (eds) 1984: *Dietro i palazzi: tre secoli d'architettura minore a Venezia (1492–1803)*, Venice.

Giannotti, D. 1540: *Libro della Repubblica de' veneziani*, Florence; ed. F. C. Polidori 1850, Florence.

Gilbert, F. 1968: Religion and politics in the thought of Gasparo Contarini. In T. K. Rabb and J. E. Seigel (eds), *Action and Conviction in Modern Europe: essays in memory of E. H. Harbison*, Princeton, NJ, pp. 90–116.

—— 1968: The Venetian constitution in Florentine political thought. In N. Rubinstein (ed.), *Florentine Studies*, London, pp. 463–500.

—— 1971: Biondo, Sabellico and the beginnings of Venetian official historiography. In J. R. Rowe and W. H. Stockdale (eds), *Florilegium Historiale: essays presented to Wallace K. Ferguson*, Toronto, pp. 275–93.

—— 1973: Venice in the crisis of the League of Cambria. In Hale 1973, pp. 274–92.

Ginzburg (ed.): see Manelfi.

Giuliani, I. 1961: Genesi e primo secolo di vita del Magistrato sopra Monasteri, Venezia 1519–1620. *Le venezie francescane*, 1–4.

Glixon, J. 1983: A musicians' union in sixteenth-century Venice. *Journal of the American Musicological Society*, 36: 392–421.

Goy, R. J. 1989: *Venetian Vernacular Architecture: traditional housing in the Venetian Lagoon*, Cambridge.

Graziato, G. 1986: *Le promissioni del Doge di Venezia dalle origini alla fine del Duecento*, Venice.

Grendler, P. F. 1969a: *Critics of the Italian World 1530–1560: Anton Francesco Doni, Nicolò Franco and Ortensio Lando*, Madison, Milwaukee and London.

—— 1969b: Francesco Sansovino and Italian popular history 1560–1600. *Studies in the Renaissance*, 16: 139–80.

449

REFERENCES

—— 1977: *The Roman Inquisition and the Venetian Press, 1540–1605*, Princeton, NJ.

—— 1989: *Schooling in Renaissance Italy: literacy and learning, 1300–1600*, Baltimore and London.

Giucciardini, F., ed. R. Palmarocchi 1932: *Dialogo del reggimento di Firenze*, Bari.

Hain, L. 1826–38: *Repertorium bibliographicum*, 2 vols, Stuttgart and Paris.

Hale, J. R. (ed.) 1973: *Renaissance Venice*, London.

Haliczer, S. (ed.) 1987: *Inquisition and Society in Early Modern Europe*, London.

HC: see Eubel et al.

Hetzer, T. 1948: *Tizian. Geschichte seiner Farbe*, Frankfurt a.M.

Hocquet, J. C. 1978–9: *Le Sel et la fortune de Venise*, I: *Production et monopole*; II: *Voiliers et commerce en Méditerranée 1200–1650*, Lille.

Hope, C. 1980: Titian's role as 'official painter' to the Venetian Republic. In *Tiziano* 1980, pp. 301–5.

—— 1983a: *Poesia* and painted allegories. In Martineau and Hope 1983, pp. 32–4.

—— 1983b: The historians of Venetian painting. In Martineau and Hope 1983, pp. 38–40.

—— 1985: Veronese and the Venetian tradition of allegory. *Proceedings of the British Academy*, 71: 389–428.

Howard, D. 1976: *Jacopo Sansovino: Architecture and Patronage in Renaissance Venice*, New Haven, Conn., and London.

Hughes, D. O. 1983: Sumptuary law and social relations in Renaissance Italy. In Bossy 1983, pp. 69–100.

Il gioco dell'amore 1990: *Il gioco dell'amore. Le cortigiane di Venezia dal Trecento al Settecento* (exhibition catalogue), Milan.

Ioly Zorattini, P. C. 1980– : *Processi del S. Uffizio di Venezia contro ebrei e giudaizzanti*, 7 vols (covering the period 1548–89), Florence.

Jacoby, D. 1977: Les juifs à Venise di XIVe au milieu du XVIe siècle. In Beck et al. 1977, I, 163–216.

Kaufmann, D., 1890: A contribution to the history of the Venetian Jews. *Jewish Quarterly Review*, 2: 297–310.

Kuntz, M. I. (ed.) 1988: *Postello, Venezia e il suo mondo*, Florence.

Labalme, P. H. 1969: *Bernardo Giustiniani: a Venetian of the '400*, Rome.

—— 1984: Sodomy and Venetian justice in the Renaissance. *Legal History Review*, 52: 217–54.

Labowsky, L. 1979: *Cardinal Bessarion's Library and the Beginnings of the Marciana*, Milan.

Lane, F. C. 1934: *Venetian Ships and Shipbuilders in the Renaissance*. Facsimile repr. Westport, Conn., 1975.

—— 1965: *Navires et constructeurs pendant la Renaissance* (rev. edn of Lane 1934), Paris.

—— 1966: *Venice and History: the collected papers of Frederic C. Lane*, Baltimore.

—— 1973: *Venice: a maritime republic*, Baltimore and London.

—— 1987: *Studies in Venetian Social and Economic History*, ed. B. G. Kohl and R. C. Mueller, London.

Lazzarini, L. 1983: Le colore nei pittori veneziani tra il 1480 e il 1580. *Bollettino d'arte*, 5: 135–44.

Lee, M., Jr 1966–7: The Jacobean diplomatic service. *American Historical Review*, 72: 1264–82.

—— 1972: *Dudley Carleton to John Chamberlain, 1603–24: Jacobean letters*, New Brunswick, NJ.

Levi, C. A. 1900: *Le collezioni veneziane*, Venice.

Lewkenor, L.: see Contarini, G.

Logan, O. 1967: Studies in the Religious Life of Venice in the Sixteenth and Early Seventeenth Centuries: the Venetian clergy and religious orders, 1520–1630. PhD thesis, University of Cambridge.

—— 1972: *Culture and Society in Venice, 1470–1700: the Renaissance and its heritage*, London.

—— 1978: The ideal of the bishop and the Venetian patriciate: c.1430–c.1630. *Journal of Ecclesiastical History*, 29: 415–50.

Lorenzi, G. 1868: *Documenti per servire alla storia del Palazzo Ducale di Venezia*, Venice.

Lowry, M. 1971: The reform of the Council of Ten, 1582–3: an unsettled problem? *Studi veneziani*, 13: 275–310.

—— 1979: *The World of Aldus Manutius*, Oxford.

Ludwig, G. 1903–5: Archivalische Beiträge zur Geschichte der venezianischen Malerei. *Jahrbuch der preussischen Kunstsammlungen*, 24 (Beiheft): 1–109; 26 (Beiheft): 1–157.

Ludwig, G. and Molmenti, P. 1906: *Vittore Carpaccio*, Milan.

Luzio, A. 1888: *Pietro Aretino nei suoi primi anni a Venezia e la corte dei Gonzaga*, Turin.

Luzio, A. and Renier, R. 1903: *La collura e le relazioni letterarie d'Isabella d'Este Gonzaga*, Turin.

Luzzatto, G. 1961: *Storia economica di Venezia dall'XI al XVI secolo*, Venice.

—— 1963: *Il debito pubblico della Repubblica di Venezia dagli ultimi decenni del XII secolo alla fine del XV*, Milan.

MacAndrew, A. 1980: *Venetian Architecture of the Early Renaissance*, Cambridge, Mass.

Macchi, M. 1849: *Storia del Consiglio di Dieci*, 2 vols, Turin.

McClure (ed.): see Chamberlain.

Mackenney, R. 1981: Arti e stato tra tardo medioevo e '600. *Studi veneziani*, n.s., 5: 127–43.

—— 1984: Guilds and guildsmen in sixteenth-century Venice. *Bulletin of the Society for Renaissance Studies*, 2.ii: 7–18.

—— 1986: Devotional confraternities in Renaissance Venice. In Sheils and Wood 1986, pp. 85–96.

—— 1987: *Tradesmen and Traders: the world of the guilds in Venice and Europe, c.1250–c.1650*, London.

—— 1990: Letters from the Venetian archives. In B. Pullan and S. Reynolds (eds), *Towns and Townspeople in Medieval and Renaissance Europe: essays in memory of J. K. Hyde, Bulletin of the John Rylands University Library of Manchester* 72–3: 133–44.

Mackenney, R. with Humfrey, P. 1986: The Venetian trade guilds as patrons of art in the Renaissance. *Burlington Magazine*, 128: 317–30.

McPherson, D. 1988: Lewkenor's Venice and its sources. *Renaissance Quarterly*, 41: 459–66.

Malipiero, D., ed. F. Longo (1564), ed. A. Sagredo 1843–4: Annali veneti dall'anno 1457 al 1500 (parts 3–5). *Archivio storico italiano*, 7: 5–720.

Mallett, M. E. and Hale, J. R. 1984: *The Military Organization of a Renaissance State. Venice c.1400 to 1617*, Cambridge.

Manelfi, P., ed. C. Ginzburg 1970: *I costituti di Don Pietro Manelfi*, Florence and Chicago.

Maranini, G. 1931: *La costituzione di Venezia dopo la serrata del Maggior Consiglio*, 2 vols, Venice.

Martin, J. 1987: Popular culture and the shaping of popular heresy in Renaissance Venice. In Haliczer 1987, pp. 115–28.

Martin, R. 1989: *Witchcraft and the Inquisition in Venice, 1550–1650*, Oxford.

Martineau, J. and Hope C. 1983: *The Genius of Venice 1500–1600* (Royal Academy exhibition catalogue), London.

Martini, G. 1986: La giustizia veneziana ed il 'vitio nefando' nel secolo XVII. *Studi veneziani*, n.s., 11, 159–206.

Mattozzi, I. 1983: Il politico e il pane a Venezia (1570–1650). *Studi veneziani*, n.s., 7: 197–222.

Mavroidi, F., ed. P. Piccinini 1989: *Aspetti della società veneziana del '500. La confraternità del '500. La confraternità di S. Nicolò dei Greci*, Ravenna.

Meersseman, G. G. 1977: *Ordo Fraternitatis: confraternite e pietà dei laici nel Medioevo*, 3 vols, Rome.

Merkel, E. 1980: Tiziano e i mosaicisti a San Marco. In *Tiziano* 1980, pp. 275–83.

Micanzio, F. tr. anon. 1651: *The Life of the Most Learned Father Paul of the Order of the Servie. Councellour of State to the most Serene Republicke of Venice . . . Translated out of Italian by a person of Quality*, London.

Modena, L., ed. and tr. M. L. Cohen 1988: *The Autobiography of a Seventeenth-Century Venetian Rabbi. Leon Modena's Life of Judah*, Princeton, NJ.

Mohler, L. 1942: *Kardinal Bessarion als Theologe, Humanist und Staatsman*, 3 vols, Paderborn.

Molmenti, P. 1880: *La storia di Venezia nella vita privata dalle origini alla caduta della Repubblica*, 3 vols, Turin. 4th edn 1927–9, Bergamo.

Momigliano-Lepschy, A. L. (ed.): see Brasca.

—— 1983: *Tintoretto Observed: a documentary survey of critical reactions from the 16th to the 20th century*, Ravenna.

Morelli, I. 1820: *Operette*, I, Venice.

Morelli, J. and Frizzoni, G. 1888: G., *Notizie d'opere di disegno*, Bologna.

Moretti, L. 1983: Portraits. In Martineau and Hope 1983, pp. 32–4.

Morosini, D., ed. C. Finzi 1969: *De bene instituta republica*, Milan.

Moryson, F. 1617: *Itinerary*, London, Repr. 1907, 4 vols, Glasgow.

Mousnier, R. 1952: Le trafic des offices à Venise. *Nouvelle revue historique de droit français et étranger*, ser. IV, 30: 552–65.

Mueller, R. C. 1971: The Procurators of San Marco in the 13th and 14th centuries: a study of the office as a financial and trust institution. *Studi veneziani*, 13: 105–221.

—— 1972: Charitable institutions, the Jewish community and Venetian society. *Studi veneziani*, 14: 37–82.

Muir, E. 1981: *Civic Ritual in Renaissance Venice*, Princeton, NJ.

Muraro, M. 1984: I conti in tasca a Lorenzo Lotto. *L. Lotto nelle Marche, Notizie da Palazzo Albani*, 13: 144–64.

Musatti, E. 1884: *Storia della promissione ducale*, Padua.

Nani-Mocenigo, F. 1909: Testamento del Doge Agostino Barbarigo, *Nuovo archivio veneto*, 17: 234–61.

Nardi, B. 1971: La civiltà veneziana del Quattrocento; La scuola di Rialto e l'umanesimo veneziano. Both in his *Saggi sulla cultura veneta del Quattro e Cinquecento*, Padua.

Neff, M. 1981: A citizen in the service of the patrician state: the career of Zaccaria de'Freschi. *Studi veneziani*, n.s., 5: 33–61.

—— 1985: *Chancery Secretaries in Venetian Politics and Society, 1480–1533*, Ann Arbor, Mich.

Newett, M. M. 1902: The sumptuary laws of Venice in the fourteenth and fifteenth centuries. In T. F. Tout, and J. Tait (eds), *Historical Essays by Members of the Owens College, Manchester*, Manchester, pp. 245–78.

—— (ed.): see Casola.

Newton, S. M. 1988: *The Dress of the Venetians 1495–1525*, Aldershot.

Niero, A. 1961a: *I patriarchi di Venezia da Lorenzo Giustinian ai nostri giorni*, Venice.

—— 1961b: La mariegola della più antica Scuola del Rosario di Venezia. *Rivista di storia della Chiesa in Italia*, 15: 329–36.

—— 1974: Ancora sull'origine del Rosario a Venezia e sulla sua iconografia. *Rivista di storia della Chiesa in Italia*, 28: 465–78.

—— 1979: I templi del Redentore e della Salute: motivazioni teologiche. In *Venezia 1979*, pp. 294–99.

NV: see Gaeta et al.

Olivieri, A. 1985: Eroticism and social groups in sixteenth-century Venice: the courtesan. In P. Ariès and A. Béjin (eds), *Western Sexuality: Practice and Precept in Past and Present Times*, tr. A. Forster, Oxford, 95–102.

Ongania, F. 1886: *Documenti per la storia dell'Augusta Ducale Basilica di San Marco in Venezia*, Venice.

Orford, Lord 1870–2: *Leggi e memorie venete sulla prostituzione fino alla caduta della Republica*, Venice.

Orlandi, G. 1976: *Aldo Manuzio editore*, 2 vols, Milan.

Padoan, G. 1978: *Momenti del Rinascimento veneto*, Padua.

—— 1980: A casa di Tiziano, una sera d'Agosto. In *Tiziano 1980*, pp. 359–67.

—— *La commedia rinascimentale veneta*, Vicenza.

Pagan, P. 1973–4: Sulla Accademia 'Venetiana' o della 'Fame'. *Atti dell'Istituto Veneto di Scienze, Lettere ed Arti*, 132, cl. Scienze Morali, Lettere ed Arti: 359–92.

Pallucchini, R. 1943: *La critica d'arte a Venezia nel Cinquecento*. Quaderni del Rinascimento Veneto, I, Venice.

Palmer, R. 1978: The Control of Plague in Venice and Northern Italy. PhD thesis, University of Kent at Canterbury.

—— 1982: The Church, leprosy and plague in medieval and early modern Europe. *Studies in Church History*, 19: 79–99.

—— 1983: *The 'Studio' of Venice and its Graduates in the Sixteenth Century*, Padua.

Panofsky, E. 1943: *The Life and Art of Albrecht Dürer*, Princeton, NJ.

Paoletti, P. 1893: *L'architettura e la scultura del Rinascimento in Venezia*, Venice.

—— 1894: *Raccolta di documenti inediti per servire alla storia della pittura veneziana nei secoli xv e xvi*, fasc. II, Padua.

Paschini, P. 1958: I monasteri femminili in Italia nel Cinquecento. In *Problemi* 1958, pp. 31–60.

—— 1959: *Venezia e l'Inquisizione Romana da Giulio III a Pio IV*, Padua.

Pastor, L. von 1891–ᅠ: *History of the Popes from the Close of the Middle Ages*, ed. F. I. Antrobus et al., London.

—— 1932: *Storia dei papi* (rev. Italian edn), II, ed. G. Mercati, Rome.

Pastorello, E. 1965: Di Aldo Pio Manuzio: testimonianze e documenti. *La Bibliofilia*, 67: 163–220.

Pavan, E. 1980: Police des moeurs, société et politique à Venise à la fin du Moyen Age. *Revue historique*, 264: 241–88.

Pavanini, P. 1981: Abitazioni popolari e borghesi nella Venezia cinquecentesca. *Studi veneziani*, n.s., 5: 63–126.

Perret, P.-M. 1896: *Histoire des relations de la France avec Venise du 13ᵉ siècle à l'avènement de Charles VIII*, II, Paris.

Perry, M. 1977: Saint Mark's trophies: legend, superstition and archaeology in Renaissance Venice. *Journal of the Warburg and Courtauld Institutes*, 40: 27–49.

—— 1978: Cardinal Domenico Grimani's legacy of ancient art to Venice. *Journal of the Warburg and Courtauld Institutes*, 41: 215–44.

Pertusi, A. 1970a: Gli inizi della storiografia umamstica nel Quattrocento. In Pertusi 1970b, pp. 269–332.

—— (ed.) 1970b: *La storiografia veneziana fino al secolo XVI*, Florence.

Pignatti, T. 1976: *Veronese*, 2 vols, Venice.

—— (ed.) 1981: *Le scuole di Venezia*, Milan.

Pirri, P. 1959: *L'Interdetto di Venezia del 1606 e i Gesuiti: silloge di documenti con introduzione*, Rome.

Pommier, E. 1959: La société vénitienne et la Réforme protestante au XVIe siècle. *Bollettino dell'Istituto di Storia della Società e dello Stato Veneziano*, 1: 3–26.

Pope-Hennessy, J. 1963: *Italian High Renaissance and Baroque Sculpture*, catalogue vol., London.

Predelli, R. 1908: Le memorie e le carte di Alessandro Vittoria. *Archivio trentino*, 23: 5–74, 129–225.

Preto, P. 1975: *Venezia e i turchi*, Florence.

—— 1978: *Peste e società a Venezia, 1576*, Vicenza.

Priscianese, F. 1540: *Della lingua latina*, Venice.

Priuli, G., ed. A. Segre 1912(I) and R. Cessi 1913(II), 1938(IV): *I Diarii*, 2nd edn. RIS XXIV.3, Città di Castello (I) and Bologna (II, IV).

Problemi 1958: *Problemi di vita religiosa in Italia nel Cinquecento. Atti del Convegno di Storia della Chiesa in Italia*, Bologna.

Prodi, P. 1973: The structure and organization of the Church in Renaissance Venice: suggestions for research. In Hale 1973, pp. 403–30.

Pullan, B. 1964: Wage-earners and the Venetian economy, 1550–1630. *Economic History Review*, ser. II, 15: 407–26. Repr. in Pullan 1968, pp. 146–74.

—— 1965: Service to the Venetian state: aspects of myth and reality in the early seventeenth century. *Studi secenteschi*, 5: 95–148.

—— (ed.) 1968: *Crisis and Change in the Venetian Economy in the Sixteenth and Seventeenth Centuries*, London.

—— 1971: *Rich and Poor in Renaissance Venice: the social institutions of a Catholic state, to 1620*, Oxford and Cambridge, Mass.

—— 1973: The occupations and investments of the Venetian nobility in the middle and later sixteenth century. In Hale 1973, pp. 379–408.

—— 1978: Poveri, mendicanti e vagabondi (secoli xiv–xviii). In C. Vivanti and R. Romano (eds), *Storia d'Italia: Annali*, I: *Dal feudalesimo al capitalismo*, Turin, 981–1047.

—— 1983: *The Jews of Europe and the Inquisition of Venice, 1550–1670*, Oxford.

—— 1985: The roles of the state and the town in the general crisis of the 1590s. In Clark 1985, pp. 285–300.

—— 1988a: The conversion of the Jews: the style of Italy. *Bulletin of the John Rylands University Library of Manchester*, 70: 53–70.

—— 1988b: Support and redeem: charity and poor relief in the Italian cities from the fourteenth to the seventeenth century. *Continuity and Change*, 3: 177–208.

—— 1990: The Scuole Grandi of Venice: some further thoughts. In T. Verdon and J. S. Henderson (eds), *Christianity and the Renaissance*, Syracuse, NY, pp. 272–301.

Pullapilly, C. K. 1975: *Caesar Baronius, Counter-Reformation Historian*, Notre Dame, Ind.

Puppalin, D. 1976–7: L'artista a Venezia: vita privata, carriera e cultura. Tesi di laurea, University of Padua (Facoltà di Magistero). Copy in BMV: dattiloscritto 65.

Puppi, L. 1973: *Andrea Palladio*, Milan.

—— 1982: *Palladio e Venezia*, Florence.

Queller, D. E. 1986: *The Venetian Patriciate: reality versus myth*, Urbana, Ill., and Chicago.

Ranke, L. von, tr. E. Foster, rev. G. R. Dennis 1908: *The History of the Popes during the Last Four Centuries*, 3 vols, London.

Rapp, R. T. 1976: *Industry and Economic Decline in Seventeenth-Century Venice*, Cambridge, Mass., and London.

Raulich, I. 1893: La congiura spagnola contro Venezia. *Nuovo archivio veneto*, 6: 5–86.

—— 1898: Una relazione del Marchese di Bedmar sui veneziani. *Nuovo archivio veneto*, 16: 5–32.

Ravà, A. 1920: Il camerino delle antigaglie di Gabriele Vendramin. *Nuovo archivio veneto*, n.s., 39: 151–81.

Ravid, B. 1976: The first charter of the Jewish merchants of Venice, 1589. *Association for Jewish Studies Review*, 1: 187–222,

—— 1978: *Economics and Toleration in Seventeenth-Century Venice: the background and context of the Discorso of Simone Luzzatto*, Jerusalem.

—— 1979: The prohibition against Jewish printing and publishing in Venice and the difficulties of Leone Modena. In I. Twersky (ed.), *Studies in Medieval Jewish History and Literature*, Cambridge, Mass., pp. 135–53.

—— 1982: The socioeconomic background of the expulsion and readmission of Venetian Jews, 1571–1573. In F. Malino and P. Cohen Albert (eds) *Essays in Modern Jewish History: a tribute to Ben Halpern*, Rutherford, NJ, Madison and Teaneck, NJ, pp. 27–55.

—— 1983a: Money, love and power politics in sixteenth century Venice: the perpetual banishment and subsequent pardon of Joseph Nasi. *Italia Judaica*, 159–81.

—— 1983b: 'A republic separate from all other government': Jewish autonomy in

Venice in the seventeenth century. In *Thought and Action: essays in Memory of Simon Rawidowicz on the twenty-fifth anniversary of his death*, Tel-Aviv.

—— 1987a: 'Kosher bread' in Baroque Venice. *Italia*, 6: 20–9.

—— 1987b: The religious, economic and social background of the establishment of the Ghetti in Venice. In Cozzi 1987, pp. 211–60.

Rodenwaldt, E. 1953: *Pest in Venedig, 1575–1577. Ein Beitrag zur Frage der Infektkette bei den Pestepidemien West-Europas*, Heidelberg.

Romanelli, G. 1982: Ritrattistica dogale, ombre, immagini e volti. In Benzoni and Zanato 1982, pp. 125–62.

Romanin, S. 1853–61: *Storia documentata di Venezia*, 10 vols, esp. IV–VII, Venice.

Romano, R. 1968: Economic aspects of the construction of warships in Venice in the sixteenth century. In Pullan 1968, pp. 59–87.

Rosand, D. 1982: *Painting in Cinquecento Venice: Titian, Veronese, Tintoretto*, New Haven, Conn., and London.

—— (ed.) 1984: *Interpretazioni veneziane: studi di storia dell'arte in onore di Michelangelo Muraro*, Venice.

Rose, P. L. 1969: The Accademia Venetiana: science and culture in Renaissance Venice. *Bollettino dell'Istituto di Storia della Società e dello Stato Veneziano*, 11: 191–242.

Roskill, M. 1968: *Dolce's 'Aretino' and Venetian Art Theory of the Cinquecento*, New York.

Ross, J. B. 1976: Venetian schools and teachers: fourteenth to early sixteenth century. *Renaissance Quarterly*, 29: 521–6.

Rossato, V. 1987: Religione e moralità in un merciaio veneziano del Cinquecento, *Studi veneziani*, n.s., 13: 193–253.

Rossi, P. 1974: *Tintoretto: i ritratti*, Venice.

Roth, C. 1930: *The History of the Jews in Venice*, Philadelphia. Repr. New York 1975.

Rovetta, G. 1626: *Salmi concertati*, Venice.

Rubinstein, N. 1973: Italian reactions to terraferma expansion in the fifteenth century. In Hale 1973, pp. 197–217.

Ruggiero, F. 1980: *Violence in Early Renaissance Venice*, New Brunswick, NJ.

—— 1985: *The Boundaries of Eros: sex crime and society in Renaissance Venice*, New York and Oxford.

Rupprich, H. 1956: *Dürers schriftlicher Nachlass*, I, Berlin.

Sabellicus, M. (Cocchi) 1487: *Rerum Venetarum ab urbe condita*, Venice. Ed. A. Zeno 1718, Venice.

Sagredo, A. 1856: *Sulle consorterie delle arti edificative in Venezia*, Venice.

Sansovino, F. 1561: *Delle cose notabili che sono in Venetia*, Venice.

—— 1581: *Venetia città nobilissima e singolare*, Venice. Ed. G. Martinioni 1663 (. . . *con aggiunta di . . . cose notabili dal 1580 al . . . 1663*), Venice; repr. with introduction by J. M. Fletcher, Farnborough 1968.

Santosuosso, A. 1973: Religious orthodoxy, dissent and suppression in Venice in the 1540s. *Church History*, 42: 476–85.

—— 1978: The moderate Inquisitor: Giovanni della Casa's Venetian nunciature, 1544–1549. *Studi veneziani*, 2: 119–210.

Sanudo, M., ed. anon. 1829: *Commentarii della guerra di Ferrara*, Venice.

—— ed. R. Fulin et al. 1879–1903: *Diarii*, Venice. Repr. Bologna 1969–70 (*DMS*).

—— ed. R. Fulin 1880: *La cronachetta di Marin Sanudo*, Venice.

—— ed. A. C. Aricò 1980: *De origine, situ et magistratibus urbis venetae ovvero La Città di Venetia (1493–1530)*, Milan.

Sarpi, P., tr. C. Potter 1626: *The History of the Quarrels of Pope Paul V with the State of Venice*, London.

—— ed. G. and L. Cozzi 1969: *Opere*, Milan and Naples.

Sbriziolo, L. 1970: Per la storia delle confraternite veneziane: dalle deliberazioni miste (1310–1476) del Consiglio dei Dieci. Le Scuole dei Battuti. *Miscellanea Gilles Gerard Meersseman*, Padua, II: 715–63.

Scarabello, G. 1979: *Carcerati e carceri a Venezia nell'età moderna*, Rome.

—— 1980: Devianza sessuale ed interventi di giustizia a Venezia nella prima metà del XVI secolo. In *Tiziano* 1980, pp. 75–84.

Scholderer, V. 1966: Printing in Venice to the end of 1481. In his *Fifty Essays in 15th and 16th Century Bibliography*, ed. D. E. Rhodes, Amsterdam.

Schulz, J. 1961–3: Cristoforo Sorte and the Ducal Palace of Venice. *Mitteilungen des Kunsthistorischen Institutes in Florenz*, 10: 193–208.

—— 1970: *The Printed Plans and Panoramic Views of Venice 1486–1797*, Venice.

—— 1978: Jacobo de'Barbari's *View of Venice*: Map Making, City Views, and Moralized Geography before the Year 1500. *Art Bulletin*, 60: 425–74.

Semi, F. 1983: *Gli 'ospizi' di Venezia*, Venice.

Sforza, G. 1935: Riflessi della Controriforma nella Repubblica di Venezia. *Archivio storico italiano*, 93.i: 5–34, 189–216; 93.ii: 25–52, 173–86.

Sheard, W. S. 1977: Sanudo's list of notable things in Venetian churches. *Yale Italian Studies*, 1: 219–68.

Sheils, W. J. and Wood D. (eds) 1986: *Voluntary Religion*. Studies in Church History, 23, Oxford.

Shuckburgh, E. S. (ed.) 1902: *Two Biographies of William Bedell, Bishop of Kilmore*, Cambridge.

Simonsfeld, H. 1887: *Der Fondaco dei Tedeschi in Venedig und die deutsch-venetianischen Handelsbeziehungen*, 2 vols, Stuttgart.

'Smarrito' (Carlo Roberto Dati) 1734: *Raccolta di prose florentine*, IV.i, Florence.

Smith, L. P. 1907: *The Life and Letters of Sir Henry Wotton*, 2 vols, Oxford.

Spencer, J. R. 1970: The Cà del Duca in Venice and Benedetto Ferrini. *Journal of the Society of Architectural Historians*, 29.i: 3–8.

Stella, Aldo, 1955: La regolazione delle pubbliche entrate e la crisi politica veneziana del 1582. In *Miscellanea in onore di Roberto Cessi*, Rome, II, 157–71.

—— 1956: La crisi economica veneziana della seconda metà del secolo xvi. *Archivio veneto*, ser. V, 58: 17–79.

—— 1964: *Chiesa e stato nelle relazioni ei nunzi pontifici a Venezia: ricerche sul giurisdizionalismo veneziano dal XVI al XVIII secolo*, Vatican City. This contains (pp. 105–318) the report of Alberto Bolognetti, nuncio in Venice 1578–81: Dello stato e forma delle cose ecclesiastiche nel dominio dei signori venetiani.

—— 1967: *Dall' Anabattismo al Socinianesimo nel Cinquecento veneto: ricerche storiche*, Padua.

—— 1969: *Anabattismo e antitrinitarismo in Italia nel XVI secolo: nuove ricerche storiche*, Padua.

Stella, Antonio n.d.: Grazie, pensioni ed elemosine sotto la Repubblica Veneta.

Monografie edite in onore di Fabio Besta nel XL anniversario del suo insegnamento, Milan, il, 715–85.

Stringa, G. 1610: *La chiesa di San Marco in Venezia*, Venice.

Tafuri, M. (ed.) 1985: *Venezia e il Rinascimento: religione, scienze, architettura*, Turin.

Tagliaferri, A. (ed.) 1974: *Relazioni dei rettori veneti*, II: *Belluno*, Milan.

Tenenti, A. 1962: *Cristoforo Canale: la marine vénitienne avant Lépante*, Paris.

—— 1967: *Piracy and the Decline of Venice, 1580–1615*, London.

Thomas, G. M. (ed.) 1874: *Capitolare dei Visdomini del Fontego dei Todeschi in Venezia (Capitular des deutschen Hauses in Venedig)*, Berlin.

Thomas, W. 1549: *Historie of Italie*, London.

Thuasne, L. 1888: *Gentile Bellini et Sultan Mohammed II. Notes sur le séjour du peintre vénitien à Constantinopole*, Paris.

Timofiewitsch, W., 1963: Quellen und Forschungen zum Prunkgrab der Dogen Marino Grimani in San Giuseppe di Castello zu Venedig. *Mitteilungen des Kunsthistorischen Institutes zu Florenz*, 11: 33–54.

—— 1972: *Girolamo Campagna*, Munich.

Tiziano 1980: *Tiziano e Venezia*, Vicenza.

Tramontin, S. 1967: La visita apostolica del 1581 a Venezia. *Studi veneziani*, 9: 453–533.

Tramontin, S., Niero, A., Musolino, G. and Candiani, C. 1965: *Culto dei santi a Venezia*, Venice.

Trebbi, G. 1980: La cancelleria veneta nei secoli XVI e XVII. *Annali della Fondazione Luigi Einaudi*, 14: 65–125.

—— 1986: Il segretario veneziano. *Archivio storico italiano*, 144: 35–74.

Tucci, U. 1957: *Lettres d'un marchand vénitien: Andrea Berengo (1553–1556)*, Paris.

—— 1973: The psychology of the Venetian merchant in the sixteenth century. In Hale 1973, pp. 346–78.

—— 1981: *Mercanti, navi, monete nel Cinquecento veneziano*, Bologna.

Ulvioni, P. 1989: *Il gran castigo di Dio. Carestie ed epidemie a Venezia e nella terraferma 1628–1632*, Milan.

Valcanover, F. 1983: *La pala Barbarigo di Giovanni Bellini*. Quaderni della Soprintendenza ai Beni Artistici e Storici di Venezia, 3, Venice.

Valeriano, G. P. 1556: *Hieroglyphica*, Basel.

Vanzan-Marchini, N. E. (ed.) 1985: *La memoria della salute: Venezia e il suo spedale dal XVI al XX secolo*, Venice.

Venturi, L. 1909: Le Compagnie della Calza: sec. XV–XVI (part 2). *Nuovo archivio veneto*, n.s., 17: 140–233. Also published as book, repr. Venice. 1983.

Vercellin, G. 1979: Mercanti turchi alla fine del Cinquecento. Il *Libretto de contratti turcheschi* di Zoane Sacra Sensale. *Il Veltro* 23: 243–76.

—— 1980: Mercanti turchi e sensali a Venezia. *Studi veneziani*, n.s., 4: 45–78.

Viario, A. 1980–5: La pena della galera: la condizione dei condannati a bordo delle galere veneziane. In Cozzi 1980–5, I, 379–430.

Vico, E. 1555: *Discorsi sopra le medaglie degli antichi*, Venice.

Wethey, H. E. 1975: *The Paintings of Titian*, III: *The Mythological and Historical Paintings*, London.

Wey, W., ed. G. Williams 1857: *The Itineraries of William Wey*, London.

Williams, G. H. 1972: The two social strands in Italian Anabaptism ca. 1526–ca. 1565. In L. P. Buck and J. W. Zophy (eds), *The Social History of the Reformation: in honor of Harold J. Grimm*, Columbus, Ohio, pp. 156–207.

Williamson, G. C. 1903: *The Anonimo*, London. Repr. New York 1969.

Wolters, W. 1961–3: Zu einem wenig bekannten Entwurf des Christoforo Sorte für die Decke der Sala del Senato im Dogenpalast. *Mitteilungen des Kunsthistorischen Institutes in Florenz*, 10: 137–45.

—— 1965–6: Der Programmentwurf zur Dekoration des Dogenpalastes nach dem Brand vom 20. Dezember 1577. *Mitteilungen des Kunsthistorischen Institutes in Florenz*, 12: 271–318.

—— 1979: Le architetture erette al Lido per l'ingresso di Enrico III a Venezia nel 1574. *Bollettino del Centro Internazionale di Studi di Architettura Andrea Palladio*, 21: 278–80.

—— 1983: *Der Bilderschmuck des Dogenpalastes*, Wiesbaden.

Wood, A. C. (ed.) 1940: Mr Harrie Cavendish, his journey to and from Constantinople, 1589, by Fox his servant. *Camden Miscellany*, 17: 12–13.

Woolf, S. 1968: Venice and the terra ferma: problems of the change from commercial to landed activities. In Pullan 1968, pp. 175–203.

Wootton, D. 1983: *Paolo Sarpi: between Renaissance and Enlightenment*, Oxford.

Wright, A. D., 1974: Why the *Venetian* Interdict? *English Historical Review*, 89: 534–60.

Wurthmann, W., 1975: The Scuole Grandi and Venetian Art, 1260 – ca. 1500. PhD thesis, University of Chicago.

Zago, R., 1982: *I Nicolotti. Storia di una comunità di pescatori a Venezia nell'età moderna*, Abano Terme.

Zampetti, P. 1969: *Lorenzo Lotto: Il 'Libro di spese diverse'*, Venice and Rome.

Zanette, E. 1960: *Suor Arcangela, monaca del Seicento veneziano*, Venice and Rome.

Zarlino, G. 158: *Sopplimenti musicali*, Venice.

Zenoni, L. 1916: *Per la storia della cultura in Venezia dal 1500 al 1797: l'Accademia dei Nobili in Giudecca*, Venice.

Zille, E. 1945: Il processo Grimani. *Archivio veneto*, ser. V 36–7: 137–94.

Zorzi, G. 1960–1: Notizie di arte e di artisti nei diarii di Marino Sanudo. *Atti dell'Istituto Veneto di Scienze, Lettere ed Arte*, 119: 471–604.

Zorzi, M. 1987: *La Libreria di San Marco. Libri, lettori, società della Venezia dei dogi*, Milan.

—— 1988: *Collezioni di antichità a Venezia nei secoli della Repubblica*, Rome.

Glossary

Acque, Magistrato, Ufficio alle   Magistrates responsible for the Venetian lagoon and inland waterways.

Auditori vecchi   A court of appeal from Venetian courts and from the judgements of Venetian governors within the Dogado.

Avogadori di Comun   Attorneys general or chief law officers of Venice, with a right of entry into every council. See II.5. They were also responsible for the registration of noble births [VI.1(b)].

Bailo   The Venetian ambassador–consul in Constantinople. He also acted as judge over civil disputes between Venetians or Venetian subjects in the Ottoman Empire. See especially VI.2(c).

Beni inculti   Uncultivated lands. Commissions charged with surveying these lands in provinces close to Venice and with examining projects for their development were established by the Senate in 1545, 1556 and 1560.

Biave, Collegio Provveditori alle (or **sopra le**)   Officials responsible for provisioning the city with grain and for supervising the bakers. *Biave* means crops, especially those (such as wheat, rye, millet) milled for bread flour.

Butt (botta, pl. botte)   A unit both of volume and of weight. Used to measure the freight capacity of a ship, it was often held to be equivalent to 10 **staia**, or approximately 0.7 of a freight ton, or about 29 English cubic feet (Lane 1934, pp. 246–8; 1965, pp. 239–43; 1966, pp. 357–8).

Camera degli Imprestiti   The loan treasury or bond office responsible for paying interest on the public debt to the state's creditors.

Camerlenghi di Comun   Magistrates who acted as public treasurers, receiving and stowing revenues in stout iron chests, e.g. from the customs and excise duties earmarked for the payment of interest on the state loan funds.

Campo (pl. **campi**)   An area of open urban space, as in Campo San Polo; also a measure of surface area, which varied in extent from one Venetian province to another.

Cantharo (p. **canthari**)   'A kintall waight being about a hundred waight and in some places, much more' (Florio 1611); 'a unit of weight . . . varying from 100 to 750 lbs in the different Mediterranean countries' (Edler 1934).

Capitolare (pl. **capitolari**)   The rule book of a Venetian magistracy, containing copies of all legislation pertaining to it and defining its powers.

Cattaveri; Ufficial al Cattaver   A magistracy of very varied functions, responsible for the recovery of public property, including buried or hidden treasure, and the goods of

460

those who died intestate; also for Jerusalem pilgrims (Newett 1907) and for pilots. These officials were placed in administrative charge of the Geto (afterwards Ghetto) Nuovo in 1516 (cf. VIII.8, 12).

Cazude, Ufficiali alle (or **delle**) Magistrates at one time responsible for exacting arrears of taxation, both tenths and *tanse*, with a 10 per cent penalty.

Censors Magistrates appointed in 1517 to seek out and punish attempts to exercise improper influence over elections (*DMS*, xxiv, cols 653–64).

Cinque Savi (or **Savii**) **alla Mercanzia** The five patrician members of the Venetian board of trade, founded in 1507 [IV.15].

Collegio The steering-committee of the Senate [II.2].

Collegio della Militia da Mar The body of magistrates in charge of naval recruitment.

Dieci Savi (or **Savii**) **sopra le Decime** Ten magistrates responsible for assessing lay residents of Venice for the tenth or *decima*, which fell chiefly upon landed property.

Ducat In most of the texts in this book the ducat referred to is the Venetian ducat of account, based on the silver currency; it was equivalent to 6 **lire** (*di piccoli*) 4 **soldi**, i.e. 124 soldi in all, or, alternatively, to 24 **grossi** or Venetian groats. For much of the time this ducat was a ghost money not represented in the coinage, although occasionally (e.g. in 1561 and 1608) silver and gold coins of the same value as the ducat of account were actually minted. However, as Coryat wrote in the early seventeenth century, 'whereas the Venetian duckat is much spoken of, you must consider that this word duckat doth not signifie any one certaine coyne. But many severall pieces do concur to make one duckat, namely six livers and two gazets, which doe countervaile foure shillings and eightpence of our money' (Coryat 1905 edn, I, 423).

Esaminador, Giudici di A law court particularly concerned with the transfer of property.

Giustizia Vecchia Magistrates concerned with the boatmen of the ferry stations and with many of the crafts; with the wages of workmen; with weights and measures; and with the just prices of various commodities, such as fruit and wood.

Governatori delle Entrate Administrators in charge of the collection of taxes, including the tenths, the taxes paid by office-holders, and the so-called 'war-moneys' of the late fifteenth century.

Grosso (pl. **grossi**) A 'coine called a grote' (Florio 1611). There were 24 grossi to a **ducat**.

Lira (pl. **lire**) In most of the texts the lira mentioned is the lira *di piccoli* or 'pound of tiny coins.' Like the old-style pound sterling before the introduction of decimal currency, the lira was divided on the l.s.d. principle: i.e. into twenty smaller units called **soldi** in Venice, while each of these was in turn divided into 12 tiny pieces known as denari. However, since there were 6 lire 4 soldi to the ducat, and the ducat was worth something in the region of an English crown (4s 8d. in Coryat's day), the Venetian lira can only have been worth 9d or 10d of English money (cf. Moryson 1907 edn, II, 154–5]. Occasionally, as in VII.8, one meets the lira *di grossi* or 'pound of groats', and each such lira, since it contained 240 **grossi** and there were 24 grossi to a ducat, was equivalent to 10 ducats. As VII.8 suggests, holdings in the state debt were reckoned in this unit in the late fifteenth century.

Livello (pl. **livelli**)   A lease; very often a personal loan disguised as a lease of property (Pullan 1973, pp. 388–92).

Marchetto (pl. **marchetti**)   A small coin worth 1 soldo (Moryson 1907 edn, II, 154–5).

Moggio   A dry measure, equivalent to 4 staia (Lane 1934, p. 245; 1965, p. 235).

Monte (pl. **Monti**)   The public loan funds – Monte Vecchio, Monte Nuovo, Monte Nuovissimo – which made up a large part of the state's debt to private persons. See IV.11–13.

Petizion, Giudici di   'Iudges of requestes', who dealt with 'causes of sales, bargaines, or contractes, by which any citizen pretendeth eyther breache of covenant or duenesse of debt' (Contarini ed. Lewkenor 1599, p. 107). See also Sanudo ed. Aricò 1980, pp. 120, 255–6.

Piovego, Giudici del   A magistracy with jurisdiction over canals, quays, bridges, public ways, and so on, and also over usury and for a time over heresy.

Procurator   The advocate or defender of a church, monastery or convent, sometimes called a proctor. For the special status and duties of the Procurators of St Mark, see II.4.

Promissione   The Doge's coronation oath [II.3(b)].

Proprio, Giudici di   '. . . whatsoever differences arise about houses, groundes, or leases, situated or lying within the boundes of *Venice* (that is, being within the lakes) are all determined by those that are called Iudges of the properties, to whose Courtes also widdowes have recourse in demandes of their dower, after the death of their husbandes' (Contarini ed. Lewkenor 1599, p. 106). They also had jurisdiction over cases referred to them by the Officials of the Night: see Sanudo ed. Aricò pp. 199, 254–5; and III.1(a).

Provveditore (pl. **Provveditori**)   A commissioner. The Provveditore all' (dell') Armata, for the fleet, and the Provveditore Generale, for the land forces, were endowed with very extensive powers as the government's principal representatives in naval and military affairs. Other Provveditori – the word was widely used – had defined spheres of administrative responsibility, as in the following list of examples (P. = Provveditori).

P. alle Biave   Supplies of corn and other crops.

P. di Cecca   The Mint.

P. di Comun   Streets, bridges, canals and public wells; some of the crafts, especially in the woollen trade; grants of citizenship to foreigners [VI.7(b)].

P. sopra i Conti   Public accounts.

P. sopra i Datii   Customs and excise duties.

P. alle Pompe   The enforcement of laws designed to restrain extravagance [IV.21–3].

P. al Sal   Salt revenues.

P. alla (sopra la) Sanità   Public health, quarantine regulations and related matters, including begging, vagrancy and prostitution.

Rason Nuove A fiscal and auditing office, responsible at one time for examining the expense accounts of ambassadors and military and naval officers, and for scrutinizing the books of some of the principal customs and excise offices.

Rason Vecchie Another such office with a variety of duties, including responsibility for the entertainment of visiting dignitaries and ambassadors. These magistrates examined the books of the governors of Venice's seaward possessions and those of Venetian consulates, leased the public fishing-grounds, sold at intervals the duty on fish 'at the post', examined the interest paid by the Camera degli Imprestiti, auctioned castles that were not garrisoned, and so on. Cf. IV.9, n. 14; IV.10, n. 33.

Rio (pl. **rii**) A canal.

Savio (pl. **savi, savii**) A general-purpose word meaning 'sage' or 'expert': used to describe the various members of the **Collegio** (Savi del Consiglio or Savi Grandi; Savi di Terraferma; Savi agli Ordini [see II.2]). Also found in the titles of other magistrates, e.g. **Cinque Savi alla Mercanzia, Dieci Savi sopra le Decime**.

Scudo (pl. **scudi**) A crown (unit of money): often fairly close in value to a **ducat**, but sometimes worth rather more. In the early seventeenth century, according to Fynes Moryson, the silver crown was equivalent to 7 **lire** (Moryson 1907 edn, II, 154–5).

Scuola (pl. **Scuole**) A religious confraternity. For the Scuole Grandi and Piccole see V.11–13 and VII. 1, 8 and 9.

Sestier (pl. **sestieri**) A district ('sixth part') of Venice [I.1].

Signoria See II.2 for the three meanings of this term.

Soldo (pl. **soldi**) A twentieth part of a lira. In 1551–65 a master builder was paid on average 29.5 soldi a day and in 1628–30 67.7 soldi a day; a journeyman in the same trade received about two thirds as much, 20.4 soldi in 1551–65 and 47.9 soldi in 1628–30 (Pullan 1964). See also VI.13, n. 23.

Sopraconsoli Magistrates concerned with persons unable to meet their obligations, who had asked for time to pay their debts; also responsible for auctioning the unredeemed pledges left at Jewish banks.

Sopraprovveditore (pl. **Sopraprovveditori**) Senior commissioners, sometimes appointed according to need to supervise the ordinary commissioners.

Stadio (pl. **stadii**) A 'measure of ground whereof be three sorts, one of Italie contayning 125 paces, eight of which make an English-mile' (Florio 1611).

Staio, staro, stero (pl. **staia, stara, stera**) A dry measure of weight and capacity, equivalent to some 83 litres or 62 kilograms, used in measuring grain and the freight capacity of ships. See also III.4(b), n. 11.

Tansa (pl. **tanse**) A personal tax falling on movable goods and assets other than landed property [see headnote preceding IV.1; and IV.8].

Ternaria Magistrates particularly concerned with the duties on oil, timber and non-precious metals, and reserving supplies of oil for the city of Venice.

Venetian style The Venetian year began on 1 March; hence, for example, 15 January 1552 Venetian style = 15 January 1553 in modern usage.

Zonta (pl. **Zonte**) A body of persons joined or ascribed to a council or to a group of officers, e.g. the Senate, or the Council of Ten [II.1, 17(a)–(b)], or the bench of one of the Scuole Grandi.

Index

INDEX

Urbino, 345
Uskoks, 100
usury, 345

Valaresso, Zacharia, 309
Valier, Agostino, 223
Valier (Valerio), Carlo, 406
Valla, Giorgio, 14, 91
Valmarana, family of, 227
Valois, Marguerite de, Duchess of
    Alençon, 406–8
Valtelline, 32
Varchi, Benedetto, 382
Vargas, Francisco, 421
Vedoa, Gasparo de (di) la (Gaspare a
    Vidua), 78, 268, 274, 407
Veggia (Veglia), 100, 151
veils, manufacture, of, 342
Vendramin, family of, 26; Andrea, 49;
    Francesco di Federico (active 1593),
    128; Francesco (Patriarch 1605–19 and
    Cardinal), 194, 227; Gabriel, 423, 428–
    9; Leonardo, 22
Veneziano, Jacometto, 425, 427
Venice, descriptions of, 4–31; dominions
    of, 31–5; foundation myth of, 4, 31;
    polemic against, 68–70, 271–2; praise
    of, 4–21, 61–2; representations of,
    397–8
Venier, family of, 26; Alberto da Ca', 170;
    Antonio, 229; Francesco (active 1482),
    220; Francesco (Doge 1554–6), 392;
    Lorenzo, 93; Nicolò, 63
Vergerio, Giambattista, 63
Vergini (Verzene, convent of) see Santa
    Maria delle Vergini
Verona, 20, 24, 34, 75, 141, 150, 222, 225,
    411, 414; monastery of San Lazzaro in,
    233
Veronese, Paolo (Paulo Caliari), 64, 232–
    6, 389, 414
Verrocchio, Andrea del, 388, 399
Vicar-general of the diocese of Venice,
    202–3
Vicenza, 34, 83, 110, 141, 150, 225, 227,
    231, 261, 269, 396, 424

victuallers, 280
Vienna, 64, 331
Vignole, 119
Villa di Piombino (Castelfranco), 251
Villarazzo (Castelfranco), 246–7
visitations, ecclesiastical, 203, 223–5
Vittoria, Alessandro, 401, 441–2
Vittorio Veneto, 30
Volta, Zuan della, and family, 420
Volte (voltae), 121, 123, 330, 405

wards, 51–2, 161
warehouses, 9, 11, 15, 107, 108, 109, 110,
    111, 167, 172, 176, 220, 269
weavers, 282
wedding festivities, 263, 264–5
wet nursing, 307–8
Wey, William, 45–6
whores, 121, 122, 123, 126–7, 189, 213,
    237; see also courtesans
widows, 161, 216, 242, 247, 250, 297, 298,
    305, 319, 320, 334
Willaert, Adrian, 376, 383
Wills and testaments, 144–5, 149, 198,
    227, 248–50, 251, 252, 268, 302, 310,
    389, 417, 418–19, 423, 434–7, 441–2
women, 22, 89–90, 178, 182, 197, 242,
    244, 245, 248–50, 254, 309, 315, 334,
    352, 380, 382, 420; as pilgrims, 63; work
    of, 19, 22, 27, 126, 205, 249, 283, 305,
    307–8, 383, 438
woodcarvers, 403–4
woodcuts, 369
woodturners, 429
woollen cloths, 29, 68, 149, 167, 171, 175–
    6, 321, 329–30
woolworkers, 293, 321
Wotton, Sir Henry, 3

Zaccaria, Dorotea, 263, 264
Zamberti, Alvixe di, 274
Zane, family of, 26; Matteo, 193–4; Zuane
    di Andrea and family, 171–3
Zante, 32, 95, 167, 172
Zara, 151
Zattere, 247